WHY DID
THE HEAVENS
NOT DARKEN?

Also by Arno J. Mayer

The Persistence of the Old Regime: Europe to the Great War

Dynamics of Counterrevolution in Europe, 1870–1956

Politics and Diplomacy of Peacemaking: Containment and Counterrevolution at Versailles, 1918–1919

Political Origins of the New Diplomacy, 1917–1918

WHY DID THE HEAVENS NOT DARKEN?

THE "FINAL SOLUTION" IN HISTORY

Arno J. Mayer

PANTHEON BOOKS · NEW YORK

Library of Congress Cataloging-in-Publication Data

Mayer, Arno J.
  Why did the heavens not darken?

  Bibliography: p.
  Includes index.
  1. Holocaust, Jewish (1939–1945) 2. Holocaust,
Jewish (1939–1945)—Causes. I. Title.
D804.3.M39 1989   940.53'15'03924   88-42621
ISBN 0-394-57154-1

Book Design by Michael Mendelsohn
Maps by James Perry
Manufactured in the United States of America
First Edition

CONTENTS

A PERSONAL PREFACE

Any student of contemporary history has an obligation to disclose his or her subjective values. This obligation is all the more imperative for a Jewish historian of Nazi Germany's genocide of the Jews who is sworn, as I am, to seek critical distance, but not cold detachment, from his subject of study. My own historical sensibility has necessarily been conditioned by my scholarly, personal, and political life experiences, which eventually moved me to try to integrate the singularity of the Jewish catastrophe into an equally singular historical epoch.

As a specialist in the recent European history, I knew that in time I would have to confront systematically what I propose to call the Judeocide. Through the years I became increasingly convinced that the unspeakable mass torment and murder of the Jews of continental Europe was one of the quintessentially distinctive events of one of Europe's darkest and most turbulent epochs. Above all, the persecution of the Jews, apart from its intrinsic enormity and significance, impressed itself upon me as a fundamental touchstone of the depth and extremity of the dislocation of Western civilization during the first half of the twentieth century.

Just as the history of war is too complex and serious to be left primarily to military historians, so the study of the Judeocide is too complex and serious to be left primarily to students of recent Jewish and German history, who treat it as an encapsulated chapter of their respective academic specialties. The wholesale and systematic violence against unarmed and essentially unresisting Jews during Europe's recent age of convulsions glaringly exposed the preconditions and mechanisms involved in crossing the thin line that divides widely accepted norms of modern civilized behavior—even in warfare—from the nether world of man's officially sanctioned willful inhumanity to man.

I should add that as a historian I also had methodological reasons for turning to the Judeocide. At a time when avant-garde professional historians continue to make a virtue of the fragmentation of their discipline and all but eliminate politics from it, the study of the Jewish disaster calls for an integrated approach and recalls the centrality of ideology, politics, and war in human affairs. Moreover, the mass murder of the Jews, more than any other single event, points up the importance of returning to the contextual study of short-term events. In the wake of Treblinka and Auschwitz it is difficult not to scorn Fernand Braudel's characterization of short-term events as mere "dust." Braudel went so far as to imply that short-term events were not worth studying since, unlike long- and medium-range events, they "traverse history as flashes of light" destined instantly to "turn to darkness, often to oblivion." *Pace* Braudel and his epigones, I have tried not only to contemplate the circumstances in which millions of Jews—along with millions of non-Jews—were reduced to "dust" in seconds of historical time but also to recapture the evanescent "light" of their torment to illuminate the historical landscape in which it occurred.

This book bears the imprint of my origins as a west European Jew. I was, like my parents, born and raised in the Grand Duchy of Luxembourg, where I spent the first fourteen years of my life. In the very early morning hours of May 10, 1940, as the armies of Nazi Germany crashed into France and the Low Countries, my parents put my sister, my grandfather, and myself in a car, and the five of us set out from Luxembourg.

The family sought safety and refuge in France. Traveling in a two-door Chevrolet, we barely stayed ahead of the fast-moving Wehrmacht and managed to avoid roads that were being strafed by the Luftwaffe. Near Verdun we experienced our first bombing raid and came within a hairsbreadth of having our flight cut short at a military control point. Except for the totally fortuitous intervention of an understanding general of the French army, we would have been interned as security risks because my seventy-four-year-old paternal grandfather was still carrying a German passport—he had been born in Bockenheim in the Rhenish Palatinate—despite his fifty years in Luxembourg.

Having been issued a special *laissez-passer* by the local military command, we drove from Verdun first to Troyes and Avallon, and then to Cannes, Montpellier, and Bagnères-de-Bigorre. A few months after the French surrender, in the early fall of 1940, we proceeded to Hendaye, on the Spanish frontier. But because my father was only thirty-nine years old, in keeping with Madrid's agreement with Berlin to bar Allied men of military age from entering or passing through Spain, the Spanish border officials turned us back.

Given my grandfather's advanced years, my parents discarded the option of crossing the Pyrenees on foot. Instead, we drove to Marseille and soon bought tickets on a boat that during the night of October 19–20 took us across the Mediterranean to Oran. In this Algerian port city we boarded the Trans-Sahara Railway in the direction of Casablanca. But on October 23 at Oujda, a Moroccan town on the Algerian border, we were taken off the train for lack of Moroccan visas. After a week in Oujda, where we attended Yom Kippur services in one of several local synagogues, a combination of diplomatic intervention and bureaucratic laxity enabled us to continue on to Rabat. We spent two months in forced residence in this political seat of Vichy France's Moroccan Protectorate, but with permission to visit Casablanca. It was there that my father on November 26, 1940, secured our American immigration visas and then illegally bought other transit visas in the manner portrayed in the film *Casablanca*.

Meanwhile, my sister Ruth was hospitalized with typhoid fever at the very moment that rumors were rife that under German pressure the local French authorities were about to prohibit the exit of all Allied males between eighteen and forty years of age. In early December 1940, after much agonizing, and following official assurances that upon her recovery my sister, together with my mother and grandfather, would have no difficulty leaving Morocco, my parents decided that my father and I should hasten ahead. Our journey took us by train through Spanish Morocco to Tangiers, and thence by hydroplane to Lisbon, where we landed on December 10. In the Portuguese capital we booked passage on the SS *Serpa Pinto*, and on December 18 sailed for New York, where we arrived in early January 1941. After taking a ship from Tangiers to Algeciras, and then the train to Lisbon, the rest of the family reached New York on the SS *Laurenco Marques* four weeks later.

Although our brief odyssey had its harrowing moments, it was nothing compared to the torment of my maternal grandparents. At the time of the German invasion they refused to leave Luxembourg, which was annexed to the Third Reich, and they remained unwilling to leave their home until after the emigration of Jews was banned. Eventually, after being interned in an abandoned monastery in the north of the Grand Duchy, my grandparents were transported on April 6, 1943, to Theresienstadt, the concentration camp located in an ancient fortified town with large military barracks not far from

Prague. At the time of their deportation my grandfather was seventy-three years old, my grandmother sixty-eight. Unknown to them, and to us, who knew about their deportation, Theresienstadt was a relative "oasis" in Nazi Germany's concentration-camp system. During the life of this camp close to 140,000 Jews must have been interned there. Of these, over half are estimated to have been sent to Auschwitz, where all but a few thousand perished. Another 32,000 inmates died from "natural" causes related to lack of heat, malnutrition, overcrowding, and medical neglect in Theresienstadt itself. The advanced age of many of the deportees who remained in this ghetto-camp accounts for this high mortality. My grandfather died in Theresienstadt on December 3, 1943. But my grandmother was among the approximately 17,000 emaciated and terrorized inmates liberated by the Red Army on May 9, 1945, exactly five years after the invasion of her native country. She had been part of a transport of ninety-seven Jews from Luxembourg, of whom eighteen survived. Shortly after her return home she told me—haltingly, prosaically, resignedly—about her life in the outer circle of purgatory, in which she never knew about the altogether incredible ghettos, concentration camps, and killing sites that were the inner circle of the Nazi hell.

The fate of my maternal grandparents prompted me to begin thinking, hesitantly and unsystematically, about the chronology and geography of the Jewish disaster, the nomenclature of the Nazi ghetto and camp system, and the different ways innocent victims were tormented and killed throughout the Third Reich's deportation universe. No less important, against the background of my own experience, the agony of my grandparents made me aware that the impact of the Jewish catastrophe was not altogether democratic, in that the odds for survival were unequal. Throughout much of the Continent, including Luxembourg, Yiddish-speaking, unprosperous, politically conservative, and religiously Orthodox Jews had a considerably smaller chance of remaining alive than more assimilated, privileged, and less religious Jews.

This is not to say that other factors besides class and status were not even more important as determinants of expulsion, relocation, deportation, and extermination. For example, especially in western Europe, Jews who were foreign nationals or stateless in their host countries were disproportionately imperiled. Still, material wealth, advanced secular education, and social integration—which were correlated with local citizenship—were frequently essential preconditions for timely emigration, escape, or hiding. Similar factors of social background significantly affected the composition of the Jewish councils and the councils of elders as well as the exercise of the collaboration that was forced upon them. In many if not most places the mainsprings of Jewish resistance were also in no small measure socially defined. The bulk of militant resisters tended to come out of the ideologically and politically conscious Communist, socialist, and Zionist left of the Yiddish-speaking working and lower middle classes.

As for my own immediate family, it was neither poor nor *grand bourgeois,* but middle-class. Fully emancipated and largely acculturated Luxembourgian Jews, we observed the High Holidays, held the yearly Seder, and celebrated Chanukah. My sister and I reluctantly went to Sunday school, and I was bar mitzvahed. In a tiny, overwhelmingly Catholic country in which there was little room for avowed, even if largely assimilated, Jews in the professions and the civil service, my father became a wholesaler, like both of my grandfathers before him. But before starting into commerce, he went to study political economy at the University of Heidelberg. It was there, while writing his thesis on Henri Fayol, one of the founders of French Taylorism, that he witnessed anti-Semitism among German university students during the early Weimar Republic. By the time he returned to Luxembourg in 1924, after having spent an additional year studying at the Sorbonne, my father had become an antifascist and a Zionist with strong left-democratic leanings. Presently, Nahum Goldmann and Victor Basch came to speak to the radical-liberal but also pro-Zionist literary society which he had organized and presided over. In the mid-thirties he also took the lead in setting up a collective farm on an abandoned estate in the no-man's-land between Luxembourg and France to train young Jewish refugees from central Europe who were to join a kibbutz in Palestine.

If we left Luxembourg in good time and never stopped to look back, it was because my father had long since recognized the innate warlike temper and anti-Semitism of the neighboring Nazi regime. He prepared both psychologically and materially for our escape, with no fixed objective except to stay out of Nazi Germany's clutches. His Zionism was an integral part of his reasoned conviction, grounded in a Popular Front perspective, that Germany would precipitate a monstrous war in which the Jews of Europe would be particularly at risk.

My experience in the U.S. Army from 1944 to 1946 finally helped me to appreciate the link my father had made between left-wing antifascism and secular Zionism. During basic training in armored warfare in Fort Knox, Kentucky, I encountered fierce expressions of anti-black racism and anticommunism, and was personally exposed to anti-Jewish outbursts. Next, instead of being sent overseas with my tank company, because of my knowledge of German I was transferred to an intelligence unit which had a dual mission: to interrogate captured generals of the German Wehrmacht and Waffen-SS about the order of battle of the Red Army and to process leading German scientists recruited to help America's postwar military buildup against the Soviets. My special assignment was to look after the "morale" of these ex-enemies, who were considered sufficiently valuable to be rushed to this side of the Atlantic. I was officially initiated into the ironies of the Cold War when I was given strict orders not to dispute any of their justifications for having served Hitler, including their favorite self-interested claim that except for persecuting the Jews, the Nazis had served their country and Europe well by saving Germany from the deadly scourge of communism and by fighting to keep bolshevism out of the European heartland. Indeed, the Third Reich's defeated generals and scientists anticipated, by forty years, the arguments of retrovisionist historians in Germany who today seek to rationalize the Nazi regime by characterizing it as intrinsically designed and essential for the struggle against the "greater evil" of Soviet communism. In any case, in 1945–46, among my charges the German scientists in particular swore that they had had no knowledge of the execrable conditions in the concentration camps and the mass killing of Jews until *after* the end of the war. At the time I could not help wondering what the German scientists who wound up on the Soviet side were telling their new captor-patrons.

In 1950, with the Cold War boiling over in Korea, and McCarthyism on the rise in the U.S.—including at Yale, where I was now a graduate student in international relations—I spent the summer in Israel, drawn there by the historical promise and possibility of a Zionist state and society independent of the two superpowers. In addition to working two months on a kibbutz of the Marxist Hashomer Hatzair, I talked with leading members of the left-wing Mapam and called on Martin Buber and Ernst Simon, outspoken advocates of a state that would be binational, democratic, and secular. Simon, professor of education at Hebrew University, had been a friend of my father's since their student days at Heidelberg. From his humanistically and religiously grounded Zionist perspective he shared with me his deep concern about the leaders of the fledgling Israeli state making a fetish of the dated Eurocentric view that Palestine was "a land without people for a people without land." Without minimizing Israel's security dilemma, both Simon and the far left of democratic Marxists took exception to the unbending policy of postindependence governments toward Israeli Arabs and the Arab states, which could only make Israel's future more and more contingent on its American connection. During my second visit to Israel in 1954 I was struck by the wisdom and prescience of these apprehensions.

During the 1950s there was no escaping the Cold War. It cast an ever longer and darker shadow over the world, including its scholarly and intellectual life. For quite a few years the atmosphere was so heavy with anxiety, even fear, that it was all but impossible to have any genuinely critical discussion of the orthodox interpretation of the Soviet-American confrontation in all corners of the globe. But by the mid-1960s and with changing political conditions, dissident historians in America began to question the quasi-official rendering of the origins and dynamics of the Cold War. I played a minor role in this effort to reappraise the tensions and conflicts of the postwar era, an effort that eventually generated a protracted scholarly and political controversy. There were, to be sure, overstatements by scholars and intellectuals on all sides of this debate. Even so, the debate was as salutary as it was inevitable, and it will never be closed.

Critical and scrupulous revision is the lifeblood of historical reflection and inquiry, and this is as true of the Judeocide as it is of the Cold War or any other momentous and perplexing historical event. After fifty years the question is no longer whether or not to reappraise and historicize the Judeocide, but rather how to do so responsibly. Three steps can advance this rethinking of the unthinkable: to abandon the vantage point of the Cold War; to place the Judeocide in its pertinent historical setting; and to use an overarching interpretative construct to explain the horrors both of the Jewish catastrophe and of the historical circumstances in which it occurred.

Discarding the residual Cold War blinders which continue to constrict our view of the Jewish disaster seems to me an essential first step. Without doing so, it is impossible to trace the nature and dynamics of the interconnection of anticommunism and anti-Semitism in the Nazi ideology and project. This interpenetration permeated *Mein Kampf* and the Nazi movement's discourse and program. It also decisively influenced Hitler's assumption of power. Furthermore, anticommunism ensnared Germany's old elites into collaborating in the consolidation of the Nazi regime and into condoning the spiraling persecution of the Jews in Germany, Austria, and Bohemia-Moravia. Thereafter, antibolshevism predisposed these same elites to support the military drive for unlimited *Lebensraum* in eastern Europe and to turn a blind eye to the savage mistreatment and massacres of Jews in the territories conquered and controlled by the Third Reich. Ultimately, Nazi Germany's dual resolve to acquire living space in the east and liquidate the Soviet regime provided the essential geopolitical, military, and ideological preconditions for the Judeocide. This fixity of purpose was the key to Hitler's obsession with the war in eastern Europe, which was the home of the bulk of the Continent's Jews and became the principal site of their suffering and destruction.

A second important prerequisite for rethinking the recent Judeocide is to set it firmly and thoroughly in the historical context of its time. Broadly speaking, in this book I relate the genesis and development of the Jewish catastrophe to the great European upheaval of the first half of the twentieth century, which included two major convulsions: World War One, with the resultant Bolshevik revolution in Russia; and World War Two, rooted in the Nazi counterrevolution in Germany, with its inherent drive toward foreign conquest. My ultimate focus and purpose is to correlate the spiraling persecution of the Jews with the changing nature and course of both the Nazi regime and the Second World War, especially in the Third Reich's crusading war against the Soviet Union.

Thirdly and finally, I conceptualize these three inseparable developments—the Nazi regime, the eastern campaign, the Judeocide—as integral components and expressions of the General Crisis and Thirty Years War of the twentieth century. This protracted European dislocation and cataclysm, which shook most of the world, reached its climacteric in 1941–45. During those four years, Nazi Germany experienced an irreversible increase of entropy in its civil and political society while fighting a life-or-death struggle with Soviet Russia, despoiling most of the Continent, and visiting its vengeful fury on European Jewry.

It is customary for an author to assume full responsibility for all mistakes, constructs, and conclusions after acknowledging the help of colleagues and friends. In this instance I invert the order of this convention with the express purpose of giving special emphasis to my own unqualified accountability for all errors, omissions, conjectures, and explanations. Nevertheless, my interpretation of the Judeocide would be even more seriously flawed than I know it to be were it not for the informed and rigorous criticism I received along the way. I am particularly indebted to Raul Hilberg, Hans Mommsen, and Pierre Vidal-Naquet. All three read the penultimate draft of my entire manuscript, except for the Prologue. Their substantive corrections, authoritative observations, and vigorous demurrals were invaluable, the more so since each of them scrutinized my text with a radically different perspective and scholarly expertise.

I am also profoundly grateful to David Abraham, Felix Gilbert,

Adrian Lyttelton, Carl Schorske, and Sheldon Wolin for their dis-
cerning reading of several of my chapters. Precisely because of our
close scholarly ties all of them were unsparingly forthright in their
critical comments. I owe special thanks to William Jordan for master-
fully and patiently guiding me in my reading and thinking about the
First Crusade. During the exploratory stage of this inquiry James
Wald sedulously assisted me with my research. Helen Wright, once
again, infallibly typed and retyped successive drafts of what to her was
a truly unsettling manuscript.

At first André Schiffrin was dubious about the wisdom and feasibility of historicizing the Judeocide, and he quite rightly remained a
demanding but judicious taskmaster every step of the way. Moreover,
with his unfailing judgment, which is the mark of Pantheon Books,
he asked Helena Franklin to edit my manuscript, which she did with
firm sagacity, circumspection, and taste. Carl Mayer made equally
discriminating suggestions for stylistic and organizational revisions.

But despite all the help I received, the research and writing of this
book was a painful, lonely, and dispiriting task. If I persevered, it was
largely because of the intense intellectual complicity of a few steadfast
friends: in the United States, Felix Gilbert, Carl Schorske, and Sheldon Wolin; in France, Maurice Aghulon, François Furet, Natalie
Sarraute, and Pierre Vidal-Naquet. Ultimately, however, my sons
Carl and Daniel sustained me most of all with their spirited curiosity
and skepticism, and without them I could not have traveled to Theresienstadt and some of the principal concentration camps and extermination sites. Above all, they and Aline were the first to realize that
at bottom the Judeocide remains as incomprehensible to me today as
five years ago, when I set out to study and rethink it.

Arno J. Mayer

Princeton and Chérence
Spring 1988

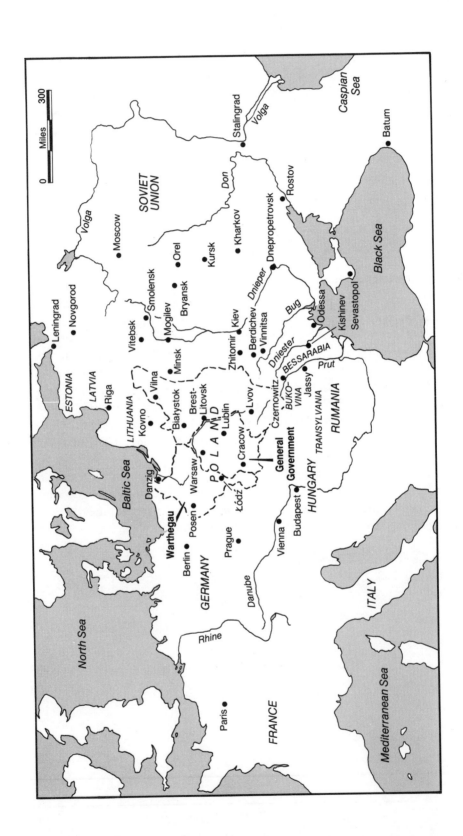

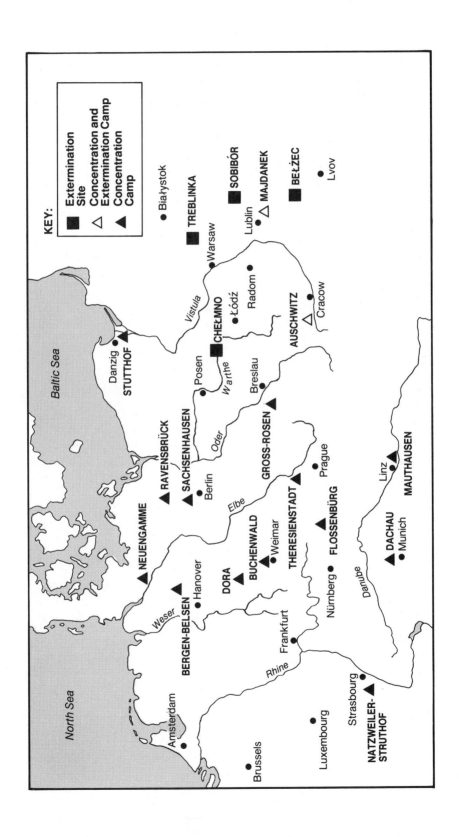

WHY DID
THE HEAVENS
NOT DARKEN?

A historical materialist . . . considers it his task to brush history against the grain. . . . The astonishment that the things we are currently experiencing should "still" be possible in the twentieth century has *no* philosophic foundation. Such an astonishment cannot be the starting point for genuine historical understanding—unless it is the understanding that the concept of history in which it originates is untenable.

> —Walter Benjamin
> "On the Concept of History"
> Spring 1940

CHAPTER I

PROLOGUE

HISTORICAL SIGNPOSTS

The mass slaughter of the Jews of continental Europe during the first half of the twentieth century was an integral part of an enormous historical convulsion in which Jews were the foremost but by no means the only victims. The large-scale and virtually indiscriminate destruction of European Jewry, perpetrated primarily by Nazi Germany, was the ultimate horror and atrocity in an exceptionally violent and savage half century of universal history. Indeed, the disaster visited upon the Jews would have been a historical impossibility apart from this cataclysm. There is thus no interpreting the recent mass murder of Jews without relating it to the singular historical context in which it was conceived and executed.

What I will call the Judeocide was set in an epoch of general crisis, with a strong tendency toward a dynamic disequilibrium in all major systems of thought and action. For Europe it was a time of extreme tension between change and resistance to change, between optimism and pessimism, between dawn and dusk. Europe's age of catastrophe was marked by a rampant instability—an intense dialectic strain—in economics, society, politics, culture, and science. The elites and institutions of Europe's embattled old regime were locked in a death struggle with those of a defiant new order: in the economic sphere merchant and manufactural capitalism against corporate and organized industrial capitalism; in civil society prescriptive ruling classes against university-trained strategic elites; in political society land-based notables and establishments against urban-based professional politicians; in cultural life the custodians of historicism against the champions of experimentation and modernism; and in science the guardians of established paradigms against the pioneers of the world's second great scientific and technological revolution.

Needless to say, this comprehensive unsteadiness and explosive stress in the internal life of Europe also had its external manifestations. It coincided with the loss of Europe's primacy in the world system and its retrenchment from overseas empire. But what was of greatest consequence for the fate of the Jews is that Europe's general crisis helped generate enormous foreign wars. In particular, it fueled the two world conflicts of 1914 to 1918 and 1939 to 1945, which between them claimed about 100 million lives, 80 million of them in Europe. By a feedback process these monstrous wars intensified and accelerated the antecedent crisis.

In the First World War some 10 million men were killed, maimed, and wounded in combat alone. There were over 2 million casualties per year, 190,000 per month, and 6,000 per day. The trench warfare on the western front was particularly horrifying. In 1916 the battle of the Somme claimed 500,000 casualties in four months, the battle of Verdun 700,000 in ten months. This immense bloodletting, which contributed to inuring Europe to the mass killings of the future, was not due primarily to the deadliness of modern weapons such as automatic machine guns and field artillery. Rather, it must be attributed to the zeal with which swarms of officers and men kept "going over the top" in the face of impossible odds. This dutiful self-immolation was a measure of the extent to which, from the outset, the war of 1914 to 1918 was a secularized "holy war," even if its ideological reason was not fully revealed and articulated until 1917. With the Russian Revolution the interpenetration of international conflict and civil war which is characteristic of times of general crisis also began to surface. Nineteen seventeen was also the year of the entrance of the United States into the war, which signaled the beginning of the end of Europe's long-standing ascendancy in the global economic and political system.

The military, economic, and social stresses of the First World War and its aftermath gravely unsettled four of Europe's six major belligerents: in Russia the tsarist regime was overthrown by a revolution of workers and peasants from below; in Germany the Second Empire bent to a democratic revolution from above; in the lands of the Austro-Hungarian Empire the Habsburg monarchy collapsed into a congeries of smaller, mostly authoritarian nation-states; and in Italy the liberal state was subverted by a fascist takeover. This radical destabilization and change in all the major continental powers, except France, went hand in hand with the thorough dislocation of Europe's intramural balance of power.

These seismic shocks growing out of an earthquake of general crisis and total war had far-reaching consequences for European Jewry. Above all, in 1917 the Russian Revolution emancipated Europe's largest and most oppressed Jewish community. Like the French Revolution, it gave a tremendous impetus to the idea and reality of the emancipation of Jews in the Christian world. Ominously, however, from the very outset antirevolutionary forces in Russia and elsewhere were tainted by Judeophobia.* From 1918 to 1921 many of the Whites in the Russian Civil War made the denunciation and persecution of Jews part of their counterrevolutionary campaign. In territories controlled by them, and especially in the wake of military setbacks, several tens of thousands of Jews were killed, mistreated, and terrorized. Not a few of the Polish and Ukrainian legions which joined the war against the Bolsheviks in pursuit of national independence resorted to this same kind of murderous scapegoating, although on a much smaller scale. Jews were also victimized in the bitter national strife that pitted Poles against Ukrainians and Lithuanians. Invariably, Jews were set upon for allegedly being in the vanguard of social and political radicalism and being inconstant in their national loyalties. In several important respects the large-scale killing of Jews in the Russian Civil War and in the national struggles following the collapse of the Romanov and Habsburg empires foreshadowed the mass murder of Jews during the Second World War.

Except in Russia, the time-honored elites of Europe survived the aftershocks of war, determined to preserve their unstable old regimes. Especially in Germany they lived to fight another day, although they were forced to relinquish some of their disproportionate political power. But there is no denying that the incumbent ruling and governing classes of all countries, without exception, were severely shaken by the chaos in eastern and central Europe, the consolidation of the Bolshevik regime, and the establishment of the Third, or Communist, International. Suddenly, they were confronted with the concrete and imminent reality of "the specter of communism" which, according to Marx and Engels, had started to haunt Europe in 1848. But contrary to their prophecy in *The Communist Manifesto,* not "all the powers of old Europe . . . entered into a holy alliance to exorcise this specter." Admittedly, revolutionary Russia was all but banned from the European and world systems, and the radical and militant left of workers and peasants was firmly controlled west of Russia. But this dual containment precluded neither intense diplomatic rivalries between

---

*When I use the term "Judeophobia," I am referring to personal prejudice. When I use the term "anti-Semitism," on the other hand, I am referring to the institutionalized forms taken by such prejudice, forms which are often but not always political, or else to the advocacy of such institutionalized prejudice. Finally, when I speak of "anti-Judaism," I am referring to hostile feelings or actions directed against the Jewish religion or Jews as adherents of that religion (i.e., to religious as opposed to "racial" prejudice).

and among the major European powers nor sharp conflicts of interest within their ruling and governing classes. While the quarantining of Soviet Russia complicated the reequilibration of Europe's balance of power, the cleavages in the power elites impeded the restabilization of Europe's civil and political societies.

The elites of non-Communist Europe were deeply divided over how best to meet the irrepressible political, social, and cultural challenges intensified by war and revolution. Sober-minded conservatives favored gradual reform as the best antidote to social unrest. Reactionaries, many of whom craved a return to a mythical and romanticized past, advocated standing firm and had fewer scruples about using repressive violence. These flexible conservatives and intransigent reactionaries, whose infighting dated from before 1914, soon backed into an uneasy relationship with outright counterrevolutionaries, who were more properly products of Europe's epoch of general crisis and war. The first and primary objective of these emergent far-rightists was to crush the organized left of industrial and agricultural workers as part of a bid for sole control of political society and cultural life. For the rest, their project was far more militant in rhetoric, style, and conduct than in political, social, and economic substance. These counterrevolutionaries, or fascists, called for a national revival, all the time putting greater stress on profound changes in attitude, spirit, and outlook than in economic and social structures. Ultimately, the formative fascists were distinctive less for their aims than for the means they forged and used to secure them. With a fiercely Manichaean perspective, they organized mass movements of the lower middle classes to engage in the kind of street politics whose hallmark was the willful and conspicuous exercise of verbal, symbolic, and physical violence. Rather than disavow or denounce the theory and practice of nascent fascism, the old elites condoned or encouraged it in the light of their own needs and interests.

The point to stress is that the resurgence of old-fashioned, theologically informed, and unforced Judeophobia and the growth of the newer kind of secular, cynically manipulated anti-Semitism were both closely linked to this drive by the internally torn but ultimately consonant right to restore, maintain, or purify the established order. During the immediate postwar upheaval this was the case not only in Russia but also in Germany and Hungary. In all three countries the composite right incited anti-Jewish hatred as part of its antirevolutionary campaign. As of that moment, and until 1945, the fascist right, usually with the tacit connivance of traditional conservatives and reactionaries, vilified Jews as the chief carriers of social and cultural subversion and the masterminds of political revolution. This

charge was grafted onto Christian Europe's age-old anti-Jewish prejudices. In fact, this new political anti-Semitism, which was a concomitant of protean anticommunism, became an important catalyst for the
reactivation of latent Judeophobia.

Anomalously in Italy, where the old elites summoned Mussolini to
take over the government in 1922, neither Judeophobia nor anti-
Semitism were much in evidence until the death rattle of the fascist
regime in 1943–44, and then only under the threat of Nazi German
guns. But nearly everywhere else in non-Communist Europe, and
particularly in eastern and central Europe, a mixture of traditional
Judeophobia and new political anti-Semitism informed the ideology
and program of the inchoate right. Above all, its fascist vanguard
used anti-Jewish appeals in preying not only on the resentments of the
endangered lower middle classes caught in the maelstrom of modernization but also on the fears of superannuated elites in the upper
classes desperate to maintain their overprivileged positions. Overall,
the fate of Europe's Jews was contingent on the evolution of Europe's
general crisis, which tended in two opposite directions. Wherever this
crisis of dynamic instability favored not reform or revolution but
reaction, Caesarism, or counterrevolution, the Jews were destined to
be in jeopardy. The third alternative of a return to normalcy—of the
crisis dying away or being resolved—was at best a remote historical
possibility.

Europe never really recovered from the Great War and the immediate
postwar turmoil. Among both the classes and the masses there was
widespread disillusionment, confusion, and distrust. The fall of the
three most awesome dynasties left a legacy of political instability. It
also resulted in the map of the Continent being radically redrawn,
which inevitably aroused irredentist rancors to be exploited by fascists and their fellow travelers.

But these psychological, political, and diplomatic strains could
have been managed and arrested, except for the fact that the protracted war had undermined Europe's economic resilience. While the
world conflict had caused relatively little material destruction, it had
taken an immense fiscal and economic toll. The ex-belligerent nations
were burdened with huge budget deficits and foreign debts. These
were all the more serious because Europe not only was losing ground
as the world's premier banker, but also was running into increasing
overseas competition and deriving declining economic benefits from
its colonial possessions. Moreover, the economic secession of Russia
and the disappearance of the Austro-Hungarian common market
impaired intra-European trade. The reparations which the Allies im-

posed on Germany merely compounded the disablement of one of Europe's pivotal economies and the dislocation of world finance and trade.

If this economic constriction and disorder became intractable it was largely for political and ideological reasons. Although there was general agreement on the urgent need for increased government revenues to reduce domestic deficits and foreign debts, the ruling and propertied classes, with their new siege mentality, blocked new tax levies, especially progressive income taxes. The laboring classes, better organized and more self-confident than before 1914, in turn refused higher indirect taxes while at the same time pressing for costly social and welfare reforms. This impasse over the sharing of the burdens and promises of yesterday's glorious war helped fire the politics of unreason, which came to focus on the volatile reparations issue on both sides of the Rhine, and beyond.

During the immediate postwar years these politically charged fiscal rigidities helped foster recession and unemployment along with acute inflation. Indeed, in key countries they impeded economic stability and growth, thus also sapping the international economy. The crash of 1929 and its global repercussions soon proved that the fiscal consequences of the war had helped turn Europe's heightened but routine economic vicissitudes into a serious structural disorder in the political economy of world capitalism.

Before that happened there was, of course, the economic recovery of 1924–29. The fact that it hinged on American loans confirmed the Old World's loss of self-sufficiency. In any case, this economic upturn fostered a precarious social peace and political accommodation throughout the Continent's danger zone. The middle third of the twenties saw not only the strengthening of the fledgling Weimar Republic in Germany and the relaxation of the authoritarian regimes in eastern and southeastern Europe but also the successful reign of the New Economic Policy in the Soviet Union. Characteristically, domestic appeasement was accompanied by the relaxation of international tensions.

This respite in Europe's general crisis was accompanied by a remission of the old Judeophobia and the latest radical anti-Semitism that had surfaced during the postwar turbulence. In fact, the Indian summer of the twenties was also the halcyon season for Jewish emancipation, acculturation, and assimilation the world over, including in Germany.

Beginning in the late twenties, however, the economic breakdown triggered a reinflammation and exacerbation of Europe's national and international disorders. The thirties saw the hardening of the Soviet regime, the drift toward fascism in the eastern buffer zone and Austria, the rise of the Popular Front in France, and the outbreak of the Civil War in Spain. The resumption of the general crisis instantly took on a global dimension with Japan's subjugation of Manchuria in 1931–32 and Italy's invasion of Ethiopia in October 1935.

But the consequences of the financial collapse that rapidly turned into a worldwide economic paralysis were most abrupt and far-reaching in Germany. The second industrial revolution and organized capitalism had advanced much further in Germany than in any other major European country, and its economy was particularly vulnerable to violent gyrations in the business cycle. Furthermore, Germany's republican institutions were too fragile to mediate and master the explosion of social discontents and political conflicts unleashed by massive unemployment, which affected over 5.5 million workers, or 30 percent of the work force and nearly 45 percent of all trade union members in 1932. For reasons of self-preservation the entrenched but internally divided power elite of big business and agriculture, seconded by the old civil- and military-service nobility, abandoned democratic for plebiscitary politics. They turned to Adolf Hitler because he, unlike them, was adept at rallying popular support for the defense of the established but endangered economic, social, and cultural order. The inveterate elites put themselves—their prestige and expertise—at the service of what Hitler portrayed as an eleventh-hour effort to save Germany from communism. Their embracing of Hitler in January 1933 was a replay of the Italian power brokers' embracing of Mussolini in October 1922. But the import of the March on Berlin was destined to be infinitely more momentous than that of the March on Rome: Germany occupied a decidedly more crucial position in the international system and the ideology of German fascism—of National Socialism—was more universalizing and creed-bound, in addition to being impregnated with anti-Semitism.

Because of the magnitude and intensity of the disorders in its civil and political society, Germany was the most critical flashpoint of Europe's seething general crisis. Its destabilization would be particularly explosive and destructive by virtue of its dual centrality. Germany was the critical hinge of the European economy, and its own depression could not help but feed into the world economy and then turn back on itself. In addition, Germany was the linchpin of the European, if not global, balance of power. With Hitler and his collaborators determined to channel Germany's domestic disorders into the international environment, the switches were set for foreign bellicosity and war. Compared to World War One, the Second World War originated even more unequivocally not in the disequilibrium in

Europe's diplomatic and military system but in the crisis of its civil and political societies. Moreover, much more than the Second German Empire before 1914, the Third Reich by the 1930s was the epicenter of that crisis and its eruption into absolute war.

The drive against the Jews originated in this same epicenter. Anti-Semitism had, of course, been one of the cardinal elements of Hitler's syncretic ideology from the very outset. It had also informed much of the political rhetoric of National Socialism during its movement phase. The Jews were used in particular as a vehicle for the attack on the invasive modernity with which the Nazis incited those who felt threatened by it. But the really grave turning point did not come until soon after Hitler was invested with power, when anti-Semitism became official state policy. Following the suppression of all political opposition, particularly the Communist and socialist left, the persecution of the Jews proceeded in tandem with the consolidation of the Nazi regime. German Jews were glaringly and publicly reviled, boycotted, deemancipated, and ostracized. They were also expelled from the professions and expropriated.

Crystal Night on November 9–10, 1938, capped this virtually unremitting cold pogrom with the desecration of nearly two hundred synagogues, countless physical assaults, and large-scale arrests. At least thirty-six Jews were killed and between 20,000 and 30,000 Jews were thrown in concentration camps. Even so, this intensified persecution was not a prelude to the predetermined mass murder of the Jews in the Third Reich—now including Austria and Bohemia-Moravia—or in the rest of Europe. The irruption against the Jews, which was officially sanctioned, was more an echo of the pogroms of the late tsarist empire than a prefiguration of the coming Judeocide. As for the Jews interned in camps, although many were mistreated, they were released within a few weeks.

After the fact, the terror of Crystal Night and its immediate sequels were used to quicken the mass exodus of Jews. At this time the Nazi aim was not to make the Jews outcasts in Germany pending their extermination. Rather, it was to make Germany *judenfrei* by harrying and driving them to flee the country. Because of the global depression and rising international tensions, the outside world kept restricting immigration, thereby impeding forcible exile and expulsion. Nevertheless, well over half of the Third Reich's Jews had been driven abroad by the time war broke out in September 1939.

To be sure, and ominously, as Europe's sea of national and international troubles grew more and more turbulent, the Jews were increasingly lashed out at. But as long as the European crisis did not erupt into general war, their persecution remained essentially unmurderous. Such was the case not only in Germany but also in Poland, Hungary, and Rumania, where this early anti-Semitic backlash was much less extreme.

The situation changed radically with the start of the Second World War, which provided many of the essential enabling conditions and motor forces for the Judeocide. The conquest of Poland brought nearly 1.8 million Jews under the control of Nazi Germany and was accompanied by the first sizable, murderous pogroms since those which had erupted after the First World War, in 1918 to 1921. The Third Reich did not, however, invade Poland in order to capture the bulk of Europe's second largest Jewish community for subsequent annihilation. Rather, Hitler seized Poland to begin and test his drive for German *Lebensraum* in the east. Moreover, the original pogroms and the victimization of Polish Jews were closely entwined with the harsh mistreatment of Polish Christians and the systematic enslavement of Poland, which included the forced relocation of Poles to make room for ethnic German settlers. At this juncture the brutal ghettoization and relocation of Polish Jews was a drastic intensification of Nazi Germany's policy of seeking to extrude—not exterminate—the Jews from the expanding Third Reich. The unlooked-for Jews of Poland were being concentrated in the expectation that subsequent military victories would secure a distant territory to which to deport the Jews of the enlarged German empire. In mid-1940 the defeat of France held out the prospect of taking over the island of Madagascar as a dumping ground, until it became clear that England, which controlled the high sea, could neither be invaded nor cowed.

The assault on Russia in June 1941 recharged and reoriented Hitler's determined but indeterminate project of deporting the Jews from the inherently predatory millenarian Reich. At that time the Soviet Union, including the lands it had secured under the Nazi-Soviet Pact, had a Jewish population of about 5 million. But once again Hitler's purpose in invading Russia was not to trap these Jews for a predetermined Judeocide. Rather, Operation Barbarossa was both a military campaign to conquer boundless living space in the east and a crusade to eradicate the Soviet regime and the Bolshevik ideology.

In line with orders issued before the attack, the invading German military and security forces searched out and killed adult male Jews who were alleged to figure prominently among the Bolshevik infidels and the political cadres of the Red Army. At the same time, throughout the Baltic countries and eastern Poland, as well as western Belorussia and the Ukraine, local superpatriots capitalized on "liberation" by Nazi German forces to vent their anti-Soviet rage in deadly pogroms against Jews.

As long as the Wehrmacht and its allied armies were triumphant, the suffering of the Jews was limited to this victimization by German security forces and local collaborationist vigilantes. This essentially unsystematic killing of Jews coincided with the expectation of a quick victory over the Red Army and a thorough liquidation of the Bolshevik regime. It was in this moment and spirit of euphoria that Nazi leaders with a special interest in the "Jewish question" envisaged the eventual evacuation of Europe's Jews farther east, perhaps beyond the Urals. Indeed, had the blitzkrieg succeeded in the east as it had in the west the year before, Europe might ironically have been spared the worst horrors of the twentieth century. The peoples of eastern Europe, notably the Slavs, would certainly have been enslaved. But they would not have been subjected to the extreme barbarization and miseries of war which began to take their horrendous toll in the fall of 1941. Likewise, the Jews, instead of being massacred, probably would have been deported to the far interior of Russia or, should England have been forced to strike a bargain, to an overseas colony.

None of this is to suggest that such outcomes would have been either benign or desirable, but it is to insist that while the Reich's conjoined war of conquest and ideological crusade were an outgrowth of the internal dynamics of the Nazi regime, it took the impasse and failure of the blitzkrieg against Soviet Russia to release the full fury of both. Certainly, Hitler and the Nazi ideology, including radical anti-Semitism, were a necessary precondition for the Judeocide. But in and of themselves they would not have been sufficient to bring it about. Without the spiraling and unsuccessful absolute war, which was in essence a crusade, the inconceivable could not have become conceivable, let alone possible and practicable. Just as in September 1941 the fatefully difficult and late capture of Kiev prompted the Nazis to intensify the brutalization of their warfare and occupation in the east, it also precipitated the transition to the systematic mass murder of Jews, beginning with the vengeful massacre at Babi Yar outside the Ukrainian capital. Hitler's ideologically and politically grounded decision to turn the failing war-cum-crusade against Soviet Russia and bolshevism into a ferocious struggle for *Sein oder Nichtsein* (life or death) entailed the pitiless torment of the Jews. Indeed, the inexorable totalization of the Second World War and of the Judeocide within it were symbiotic in their origin and dynamics, and both reached their terrible culmination in eastern Europe.

For Europe, World War Two was an even greater enormity than World War One in terms of death, material devastation, destruction of wealth, and psychological trauma. In addition, the second war spelled the end of central and western Europe's economic, military, and colonial supremacy in the world system.

Overall, World War Two claimed at least 50 million dead, the overwhelming majority of them in Europe. There were about 20 million battlefield casualties, 15 million of them Europeans. About half of the European soldiers killed were Russians. These included over 3 million Soviet officers and men who were murdered or died after capture by the Wehrmacht, making them as much political as military victims. The battles of Leningrad and Stalingrad in 1942 corresponded to those of the Somme and of Verdun in 1916, except that in addition to shifting the center of the bloodletting to the east, they took the lives of a high but as yet uncertain number of noncombatants.

In fact, the huge toll of civilian lives was one of the chief characteristics of the Second World War. Easily over 50 percent and probably closer to 70 percent of all the dead were noncombatants. Among Europe's 18 million civilian war dead, the bulk were Russians and Poles, without counting Russian and Polish Jews. Except in Germany, only a relatively limited number of civilians died or were wounded as a direct consequence of military actions, such as the shelling and bombing of cities and the strafing of open roads and fields. By far the greatest number of the "unknown noncombatants" of the Second World War perished from undernourishment, disease, forced labor, deportation, and resettlement, as well as in massacres, executions, and gassings.

From 1939 to 1945, unlike during the Great War of 1914 to 1918, Europe suffered not only an enormous loss of life but also widespread devastation. The chief battle zones were ravaged and, thanks to the use of air power, many major cities were severely damaged, several of them all but razed. Again, the destruction was far greater in eastern Europe, including eventually eastern Germany, than farther west. Not that western combat areas and cities escaped it altogether. But the contrasting fate of the capitals of France and Poland may be taken as symbolic of the concentration of the desolation of war in the east. While Paris emerged unscathed from the war, Warsaw was left in utter ruins. The Polish capital suffered three separate German assaults, each of which killed mostly civilians: the terror bombing in September 1939; the liquidation of the Jewish resistance and ghetto in 1943; and the repression of the nationalist uprising in 1944. Warsaw's ordeal and destruction were unsurpassed.

More generally, the western regions of the Soviet Union and much of Poland—the chief battlegrounds of the Wehrmacht's life-or-death struggle with the Red Army—survived as a mere wasteland, having suffered well over one half of Europe's total material ruination. Nazi Germany's scorched-earth practices and modern-day pillage, which were not uncontrolled but carried out on deliberate command, were particularly lethal and were all but limited to the east. In any case, in the east most roads, bridges, railway tracks, waterways, and ports were wrecked or damaged. Thousands of cities, towns, and villages were laid waste, including their factories, schools, and libraries. Throughout the occupied eastern territories the Germans not only commandeered forced hard labor but also plundered livestock, horses, raw materials, foodstuff, and rolling stock.

The Judeocide erupted and was systematized in this context of monstrous death and destruction, and it was carried out in a setting and atmosphere weighted down with the miseries of war. It must be remembered that this climate of pervasive violence and suffering was beyond compare in eastern Europe, which was the home of the vast majority of continental Jewry and became the site of its doom.

In some respects the experience of the Jewish minorities was much the same as that of the majority populations. Jews fought and died for their countries and ideals. They were victims of air raids and shared in all the trials and tribulations of war. Jews were also impressed for forced labor both locally and far away from home, and they were hounded and executed for being real or suspected members and helpmates of the resistance.

But for the Jews, such "normal" suffering was the exception, not the rule. The main body of European Jewry was forced to endure torments of another order entirely. Unlike their fellow countrymen, Jews were stigmatized and ostracized. Only Jews were locked into congested and squalid ghettos in their native cities or in cities to which they were deported from near and far. At all times material conditions—provisions of food, fuel, and medicine—were incomparably worse inside these ghettos than in the cities in which they were located. While the ghetto-dwellers in Warsaw and Łódź were reduced to extreme destitution, the Christian populations outside the ghetto walls lived on tolerable rations. Similarly, in concentration and work camps the ill-treatment of Jews exceeded that of most, if not all, other groups. In both ghettos and camps the Nazis willfully decimated Jews by malnutrition, sickness, and hyperexploitation.

There is, of course, no denying that non-Jews were also deported and massacred in large numbers. But the nature of their affliction was distinctly different. Most of the non-Jewish civilians who were conscripted and deported for compulsory labor, including the political prisoners among them, were men and women in the prime of life whose labor power tended to be valued and spared. By contrast,

Jews—and Gypsies—were deported for forced labor regardless of age, sex, and health, with murderous consequences.

As for the massacres of non-Jewish civilians, they were not an end in themselves, nor were they purely ideological in purpose. Almost invariably such mass killings were intended to further real even if warped military and political purposes. Typically, they were reprisals for acts of sabotage or for the assassination of German officers or security officials. Reprisals were much less common in the west than the east, which was subjected to a hostage system. But no matter where, the selection of hostages was arbitrary and often included women and children. The Nazis carried out their retaliations in situ and in public with a view to terrorizing the population at large and deterring would-be resistance fighters and their helpers. The wholesale punishment of Lidice near Prague and Oradour-sur-Glane near Limoges were typical of such instrumental massacres. Most of the women and children of Lidice were deported to Germany after being forced to witness the murder of the entire male population. The women and children of Oradour-sur-Glane were burned and shot to death along with the men.

But such conflict-related massacres of unarmed and unresisting civilians were sporadic and irregular compared to the massive and systematic wrack of the Jews—men, women, children, infants, the sick, the elderly. Although not a few Jews were also seized and executed as part of wanton security operations, the overwhelming majority were killed outright or were worked, starved, or otherwise driven to death for reasons essentially unrelated to military and political security. Unlike all the other civilian victims of retaliatory terror, the Jews were demonized and turned into scapegoats not for real or alleged acts of hostility against specific German targets but for incarnating the nemesis of the Nazi pretense. At the same time, though Hitler proclaimed *urbi et orbi* that the Jews would be terribly punished, the worst of this "retribution" was carried out in secrecy. Because the torment of the Jews in the Warsaw ghetto and at Auschwitz was not completely secret, separate, and distinct, it was to some degree instrumental and similar to that of Gentiles. By contrast, at Treblinka and the other three quintessential killing sites, the torment of the Jews was totally isolated and concealed, and therefore intrinsically unique.

Prima facie the catastrophe which befell the Jews during the Second World War was unique in its own time and unprecedented in history. There are strong reasons to believe that the victimization of the Jews was so enormous and atrocious as to be completely outside the bounds of all other human experience. If that is the case, what the

Jews were subjected to will forever defy historical reconstruction and interpretation, let alone comprehension. It may well be that only survivors who actually passed through the fiery ordeal of the killing sites, ghettos, and camps are in a position to speak to it: they alone can penetrate to the innermost feelings, thoughts, and agonies of the victims; they alone can provide authentic testimony about the unspeakable brutality of their oppressors and the atmosphere of pervasive inhumanity generated by them.

Such eyewitness accounts are indispensable for any interpretive reading of the Judeocide. It is not to depreciate their historical value to insist, however, that they are neither complete nor in themselves sufficient. Naturally, as they cast their eyes back, the survivors of the Jewish torment cannot be expected to see the chronology of their own experiences and the historical context in which they unfolded. Furthermore, as they evoke their remembrances, these are bound to be shaped and selected in the light of later events and understandings. In particular, they cannot help but be informed by the tenets and metaphors which have structured the subsequently crystallized collective memory and vision of the Jewish catastrophe. Remembrances are also likely to be adapted to fit the narrative designs in which this catastrophe is recounted.

But despite these unexceptional limitations, the reminiscences of the survivors nevertheless remain an essential source of information and insight for anyone pondering the Jewish disaster. They also help to preserve and pass on its memory for later generations. The anguished recollections of survivors have been woven into a liturgy for what has evolved into a cult of remembrance, with its own ceremonies, holy days, shrines, monuments, and pilgrimages. The laudable purpose of this ritual memorialization is to make sure that neither Jews nor non-Jews forget or normalize the recent suffering of the Jews.

But gradually, even if unwittingly, this cult of remembrance has become overly sectarian. More and more, it has helped to disconnect the Jewish catastrophe from its secular historical setting, while placing it within the providential history of the Jewish people to be commemorated, lamented, and restrictively interpreted. Its reification has found expression and consecration in the religiously freighted word concept "the Holocaust," a term whose standard meaning is a sacrificial offering wholly consumed by fire in exaltation of God. The embryonic creed of "the Holocaust," which has also became an *idée-force*, has taken the reflective and transparent remembrances of survivors and woven them into a collective prescriptive "memory" unconducive to critical and contextual thinking about the Jewish calamity. A central premise is that the victimization of the Jews at the hands of

Nazi Germany and its collaborators is absolutely unprecedented, completely *sui generis*, and thus beyond historical reimagining.

Of course, when confronting aberrant and impenetrable events in the past, many of the defects which limit and distort the vision of the inward and cloistered eye of memory also truncate and skew the vision of the external and shortsighted eye of history. Like the recorders and custodians of memory, those of history select, circumscribe, and angle their readings of the past under the ubiquitous sway of hindsight. Indeed, historians normally take account of the paradigmatic orthodoxies and narrative requirements of their craft and time, and they do so in the light of the political climate of their day.

Compared to the Muse of memory, however, the Muse of history is sworn to certain ideas and rules for recording and interpreting the past. Since the Enlightenment, historians have shared certain commonsense notions of causality and accuracy. They have also presumed the past to be accessible by virtue of being profane, not providential. In addition, rather than give free rein to their subjectivity, they are supposed to master it. At a minimum, historians are expected to avow their own prejudices and to probe those of their sources. No less important, they invite critics, both friendly and hostile, to verify the authenticity and reliability of their evidence as well as to debate the logic of their constructions and the coherence of their explanations. Historians must also develop a lateral and wide-angled vision, for they are enjoined to probe for linkages between events that were unclear or unknown to contemporaries.

It is striking that the foremost contemporary chroniclers of the recent Jewish disaster, unlike those of earlier times, recorded their eyewitness observations in the spirit of Enlightenment history. No retrospective memoir, literary work, or historical analysis can match the precision and penetration of Emmanuel Ringelblum's *Notes from the Warsaw Ghetto,* of Adam Czerniaków's *Warsaw Diary,* and of the collectively kept *Chronicle of the Łódź Ghetto, 1941–1944.* These three firsthand chronicles, written inside the cities of the dying and the dead, were framed with distinctly modern ideas of facticity, chronology, and context, and also of the dynamics of collaboration and resistance under conditions of extreme powerlessness. More remarkable still, they registered the impact of the course of world history, particularly the war, on the daily life and fate of the ghettos.

At the core of the modern idea of history is the axiom that historical praxis and interpretation are neither static nor consensual. There are constant changes in concept, method, technique, and evidence which along with changing times keep stimulating new as well as critical questions, hypotheses, and reappraisals. Whereas the voice of memory is univocal and uncontested, that of history is polyphonic and open to debate. Memory tends to rigidify over time, while history calls for revision.

To revise the conventional rendering and interpretation of the Judeocide is to revise the conventional rendering and interpretation of the international conflict to which it was so closely tied. Since the one cannot be rethought apart from the other, a framework that can handle the common source and driving power of their shared enormity is required. Ultimately, the immensity of both the absolute war and the catastrophe visited on the Jews was grounded in the interfusion of politics and ideology in a time of general crisis. This premise runs counter to the postulate that the violence and brutality of 1914 to 1945 were uniquely modern and essentially unprecedented.

Appearances notwithstanding, the efficacy of advanced weapons, communications, and bureaucracies was neither the principal nor sufficient cause for the appalling destructiveness of the two world wars. Paradoxically, in 1914 and again in 1941 the latest instruments and techniques of warfare made history with their failure, not their success: the miscarriage of the Schlieffen Plan led to the gory trench warfare on the western front; the miscarriage of Operation Barbarossa resulted in the savage life-or-death struggle on the eastern front. Both world conflicts were dominated by mass warfare in which manpower, not weapon power, remained supreme. The newest arts of war merely intensified and prolonged the fighting whose deadly fury was fired not by military logic but political reason (or unreason). The harrowing and endless battles of the Somme and of Leningrad, of Verdun and Stalingrad, were not products of modern military strategy and science. These and other battles were essentially conventional, and they could have been cut short if it had not been for the ideological rationale behind them. That modern weapons were not decisive is also clear from the fact that relatively few of the millions of civilian victims of the international and civil wars of the first half of the twentieth century were killed by such unconventional methods of contemporary warfare as armored charges and aerial bombardments.

Similarly, the availability and efficient use of the latest instruments, techniques, and agencies of civil violence do not account for the enormity of the Judeocide. There is, of course, no denying the modernity of the mechanisms of destruction: the highly organized character of the bureaucratic apparatus; the motorization of the *Einsatzgruppen* (special SS task forces); the utility of the railway system; and the capacity of the crematoriums. But while this rampant functional rationality contributed to the unprecedented magnitude of the Jewish catastrophe, it was not its immanent mainspring. To overemphasize the modernity and banality of the killing process is to risk diverting attention from its taproots, purposes, and indeterminacies. Just as the latest weapons were not needed to feed the fury of the two world wars, so the latest technical and bureaucratic skills were not essential to feed the fury of the Judeocide. As previously noted, the massacre of Babi Yar outside Kiev reveals that the same ideological zeal which fired Nazi Germany's radicalization of its absolute war against the Soviet Union also fired the radicalization of its war against the Jews. The two processes were part of a single causal nexus, and neither the one nor the other was, in the main, made possible or driven by the modern technology and bureaucracy of violence.

To grasp the underlying motor forces of these intertwined enormities, the absolute war and the Judeocide, it may help to ponder comparable historical processes in the distant past. R. G. Collingwood quite rightly insisted that such retrospection was indispensable to uncover "the less obvious features hidden from a careless eye in the present situation." The General Crisis and Thirty Years War of the seventeenth century and the First Christian Crusade of 1095 to 1099 and its sequels seem particularly apposite and revealing. To probe homologous events in former times is to isolate essential similarities and differences with kindred historical processes of later times. It is also to strive for critical distance, to be achieved by standing both outside and within the living past.

The general crisis of the seventeenth century, not unlike that of the twentieth, touched all major aspects of civil and political society, of cultural and intellectual life. Such moments of crisis are uncommon, short-lived, and convulsive. Characteristically, general crisis spills over regional and national boundaries to run in international veins. In the seventeenth century, as in the twentieth, it took different forms in different countries. Invariably, however, it gave rise to destabilizing tensions between state and society.

The first half of the seventeenth century was one of Europe's greatest watersheds. It was the epoch of the ascendance of mercantile capitalism, standing armies, and tax-collecting bureaucracies; of the breakthrough into modern physics, mathematics, and applied sciences; of the glorious revolution in literature and the performing arts; and of the radical renewal of philosophy, ethics, and law. These new departures were interconnected, although the exact manner, intensity, and sequence of interaction remain problematic. They were also fiercely contested by champions of vested interests and orthodox ideas who enlisted obscurantist forces in their efforts to stem or reverse the course of history. The irrepressible clash between Protestantism and Catholicism, particularly its increasing politicalization, was both cause and effect of Europe's great unsettlement, which resulted in concurrent but uncoordinated social and political upheavals in several countries.

Epochs of general crisis are also times of general war. The linkages between deep-rooted domestic dislocations and chronic international conflicts are indeterminate but intense. While the scourging impact of unbridled warfare on crisis-torn societies is transparent, the reverse process is far less so. It stands to reason, however, that in times of general crisis the upward spiral of war owes less to diplomatic and military imperatives than to impulses generated by the dynamic instabilities in civil and political society. Such internal driving forces make for absolute war which, being charged with ideological fervor, is fought without compromise for ill-defined and unlimited objectives. It follows that any war of this nature is not only a spur to social and technological progress but also, or above all, a forcing bed for ineradicable crimes against humanity and for historical regression.

Between 1618 and 1648 Europe was wracked by a series of wars which retroactively were named and conceptualized as the Thirty Years War. This essentially seamless conflict was freighted with the religious passions stemming from the great schism in Christianity. Although the struggle between Protestants and Catholics was nearly a century old, religious emotions remained strong and, above all, inflammable. In addition, the trans-European impulses and conduits of general crisis carried the fire of religious division into interstate conflict. Civil strife and foreign war were impossible to keep apart, with the former inviting external intervention.

The religious factor contributed significantly to the singular destructiveness and ferocity of the first Thirty Years War (the second one being the strife which tore Europe apart between 1914 and 1945). Not that this conflict was purely or primarily religious. For the leaders of the two opposing coalitions, which were not religiously homogeneous, secular objectives and religious motives were inseparable. Clearly, crowned heads and their chief ministers and generals pursued temporal goals and interests, guided by the newly formulated principles of the balance of power. Cardinal de Richelieu, Louis XIII's chief minister, was the most astute practitioner of this realpolitik. After breaking the Protestant party inside France, he took Catholic France into an alliance with Protestant Sweden in order to check the Catholic Habsburgs' bid for European hegemony. There were also instances of men of power turning religious fanaticism to political account. But overall, religion was not merely a tool or a sham. The elites and the lower orders shared a worldview which precluded separating the profane and sacred spheres in both private and public life. Doubtless there was more excitability among the masses, and the classes were not beyond exploiting it. At any rate, religion sanctioned and incited the use of extreme violence for ends that were perceived to be both sacred and profane.

During the first Thirty Years War some 1 million men were killed in action or died from battle wounds. The limited size of the mercenary armies accounts for this relatively "small" number of military casualties, particularly compared to the much larger number of civilians who lost their lives. An estimated 8 million perished from famine and disease. This figure is the more staggering since the population of the territories of the Holy Roman Empire, which were in the eye of the storm, was only about 60 million. Large areas of central Europe were laid waste by troops living off the land, looting, and running riot, partly in order to ensure their own survival. Rural areas took the brunt of the punishment. Entire villages were destroyed outright or died out when their inhabitants fled. In the 1630s well over half of the population of Brandenburg was wiped out by disease. The population of Bohemia, where the blaze started, was also cut in half, and over 80 percent of its villages and hamlets disappeared, many of their dwellers running for their lives, most of them in vain. In *Mother Courage and Her Children* Bertolt Brecht, relentless explorer of the living past, captured the fate of these forlorn refugees who crisscrossed the Continent's wasteland, desperate to stay ahead of "the Hyena of War."

Although the countryside was hardest hit, the towns and cities of the German lands were not spared, losing perhaps one-third of their population. Marburg and Munich were struck, and so was Augsburg, the home of the Fuggers. But by all accounts the destruction of Magdeburg was both unequaled and paradigmatic.

Located on the middle Elbe, Magdeburg was a major commercial center and vital strategic point in north-central Germany. It was invested by General Count Johannes Tserclaes von Tilly, one of the most effective but also most ruthless commanders on the imperial Catholic side. After sustaining considerable losses during an unexpectedly long siege, Tilly's troops finally managed to storm the city on May 10, 1631.

At the opening of a new era, in 1791, Friedrich Schiller portrayed this capture of Magdeburg with stark but also heartrending realism that remains unexcelled to this day. Poet laureate and historian of the German Enlightenment, Schiller saw through to the mechanisms of the "savage cruelty" visited upon the city and its "devoted citizens."

While he dwelled on the "brutal appetites" of the multinational troops, he also made a special point of stressing that Tilly, ignoring the scruples of several of his own officers, did nothing to restrain them once they were inside the city gates.

Here commenced a scene of horrors for which history has no language—poetry no pencil. Neither innocent childhood, nor helpless old age; neither youth, sex, rank, nor beauty, could disarm the fury of the conquerors. Wives were abused in the arms of their husbands, daughters at the feet of their parents; and the defenceless sex exposed to the double sacrifice of virtue and life. No situation, however obscure, or however sacred, escaped the rapacity of the enemy. In a single church fifty-three women were found beheaded. The Croats amused themselves with throwing children into the flames; Pappenheim's Walloons with stabbing infants at the mother's breast. . . . These horrors lasted with unabated fury, till at last the smoke and flames proved a check to the plunderers. To augment the confusion and to divert the resistance of the inhabitants, the Imperialists had, in the commencement of the assault, fired the town in several places. The wind rising rapidly, spread the flames, till the blaze became universal. Fearful, indeed, was the tumult amid clouds of smoke, heaps of dead bodies, the clash of swords, the crash of falling ruins, and streams of blood. The atmosphere glowed; and the intolerable heat forced at last even the murderers to take refuge in their camp. In less than twelve hours, this strong, populous, and flourishing city, one of the finest in Germany, was reduced to ashes, with the exception of two churches and a few houses. . . .

Scarcely had the fury of the flames abated, when the Imperialists returned to renew the pillage amid the ruins and ashes of the town. . . . On the 13th of May, Tilly himself appeared in the town, after the streets had been cleared of ashes and dead bodies. Horrible and revolting to humanity was the scene that presented itself. The living crawling from under the dead, children wandering about with heart-rending cries, calling for their parents; and infants still sucking the breasts of their lifeless mothers. More than 6,000 bodies were thrown into the Elbe to clear the streets; a much greater number had been consumed by the flames. The whole number of the slain was reckoned at not less than 30,000.

It does not detract from Schiller's timeless insight to suggest that he no more than hinted that the furor was something more than an authorized army riot.

The sack of Magdeburg was neither within the norms for the (mis)treatment of captured cities nor purely adventitious. The eruption of "ruthless barbarity" was ideologically conditioned. Magdeburg was a prominent seat of German Protestantism. It was seen as such by General Tilly, who was a staunch Catholic. It was seen in these same terms by Gustavus Adolphus (Gustavus II), an equally staunch Protestant. King of Sweden, Gustavus Adolphus was the principal foe of the Habsburgs and chief protector of Protestantism in central Europe. It was to forestall his coming to the rescue of Magdeburg that Tilly had rushed to seize the city.

Tilly and Gustavus Adolphus, each in his own way, were playing for high secular stakes. But both also were secure in their belief that God sanctioned their respective missions and consecrated their respective swords. In real as well as symbolic terms the place of the church in civil and political society remained a paramount issue for them and their supporters. The maxim *Cuius regio, eius religio* (He who owns the land determines the religion) was as much an expression of calculating statecraft as of religious intolerance. The destruction of Magdeburg was the most salient and concentrated manifestation of the physical and mental torment, especially of civilians, stemming from the interfusion of warfare and religion during the first Thirty Years War.

There is no more perceptive contemporary chronicle of this ideologically fueled physical and mental torment than the etchings of Jacques Callot, one of the greatest engravers of his time. In 1632–33, possibly under the impact of the widely known wrack of Magdeburg, Callot made two series of drawings, or a total of twenty-four plates, titled *The Miseries and Calamities of War*, which focused almost exclusively on the agony of civilians. He stood in the tradition of Bosch and Brueghel, except that there was nothing fantastic, burlesque, or macabre about Callot's graphic account of the beast in man and of hell on earth. With wrenchingly unaffected strokes he concretized and decried the outrages of the *soldatesque* of the first Thirty Years War: executions, torture, the burning of homes, pillage, rape. But Callot, unlike Schiller sixty years later, also highlighted the religious side of the fury. He depicts the burning of a church, the devastation of a monastery, the cowing of a priest, and the abuse of a nun. Himself a Catholic from the ravaged Franche-Comté, Callot fixed on the profanation of his own faith. But there was nothing sectarian about his account. This is evident from his cynical rendering of a priest brandishing a small crucifix as he climbs a ladder to reach twenty crippled bodies dangling from two branches of a cross-shaped tree. In Callot's vision Christianity's enemy brothers both embraced the same creed of holy war, a creed which was a legacy from the First Crusade.

· · ·

The idea and practice of holy war predated the great schism in Christianity. It grew out of the First Crusade of 1095 to 1099, which before long was mythologized into the positive archetype for all later variants of holy war. Heretofore, the Church had only haphazardly and unceremoniously sanctioned the exercise of violence, thereby condoning a gradual barbarization of Christianity. But this changed dramatically in 1095, when Pope Urban II summoned the faithful to go forth to free the Holy Land from Moslem misbelievers. The pontiff promised redemption to those taking the cross, and also assured them that their swords would be consecrated. Two major groups started out on the unfamiliar road to Jerusalem. One took the form of a military expedition of knights and their retainers, the other that of a popular pilgrimage.

This dual crusade sprang from dislocations within medieval society. Although most would-be soldiers of God were swept along by religious faith, they were also driven by personal motives and interests. Moreover, the crusade served to turn internal ideological stirrings and social tensions against an external enemy. There was no clear and present danger from afar, since Moslem ideas or zealots were not about to sweep over the European heartland. In any case, in an outburst of eschatological expectation and apprehension, many thousands of both true and opportunistic believers from among the higher and lower social orders answered the papal summons in several regions of western Europe.

The knights of Christ needed four years to prepare their crusade and make their way through central Europe and Asia Minor to the Holy Land. They and their vassals were accompanied by prominent clerics, who exhorted them to keep the faith. While this *militia Christi* committed many holy murders and atrocities along the way, these were negligible compared to those they perpetrated during the liberation of Jerusalem, the culmination of the First Crusade.

On entering the Holy City on July 15, 1099, the soldiers of God were seized by "divine" fury against all infidels. Even during the first day "they shed . . . [an] incredible amount of blood," putting both men and women to the "naked sword." But according to the *Gesta Francorum,* an anonymous eyewitness account, the truly "wonderful sights" were only to be seen a few days after the capture of the city.

> Some of our men (and this was merciful) cut off the heads of their enemies; others shot them with arrows, so that they fell from the towers; others tortured them longer by casting them into the flames. Piles of heads, hands, feet were to be seen in the streets of the city. It was necessary to pick one's way over the bodies of men and horses.

But these were small matters compared to what happened at the Temple of Solomon. . . . If I tell the truth [about what happened there], it will exceed your powers of belief. So let it suffice to say . . . that men rode in blood up to their knees and bridle reins.

As for the number of dead, this same witness testified that "no one knows their number except God alone," while Fulcher of Chartres, another contemporary chronicler, affirmed that the true number would never "be determined since large numbers can only be estimated." Meanwhile, the streets of Jerusalem were "filled with corpses." In order to eliminate the "great stench" and prevent an epidemic, the Christians ordered the "living Saracens . . . [to drag] the dead" outside the city gates, where they were forced to stack them in "funeral pyres" in the shape of "pyramids." Apparently, corpses were cut open in the search for gold coins and the elderly and the sick were the first to be killed.

By all accounts, an equally pitiless fate (alluded to in the quotation above) awaited the Jews of Jerusalem, many of whom had fought alongside their Moslem neighbors. Fearing the worst, they had assembled in the city's main synagogue for safety and prayer. After surrounding the Temple and blocking all exits, the servants of the Christian God set the sanctuary on fire. The Jews who were not consumed by flames were hunted down and put to death in the same spirit in which the Saracens were being slaughtered.

But this massacre of the Jews in the Holy City was neither the most characteristic nor the largest assault on Jews during the First Crusade. Whereas in Jerusalem Jews were murdered along with Moslem unbelievers, in central and eastern Europe their fate was altogether singular. Not that it remained so for long, since in due time it turned out that the Jews were merely the first of a long line of "infidels" to be persecuted inside Christian Europe. Indeed, the attack on the Jews set a disastrous precedent, depositing a fatal poison in the European psyche and imagination.

The First Crusade's popular host was the trailblazer for this internal holy war against the Jews. Although the religious and secular leaders of this sprawling legion, like those of the knightly army, were well-born, its rank and file originated among the lower, if not lowest orders of medieval society. Harkening to the magic and contagious call of Jerusalem, they set forth with little preparation and without any sense of the distances and perils of the journey ahead. Before long, the extreme rigors of an apparently endless and aimless trek led many true believers to fall under the spell of such self-appointed prophets as Peter the Hermit and Count Emicho of Leiningen, who urged that the sanctified fury and sword be turned against the Jews. Whereas the *populus* was baffled by talk of the distant Moslem infidel and the defiled Holy City, it responded to diatribes against the Jewish misbelievers in their "very midst," who were traduced as Christ-killers.

Presently, the errant popular zealots of Christ, who were the vanguard of the First Crusade, veered from their meandering course to distant Jerusalem, and instead proceeded toward nearby cities along the Rhine and Moselle rivers to massacre Jews without regard for age, sex, health, and status. This region was home to central and western Europe's culturally and economically most vibrant Jewish communities. Between May 3 and May 29, 1096, the essentially undisciplined pilgrims vented their holy rage on the Jews of Speyer, Worms, and Mainz. These were by no means the only cities whose Jewish citizens were set upon. But these three unprovoked onslaughts, which went from bad to worse, are best documented and became archetypal of the Jewish torment of the future.

In Speyer, according to the firsthand chronicle of Solomon bar Simson, "eleven holy souls" who refused baptism were murdered, although the other Jews were "saved by [the intercession of] the local bishop without defilement." The attack in Worms was much more ferocious, and local Christians were less effective or resolute in shielding their Jewish neighbors. After looting and desecrating the Torah scroll, the rampaging crusaders proceeded to commit mass murder. They "stripped [the Jews of Worms] naked, dragged them along, and cast them off, sparing only a small number whom they forcibly baptized in their profane waters." Some Jews "chose to be slain to sanctify the Name"; others "took their own lives." The death toll "was approximately eight hundred—and they were all buried naked."

The apogee of this first Church-sanctioned mass homicide of Jews within Europe (in which no Christians were killed) came during the last week of May 1096 in Mainz, just north of Worms.

> . . . Count Emicho, the oppressor of all Jews . . . showed no mercy to the aged or youths, or maidens, babes, or sucklings—not even the sick. And he made the people of the Lord like dust to be trodden underfoot, killing their young men by the sword and disemboweling their pregnant women. . . . On a single day . . . one thousand and one hundred holy souls were killed and slaughtered, babes and sucklings who had not sinned or transgressed, the souls of innocent poor people.

After noting that "no one was found to stand in the breach," bar Simson lamented, "Why did the heavens not darken and the stars not withhold their radiance, why did not the sun and moon turn dark?"

Beginning with the testimony of bar Simson and other survivors and their descendants, Jewish voices forged a memory and commemoration of the inscrutable massacre of Mainz that made it concordant with the providential history of the Jews, rooted in the Old Testament. Probably, the option of baptism never was more than marginal, since the crusaders' purpose was evidently to kill infidels, not convert them. But to make this option central to the crystallizing myth was to extol those who refused conversion and "extended their necks for slaughter and offered up their pure souls to their Father in Heaven." At the same time the torment of the Jews of Mainz was hallowed and placed within the continuum of Jewish history, it was severed from the messianic groundswell of the holy war against Islam and the unstable situation in the Rhenish cities, both of which had a decisive influence on the Jewish disaster.

But the self-projection of the victims had far less wide repercussions than that of their murderers. As one of the great political innovators of all time, Pope Urban II legitimated, consecrated, and glorified the laity's use of the sword for the defense and propagation of the faith. This is not to say that by sacralizing the sword the holy father either prescribed or foresaw the massacres of Jerusalem and Mainz. Nevertheless, his warrant was so broad as not to preclude any excesses. In addition, the pope's sanction was reinforced by the *principes* of the Crusade—noblemen, knights, bishops—who ordered or condoned the atrocities committed by primitive zealots.

Although infamous, these atrocities were epochal not so much in and of themselves as by virtue of their subsequent acceptance and representation. Neither Urban II, who died in 1099, nor any of his successors censured or proscribed them. On the contrary, instead of expressing misgivings, clerics glorified the armed pilgrimages, including the liberation of Jerusalem. They were inspired to do so by the eyewitness account of Raymond of Aguilers, who reported that the *milites Christi* had "rejoiced and exulted" to see the Holy City "filled with the blood of the unbelievers," convinced that "it was a just and splendid judgment of God." Indeed, churchmen fulfilled Aguilers' prophecy that the ides of July 1099 would "be famous in all future ages." With time, clerics and poets helped whitewash the massacres by exalting the chivalrous heroes and humble martyrs of the events triggered by Pope Urban's summons. The First Crusade became the prototype for those that followed in the twelfth and thirteenth centuries and which were similarly directed to the Near East. Because the Church made recourse to the sword meritorious and redemptive, the crusades left a deep mark on the mentality and culture of Christian

Europe. They also began to mark its politics, as the Church turned to using the sacred sword against misbelievers within Europe and increasingly did so in collaboration with civil authorities.

While the massacre at Mainz, unlike that at Jerusalem, was never glorified, it became a model for dealing with misbelievers nearer home. Now that the Church was militant and triumphant it was in no mood to tolerate the challenge posed by the Cathars, especially the Albigensians. Determined to bend to its will these dualistic Christian sects centered in southwestern France, the Holy See initially resorted to exhortation and the threat of excommunication. But it was like preaching to the winds. Finally, in 1209 Pope Innocent III, who had recently launched the Fourth Crusade against the faraway Moslems, ordered an internal crusade against the Albigensians. Those taking the cross in Europe were guaranteed the same remission of sins as those taking it to the Near East. Although this internal crusade continued off and on for twenty years, it reached its horrifying peak early on, with the sack of Béziers on July 22, 1209, about a century after the sack of Jerusalem. Under the leadership of four bishops and several scores of French counts and barons, a host of about 10,000 soldiers of Christ and 10,000 camp followers invested the city. When the citizens of Béziers refused to abjure their faith and made a stand, the fanaticized crusaders stormed the city.

Without premeditation, but also without restraint by its clerical and secular leaders, the *militia Christi*, or knights of Christ, raised a storm of death and destruction. Terrified, the populace rushed into the churches for refuge and prayer. But the holy fury knew no limits and was altogether indiscriminate. The invading zealots set fire to the church of Sainte-Madeleine, burning alive the 3,000 men, women, children, and priests who had crowded into it. In the midst of the frenzy, when asked how to tell apart true Catholics and dangerous heretics, Arnaud-Amaury, the papal legate assigned to the crusade, allegedly answered, "Kill them all, God will recognize his own." But even if this retort is apocryphal, Arnaud-Amaury's report to Pope Innocent III was authentic: "Without regard for sex and age, nearly 20,000 of these people were put to the edge of the sword." The bulk of the population was slaughtered, and much of Béziers was left in ruins. There were no official gestures of mercy, no words of sorrow.

The virulence and scale of the inland crusade abated after the sack of Béziers, largely because hearing of it was enough to terrorize most of the Languedoc. Instead, special ecclesiastic tribunals were set up to ferret out and punish heretics who refused baptism. A large but uncertain number of Cathars and other misbelievers were consequently burned at the stake. In 1233 Pope Gregory IX institutionalized this Inquisition, which was to weigh on Christian Europe and Spanish America until early modern times. It was the joint work of, on the one hand, local bishops and inquisitors appointed by Rome from among the Dominican and Franciscan orders, and, on the other hand, civil authorities who did the bidding of the Church until they managed to bring the tribunals under their own sway. In the nascent synergy of church and state, the secular agents, which were responsible for the exacerbation of the Béziers massacre, gradually gained the upper hand.

The Inquisition did not victimize the Jews until the late fifteenth century in Spain, although beginning with the massacre of thousands of Jews in cities throughout the peninsula in 1391, the Jews of Spain were under nearly constant duress. As a result, large numbers of them chose baptism. When the state-sponsored Spanish Inquisition began to persecute them, about 50,000 of Spain's 200,000 Jews were *conversos*, who were widely reviled as *marranos*, or swine. While some of these new Christians had converted voluntarily and were fully assimilated and acculturated, others had done so against their will, and many were suspected of remaining secretly faithful to Judaism. Although the state-sponsored Spanish Inquisition investigated over 150,000 cases, most of the 2,000 victims who were burned at the stake were *marranos*, all of them accused of false-heartedness in their Christian beliefs and practices. In 1492 Isabella I and Ferdinand V issued an edict expelling the Jews from Spain. About 100,000 soon crossed into Portugal for a temporary stay. Another 50,000 set sail from Spanish Mediterranean ports for North Africa, the Ottoman Empire, and Italy, where they were welcomed. Some of the refugees suffered shipwreck; others were robbed and physically assaulted during their journey. As for the *marranos*, they came under increasing pressure to become "true Christians" or get out, which many of them did. Primarily by virtue of this forced emigration, Spain became all but *judenfrei*. The expulsion of the Jews, like that of the Moors, was an act of government, marking the fusion of scepter and miter. The secular powers achieved ascendancy at the same time they became the champion and protector of the established church.

At almost this very moment a religious reform movement exploded which then developed into the great and irreparable schism between Protestantism and Catholicism. As was to be expected, the papacy and the local churches saw the incipient Protestants as heretics. The excommunication of Luther in 1520 and his refusal to yield obedience turned out to be the first step toward endless confessional struggles intertwined with civil conflicts and foreign wars.

Not only the Catholics but also the Protestants embraced the idea and practice of sanctified violence. They saw each other as irreconcilable adversaries—as infidels—to be won over or subjugated. Both considered holy war good and necessary to defend or propagate the faith. Their shared Manichaean mentality precluded compromise as they charged each other with sacralized swords and invoked the same enabling passages from the Old Testament. Had Luther and Calvin renounced and denounced the creed of sacred violence, it might have lost its potency. But both of them needed secular champions and protectors whom they felt they could trust to shoulder a divine mission. Though he was referring to self-defense at the time, Luther justified the Christian soldier who, as God's proxy, "hangs, tortures, beheads, slays, and fights."

Even if by the dawn of early modern times the institutions and rewards which had played a key role in the original crusades had receded into a distant past, the idea of the sanctity and nobility of fighting for the Lord remained deeply embedded in the European consciousness and imagination. The Church, of course, never ceased to exalt the time of the crusades as one of its finest hours. But no less important, Europe's intelligentsia and artists continually extolled the crusades as the purest and most majestic expression of Christianity. Poets, painters, sculptors, and musicians transfigured them into an epic of dramatic episodes, triumphant leaders, and heroic martyrs. The history of chivalry and the crusades being inseparable, they seized upon the mounted knight as the model soldier of Christ, thereby contributing to the ascendancy of the nobility, whose political role became ever more crucial. Although troubadours, trouvères, and minnesingers inveighed against certain abuses of the internal crusades in Europe, there was little if any criticism of the crusading idea and movement as such. Artists, not unlike churchmen, romanticized the holy warrior and his sacralized deadly weapons.

The religious and secular leaders of the sixteenth and seventeenth centuries appropriated and inflamed this collective pretense, not to say memory. As previously noted, even with the considerable tempering of fanaticism, the opposing sides in the first Thirty Years War continued to be driven by a blinding religious passion. Both Gustavus Adolphus and Tilly considered themselves invested with a mission that was at once divine and temporal, and may be said to have seen and carried themselves as latter-day crusaders.

Notwithstanding the horrors, miseries, and terrible costs of the religiously infused warfare of the Thirty Years War of the seventeenth century, the myth and lore of holy war—of crusading war—were not discredited. They persisted under the surface, to be revitalized and exploited three hundred years later, during the General Crisis and Thirty Years War of the twentieth century.

As indicated earlier, the epoch of 1618 to 1648 has important likenesses with that of 1914 to 1945. In both, the traditional foundations of Europe were shaken by a general crisis in civil and political society which was at once cause and effect of total and monstrous war. The first half of the seventeenth century had the dubious distinction of being the bloodiest and most destructive half century on record, until it was surpassed by the first half of the twentieth. Of course, there are not only profound resemblances between these two historical moments but also essential differences. One of these dissimilarities stands out above all others. Whereas the General Crisis and Thirty Years War of the seventeenth century marked the last phase of the ideological struggle between Catholicism and Protestantism, the General Crisis and Thirty Years War of the twentieth century marked the climacteric of the ideological struggle between fascism and bolshevism. To borrow and adapt an image from Jacob Burckhardt, while the first half of the seventeenth century was "bigoted," with realpolitik ascendant, the first half of the twentieth was "fanatical," and therefore distinctly more destructive and brutal. Of course, as we saw, the first Thirty Years War was anything but free of the horrors of religiously charged warfare: the sack of Magdeburg in 1631 was merely the most harrowing and dramatic evidence of its ideological fury. But this and other willful infamies were unsystematic and scattered compared to those of the second Thirty Years War.

Europe's second epoch of general crisis and war became so uniquely violent by reason of the conjunction of total war and ideological crusade in the Third Reich's eastern campaign against the Soviet Union. The Nazi drive against the Jews was embedded in this war-cum-crusade. When its eastern campaign bogged down in the late fall of 1941, Nazi Germany radicalized the conduct of the war against the Soviets and the crusade within it, fixing on the Jews for slaughter as the most hated and accessible member of the "common enemy"— "Judeobolshevism"—which they constantly invoked. In many essentials the vengeful ideological fury thus deflected against the Jews of Europe, particularly of eastern Europe, during the *Glaubenskrieg* (doctrinal war) of 1941 to 1945 paralleled the sacred fury turned against the Jews of western and central Europe during the original crusade of 1095–99 against the Moslem infidels in the Holy Land.

To contemplate the sack of Magdeburg in 1631 and the massacre of the Jews in Mainz in 1096 is to realize that neither the brutalities and miseries of the first Thirty Years War nor the Judeocide of the

First Christian Crusade were contingent on sophisticated instruments and techniques of violence. In fact, the actual deadliness of the weapons and the methods of destruction were inconsequential. What was decisive was their sacralization and their use by warriors serving a "holy" cause and prone or authorized to view and treat their enemies as less-than-human misbelievers deserving of depersonalized killing. A similar historical process was at work in the twentieth century, which saw what was in the nature of a fused second Thirty Years War and Crusade.

The two thirty years wars had several major correspondences. In terms of the international system, the issue in both cases was the bid of a major power for continental hegemony, a bid which was opposed by ideologically inconsistent military coalitions. As champions of the balance of power, Richelieu and Gustavus Adolphus were as incongruous a pair as Winston Churchill and Joseph Stalin. In one case central Europe was in the eye of a hurricane; in the other case eastern Europe was. Both times the bloodletting was enormous and there were more civilian than military casualties, "the Hyena of War" accounting for much of the suffering and horror.

As for the outcomes of the two conflicts, they also had much in common. In 1648 the checkmate of the Habsburgs' hegemonic and centralizing pretensions was translated into the continuance of Germany as a collection of over two hundred virtually autonomous territorial states whose rulers wielded authority on the principle of *Cuius regio, eius religio.* In 1945 the defeat of the drive for European mastery by a belatedly united Germany resulted in its being divided in two halves, each of which had its own inviolable civil religion.

In every other respect, however, the consequences of the second General Crisis and Thirty Years War were more far-reaching, and the watershed was more radical. In the seventeenth century Europe simultaneously reordered and enlarged its imperial reach; in the twentieth it lost its world primacy and overseas empire. Internally, in both halves of Germany and of Europe, the discontinuities in civil and political society were much greater after the Yalta-Potsdam settlement than after the Treaty of Westphalia. Throughout most of Europe the old regime was either decimated or cast off by 1945. In eastern Europe, which after 1648 had experienced major social regressions, this most recent break took the form of a thorough recasting of political, economic, and social institutions, with changes in high culture and mental structures following at a much slower pace. In central and western Europe less of the old order had persisted far into the twentieth century, but much of what survived was excised. The contrast between 1648 and 1945 was most striking in the cultural sphere: whereas the triumph of the baroque marked a reconstitution and reaffirmation of ancient and honorable artistic idioms and values consistent with essential continuities in civil and political society, the triumph of post-Impressionist modernism broke the chain of historicist traditions which had informed central and western Europe's official cultures over the past four hundred years.

The two thirty years wars have essential family resemblances even if the motor forces, costs, and outcomes of the second were more extreme than those of the first. When the "great world-historical" moment of the seventeenth century recurred three hundred years later, it was a tragedy worse than the original one. Evidently, Germany was the seedbed of the greater intensity of the cataclysm of the twentieth century. Instead of being the principal pawn and prey of the European crisis, as it had been in times past, Germany was its nerve center. As previously noted, Germany was the hub of the chronically and dynamically unstable capitalist world economy and the European balance of power. This dual centrality was all the more crucial because Germany was also saddled with more severe internal strains and stresses than any other major European power. The tensions stemming from the contemporaneousness of institutions and mentalities rooted in vastly different historical periods became particularly explosive, with the National Socialists feeding on the "pent-up rage" that was seething in many outdated and imperiled segments of civil and political society. Hitler embodied, incited, and disciplined this rage, transmuting it into an apocalyptic movement against modern times. While he drummed up mass support for Nazism among those in the middle orders of German society who were or felt themselves victims of modernization, he found his essential collaborators among members of the old elites who were moved less by political faith than by material and personal interest. With their help he forged a project in which technological and bureaucratic modernity was interwoven with a regressive purpose.

The pivotal importance of Hitler, who had no counterpart in the seventeenth century, is evidence of the peculiar intensity of Germany's internal crisis. According to Max Weber, "times of psychic, physical, economic, ethical, religious, and political distress" are the breeding ground for "natural leaders . . . of specific gifts of body and mind . . . [which are] believed to be supernatural, not accessible to everybody." In Weber's construction, to "gain and maintain" his authority a charismatic leader needed to constantly "keep proving himself" to his followers. He could do so either as a "prophet . . . performing miracles," or as a "warlord . . . performing heroic deeds."

Hitler was both prophet and warlord. He repeatedly proclaimed himself a seer with a divine mission. He was, of course, a wrathful prophet who saw the world as polarized between friend and enemy, good and evil. Though profoundly irreligious, in public he often claimed to serve the Almighty and asked for his guidance. Likewise, despite his contempt for Christianity, and particularly for its Catholic branch, Hitler styled many aspects of the Nazi movement after the Catholic Church. He purposefully adapted key elements of its nomenclature and modus operandi for his secular religion and church: hierarchy, ritual, dogma, martyrology, catechism, proscription, and index. Although systematized with bureaucratic rationality, this religious posture and profession was not mere pretense. It was intrinsic to the idea and practice of National Socialism. Until 1933 it informed the mobilization of the Nazi movement, thereafter the life and demise of the Nazi regime.

Hitler's striking diplomatic and military exploits—his "heroic deeds"—served as the "miracles" that bolstered his prophetic standing and acclaim. Conversely, his pseudoreligious conceit and zeal animated his war-making. This became most evident during the war against the Soviet Union. By naming the eastern campaign Operation Barbarossa, Hitler indicated that he saw elective affinities between Friedrich Barbarossa (Frederick I) and himself. Barbarossa was the German Emperor who in the twelfth century, in addition to setting his sights on eastern Europe, had forced his own anointment before taking the cross to the Holy Land. For Hitler to preach a crusade against the Bolshevik regime and ideology was not to mask but to sacralize his own geopolitical designs and weapons. The premeditated field orders issued to the officers and men of the Third Reich's eastern armies and security forces leave no doubt that they were sent to fight a "holy war." This is corroborated by the central role assigned to the Waffen-SS, the latter-day legion of "holy warriors" sworn to the twisted cross. In addition, the Nazis loudly proclaimed that the war against Soviet Russia was a *Glaubenskrieg* against "Judeobolshevism," which initially earned them considerable sympathy and support among conservatives, reactionaries, and fascists throughout much of the Continent.

The torment of the Jews was contingent on the course of this war-cum-crusade. As noted before, during the initial triumph of Barbarossa in the summer of 1941 the Jews were persecuted primarily as part of the "common enemy"—"Judeobolshevism." Nazi Germany did not cross the threshold to the willful and systematic mass murder of Jews until the war-cum-crusade ran aground. The impasse and ultimate failure of the imperative and vainglorious war against the Soviets in the east first tarnished and then ruined Hitler's charismatic claim as warlord. As if by reflex, the führer became more and more the enraged prophet predicting, indeed vowing, the retributive annihilation of the Jews, and warning that an irruption of bolshevism into central Europe would spell the doom of Western civilization. Hitler began to thunder forth his avenging fury and apocalyptic warnings at the same time that the leaders of the Third Reich resolved to turn the war—particularly the war against the Soviets—into a life-or-death struggle, whatever the cost. The Jewish catastrophe was forged in the crucible of this irreversible but failing *Glaubenskrieg*. This secular crusade provided the mastery of space, the corridor of time, and the climate of violence the Nazis needed to perpetrate the Judeocide.

PART ONE

CHAPTER II

THE GOLDEN AGE

It is one of the great paradoxes and cruel ironies of recent times that the most calamitous epoch in the turbulent history of the Jews of Europe followed upon or grew out of the phase of their greatest emancipation, acculturation, and assimilation. But the remarkable improvement in the condition of European Jewry did not occur in a vacuum any more than its eventual cataclysmic reversal. Rather, the prodigious upturn in Jewish fortunes began with the French Revolution and the Napoleonic Wars and progressed in tandem with the difficult and fitful advance of political democracy, economic liberalism, and social reform. Although the calendar and rhythm of change for the better differed from country to country, by 1914 Jews enjoyed full civil and political rights throughout western, central, and northern Europe.

Of course, the removal of legal and political disabilities was much easier and more complete than the elimination of deep-rooted individual, social, and institutional discrimination. Besides, there were recurrent attempts to turn back the clock of emancipation and assimilation. In particular, a new breed of conservatives—the Stöckerites in imperial Germany, Karl Lueger and Georg Ritter von Schönerer in cisleithan Austria-Hungary, and the anti-Dreyfusards in Republican France—directed much of their hatred of the modern world against the Jews. But just as the chancellors of the late Hohenzollern and Habsburg empires were fundamentally unlike Hitler, so the political anti-Semitism of the last quarter of the nineteenth century had nothing except its populist ferment in common with the systemic anti-Semitism of the Third Reich. Nor did Captain Alfred Dreyfus's spurious indictment for treason presage Vichy France's complicity in the "Final Solution" some fifty years later. Traditional conservatives, radical democrats, and mainline socialists effectively drove back the new-model anti-Semitism of the *fin de siècle*. The successful campaign to vindicate and free Dreyfus, followed by the republicanization of the French army, was symbolic of this reflux. Notwithstanding Theodor Herzl's pessimistic view of the Dreyfus affair, there is no denying that afterward the Jews entered the era of their most complete emancipation and assimilation to date, an era which lasted until the early 1930s throughout central Europe, and until the outbreak of war in 1939 in western, southern, and northern Europe. Evidently, then, there was nothing inevitable about the conversion of residual religious and cultural anti-Judaism into militant secular and political anti-Semitism. It could be contained, but increasingly only with the support of the democratic and socialist left, which was the chief rampart against the flood tides of illiberalism.

The Russian Revolution and the First World War fired the emancipation of the Jews in eastern and east-central Europe, much as the French Revolution and the Napoleonic Wars had done for their counterparts in the West. Particularly in Russia, site of Europe's last blood libel in 1911, the year 1917 saw the lifting of all anti-Jewish disabilities. Having unlocked both the ghettos and the Pale of Settlement, the Soviets proceeded to provide access to higher education as well as to careers in industry, the professions, and public service. The governors of the successor states of the defunct Romanov and Habsburg empires, followed by Rumania, eventually took some of the same steps, less under the influence of Lenin than of Woodrow Wilson.

Again, there remained a substantial residue of intense individual Judeophobia and institutional anti-Semitism, which counterrevolutionaries and reactionaries willfully exploited during the end-of-the-war crisis: the Whites capitalized on it in the Russian Civil War, the Magyar old guard in the Hungarian Civil War of 1918–19, and the Polish superpatriots in the Russo-Polish War of 1919 to 1921. Significantly, in each case far-rightists played on the tried specter of revolution, updating and invigorating it with the bogus threat of "Judeobolshevism." If contemporary Europe ever had a rehearsal for the "Final Solution," it was neither the flare-up of bloodless political anti-Semitism in imperial Germany nor the anti-Semitically infused political assassinations in the Weimar Republic, but the indiscriminate persecution and slaying of Jews during these closely entwined civil and national conflicts in the wake of the Great War in eastern Europe. However, this huge wave of political anti-Semitism receded, not to rise again until the general crisis overheated in the 1930s. Meanwhile, defeated in the Russian Civil War, prominent Whites emigrated, notably to Germany, with the bugbear of "Judeobolshevism" and the spurious *Protocols of the Elders of Zion* in their ideological baggage.

In view of the marked acceptance and advancement of the Jews in Soviet Russia and Weimar Germany, and notwithstanding the eruption of anti-Semitism during the postwar turmoil, the first three decades of the twentieth century were a time of unprecedented opportunity and freedom from oppression for the Jews of Europe. During this era legal and political enfranchisement, combined with increased access to a wider range of careers, paved the way for accelerating acculturation and assimilation. More and more Jews felt that the remaining restrictions and prejudices were fast-fading archaic vestiges, and that their children and grandchildren would soon cease to be strangers in their own lands. During these halcyon years Europe's Jewish communities lost much of their separateness, which through the ages had been partially self-chosen. The rate of religious nonobservance, voluntary conversion, and intermarriage rose sharply, particularly in big cities. At the same time, attendance at denominational heders and yeshivas declined in favor of enrollment in public schools. Likewise, judging by the ardor and valor with which Jews fought and died for their homelands during the Great War, the reality and expectation of continuing acceptance in Gentile civil and political society fostered intense patriotism.

Only a relatively small but influential group of what might be called "integral" assimilationists, most of them of great wealth or education, rejected their own cultural and religious past in their bid for complete integration. A much larger number of Jews sought full participation in the wider secular society around them without denying their heritage and compromising their identity. These "limited" assimilationists held fast to their religious and cultural traditions even as they sought to improve their economic opportunities and to encourage their sons to prepare for careers in fields other than petty commerce and manufacture. Having jettisoned distinctive ethnic speech, dress, and customs, but having not yet gained access to political society, many upwardly mobile Jews became avid consumers and patrons of Europe's dominant high culture. In fact, for them acculturation was a key strategem for gaining admission to the ruling and governing class. While breaking into Gentile culture and society, many of these assimilationists also sought to influence consistories to relax what they considered the excessive religious orthodoxy and social insularity of Jewish communities.

By respectively denying and diluting their Jewishness, the integral and limited assimilationists stood apart from the vast majority of the third major component of European Jewry, the Ostjuden, who lived in, had come from, or whose families had come from, eastern Europe. To mention them last is to risk understating their importance. At the base of the pyramid of European Jewry, the eastern Jews were by far the most numerous, the poorest, and the most sealed off. They constituted the main body of Europe's large Jewish communities, except in France and Germany. But even there they became a critical mass after 1918, with the arrival of refugees from eastern Europe. Particularly in Germany, not only Gentiles but also many Jews decried the seemingly endless flow of alien immigrants out of the congested ghettos of the geographically neighboring but culturally distant Pale.

At the time, most assimilated and assimilating Jews viewed their unacculturated eastern coreligionists with a mixture of apprehension, shame, and disdain. On the whole, the former scorned rather than valued the latter's distinctive religious, social, and cultural ways. Europeanized Jews disparaged the shtetls and ghettolike city districts of eastern Jews west of the Vistula as stale, oppressive, and dirty, and among themselves referred to their residents as *Polacken, Galizianer, die Frommen,* or "the others." Indeed, most assimilated and acculturated Jews saw the eastern Jews as flaunting archetypal traits and habits that they themselves had long since forsworn. Not a few of "the others" continued to grow untrimmed beards and side curls *(payes),* to wear black caftans and white socks, to speak Yiddish, and to ignore Christian Europe's high culture. Theirs was a fortress mentality, forged to protect their singular universe from a surrounding world they perceived as immutably hostile. Thus, the eastern Jews made little effort to breech the invisible walls of isolation and discrimination surrounding them.

Of course, the Jewish ghettos, whether inside or outside eastern Europe, were neither monolithic nor static. They harbored a growing middle class which evaded or resisted the iron grip of tradition. In addition, young men continued to leave the ghetto for work or study in cities near and far, where they were exposed to the possibility of assimilation and acculturation. With time, by eroding the viability of the petty commerce and manufacture which provided the ghetto's economic lifeblood, both capitalist and socialist modernization quickened the pace of this exodus. An ever larger number of Jews settled in urban areas whose environment accelerated the crumbling of even the hardest "cake of custom."

Although the epicenter of this century's assault on European Jewry was located in Berlin, ultimately the Jews of Germany were not as severely decimated as the Jews of eastern Europe. In large part, this was so because nearly half of Germany's Jews—250,000—managed to emigrate before the outbreak of war in September 1939, and hence before the start of the "Final Solution" two years later. But because at the outset the anti-Semitic assault of the Nazis was directed against the Jewish community in Germany, it is important to have a clear sense of its makeup and situation.

Although Poland and Soviet Russia, with 3.2 and 2.5 million Jews respectively, had by far the largest Jewish communities in Europe, Germany had the most sizable Jewish community of any of Europe's modernized nations. In 1925 there were slightly over 550,000 Jews in the Weimar Republic, or just short of 1 percent of Germany's total population. This minority was heavily urban: about 70 percent lived in cities of over 100,000, and another 15 percent in cities between 10,000 and 100,000. Berlin alone claimed about 170,000 Jews, or close to one-third of all the Jews in Germany. By virtue of their concentration in big cities, the Jews were highly visible, the more so because they tended to cluster in distinct residential sections. In addition, they had an unusual occupational structure. Few of them were wage-earning artisanal or industrial workers, and even fewer were agricultural laborers or farmers. About three-quarters of all working Jews—compared to one-quarter of all working non-Jews—earned their living in trade and commerce (including small-scale manufacture), the professions, and banking. They were heavily overrepresented in trade and commerce, especially in the consumer-goods sector, in which over half of them were self-employed, three-quarters of these as retailers. In this sector, and most particularly in textile and clothing manufacture, the majority of Jews were owner-operators or employees of small or medium-sized firms. Accordingly, Jews owned about 40 percent of Germany's wholesale textile firms and about 60 percent of all wholesale and retail clothing establishments. Their weight in retailing, notably of clothing and outerwear, was all the greater because by the late twenties Jewish department and chain stores, whose personnel was also heavily Jewish, accounted for close to 80 percent of the turnover in large-scale merchandising.

Even so, the Jews had little influence in the German economy as a whole, and they were of no great importance in Germany's powerful business elite. To be sure, they held a few commanding posts in the large-scale production of textiles and ready-to-wear, electrical equipment, and chemicals. But they were at best on the margin of heavy industry. Likewise, although the heads of a few great Jewish banking houses continued to be men of influence, notably in Berlin and Frankfurt, they were no longer as influential as the directors and top executives of large corporate financial institutions.

Publishing was the only industry in which Jewish houses were paramount. This was true in both book and newspaper publishing.

Significantly, this world of the printed word—like that of filmed images—had close ties to Weimar's unattached intelligentsia, in which Jewish journalists, literati, and artists figured prominently. These Jewish men of letters, of whom there were many, achieved the same éclat as the Jewish members of the professions. In the early 1930s at least 10 percent of all physicians and 15 percent of all lawyers and notaries were of Jewish origin. These percentages rose to over 40 percent and 50 percent in Berlin.

Evidently, the Jewish community was torn by the same *Gleichzeitigkeit des Ungleichzeitigen* (simultaneity of the unsimultaneous, or the coexistence of elements derived from vastly different historical eras) as the rest of German society: a minority were wealthy businessmen and professionals, most of them fully assimilated and even converted; a much larger stratum consisted of middle-class merchants, professionals, and literati, increasingly acculturated and secularized; and a multitude of petty bourgeois shopkeepers, wholesalers, and peddlers deeply attached to traditional Jewish culture and religion completed the picture.

This lower middle class included many *Ostjuden*. While at the turn of the century only about 7 percent of the Jews in Germany were recent immigrants from eastern Europe, by 1933 this proportion reached almost 20 percent, or 110,000, of whom fewer than 5 percent were naturalized. As a rule, these *Ostjuden*, half of whom were Polish nationals, were drawn to the big cities, until in the late twenties they formed close to 30 percent of all Jews in Berlin, over 25 percent in Munich, 60 percent in Dresden, and nearly 75 percent in Leipzig.

In these and other cities—above all in Saxony and the northwest—the *Ostjuden* were not only at the bottom of the Jewish community's social hierarchy, they were also excluded from the inner circles of most consistories. Germany's native and established Jews were disquieted by these newcomers, not least because they feared that they might arouse anti-Semitism and complicate the course of integration.

While in the cities the most recent immigrants from the east, not unlike recent arrivals from German villages and towns, lived in a ghettolike world of their own, long-established Jews generally took pains to break into Christian society. During the short life of the Weimar Republic, at least 20 percent of their offspring chose non-Jewish brides or grooms, and at most 25 percent of the children of mixed marriages were raised within the Jewish religion. The rising rate of intermarriage and conversion coincided with declining attendance at religious services and classes. Although compatible with the continuation of a Jewish cultural identity, this gradual defection from the synagogue went hand in hand with an ever more intensive acculturation and patriotism, fostered by university education. During the high noon of Weimar close to 5 percent of all university students were Jewish, and so were 5 percent of the professors. In the capital, depending on the discipline, the percentages were significantly higher.

Compared not only to the rest of Europe but to the United States as well, Weimar Germany provided Jews with considerable opportunity for political activity and public service. They had, of course, been present at the creation of the republic. Even before 1914, under the late Second Empire, some of whose diehard conservatives had either condoned or embraced political anti-Semitism, these Jewish middle classes had backed parliamentarization as advocated by left National Liberals, Progressives, and Social Democrats. Not surprisingly, therefore, during the end-of-the-war crisis they supported the removal of the autocratic monarchy in favor of a republic. In January 1919 the lion's share of the Jewish vote went to the Democratic Party, Weimar's most authentic but also ill-starred liberal-progressive party. As late as 1930 the Staatspartei, this party's successor, still held a quarter of this vote. But by then, shocked by the eruption of anti-Semitism in both the old and the new right, most Jews, even conservative Jewish businessmen and professionals, had turned to the established socialist party, the Social Democratic Party (SPD), if only for lack of alternative. Just as before 1914 the socialists had placed the democratization of the Second Empire ahead of social reform, so as of the late twenties they gave first priority to defending the embattled Weimar Republic, the essential bulwark for continuing Jewish emancipation.

Certainly, Jewish men of ideas had started to join the socialist movement well before the Great War. They became particularly active as party journalists, though a number of them also became SPD deputies in the Reichstag. Eager to topple the old regime, when the party suffered a schism in 1917, such leading Jewish parliamentarians as Eduard Bernstein, Kurt Eisner, Hugo Haase, and Rudolf Hilferding joined the new Independent Social Democratic Party (USPD), a left splinter. During the post-Armistice unrest Rosa Luxemburg, Karl Radek, and Paul Levi spearheaded the Spartacists, the nascent Communist party, and all three had Jewish origins.

There is no denying that Jewish leftists contributed their share to the radicalization of German politics. In 1918–19 they were conspicuous actors not only in Berlin but also in Munich. Following Eisner's assassination, such Jewish literati as Gustav Landauer, Erich Mühsam, and Ernst Toller helped guide the Bavarian People's Republic, headed by Eugen Leviné. The Spartacists having been curbed in the capital in January 1919, it was the turn of the Munich Commune to be crushed four months later. As for the USPD, it was moribund by midyear as well, though it recovered some strength in 1921–22. The "revolution from above" quite easily brought the "revolution from below" to heel, along with its Jewish energizers, several of whom were murdered.

Smarting from this misadventure, radical Jewish intellectuals and literati retreated from the rough-and-tumble of the political arena to the politics of radical journalism and countercultural gesture. And throughout the postwar turbulence, most left-wing Jewish politicians with experience and expertise remained loyal to the majority Social Democratic Party, to which a chastened Bernstein soon returned. The SPD continued to be open to Jews and to stand against manifest anti-Semitism throughout the Weimar era. Otto Landsberg was Friedrich Ebert's minister of justice and Hilferding served first Gustav Stresemann and then Hermann Müller as finance minister. But above all, throughout the entire period close to 10 percent of all Social Democratic deputies, 10 percent of all delegates to the SPD congresses, and 10 percent of all party members were of Jewish origin. Of the 121 socialists elected to the Reichstag in November 1932, 10 were of Jewish descent—down from 17 of 153 representatives in 1928. In addition, Jews held important positions in the party press as well as in socialist women's, student, and teacher associations. There were also quite a few Jews among the SPD's economic, financial, and legal experts. During the twenties, while the membership of the Communist Party was less than 1 percent Jewish, about 10 percent of its leaders and cadres were Jewish-born.

There were many fewer Jews in leading positions in other major parties, with the result that only 2 to 3 percent of the Reichstag deputies were of Jewish ancestry. It is worth noting, however, that this was twice to three times the ratio of Jews in the total population. Be that as it may, and irrespective of political coloration, hardly any deputies or high bureaucrats of Jewish lineage were *Glaubensjuden* (practicing Jews), advertised their Jewishness, or endorsed Zionism.

Until the onset of the Great Depression, and even down to January 1933, Weimar Germany was in the forefront of Jewish emancipation, acculturation, and assimilation. This is not to say that Germany was free of anti-Semitism. Especially in the immediate postwar years, and again after the economic crash, there was an upswing of strident Jew-baiting on the far and new right, particularly in the student fraternities. This politically orchestrated anti-Semitism capitalized on undercurrents of age-old anti-Judaism and Judeophobia that appeared to be no stronger in Germany than elsewhere in Europe. In any event, in the 1920s anti-Semitism became unusually rampant in Germany, with new populist parties and associations (Deutschnationale Volkspartei; Deutschvölkische Schutz- und Trutzbund; Deutschvölkische Freiheitspartei) making it part of their political creed. But this was so largely because both wellborn notables and *völkisch* firebrands resorted to Jew-baiting in their campaign to destabilize and topple the fragile Weimar Republic, whose legitimacy they had never accepted. For them, to vilify the "Jewish Republic" and the Jews was to attack a democratic and social reformist project destructive of the old Germany.

The profile of France's Jews was not radically different from that of Germany's. To be sure, legal emancipation had a longer life and, as shown by the defeat of the anti-Dreyfusards, a broader and deeper base of political support in France than in Germany. Moreover, as it was geographically and culturally at a greater remove from the Pale of Settlement, until the Great War the Third Republic had a smaller inflow of *Ostjuden* than the Second German Empire. In 1919 the Jewish population of France, including Alsace and Lorraine, was around 150,000, but by the outbreak of World War II it had risen to 350,000 in a population of about 40 million. This rapid and substantial growth of French Jewry was due to two waves of newcomers. The first wave consisted of refugees from the turmoil of east and east-central Europe after 1918, and it swelled the proportion of *Ostjuden* in France. After the Nazi takeover in Germany in 1933, a second wave brought fugitives from central Europe, most of them middle-class and assimilated. In addition, some 400,000 Jews stopped in France, on their way to safer havens.

In 1939 by far the largest number of Jews in France were centered in and around the French capital: 200,000 of them, or over 60 percent, lived and worked in Paris. Of the 150,000 Jews within the city limits, 45,000 were of French, especially of Alsatian stock, 15,000 were of Sephardic lineage from North Africa, and 90,000 were relatively recent arrivals. All but 5,000 of these last were from eastern and east-central Europe. Clearly, in Greater Paris the native-born Jews were heavily outnumbered by newcomers from eastern Europe, nearly all of them in straitened circumstances.

The old-guard Jews occupied the top reaches of the economic, social, and cultural hierarchy of the Jewish community. Especially in Paris, they were a world unto themselves, with more links to Christian society than to the foreign, less well-to-do, and more religious Jews of the Marais (the Jewish quarter). Among the socially prominent Jews the bankers stood out, and among them the Rothschilds. Close to a quarter of the working native Jews of Paris were lawyers, physicians, dentists, and educators. About half were active in retail and wholesale commerce, particularly in apparel, leather goods, and jewelry. Another 20 percent were manufacturers. In both commerce and manufacture long-settled Jews operated and managed firms that were larger and more favorably located than the shops of recent arrivals.

Most indigenous Jews were fully assimilated and acculturated, and, like Captain Alfred Dreyfus, wished to merge into French culture and society. In this as in most other respects they were the model for the sons and daughters of the ghetto Jews, many of whom went to the public schools of the Third Republic as the only way out of the traditional world of their fathers.

During the Great War as well as between the wars, the assimilationists were intensely patriotic. They were also good republicans, dividing their support between the traditional right and the moderate left. During the early 1930s quite a few French citizens of Jewish faith were more fearful of the far left than of the radical right, with the result that some of them actively sympathized with the Croix de Feu, an ultraconservative veterans' movement. The bulk of the Jewish *grande bourgeoisie* and business middle class, however, identified with the Fédération Républicaine, the main party of the traditional right, and the Radical Socialist Party, the bulwark of the parliamentary regime. They are also likely to have identified with Georges Mandel, a prominent ultrapatriotic deputy of Jewish descent (although he denied his origins). Mandel had first made his mark as chief assistant to Prime Minister Georges Clemenceau during the Great War. After 1934 he held several important cabinet positions and became France's would-be Churchill, loudly forewarning of the Nazi danger, but without denouncing Hitler's anti-Semitism.

As of 1936, with many French conservatives favoring the appeasement of fascism abroad as part of their bid for power at home, even fully assimilated and well-to-do Jews had to reconsider their political allegiances. Naturally, many opposed the Popular Front for threatening their class interests. They felt no less irked by the prominence of Jews in left-wing politics, charging them with feeding the flames of anti-Semitism. Though Léon Blum, the socialist leader who headed two Popular Front governments, was highly assimilated and acculturated, he openly avowed his Jewishness. Blum quite artlessly chose two Jews, André Blumel and Jules Moch, to be close assistants. His two cabinets also included not a few ministers and under secretaries of Jewish origin. In any case, disconcerted by the fascist temptation within French conservatism, as expressed in the hectoring slogan "Better Hitler than Blum," the established Jews moved left, much against their own will.

Of course, not all socially and culturally integrated Jews were quite so late and reluctant to move to the left. Large sectors of the Jewish intelligentsia and the professional middle class quite early and naturally joined the popular front against international fascism and in defense of the republican regime. Significantly, Victor Basch, a highly respected Jewish professor of philosophy at the Sorbonne, headed the prestigious League for the Rights of Man, which was in the vanguard of the antifascist mobilization.

There is no denying that in France Jews occupied pivotal and exposed positions in government as well as in mass movements of the left. Surely, this broadly accepted Jewish presence deserves as much attention as the turbulent political anti-Semitism on the far right, which was effectively contained until the fall of France in June 1940. Blum was, after all, the first self-avowed, even if fully assimilated, Jew to become prime minister in Europe, or indeed in the world.

Most French Jews who were on the left were carried there by the quest for social justice rather than for legal and political rights, which seemed secure. Most of them were neither native to France nor economically well off. Rather, they were relatively recent arrivals from eastern Europe earning a precarious living as artisans, minimanufacturers, and petty merchants in the traditional consumer-goods sector. They either brought their trades with them or acquired them in the Jewish quarters of Paris and provincial towns. Economically, the first and second generation immigrants and citizens quite easily fitted themselves into the French economy, in which small-scale manufacture and commerce were still vigorous. Ironically, although Paris had been the pioneer in large-scale retailing, the department and chain stores of the French capital were not Jewish, as they were in Germany and England, which deprived local anti-Semites of a favorite rallying cry.

At any rate, most of the Jews of eastern European origin eked out a modest and difficult living, which was undercut in times of economic adversity. Well before the Great Depression the Ostjuden turned to the socialist and Communist parties and trade unions, some of them inspired by personal experiences in the Bund, prerevolutionary Russia's large Jewish social democratic workers' party, others by memories of it. Certainly, they were not about to follow upper-class Jews in their rightist or centrist politics. Quite apart from not sharing the same material interests, France's two major Jewish communities were culturally and socially estranged. While the established Jews helped and patronized the eastern Jews with charity, the latter took pride in their rich cultural and religious heritage. Their sense of Jewish distinctness and coherence predisposed them to react intensely and instantly to the danger of the protofascist leagues at home and the Nazi danger abroad. The more prominent and acculturated Jews were much slower to apprehend the perils which threatened to engulf even them.

In England the Jews were also highly assimilated, but no more so than in Germany and France. The new political anti-Semitism of the *fin de siècle* was all but stillborn, and in the thirties Sir Oswald Mosley's fascist movement was nipped in the bud.

Nonetheless, a large residue of traditional distrust of Jews remained. Even if this age-old Judeophobia never broke to the surface, it did leave a mark on government policy in the 1930s. As it turned out, the British ruling and governing class was not put to the test: because England was never invaded and occupied, it never came face to face with Nazi officials demanding the delivery of Jews for deportation to the east. Just as British civil and political society was spared the fratricidal strife between collaborators and resisters which raged on the Continent, so the Jews of England were spared the fiery ordeal that ravaged their coreligionists across the Channel.

England had never really been in the vanguard of Jewish emancipation. Having been banished from the country in 1290, Jews were not allowed back in until the second half of the seventeenth century. The last civil and political disabilities were not removed until 1866, when a revised Parliamentary Oath Act, time and again rejected by the House of Lords, finally enabled Jewish MPs to take their seats in the House of Commons without denying their faith. This last hurdle, not unlike earlier ones, was cleared away by the Liberal Party, to which the Jews were tied. But soon economic and social considerations prompted Anglo-Jewry to move closer to the Tories.

This swing to conservatism was reinforced by a radical transformation of the Jewish community. In the mid-eighties England had only 65,000 Jews, of whom over 46,000 lived in London. Three-quarters of them were engaged in trade, commerce, and the professions, and most of them were well established and relatively well-off. But then during the next thirty years, up until 1914, the Jewish population increased nearly fivefold, to reach 300,000. At least 150,000 of the newcomers were refugees from the Russian pogroms of 1881 and the early twentieth century. Practically all these *Ostjuden* were or became artisans and petty merchants, spoke Yiddish, and were steeped in religious and cultural tradition. Close to 75,000 of them settled in the East End of London, the rest in Jewish districts in Leeds, Manchester, and other industrial cities.

Fearful that this flood of aliens would incite Judeophobia and complicate assimilation, the Anglo-Jewish establishment, working through both political parties, supported legislation to limit the entry of immigrants from eastern Europe. The established Jews kept their distance from the eastern Jews, though they did set up relief organizations to help the many paupers among them. One of their primary concerns was not to endanger their own acceptance in British society. Unlike in Germany and France, the sons of successful businessmen were slow to gain admission to the elite universities and professions. It was easier for Jewish business magnates to take the political route into the establishment. They began to obtain their share of ennoblements, and by 1906 sixteen highly Anglicized but unconverted Jews sat in the House of Commons, four of them Conservatives, the others moderate Liberals. While far from enthusiastic about a Jewish homeland in Palestine—except as a sanctified dumping ground for disconcerting Ostjuden—prominent established Jews reluctantly supported the Balfour Declaration.

The scions of Anglo-Jewry found themselves more and more embarrassed by the "East Ends," as the poorer Jewish quarters of English cities were called. Not that these kept expanding. The influx of working- and lower-class Jews from eastern Europe fell to a mere trickle between the wars. At the same time, although first- and second-generation eastern Jews continued to make the Jewish districts their place of work and business, many of them moved their homes elsewhere. The result was that the resident population of London's East End declined from 125,000 in 1900 to 85,000 in 1929, and the Jewish sections of Leeds, Manchester, and Glasgow had a similar evolution. This decline continued despite the 50,000 to 60,000 Jews who crossed the Channel in the 1930s, raising Britain's Jewish population to 385,000, and London's to 235,000. This was so because most of these new arrivals were refugees from central Europe (Germany, Austria, Czechoslovakia), which meant that they were assimilated, educated, and comfortable businessmen and professionals who had no intention of settling among ghetto dwellers.

Between the wars, and especially after 1929, England's Jewish ghettos were trapped in poverty, with the unemployment rate well above 10 percent. They were crammed with small and squalid workshops manufacturing clothing, furniture, footwear, hats, and furs. In 1932 close to 25 percent of London's Jewish male work force labored in the clothing trade, as did 50 percent of all working Jewish women. The 6,000 to 8,000 Jewish artisans making furniture accounted for half the labor force in that industry. Jews were also heavily engaged in retail and wholesale commerce. The typical firm in both manufacturing and distribution was small, which was in line with the size of firms in these two branches of the national economy as a whole. Low profitability compounded by chronic depression pushed second- and third-generation males out of modest family businesses into ordinary white-collar jobs.

Not surprisingly, the resident workers and petty traders of the East Ends, as well as those who kept close ties to them from afar, became the principal supporters of left Zionism and the Labour Party. Under their pressure the move to the left, begun during the Great War, lasted through 1945. Benefiting from the expansion of the male franchise in 1918, the poorer Jews joined Labour's uphill struggle for greater economic and social justice. They were also drawn to Labour by its call for the implementation of the Balfour Declaration, which was being criticized and sabotaged from within the ruling Conservative Party. As of the mid-twenties, Jews became increasingly active on behalf of Labour, which inherited the emancipationist aura of the dying Liberal Party.

This upswing of left Zionism and laborism in the East Ends profoundly troubled the Anglo-Jewish establishment. Forever sensitive to the risk of Jews being suspected of dual loyalty and militant leftism, they reacted by redoubling their allegiance to the Conservative Party, and in 1935 half of the Jewish MPs were still elected on the Tory ticket. By then, however, they were increasingly embarrassed by those conservative elements in and out of government whose avowed or tacit anti-Semitism predisposed them to sympathize with fascism, to press for the appeasement of Mussolini, Franco, and Hitler, and to restrict Jewish immigration to Britain and Palestine. Anglo-Jewry gradually loosened its ties to the Conservatives, particularly now that Labour had come to stand foursquare against fascism, appeasement, and the closing of Palestine. Reluctantly, English citizens of Jewish faith had to concede that just as in the nineteenth century the Liberal Party had been the chief architect of emancipation, so now Labour had emerged as the surest protector of Jews at home and abroad. Conservatives in Britain, like their counterparts on the Continent, were far less consistent, timely, and resolute opponents of fascism and anti-Semitism than the composite left.

To be sure, Winston Churchill, who succeeded Neville Chamberlain as prime minister on May 10, 1940, was a dyed-in-the-wool Conservative. Viscerally anti-Communist, Churchill had sympathized with both Mussolini and Franco, and remained unbending in imperial questions. If he finally became England's most resolute opponent of appeasement and Nazi Germany, his reasons were as much geopolitical as ideological. Paradoxically, to defeat Nazi Germany's bid for continental hegemony, he had to collaborate with the Labour Party at home and the Soviet Union abroad, both of which he detested. Above all, Churchill had to make Clement Atlee, the Labour leader, his deputy premier in order to mobilize the homefront for a war that, despite himself, assumed an economically and socially progressive character. The Jews of England contributed, disproportionately, to the popular landslide that in 1945 swept Churchill and the Tories from power in favor of Labour. Of the fifty-nine Jewish candidates who stood for election then, twenty-eight were returned, and among these there was not a single Conservative.

Italy eventually, in 1943, did have to bend to the will of Nazi Germany, and the rearguard of Italian fascism did become complicit in the deportation of Jews from Rome. Until then, however, the Jews of Italy were perhaps the most accepted and assimilated in the world, even during much of the fascist regime. Indeed, within about two decades in the mid-nineteenth century, Italy had changed from being the least to the most hospitable environment for Jews: the first step was the emancipation of the Jews of Rome in 1848, the last the removal of all remaining disabilities in 1870. Clearly, Jewish emancipation proceeded in conjunction with the liberation, unification, and liberalization of Italy.

Having lived among Italians since antiquity and being fully assimilated, the Jews had relatively little difficulty finding acceptance. In Italy, unlike in other European countries, there were few differences of language, culture, or tradition, aside from religious nonconformity, to set them apart. The Jews who had fled to Italy from Germany and Spain in early modern times had long since been absorbed. In addition, the Jewish trek out of eastern Europe after 1880 had bypassed Italy almost completely, with the result that there was no influx of Ostjuden to disrupt the homogeneity, assimilation, and social ascent of Italian Jews, who never numbered more than 40,000. Clearly, Italy offered little fertile ground for the growth of the new political anti-Semitism of the late nineteenth century.

By then Jews had long since started to make their way into the Italian establishment. In 1894, 15 Jews sat in the Chamber of Deputies, though that number was down to 9 in 1921. That same year 19 of the Senate's 350 members were of Jewish descent, a sign of the favor of the Crown, which appointed the members of Italy's upper house. Prewar Italy also had two prime ministers of Jewish origin. Luigi Luzzatti, a prominent economist and a parliamentary deputy from 1870 to 1914, served repeatedly as finance minister before becoming prime minister in 1910, and concluded his distinguished career as a senator. Sidney Sonnino, for his part, had two short terms as premier in 1906 and again in 1909–10, prior to becoming foreign minister from 1915 to 1919, when he fought for maximum territorial gains for Italy.

It is worth noting that, although of Jewish descent, Luzzatti and Sonnino were not observant Jews. While Luzzatti prided himself on being a freethinker, he made no secret of his having been born into a Jewish family. He stood squarely against religious bigotry, and whenever denounced for his Jewishness, Luzzatti, with his head held high, proudly asserted his origins. Sonnino, half-Jewish but raised as a Protestant, was rather less forthright about his background, and less inclined to do battle for mutual tolerance. But perhaps he was more typical than Luzzatti of the other assimilated Jews who occupied high positions in Italy's political society early in this century: Leone Wollemborg, minister of finance from 1900 to 1903; General Giuseppe Ottolenghi, minister of war in 1902 and 1903; and Giacomo Malvano, the permanent under secretary of the Foreign Ministry. All of these were liberal and flexible conservatives in the age of Giovanni Giolitti's cooptive reformism, except for Sonnino, who became a rigid conservative in both domestic and foreign affairs. Giuseppi Emanuele Modigliani and Claudio Treves, the two Jewish leaders of Italy's socialist movement, were reformists or revisionists, not revolutionaries. They, too, had fully blended into their milieu, as had the many Jewish members of the professions, the intelligentsia, and the academic community.

Significantly, while anti-Semitism became an important component of the counterrevolution in most of Europe, this was not the case in Italy, the cradle of fascism. To be sure, from 1917 to 1919 Mussolini repeatedly denounced the Jews for their involvement in the Bolshevik revolution in Russia. But he soon stopped ringing the tocsin of "Judeobolshevism," probably because he doubted its usefulness in Italy and out of regard for the Jews in his entourage. While Jews of liberal and socialist persuasion were hostile to fascism, those with conservative convictions and economic interests supported Mussolini for his supernationalism and anti-Communism. Accordingly, there were five or six Jews in the vanguard of Italian fascism, three of the early martyrs of Mussolini's countermovement were Jewish, and there were some early Jewish paymasters as well. Over two hundred Jews are said to have participated in the March on Rome, and easily three times that number were registered party members soon thereafter. Aldo Finzi, a Jew, became under secretary of the interior in Mussolini's first cabinet. In July 1932 il Duce made Guido Jung, another Jew, his minister of finance, thereby also raising him into the Grand Council. Although Jung lost his cabinet post in 1935, he served in the Chamber of Deputies until 1938, when he retired to his native Sicily. Gino Arias, a Jewish lawyer, wrote for *Il Popolo d'Italia*, the main party newspaper, and a number of military officers of Jewish origin served in important command positions, some of them in the Abyssinian campaign and the Spanish Civil War. It was not until 1938, when the government issued the Law for the Defense of the Race as well as a series of anti-Semitic decrees, that Jews began to be systematically barred and removed from high public office. But until the fall of 1943, when the Germans took over, none was put in prison, deported, or killed.

In civil society, despite certain exclusionary measures, Jews remained unmolested up to that same moment. They could keep their posts in universities and academies and were free to practice the professions. Like many Gentile Italians, Jews in fact benefited from the industrial growth stimulated by Mussolini's diversionary and imperialist military ventures.

By and large, especially considering the importance of Rome's alliance with Nazi Germany, Mussolini's attitude toward Italian Jews remained relatively benign. Ignoring his own hard-liners, the duce left the exit doors wide open, and his military and civil administrators in annexed and occupied territories made a point of shielding both indigenous and foreign Jews.

While the Great War had a progressive impact on the condition of Jews throughout central, western, and southern Europe, the same was not the case in eastern and east-central Europe. In fact, from the perspective of the recent history of European Jewry, the conflict of 1914–18 divided this ill-starred region of the Continent into two radically separate zones. One zone comprised Poland, Rumania, and Hungary; the other, Russia.

While reborn Poland and greater Rumania acquired large numbers of unwanted Jews with the territories that they reclaimed or acquired from their neighbors after World War One, newly independent but truncated Hungary lost many of its unvalued Jews along with the lands that it was forced to cede. These three nations, combined with the three Baltic republics severed from Russia—Lithuania, Latvia, Estonia—contained over 4 million Jews. Between the wars the vast majority of these Jews remained largely segregated and unacculturated, as well as subject to the vicissitudes of chronically ailing economies. Although legally emancipated, they feared that the authoritarian governments and unreconstructed ruling and governing classes of their homelands would backslide at the first sign of crisis. Their fears were borne out in the 1930s, once mounting domestic and international strains sparked a resurgence of anti-Semitism in regimes increasingly susceptible to fascism. Accordingly, the Jews of Europe's most unstable and perilous geopolitical region were scourged by a blend of traditional Judeophobia and new political anti-Semitism before becoming the prime victims of Nazi Germany's murderous fury.

In the second zone of eastern Europe, conditions were radically different. The Russian Revolution brought with it the instant emancipation of what until 1917 had been Europe's largest and most oppressed Jewish population. With the loss of the Baltic, Polish, and Bessarabian provinces, Russia's Jewish population was reduced from over 5.2 million to 2.7 million, which still left the Soviet Union with the Continent's second-largest Jewish community, immediately after Poland. Following the removal of all legal disabilities, the integration of the Jews of Russia proceeded in conjunction with the general transformation of political and civil society, with the result that within a quarter century the level of assimilation and acculturation approached that of the Jews of central and western Europe. Of course, because of the Bolsheviks' frontal assault on all organized religion, this breakneck integration entailed a more rapid crumbling of the religious foundations of Jewish culture in Soviet Russia than in any other country.

Russia's provisional government, under Alexander Kerensky, took the first essential step toward Jewish emancipation by proclaiming the liberation of all minorities. A decree dated April 2, 1917, repealed "all restrictions imposed upon the rights of Russian citizens by legislative acts . . . based upon their adherence to a particular religious faith, religious sect, or nationality." After their seizure of power the Bolsheviks continued in this same vein. On November 15, 1917, at Lenin's urging, the Council of People's Commissars reaffirmed and specified the abolition of all inequalities based on religion and nationality. By July of the following year, with the Whites playing on age-old animosities against the Jews to rally popular support for the counterrevolution, Lenin signed a decree calling on "all the Soviets to adopt firm measures in order to uproot the anti-Semitic movement" and to outlaw "pogromists and those who incite pogroms by their agitation." To be sure, it would take more than an official ukase backed with penalties to eradicate deeply ingrained anti-Jewish prejudices, notably in the towns and villages of the Ukraine and Belorussia. Still, the Bolshevik regime did proscribe public anti-Semitic speech and agitation, and the improved status of Jews was one of the most striking accomplishments of the Russian Revolution.

Early in the Civil War several Red Army units apparently victimized Jews in the Ukraine. But such incidents seem to have been the exception, and ceased altogether once the High Command imposed its authority as part of the consolidation of power in Soviet-controlled territories. In any case, the top political and military leaders of the fragile Bolshevik regime firmly condemned rather than condoned or encouraged anti-Jewish outbursts, whether military or civilian.

By contrast, the chiefs of the Ukrainian nationalists and the Whites either inflamed the anti-Jewish feelings of their troops and followers, or else failed to curb them. Certainly, Simon Petlura, the Ukrainian hetman, did little to check the pogroms and anti-Jewish army riots that swept the provinces under his control in 1918–20. Admittedly, General Anton Denikin, the commander in chief of the volunteer armies in the south, sought to bridle his *enragés*. He did so primarily to placate Woodrow Wilson and Lloyd George, who were said to make additional Allied aid conditional on self-restraint in the anti-Bolshevik camp. But just as Denikin claimed to be unable to keep large landowners from seizing back their lands from peasants, so he appeared powerless to stop his officers and men from perpetrating atrocities against Jews. In Siberia, meanwhile, Admiral Alexander Kolchak, the nominal supreme ruler of Russia, remained an undisguised ideological warrior who publicly endorsed the *Protocols of the Elders of Zion*. On the whole, the Whites presented their struggle to restore the old regime and the late empire as a selfless crusade against Jewish, godless, and barbaric communism. Members of the old ruling and governing classes, including high Russian Orthodox clerics, pressed this cause at the headquarters and in the outlying precincts of the counterrevolution.

In the Russian Civil War—as in all civil wars—fanaticism and ruthlessness were characteristic of *both* sides. But the Ukrainian anti-Bolsheviks and the Whites easily surpassed the Reds in brutalizing and slaughtering innocent civilians, and these included a disproportionately large number of Jews. In 1918–19 over 1,200 Jews were fatally assaulted in the Ukraine alone, and these transgressions continued in 1920, though at a reduced pace. The Jews were also victimized by the Polish armies, notably in Belorussia, during the Polish advance into Russia that was part of the Allied intervention in support of the Whites. According to the best and most conservative estimates, between 30,000 and 50,000 Jews, nearly all males, were slain in these pogroms and army riots. Easily that many again eventually died of injuries. All this time countless others suffered extreme material and psychological damage. Most of this destruction was centered in the former Pale of Settlement, which was destined to become the principal locale for the "Final Solution" some twenty years later.

Jews played an active role in the composite reformist and revolutionary movement that broke to the surface once military overexertion and defeat cracked the foundations of the tsarist regime. In particular, they figured prominently among the leaders not only of the Bolshevik Party but also of the Menshevik and Social Revolutionary parties. The champions of the old order seized upon this fact to denounce the revolution as a Jewish-inspired and directed plot.

Although Jews played a significant role in the leadership of the opposition parties, they provided little of the social base for revolt. Many of the prominent Jewish radicals had turned their back on the culture and language of their native milieu, which probably made it more difficult for them to rally "their" people. Besides, the economic and social program of the left-wing parties was not designed to appeal to the bulk of Russian Jewry, which was neither proletarian nor peasant, but lower-middle-class. Certainly, before 1917–18, few Jews joined or supported the Mensheviks and Social Revolutionaries, let alone the Bolsheviks.

To the extent that Jewish artisans and workers engaged in radical political and syndical action, they did so primarily through the Bund. Closely tied to the Menshevik Party, the Bund stood for a social democratic society with equal rights and cultural autonomy for Jews. In late 1917 the Bund counted well over 30,000 members, making it perhaps Russia's largest left-wing political organization. Like the leaders of the other radical opposition parties, most leaders of the Bund opposed the Bolshevik seizure of power not only because they feared a counterrevolutionary backlash but also because they disagreed with Lenin's domestic program and policies.

Actually, instead of supporting the left, most politically conscious Russian Jews were drawn to Zionist and Orthodox Jewish organizations, which were socially and culturally conservative. Many also backed the Cadets, or Constitutional Democrats, who constituted the core of the loyal democratic opposition to the autocracy.

It was not until after the start of the Civil War and the Allied intervention on the side of the Whites that Jews of all classes and persuasions began to rally around the beleaguered Bolshevik regime. They did so for fear that the defeat and overthrow of the Soviets would bring on the restoration of an *ancien régime* certain to revoke the edict of Jewish emancipation and to condone, if not sponsor, pogroms. Indeed, it took the anti-Jewish massacres and excesses of the White Guards, the Ukrainians, and the Poles to swing the Jews behind Lenin and Trotsky. This was particularly the case in the Ukraine and Belorussia, where young Bundists rushed to enlist in the Red Army, thereby forcing the hand of their leaders.

As previously noted, the contraction of Russia's western borders reduced Russia's Jewish population from 5.2 million to 2.7 million. But except for this numerical decrease and the economic hardships of the war and revolution, the condition of the Jews of Russia remained unchanged until after the Civil War and Allied intervention, when it improved radically and quickly.

In 1914, while the Jews accounted for slightly over 4 percent of Russia's total population of 130 million, 90 percent of them were concentrated in the fifteen European provinces of the Pale of Settlement stretching from the Black Sea to the Baltic coast. While they constituted about 11 percent of the total population of this Pale, which was heavily rural, they made up close to 40 percent of its urban population. At most, 3 percent of the Jewish labor force worked in agriculture, compared to over 30 percent in petty commerce. Jews were above all ensconced in traditional manufacture. Of the close to 660,000 Jewish laboring men in the Pale, only about 10 percent were factory workers, while most of the remaining 90 percent were artisans in small and technologically outdated workshops. Nearly all firms were owner-operated with the help of one or two apprentices.

The bulk of Russian Jewry was lower-middle-class, concentrated in petty manufacture and trade primarily for and within the Jewish community, much of it impoverished. Although the great emigration of the prewar decades alleviated the stress of daily life, about 30 percent of Russian Jews received relief from Jewish welfare agencies. Over 95 percent spoke Yiddish and lived in cloistered communities whose organic culture was half religious and half secular.

Capitalist modernization began to erode the economic viability and cultural self-containment of these communities well before the Great War. More and more young Jews learned Russian, acquired new skills, and either looked or stepped beyond the Pale as they sought to fashion less impoverished and sectarian lives for themselves. Still, it was not until the Bolshevik regime quickened the pace of state-controlled modernization that the life of Russian Jewry began to be strikingly transformed. As of 1921 the push and pull of rapid economic growth and diversification hastened the "normalization" of the Jewish communities in Belorussia and the Ukraine to the east of the new Poland. With the end of ethnic discrimination Jews took jobs in factories, joined agricultural communes, and began to work in the rapidly expanding state apparatus as technicians, engineers, administrators, doctors, and academics. Though at the price of political compliance, many Jews of petty bourgeois and working-class origin, along with scores of non-Jewish Russians of similar background, applied for positions formerly closed to them, eager to improve their economic situation as well as to enhance their geographic and social mobility.

From 1926 to 1939 the Jewish population rose from 2.7 million to slightly over 3 million, less by virtue of a high birth rate than a rapidly falling infant-mortality rate. During the same fifteen years, except for a momentary upturn, the number of Jews on the land remained stable. Despite the efforts of the Commission for the Rural Settlement of Jewish Toilers, less than 6 percent of all Jews made their living from agriculture. But in most other respects the Jewish occupational structure was radically changed. The number of petty shopkeepers and peddlers rapidly declined. Although 15 to 20 percent of all working Jews were still self-employed artisans, by the late 1930s many of them belonged to cooperatives. About 70 percent of all gainfully employed Jews now earned wages and salaries, half of them as skilled workers, technicians, and managers in the fast-growing industrial sector. Overall, the percentage of employed Jews who were handworkers remained roughly unchanged since before 1914 at 20 percent. By comparison, the proportion of Jews working in white-collar positions rose from 7 to over 37 percent, and that of Jews in the professions from 3 to nearly 13 percent.

This prodigious transformation of the Jewish work force was closely related to the restaffing and expansion of the state apparatus, as well as to the development of party agencies. Having proven their reliability and usefulness during the Civil War, and with the Soviets determined to promote their "normalization," Jews were hired to fill many of the government vacancies created when incumbent officials resigned, went into exile, or were purged. In addition to filling this vacuum, Jews studied to qualify for the countless openings in the burgeoning state and party apparatus. As of the late twenties, close to 8 percent of all government employees were Jewish. A disproportionate number of Jews came to hold posts in the secret police and to serve as political commissars in the armed services. They not only occupied lowly official jobs but were also appointed to high-level and conspicuous positions which called for unimpeachable political loyalty, if not party membership.

This profound vocational mutation fostered both geographic and social mobility. By 1939 over 1 million Jews, or easily one-third of the total, lived outside the former Pale. The overwhelming majority of Soviet Jews became city rather than shtetl dwellers. A full 40 percent were concentrated in six major cities, where they lived not in separate Jewish districts but in integrated neighborhoods.

The Jews who moved ahead professionally and moved out of the former Pale were also in the vanguard of assimilation and acculturation. Between 1926 and 1939 the proportion of Russian Jews declaring Yiddish to be their first language was reported to have fallen from 72 to 41 percent. At the same time, mixed unions soared to over 15 percent of all Jewish marriages in the big cities within the former Pale, and to 25 percent outside. Russification and Sovietization were particularly pronounced among Jews going to universities, who made up between 13 and 15 percent of the student body. About 45 percent of all medical students in the Ukraine and Belorussia were Jewish, as were 11 percent in the Russian Republic. Between the wars Jewish enrollments kept rising in both absolute and relative numbers not only at universities but also in higher technical and vocational schools.

The integration of Russian Jews was driven forward by the push of chronic poverty intensified by war, revolution, and civil war, and by the pull of the unexpected opportunities opened up by the emancipation of 1917. In turn, the Soviet government channeled the process along lines compatible with its inchoate revolutionary project. In early 1918 it set up the Yevsektsia to create and direct special sections for Jewish affairs inside major state and party organs. Staffed by Jews of Bolshevik persuasion, these sections had a triple assignment: to undermine, if not destroy, all traditional loyalties, institutions, and conventions; to foster support, not to say zeal, for the Bolshevik regime and purpose; and to promote the fundamental reshaping of Russian Jewry.

Yevsektsia's Jewish activists were divided between those favoring the wholesale assimilation of Jews into Soviet Russian life and those advocating the development of a separate Jewish culture without religious moorings. At the outset, however, both factions were resolved to press the new regime's general drive against all centers and institutions of non- and anti-Bolshevik power within the Jewish world. In the noneconomic sphere the first and easiest task was to help close down Jewish political parties and organizations. This instant operation was followed by the much more difficult and long-term war of attrition against organized religion and religiously infused cultural activities, especially in the provinces. Yevsektsia's sections forced the closing of synagogues, heders, yeshivas, and voluntary associations. This drive to choke off religious life was combined with the promotion of a profane Yiddish subculture divested of its collective mneme and the Hebrew language.

During the 1920s this secularizing enterprise made some headway, as measured by the growing number of Yiddish schools, publications, and performing ensembles. But by the late twenties, the push to create a genuinely autonomous and thoroughly secularized Yiddish culture was exhausted. Backed by the government, the assimilation-ists had gained the upper hand over the autonomists in the Yevsektsia sections, with the result that the new Yiddish establishments increas-ingly became agents for the regime's depluralizing educational and cultural programs. This shift was justified and facilitated by the fact that rather than enroll their children in Yiddish schools, more and more Jewish parents chose to send them to regular schools with a view to improving their life chances. The religious Jews alone stood apart, rejecting both the assimilationist and the autonomist nostrums.

At the end of the decade the Soviets began to intensify their strangulation of Jewish nonconformity along with that of all other religions and national minorities. They now used administrative, fis-cal, and police measures to curtail religious training, worship in syna-gogues, and Hebrew instruction. There is no denying the mounting official pressure for compliance and conformity. Even so, except for the use of coercion, the religious and cultural de-Judaization of Soviet Jewry, like its occupational and social transformation, was part of the press for Jewish "normalization" which was common to all of Europe.

Certainly, whatever the Bolshevik proscriptions and compulsions, they were animated by militant materialism rather than anti-Semi-tism. No steps were taken to reduce the very considerable presence of Jews in state and party. As previously noted, Jews held a dispropor-tionate number of government posts at all levels. Starting in 1917, they played an equally considerable role in the Bolshevik Party. In August of that year six out of the twenty-one members of the Central Committee were Jewish: Kamenev, Sokolnikov, Trotsky, Uritsky, Zinoviev, and Sverdlov. Until 1926 Zinoviev was head of the Comin-tern and Trotsky remained one of the regime's strongmen, bidding for first place. Between the early twenties and the late thirties Jews accounted for between 4 and 5 percent of the party membership, and they were no less well represented in the party apparatus and in key organs of state.

During the years 1926 through 1929 Trotsky was, of course, driven first from the Central Committee, then from the Politburo, and finally from the country as well. But anti-Semitism was at best inciden-tal to his fall, which was occasioned by the struggle for supremacy within the party. Kamenev and Zinoviev, who sided with Trotsky against Stalin, deserted the former in good time and managed to persevere until 1936, when they were liquidated in the political purge. Hundreds of Jewish officers and political commissars of the Red Army perished in the great military purge of 1937–38, which decimated the Soviet officer corps and consumed at least 30,000 lives. Among the Jewish victims were the chief of the army's political directorate, the commander of the military district of Leningrad, and the chief of civil defense. But while anti-Jewish prejudice may well have entered into the selection of Jews to be killed in the bloody purges and to be removed from important posts in state and party, Stalin's terror was not directed specifically, principally, or disproportionately against Jews. It was a measure of the sweeping forced-draft change in the condition of Soviet Jewry that by the mid-thirties about 4 percent of the officer corps and 8 percent of the political commissars were of Jewish ancestry. The purges neither significantly changed the Jewish presence in the Red Army nor stopped the promotion of Jews to high-ranking positions. Similarly, Stalin's dismissal, in May 1939, of Maxim Litvinov, the Jewish commissar of foreign affairs, was a maneuver in world politics and did not presage an anti-Jewish purge of the Foreign Office and the diplomatic service. Indeed, the Jews retained their historically unprecedented place in Russia's bureaucracy and armed services, and also their unexceptional position in the Bolshevik Party. This was in stark contrast with the acute deterioration of the condition of Jews in eastern, east-central, and central Europe.

CHAPTER III

THE EAST EUROPEAN
RIMLAND

During the General Crisis and Thirty Years War of the twentieth century, the Jews of east-central Europe suffered a fate of unique cruelty in terms of both Jewish and world history. The condition of these eastern Jews was distinctly less favorable and less affected by modern reforms than that of the Jews of western and central Europe and also, after 1917, than that of the Jews of the Soviet Union. Between the wars Soviet Jewry achieved parity with, and in some respects surpassed, the Jews of central and western Europe in acculturation and assimilation. To be sure, this forced-draft integration, which was fueled by a massive economic and professional restructuring, was accompanied by a massive erosion of religious and cultural Judaism. Even so, during the interwar years, and increasingly during the 1930s, the steady improvement in the condition of Soviet Jewry must have impressed the Jews of east-central Europe, whose situation remained precarious by comparison. Imperiled by economic deterioration and fascist anti-Semitism, even Orthodox and traditional eastern Jews, who intended to preserve their religious and cultural heritage, could not close their eyes to developments in atheistic Russia. As of the mid-1930s the situation of east-central European Jews became uncommonly precarious because the governments of their host countries reverted to active illiberalism and because they were located in a strategic zone which became the principal point of friction between Nazi Germany and Soviet Russia.

In east-central Europe, as in Germany, the fate of the Jews was neither predestined nor unilinear. Starting in 1917, the fall of the Romanov, Habsburg, and Hohenzollern empires brought a distinct relaxation of both official and informal discrimination. At the same time, both the example of the Russian Revolution and the support of Woodrow Wilson for self-determination emboldened the champions of reform and liberalization in a region burdened with intense national, ethnic, and religious antagonisms. To be sure, in several places and circumstances Jewish communities suffered disproportionately during the end-of-the-war crisis. Jews were especially at risk in regions where struggles between progressive and conservative social forces intersected with diplomatic and military conflicts over national borders. In particular, conservatives charged Jews with national disloyalty to advance their own political cause. But Jews were most in danger wherever social and national conflicts were, in addition, tied to the ideologically charged drive to contain Bolshevism.

Even so, after considerable suffering in the end-of-the-war crisis, the Jews gained their civil and political rights in renascent Poland and Lithuania, as well as in newborn Latvia and Estonia. Similarly, by 1923 the Rumanian government emancipated its Jews, including the Jews in its newly acquired territories. Although Jews had long since secured their civic rights and individual freedoms in the lands of the defunct Dual Monarchy, these liberties were enlarged in all the successor states. Between the wars the Jews of east-central Europe benefited from legal emancipation as well as from a lessening of informal and customary discrimination. Naturally, the apogee of this advance came during Europe's brief moment of relative economic, political, and diplomatic stability, which in the second half of the 1920s favored far-ranging nonconformity and tolerance. At all times the improvement of the Jewish condition was contingent on fragile domestic compromise and international tranquility. In the event, this improvement fell considerably short of the hopes inspired by Lenin's revolutionary catechism and Wilson's progressivist gospel. As if in anticipation, the Balfour Declaration, which was forged during the same world-historical turning point as the manifestos of Lenin and Wilson, became a kind of insurance against the possible miscarriage of this overdue emancipation of eastern Jewry.

Three characteristics of the new and reborn nations of east and east-central Europe account for their halting and unsteady emancipationist course: the superannuation of their civil and political societies; the vulnerability of their international position; and the distinctiveness of most of their large Jewish populations. Any one of these three characteristics by itself would not have been fatal. But the combination of all three created insuperable obstacles to the emancipation and assimilation of the millions of Jews trapped in the perilous east European rimland.

Along with the countries of the Iberian Peninsula, the countries of this rimland remained prime bastions of Europe's fading old order, rooted in preindustrial economies. Their ruling classes were dominated by landed nobles and gentrified middle classes; their governing classes by civil and military service nobilities; their foreign-policy establishments by titled diplomats and political generals; and their hegemonic institutions (churches, universities, academies, museums) by traditional mandarins. As for their political societies, they were essentially authoritarian.

Economically and socially, the lands stretching from the Baltic to the Balkans and separating Russia from central Europe were thoroughly "unmodern." Except for the Bohemian-Moravian half of Czechoslovakia and the disputed Silesian province of Poland, this deep and strategic buffer zone was predominantly agricultural. It was overpopulated, with an impoverished, underemployed, and inefficient peasantry, large segments of which were illiterate. During the interwar years old ruling classes all but blocked land reform, leaving smallholders and agricultural workers at the mercy of landlords and large estate owners. In Poland, Rumania, and Hungary, as well as in the Baltic and Balkan states, between 75 and 80 percent of the population continued to live in villages and rural towns. Cities, factories, and mines were like small clearings in vast agrarian domains. Even as late as 1938 the eastern rimland produced barely 8 percent of the industrial output of non-Communist Europe, Czechoslovakia by itself accounting for one-third of this. Not surprisingly, in these unchanging civil societies landed, bureaucratic, and ecclesiastic notables were dominant in the ruling classes. Of course, the old elites needed and used the economic services of the bourgeoisie, in which Jews figured prominently. But they were also careful to keep the members of this claimant class, which craved social acceptance, out of the innermost establishment.

The political societies and governing classes of east-central Europe were also of another time. Monarchy was the dominant state form. Czechoslovakia and Poland were the only republics south of the Baltic, and Poland was run by a military caste. Admittedly, the kings of Rumania, Bulgaria, Yugoslavia, and Greece were not crowned despots. Nonetheless, as *kings in politics* they wielded enormous power by both law and common practice. The same was true of the regent of Hungary: Admiral Miklós Horthy sought to disguise his nation's want of a dynasty and a navy by riding a white charger, presiding over a vast gentry, and reinvigorating a dormant dueling code. At any rate, the heads of state of east-central Europe commanded their armies, packed their upper chambers, swayed their civil bureaucracies, and changed their chief ministers almost at will.

Of course, neither kings nor officers governed by themselves. They were pivots of small political classes or oligarchies drawn from military and civil-service castes and connected to longstanding social and religious establishments. As in all such old regimes, the bourgeoisie cut an even smaller figure in the governing than the ruling classes—in political than in civil society. In east-central Europe the upper middle class of business and the professions was particularly powerless because the Jews, who were prominent in its ranks, were all but debarred from the political arena, including from government service.

Although the governing elites of these nations tolerated a fair degree of party politics and parliamentary debate in times of normalcy, they were quick to restrict democratic freedoms in times of stress. In fact, from the outset they were open to the fascist temptation, taking Mussolini as their model. To be sure, as dyed-in-the-wool conservatives they distrusted the duce's populism, not least his passion for the politics of the piazza. They, for their part, managed to seize and solidify power in traditional ways: confident of the army and the police, they saw no need to activate the plebs in the streets. Even so, they admired Mussolini for fusing the appeals of supernationalism and antibolshevism. They were no less impressed that after blackmailing Italy's governing and ruling classes into investing him with power, Mussolini made his peace with them. Although he left the monarchy, the army, the bureaucracy, and the church essentially intact, Mussolini proceeded to smash parliament, political parties, and trade unions. Until the early 1930s, the traditional conservatives of eastern Europe were distantly respectful of the fascist experiment in Italy even as they nervously watched their own critics on the far right, who were forging political formulas which were both defiantly populist and fiercely anti-Semitic.

The postwar territorial settlement of eastern and east-central Europe did not eliminate age-old linguistic, cultural, and religious antagonisms. On the contrary, these discords fueled an epidemic of international conflicts that sharpened the illiberal bent of the old regimes. Between 1917 and 1921 the borders of all countries in the region were shaped or reshaped with territories carved out of four prostrate empires. The Austro-Hungarian and Turkish empires disappeared altogether, while the deimperialization of Russia and Germany was partial and temporary. The overall effect was a major dislocation and vacuum in the international system. On the one hand, this great unsettlement facilitated the generous foundation of Czechoslovakia and Yugoslavia, the overexpanded rebirth of Poland, and the inordinate aggrandizement of Rumania. On the other hand, it allowed for the drastic cutback of Hungary and Turkey, as well as Bulgaria, leaving all three dissatisfied with their reduced frontiers.

Although the principles of self-determination and ethnic equity supposedly guided the drawing and redrawing of borders, in the final analysis the new political map of east-central Europe bore the imprint of the interests and preoccupations of the major victors of the Great War. No doubt, the Big Four meant to shackle Germany, which despite its military defeat and political turmoil remained the Continent's most potent power. But their resolve to curb and punish Germany was tempered by their concern for the stability of the fledgling Weimar Republic. The new governors in Berlin became expert not only at frightening the victors with the specter of revolution in central Europe but also at impressing them with the importance of Germany, the pivotal *Land der Mitte,* for the containment of both the Soviet Union and bolshevism. Starting with the Paris Peace Conference, this quarantining of the Russian Revolution became the principal obsession of non-Communist Europe.

In particular, the leaders of Poland and Rumania, for their own domestic reasons, cunningly capitalized on the Big Four's fear of bolshevism to claim inflated borders in clear violation not only of the nationality principle but also of the most elementary rules of diplomatic prudence. They looked above all to France, where triumphant but unconfident conservatives declared the Allied victory a pyrrhic one. Afraid of an early German recovery and revival, Paris desperately needed allies to replace Moscow as a counterweight to Berlin and to serve as a cordon sanitaire between revolutionary Russia and central Europe.

At any rate, the leaders of France—President Raymond Poincaré, Premier Georges Clemenceau, and Marshal Ferdinand Foch—pressed the peacemakers to award Poland western Prussia, Posnia, and southern Silesia, which in ethnic terms were essentially German. They also encouraged and helped the conservative nation-builders in Warsaw to intervene in the Russian Civil War, their minimum objective being the eastward enlargement of France's newfound eastern ally. After Poland's narrow victory over the Red Army, and with the blessings of Paris, in 1920–21 Marshal Józef Piłsudski and Jan Dąbski extended the borders of their reborn nation well over a hundred miles beyond the proposed Curzon Line, deep into Belorussia and the Ukraine. These territories nearly doubled the size of Poland, making it the linchpin of the new European security system designed to simultaneously keep apart and hedge in Germany and Russia, the two momentarily disabled giants. Even as Polish maximalists decried the insufficiency of this territorial overreach, it sowed the seeds of a congenital weakness, for resurgent Poland was destined to be torn by centrifugal forces. Out of a total population of 27 million, fully one-third, or 9 million, were non-Poles, whose integration promised to be both difficult and slow. Among these there were 4 million Ukrainians and 1 million Belorussians. Besides defying their unwanted overlords, these Slavic minorities, notwithstanding their antagonism toward Russia and bolshevism, were a ready cause or pretext for future Soviet irredentism. The minority of 1 million Germans along Poland's western borders constituted a similar risk. In addition, the new Poland comprised about 3 million Jews, who accounted for over one-tenth of its total population and one-third of its minority population. But unlike the Slavic and German minorities, the Jews were without a potential external protector. This made them doubly vulnerable, since, as we shall see, the Jews were to be exposed to the charge that they were unassimilable aliens in the service of Judeobolshevism.

Rumania's seasoned political class, led by Ion Bratianu, was equally grasping and confident of French support. It was unexceptional that as one of the victors Rumania should have taken the southern Dobruja from defeated Bulgaria. But this acquisition was insignificant and innocent compared to that of the much larger territories acquired in another cause. For their help in rolling back Soviet Russia and crushing the Hungarian Soviet Republic, the Rumanians were allowed to keep possession of Bukovina, Transylvania, and Bessarabia. All in all, the old Rumania of 1914, or the Regat, more than doubled its territory and population. A full quarter of its population of over 15 million was now non-Rumanian. Among the minorities there were some 1.5 million Magyars, most of them in Transylvania, taken from Hungary. Greater Rumania also included 400,000 Russians and 600,000 Ukrainians, the bulk of them in Bessarabia, taken from the Soviet Union. As for Rumania's Jewish population, with the territorial extension it rose from about 450,000 to about 760,000.

Hungary's postwar reshaping was the opposite of Rumania's. Its territory contracted by about 30 percent and its population by about 40 percent, to some 8 million. In the process Hungary all but lost its multiethnicity to become 90 percent Magyar. Its Jewish population was reduced from 750,000 to 440,000 and assumed a distinctly less "eastern" profile.

Taken together, Poland, Rumania, and Hungary counted over 4 million Jews, most of them unassimilated and unacculturated strangers in their homelands. Unfortunately, Europe's largest Jewish communities were long established in civil and political societies whose internal infirmity was aggravated, if not largely caused, by their location in the Continent's most imperiled geopolitical zone. This conjunction heightened the historical predicament of the Jews, including their exposure to scapegoating. Nothing was easier for conservative leaders eager to expand national borders and consolidate their own power than to accuse Jews of being antipatriotic, pro-Soviet, or subversive. In the disputed territories of the Baltic, Belorussia, the Ukraine, and Bessarabia, some Jews certainly had more sympathy for the Soviet Union than for Poland or Rumania, just as in Transylvania some Jews favored staying with Hungary. Here and there, Jews—like others— had collaborated with Soviet troops and authorities before these were forced to retreat. Some collaborated out of conviction; others acted out of expediency, which often proved to be miscalculated. But this is not to say that even those Jews who welcomed the Russians were traitors or revolutionaries. In what were extremely fluid circumstances, the parameters of loyalty were still confused. Yet at a time that leaders demanded instant nationalist allegiance, if not zeal, there was little tolerance for equivocation. By and large, the Jewish communities were like buoys in tempestuous seas, in danger of being torn from their moorings. In such turbulent weather eastern Jews were apt to look to incumbent rulers rather than opposition parties to protect their interests.

Aware that these interests were now very much at risk, Jewish notables rushed to the Paris Peace Conference to help convince the Big Four to design international instruments to require the governments of the new and newly recreated nations to respect the human rights of their large ethnic and religious minorities. Woodrow Wilson and Lloyd George in particular rose to the occasion once it became evident that these minorities were the prime victims of many pitched battles for the possession or repossession of contested lands. The worst excesses occurred in Eastern Galicia, in the western reaches of the Ukraine and Belorussia, and in southern Lithuania. Although the Jews were not the only ones to suffer from the military and civil atrocities accompanying the Polish liberation or conquest of these territories, they certainly suffered more than their share.

During the winter of 1918–19 there were several anti-Jewish outbreaks in both halves of Galicia. In the western half, notably in ethnically Polish territories formerly under Austrian rule, such onslaughts were fired by end-of-the-war shortages and executed with the complicity of police and army units carried over from the Habsburgs. While only a few Jews were killed in these pogroms, many more were wounded, plundered, and humiliated. Significantly, in several cities, including Cracow, liberal-minded provisional authorities encouraged Jews to organize their own militias and even supplied them with arms.

While most anti-Jewish outbursts in Austro-Poland were part of an essentially homegrown right-wing reaction against real or imagined social dangers, they were not part of the crusade against "Judeobolshevism."

The situation was distinctly different farther east, in East Galician areas contested by Ukrainian nationalists and throughout Polish territories formerly controlled by tsarist Russia, and beyond. There the assaults on Jews were a by-product of military operations inspired by both ultranationalism and antibolshevism. Starting in early November 1918, Poles and Ukrainians were locked in battle over possession of northeastern Galicia. While Jews were harassed in several towns "liberated" by the Poles, in Lvov they suffered a massive pogrom. A faction of the Polish military charged that in the battle for this city, which was about one-third Jewish, Jews had either sided with the Ukrainians or adopted a neutral position favorable to them. In addition, and incongruously, the Jews were accused of being Bolsheviks. To punish the Jews for their alleged misdeeds, starting November 22, 1918, after the local Jewish constabulary was forcibly disbanded, Polish legionnaires and vigilantes sacked Lvov's Jewish quarter. During two days of wild violence at least 70 Jews were killed and about 450 wounded. In addition, three synagogues and many times that number of homes and shops were set on fire and plundered. As is characteristic of moments of nationalist intoxication, just as the Polish ultras vastly exaggerated the "disloyalty" of the Jews, so Jewish extremists, with better reason, overstated the number of the pogrom's victims, claiming that the dead and wounded ran into the thousands.

Starting in February 1919, Polish military units moved into Belorussian and Lithuanian territories. The hastily improvised Polish divisions included officers and men who, having fled westward, proposed to reclaim their lost homes and properties. Together with Polish superpatriots, these émigrés inculcated the advancing armies with a fanatical hatred of the Soviets and their ostensible local supporters, notably leftists, insurgent peasants, and Jews. Not surprisingly, the "liberation" of quite a few cities and towns was followed by wanton raids against suspected Bolsheviks, many of them Jews. The Jews were set upon as often for their alleged radicalism as for their alleged collaboration with national enemies. As part of this irregular political warfare, in the spring of 1919 Polish "freedom fighters" killed thirty-five Jews in Pinsk, fifty in Vilna, and thirty in Lida. These cities were heavily Jewish, and in all of them these murders were combined with arson and plunder, as well as with the desecration of either synagogues or holy scrolls. Clearly, the military campaign to annex ethnically non-Polish districts went hand in hand not only with the brutal "pacification" of Belorussians and Lithuanians but also with outrages against Jews.

This link was equally evident in the Russo-Polish War of 1919–21, following the signing of the Versailles peace treaty. In collusion with the French, the Poles launched a major drive against the Soviets, loosely collaborating with Simon Petlura, hetman of the Ukrainian armed forces in the south, and General Bulak-Balokhovitch in Belorussia. The principal Polish legion was commanded by General Józef Haller, who had close ties to the French General Staff and was known for his anti-Semitism, which many of his officers shared. Like the Whites and Petlura in the Russian Civil War, the invading Polish divisions meant to slay the dragon of "Judeobolshevism." Time and again, after the capture of cities and towns with large Jewish populations, local Jews were persecuted for having "collaborated with the enemy." In August 1919 thirty-two Jews were killed in Minsk, which was close to 40 percent Jewish.

But the worst outbreak of anti-Jewish violence in the Russo-Polish War—indeed, in the interwar years—still lay ahead. At first, the Poles had little difficulty penetrating deep into the Ukraine in their daring drive to bring down the Bolshevik regime. Before long, however, they found their lines vastly overextended. Lenin and Trotsky seized their opportunity not just to push back Piłsudski's forces but to try to break through Poland into central Europe, undoing the cordon sanitaire along the way. By July 1920 the Red Army, led by the ex-tsarist General Mikhail Tukhachevsky, had advanced to within a few miles of Warsaw. This unexpected show of Soviet power shook not only Poland's untried military and political elite but also its Catholic episcopate, which had extolled the war of conquest and the campaign against "Judeobolshevism." Soon a wave of murderous pogroms hit Białystok, Siedlce, Minsk, Lukow, and other cities. In addition, special courts-martial convicted Jews of spying and ordered several summary executions. Even Jewish officers sworn to the Polish cause were disarmed and deported to a camp at Jablonna, near Warsaw. This anti-Jewish frenzy did not subside until late August 1920, when the tide of battle once again turned in Piłsudski's favor. Soon the Red Army was in headlong retreat. By October, in exchange for an end to the war, the Soviet leaders ceded Poland a zone of between 125 and 185 miles east of the proposed Curzon Line without regard for ethnic and historical considerations.

The legacy of the bloody battles for control of parts of the former Pale of Settlement was heavy indeed. Hereafter, the borders between the Soviet Union and *all* its European neighbors were mined with hostility and suspicion. In diplomatic terms Russia was reduced to a dissatisfied great power with militarily vulnerable frontiers. On the other hand, having taken non-Polish lands—above all from defeated Russia and defeated Germany—the Second Polish Republic emerged as a satiated minor power resolved to defend an adventitiously favorable status quo. Much the same was true of Rumania, which had seized Bessarabia from Russia and Transylvania from Hungary.

These forced territorial arrangements had important domestic consequences as well. Traumatized by foreign intervention, territorial amputation, and the cordon sanitaire, Bolshevik leaders retreated into building socialism in one country. Although their rhetoric remained international, their policies increasingly bore the mark of their fortress mentality. At the same time, the conservative regimes and political classes of Poland and Rumania strengthened their position by securing expanded but internationally sanctioned frontiers. Dizzy with success, they were not likely to protect and promote the human rights of their large minority populations, especially in times of crisis.

There is no denying the persistence of age-old and deep-seated Judeophobia throughout east and east-central Europe. But this does not mean that it was stronger there than elsewhere in Europe or that it alone was sufficient to prevent full and lasting Jewish emancipation between the wars. A host of other factors were also involved: on the one hand, entrenched structural obstacles, such as political illiberalism, economic underdevelopment, ethnic involution, and religious obscurantism; on the other, contingent complications such as contested national borders, vast and restless minority populations, the imminence of bolshevism, and the rise of fascism. These two sets of factors conspired to complicate the democratization and economic advance of the host nations, which were essential preconditions for the improvement of the Jewish condition within them. There were two contingencies of an international nature that exacerbated the situation still further: the fluctuations at the core of world capitalism, which disproportionately harmed the dependent east European economies; and the mounting restrictions on immigration by the developed countries, above all by the United States, which was particularly detrimental to the Jews. Apparently, the chronic predicament of the eastern Jews was inseparable from the congenital deficits of liberal democracy and capitalism throughout east-central Europe.

This, then, was the inauspicious habitat of Europe's largest concentration of Jews, which comprised the world's most vital centers of cultural and religious Judaism. Although there were important pockets of acculturation and assimilation in the main cities, the traditional profile of the east-central European Jews remained essentially intact through the interwar years. Most spoke Yiddish, were religiously observant, and limited their contact with the outside world. They earned their living as independent artisans and shopkeepers, of lower-middle-class status, who lived and worked in towns and cities, where they also stood out in the professions.

By local standards, the Jews of east-central Europe were not economically underprivileged. On average, their per capita income was considerably higher than that of non-Jews. Not that they, any more than most Gentiles, were prosperous. Certainly, large sections of eastern Jewry lived in poverty. Probably, there were greater differentials of income among Jews than Gentiles, partly because disproportionately more Jews made their living from nonmanual rather than manual labor. In many Jewish communities there was a huge gap in income and living standard between a small layer on top and the great mass below.

Jews continued to be overrepresented among petty shopkeepers and big merchants. They were also in the forefront of manufacture and industry, which meant that they led the way in providing employment for non-Jewish workers. In east-central European societies Jews were by no means obstacles to industrialization as anti-Semites sometimes maintained. Nor were they economic parasites—another accusation leveled against them—the less so since many Jewish small shopkeepers and peddlers catered to fellow Jews.

The Jewish population of Poland may be taken as typical of the Jews of east-central Europe between the wars. From 1919 to 1939 Jews accounted for about 10 percent of the population of Poland: in 1921 they were 2.8 million out of 27 million; in 1939 3.5 million out of 35 million. The increase in absolute numbers was due to a high birthrate as well as a decline of infant mortality and emigration.

Whereas overall the population of the new Poland was heavily rural, the Jewish population was heavily urban. Taking Poland as a whole, at most 25 percent of all Jews lived in villages, a percentage that was substantially lower in the central provinces. Although the Jews made up only 10 percent of the total population, they constituted over 27 percent of Poland's city and town dwellers. Over one-quarter of the Jewish population was concentrated in the nation's six major cities. There were 350,000 Jews in Warsaw, which meant that Poland's capital and largest city was close to one-third Jewish. The percentage was the same in Łódź, Poland's second city and leading industrial center, where 202,000 out of 605,000 inhabitants were Jewish. Except for Lvov, the cities east of the Curzon Line were much smaller. But the Jewish populations of these towns were proportionately larger, ranging from 42 percent (21,000) in Grodno to 63 percent (20,000) in Pinsk. In each city and town, the Jews lived in separate residential districts, where most of them worked as well.

The urban bias was equally pronounced in Rumania and Hungary. In 1930 Rumania counted about 750,000 Jews, or slightly over 4 percent out of a population of 18 million. Although they accounted for only about 15 percent of Greater Rumania's urban population, the cities and towns of Bukovina, Moldavia, and Bessarabia were between one-quarter and one-third Jewish. Czernowitz, Jassy, and Kishinev, the capitals of these provinces, were close to half Jewish. As for Hungary, after the Treaty of Trianon it had about 450,000 Jews or roughly 5 percent in a population of about 9 million. Not quite half of these Jews lived in Budapest, where they constituted at least one-fourth of the total population.

Unlike the Christian populations, the Jews as a rule made their living outside the agricultural sector, in manufacture, commerce, and the professions. In Poland nearly one-half of the labor force in textile, clothing, and shoe-manufacturing was Jewish, and so was about one-fourth of the labor force in food-processing. The Jewish working class consisted almost exclusively of artisans toiling in consumer industries, the overwhelming majority of them either in small workshops or in one-man shops and in their own homes. To the extent that Jews were wage earners in large-scale establishments, they were employed not in industrial plants or coal mines but in textile mills, some of which were Jewish-owned.

The line between manufacture and commerce was blurred, since many independent artisans produced for sale in their own stores. In Poland 55 percent of all petty shopkeepers were Jewish, about 10 percent of them plying their trade in villages. The percentage of Jewish shopkeepers was highest in the eastern regions. Twenty-seven percent of all actively working Jews were petty merchants, the overwhelming majority of them self-employed, with family rather than hired help. Between them artisanal workers and small shopkeepers comprised over 75 percent of all gainfully employed Jews in Poland, and their income and living standard compared favorably with those of non-Jews in these same callings.

The occupational profile of the Jews of Greater Rumania was roughly the same. But that of Hungarian Jewry was significantly different. Having lost many of its traditionally oriented Jews with the territories ceded to Rumania, Hungary was left with a Jewish community with a profile closer to Germany's than Poland's. This was particularly true of the Jews of Budapest.

In Poland, Jews were nearly entirely excluded from state employ-ment, including the postal service, the government-owned railroads, and the national manufactures of liquor, tobacco, and matches. Few Jews were army officers, judges, or physicians in the public health service. They were also all but shut out of municipal jobs, even in cities and towns with large Jewish populations. There were few Jewish schoolteachers in either primary and secondary schools or in institu-tions of higher learning. Jews were equally excluded from public service in Rumania and only slightly less so in Hungary.

In turn, Jews were heavily overrepresented in the professions. In Poland easily half of all physicians and lawyers in private practice were Jewish. In addition to roughly 10,000 Jewish physicians and lawyers, there were at least as many private teachers, most of them narrowly educated and poorly paid Orthodox *melamdim*. Because of the closure of the public sector, many Jews entered these and other independent professions, in which not a few of them lived on the margins of poverty. Even so, Jews continued to seek university degrees. In the early twenties about a quarter of all students enrolled in Polish univer-sities were Jewish. By the end of the decade, when 32,000, or 40 percent, of Poland's university graduates were Jewish, the proportion of Jewish students was down to 20 percent, in part due to restrictive quotas. This percentage was halved during the crisis of the 1930s, which saw an escalation of discrimination.

There were similar developments in both Rumania and Hungary. In prewar Hungary nearly 30 percent of all registered university stu-dents were Jewish, and there were nearly as many Jews as non-Jews in the medical and legal professions. Although by 1930 the propor-tion of Jewish university students generally was down to about 10 percent and that of Jewish medical students to 23 percent, the propor-tion of Jewish doctors and lawyers was respectively 50 and 55 percent, and that of Jewish engineers 30 percent.

In socioeconomic terms, the Jewish communities of east and east-central Europe were intensely lower-middle-class, the more so since their working classes were artisanal rather than proletarian and their professional classes had sharply limited upward mobility. But whereas this composite *Mittelstand* was the choice recruiting ground for fascist movements in central and western Europe, this was much less the case in the eastern reaches of the Continent, where large sectors of the lower middle classes were less superannuated and endangered, and therefore less open to the politics of resentment. In addition, once the local fascists embraced anti-Semitism, the lower middle classes lost much of their counterrevolutionary potential, for the exclusion of the numerous Jewish petty bourgeoisie greatly limited their potential appeal. Besides, unlike their western European counterparts, who reviled Jews as pernicious capitalists and department store owners in the big cities, eastern European fascists vilified them as usurious moneylenders and shopkeepers in the countryside. In east-central Europe the urban potential of fascism was likewise undercut by traditional conservative rulers who pandered to job- and status-seeking university graduates by restricting the access of Jews to the universities, the professions, and the civil service. All this time the old elites, who condoned age-old Judeophobia, continued to enlist the services of Jewish finance and industry, which remained readily available to them.

Obviously, the Jewish communities of east-central Europe were not homogeneous. Like all large ethnic minorities, they were riven by intense class and cultural schisms, which gave rise to acute internecine political divisions. Not all Jews were poor, and far from all adult Jewish males steeped themselves in the Torah or cast themselves in the likeness of holy *zaddiks*. Between the wars more and more young Jews sought to break loose from the ghettos and shtetls. Ambitious businessmen in particular broke away, as did restive members of the professions and the intelligentsia. Susceptible to the promise and reality of the Enlightenment and Haskalah, a majority of Jews probably silently approved of these secessionists. Similarly, many of the leftists among the defectors sympathized with communism and Soviet Russia because they expected the Russian Revolution to complete the work of the French Revolution. Although many east-central European Jews were Zionist supporters or sympathizers, relatively few ever considered settling in Palestine, at least until the thirties. By no means all Jews were straining to emigrate, the vast majority of them remaining firmly attached to their host countries, which were their homelands. While the Bund defiantly demanded national and cultural autonomy for a Jewish socialist commonwealth in Poland, the Aguda, the anti-Zionist Orthodox party, practically infeudated itself in exchange for the unhampered but oppressive exercise of religious self-determination.

Between the wars east-central European Jewry did not undergo an unremitting cold pogrom, portending catastrophe. Emancipation progressed significantly if haltingly not only from 1917 to 1919, but again from the mid-twenties to the early thirties. This advance was as authentic as the anti-Jewish eruptions from 1919 through 1921 and after 1933. Just as far from all Jews were alienated from their host countries, far from all Gentiles of the area were consumed by anti-Judaism and Judeophobia. Because of the continuing sway of the unreconstructed Christian churches, traditional Judeophobia may well have been more pervasive among the masses and classes of the eastern marches than of any other region of Europe with large Jewish populations. But this is not to say that this age-old prejudice was inherently more lethal than the new kind of political anti-Semitism arising in more developed countries, where it may have been less endemic. Certainly, radical liberals, socialists, and Communists opposed Jew-baiting as part of their larger struggle against the old order.

In east-central Europe, like everywhere else, the curve of anti-Jewish hostility closely correlated with the fever chart of general economic, political, and diplomatic developments. Admittedly, the conservative ruling and governing classes of the rimland were more prone to resort to overt anti-Jewish rhetoric and measures than their counterparts in the rest of Europe. But this was so essentially because they presided over relatively illiberal civil and political societies which were contemptuous of the human rights of all minorities, including the Jewish minority. No doubt the abuse of the Jews was more salient and frequent throughout most of east-central Europe than elsewhere in Europe. But notwithstanding its greater immanence, until 1933 this intolerance was not uniquely fatal precisely because it was archaic and consonant with traditional societies and mentalities. Characteristically, in addition to being among the most brazen disseminators of religiously based anti-Judaism, churchmen were active in the fascist movements which purveyed local variants of the new-model, profane anti-Semitism that was surfacing all over Europe. The men of the cloth helped recast the age-old decalogue of anti-Judaism by replacing the old charge of blood libel with the politically contrived charge of "Judeobolshevism." The objective was to transmute, not lessen, ostracizing diabolism.

During the years of European prosperity and stability pump-primed by American bank loans, as part of a general relaxation the old regimes relented in their treatment of minorities. Both physical and verbal violence against Jews subsided, and the governments of Poland, Rumania, and Hungary ignored, relaxed, or even rescinded the recently enacted admission quotas for higher education. Not all restrictions disappeared. But the remaining quotas, which were half-tacit, were not so different from the unspoken quotas in effect in many countries, including in the United States. If many east-central European Jews lost economic ground, even during the relatively prosperous years, they did so as a consequence of the overall decline of petty manufacture and trade rather than because of discriminatory measures.

Meanwhile, acculturation proceeded apace. Although the lower and rural strata continued to speak Yiddish, a growing number of educated and middle-class Jews abandoned their ancestral language for that of their host countries. This linguistic adaptation, fostered in public schools, often triggered a desire for further assimilation. By the late 1930s in Poland approximately 10 percent of all Jews were Polonized, most of them men of wealth, intellectuals, or artists. Among assimilated urban Jews intermarriage was not uncommon, and by the late twenties there were also an estimated 2,000 to 3,000 conversions yearly. The rate of mixed marriages and conversions was considerably higher in Hungary than in Poland, especially in Budapest.

The new Poland was endowed with a democratic constitution providing for an independent parliament. The first Sejm, or lower chamber, was elected in 1919, the second in 1922. Although both elections were held under unsettled conditions and a complicated franchise, they were relatively free and fair. Since independence had been secured by diplomatic and military means without a social and cultural upheaval, the landed and ecclesiastical elites in particular retained the loyalty of large sectors of the rural electorate. The forces of order also benefited from the militarization of postindependence politics as well as from the ultranationalism and antibolshevism stirred up by the war with Russia. At least 50 percent of the deputies elected were of the right and the center right, and many more closed ranks with them at the slightest challenge from the left. The strength of the parties of the left and of the minorities was not negligible, since they counted, respectively, 25 and 22 percent of the house. But the two camps were sometimes at odds and torn internally as well. In 1919 Jewish voters returned thirteen deputies on Jewish tickets, and six of these deputies professed Zionist sympathies. Three years later they elected thirty-five deputies, seventeen of them of varying Zionist persuasions. By then Poland had incorporated eastern lands with large Jewish communities, including Eastern Galicia, the center of Zionism. Thus, although the thirty-five Jewish deputies formed a single delegation within the Diet, it was riven by intense ideological, regional, and factional discords that compounded its intrinsic fragility. Meanwhile, by supporting a profusion of Jewish parties, which remained politically isolated, the Jews may unintentionally have helped the forces of the old order, which were fundamentally antiparliamentary. Since the Jewish vote was heavily urban—35 percent of Warsaw's electorate was Jewish—it might have gone to strengthen the radical democratic and socialist forces if it had not been diverted into sectarian channels. The liberal potential of the Jewish vote was reduced still further by the resolve of conservative and orthodox Jews, in particular the leaders of the Aguda, to collaborate closely with the authoritarian power brokers.

Only the Bundists made a concerted effort to bolster the fledgling forces of genuine parliamentarism and effective party politics.

Ultimately, however, the choice facing Poland may never really have been between democratic and authoritarian government but between varieties of authoritarianism that shared many family resemblances. Whatever the differences between Piłsudski's Sanacja and Roman Dmowski's Endecja, these rival conservative camps were ultranationalist, antileftist, anti-Bolshevik, antiparliamentary, and respectful of the Catholic Church. But while both Piłsudski and Dmowski had fascist leanings and admired Mussolini, only Dmowski encouraged Jew-baiting and completely truckled to the landed element. As of 1923, there was increasing talk of a coup d'état or a pronunciamento to establish a right-wing clerical dictatorship with a sharp anti-Semitic edge.

Following the peace treaty with the Soviet Union in March 1921, successive governments put an end to all anti-Jewish excesses as part of a turn to national conciliation and reconstruction. Certain new fiscal and economic measures were particularly hard on the Jews, who soon paid 40 percent of all direct taxes. But the government adopted these measures not to punish the Jews but to satisfy landed and church interests bent on shifting the tax burden to the nonagrarian and urban sectors of the economy, in which the Jews were dominant. As previously indicated, despite quotas, Jewish access to higher education was relatively open. Also, state schools began to exempt Jewish students from taking examinations on Saturdays, and the army considered providing kosher food for Jewish conscripts.

In May 1926 Piłsudski staged a coup with the help of disgruntled soldiers and workers. Unlike Mussolini, he challenged and split the establishment, spilling blood in the process. He also scorned the duce's political and populist theatrics. But despite significant differences in ideology, method, and purpose, the March on Warsaw had much in common with the March on Rome, and Piłsudski, like the duce, dispensed with anti-Semitism. In fact, precisely because he was presumed to have preempted a takeover by Dmowski's far more reactionary and anti-Semitic forces, not only the Socialists but also all the Jewish deputies ratified Piłsudski's seizure of power. At the outset even the half-legal Communists supported Marshal Piłsudski as the lesser evil.

Curiously enough, it looked as if in Poland, as in Soviet Russia, it would take an iron official hand to reduce the residues of Judeophobia, and to check their irruptions. But whereas in Russia this campaign was tied to a policy of radical economic, social, and cultural change favorable to Jewish acculturation and assimilation, this was not the case in Poland. Soon after his takeover, Piłsudski launched a project of conservative nation-building. He enlisted the support not only of the agrarians and the church but also of the Jewish business and professional classes and the Aguda, which opposed Jewish secularization. As if in exchange, Piłsudski proposed to curb and isolate the Socialists, his former confederates, as well as the Bund and the left Zionists. By tying his project to the established economic and social interests, notably to the landed estate, Piłsudski stymied the growth of the Polish economy. In turn, the condition of the Jews could not improve partly because the safety valve of emigration was nearly closed by the restrictive policies of the outside world. There was a similar economic and social immobility in the other east European nations, with the same consequences for the Jews—except in Czechoslovakia.

The Great Depression intensified this impasse, so dangerous for the Jews. Almost overnight, unemployment and underemployment soared, creating massive poverty and destitution. Probably, the Jews suffered disproportionately. The urban and nonagrarian sectors, in which they were so heavily concentrated, were most severely hit. As independents and employees of small firms, most Jews did not qualify for welfare support, which was in any case minimal. Also, being barred from the civil service, Jews did not benefit from the security of employment in the public sector. Overall, however, in strictly economic terms, the Jews were only marginally worse off than Gentiles, in part because they had better communal support systems.

Even so, the plight of the Jews was further aggravated by virtue of their becoming the victims of boycotts, pogroms, and quotas. At first, these renewed transgressions against the Jews were of a "wildcat" nature. But soon, because of acute dissension within the old elites over how to manage the growing crisis and how to domesticate their would-be fascist helpers, they were intermittently and selectively sanctioned by higher authorities.

There was widespread agreement that government needed to be hardened in the face of rising social and ethnic tensions. As early as 1932, Regent Horthy instructed Premier Gyula Gömbös to further emasculate the powers of the Hungarian parliament. In early 1935 Tsar Boris III, backed by the military, took charge in Bulgaria. Shortly before his death in April 1935, Marshal Piłsudski gave Poland a new constitution strengthening the executive which turned out to be tailor-made for the political colonels who succeeded him. Finally, in February 1938 King Carol II, in league with his generals, took over in Rumania, and then promulgated a new corporatist constitution.

While Hitler's ascent in Germany set the tone for this political hardening, it was fired by essentially internal developments.

Throughout east-central Europe the traditional ruling and governing classes succeeded in maintaining themselves without calling in the fascists or being superseded by them. Not that the irruptive far right did not make itself felt. But the old elites, in addition to tightening their control of the state, again became stridently nationalist and anti-Communist in their own right. This fascist suffusion of the old order was a function of the logic of the internal divisions and frailties of conservatism in a time of crisis rather than of the overweening strength of the radical right. Accordingly, instead of liquidating their fascist challengers, the established political classes preferred to bridle them, perhaps to keep them available for future use.

Anticommunism and anti-Semitism became the chief trademarks of this radicalization of conservative politics. The left and the Jews were particularly easy prey. Given the low level of industrialization and the left's failure to speak to smallholders and agricultural workers, the Socialists and Communists were weak in addition to being poised against each other. Even so, these "enemy brothers" served to cement the composite right, which accused them, indiscriminately, of being carriers of "Judeobolshevism" guided from Moscow.

Jew-baiting served a similar purpose. The Jews were an even more serviceable surrogate target than the Reds. They were, of course, the most culturally and religiously distinctive strangers in their own lands. In addition, they were vilified as perennial Shylocks, dangerous revolutionaries, subversive intellectuals, profane artists, and cunningly indispensable business and financial magnates.

Poland, unlike Rumania and Hungary, was spared a separate fascist movement, largely because fascist ideas and sentiments had permeated the two major conservative parties, but most especially the Endecja. In any case, armed with the new constitution, Marshal Edward Śmigly-Rydz, Piłsudski's successor, and Colonel Józef Beck, Poland's influential foreign minister, moved the government further to the right. Attuned to the fascist upsurge around them, they resorted to political anti-Semitism as a diversion from insoluble economic problems and as a lightning rod for swelling popular frustrations. Quotas in higher education were stiffened and enforced. More and more voices within the establishment called for a boycott of Jewish merchants, manufacturers, and professionals. Several officials echoed the rising cry that since most Jews were either parasites or Shylocks they should be forced out of the country.

Piłsudski's successors in government sought to contain and pacify their own extremists by meeting them partway. Characteristically, in

March 1936 they engineered the passage of a bill restricting *shechita*, the Jewish ritual slaughter of animals, rather than outlawing it altogether. Here and there, members of the squirearchy, fearing peasant uprisings, aided and abetted the anti-Jewish agitation, whose center of gravity was in rural rather than urban Poland.

This escalation of anti-Semitism went hand in hand with an intense upsurge of superpatriotism and anticommunism. In this right-wing ideological amalgam the outcry against "Judeobolshevism" was turned against the Jewish left at home and Soviet Russia abroad. Anti-Semitism also promised to facilitate a diplomatic rapprochement with the Third Reich, whose new politics impressed Poland's governing class. Colonel Beck disguised neither his philo-Nazism nor his virulent antibolshevism.

The Catholic hierarchy openly supported and legitimated the strident verbal campaign against the Jews, though it was careful to reject recourse to physical violence. In 1936 Cardinal August Hlond, the new primate of Poland, set the official tone in a widely disseminated pastoral letter which artfully wove strands of the new political anti-Semitism into the long-standing dogma of Judeophobia.

> It is an actual fact that the Jews fight against the Catholic Church, they are free-thinkers, and constitute the vanguard of atheism, bolshevism and revolution. . . . It is also true that the Jews are committing frauds, practising usury and dealing in white slavery. It is true that in the schools the Jewish youth is having an evil influence, from an ethical and religious point of view, on the Catholic youth. . . . One does well to prefer one's own kind in commercial dealings and to avoid Jewish shops and Jewish stalls in the markets, but it is not permissible to demolish Jewish businesses. One should protect oneself against the influence of Jewish morals . . . but it is inadmissible to assault, hit or injure Jews.

Other prominent prelates, including Adam Lapieha, the archbishop of Cracow, issued similar epistles. The Church propagated the gospel of conjoined anti-Judaism and antibolshevism not only from its pulpits but also through its daily and periodical press.

From mid-1935 and into the second half of 1938, hundreds of individual Jews were humiliated, pillaged, and assaulted. There were also several organized pogroms, notably in towns and villages of central Poland, in which Jews were killed and wounded, though the exact number of casualties remains uncertain. In most respects these assaults were reminiscent of those of late imperial Russia. The public authorities delayed restoring order until after considerable damage was done, and the assailants either went free or received light sentences. All this time the government continued to condone economic boycotts. It also silently approved the ultranationalist students and rectors who forced Jewish students to sit on separate ghetto-benches on the left side of classrooms in many institutions of higher learning, leading to a radical drop in the number of Jews attending universities and polytechnic institutes. The rhetoric and practice of Polish anti-Semitism remained relatively inchoate, however: it was far from systemic and murderous. In short, it was more an echo of past persecutions than an augury or embryo of future massacres.

Certainly, not all Poles hated the Jews. Individual Poles of all stations and callings came to the rescue of innocent victims and many more demurred without, however, actively protesting. Some fifty faculty members combined to take exception to the establishment of the ghetto-benches and the harassment of Jewish university students. But the loudest and strongest public protest came from the organized left. Needless to say, the left itself was beleaguered and knew itself to be a principal target of the renewed victimization of the Jews. In any case, the left wing of the Peasant Party and in particular the Communist and Socialist parties denounced the anti-Jewish transgressions and exposed their hidden social and economic objectives or consequences. Beginning in the fall of 1936 the clandestine Communists issued manifestos declaring that the ongoing crisis could not be resolved by blaming the Jews, and condemning the strategy of sanctioning pogroms in order to curry the favor of the most reactionary and darkest forces in Polish society. The Socialists, for their part, proceeded to cooperate more closely with the Bund. To be sure, they refused to run on joint slates with their Jewish comrades for fear that such an open identification would be counterproductive. In late 1938 and early 1939, however, Socialists and Bundists informally but effectively collaborated in the local politics of major cities.

This outstretched hand from the left pulled many young Jews into the left opposition at the same time that it changed the political landscape within the Jewish community. There was a massive defection from Zionism to the Bund: in the last prewar municipal elections in Warsaw, the Bund and the Socialists not only reclaimed ground from conservatives of all stripes but the Bund captured 79 percent of the vote in the Jewish districts, giving it seventeen seats to only one for the Zionists. In Łódź the Socialists and the Bund secured an absolute majority and elected a Socialist mayor. There were many reasons for the swing away from Zionism: the reduction after 1935 of the immigration quotas which the British set for entry into Palestine; the government's advocacy of the mass emigration of Jews to the Holy

Land, which Jews saw as an anti-Semitic policy; and the effort by certain Zionists to belittle the importance of the Socialists joining with Bundists in strikes and demonstrations against the anti-Semitic excesses of 1936.

Just as in Poland the relatively benign Piłsudski wing of national conservatism yielded to hardliners in the face of mounting difficulties at home and abroad, so in Hungary, Regent Horthy facilitated the replacement of inveterate conservatives by their considerably more intransigent challengers on the right. In 1920, in the aftermath of the Béla Kun regime and the Trianon Treaty, the Magyar reaction had made a special point of introducing a *numerus clausus* reducing Jewish enrollments in higher education with a view to protecting career access for Christians and precluding the resurgence of a left-wing Jewish intelligentsia. While this quota was all but ignored by the moderate governments of Premier István Bethlen during the twenties, it was reactivated and expanded in scope as part of the turn to the right in the thirties. In 1938 parliament voted almost without opposition to limit the proportion of Jews in key sectors of Hungary's economic and cultural life to 20 percent by 1943, notably in the big cities, but especially in Budapest. Jewish war veterans and their relatives, as well as converts to Christianity, were not to be counted toward the Jewish quota.

This discriminatory law signaled that in the shadow of Nazi Germany's deemancipation of Jews Hungary's ruling and governing class proposed to increase the restriction of Jews in civil and political society. Leading Bethlenites and church leaders gave their blessing, presumably in order to forestall tougher measures being urged by rightist extremists determined to promote a counterrevolution inside Hungary along with a radical revision of Hungary's borders under the inglorious Trianon settlement.

As previously noted, the largest communities of European Jewry were crowded into unstable and inhospitable countries which had largely arbitrary and insecure borders and were located in the Continent's most strategically hazardous geopolitical zone. Once Hitler set his sights on the conquest of living space in the east, this zone stretching from the Baltic to the Black Sea assumed altogether critical importance. In addition to their intrinsic value for the projected Thousand-Year Reich, the countries of east-central Europe were the indispensable military staging ground for expansion farther east.

Just as after 1918 the Allies had considered Poland the key first to the overthrow and then to the containment of bolshevism, so now Hitler focused on Poland as the essential passageway for his own showdown with bolshevism and drive to the Urals. He saw Poland as providing a large terrain for military deployment behind a wide-stretched forward salient ideally suited for attack. In addition, Hitler had reason to expect that the government in Warsaw might fall in with his plan, given its protofascism at home and sworn enmity with Russia abroad.

The Polish leaders, for their part, were caught in a complex and unenviable predicament, much of it of their own making. Poland alone had long and intensely disputed borders with *both* Nazi Germany and Soviet Russia. It also commanded the most strategic corridor between these two giants. While the founding fathers of the new Poland had meant to build a nation capable of staving off both major neighbors, by the mid-thirties their successors must have realized that they had been left with an overextended and therefore poisoned legacy. Would the government of the colonels make a virtue of necessity and seek a rapprochement with Soviet Russia in order to deter Nazi Germany from moving eastward? Domestic as well as external factors argued against such a move. Above all, it would be difficult to reconcile Poland's internal swing to the right with an overture to Stalin. Ideologically, Foreign Minister Beck had greater affinities with Berlin than Moscow, not least because of his concern for the existing social order, particularly in the agricultural districts of eastern Poland. In this sense, Poland's strongmen had much in common with the leaders of England and France, many of whom were also more anti-Soviet than anti-Nazi. Even after reluctantly giving way at Munich, the Allies continued to fight shy of an agreement with Moscow, thereby encouraging the Poles to do likewise. And once London and Paris declared that they would stand with Warsaw in case of a German attack, Poland's leaders chose to believe that this guarantee, by itself, would be sufficient to deter Hitler.

Needless to say, the distended eastern border of 1921 weighed heavily in the balance: Polish decision-makers recoiled from diplomatic and military cooperation with Stalin for fear that in exchange he would sooner or later reclaim tsarist Russia's Belorussian and Ukrainian territories—which he would certainly have done. Accordingly, Warsaw balked at allowing Soviet troops to cross Polish territory to engage the Wehrmacht, convinced that they would never withdraw behind the borders fixed by the Treaty of Riga. Meanwhile, Beck continued to treat possession of both Danzig and the Corridor as a matter of national honor and survival. He did so even after it became clear to him, as it was to Hitler and Stalin, that Nazi Germany's acquisition of both territories was only part of its overall plan to make Poland not only its first major conquest but also the prime bridgehead for the invasion of Russia and the seizure of *Lebensraum* farther east.

Although Rumania had no border with Germany, its political and diplomatic position was similar to Poland's. King Carol hardened his regime at the same time that he staked his reign on maintaining the integrity of Greater Rumania. Accordingly, Bucharest outdid Warsaw in closing the door to any kind of cooperation with Moscow. Carol preferred to trust Rumania's extortionate frontiers to collaboration with ideologically congenial Nazi Germany, the chief challenger of the European status quo. Of course, he also meant to propitiate Hitler as a hedge against irredentist Hungary's becoming Germany's privileged ally. But again, both Stalin and Hitler realized that much more was involved than the contested borders of Rumania and Hungary.

Meanwhile, England and France did little to encourage or force the governments of Poland, Rumania, and Hungary to reconsider their pro-German tilt. Yet the British and the French were not exactly innocent or helpless bystanders. The responsibility of their ruling and governing classes dated from the years 1917 to 1921, when they had mediated the establishment of the ramshackle and ill-starred new order in the eastern buffer zone. During the general crisis of the 1930s their obsession with the containment of Soviet Russia and the left generally predisposed them to countenance recourse to the authoritarian or fascist antidote to disorder. Allied appeasement of Hitler, Mussolini, and Franco could not help but embolden the Polish colonels, King Carol, and Admiral Horthy to continue preferring Hitler to Stalin.

The conjuncture of events of the late thirties was catastrophic for the Jews of the eastern marches, in that they were all but abandoned. Locally, they could count on only the support of the left, which was barely less powerless and beleaguered than they were themselves. There was little more to be hoped for from abroad. Anglo-French appeasement of Germany and the unfaltering quarantining of Soviet Russia helped to turn all of central and east-central Europe into a vast zone of deemancipation and persecution. In addition, with the general crisis ravaging most of the globe, the outside world ceased to provide "a refuge for the oppressed, a refuge in time of trouble."

The Nazi-Soviet Pact must have struck the Jews of east-central Europe as further proof that they were condemned to face another dark age of oppression. The last illusions were falling. Stalin hastened to make a diplomatic deal with Hitler, thereby destroying what remained of the united front against the fascist presumption. Many Jews must have feared that Stalin, having struck a deal with Hitler, would take the additional step of revoking the recent emancipation of Russian Jewry. They were unlikely to fathom Moscow's strategy of gaining time and space for the inevitable Nazi-Soviet showdown of the near future.

It was not until after the fall first of Poland and then of France that the unintentionally and fortuitously redeeming features of Stalin's appeasement of Hitler came into view. By securing eastern Poland in exchange for his perfidious neutrality, Stalin momentarily kept 300,000 Jews from falling under the Nazi heel. A week after the surrender of France and in accordance with his secret compact with Berlin, Stalin took possession of Bessarabia and northern Bukovina. In the process, 300,000 Jews were removed from Rumanian jurisdiction. For the moment, for the eastern Jews, the Soviet Union's Machiavellian diplomacy was not entirely without benefit.

Had the destruction of European Jews been Hitler's paramount objective or constant obsession, he might well have pressed Stalin to transfer the Jews of eastern Poland to German control, and had Stalin been a sworn anti-Semite, he might not have spurned such a proposal. Of course, with his consummate slyness Hitler may have refrained from making such a demand, confident that he would seize these forfeited Jews, and many more, with his subsequent conquest of Soviet lands. Most likely, however, neither Hitler and Ribbentrop, nor Stalin and Molotov, so much as gave a thought to the Jews as they struck their nefarious bargain.

In any event, the Nazi-Soviet Pact and the German conquest of Poland put an end to the ill-founded territorial arrangement in the east-central European rimland that had been contingent on the temporary weakness and grudging acquiescence of both Russia and Germany. Greater Poland was now unevenly divided between them, with by far the larger part of the country and the larger number of Jews going to Germany. As for Greater Rumania, it was forced to retrocede the territory it had taken from Russia. Although Germany had no territorial claims on Rumania, by virtue of its hegemony in Danubian Europe, it all but dictated Bucharest's border revisions. On August 30, 1940, Ribbentrop and Galeazzo Ciano mediated Rumania's return of northern and eastern Transylvania to Hungary. Horthy thus recovered two-fifths of the territory and the 2.5 million souls ceded to Rumania in the Treaty of Trianon. Having also had to yield southern Dobruja to Bulgaria, Greater Rumania was reduced by one-third of its territory and population. The consequence of this diplomatic debacle was the resignation of King Carol in favor of his son Michael, who kept General Ion Antonescu as his strongman. Determined to restore Rumania's grandeur, especially at the expense of Russia, the protofascist Antonescu sought to march with Berlin, which was about to become the Continent's supreme arbiter. So did Admiral Horthy, since with Hitler's accord Hungary recovered much of Slovakia and Ruthenia from Czechoslovakia before repossessing about half of Transylvania and half of the lands yielded to Yugoslavia in 1919. Naturally, along with its lost territories Hungary regained most of its lost but not exactly regretted Jews.

To fall in with Nazi Germany entailed a continuing rightist radicalization detrimental to the Jews. In Rumania, although Antonescu brought Horia Sima's fascist Iron Guard to heel in January 1941, he nevertheless left it considerable scope for action. In keeping with this complicity, his government toughened and enlarged upon certain discriminatory measures, thereby increasing the Jewish community's sense of insecurity. And as previously noted, in Hungary the Horthy regime pushed the discrimination against Jews in certain professions and sectors of the economy, although without troubling either the Jewish business bourgeoisie or the converts from Judaism.

Still, while anti-Semitism made considerable strides in General Antonescu's Rumania and Admiral Horthy's Hungary, it did not become murderous until after both countries became Nazi Germany's satellites in the war against the Soviet Union. It should nevertheless be noted that the old regimes of Rumania and Hungary were not coerced into participating in the eastern crusade against bolshevism. They did so of their own accord and in pursuit of their own interests, both domestic and foreign. Collaboration with Nazi Germany braced rather than dictated or defined their projects.

CHAPTER IV

THE SYNCRETISM OF
MEIN KAMPF

Anti-Semitism was a cardinal postulate of the *Weltanschauung* which fired the rise of the Nazi movement as well as the consolidation of the Nazi regime and its drive for the mastery of Europe. But although anti-Semitism was an essential tenet of the Nazi worldview, it was neither its foundation nor its principal or sole intention. Anti-Semitism was one of several central creeds of an essentially syncretic ideology, the others being social Darwinism, the geopolitics of eastern expansionism, and anti-Marxism. While these four articles of faith were closely enmeshed and eventually crystallized into an indivisible belief system, within this system their position and importance in relation to each other varied with time, place, and circumstance.

The ideology of nazism was not simply a random collection of ideas with a familiar philosophic lineage. It was also the product of a political practice, which was truly novel. Both doctrine and practice were shaped and calibrated in a tempestuous historical moment and a concrete sociopolitical context. Nazi leaders and publicists produced and tailored their central canons with a view to courting many different publics.

The ideological discourse of National Socialism was not confined to the written and spoken word. It was also expressed through symbols, gestures, uniforms, rituals, sounds, and rallies. These nonwritten and nonspoken idioms had a life of their own and many of them took shape before Hitler composed and published *Mein Kampf* and before senior Nazi leaders delivered their carefully staged homilies.

The Nazi *Weltanschauung* was deeply rooted in the conservative and reactionary ideas that had surfaced in central Europe during the second half of the nineteenth century. The basic thrust of these ideas was to negate reason, science, and progress in favor of irrationalism, intuition, and a return to an idealized past. This wholesale rejection of the Enlightenment was articulated by social critics who were terrified by the ever more rapid waning of the old regime of aristocratic society, time-honored high culture, and elite politics.

Friedrich Nietzsche was the most profound and lucid member of this deracinated intelligentsia, which also included Paul de Lagarde, Julius Langbehn, and Houston Stewart Chamberlain. Alienated from the contemporary world, these nonacademic men of ideas railed against liberal democracy and industrial capitalism; against Marxism and organized labor; and against the philistine bourgeoisie and the culture of modernism. With the notable exception of Nietzsche, the new conservatives denounced the Jews as the prototypical subverters of the old order, primarily on account of their allegedly protean links to modernity.

The *nouveaux philosophes* of those days also interspersed their bitter negation of the present and future with strident maxims and disquisitions about "the survival of the fittest," "the will to power," the virtue of elitism, the wholesomeness of rural life, and the ideal of classical art. Theirs was a call to eliminate the corrosion of material greed, political artifice, and cultural iconoclasm by restoring the primacy of honor, sacrifice, and reverence.

After 1918 incipient National Socialists appropriated key elements of this neoconservative stance, which they declared had been vindicated by Germany's inglorious defeat and postwar convulsions. Almost unwittingly, they radicalized both the text and the temper of the irrationalist doctrine. Unlike their spiritual precursors, who had theoretical or philosophic pretensions, the early Nazis were engaged in political struggle, not in intellectual disputation. The old social critics had spoken to educated and elite audiences with pedantic books, abstract arguments, and sober voices. By contrast, the fledgling Nazis and their ilk addressed popular audiences with fiery words and pamphlets intended to overdramatize the troubles of their time as well as to unmask and vilify those allegedly responsible for them. As Georg Lukács put it, to move the ultraconservative discourse out of the private studies, salons, and cafés of the staid Second Empire into the beerhalls and streets of the turbulent Weimar Republic was to transform it into an ideology of political combat.

The improvisers of National Socialism appropriated the irrationalist beliefs, attitudes, and phrases of their forerunners as they set out to specify the targets and victims of their political insurgency. In their hands the critique of liberal democracy and capitalism became a venomous indictment of the Weimar Republic and its economic order; the critique of materialism, Marxism, and organized labor a fierce excoriation of German communism and Russian bolshevism;

and the critique of cultural heterodoxy a scathing denunciation of abstract and expressionist art. While the doctrine of social Darwinism was perverted into a warrant for the conquest of *Lebensraum*, the axiom of a pastoral Arcadia was turned into the mystique of *Blut und Boden* (blood and soil). As for the equivocal tropes of "the will to power" and "the *Übermensch*," they were conflated into a sweeping imperative for all-out domination over civil and political society in Germany as well as over "inferior" peoples in eastern Europe.

The catechism of anti-Semitism was radicalized and particularized as part of this sweeping transformation of the new conservatism. Heretofore, the defamation of the Jew had been couched in the traditional, essentially abstract language of theologically based and colored social, economic, and cultural anti-Judaism. After the war the trailblazers of National Socialism inflamed the rhetoric of this *odium theologicum* by using phrases and images drawn from demonology, racial biology, and parasitology. At the same time that they transmuted the vernacular of Jew-baiting, they concretized their attack, holding the Jews responsible for the November revolution, the Munich *Räterepublik*, the Versailles *Diktat*, and the plague of bolshevism. The Nazis also denounced the Jews as the mainstay of parasitic capitalism and the masterminds of the modernist subversion of classical culture.

There is no denying the importance of the legacy of the new conservatism of the late nineteenth century for the pioneers of National Socialism. During the early interwar years they not only usurped its moral and cultural pretensions to ennoble their political virulence but also drew upon its ideas and rhetoric to fashion their political formulas. But ultimately the availability of the spirit and thought of the new conservatism was less consequential than its reception and perversion by the Nazis.

The character of the new conservatism was such that it was easily distorted. It had neither a central postulate nor a systematic structure, and its mode of argument was discursive and aphoristic. Because of its brittle foundation, the new conservatism was open to selective appropriation, distortion, and debasement.

Nonetheless, if the Nazis became past masters at appropriating and manipulating ultraconservative ideas, it was largely because Germany provided an exceptionally favorable terrain for their implantation and dissemination. Germany was not only Europe's eternal *Land der Mitte*, with fertile soil for the propagation of the specious syllogism of geopolitics. It was also, or perhaps above all, what Ernst Bloch called Europe's "classic country of unsimultaneity [*Ungleichzeitig-*

keit]," the ideal seedbed for fascism. After unification in 1870, and with mounting speed and intensity, the new German nation experienced the strains and stresses of uneven economic, social, and cultural development, in which the pace was set by an uncommonly rapid industrialization, urbanization, and bureaucratization. By the turn of the century the Second Empire had become Europe's most advanced industrial and capitalist society.

Nonetheless, in many important, possibly decisive, respects Germany remained an old regime, even after 1918, under the Weimar Republic. Germany's breakneck capitalist modernization was fitted into preexisting social, cultural, political, and military structures. Although this racing modernization overstrained some of these structures and warped the mentalities of some of their social carriers, by and large the long-established world persisted. In Germany's ruling and governing classes not only did the landed aristocracy of East Elbia keep most of its influence and power, but so did the higher echelons of the bureaucracy and the officer corps. The leaders of these three estates set their own dated terms for the admission of bourgeois businessmen and professionals to their relatively closed establishment. Even under the Weimar Republic the old elites continued to more than hold their own, in large part because they knew how to play on the conflicts of interest and social fears which agitated the business and professional classes. Eventually, Germany's elites were so weakened by internecine discords that as a last resort they called on Hitler to provide them with the popular support they needed to restabilize their endangered positions.

Hitler's popular support derived from yet another group whose roots—and outlook—were fixed in the past. It consisted, above all, of small but independent peasants, artisans, and shopkeepers. This composite lower middle class, which also included salaried white-collar workers, felt intensely threatened by both organized capitalism and organized Marxism. Large sectors of Germany's *Mittelstand* were nostalgic for other times, to which they hoped to return. The petty bourgeoisie, always anxious about their status, and according to Bloch filled with an "amorphous pent-up fury," became the reserve army of resistance to change. While this fury was latent in periods of normalcy, it threatened to erupt in times of crisis, fueled by a burning passion for "duty, *Bildung*, status, . . . home, soil, and *Volk.*"

Bloch postulated that in Germany the "simultaneity of the unsimultaneous" was so deep and pervasive that "no Nietzsche was needed for the antithesis of blood and intellect, ferocity and morality, frenzy and reason to develop into a conspiracy against civilization." The peculiar German ideology was unthinkable apart from the peculiar soil of the "classic country of unsimultaneity" in which it took root. The diffusion and appropriation of this ideology—of this new conservatism—were conditioned by this same ambience.

As of the last quarter of the nineteenth century anti-Semitism became an overt issue in the preachings of literati and politicians seeking to mobilize the real or self-styled losers of capitalist industrialization to hold and drive back the forces of modernity. In the manifestos of these hate-mongers the Jews became convenient scapegoats for the dissolution and defilement of an idealized and regretted past. Hitler made this retrogressive project his own. By casting the Jews as the principal agents—the "demons"—of economic, social, and cultural change, Hitler made them the surrogate *victims* of his counter-attack against polymorphous modernity, which was his ultimate *target.* This mutation of unorganized and fitful Judeophobia into political and systematic anti-Semitism went hand in hand with the transformation of the new conservatism into revolutionary counter-revolutionism. Early in his political career Hitler discovered himself to be "a revolutionary against the revolution," and he commended himself as such to would-be political allies. In this respect he was at one with Mussolini, except that unlike the duce he integrated anti-Semitism into his fascist formula.

In due time key business leaders supported collaboration with Hitler, prompting Max Horkheimer to assert "that whoever refuses to discuss capitalism should keep silent about fascism." There is no denying that influential industrialists and bankers, consumed by an obsessive hatred of socialism and fear of bolshevism, condoned the rise of National Socialism and facilitated Hitler's accession to power.

But while big business at critical moments encouraged the Nazi defiance, it was not its prime mover. Even if the bourgeoisie of industry, banking, and trade had not been internally divided, it would have been in no position to establish its own political ascendancy. No doubt it wielded enormous economic power during the Great War and between the two wars. But in all other respects—social, cultural, political—the bourgeoisie remained the junior partner of the feudal element and its confederates.

The composite bourgeoisie was too torn, weak, and ambivalent to wield as much influence as the power elite of the land, the bureaucracy, and the army, especially since this same elite also kept a firm hold on the churches, universities, and academies. While the bourgeoisie certainly aided and abetted the transfer of power to Hitler, it could not have cleared the way for it by itself or against the will of its senior partners. Fascism prevailed in Germany less because some sectors of big business used it as a stratagem to save capitalism than because the old elites resorted to it to preserve their superannuated positions of class, status, and power.

Perhaps Horkheimer's dictum should be revised to say that whoever refuses to discuss capitalism and its symbiotic relationship with the forces of the old order should keep silent about fascism. Particularly in times of serious economic crisis, without state aid capitalism was helpless in the face of the socialist and Communist challenge, and also of foreign competition. After 1929 the instability of Weimar's cabinets benefited the presidency, the army, the bureaucracy, and the judiciary. Since these organs of government were the chief strongholds of the world of yesterday, the old elites became Germany's designated power brokers. But they, too, had a large chink in their armor, disabling them for both democratic and plebiscitarian politics: Hitler had sapped their popular support, as measured by the inroads of the National Socialists into the electoral base of traditional conservatism. There was no way for the old elites to make good this deficit, particularly since their uneasy bourgeois associates were equally unsuited for the practice of Bonapartism.

Accordingly, in January 1933, to avert disaster, Germany's divided antidemocratic ruling and governing circles pulled together to exploit nazism for their own ends. By then Hitler had seen to the eruption of the "pent-up fury" of the lower middle classes. Clearly, like his political sponsors in the corridors of power, his popular supporters in the streets and at the polls were oriented toward the past. Hitler commended himself to both classes and masses with an ideology saturated with archaic and magical tropes. This is not to say that he dismissed or minimized the role of classes, interests, and objectives rooted in the historical present. Nor is it to suggest that once in power Hitler remained beholden or subservient to his political godfathers, though he never entirely forsook them. But it is to insist that National Socialism was at once a program and an ideology. Its core program— to overthrow the Weimar regime, to smash the organized left, to cut back unemployment, and to break the shackles of Versailles—rallied the full spectrum of conservatives, reactionaries, and counterrevolutionaries, both high and low. But this multipartisan policy, entailing a vague but firm commitment to autocratic government, was enveloped in a *Weltanschauung* that was a religion in a secular guise, with a distinctive decalogue, clergy, ritual, and teleology. Whereas the Nazi program was in large part coherent and calculated, its ideological integument was intrinsically irrational and impulsive. Of course all concerned reacted to both program and ideology, which were synergetic. At the outset, however, the old castes and the lower middle classes were more enthusiastic about the new religion than the bourgeoisie.

The ideology of nazism was passéist. Its projected millennium was furnished with symbolic bric-a-brac culled from Germany's remote ages. The Nazi vision of the present and future was essentially parochial, untouched by universal criteria of truth and knowing, which Hitler repudiated.

Hitler's millenarianism was no less powerful for being narrowly exclusive. The chimera of the Thousand-Year Reich was decked out in historical and symbolic motifs selected from Germany's past. Although the Nazi project was inherently gnostic and apocalyptic, it was also fundamentally nationalistic. Indeed, the secular faith and political messianism of nazism were built on the bedrock of extreme and expansionist nationalism. Both the charismatic prophet and the proselytizing message of this pseudoreligion were singularly German, drastically circumscribing its appeal abroad. Much the same was true for the crusading drive for eastern *Lebensraum*, since it was grounded in a legendary mission to protect the holy German empire from barbarians and infidels, which the Nazis regenerated in a de-Christianized and imperialist form. They authenticated the nonuniversalist character of their latter-day imperial pretense with their specious social Darwinist and racist lore.

No matter how this-worldly and parochial, nazism had all the earmarks of a religion. Its faith and canon were institutionalized in and through a political movement which bore some resemblance to a hierarchical church. The self-appointed head of this church, the führer, exercised strict authority over a ranked political clergy, as well as over a select order of disciples, with all the initiates wearing uniforms with distinct emblems and insignias. During both the rise of nazism and the life of the Nazi regime, this clergy acted as both the celebrants and the congregations for a wide range of cultic ceremonies, some of which took place in sacred shrines and spaces. Most of these ceremonies were conspicuously public and massive, their purpose being to exalt, bind, and expand the community of faithful. There were, in addition, more exclusive rites for chosen groups of true believers. But whatever the size and nature of the congregations of these cults, the latter had their own liturgical forms, complete with symbols, incantations, hymns, and sermons.

Just as the Nazi ideology could not be understood apart from the circumstances and purposes which gave rise to it, so it could not have been put into practice without the peculiar institutions through which it was propagated. Had it not been for these conditions and

institutions, Hitler's *Mein Kampf* would have been of no greater
political consequence than the writings of the right-wing paralogi-
cians of the late nineteenth century. Almost from the very beginning
the Nazi discourse could neither be read nor heard in and for itself.
Its maxims and watchwords were freighted with meanings derived
from the pseudo-religious cult that sanctified and propagated them.
By creating an emotionally charged atmosphere—for both believers
and unbelievers—this cult affected the ways in which the written and
spoken words of the Nazi ideology were read, heard, and experienced.
The Manichaean persuasion of nazism would have remained inert
and harmless if it had not been animated by collective rituals of
uncommon arrogance, hatred, and frenzy. This calculated release and
officially authorized display of "pent-up fury" embodied and amplified the violence of the written and spoken words.

Hitler viewed ideas in instrumental terms. He dismissed general principles unless they lent themselves to appropriation and manipulation
in his homespun political homilies, which gradually, after much testing, hardened into a coherent doctrine, set down in *Mein Kampf.* In
this manifesto—this National Socialist manifesto—Hitler laid bare
the premeditation with which he fabricated his ideological weapon.
As he stated himself, *Mein Kampf* was intended to propound a *Weltanschauung* whose general principles would be sufficiently vague to
"become the banner" of a political movement, which he saw developing into a "fighting fellowship of faith, unified in mind and will." At
the same time, it was meant to translate the "general conceptions"
of this worldview "into a political program." Hitler cast even this
political program in the form of a "faith" or a "credo," encapsulated
in "brief, precise, sloganlike" statements of "certain ideas" of the
overarching worldview. He maintained that "what dogmas are for
faith, party principles are for the political party in process of formation."

In *Mein Kampf* Hitler conceived the Nazi *Weltanschauung* as a
contraposition to the Marxist doctrine, which he considered "the
concentrated intellectual essence of today's universal world-concept."
For him, international Marxism was the final culmination and distilla-
tion of the Enlightenment, the initial wellspring of the modernity that
fired his burning hatred, fear, and aggression. In fact, Hitler stressed
that "without the underlying foundation of . . . [this] generally preexisting poisoning" the Marxist idea of class and equality would have
been stillborn. Since the bourgeois and Marxist projects discharged
essentially the same poisons, their worldviews differed "only in degree
and in personalities." According to Hitler, "the Jew Karl Marx,

. . . with the sure eye of the prophet, had recognized the essential poisons in the slough of a slowly decaying world," only to use them to quicken the ongoing rot for the benefit of "his race."

As self-styled counterprophet, Hitler put forward a worldview that recognized "the value of race" over class and the "aristocratic principle within the people" over "the idea of the majority." Not unlike "the Marxist party organization [which] clears the road for internationalism," this opposing ideology needed a fighting instrument "to assert itself in battle."

Hitler proposed to make the masses, not the classes, the social carriers of this organization. To counter the "fifteen million Marxists, Democrats, Pacifists, and Centrists," he meant to rally the people primarily with the nationalist, not the racist idea. Accordingly, Hitler fixed "the nationalization of the masses" as the "highest aim" of the Nazi movement. But since this ambitious goal could not be achieved by "half measures," he proposed to infuse this national awakening with "the whole vehemence inherent in extremes," to be applied with "ruthless and fanatically one-sided concentration."

Nationalism became a central tenet of the political faith that was to pit the nascent "*idealistic* Reich" against the "arithmeticians of the present *realistic* Republic." Taking the ways of the Catholic Church as his model, Hitler prescribed not only a "tenacious adherence to dogma" but also an aggressive propagation of the faith, driven by "fanatical intolerance." In a distant past, when building "its own altar," Christianity had not hesitated to "destroy the altars of the heathen."

From the expansion of the Christian faith and church, Hitler claimed to have learned that the drive against an opposing worldview required violence combined with the "driving power of a basic intellectual conception . . . and a definitive intellectual conviction." Indeed, unless such a campaign were rooted "in a fanatically intense *Weltanschauung,*" brute force would be "vacillating and uncertain," and ultimately self-destructive. To date, the battle against Marxism had been ineffective because without unshakable principles force could only be applied defensively and haltingly. To turn the tide, the enemies of Marxism would have to adopt a political faith and "exchange the catchword of weak and cowardly defense for the battle cry of bold and brutal attack."

This offensive could only be carried by the "broad masses of the common people," to be mobilized in the streets rather than through the parliament. To this end, Hitler urged recourse to "the magic power of the spoken . . . [rather than] the written word," in imitation of predecessors who had produced the "great religious and political landslides of history," including the volcanic eruption of Christianity. If Marxism had a firm hold on "the broad masses," it was not because these had read "the formal, written product of Jewish brainwork . . . and the Marxist Church Fathers." Actually, Hitler maintained, less than a hundred out of a hundred thousand German workers were familiar with the basic works of Karl Marx. Besides, these were written "not for the broad masses . . . but for the intellectual leadership of the Jewish machine for world conquest." The millions of workers who rallied to Marxism did so because they were carried along by an "enormous wave of oratorical propaganda" created by "the tireless and truly tremendous . . . work of ten-thousands of tireless agitators."

Hitler did not expect every fighter for the Nazi worldview to master the "ultimate ideas and reasoning of the movement's leaders." All he wanted was for the rank and file, like the soldiers of an army, to be taught "rigid discipline and fanatic belief in the justice and strength of their cause." To achieve this objective, propagandists would have to work on the emotions rather than the reasoning faculties of the great masses. They would also have to adopt "a deliberately subjective, one-sided attitude" on only a few salient issues, mindful that the absorptive capacity of the masses was "very limited, their understanding small, and their forgetfulness great." In *Mein Kampf* Hitler made it clear that Nazi propaganda would be "confined to a very few points." These would be expressed in simple slogans, to be repeated over and over, with a view to unleashing "a storm of hot passion."

Similarly, to be effective in the life-and-death struggle of opposing worldviews, it was all-important to focus sharply "on a single adversary." Hitler considered it "part of a great leader's genius to make even widely separated adversaries appear as if they belonged to one category." Apart from increasing "the magnetic attraction of a movement," this concentration on an archenemy was necessary to foster solidarity. To target a multiplicity of foes would be to leave room for self-doubt and "objectivity" among the faithful.

This fixation on a single sworn enemy was congruent with the exclusivity of the fighting movement and its worldview. Just as this movement was not simply one "party among others," in that it "imperiously demands complete and exclusive" loyalty, so its creed expressed a "hellish intolerance" for the enemy. Hitler affirmed that whereas ordinary political parties faced adversaries and were open to compromise, "world concepts proclaimed their infallibility," which was not negotiable. This unconditionality marked Hitler's affirmation in *Mein Kampf* that "with the Jew there can be no coming to terms, but only the implacable 'either-or.' "

. . .

"The Jew" occupied a significant place in *Mein Kampf*. He appeared in many different guises: the antithesis of the German Aryan, the purveyor of modernity, the prime mover of parasitic capitalism, the agent of Marxist subversion, and the master of Bolshevik Russia. It seems as if Hitler, determined to provide the Nazi movement with a single enemy, seized upon "the Jew" as best suited to make "widely separated adversaries appear as if they belonged to but one category."

In Hitler's conception the Jews were totally different from other peoples, their distinctiveness being in important ways racially determined, and therefore constant and immutable. But Hitler also stressed the ability of the Jews to maintain their unity and separateness by virtue of their special "intellectual qualities" and "religious bonds." In *Mein Kampf* he attached particular importance to the Jewish religion, whose teachings he alleged to be "primarily a rule to keep the blood of Jewry pure."

To Hitler the most characteristic fact about the Jews, the one that made them what they were, was their not having a "territorial state of their own." He denounced them for lacking the "productive capacities" and selfless idealism needed to build and preserve a state, yet he also damned them for excelling at compensating for their rootlessness. Through the ages, because of their "mania for self-preservation" and their "infinitely tenacious will to live," the Jews had devised countless stratagems for survival. Wherever they went, they fought "first for equal rights and then for superrights," always with the aim of perfecting their weapons of "cunning, intelligence, astuteness, knavery, [and] dissimulation [which were] rooted in the character of [their] folkdom." Hitler charged the Jews with appropriating the skills of Gentiles and exercising them with "naked egoism" for their own material benefit.

In the last analysis, he said, the Jews were parasites "on the body of other peoples." As such, they fed on the weaknesses and miseries of host nations, thereby sapping their strengths. Having devitalized or destroyed their prey, the Jews would move on to exercise their destructive force in other vulnerable lands. Repeatedly reviling "the Jewish parasite" for constantly "seeking new soil for his race to live on," he couched his denunciation as much in social as in racial terms. If anything, this unstudied confusion increased the effectiveness of his attack on "the Jew" by making it easier to portray him as the proverbial single enemy.

Mein Kampf was permeated with the language of parasitology. Hitler attributed the defeat of 1918 to "a whole series of manifestations of disease and its germs" dating back to before the war. Fortuitously, the "acute form of the collapse" exposed this "creeping disease," which would otherwise "have become chronic," destroying the nation "more slowly, perhaps, but all the more surely." Hitler claimed that while man was helpless and resigned in the face of insidious diseases like tuberculosis, he had learned "to master the plague," which struck violently, causing "fearful waves of deaths." In like manner, "the diseases of peoples" were fatal unless they took "the form of catastrophes," which prompted society to react "with ruthless energy."

Hitler singled out the Jews as the chief carriers of the deadly bacilli that were consuming Germany. Starting before 1914, the Jews had helped to spread the "carrion virus of Marxist ideas," the most dangerous of all the poisons. Had Germany had a "responsible national government" during the war, it would have "kept twelve to fifteen thousand of these Hebrew corrupters of the people under poisonous gas, as hundreds of thousands of our very best German workers . . . on the battlefield had to endure it." Indeed, the timely elimination of a few thousand "traitors, parasites, usurers, and swindlers" might have saved many times that many "real Germans of great value for the future." Instead, these Jewish "poisoners" were left free to continue their contamination, which was pervasive. The Jews were "disease carriers of the worst sort" in the cultural world as well, producing "literary filth, artistic trash, and theatrical nonsense." They infected the people "with an intellectual pestilence worse than the Black Death of ancient days."

In the present world, Jews were dangerous above all by virtue of being the founders and organizers of Marxism, which had scored its greatest triumph with the Bolshevik revolution and regime in Russia. According to Hitler's manifesto, just as the Jews had once used "the bourgeoisie as a battering ram against the feudal world," so they were now "using the worker against the bourgeoisie." Of course, by practicing "parliamentarism," which was as "dirty and untrue" as the Jews themselves, bourgeois democracy provided a fertile soil for the spread of the Marxist "world plague" and "pestilence." But at this time the Jews were using organized Marxism in their fight to replace the rule of democracy with that of the dictatorship of the proletariat. In this latest drive for power "the democratic popular Jew is becoming the bloody Jew and tyrant over the people." His true face was showing through in Russia, where he "killed (sometimes with inhuman tortures) or starved to death with truly fanatical savagery close to thirty million people." In his *Secret Book* Hitler pointed to "the Jewish struggle for hegemony in Russia" as a forewarning to Europe's established elites, insisting that "with the help of the Bolshevik revolution the Russian upper classes and . . . national intelligentsia were murdered and completely extirpated amid inhuman agonies and atrocities." The final consequence was the "denationalization" as well as the "promiscuous bastardization" of the Russian people. As he sounded the alarm about the danger of this "bloody Bolshevization" sweeping over the Continent, Hitler noted that "after the death of the victim, the [Jewish] vampire itself also will die sooner or later."

For Hitler "the two perils . . . of Marxism and Jewry" were fused to the point of being inseparable. Together they formed the antipode as well as chief enemy of his National Socialist faith and dogma.

> The Jewish doctrine of Marxism denies the aristocratic principle of Nature, and sets mass and dead weight of numbers in place of the eternal privilege of strength and power. Thus it denies the value of personality in man, disputes the significance of nation and race, and so deprives mankind of the essentials of its survival and civilization. Marxism as a foundation of the universe would be the end of any order conceivable to man. . . .

In keeping with his apocalyptic outlook and his need for a single enemy, in *Mein Kampf* Hitler warned that "if by help of his Marxist faith the Jew conquers the peoples of the world, his crown will be the burial wreath of mankind [and] our planet will again move uninhabited through the ether, as it did millions of years ago." As if to invest his own mission with a higher sanction, Hitler invoked "the spirit of the Almighty Creator" and professed that "by resisting the Jew I am fighting for the Lord's work."

The social Darwinist imperative, in addition to underpinning Hitler's dogma on the Jews, also informed his dogma on *Lebensraum* in eastern Europe. He maintained that just as throughout history individual men—and rootless Jews—struggled for existence and self-preservation, so did states and nations. According to *Mein Kampf* the precondition for the beginning of civilization was the "availability . . . , conquest, [and] subjugation . . . of inferior races." In a distant past "the conquered man . . . drew the plow" for the Aryan, whose instinct for self-preservation was coupled with a willingness to subordinate and sacrifice "his own ego to the life of the community." Ever since, international politics had been a life-and-death struggle in which the triumph of one nation meant the rape and conquest of another. For Hitler, states were locked in a perpetual struggle for survival, contingent on *Lebensraum*. Foreign policy had no real autonomy. It was governed by the same Hobbesian laws as domestic politics, with which it formed a seamless web.

Like Hitler's animus against the Jews, his obsession with *Lebens-raum* was intrinsically antimodernist, not to say archaic. At bottom, Hitler championed a foreign policy congruent with his hostility to industry, labor, and city. He embedded his critique of German foreign policy since 1870 in a comprehensive assault on modern Germany. Hitler charged that by pursuing "the phantasm of world economic conquest" past governments had served the runaway industrialization that was corrupting the nation. This "ill-conceived foreign policy" hastened the fatal decline of the "peasant class," which was being supplanted by the "mass of the proletariat." Given Germany's "stupendous" population growth, the result was "the violent contrast between poor and rich . . . and the political division of classes," especially in the turbulent cities. But worst of all, *Weltpolitik*, or global politics, including the bid for overseas colonies, forced the country's "commercialization and industrialization" to such a degree that economics "became the ruling mistress of the state [and] money became . . . the false Mammon [for whom] incense was being burned." Unfortunately, even Kaiser William II had sanctioned this "rule of money . . . by bringing the nobility under the influence of the new finance capitalism." Starting before 1914, the "personal form of property" was crushed by corporations and stock exchanges which furthered the "internationalization of the German economic structure," and hence its vulnerability to foreign powers.

Hitler insisted that instead of concentrating on "a colonial and commercial policy" Germany needed to adopt a "territorial policy." In addition to securing "new land for the transplantation of the overflowing population," such a policy would help to arrest Germany's decay by preserving or restoring a "healthy peasant class." For Hitler a sound peasantry was the best antidote to the nation's "social ills." By insuring the supply of "daily bread," peasants would also check the growth of industry and trade, and hence the nation's dependence on imports.

In light of Germany's swelling population there were only two alternatives. One, which was unacceptable, was to allow the country's "inadequate living space" to continue being turned into ever greater "work centers" that were "like abscesses in the national body in which all evils, vices, and diseases seemed to unite," making them breeding grounds for "international Jewish racial-maggots." The other was to secure the additional *Lebensraum* without which the German nation and people could not survive and prosper. It was up to the "racial state" to use foreign and military policy to "remove the disparity between our population and the scope of our territory." Of course, "national leaders" would have to use "domestic policy . . . to forge the sword" with which to execute their foreign policy of "land and soil," the sword being the "pathbreaker for the plough."

In sum, in *Mein Kampf* Hitler vowed that German foreign policy would be "determined by the necessity to secure the space necessary to the life of our people." Such a territorial policy could not help but be radically different from the "border policy" of the Weimar Republic's bourgeois cabinets, which called only for "the restoration of the frontiers of 1914." These boundaries were incomplete in terms of both "German nationality" and "military-geographic fitness," so that even if they were reclaimed, they could not justify the sacrifices of the last war.

As for the geographic direction of the new territorial policy, Germany could only expand in Europe, "not in the Cameroons," and in Europe it could only do so "at the expense of Russia." Had the leaders of the Second Empire realized this before 1914, they would not have simultaneously backed Vienna and pursued *Weltpolitik*, thereby alienating both St. Petersburg and London. Instead, Germany would have offered England a free hand overseas in exchange for a free hand with Russia, the traditional rival of the British Empire.

Hitler maintained that although the collapse of the Habsburg and Romanov empires had drastically changed the European system and the world order, there remained a solid basis for Anglo-German cooperation. Germany was no longer handicapped by the Austrian connection. In turn, England needed an ally to help steady the Continent and contain bolshevism, freeing London to concentrate on its naval and economic rivalry with the United States. The main obstacle was a rift inside England: whereas "official or rather traditional British statesmanship" was eager to collaborate with Germany, "the Jewry of finance," centered in London and New York, pushed for Germany's "complete economic destruction . . . [and] political enslavement," which was contrary to England's real interest. Jewish finance and its "Marxist soldiers" were in the forefront of a drive to internationalize the German economy. Their objective was to quicken the modernization and Bolshevization of this economy with a view to "breaking the backbone of the German National State." Jewish interests similarly worked against an Anglo-Japanese rapprochement.

No effort should be spared to reach an agreement with England, not least in order to outflank France, whose enmity was intractable. But attention should be focused, above all, on Russo-German relations, which were both the "most critical business in German foreign policy . . . [and] the test of clear thinking and correct acting . . . for the young National Socialist movement." In his manifesto Hitler made a special point of emphasizing that Berlin's Russian policy was the key to Germany's domestic and international rebirth. In characteristically archaic terms he stressed that the time had come for a new German empire to resume the eastward march of the "Knights of the German Order, to give sod to the German plow by the German sword, and to win the daily bread of the nation." To do so would require a radical change.

> Thus we National Socialists put an end to the prewar tendencies of our foreign policy. We begin the work where it was left six hundred years ago. We stem the eternal Germanic migration to the South and West of Europe, and direct our eyes towards the land in the East. We finally put an end to the prewar colonial and trade policy and change over to the land policy of the future.

Hitler repeated that as he probed for "new land and soil" for Germany he could "think only of Russia and the border states that are subject to her."

Geopolitics dictated this course. The east alone could provide the German people with "sufficient living space for the next hundred years," while simultaneously making Germany "a decisive power on the land, . . . which presupposes great military power." Germany could then also afford to allow its "naval power . . . [to] recede into the background," which would reassure England.

But there were also compelling political and ideological reasons for turning east. As if willed by "Fate," the Bolshevik revolution had weakened Russia by removing "the Germanic upper stratum," its essential "state-forming force." Being racially inferior, the Slavs were incapable of building and preserving a state by themselves. Of course, the Jews had filled the void and were running Russia. But since the Jews invariably were "a ferment of decomposition" rather than "an element of organization," they would leave the "gigantic Empire in the East ripe for collapse" and for German conquest.

An alliance with Russia was out of the question. Even if a truly "national element" resurfaced there, it would "be madness" to join forces with Moscow. Since the Western powers would never tolerate a Russo-German bloc, Germany would risk having to fight a war on its own soil and by itself, except for the support of an antiquated Russian army lacking "technical armaments" and motor power. Such a conflict could only spell "the end of Germany."

As for an entente with the Bolshevik regime, it would be even riskier than with a traditional Russia. Of course, the "present rulers" in Moscow had no intention of making and honoring an alliance. But above all, from Germany's standpoint, there could be no collaborating with a nation whose leaders were "bloodstained criminals . . . [who had] killed and rooted out millions of [Russia's] leading intelligentsia in a wild thirst for blood . . . [and] exercised the most cruel tyranny of all times." Besides, Soviet Russia's leaders were linked with international Jewry, which was bent on imposing "its bloody suppression upon the whole world." In Hitler's view, as articulated in *Mein Kampf*, since "Russian bolshevism represents the twentieth-century attempt of the Jews to gain world dominion . . . the struggle against the Bolshevization of the world by the Jew necessitates a clear attitude toward Russia."

Under the circumstances, rather than making overtures to the Soviets, Germany should prepare to conquer Russia's "gigantic land area," which the Jews would be incapable of forging into a state. It was Germany's "good fortune" that it could move into this vacuum without too much effort. By so doing it would at one and the same time forestall the formation of a second major continental power on Germany's own borders and carry through the territorial policy of guaranteeing "every individual descendant of our people his own piece of land and soil for centuries to come." Hitler knew no holier "right" than to take possession of the "soil which one wants to till oneself" and no holier "sacrifice" than to "shed blood" for it.

Hitler's geopolitically and racially informed imperative for *Lebensraum* in the east was of one piece with his antimodernist and anti-Semitic project inside Germany. Of course, to extend German power through eastern Europe deep into Russia was to bid for the mastery of Europe. It would seem, however, that this territorial policy was not conceived as a calculated first step toward world domination. On the contrary, Hitler intended continental imperialism to be a retreat from *Weltpolitik*, and to facilitate a contraction of those sectors of Germany's economy and society which he felt supported it. Although he had no intention of dismantling big industry and finance, he proposed to bend and reshape them to fit the needs of his territorial policy. By implication, this meant reducing the export sectors of the economy in favor of the heavy industry essential to modern warfare, whose economic and technological requirements Hitler appreciated.

The fact that Russia was ruled by a Bolshevik regime increased the ideological charge and fixedness of Hitler's eastern-oriented territorial reach. The conquest of living space would be combined with an assault on the chief citadel of the opposing worldview. This anti-Marxist and anti-Bolshevik intention gave a pseudoreligious consecration to the sword and the plow of the revived *Drang nach Osten* (drive to the east). The renascent "Knights of the German Order" would march under the dual banner of supernationalism and anticommunism.

As previously noted, anti-Marxism and anti-Semitism were closely but indeterminately interwoven in Hitler's justification for the conquest of *Lebensraum* from Russia. He saw and portrayed the Jews as controlling the Soviet government and the Moscow-based Third International, and charged them with using both to advance their own bid for world domination. Yet in the same breath in which Hitler made Jewry out to be infinitely powerful and cunning, he scorned the Jews of the Bolshevik regime as being unfit to rule. Rather than fearing the Jews of Moscow, he expected them to further the decomposition of Russia and thus clear the way for easy conquest. In *Mein Kampf* there is nothing to suggest that the drive to the east was intended to decapitate the "Jewish octopus" or to seize Europe's principal reservoir of Jews, located in Poland and Russia.

Mein Kampf's fantasy of a "Jewish-Bolshevik" conspiracy echoed the fabrications of the *Protocols of the Elders of Zion*. Brought to Munich by White émigrés from the Russian Revolution, this forged document purporting to be a Jewish manual for world conquest was of another time and place. It reflected the essentially religious and cultural anti-Semitism of the late tsarist empire, which had taken the form of residential restrictions, quotas, blood libels, and pogroms. Influenced by Alfred Rosenberg, a Baltic German driven out of revolutionary Russia, Hitler appropriated the idea of the ubiquitous, clannish, grasping, and conniving Jew from the *Protocols*. In his rendering, this eternal Jew had taken to exploiting bolshevism, both national and international, as part of his most ambitious and daring bid for power to date. Not unlike anti-Marxism and antibolshevism, this anti-Semitism both suited and stimulated Hitler's *Drang nach Osten*.

Anti-Semitism permeated Hitler's worldview and project. It was also consonant with his interpretation—and execration—of the corruption of the modern world. But while Hitler condemned the Jews as the chief disease-carrying poisoners and parasites of contemporary society, he struck out through them against the processes and forces of emancipation and modernization, which for him were the ultimate source of pollution. Indeed, if Hitler's worldview had an epicenter, it was his deep-seated animosity toward contemporary civilization, and not his hatred for Jews, which was grafted onto it.

Just as anti-Semitism was not the core of Hitler's presumption, it did not have precedence over his other dogmas, particularly anti-Marxism and antibolshevism. Although infused with Jew-hatred, they were not mere screens or surrogates for it. Hitler was obsessed with two imagined threats: the Marxist-cum-Bolshevik "octopus" and the

Jewish world conspiracy. He did not put one ahead of the other. They were twins, even if not identical twins. Both were at one and the same time incarnations and agents of decay, and both were to be extirpated. Hitler also invoked anti-Marxism and anti-Semitism, separately and jointly, to give a quasi-religious impetus to the imperative for eastern *Lebensraum*, which like them was inherently autonomous. All three tenets—anti-Semitism, anti-Marxism, and eastern expansionism—were pervaded with antimodernism, and all three furthered the eschatological momentum of the Nazi movement. Of course, inwardly anti-Semitism may have been Hitler's core idea and all-consuming passion. But before 1933 neither his public discourse nor the creed and ritual of the Nazi movement put it first, or were perceived as doing so.

Anti-Semitism did not play a decisive or even significant role in the growth of the Nazi movement and electorate. The appeals of nazism were many and complex. People rallied to a syncretic creed of ultranationalism, social Darwinism, anti-Marxism, antibolshevism, and anti-Semitism, as well as to a party program calling for the revision of Versailles, the repeal of reparations, the curb of industrial capitalism, and the establishment of a *völkisch* welfare state.

Not unlike the Nazi ideology as a whole, anti-Semitism was multifaceted. There was, to be sure, the racially weighted anti-Semitism promulgated by Hitler. But because it was so novel, incoherent, and extreme, it may initially have been less prevalent and consequential than the more traditional form of theologically leavened economic, social, and cultural Judeophobia. Large sectors of the beleaguered *Mittelstand* were particularly susceptible to this customary Jew-baiting, and so were frustrated university students and professionals.

More than likely most of the Germans who joined and supported the Nazi movement, or sympathized with it, did so without regard to its political and racial anti-Semitism, or in spite of it. But once drawn into or close to the fold, they embraced or assumed it along with nazism's other articles of faith and political promises. This assent or connivance was facilitated by latent Judeophobia, which predisposed many constituencies in Germany to concede the legitimacy of taking up what was euphemistically referred to as the "Jewish question." Formulated by conservative and reactionary publicists and politicians during the Second Empire, this "question" centered on how to curb the Jews who were said to have become unduly influential and subversive in civil and political society. Their main proposal was to promulgate quotas to limit the access of Jews to universities, the professions, and the civil service. Beginning with the great economic emergency in 1929, the Nazis' stentorian assault on Jewish bolshevism and Jewish plutocracy made such measures appear moderate and reasonable by comparison and may thus have helped to gain acceptance for them.

But in the last analysis this normalization of anti-Semitism owed as much to Germany's traditional elites as to the Nazi leaders and their petty bourgeois followers. Many members of the upper and conservative classes in and out of government shared too many of the basic values and objectives of the National Socialist movement to take exception to its increasingly sweeping and violent Jew-baiting. They were at one with the Nazis in their hostility to communism, socialism, organized labor, the Versailles *Diktat,* the Weimar Republic, and Bolshevik Russia. Panic-stricken by the consequences of the Great Depression, high civil servants and officers became increasingly disposed to overlook, if not countenance, even the worst political and rhetorical excesses of the Nazis, and so did prominent businessmen, agrarians, professionals, churchmen, and academics. Not that significant numbers of Germany's upper ten thousand actively supported or joined the Nazi Party. But they and their political spokesmen were so determined to turn the "nationalization of the masses" to their own advantage that they closed their eyes to the deep moral and political gulf between themselves and the Nazis. As part of this indulgence for the unrestrained politics of unreason, the German elites blinked at the irruption of the new anti-Semitism, which they downplayed and expected to fade away. Besides, they did not attach a high priority or urgency to the "Jewish problem." In the meantime, they covered the miasmic scourge of anti-Semitism with their prestige and silence.

PART TWO

CHAPTER V

THE FOUNDING AND CONSOLIDATION OF THE NAZI REGIME

MAINSPRINGS OF DEEMANCIPATION

That Hitler and the National Socialists were anti-Semitic is beyond question. It is no less certain that soon after they were in partial or full control of the German government they began to deemancipate the Jews. Before too much longer they began to use a combination of economic, political, and social pressure as well as terror to drive them to emigrate. But this is not the same as saying that this disenfranchisement, exclusion, and forced emigration were so many cunningly calculated preliminary steps toward the predetermined final goal of extermination. To posit that the forced emigration or flight of German Jewry was a prelude to the murder of European Jewry is also to posit that Nazi Germany—or Hitler—went to war to dominate the Continent and perhaps the world in order to capture the maximum number of Jews for slaughter.

There is no evidence to support the view that the destruction of the Jews was the primary motive and purpose of Hitler's pursuit of power and determination to go to war. The causes and driving forces for the Judeocide were infinitely more numerous and complex. Although the anti-Semitism of Hitler and the Nazis was hard-set, it could not have become genocidal without a whole series of enabling and catalyzing contingencies, which ultimately included the opportunistic conquests and irreversible insufficiencies of an ideologically immutable warfare state.

The most crucial of these contingencies was the deep-seated convergence of interests and compatibility of values between, on the one hand, the cartel of traditional conservatives and reactionaries, and, on the other hand, Hitler and the National Socialist movement. Against the background of the most severe economic and political repercussions of the world depression anywhere in Europe, both sides were equally extreme in their hostility to the left as well as in their resolve to bury the Weimar Republic and the Versailles Treaty. The "Jewish problem" was not an issue in the political maneuvers and negotiations that culminated in the incumbent conservative elite calling on Hitler to become chancellor of Germany. In coming to terms the principals did, however, share the unspoken assumption that Germany faced a "Jewish question" and that it would be both necessary and legitimate to deal with it as part of an all-out effort to resolve the nation's general crisis. The callow Nazis were certain to press for a sweeping deemancipation, while the old ruling and governing classes would probably settle for the adoption of a *numerus clausus* for Jews in the civil service, the professions, and higher education. In any event, while anti-Semitism was certainly an important ideological cement binding together the rival factions of the Nazi movement, it was not one of Hitler's major or decisive electoral appeals. Moreover, not anti-Semitism but a combination of anticommunism and ultranationalism constituted the brick and mortar for the factitious collaboration between Nazism and conservatism in both political and civil society. In the crunch of 1932–33, the "Jewish question" was not at the top or center of their joint preoccupations.

On becoming chancellor on January 30, 1933, Hitler headed not an all-Nazi but a coalition cabinet of "national concentration." The traditional conservatives in this government had close links to Field Marshal Paul von Hindenburg, the aged president who had finally yielded to their counsel, if not pressure, to appoint and ordain Hitler. Although there were scattered and spontaneous anti-Semitic incidents during Hitler's first two months in office, his government and political movement concentrated on hounding leftists, not Jews. In fact, the political and syndical left remained the principal target of brutal repression well past the time of the definitive consolidation of the new regime in July-August 1934. The non-Nazi cabinet ministers actually were even more willing than Hitler to use violence to destroy the left as part of their unconscionable bid to restore a populist variant of the pre-Weimar authoritarian order by enlisting the services of self-proclaimed barbarians.

Although only four of the twelve members of the coalition government were certified Nazis, they arrogated disproportionate power to themselves. Hitler was clearly in command, not least because he had the popular support that his conservative associates knew full well they could not muster on their own. After Hitler, the most important Nazi in the Cabinet was Dr. Wilhelm Frick, the former interior minister of Thuringia. A faithful member of the party and a skilled bureaucrat, Frick took over the strategically important Reich Ministry of the Interior, in which he served for ten years. While Hermann Göring became minister without portfolio and commissioner for aviation, at the outset his inordinate power stemmed from Hitler's also having put him in charge of the Prussian Interior Ministry, Police, and Gestapo. On March 3 the new chancellor formally appointed Dr. Joseph Goebbels, the gauleiter of Greater Berlin, to head Germany's—indeed Europe's—first Ministry of Popular Enlightenment and Propaganda.

These four relative neophytes were allied with eight experienced conservatives who needed but distrusted them and their fiendish populism, which they were confident of bridling in due time. Of the eight conservative cabinet members, five were nobles with an aristocratic aura about them; four were holdovers from the von Schleicher and von Papen cabinets; and five remained in Hitler's government for over four years, two of them until 1945. Four of the non-Nazi ministers were so-called "professionals," one was a right-wing Catholic, and three were members of the German National People's Party (DNVP, or Nationalist Party).

Except for Hitler himself, and given Göring's patrician lineage and pseudoaristocratic swagger, Franz Seldte was the only "commoner" without a university education in the cabinet. A manufacturer from Magdeburg, Seldte had been wounded and decorated in the Great War. This *Kriegserlebnis,* or war experience, prompted him to found and lead the Stahlhelm, a sprawling paramilitary formation of far-rightist war veterans. Although the superpatriotic Stahlhelm originally marched in step with the Nationalist Party, as of 1928 it moved closer to the Nazis in both outlook and tactics. Soon after becoming minister of labor, a post he held until April 30, 1945, Seldte reluctantly merged his veterans' organization into the Nazi movement, notably into the SA.

The five aristocrats in the cabinet were Franz von Papen, vice chancellor and reich commissar for Prussia; Baron Konstantin von Neurath, foreign minister; Count Lutz Schwerin von Korsigk, minister of finance (until May 23, 1945); Baron Paul von Eltz-Rübenach, minister of transport and postal service; and General Werner von Blomberg, minister of the armed forces. All five had solid roots in the preindustrial establishment of the land-based civil and military service nobility. Although they were non-Nazi, they were scarcely nonpartisan or unpolitical state servants.

Alfred Hugenberg, the minister of economics, food, and agriculture, was a notable of another sort. Chairman of the Nationalist

Party, he was a self-made man who had amassed his fortune first as a top executive in the Krupp combine and then as a mass-media mogul. Though a powerful spokesman for big business, Hugenberg was anything but an absolute bourgeois. A reactionary Pan-German with monarchist leanings, he gradually but clumsily adopted right-populist tactics, and finally became one of Hitler's chief fellow travelers. Caught between Hitler, who was wary of his independent power base, and the aristocratic notables, who disdained his radical conservatism, Hugenberg was forced out of the government within five months.

Clearly, Hitler was surrounded and helped by men who were not of his own ilk, and his very respectable conservative cabinet ministers were but the tip of a massive iceberg of collaboration. Although the higher echelons of the civil and military bureaucracy did not actively aid and abet the Nazi rise to power, they did nothing to hamper or obstruct it. Indeed, they became compliant collaborators, thereby providing not only an essential framework of continuity but also a nimbus of legitimacy. Civil servants and army officers, both high and low, cooperated quite readily, as did most of the magnates of industry, banking, and agriculture. Intellectuals, academicians, and clerics did likewise. Along with judges and lawyers they generally remained silent in the face of egregious violations of civil rights and liberties immediately before and after Hitler's accession to the chancellorship on January 30. University professors behaved in much the same way, in that they did not protest breaches of academic freedom.

This wholesale collaboration was not secured by force or violence. The old ruling and governing classes freely came together around Hitler because they shared many of his objectives at home and abroad. Like him, they wanted to regenerate Germany, which meant, to begin with, overthrowing the Weimar Republic in favor of an authoritarian regime. They were, of course, far from agreed, even among themselves, on essential questions of foreign, military, and cultural policy. Notwithstanding a shared fear of possible Nazi leveling, the old elites were also intensely divided over social and economic questions. Even so, conservatives, reactionaries, and counterrevolutionaries were joined by one strong, if negative, common denominator: the resolve to destroy the organized left. Whatever reservations Hitler's collaborators may have had about his verbal and political excesses, they condoned or supported them provided they were turned against Marxism in any of its guises—communism and socialism at home, and Soviet bolshevism abroad. As previously noted, Hitler gave top priority to persecuting not the Jews but the left, and he did so both out of personal conviction and because he calculated that by so doing he could rally broad support among the old elites, whom he meant to entrap. Indeed, he used the suppression of the left to legitimate the politics of violence and unreason which enabled him to set up a one-party state and to wear down real and imagined internal enemies at will. By condoning if not encouraging the crushing of the organized left, Hitler's otherwise cunning collaborators unwittingly helped clear the way for the Nazi drive against the Jews, who at the outset were persecuted for political, intellectual, and cultural radicalism rather than for their ethnicity or race.

On February 1, 1933, two days after he was elevated to the chancellorship, Hitler issued a declaration blaming the Marxist parties for the misery of Germany and insisting that especially the Communists and their fellow travelers were exploiting it for their own destructive ends. In the name of the new government, and invoking Christian values, he vowed that since "one year of bolshevism" would complete the nation's ruin he would not tolerate "the red flag of destruction" being planted in the heart of Europe. Two days later Hitler told the commanders of Germany's armed forces of his resolve to "exterminate Marxism root and branch" and to use radical methods to "eliminate the cancerous ravages of democracy." After reassuring the Reichswehr, or regular army, that "Nazi organizations" had the struggle against internal enemies well in hand, he urged Germany's generals to remain "unpolitical and nonpartisan." And as if to tempt them, the führer promised that once consolidated, his government would turn to "conquering new export possibilities or, more likely, new *Lebensraum* in the east, which would be ruthlessly Germanized."

On February 20 Hitler and Göring addressed a group of twenty-five leading industrialists and bankers. Again, the message was the same. Harkening back to Bismarck, who had warned that liberalism would become the "forerunner of Social Democracy," the chancellor charged that in the present situation a host of subversive forces were acting as "forerunners of bolshevism." Since economics and politics were inseparable, a firm political order was an essential prerequisite for economic and fiscal recovery. The nation was about to vote again, for the fifth time in five years, and this was, Hitler emphasized, the last chance to secure stability through legislative elections. Should the outcome be inconclusive, the electoral road would have to be abandoned, for "there is no going back." Hitler spoke for both himself and the assembled leaders of the business community when he insisted that there could be "no internal peace until Marxism is finished off," and that this would have to be the primary objective, "no matter how hard the fight." Should communism not be defeated at the polls, it would have to be vanquished with "other weapons, which might claim heavier casualties."

Göring, who had summoned some of Germany's most powerful economic leaders to this meeting at his residence, was the next to speak. Like Hitler, he reassured them that capitalism would be safe, provided political conditions were stabilized. For that reason the upcoming elections, fixed for March 5, would be critical, especially since they would be the last "for five years, if not a hundred years." Since many business magnates both countenanced and dreaded yet another frenzied election, Göring promised that whatever the outcome, the "distribution [of seats] in the Cabinet between the NSDAP [Nazi Party] and the DNVP would remain unchanged." Before adjourning, the spokesmen for major branches of industry pledged 3 million marks for a special election fund to be administered by Hjalmar Schacht, the prominent conservative nationalist who had facilitated the nascent collaboration between Hitler and big business and in March was reappointed to the presidency of the Reichsbank.

Göring, in addition to being close to Hitler, had the whip hand in Prussia, far and away Germany's largest and most populous state, with Berlin as its capital. Bent on setting the pace, he hastened to purge Prussia's civil service and to use its police force to restore the order which the Nazis themselves had done so much to undermine. On February 17 he issued a circular instructing the police to "proceed forcibly against the terrorist acts and assaults of Communists, and not to hesitate to make use of firearms." Göring assured Prussia's 54,500 policemen that should they have to shoot, he would fully "cover their actions" and warned them against being inhibited by "false scruples." Five days later, on February 22, Göring nearly doubled his police force by making members of the SA, the SS, and the Stahlhelm auxiliary police agents, with the right to bear side arms.

Instead of restraining Hitler and the Nazi ministers, the conservatives in the Cabinet supported, not to say encouraged, them in their indiscriminate assault on the Weimar constitution and above all on the supposedly ubiquitous and pernicious left. They were so eager for the suppression of the Communists, socialists, trade unionists, and *Kulturbolschewisten* that they condoned the destruction of what remained of the *Rechtsstaat*. In the process, the old elites kept lending credence to the wild exaggerations of the left's strength and militancy, which Hitler used to frighten undecided voters and to present himself as the savior in the face of imminent chaos and revolution.

The Reichstag fire of February 27 and the events that followed proved, if proof was needed, that there was no popular front of resistance to make a stand against the preemptive counterrevolution launched and directed by Hitler, with the connivance of the traditional right. It is immaterial whether in starting this blaze Marinus van der Lubbe, the Dutch anarcho-Communist, acted on his own or in concert with the SA, either knowingly or unintentionally. What mattered was that the new chancellor was generally perceived as having moved quickly and skillfully to turn the fire to political account, thereby both impressing and intimidating his conservative associates. Even though they had heretofore scorned the Reichstag as a symbol of the political deficiencies of the hated Weimar Republic, the Nazi leaders now posed as its protectors, not to say its avengers, insisting that this act of arson amply vindicated their predictions of Communist terror. With the building still smoldering, Hitler easily convinced the conservative Cabinet members and President von Hindenburg to approve the second of a series of emergency decrees suspending fundamental personal rights and constitutional guarantees, ostensibly to better "protect the people and the state."

Armed with this additional conservative empowerment, the Nazis stepped up their drive against leftists. Göring ordered the arrest of all Communist deputies in the Reichstag and the Prussian Diet in the capital. He also ordered the closing of the offices, newspapers, and meeting halls of the Communist Party (KPD) throughout Prussia. In the Reich as a whole, about four thousand Communist officials and party members were arrested within a matter of hours, while the SA and the SS harassed Social Democrats and other anti-Nazis as well.

On March 3, two days before the balloting, Göring divulged his own political strategy in a statement giving the crux of nazism's political formula. He boasted that instead of fighting a defensive campaign pervaded with "bourgeois civility and faintheartedness" he was "attacking on a broad front," without regard for legal niceties. In this "war to the death" against communism, Göring proposed "to destroy and to exterminate, nothing less." Rather than rely exclusively on regular "police powers," as was the practice in bourgeois states, he looked to the Brownshirts (SA) to help bring the Communists to heel.

With these blustering assertions justifying political arrests, street brawls, and mass demonstrations, the Nazis abandoned the pretense of formal legality. They stripped away the cloak of law that usually is needed to make coercion palatable to conservatives. Even so, the old elites, both in and out of government, continued to whitewash the verbal and political aggression of the Nazi leaders much as Göring and Frick "covered" the lawless violence of the police and the SA.

The election of March 5 was remarkable by any standard. Counting the two presidential elections of 1932, this was the seventh in five years. Even so, the rate of participation was higher than ever before: 39.3 million citizens went to the polls, or close to 90 percent of all eligible voters. Despite all the terror and intimidation, the left held fast. Since the election of November 6, 1932, the Social Democratic Party (SPD) lost only 2 percent of its popular vote and one parliamentary seat, leaving it with over 7 million supporters and 120 deputies. Although the Communist Party lost 19 seats and 1 million votes, or 4.55 percent of its following, it nevertheless received close to 5 million votes and elected 81 deputies, most of them in jail or in exile. Between them, the fatally incompatible Social Democrats and Communists captured slightly over 30 percent of the electorate and 202 out of a total of 647 Reichstag seats, or 17 seats short of one-third of parliament. As for the two principal Catholic parties, the Zentrum, or Center Party, and the Bavarian Peoples' Party, they, too, held their own, securing 14 percent of the vote and 92 seats. The Center Party was, of course, by far the largest of these two. Despite a slight drop, it retained 4.5 million voters, or 11.2 percent of the total, giving it 73 deputies, a gain of 3 over the preceding legislature.

In one sense it might be argued that taken together the Communists, socialists, and Catholics constituted an internally divided opposition bloc of nearly 45 percent of the electorate and of all Reichstag deputies. But the political Catholics cannot really be lumped with the would-be opposition. To be sure, they did not vote for the Nazis. But after 1928 large numbers of them, and many of their leaders, espoused some of the principal tenets of Hitler's program, and their latent Judeophobia made them view Nazi anti-Semitism with indulgence. Whatever the residual strength of democratic and left-reformist Catholicism, Monsignor Ludwig Kaas, the head of the Zentrum, never even considered leading his followers into opposition. In short, the Center Party had fewer affinities with the Social Democrats, not to mention the Communists, than with the Nationalists. Once it rallied to Hitler, it did so despite his contempt for Christianity, which he counterbalanced with indications that he wished to keep open his lines to the Catholic and Protestant churches, as well as to the Vatican.

As for the Nationalist Party, it never really recovered the ground it had lost to Hitler in 1928. On March 5 the Nationalists secured only 3.1 million votes, or 8 percent of the popular vote, leaving them with a mere fifty-two seats. By contrast, Hitler's National Socialists, or Nazis, gathered 17.3 million votes, 43.9 percent of those cast, giving them 288 deputies.

Clearly, then, the Nazis did not win an absolute majority by themselves, but such an outcome would in any case have been extremely unlikely in a multiparty system. What is so striking is that with their blatantly violent ideology, program, and tactics they managed to secure by far the largest popular vote of any party, primarily by mobilizing the lower middle classes for their cause. In addition, supported by the Nationalists, their bona fide partners, the Nazis could rightfully claim to speak for the majority: 20.4 million out of 39.3 million voters, or 51.9 percent of the total, and 340 out of 647 Reichstag seats. Although the popular and parliamentary margin was slim, it was enough to project a semblance of democratic legality that assuaged many a troubled conscience in the establishment. In actual fact, by breaking the law it claimed to uphold, the coalition government acquired control of the lower house: the 81 Communist deputies were in jail, in hiding, or in exile. Of the 120 socialist representatives, 10 were in prison and 16 had either gone underground or fled abroad. Even so, the Nazis stepped up their drive against leftists, still portraying them as an unremitting clear and present danger. On March 10, Hitler called on the party, the SA, and the SS to continue giving first priority to "the destruction of Marxism."

At the same time they increased the level of coercion, the Nazis redoubled their efforts to present themselves as the chosen heirs and agents of Germany's hallowed national traditions. To this end, Hitler decided to make a special occasion of the investiture of the new parliament. He charged Goebbels with inventing and orchestrating the imagery and symbolism of what was to become a spectacular national celebration. The day chosen was March 21, the anniversary of Bismarck's inauguration of the first all-German Reichstag in 1871. The main activities would take place in Potsdam, the cradle of the Hohenzollerns, the dynasty whose name was synonymous with Prussia's legendary glories.

The first act of the syncretistic ceremony designed to reconcile and unite the old and the new Germany was a carefully staged meeting of the two principals on the steps of Potsdam's Garrison Church, where Frederick the Great was buried. For the occasion Hitler wore tails and carried a top hat, while Hindenburg wore his field marshal's uniform and clutched his military baton. After shaking hands, they advanced, together, into the church. As in late imperial times, the choir and galleries were filled with diplomats, generals, admirals, and other dignitaries, many of them in colorful attire. The members of the government sat inside the chancel facing the marble altar. The pews behind them, in the nave, were reserved for the Reichstag deputies of the Nazi, Nationalist, and Catholic parties. The Socialists stayed away, and the attendance of Communists was proscribed.

Characteristically, the Nazi deputies wore their brown-shirted uniforms. No less significant, while in the old imperial box a chair was pointedly left empty for Kaiser William II, his son occupied the seat immediately behind it. Wearing a Death's Head Hussar's uniform, with its high fur cap, former Crown Prince Frederick William, who nurtured hopes of a Hohenzollern restoration, was accompanied by his wife Cecilie of Mecklenburg, who made no secret of her Nazi sympathies. With bells tolling and the organ pealing, Hindenburg and Hitler continued to move down the aisle, with Hitler trailing behind ever so slightly as a mark of respect for his venerable partner, who had both appointed and cleansed him. Presently, the president stopped, momentarily, before the imperial box, just ten feet from his own seat of honor, to raise his marshal's baton in homage to the ex–crown prince.

After an invocation by Otto Dibelius, eminent Evangelical leader and general superintendent of Brandenburg, President von Hindenburg delivered a brief address. He urged the members of the new Reichstag to rally around the cabinet, the recent elections having given it "a clear popular majority" and providing it "with the constitutional foundations for its labors." Hitler spoke at considerably greater length. But except for his praise for "this marriage of the symbols of ancient grandeur and new-wrought strength," what he said was less important than the setting in which he delivered an essentially innocuous address. Not only during his oration, but also before and after it, Hitler ostentatiously paid obeisance to Hindenburg. At the end of the ceremony and before the recessional, the field marshal descended into the church vault to deposit two wreaths on the sepulchers of Frederick William I and Frederick the Great.

The second act of the inauguration took place outdoors. From a platform near the Garrison Church, Hindenburg, Hitler, and his Cabinet reviewed an imposing military parade. Again, on the reviewing stand Hindenburg and Prince Frederick William were at least as conspicuous as Hitler, and neither of them hesitated to salute the irregulars of the SA, SS, and Stahlhelm who marched past them in the train of infantry and mounted cavalry units of the regular Reichswehr. On nearby public buildings and streets, in keeping with this coupling of a chimerical past to a perilous future, the black, red, and gold flag of the defunct republic had been replaced with the black, white, and red colors of the renascent empire and the swastika banners of nazism.

The third act of the civil ceremony came late in the afternoon, with the first sitting of the new parliament in the Kroll Opera House, the temporary home of the Reichstag. As leader of the largest parliamentary delegation, Hermann Göring was in the presiding chair. After reviling the Weimar Republic for having betrayed the spirit of Potsdam, he vowed that the new Reichstag and government would reclaim that spirit by "restoring the Reich to its past greatness, dignity, honor, and freedom." While Hindenburg was not in attendance, the ex–crown prince, now wearing a general's uniform, was in the center box reserved for honored guests. When Hitler entered the chamber to take his seat with the Nazi delegation, Frederick William rose to shake the führer's hand and to give the Nazi salute. To dramatize the break with Weimar's parliamentary dawdling, Göring took less than ten minutes to push through the election of the officers of the new legislature. Inevitably, the Social Democrats were relegated to the far left of the chamber, where the Communists formerly sat.

The impresarios of this ceremonial transfer of power arranged to close Potsdam Day with one of the great works in Germany's cultural tradition. Wilhelm Furtwängler conducted a gala evening performance of Richard Wagner's *Die Meistersinger* at Berlin's Staatsoper. Members of Germany's ruling and governing class eagerly sought invitations to an occasion that was designed to glorify Hitler, his retinue, and his conservative collaborators.

Throughout Germany millions were touched by this dramaturgy of power. Goebbels arranged for the main events to be broadcast over nationwide radio. Many cities and towns staged satellite ceremonies and demonstrations. During the day there were parades by soldiers, Brownshirts, Stahlhelm veterans, and members of student fraternities. Nazi enthusiasts also staged nocturnal torchlight parades, which by now were a hallmark of their frenzied politics of acclamation and intimidation.

Within two days, on March 23, the Reichstag convened for its first working session. By then the setting in and around the Kroll Opera House had been changed to reflect the new realities of power. SS formations surrounded the building, while inside SA men stood along the walls of the corridors and the chamber. Nazi emblems crowded out all other symbols. Hitler mounted the speaker's platform in his party shirt and breeches to ask the assembled deputies to vote a five-part Enabling Act empowering him to govern by decree. He disclaimed any intention of "abolishing" parliament and stressed that the emergency powers would run for only four years, the life of this Reichstag.

But even without such specious assurances the passage of the Enabling Act was a foregone conclusion. While the Nazis and the

Nationalists had a bare majority by themselves, they were supported by the Zentrum, which thought to make the best of a desperate situation, perhaps by exerting influence from within the incipient system. Since they were under arrest, in hiding, or in exile, the Communist deputies were not present to voice their opposition. Ninety-four Social Democrats alone tempted Providence by attending the sitting to speak and vote against the *coup de grâce* to what remained of Weimar constitutionalism.

Although the Social Democratic leaders expressed their dissent, they did not issue a call to resistance. In fact, ever since January 1933 they had gone out of their way to restrain those of their followers who advocated mass protests, demonstrations, and strikes. While remaining determined to uphold electoral politics and parliamentarism, the Social Democrats became more and more confounded and resigned. Whereas they, like the Communists, continually underestimated the resolve and efficiency of their enemies, the Nazis systematically and willfully overstated the strength and militancy of the left.

Between January 30 and March 23 the fledgling regime's reign of terror was turned first and foremost against the Communists. Since it was not prepared for resistance, partly because of its largely self-inflicted isolation, the Communist Party was broken in no time. With few exceptions the more than four thousand men and women arrested immediately after the Reichstag fire were members of the party. While the Communists were the chief victims of this campaign of repression and intimidation, in which the vigilantes of the SA and the SS played an important role, the workers' movement as a whole was its ultimate target. To be sure, the Nazis never relented in their persecution of Communists. But just as the emergency decree of February 28 triggered the raids against them, so the Enabling Act of March 23 was followed by the siege and repression of the Social Democratic Party and its affiliates. Within three months the Reichsbanner (the largely Social Democratic republican defense organization), the powerful free trade unions, and, finally, the SPD itself were outlawed. At the same time that he crushed the organized left, Hitler cajoled the workers by appropriating May Day for the regime's new-wrought ceremonial calendar.

In the face of rising pressure the Zentrum disbanded and the bishops repealed their ban against Catholics joining the Nazi Party. With this self-liquidation all autonomous political activity came to an end. It was accompanied by a second wave of arrests. By the end of July 1933, or within six months of Hitler's takeover, Germany counted close to 27,000 political prisoners, nearly 15,000 of them in Prussia, 4,000 in Bavaria, and 4,500 in Saxony. Although the Communists and their suspected sympathizers continued to be heavily overrepresented among these internees, they were now joined by a considerable number of socialists and a scattering of defiant political Catholics and left democrats. Those taken into protective custody included such prominent cultural figures as Egon Kisch, Erich Mühsam, Carl von Ossietzky, and Ludwig Renn. There were relatively few Jews among these early prisoners of the Third Reich, and all of them were arrested for being left-wing politicians, lawyers, or literati.

Germany's jails were not equipped to accommodate such a large flood of prisoners. In the rush of events the regular police as well as the SA and the SS converted empty buildings, including old fortresses, into makeshift detention centers, mostly in and near major cities. Particularly in the facilities run by the SS, Hitler's praetorian guard, prisoners were severely mistreated. That this abuse was not incidental and unwitting became clear with the establishment of special concentration camps whose rules and procedures reflected the naked brutality intrinsic to the Nazi project.

Dachau was the first concentration camp to be set up and soon became the prototype for a new species of penal institution. Heinrich Himmler, the then police chief of Munich, announced the establishment of a "concentration camp for political prisoners" near Dachau on Monday, March 20, 1933. The press carried this announcement on Tuesday, March 21, the "day of national resurgence" at Potsdam. The plan was "to concentrate, in one place, not only all Communist officials but also, if necessary, the officials of the Reichsbanner and of other Marxist formations who threaten the security of the state" and who would in time overtax the regular prison system. The inmates would be guarded jointly by the regular police and the SA. The first contingent of two hundred prisoners, all of them Communists, arrived in Dachau on Wednesday, March 22, the day preceding the passage of the Enabling Act.

Dachau on the Amper is ten miles northwest of Munich, the capital of Bavaria and birthplace of nazism. The site was an old munitions plant located between the commune of Prittlbach and the village of Etzenhausen. Local officials and businessmen pressed the vacant facility on Himmler, hoping that the projected camp would stimulate economic recovery in the surrounding region. The original plan was to build twenty barracks, each to hold 200 to 250 men, for a total of about 5,000 prisoners. Some contractors were eager to build barracks. Others offered to manufacture beds, uniforms, and blankets, as well as to provide food and laundry services.

The first commandant of Dachau was SS Sturmbannführer (Major) Hilmar Wäckerle. Within three weeks the Munich police

announced that "four Communist prisoners had attempted to escape
. . . and, after they had ignored an order to halt, the guards had
opened fire, killing three of them and seriously injuring the fourth."
Evidently, the camp was run with an iron hand well before SS Gruppenführer (Lieutenant General) Theodor Eicke took over from Wäckerle in late June 1933, by which time Dachau had 2,000 inmates. But
Eicke then proceeded to conceive and systematize the merciless and
dehumanizing penal regimen which became characteristic of the incipient concentration-camp system.

This large-scale political repression, which was half "wild" and half
"legal," was one of the most distinctive features of the first six months
of Hitler's chancellorship. There was absolutely nothing secret or
hidden about it. After all, the arrest of the 27,000 political prisoners
was intended to cow many times that number. The führer's conservative coadjutors and supporters certainly knew about the nature and
extent of the persecution, including the mistreatment of prisoners by
the SA and the SS.

Whereas before January 30, 1933, when Hitler became chancellor,
conservatives had condoned the violence and lawlessness of the
Nazis, after that date they became complicit in legitimating it. There
is no denying that they were beguiled by the pomp and circumstance
of Potsdam Day and that they fell victim to their arrogant belief that
they could outmaneuver and rein in their upstart partners. But ultimately it was their *grande peur* of the left that motivated the old elites
to continue collaborating in the destruction of parliamentary government and of the rule of law. In the process, they helped create the
essential preconditions for the deemancipation of the Jews. For them
as for Hitler, the "Jewish question" was incidental to the founding of
the new regime, the strangulation of the left, and the struggle for
primacy within the still unformed Hitler-Papen coalition.

Throughout their rise to power the Nazis made the Jews prominent
targets of their violence and abuse. Even if the Jews never became the
sole or preeminent villains in their demonology, they were nevertheless one of their most hated chosen enemies. Yet although in many
parts of Germany party activists continued to revile the Jews after
January 30, 1933, the new government did not at first do so. During
the weeks and months immediately following Hitler's takeover, the
emphasis was on destroying Germany's spectral *Gesamtmarxismus*,
beginning with the Communists. This persecution was intended to
smash what remained of an independent parliament and a relatively
autonomous judiciary, two important bulwarks of Jewish emancipation. This is not to say that Hitler swept away constitutional safe-

guards with the fixed purpose of facilitating the persecution of the Jews. Nevertheless, the removal of these safeguards was a necessary precondition for what was to follow.

The first concerted anti-Jewish measures came around April 1, 1933. By then the government had detained thousands of political prisoners and was preparing to move against the non-Communist left and all remaining real or imagined internal enemies. A second major wave of arrests was in the offing and both the SA and the SS were overrun by new members. While Hitler pressed to consolidate the new regime, and his primacy in it, he had to keep a careful eye on his two major loyal oppositions. On the one hand, although he had continuing need for the active support of the conservative elite, including von Hindenburg, he had to be careful not to yield additional power to them. On the other hand, he needed to keep reassuring his own zealots who resented his ostentatious cooperation with the old right. Whatever the autonomous force of Nazi anti-Semitism, the attacks against the Jews remained contingent on the regime's cardinal needs and constraints.

The linkage between the drive to root out *Gesamtmarxismus* and the destruction of constitutional and personal liberties was not immediately apparent, partly because influential opinion-makers in and out of Germany welcomed the repression of the left. Perhaps it is not too surprising that it took the economic boycott of the Jews on April 1 and the subsequent discriminatory decrees against Jews in the professions to begin awakening Europe's, including Germany's, traditional elites to the pernicious nature of the Nazi regime. The book burnings of May 10 also contributed to this sobering process. By then, however, the situation had become close to irreversible.

Most German Jews were equally slow to grasp the implications of Hitler's attack on the left and to join in the defense of political forces and institutions vital for their own protection. Admittedly, from 1928 to 1933 Jews had voted in ever greater numbers for the Social Democratic Party, which had become the only substantial support for the dike holding back the floodwaters engulfing the fragile Weimar Republic. But they had done so primarily for lack of any other alternative. The bourgeois-liberal Staatspartei was moribund, while the Catholic Center party was an unlikely intercessor for the Jews, especially now that it was being pulled further to the right. At any rate, Jews had voted for the Social Democrats less out of socialist conviction than because the party stood against anti-Semitism and included several Jews among its leaders. For many well-established Jews, however, this fellow-traveling was distasteful, and they preferred the Nationalist Party. The members of the Deutsche Staatsbürger Jüdischen

Glaubens and its sympathizers were not only intensely patriotic but also socially and culturally conservative. After January 30 these "German citizens of Jewish faith" kept their distance from the hounded left, hoping that the new Cabinet would confine itself to cracking down on dangerous Communists and militant Social Democrats, whom they scorned. Until Crystal Night in November 1938 many middle-class Jews, like many of their non-Jewish counterparts, expected that political and economic exigencies would prompt Hitler to curb his overzealous lieutenants.

Not that all Jews were so sanguine about the future or minimized the importance of the first anti-Semitic measures. About 60,000 Jews left Germany in 1933–34. These early emigrants were primarily well-to-do merchants as well as academics, literati, and artists. As a rule, only the intellectuals among the émigrés, who had been the first to lose their posts and livings, were disinclined to consider going back under Hitler. They were both bewildered and scarred by the failure of the Gentile intelligentsia and academic community to protest their dismissal and the book burnings. Since most of Germany's Jewish scholars and intellectuals were ultra-assimilated and acculturated, the auto-da-fé of May 10 scandalized many of them less for traducing Jewish authors and their works than for desecrating European scholarship and culture generally. Besides, the first of the nine categories of branded books included volumes preaching "class conflict and materialism," and the book-burners proceeded to exorcise this greatest of all heresies by giving the writings of Karl Marx and Karl Kautsky "over to the flames." But by now it was clear that like the persecution of the political left, the attack on Marxist and Jewish authors was aimed at a much larger target.

Whereas the political opposition was suppressed methodically and with lightning speed, the persecution of the Jews proceeded by fits and starts. In the beginning the aim was neither to massacre the Jews nor to expel them from Germany overnight. Instead, the objective was to drive them out of the country gradually. After being legally and politically deemancipated, the Jews were to be squeezed out of the professions, the civil service, higher education, business, and banking. In addition, the Jews were to be driven back into total isolation. The threat and reality of mounting economic impoverishment, social ostracism, and personal humiliation were expected to quicken their forced exodus.

While none of Hitler's conservative partners had qualms about persecuting leftists, some of them were troubled by the persecution of the Jews. Although most had no objection on principle to reducing the place of Jews in German society, and made no joint or public protests, they did make individual efforts to restrain the Nazis. They did so largely because their own world intersected with that of the Jewish upper and middle classes through intermarriage as well as in business, the professions, the universities, and the realm of high culture. Under the circumstances, it was difficult for the old elites to lend themselves to the wholesale pillorying of Germany's Jews, so many of whom were known to them and had important international connections and reputations which brought honor to their country. Not unlike some of the Jewish notables, they were prepared to condone the persecution of Jewish Marxists and the exclusion of unassimilated Ostjuden, and even to overlook the discussion of quotas for higher education and the professions. But Hitler and the true believers in the party, the SA, and the SS meant to cast their net much more widely. Before too long, well-placed Germans would or could do no more than help an occasional member of the Jewish upper or middle class. Though honorable, such personal and private intercessions were inconsequential.

The government did not issue a general proclamation deemancipating and proscribing the Jews. Apart from following no premeditated design or timetable for "solving" the "Jewish problem," Hitler was mindful of familiar political cross-pressures in tackling it. He took account of the militant activists in the party and the SA who were impatient to malign the Jews. The führer also listened to party strategists who advocated using anti-Semitic measures to divert the attention of sectors of the lower middle classes which were looking for instant but unrealizable social benefits. Then again, there were close party confederates and conservative collaborators who counseled caution for fear of adverse political and economic reactions abroad.

Ultimately, Hitler decided on the timing and scope of the first strikes and measures against the Jews. As of this moment anti-Semitism ceased to be the responsibility of local and regional party leaders and became a matter of state policy, to be decided by him. Until 1939, while strengthening his hold on power and preparing for war, Hitler did not adopt a clear or consistent line toward the Jews. Now and then he stood behind Julius Streicher, gauleiter of Franconia and editor of the violently anti-Semitic weekly Der Stürmer, and Goebbels, who urged a frenzied anti-Jewish campaign, complete with pogromlike assaults reminiscent of the days of old. At other times he backed Göring, Himmler, and Reinhard Heydrich, at this time one of Himmler's chief assistants, who advocated applying ever stronger pseudolegal and systematic pressures to force the Jews to leave Germany. Although Hitler repeatedly authorized pogroms, on balance he favored the rational-bureaucratic (in Max Weber's sense) approach as easier to control and more effective.

The first full-sized aggression against the Jews occurred on April 1. During the week after the passage of the Enabling Act, Streicher and Goebbels convinced Hitler to authorize a protracted boycott of Jewish businesses and professionals. But when Hitler informed his Cabinet of the projected action, his conservative partners demurred. Konstantin von Neurath, Schwerin von Krosigk, von Eltz-Rübenach, and even Vice-Chancellor von Papen warned of the likely diplomatic, legal, and economic costs of such a boycott, and Schacht, the president of the Reichsbank, supported their position. Perhaps their demurral also reflected their apprehension that an attack on the Jews might become the first step toward a "second revolution" in favor of so-called left nazism. At any rate, von Neurath, the foreign minister, prevailed on von Hindenburg to intercede with Hitler. Although the führer refused to back off altogether, he did agree to limit the boycott to a single day.

The manifesto announcing a boycott for April 1 presented it as a defensive counteraction against a Jewish-inspired campaign for an international boycott of German products, detrimental to German workers. It stated that compared to the Bolshevik revolution, which had taken "over three million lives," Germany's national revolution had "barely harmed" any of its Jewish-Marxist enemies. Even so, "the Communist and Marxist criminals and their Jewish-intellectual instigators who had scurried abroad, with their capital, were orchestrating an unconscionable and treasonable hate campaign" against the German people. Ultimately, however, the "Jews among us," not the émigrés, were responsible for spreading flagrant "lies and calumnies," and it was up to them to "condemn the liars of the outside world." The upcoming boycott would be directed against the German Jews for failing to set the record straight. Evidently, the Jews in Germany were to be held hostage for any and all hostile foreign criticism, which in turn was blamed on Jewish émigrés from Germany and on world Jewry.

Jews outside Germany were certainly denouncing Nazi outrages in general and anti-Semitic transgressions in particular. Albert Einstein was among the first to stand up and be counted. Given his stature, his words and actions carried far. As a confirmed left-leaning humanist, democrat, and pacifist, Einstein had long since recognized the explosive danger of nazism, which he now expected would feed on the Great Depression. He happened to be in the United States on January 30, 1933, when the Nazi takeover confirmed his worst fears.

Although Einstein decided not to return to Germany in late February, he waited until March 10, after the elections, to make his decision public. Meanwhile, he issued several statements criticizing Hitler's government for abolishing political freedoms and the principle of equality of German citizens before the law. Einstein denounced "the acts of brutal force and suppression which were directed against all free men as well as against Jews," and voiced the hope that every friend of civilization would rally in time to "save Europe from relapsing into a barbarism of a distant past." To lend additional weight to his protest and warning, on March 28 he resigned from the Berlin (Prussian) Academy of Sciences and renounced his German citizenship. At the insistence of the Ministry of Science, Culture, and Public Education, the secretary of the academy censured Einstein for joining the atrocity-mongers in America and Europe and accused him of violating the unpolitical status and ethos of the academy. This declaration was published in the German press on April 1, to coincide with the anti-Jewish boycott.

But the principal pretext for this first quasi-official strike against the Jews was an altogether more collective and sectarian protest than Einstein's. Alarmed by ominous forewarnings in Streicher's *Der Stürmer*, on March 20 a committee of prominent American Jews, under the leadership of Rabbi Stephen S. Wise, called a mass meeting for March 27 in New York's Madison Square Garden, to be coordinated with rallies in eight other major American cities. The objective was to take a stand against the new German government's wild anti-Semitism, which took the form of unrelenting verbal aggression, sporadic physical assaults, and the arbitrary dismissal of scholars and civil servants. During the week preceding the scheduled meetings Jewish notables pressed the State Department to make representations in Berlin and threaten a trade boycott. They also enlisted the support of church and labor leaders.

Mindful of the scruples of traditional conservatives, Göring called in the leaders of Germany's four major Jewish organizations, each representing a different branch of German Judaism. After raging against what he claimed was vicious propaganda about anti-Semitic atrocities in the foreign press, Göring admonished them to put a stop to this slander and to see to the cancellation of the New York rally. At his urging, a deputation of three Jewish leaders rushed to London. There they conferred with leaders of the Anglo-Jewish community and telephoned Rabbi Wise in an eleventh-hour effort to head off the mass demonstrations. At the same time, Secretary of State Cordell Hull, after checking with the U.S. embassy in Berlin, informed Wise that the German government was about to curb anti-Semitic excesses.

Although Wise hesitated, momentarily, he finally stood fast and the meetings took place as planned. In turn, Hitler decided to go through with the one-day action.

Meanwhile, preparations had been going forward in Germany. Streicher presided over a fourteen-member committee charged with organizing and directing the boycott. Adolf Hühnlein and Heinrich Himmler represented the SA and the SS, which were to form action groups throughout the Reich. But most of the other committee members were spokesmen for the special-interest associations of the Nazi movement, including Jakob Sprenger for the civil servants, Dr. Theodor von Renteln for the small businessmen, Dr. Hans Frank for the jurists, and Dr. Gerhardt Wagner for the physicians. The composition of this task force leaves little doubt about the social carriers and purposes of the operation. As for the Nazi cabinet members, including Goebbels, they remained on the sidelines, careful not to implicate the government directly.

For the appointed day Streicher issued a proclamation urging support for the counterattack on "the Jewish agitation for a boycott and against [alleged] atrocities." International Jewry was said to be incensed because "the national revolution had smashed the old system and wrecked Marxism." Intent upon turning foreign opinion against Germany, the Jews were supposedly flooding the world with monstrous lies: that in the new Reich Jews were being "cruelly tortured to death, that their eyes were being gouged out, their hands chopped off, their ears and noses cut off, and . . . their corpses . . . hacked to pieces." In addition, the proclamation went on, Jews were spreading tales about "Jewish women being brutally killed and Jewish girls being raped under the eyes of their parents." The German Jews were inciting their *Rassengenossen* abroad to press for an economic boycott calculated to "increase the misery of the unemployed in Germany by ruining German exports." To retaliate, German citizens were being asked "to cease patronizing Jewish shops and department stores, to stop retaining Jewish lawyers, and to avoid Jewish doctors." According to Streicher, since it was to be in the nature of a warning, this "defensive boycott would be of a strictly economic nature, and would not be directed against the person or life of the Jew." In turn, the party executive now called for mass meetings to demand that quotas be set to limit Jews in higher education and the professions to their proportion in the general population.

On Saturday, April 1, from 10 A.M. until 7 P.M., uniformed SA men were posted outside Jewish stores and offices. The Brownshirts, many of them flaunting rifles, placarded store fronts, picketed doorways, and taunted Jewish shopkeepers as well as would-be customers. Characteristically, even where these vigilantes smashed shopwindows or assaulted individuals, the regular police either looked on or vanished. Likewise, few if any ordinary Germans stepped forward to restrain or reprove the blackguards of the SA and the party, perhaps because by this time the will to resist and the political climate in which resistance might be expressed had been destroyed. Nor did churchmen, magistrates, or intellectuals remonstrate.

There was little physical violence. On the whole, the boycott was orderly in the centers of major cities, most department stores having closed for the day. Away from these centers and in smaller towns, the atmosphere was considerably more turbulent. Yet despite years of anti-Semitic agitation, the boycott did not trigger pogroms. The public response was lukewarm at best. Evidently, there was less support for street violence against Jewish shops and department stores than there proved to be for the statutory curtailment of Jews in the civil service, the professions, and higher education. Perhaps this is not altogether surprising, for government servants, university students, and disillusioned degree-holders continued to be overrepresented among Nazi enthusiasts and activists.

A considerable number of civil servants had joined the National Socialist party before January 1933. Naturally, with Hitler at the helm, they literally flooded into different Nazi organizations, including the SA reserve. Probably, most officeholders were motivated less by ideological conviction than by their concern for job security and advancement. But whatever their reasons, they became willing, if not eager, servants of the new regime.

Nevertheless, Hitler and his closest associates were determined to purge the bureaucracy in order to make it more loyal and submissive to the new Reich than it had been to the Weimar Republic. Almost immediately after taking office Frick and Göring began to dismiss or retire officials pledged or sympathetic to the Weimar regime. By the end of March 1933 hundreds of officeholders had been discharged, among them a good many Jews. Some of these Jewish officials were removed for their liberal or social democratic beliefs, others simply for being Jewish. In Breslau, Leipzig, Frankfurt, and Berlin local Nazis, notably jurists, pressed for the ouster or lockout of Jewish judges and lawyers.

On April 7, six days after the boycott, decrees "Restoring the Professional Civil Service" and "Regulating the Admission to the Bar" regularized this purge. These decrees are infamous as the first government measure since 1870 to include an explicitly anti-Semitic paragraph. The conservatives surrounding Hitler must take some of the blame. There was wide agreement among them that Jews were too numerous and prominent in the state service and the liberal professions. But rather than allow the canaille to drum out the Jews arbitrarily, Hitler's coalition partners preferred to restrict them legally. To oblige certain conservatives, in particular von Hindenburg, the discriminatory articles concerning civil servants were mitigated: officials of "non-Aryan descent [*Abstammung*]" were to be retired with a pension, not fired, while those who had entered the state service before August 1, 1914, could stay on provided they had been frontline soldiers during the Great War or had had a son or father killed in action.

The formula "non-Aryan" was generally taken to designate only Jews. But it was so vague as to create extreme confusion, and within four days the government issued a clarifying amendment: an official would be considered non-Aryan if one of his parents or grandparents practiced the Jewish religion. This criterion—one of "cultural" rather than "racial" identity—was difficult to verify. In any case, it began to be applied in both the state bureaucracy and the professions.

The new regime was particularly eager to subdue the courts and the bar. On the whole, the Nazis had less reason to worry about the judges, many of whom had been gravediggers of Weimar, than about the lawyers, who had worked to consolidate and expand civil rights. Besides, there was a surplus of lawyers, and Jews were disproportionately represented in the legal profession. In 1931–32 in Prussia 3,378 out of 11,814 lawyers and 2,946 out of 6,224 notaries were Jewish. Within less than a year the decree pertaining to the bar, especially its Aryan clause, helped reduce the number of Jewish lawyers and notaries to 2,066 and 884 respectively. But these provisions, which amounted essentially to a quota system, failed to satisfy the *enragés* of the legal profession, who wanted Jewish lawyers prohibited from representing Gentile clients.

The pattern and rhythm of calculated discrimination were similar in the medical profession, with Jewish doctors and dentists being forced out of the national health service. Before the end of April the quota for Jewish students in the legal and medical faculties was fixed at 1.5 percent.

Jewish members of the intelligentsia and Jewish university professors were perhaps the first to come under intense pressure. There were, of course, more leftist radicals among the former than the latter. To be sure, compared to the guild of lawyers and doctors, the corps of professors and academicians counted few Nazi zealots among its members. But German scholars and scientists did not stand up for unfettered teaching and research, either collectively or individually. Few Gentile faculty members took a public stand, resigned, or went into voluntary exile in response to the suspension or dismissal of their Jewish colleagues for political or ethnic reasons. Instead, they silently accepted, not to say countenanced, such measures. They were equally passive in the face of the increasing violations of freedom of speech and of the press in general, including the book-burnings on May 10, 1933. Not one of Germany's twenty-three universities, eleven academies of science, and ten technical colleges (Technische Hochschulen) became a center of dissent, let alone of protest or resistance.

As for university students, they were very much disposed to collaborate actively. By the late twenties, many if not most of them were either declared ultraconservatives or romantic partisans and sympathizers with nazism. At leading universities substantial numbers of them brazenly abused and boycotted liberal or Jewish professors. Eventually, it was these far-rightist students who organized book-burnings and led torchlight parades from university buildings to the flaming pyres in nearby squares. But the faculty members and rectors were anything but innocent. Through the years few of them had tried or dared to reprove these nihilistic rebels. Nor had they addressed the larger academic and political issues raised by this fronde. In particular, they had failed to challenge the canting ideology and practice of the unpolitical university and professoriate in Germany. Besides the dons and administrators who ignored or made light of the surging political intemperance both within and outside the academy, there were some who approved of it. On March 3, 1933, three hundred high school teachers issued a statement supporting the Nazis in the upcoming elections. In April and May the executive committees of the association of high school teachers and the organization of university professors pledged their loyalty to the fledgling regime.

On May 27, just two and a half weeks after the first book-burnings, Martin Heidegger was installed as the new rector of Freiburg University. Instead of denouncing the ongoing perversion and exploitation of the ostensibly unpolitical university for political ends, he used his inaugural address to validate and celebrate the new turn in Germany's destiny. Though glaring for its moral perversity, this paean to the nascent new order by one of the nation's most eminent philosophers was no less supererogatory than the oath of allegiance to Hitler which seven hundred university and college professors signed in November 1933. By then most university rectors had either made obeisance or been replaced by willing collaborators. However, the great speed and extent of the dismissals in higher education was not due

to administrative intimidation or coercion but to the unforced compliance of faculty members who had taken umbrage at Weimar's
libertarian and reformist intellectual and cultural atmosphere. During
this first year of the Hitler-Papen coalition, close to 15 percent of the
faculty was removed, including 11 percent of all full professors. While
20 percent of these academics were ousted or suspended for political
reasons, the majority of the other 80 percent were driven out for
being Jewish or half-Jewish. Among those who were discharged or
"chose" to resign, there were nearly 500 professors of all ranks, nearly
600 untenured instructors, and about 230 associates of scientific
institutes. The hardest hit were the universities of Berlin and Frankfurt, each of which lost 32 percent of their faculty. The ousters ran
to between 18 and 25 percent at Göttingen, Freiburg, Breslau, and
Heidelberg. The law faculties were in the forefront of this purge, in
that 78.5 percent of the teachers dismissed or retired from them were
"non-Aryans."

Most of the victims of this nationwide persecution went into exile.
Few if any of them were put in concentration camps, and none were
killed. It is not clear how many Jews were dismissed for being Jews and
how many for political and intellectual reasons as well. For the time
being, Jews continued to hold teaching and research positions and to
practice their professions, in part because the Aryan paragraphs were
sufficiently elastic to be circumvented. The result was that a considerable number of Jewish professionals, along with many of their wholly
assimilated coreligionists, considered the discriminatory practices
half-hearted and temporary. This optimistic assumption was reinforced by a remission in the persecution of Jews in 1934 and during
the first half of 1935. At this point it looked as if the storm had
subsided or passed, and about 10,000 of the 60,000 Jews who had left
Germany returned home.

By the first half of 1934 Hitler had gone a long way toward breaking
all political resistance, centralizing the one-party state, regimenting
the bureaucracy, propitiating the armed forces, reassuring the Christian churches, shackling higher education, and intimidating the vis-
ual and performing arts. Probably to his own surprise, he did not
meet with concerted resistance from any quarter. Nevertheless, Hitler
and his lieutenants set up a string of concentration camps not only
to suppress and deter dissidents but also to signal the constancy of
their politics of the mailed fist. These camps gave a raison d'être to
the SA and SS, which, having furthered the cause of nazism by
physical and symbolic violence, were uneasy about their mission and
status following the consolidation of power.

The SA, headed by Ernst Röhm, was a considerable force to reckon with. Its membership rose from 30,000 in the fall of 1929 to about 300,000 at the time of Hitler's accession. During the next five months the membership increased to 500,000, and it reached over 2 million by the end of 1933. The integration of the Stahlhelm into the SA accounted for one-half of this total. Whereas until January 1933 most storm troopers had also been party members, this ceased to be the case thereafter, when opportunists rushed to join. Although the party continued to finance the SA and provide the uniforms, these new hirelings, including many of the veterans from the Stahlhelm, were responsible for a considerable ideological dilution. Probably over 50 percent of the rank and file were workers, the vast majority of them unemployed. The leadership of the SA, however, continued to be drawn predominantly from the lower middle classes, the quintessential social carriers of the Nazi movement.

Röhm's special militia was outsized, certainly compared to the still limited regular army. But because of the sudden influx of so many ideologically and militarily raw recruits, and also because of the shortage of trained leaders, the SA was volatile. Just the same, Röhm commended the SA as the only reliable instrument for consolidating Hitler's power and advancing the Nazi project. His viewpoint was essentially domestic, with little appreciation for foreign-policy objectives and military requirements. Röhm neither understood nor trusted the logic of building a new Germany through war and expansion. He was skeptical of the primacy of foreign policy, whose built-in constraints of time dictated Hitler's domestic strategy of sparing and collaborating with the army, big business, and large-scale agriculture. Röhm demurred, urging a reversal of priorities. Although he had no coherent program of his own, he did advocate supplanting the Reichswehr with the SA. He also envisaged curbing organized capitalism in favor of small-scale agriculture, industry, and trade. At any rate, Röhm came to be seen as preparing and positioning the SA to become the vanguard for a permanent counterrevolution by and for the middle and lower orders of the Nazi movement. Not too surprisingly, both inside Germany and in the outside world this constellation was widely perceived to be the *locus classicus* of populist and pogromist anti-Semitism, which was generally considered much more intractable and pernicious than the rational-bureaucratic variety increasingly championed by the SS.

The SS soon evolved into one of the principal rational-bureaucratic agencies for the implementation of the Nazi project. In this respect, the SS was comparable to the Reichswehr. To be sure, unlike the time-honored army, and notwithstanding its own archaic core, the SS was a radically new and historically unparalleled formation. But this did not preclude the army and the SS from eventually cooperating in the use of ultrarational means and methods for fundamentally irrational ends. As a first step, however, the SS needed to expand and solidify its position within the infant party state, and unlike the SA, it would do so alongside the army, not in competition with it.

The SS began as Hitler's praetorian guard, attached to the SA. In January 1929, when Hitler appointed the twenty-eight-year-old Heinrich Himmler as its chief, the SS counted less than 300 members. Four years later, on January 30, 1933, the number of SS men had risen to about 50,000. In the meantime, Himmler had created an unofficial security police, the future SD, as a separate branch of the SS, which was the first step in transmuting it from a bodyguard for important Nazi leaders into a security force to protect the party. Immediately following the Reichstag fire, Göring temporarily gave official status to the SS of Prussia by deputizing its members to participate in the war against the Communists. In an atmosphere of enthusiasm mixed with opportunism, the membership of the SS rose to 100,000 by midyear and to 200,000 before the end of 1933. By then Himmler had taken command of the police forces of all the states except Prussia, and in mid-1934 he declared the unofficial SD the party's official counterintelligence corps.

In three respects Himmler's approach was radically different from Röhm's. His aim was to penetrate rather than supplant the old state apparatus, notably its police and internal-security organizations. In addition, as he expanded the membership and the reach of the SS, Himmler was careful to foster its elite status and image. Accordingly, because of the rush to join the SS after Hitler became chancellor, he closed admissions for a few months in order to define selection principles and weed out undesirables. Lastly, Himmler made a point of having all SS men swear a special oath of loyalty to the führer. This solemn pledge was designed not only to promote a sense of exclusiveness but also to signal to Hitler and others that unlike the SA, the SS meant to serve rather than challenge the führer's hardheaded compromises with the old elites.

Until January 1933 the SS had been composed of former members of the Freikorps and seasoned party veterans, as well as disgruntled professionals and a scattering of aristocrats. As of March 1933, with the rush of new applicants, the social composition of the SS changed radically. As we saw, in 1933 unemployed workers flooded into the SA, although its leadership remained basically lower-middle-class. By comparison, the SS had a considerably higher social and educational profile. While the rank and file generally came from petty-bourgeois backgrounds, the middle and higher echelons were increasingly drawn from the upper middle class of professionals, businessmen, and landowners, as well as from the titled nobility.

The scattering of aristocrats who had joined the SS before 1933 were now joined by scores of their own kind. Among the descendants of prominent noble families who signed up and lent the SS their prestige were the Archduke of Mecklenburg; the princes Waldeck, von Hessen, and von Hohenzollern-Emden; the counts Bassewitz-Behr, Stachwitz, and von Rödern; and the barons von Geyr, von Malsen-Ponickau, and von der Goltz. These and other members of noble families, both titled and untitled, were destined to provide the SS with a not insignificant number of its leaders. By the late thirties close to 19 percent of the SS's full generals, nearly 10 percent of its lieutenant generals, 14 percent of its brigadier generals, and 9 percent of its colonels came from the nobility. The aristocrats had become nearly as prominent in the SS as they continued to be in the regular army and the government bureaucracy.

While aristocrats contributed prestige and military know-how, increasing numbers of university-educated professionals, notably lawyers, joined to contribute their administrative and technical expertise. Businessmen soon began to make regular financial donations.

Without a doubt, individual aristocrats, professionals, and businessmen were moved to become members of the SS by a combination of self-interest and idealism. But Himmler also seduced them by playing on their craving to be part of an elite sworn to regenerate Germany without any of the leveling advocated and represented by the brown-shirted SA. Accordingly, Himmler conceived the black uniform, the death's-head emblem, and the profession of the Germano-Aryan faith to give novices the sense that they were joining a secular order of the elect. While many of the German notables who joined settled for honorary or associate membership, all of them bought their uniforms, or had them finely tailored.

Covered by the prestige of wellborn and well-educated converts, the policemen and junior army officers who joined the SS full-time proceeded to design and implement a singularly extralegal and repressive system of internal security. During the first year of Hitler's chancellorship the rapid expansion of the SA and the SS coincided with the equally rapid establishment of unofficial detention centers for the 80,000 to 100,000 political prisoners arrested in 1933, of whom no more than 27,000 were detained at any one time. Before long, top Nazi leaders themselves recognized the need for controlling and regularizing this dual growth, which was unrelated to the "Jewish problem." From the outset this rationalizing drive benefited Himmler's SS, which was seeking to help build the party state.

Early in 1933 most of the political arrests were carried out by regional and local henchmen of the SA and the SS, and it was they who set up about forty makeshift camps for the preventive detention of political prisoners in different parts of Germany. Just as in February and March Göring had set the pace in arresting and purging anti-Nazis, so in October 1933 he led the way by ordering that the improvised camps in Prussia be reduced in number and streamlined. Within less than a year there remained only four major camps in Prussia: Papenburg for the district of Osnabrück; Sonnenburg for Frankfurt on the Oder; Lichtenberg for Merseburg; and Brandenburg for Potsdam. In Saxony three camps were kept in operation to service the major urban centers of that state. Fuhlsbüttel near Hamburg performed the same function in that region. The SS rather than the SA took charge of these installations at a time—late 1934—that the number of political prisoners was drastically reduced to well below 10,000.

All this time Himmler continued to push the construction and development of Dachau as a model of a new type of camp for political prisoners, to be run by the SS. Because SS Major Wäckerle, the first commandant, ran the camp with the uncontrolled violence characteristic of the years of struggle, in June 1933 Theodor Eicke was sent to take his place. Eicke instantly set to work stiffening the regulations for the treatment of inmates and the conduct of the guards. On October 1, 1933, he issued what eventually became the standard code for the enforcement of "discipline and order" for concentration camps. Depending on the nature and gravity of the infraction, it prescribed death (by shooting, execution, or hanging), corporal punishment, solitary confinement, or exhausting physical labor. Eicke required the SS guards to swear to apply these regulations ruthlessly and without mercy.

The concept and practice of the penal regimen at Dachau must have impressed Himmler. By January 1934 he promoted Eicke to the rank of brigadier general in the SS. In the spring Himmler moved to Berlin to take over the Prussian Gestapo and to organize a central office to direct and oversee all the camps under SS jurisdiction. Apparently, he considered asking Eicke to join him as coordinator of the embryonic concentration-camp system, confident that he would imbue it with the harsh spirit and iron discipline of Dachau. This was on the eve of Hitler's preemptive strike against Röhm, which turned on the dutiful cooperation of the SS—of Himmler, Heydrich, and Eicke.

Hitler was still torn between two poles: on his left, the restless true believers, who presumably came together around Röhm and the sprawling SA and were beginning to press for a "second revolution"; on his right, the traditional conservatives, who were bent on stabilizing the new regime in the interest of social order and diplomatic credibility. Of course, Hitler had no qualms about cowing his coalition partners with the specter of a second revolution. But basically he shared their concern for the maintenance of the economic and social status quo, which he considered the soundest and handiest foundation for his single-party welfare and warfare state. As early as July 1, 1933, the führer had warned SA and SS leaders that he would "suppress every attempt to disturb the existing order as ruthlessly as I would deal with a second revolution, which could only lead to chaotic conditions." A few days later he had gone before an assembly of Reich governors (Reichsstatthälter) to declare that the revolution could "not be allowed to become . . . a permanent state of affairs." Instead, the "revolutionary currents that have been released need to be guided into the safe channels of evolution." Attentive observers in and out of Germany, including many Jews, welcomed these and similar pronouncements as confirmation of Hitler's resolve to check his own militants.

Notwithstanding Hitler's exhortations and threats, the lingering economic crisis continued to fuel populist disapproval of his collaboration with industrialists, agrarians, generals, bureaucrats, and clergymen. Meanwhile, more and more conservatives, among them von Schleicher and von Papen, grew impatient with the continuing agitation for a radical renewal by Nazi extremists. In mid-June 1934 von Papen, who coveted the presidency, took it upon himself to offer a public warning against "a second wave [which] might be followed by a third" and to caution that "whoever threatens to use a guillotine is likely to be its first victim." Taking note of the clamor for "socialization" among the Nazi zealots, von Papen asked whether Germany had "gone through the anti-Marxist revolution in order to carry out a Marxist program?" In his view the time had come to stop "the movement" and reinforce "a solid social structure," for real development was impossible in the midst of "endless eruptions." Von Papen issued this self-serving admonition against a second revolution at Marburg University without taking note of local faculty dismissals, let alone of political arrests, which were the consequence of the "first revolution" he had helped engineer and legitimate.

Hitler had one absolute priority: to harness Germany's industrial-military complex for instant reemployment and rearmament. Accordingly, he was not about to reverse the conservative tilt of his consolidation of power. While Hitler remained confident of his own ability to outwit the old elites, he became increasingly uneasy about Röhm's defiance. In addition to insisting that the SA should replace or match the Reichswehr, even at the risk of weakening Germany militarily, Röhm exposed Hitler's tergiversation and challenged his unconditional leadership.

Much about the St. Bartholomew's Day massacre (Night of the Long Knives) of June 30, 1934, remains obscure. There continues to be considerable uncertainty about not only the trigger for the carnage but also the exact identity of the eighty-eight victims. Unquestionably, the leadership of the SA was decimated. After refusing to end his own life, Röhm was shot by Theodor Eicke and SS Major Michael Lippert, his adjutant. Although Gregor Strasser had withdrawn from politics and the party, he was murdered, probably to remove any possible rallying point for the populist militants within the movement. General Kurt von Schleicher, his wife, and his close associate General Kurt von Bredow were slain, and so were two of von Papen's closest associates, including Edgar Jung, who had drafted his Marburg address. But the vice-chancellor himself got off with temporary house arrest, probably thanks to the protecting hand of von Hindenburg. Among those killed there were a number of other conservative Catholic politicians with roots in Bavaria, scene of most of the bloodshed.

When Hitler addressed the Reichstag on July 13 to justify his action, he charged his victims with having defiled the noble cause of nazism with their homosexuality, drunkenness, and corruption. But he also claimed to have warded off an imminent uprising by "revolutionaries who favored revolution for its own sake and advocated making it a permanent condition." In fact, Hitler simultaneously struck out in two directions. By liquidating Röhm and his camarilla he brought to heel the SA and intimidated all the *enragés* in the Nazi Party and movement. With the murder of von Schleicher and von Bredow, as well as with the humiliating removal of his own vice-chancellor, he intimidated his conservative collaborators, the more so since von Hindenburg and, above all, the Reichswehr, readily acquiesced.

At the same time, the SS came into its own. Himmler and Heydrich directed the entire massacre. Nearly all the killing was done by a small number of SS men, among them Eicke and Lippert and some of their guards at Dachau. By ordering and trusting the SS to act as his principal executioner, Hitler acquired an awesome instrument of repression and terror. Himmler took Röhm's place, determined to harness and discipline the Nazi fury in support of Hitler's drive for absolute political mastery at home and his preparation for waging aggressive war abroad. Himmler knew only too well that the Night of the Long Knives was not the Thermidor of a far-reaching revolution from below. He quite rightly saw it as a sign of the further hardening of a counterrevolution from above, contingent on maintaining and exploiting Germany's economic, social, bureaucratic, military, and religious establishment for the radical transmutation of its politics, culture, and foreign policy, in accordance with the syncretic ideology of nazism.

Himmler and Heydrich forged and offered a police and security force suitable for this purpose. The SS, unlike the SA, had few populist impulses of its own, and there was nothing spontaneous, improvised, or undisciplined about its methods. Himmler, who also became master of the Gestapo, was an impassive technician of violence, whose mode of operation was deliberate, systematic, and efficient. Characteristically, in early July he appointed Röhm's assassin Eicke inspector of concentration camps and chief of SS Camp Guards, with offices in Berlin, and promoted him to *Obergruppenführer*, or lieutenant general, the second-highest rank in the SS. Whereas Röhm had been proficient in raising and commanding the popular followers and storm troopers of nazism during its movement phase, Himmler was ideally suited to be the grand master of an elite corps of disciplined believers and executioners for its regime phase. Hitler himself realized this, and eventually claimed that he had "found his Loyola."

The collaborationists who had urged Hitler to curb the intractable SA felt reassured. Perhaps they deplored the brutality and treachery of the massacre, notably the murder of two of their own generals and a score of politicians from within their ranks. They ultimately accepted it, however, as the price they had to pay for the hoped-for conservative restabilization. Even many—perhaps most—Jews failed to realize that Hitler and his innermost circle were neither calculating Thermidorians nor confirmed revolutionaries, but habituated ethical nihilists.

Encouraged by their easy and unbroken successes, the Nazi leaders kept alternating and mixing moderation with extremism in pursuit of a project that, notwithstanding its many inconsistencies, had an unalterable core. Hitler and his associates remained set in their anticommunism and anti-Semitism, as well as in their resolve to expand in the east. Even after the suppression of the left in the first half of 1933, the campaign against the Jews continued to be contingent, no less so following the consolidation of power, when the preparation for war became the first priority. This primacy of foreign policy accounts for

Hitler's persisting in his grand accommodation with the magnates of business, agriculture, the armed services, and the higher civil service. Hitler was driven by a sense of urgency, since he knew that his drive for European hegemony would be a race against time. Rather than waste time and resources recasting the German establishment—which the Nazis never really intended to do in the first place—the führer meant to harness the old power elite for many of the pressing purposes he and they had in common.

By 1935 Hitler had reassured the economic and military elites that collaboration was perfectly compatible with their own self-interest and relative autonomy. Big business and finance were cheered by the quick pace of economic recovery. Between January 1933 and mid-1935 unemployment was reduced from 6 million, or nearly 30 percent of the work force, to 2 million, or slightly over 10 percent of the work force. Clearly, there was a rapid upturn in production and demand as well as in profits. Of course, the state played a major role in bringing about this economic miracle. On the whole, the business community applauded the government for breaking the trade unions and for financing public works, such as railway and autobahn construction. At the same time, certain branches of industry and banking were wary of exchange, fiscal, tariff, and price controls. However, many of these controls went back to before 1933 and were not incompatible with the preservation, if not strengthening, of organized capitalism in times of acute economic and fiscal stress, and also of war. Although weapons production did not go into high gear until 1936, by then it was understood that business would readily accept state regulation in exchange for the economic and social benefits of rearmament.

In the meantime, the army was no less heartened than the business community. The liquidation of Röhm and the taming of the SA encouraged the generals to fine-tune their plans to triple the size of the Reichswehr from twenty-one to between thirty and thirty-six divisions, and to provide these divisions with the latest equipment. The buildup of the air force was also begun. On February 26, 1935, Hitler officially established the Luftwaffe as an independent third branch of the armed services, alongside the army and navy. By announcing that Göring was in charge of the air force, he intended to impress the German military as well as the European chancelleries with his resolve to continue breaking the chains of Versailles, a process he had begun in October 1933, when Germany had withdrawn from the League of Nations.

Hitler exulted in the outcome of the plebiscite which on January 13, 1935, returned the Saar to Germany and on March 16 he announced the reintroduction of general conscription. To be sure, in April Great Britain, France, and Italy chided Germany for unilaterally canceling international treaties. But on June 18, 1935, England signed a naval treaty with the Third Reich, thereby implicitly accepting the legitimacy of Germany's one-sided revisions of the peace settlement. London's appeasement discouraged both Rome and Paris from taking a stronger stand.

Meanwhile, a major change of policy was under way in Moscow. Both Stalin and the Communist parties of Europe were shaken by the ease and speed with which the German Communist Party had been destroyed and the Nazis had tightened their grip on power. Desperate to break out of its diplomatic isolation, the Soviet Union joined the League of Nations less than a year after Germany walked out. Stalin now also urgently sought a military alliance with France. At the same time, the French Communist Party had been sobered by the failure of the German left to unite in defense of Weimar. It now pressed for a popular front with Socialists and Radical Socialists in support of the Third Republic, which faced a swelling right-wing *fronde.* The foreign-policy imperative of Stalin and the political exigency of Maurice Thorez, the leader of the French Communist Party, soon converged to produce a radical change in Communist strategy, both international and national. The shift from an aggressive and unilateral *politique du pire* to a collaborative policy in defense of Soviet Russia and of "bourgeois democracy"—in France and Spain to begin with—was confirmed at the Seventh Congress of the Communist International (Comintern Congress) in Moscow in late July 1935.

This nascent front of resistance was the essential backdrop for the Seventh Congress of the Nazi Party in Nuremberg on September 10–16, 1935. It also triggered and informed the racial laws—the Nuremberg Laws—passed on September 15 by the Reichstag, which Hitler had summoned to meet in the same city and ambience as this party rally.

This so-called "Congress of Freedom" was meant to trumpet forth "the struggle of the National Socialist movement against the Jewish world revolutionaries" who had recently met in Moscow. The rally in Nuremberg was billed as the "answer," the "retribution," and the "antipole" to the rally in Moscow. As such, it claimed to speak for "all of Europe . . . and for European culture." In his opening proclamation, read by Gauleiter Adolf Wagner, Hitler told the party faithful to be proud to have been "the principal theme" of the Comintern Congress which "quite rightly" considered Nazi Germany "the chief obstacle to the expansion and realization of Bolshevik designs in

Europe." As National Socialists, they would continue to stand firm, especially now that "in Moscow the Bolshevik Jew was once again threatening the world with destruction."

Goebbels spoke in the same vein. He, too, denounced the recent meeting of the Comintern, which was an "apparatus for the destruction . . . of all European peoples and states." By leading the battle against "the Bolshevization of the world," the National Socialists were, he maintained, both serving Germany's national interest and assuming a "world mission" on behalf of all *Kulturvölker*. Goebbels insisted that not only "posterity but also the present world" should hail the führer for rescuing Western culture from the "abyss of total destruction" by saving Germany from bolshevism. He alleged that in Russia "godless . . . [and] anticultural" bolshevism had killed over 1.8 million people, including "6,000 teachers and professors, 8,800 physicians, 54,000 officers, 260,000 soldiers, 105,000 policemen, 48,000 gendarmes, 12,800 bureaucrats, 355,000 intellectuals, 192,000 workers, and 815,000 peasants." According to Goebbels, by 1930 "30 bishops, 1,600 clergymen, and 7,000 monks had been killed, [while] 48 bishops, 3,700 clergymen, and 8,000 nuns were in jail." Besides, in 1921–22 over 5 million Russians had died of starvation.

Goebbels then asked "who has invented this madness, who has translated it into reality in Russia, and who is trying to make it triumph in other states?" If National Socialism was altogether "uncompromising in [its] struggle against Jewry" it was because "the Bolshevik international is, in reality, a Jewish international." The Jews "invented Marxism" and "pulled the strings" of this "deviltry," bent on "exploiting the basest human instincts" in order to advance their own interests.

When Alfred Rosenberg stepped forward to speak, he offered his own answer to the questions raised by Goebbels. In his view, there was no way to fathom bolshevism, which was "a world historical phenomenon," without understanding that there were "parasites not only in the plant and animal kingdom but also in human life." Moreover, this parasitism was not acquired but "inborn." Precluding all "creative work," it was a function of the purity of the Jewish blood, "prescribed by his religious laws." This religious code was the ultimate source of "the cultural corrosion, economic corruption, and political agitation" of the recent past. Taking a "large and worldpolitical view, bolshevism is the culmination of this Jewish penetration into European culture and politics."

As for how to fight the bolshevism emanating from Moscow, Germany was showing Europe the way. Rosenberg claimed that under the führer's leadership the National Socialists had built a dam to break what Goebbels called the "flood of Asiatic-Jewish filth." He asserted that although communism had been stamped out in Germany, it was necessary to continue reducing the Jewish influence in the Reich's economy and public life. Hauptamtsführer Dr. Gerhardt Wagner, the Reich medical leader, assured the congress that this *Ausschaltung,* or exclusion of the Jews, was being carried forward by stages. Judging by "the return of Jewish emigrants to Germany this last year," certain Jewish circles construed this gradual approach, which took account of "practical possibilities," as a sign that National Socialism was about to forswear one of its "fundamental beliefs." That this was not the case should be clear from the change in "the racial composition" of the medical profession in Berlin during the past twelve months.

The Nuremberg Laws were intended as an extension of what Hitler called "the legal regulation of the problem." In addition to justifying the proposed legislation as a response to the hostile agitation of the Comintern and of international Jewry, he invoked recent spontaneous "defensive actions" against Jews by indignant citizens and party veterans.

During the first half of 1935 there had indeed been a flare-up of popular anti-Semitism, particularly in several towns and cities of southern Germany. Protestant Franconia was part of the heartland of nazism and Nuremberg, its capital, was the seat, if not the fiefdom of Julius Streicher, gauleiter of the province and editor of *Der Stürmer.* This yellow paper's constant vilification of the Jews kept stoking the anti-Semitism of zealous and disgruntled party members. But such eruptions of popular anti-Semitism were not pronounced enough to sway the Nazi leadership. The nascent front of resistance centered in Moscow, rather than the incidental outbreaks of popular anti-Semitism in southern Germany, prompted the Nazi leaders to feature the "Jewish question" at the Nuremberg rally in the early fall of 1935.

It also gave their anti-Semitic rhetoric a new inflection. With communism crushed inside Germany the Nazis proceeded to make bolshevism—Russian, European, universal—the new focus and target of their verbal furor. Whereas heretofore they had rallied conservative Germany with their relentless drive against *Gesamtmarxismus,* they now proposed to rally conservative Europe with their call to arms against *Gesamtbolschewismus.* By portraying the Jews as the chief engineers, carriers, and exploiters of bolshevism, the Nazis also enlarged the audience for their anti-Semitic diatribes. Until now they had geared their anti-Semitism essentially for home consumption, partly because except for eastern Europe, the outside world had remained unreceptive. By grafting their Jew-baiting onto their antibolshevism, the Nazis attempted to make their anti-Semitism appear less eccentric and more politically grounded.

The Reichstag had been summoned for a special meeting in Nuremberg for both practical and symbolic reasons. The city provided a uniquely rich historical setting and was intimately associated with the growth of the Nazi movement. To have the deputies convene in Nuremberg during the rally was to stress the tightening symbiosis of party and state, as well as to underscore that politics was also, importantly, pageantry and gesture.

The meeting was held in the large hall of Nuremberg's Kultur-vereinhaus on Sunday evening, September 15. By then the spectacle, swagger, and speechmaking of the Party Congress were over, save for next day's celebration of the armed forces, which took the form of a mammoth military parade, the first since the return of conscription. Not only the deputies were there, but also the usual complement of diplomats, dignitaries, and journalists. Hitler arrived in the company of all his Cabinet members. After raging about the continuing mortification of the loss of Memel, which was taken from Germany at Versailles, the führer contrasted the peaceful intentions of the Third Reich with the recent decision of the Bolshevik International, meeting in Moscow, "to openly and systematically foster revolution and incite hatred abroad." Hitler added that, as always, on the whole "Jewish elements are the chief agents" of this campaign of "hatred and subversion." He claimed that in America, Jews had desecrated a German flag, thereby insulting the German nation, and Jewish elements were again calling for an economic boycott of Germany. Hitler called on the Reichstag to approve the bill that he hoped would put an end to this Jewish agitation. The proposed "legal . . . and secular" measures ostensibly were intended to establish a modus vivendi with the Jewish people.

It was left to Göring to introduce the two measures to be voted on by the Reichstag. The first was to make the swastika, the foremost party emblem, the core of the official flag of the new nation, empire, and army. According to Göring, the struggle for the rebirth of Germany was also a "battle of symbols." Fortunately for the world, in Germany the "blood-red flag" with the swastika had recently won out over the "blood-red flag" with the "Soviet star." But the swastika was also "the holy symbol" of the fight against the "Jews as race defilers," which meant that hereafter Jews would not be allowed to "fly or display the imperial or national colors."

While this flag law was a scheduled item on the prearranged agenda of this unusual session of the Reichstag, the racial law was an eleventh-hour improvisation. Apparently, Hitler at the last minute decided against delivering a major and strident foreign-policy address, leaving the widely publicized Reichstag spectacular without a program worthy of the occasion. In search of a substitute act for the finale of their dramaturgy of power, the top Nazi leaders seem to have fastened on the idea of traducing the Jews. On September 13 Frick, the interior minister, summoned several of his experts on the "Jewish question" from Berlin to Nuremberg. Under his direction, but in consultation with other Nazi leaders, including Hitler, these advocates of legal and partial deemancipation drafted several versions of a racial law of varying degrees of stringency. Following hectic consultations and with Hitler's approval, Göring took the mildest of the drafts to the Reichstag.

The racial legislation consisted of two separate acts. The first specified that only "a citizen . . . of German or kindred blood" had the capacity and right "to serve the German people and Reich," and that only such citizens were entitled to exercise "full political rights." The second prohibited both marriage and extramarital sexual relations between Jews and full citizens, and also prohibited Jews from employing maidservants of German blood and under forty-five years of age in their households.

The Reichstag ratified the "Reich Flag Law," the "Reich Citizenship Law," and the "Law for the Protection of German Blood and Honor" with boisterous enthusiasm and without debate. The deputies, many if not most of whom were party members, were likely to have been under the spell of the grandiose spectacle and fiery rhetoric of the last three days. They did not pay close attention to the wording of the racial laws, which were incitive but vague. By voting these laws, they acclaimed the overall Nazi presumption and vicariously participated in a cold pogrom. For Hitler and Göring the Nuremberg Laws were an extension of the rational-bureaucratic anti-Semitism inaugurated in April 1933 with the decrees limiting the place of Jews in the civil service and the professions. Judging by some of the speeches at the rally, the regime was moving from the restriction to the exclusion of Jews. The laws of September 15, 1935, immediately deemancipated the Jews, denying them all political, civil, and legal rights. Hereafter, they would have no recourse or protection against the arbitrary whim and power of the party-state poised to restrict, ostracize, and expatriate them.

The original Nuremberg Laws were ambiguous. According to the preamble, their purpose was to protect the purity of German blood, which "the Jew" was said to be defiling. But the text did not spell out who was to be considered a Jew, thereby causing considerable confusion. The Nazis had run into this problem once before, when the definition of "non-Aryan" in the civil-service decree of April 7, 1933, had been so imprecise that the authorities had issued a clarifying amendment within four days. The Nuremberg legislation was similarly elaborated on November 15, 1935, in a directive governing the application of the "Citizenship Law." This directive specified that the law applied to any "full Jew" with at least three "fully Jewish" grandparents, as well as to any "half-Jew" who belonged to the Jewish religious community and was married to a Jew. Although the directive used the formula "Jewish as regards race" twice, it defined a fully Jewish grandparent as one "belonging to the Jewish religious community." Thus, religious affiliation and not blood remained the ultimate criterion. In any event, except for individuals with only one Jewish grandparent, from now on all Jews were stripped of their political and civil rights. They were also barred from public service, with the result that the Jews who had stayed on after April 1933 were dismissed effective December 1935, the exemptions for service in the Great War being canceled.

Except for fanatical proponents of Nazi racial mythology, the Nuremberg Laws were not a matter of exceptional interest or concern. Once again many Gentiles and Jews were reassured by a seemingly legal handling of the "Jewish question," which might be expected to forestall wild outbursts of anti-Semitism. Although the Jews were reduced to "subjects" of the Reich, or to second-class citizens, the government appeared ready to guarantee their minority status. The deemancipation, however painful and barbarous, made the condition of the Jews seem less uncertain and arbitrary. Although the Nuremberg Laws were potentially cancerous, at the time they were certainly not perceived as such, and they did not significantly speed the exodus of Jews from Germany. To be sure, a growing number of Jewish businessmen and bankers proceeded to sell out at a sacrifice and to arrange for Gentile strawmen to run their firms. Also, Jewish professionals became increasingly dependent on Jewish clients. On the whole, however, the blood law did not totally cripple the economic life of the Jews.

For nearly three years after the passage of the Nuremberg Laws, while the Jews were subjected to continuing verbal abuse and occasional physical assaults, no further "legal" measures were taken against them. As part of their effort to make the Olympic Games of 1936 a showcase for Germany's national renewal and economic recovery, the government temporarily muffled all public displays of anti-Semitism without, however, modulating their strident antibolshevism.

To be sure, immediately after the Olympics, at the Eighth Party Congress in Nuremberg from September 8 to 14, 1936, the rhetorical assault on the Jews was resumed. Significantly, however, the Nuremberg Laws did not figure prominently in the renewed explosion of Jew-baiting. In his report on "Racial and Population Policy," Dr. Gerhardt Wagner stressed that half-Jews now needed special permission to marry non-Jews, and Dr. Hans Frank invoked the Nuremberg edicts in his report as *Rechtswahrer,* or warder of the law. But the principal theme of this monstrously spectacular week-long rally was not anti-Semitism but antibolshevism.

The main speakers intensified the anti-Semitic charge in their tirades against *Gesamtbolschewismus,* harangues of a type heard also during the previous year's rally. Portraying the Spanish Civil War as the confirmation of their recent forewarnings about the boundless Bolshevik threat, the Nazi leaders used this 1936 Congress to once again counterpose bolshevism and National Socialism as "the great thesis and antithesis of this century." According to Hitler, the world had seen no comparable crisis "since the rise of Christianity, the triumphal march of Islam, or the Reformation." Bolshevism was a *Weltpest,* or universal pestilence, which called for an "immunization" drive as well as for "a concerted struggle against the international carriers of this bacillus." For Goebbels this "infernal" plague needed "to be *ausgerottet* [exterminated] [in a] world struggle for which Germany was sounding the charge."

Hitler stated that the differences between bolshevism and National Socialism were so "extreme" as to be altogether "irreconcilable" and "unbridgeable." He claimed that even in Germany his "warnings and predictions" about this polarization had once been dismissed as "the ravings of a maniac," and his "prophecy had been ridiculed." And yet, only "prophets" had the rare gift of seeing "the causes and the fixed motion" of disparate critical events that were fated to clash. With naked presumption Hitler declared that the present world was "fortunate to have a prophet who was not a literateur but a politician."

The Nazi leaders stressed that there was, of course, no fighting Marxism and bolshevism without understanding them, which meant facing up to the pivotal role of the Jews. All of Europe needed to realize that, having invented the Bolshevik madness, the Jews were masterminding it from Moscow in their bid for world domination. At the 1936 Party Congress, Hitler, Hess, Goebbels, and Rosenberg took turns portraying the Comintern, the general headquarters of world bolshevism, as Jewish-dominated. The Nazi leaders also claimed that the Jews constituted "98 percent" of the political and administrative leadership of the Soviet Union, which meant that ultimately the "dictatorship of the proletariat in Soviet Russia . . . is a dictatorship of Jewry." According to the Nazi demonology, which both exploited and distorted demonstrable facts, the entire Soviet power structure was replete with Jews. To begin with, they maintained that Lazar Kaganovich, who was not only Stalin's right-hand man and first deputy but also his brother-in-law, headed a Jewish clique at the apex of the regime. In addition, the Nazis pointed out, his brother Michael Kaganovich was deputy commissar for heavy industry. Jews also occupied key positions in the Commissariat for Internal Affairs, including the Security Service, or GPU, as well as in the Commissariats for Domestic Commerce, for Food, and for Heavy Industry, including arms production. Being unfit for military and strategic affairs, the Nazis argued, Jews were of course rare among the officers and soldiers of the Red Army. But they more than made up for this underrepresentation by controlling the all-powerful political administration of the Red Army, which was under the command of Jan Gamarnik. As for the Soviet Union's foreign policy and diplomacy, the Nazis insisted it was totally in Jewish hands. Not only was the foreign commissar, Maxim Litvinov, Jewish, but so were the chief ambassadors and foreign-trade officials. According to this view, Jews also directed Bolshevik Russia's cultural and artistic life, and led the assault on Russia's Christian churches.

The Jews were also portrayed as the leading operatives of the Third International, which executed the orders of the allegedly Jewish-controlled government in Moscow. Nazism's chief platform orators insisted that, judging by recent developments in Spain, the decisions of the Seventh Comintern Congress held in July–August 1935 had to be taken seriously. Goebbels fantasized that since that meeting "well over one hundred Communist revolts" had taken place in different countries, including in France, Poland, Greece, Brazil, Argentina, Uruguay, Paraguay, Chile, and China. All of them, he said, were centrally directed, and now large parts of the world were in danger of being engulfed by full-scale civil war of the sort that was raging on the Iberian Peninsula. Goebbels falsely claimed that the uprising in Spain was a Bolshevik insurgency, directed and financed by agents of the Comintern, most of them Jews. He maintained that the ground had been prepared for them by descendants of the *marranos*, the Jews who had converted to Catholicism to avoid expulsion from Spain in the fifteenth century. According to Rosenberg, these underground Jews had waited until now to take their vengeance by becoming "the leaders of the allegedly liberal revolution" which primed Spain for "the ascendancy of Soviet Jews."

At the 1936 Nuremberg rally, even more than at the previous year's rally, the diatribe against the Jews was bound up with Hitler's intense disquiet about developments in France and the radical turnabout in Soviet policy. Berlin's intervention in Spain was to a considerable extent calculated to embarrass Paris. No doubt the Nazi leaders were tempted to portray Léon Blum and his Popular Front government as the newest link in the Jewish world conspiracy. But they prudently refrained from doing so, leaving less official voices to disseminate this fable. Instead, Hess and Goebbels denounced the Comintern for what they believed was its new and insidious Popular Front policy of implanting "Trojan horses" throughout Europe, notably in Spain but above all in France. In the elections of April and May 1936 the French Communists nearly doubled their vote, increasing their number of deputies from twelve to seventy-three. There was also a dramatic growth in the membership of the French Communist Party and its affiliated trade unions, as well as in the circulation of L'Humanité. The Nazi leadership charged that since Europe's democratic governments were in large part responsible for the Popular Front in Spain and France, the bourgeoisie was clearly blind to the fact that the Comintern's new course was nothing but a "tactical compromise" in bolshevism's "uncompromising" quest for power. As Hitler put it, in Germany the removal of these fainthearted "champions of a bourgeois world" had been an essential prerequisite for the showdown with Marxism. Indeed, there was no way of "striking at the real enemy without first fighting one's way through this bourgeois slime."

The "Trojan horse" in Paris was doubly dangerous because of the projected Franco-Soviet military pact, which would supplement the Soviet-Czechoslovak pact of 1935. By securing the use of Czech airfields and airstrips, the Red Army moved its planes to points "20 minutes from Dresden, 11 from Chemnitz, 9 from the Silesian industrial basin, 42 from Berlin, 9 from Vienna, 17 from the armaments plants in Steyr, 27 from the industrial basin of the Steiermark, and . . . 6 from Budapest." Goebbels warned that with bases in Czechoslovakia and France the Soviets would become a serious military threat to all of Europe.

By now Hitler was obsessed with the urgency of preparing Germany for war, lest it become too late to turn the military balance in the Reich's favor. In August 1936 he himself took an active part in drafting the justification for the first Four-Year Plan, which he presented to the Cabinet on September 4 and announced at the party rally four days later.

Hitler's chief premise was that a showdown with Soviet Russia was inevitable. The Bolsheviks had used successive five-year plans to modernize the Russian economy and build up the Red Army, and they could not be given another ten or fifteen years to press on with their military preparations. Should Soviet Russia and bolshevism, which were bent on aggression, overwhelm Germany, the consequence "would not be a Treaty of Versailles but the final destruction if not extermination of the German people" (die entgültige Vernichtung, ja Ausrottung des deutschen Volkes). Not only Germany but all of Western Europe would suffer "the most gruesome catastrophe" since ancient times.

Germany was both overpopulated and deficient in critical resources. Hitler considered it the duty of political leaders, therefore, "to once and for all solve . . . Germany's Lebensnot . . . through the expansion of Lebensraum, so as to command [a secure] supply of raw materials and foodstuffs for our people." Whereas in theory this objective might be achieved by increasing exports, in practice this was not possible. According to Hitler, foreign-exchange earnings would never be sufficient to pay for both foodstuffs and raw materials, and under "no circumstances" could food be procured and secured "at the expense" of imports essential for rearmament. Therefore, the first priority was "to prepare for war in peacetime," which could not be done by simply "stockpiling raw materials and foreign currencies." Regardless of cost, Germany had to push for complete self-sufficiency in basic materials, including synthetic fuel and rubber.

This, then, was Hitler's rationale for the Four-Year Plan with the twofold goal of making both the German army and the German economy ready for war within four years. The Reich's inner circles understood that the thrust for autarky-cum-Lebensraum was essentially directed toward the east, against Soviet Russia, and not overseas. This project came as no surprise to those familiar with the central foreign-policy postulates set forth in Hitler's Mein Kampf.

The appointment of Göring, on October 18, 1936, as commissioner for the Four-Year Plan underlined the fact that the preparation for war now had the highest priority. Göring was widely perceived not only as the second most powerful man in the regime but also as the mediator of Hitler's purposeful collaboration with big business, agriculture, and finance, notably with those sectors favoring the drive for autarky and eastern expansion. A mixture of ideology and self-interest motivated their cooperation, so that both sworn adherents of nazism and calculating magnates welcomed the new course.

Meanwhile, Himmler's meteoric rise continued. On June 17, 1936, Hitler appointed him Reichsführer or supreme chief of the SS as well as chief of the German Police. Within less than ten days, on June 26,

Himmler named Reinhard Heydrich to head both the Secret State Police, or Gestapo, and the Criminal Police. He also asked Heydrich to stay on as head of the party's Sicherheitsdienst (SD), or security service. Himmler and Heydrich, in their own persons and offices, embodied the continuing fusion of state, party, and SS.

By this time Himmler had gone far to "rationalize" the concentration camps, bringing all of them under the control of the SS. His man Eicke was in command of all camp commanders, inspectors, and guard units. Between late 1935 and the fall of 1936, Oranienburg, Fuhlsbüttel, Esterwegen, and Columbia-Haus were closed. At the same time, the total number of inmates was reduced to about seventy-five hundred. By the summer of 1937 all political prisoners were concentrated in four camps: Dachau, near Munich, for southern Germany; Sachsenhausen, near Berlin, for eastern, northern, and central Germany; Buchenwald, near Weimar, for western and northwestern Germany, Saxony, and Thuringia; and Lichtenberg, near Hof, for women. The number of camps and of inmates would remain essentially unchanged until the annexation of Austria and Czechoslovakia.

This consolidation went hand in hand with a stricter regimentation of the camp system. The Dachau regimen for prisoners was extended to the other camps at the same time that the training and discipline of the camp guards were standardized. As of March 29, 1936, the guard companies became known as *Totenkopfverbände*, or Death's Head detachments. By mid-1937 Eicke concentrated these barbarous SS volunteers in three regiments, each with between 1,000 and 1,500 men: the Oberbayern regiment at Dachau, the Brandenburg at Sachsenhausen, and the Thüringen at Buchenwald.

There can be no doubt that during the first few years of the regime the express function of both the older detention centers and the new concentration camps was to exercise political control and promote terror. Unwittingly, even the inmates who were released served this purpose, in that they helped spread the fear of the dreadful conditions and mistreatment they had experienced. The concentration camps became a permanent fixture of the political and psychosocial landscape of the Nazi regime only well after all internal opposition had been crushed. In time, these camps took on new functions congruent with the shift from domestic consolidation to foreign expansion and rearmament, as well as with the idea of using camp labor to help construct monumental buildings designed to glorify the nascent Thousand-Year Reich. This adaptation of the concentration camps was not in any way connected with "solving" the "Jewish problem."

The high command of the conjoined SS and police—Himmler,

Heydrich, Eicke, Oswald Pohl—proposed to gear the still rudimentary concentration-camp system to be of use to the Nazi Behemoth. Unemployment had all but disappeared by the time forced-draft rearmament got under way. In the face of a certain labor shortage, the idea took shape that the camps could serve as both political prisons and work compounds. As of late 1936, the security forces targeted a broad range of "marginal," essentially nonpolitical individuals for permanent internment and exploitation in the camps: beggars, criminals, scofflaws, drunkards, loafers, vagabonds, Gypsies, and religious sectarians.

Additional concentration camps were about to be established, and they were designed with economic production and war in mind. Both Sachsenhausen and Buchenwald, which opened in August 1936 and July 1937 respectively, were located and adapted for the production of construction materials, primarily for Hitler's grandiose architectural schemes, to be executed by Albert Speer. Furthermore, as early as June 1936 Eicke argued that future concentration camps should be large enough to hold potential antiwar activists. Originally, Buchenwald was planned for 3,000 inmates. But in late October its capacity was doubled, since Eicke insisted on the urgent need for concentration camps to be built to meet the requirements of war. Similarly, early in 1937 Himmler envisaged a major increase in both the camp population and the Death's Head detachments. By the time the war began the number of inmates had risen to about 20,000, which now included the internees of Mauthausen near Linz, a camp founded shortly after Austria's annexation. Between them Dachau, Sachsenhausen, and Buchenwald held about 15,000 of these prisoners, half of them consisting of the so-called "asocial elements" interned for forced labor.

Needless to say, the pool of concentration-camp labor was too small to make a dent in Germany's inordinate manpower needs. By 1937 the expansion of the army and of weapons production began to significantly strain the economy. The Nazi regime now faced the prospect of serious labor deficits, inflationary pressures, and, above all, shortages of industrial raw materials. From a liberal-imperialist perspective Hjalmar Schacht, president of the Reichsbank, once again urged stepping up the export of manufactured goods and capital to pay for the import of critical commodities. But he came up against Göring, who was more inclined to stay on an essentially autarkic course contingent on expansion into eastern Europe, with its vast reservoirs of cheap oil, minerals, food supplies, and labor.

Presumably, Hitler knew that his Four-Year Plan was driving Germany's political economy to the verge of a critical crunch when he met his top four generals and his foreign minister on November 5, 1937, to outline his world policy. On this occasion he left no doubt that his bid for European hegemony hinged on the conquest of *Lebensraum* in the east which in turn necessitated the destruction of Bolshevik Russia. None of this was new, except that Hitler now thought that the showdown would have to come no later than between 1943 and 1945, when the military balance would turn against the Third Reich. He also indicated that he would look for an early opportunity to move against Austria and Czechoslovakia on his way eastward.

Field Marshal Werner von Blomberg and General Freiherr Werner von Fritsch, as well as Baron Konstantin Freiherr von Neurath, expressed certain reservations about deliberately preparing and heading for war without first exploring diplomatic avenues to restore Germany to a position as *primus inter pares* in the European system. They were haunted by the specter of another two-front war. Determined to press on, and impatient with such equivocators, Hitler carried out a major government shake-up between December 1937 and February 1938. Although he kept Schacht at the Reichsbank, he forced him to yield the Ministry of Economic Affairs to Walther Funk. A tested party regular, Funk was sure to work closely with Göring, now responsible for the implementation of the Four-Year Plan and commander in chief of the air force. Similarly, von Neurath was dismissed from the Foreign Ministry in favor of Joachim von Ribbentrop, an early convert to nazism.

But Hitler was determined, above all, to surround himself with tractable military men. He cashiered von Fritsch, the commander in chief of the army, giving his post to General Walther von Brauchitsch. Hitler also removed von Blomberg from the Ministry of War, which he dissolved. The führer decided to take command of all the armed forces, thereby making himself commander in chief in addition to president and chancellor. To help him exercise his supreme military authority, Hitler appointed General Wilhelm Keitel chief of the revamped High Command of the Armed Forces (OKW) and General Alfred Jodl chief of the General Staff. Keitel and Jodl, who were chosen for their ideological pliancy, promptly retired or reassigned about forty senior officers of questionable reliability or enthusiasm.

This latest removal of traditional conservatives from key leadership positions should have disabused non-Nazi collaborators in and out of government about the extent of their restraining influence, let alone power. Yet few if any went into internal exile or opposition. Even when discharged dishonorably or unceremoniously, virtually all remained ready to serve their master: just as in 1934 von Papen had

CHAPTER VI

EXPANSION AND WAR, 1938–40

CATALYSTS FOR FORCED EMIGRATION, GHETTOIZATION, AND DEPORTATION

From 1933 to the end of 1937 the founding and solidification of the Nazi regime resulted in the deemancipation of German Jewry. As of 1938, when the regime turned to territorial annexation and aggressive war, it also turned to the forced emigration, ghettoization, and deportation of Jews. Foreign expansion and war intensified the war against the Jews. This anti-Jewish drive was not self-contained, nor did it develop by successive stages which were predetermined and inevitably culminated in mass extermination. If the Third Reich was characterized by any organic development toward a fixed goal, it was the immanent growth of a Behemoth conceived in the collaboration between Hitler and the old elites and contingent on war-making and foreign conquest. In turn, given Germany's geopolitical location and Hitler's obsession with *Lebensraum* in the east, the Behemoth could only expand in a direction that would entail a radical change in the configuration and treatment of the "Jewish question."

Between 1938 and 1940—and thereafter—each annexation and conquest brought a collateral increase in the number of Jews under German control, ever more of them unassimilated, unacculturated, and poor. The Jews of Austria and Czechoslovakia, followed by those of Germany, were put under mounting pressure to emigrate. In time, those remaining in these three countries were increasingly isolated, and eventually a small number of them were deported, some of them to satellized unoccupied France, others to conquered Poland. The Jews of Poland were the first to endure the full consequences of falling under the heel of the Nazi warfare state. In addition to being battered by war-related pogroms during the invasion, they were concentrated, ghettoized, and relocated to the eastern reaches of German-occupied Poland, not too far from the Soviet border.

There was at this point no intention or plan to exterminate the

159

Jews. But the urge to unburden the expanded core of the expansionist Third Reich of what were now millions of Jews increased at the same time that the prospects of being able to do so declined. Not only was far-eastern Poland ill suited to absorb vast numbers of Jews, but the state of war all but closed off most previous channels of emigration and flight. This impasse gave rise to a project to transport 4 million European Jews overseas, for forced residence in Madagascar. But this comprehensive plan was stillborn because England, which controlled the high seas, refused to surrender or negotiate an accommodation.

Almost from the outset Nazi Germany's anti-Semitic drive was the most intense and strident in Europe since 1789. Even so, it is worth noting that until 1938, and notwithstanding many incidents of random coercion and intimidation, there was little orchestrated physical violence and few Jews were actually killed. By comparison, the Jewish persecutions in tsarist Russia between 1880 and 1914 had been much more deadly. Likewise, after the end of the Great War, Jews had suffered large-scale massacres at the hands of Russian and German counterrevolutionaries as well as of Ukrainian and Polish ultranationalists. While the bloody pogroms of the late Romanov empire had been part of the chronic convulsions of a failing *ancien régime,* those of 1918 to 1921 had been part of the violence of intensely fought civil and national conflicts characteristic of a furious era of general crisis and war. But, above all, the bulk of these anti-Jewish outbreaks occurred in regions of the Continent that were essentially unmodern and undemocratic, and in which Jewish emancipation was either nonexistent or incipient and contested.

Nazi anti-Semitism exploded in a civil and political society that was—or had been—altogether more modern and liberal. But German society was also riven by the stresses and strains of an acute "simultaneity of the unsimultaneous" ultimately favorable to historical regression. There is no question but that in Germany the assault on the Jews was grafted onto a violent backlash against democratic liberalism, advanced capitalism, and cultural modernism. All three had been critical pillars and vehicles of Jewish emancipation. Even while bloodless, the brawling harassment of the Jews by the Nazis struck most contemporaries as at once egregious and unreal, in particular because it erupted in one of the world's most advanced outposts of Jewish emancipation, acculturation, and assimilation. The German Jews themselves refused to believe that the Nazi regime would disenfranchise, ostracize, and humiliate them to the point of driving them out of the country—out of their *Heimat.* If during the first five years of the Third Reich only about 22,500, or 5 percent, of Germany's

500,000 Jews emigrated each year, the reason was this incredulity combined with a sense of absolute belonging, and not the difficulty of finding refuge abroad. Most Jews outside the Reich had similarly discounted the Nazi design for expulsion.

The year 1938 was to be hard for both Gentiles and Jews who until now had tried to ignore the Nazi furor or had been bewildered by it. The year began with Hitler and his acolytes taking full charge of the armed forces, the Foreign Office, and the Ministry of Economic Affairs, with the old elites readily acceding to this final "purge." Having gathered all the reins of government in his hand, the führer became even more daring than before. On March 12, 1938, he consummated the *Anschluss*, or annexation, of Austria. Of course, Hitler acted unilaterally. But because his troops did not have to fire a single shot and were wildly cheered as they marched into Vienna, he managed to create the impression that the Austrians had invited him in— which was close to the truth. The fact that the Austrian army laid down its arms and that London and Paris, giving no heed to Moscow, failed to issue a credible remonstrance further confounded those rare conservatives in Germany who even after the brazen but triumphant reoccupation of the Rhineland and intervention in Spain continued to counsel caution. They kept insisting, in vain, that the Reich needed additional time to prepare to remove the remaining iniquities of the Versailles *Diktat*, to strike for *Lebensraum* in the east, and to reach for European hegemony.

By both temperament and calculation Hitler was racing against time. He excelled at creating a sense of perpetual movement and accomplishment to compensate for his specious legitimacy and incongruous social program. Pursuing an activist world policy was the best way of stoking this diversionary momentum. In fact, domestic and foreign policy were closely enmeshed. Forced-draft rearmament contributed not only to continuing prosperity but also to diplomatic swagger and success.

Even before the *Anschluss* of Austria Hitler had ordered the High Command to prepare contingency plans for the conquest of Czechoslovakia, an essential stepping-stone to the east. In the wake of his easy triumph in Vienna, the impatient chancellor decided to force the pace still further. Confident of Germany's military head start and playing on the political and diplomatic divisions of the other powers, Hitler sought to provoke a situation that would allow him to launch Operation Green, the blitzlike military occupation of Czechoslovakia. Much to his own surprise, the incoherence and irresolution of the Big Powers were even greater than Berlin had anticipated. Even the government of Poland, which was marked for conquest, prepared to concur in the dismemberment of Czechoslovakia in exchange for Teschen. Unwilling to accept—or pay for—Stalin's proffered cooperation, on September 29, 1938, an eager Neville Chamberlain and an uneasy Édouard Daladier rushed to Munich to sacrifice the Sudeten territory of northern Czechoslovakia less for "peace in their time" than for time to improve their diplomatic and military preparedness.

But Hitler, intent on pressing his advantage, kept this pause to a strict minimum. He was not about to allow a rump Czech state and the Carpathian Mountains to impede Germany's drive to the east. Immediately following the Munich Summit the führer repeatedly called on the Wehrmacht to stand ready to finish off the rest of Czechoslovakia. Once again, however, there was no need to speak with guns. Exploiting the strife between Czechs and Slovaks, as well as the impasse between the Soviet Union and the Western Powers, on March 15, 1939, Hitler peremptorily ordered the occupation and annexation of the two Czech provinces of Bohemia and Moravia.

The *Anschluss* of Austria and the destruction of Czechoslovakia demonstrated that Berlin was determined to continue using a lethal mixture of diplomatic bluster, political subversion, and military intimidation to secure its expansionist foreign goals. But such seemingly nonviolent masterstrokes of international politics were also calculated to reinforce the party-state. In addition to awing further the Reich's generals and diplomats, the easy incorporation of Austria and the rape of Czechoslovakia enabled the SS to enlarge its apparatus and sharpen its ethos. Indeed, the constantly increasing role of the SS in the Nazi regime was a concomitant of foreign expansion and conquest. The Blackshirts found their natural habitat beyond the borders of the Reich, where they were free to operate with complete impunity. Himmler certainly counted on this moving frontier, especially in the east, as he forced the buildup and training of the general SS and the Death's Head formations. By early 1938 both constituted a large reservoir of reliable political soldiers ready to be tapped for duty abroad, and so did the security services of the police and the party. To be sure, the SS and the SD had been forged to crush and terrorize internal enemies and outcasts. But whatever their immediate purposes, their ultimate mission was to pacify, exploit, and subjugate conquered peoples and lands.

Characteristically, special mobile units of the security services inconspicuously moved into Austria in the wake of the Wehrmacht. Their assignment was to hunt down sworn or potential enemies of the Reich among German émigrés, Freemasons, Jews, Catholics, and members of the Second and Third International. Directly responsible to Himmler and working from prepared lists, these squadrons, organized by Heydrich, conducted searches and made numerous arrests during the first week of occupation. Before long, they were replaced by regular units of the Gestapo, the Kripo (Criminal Police), and the SS. No later than mid-1938 the SS started a concentration camp in Mauthausen, located on the Danube near a stone quarry, sixteen miles southeast of Linz. Mauthausen counted 900 inmates by the end of the year, and three times that many a year later.

The modus operandi was the same when Heydrich's men followed the Wehrmacht into Bohemia-Moravia. By then the mobile spearheads of the Reich's security forces began to be referred to as "Einsatzgruppen." As in Austria, they were charged with ferreting out politically hostile individuals and organizations in total disregard of legal conventions. The stress was on arresting local Communists and left-wing émigrés from Nazi Germany. Following the occupation of Prague, about 4600 persons were arrested, over 200 of them for extended terms. The mobile Einsatzgruppen as well as the fixed security forces that took over from them were answerable to Himmler and Heydrich, not to the field command or military government of the Wehrmacht.

This irruption of political soldiers into Austria and Czechoslovakia was in no way connected with the persecution of Jews as Jews and the erratic effort to tackle the "Jewish question." Paradoxically, with every annexation and conquest the Third Reich acquired additional Jews, thereby running counter to the drive to make Germany *judenfrei*. This contradiction undoubtedly went unnoticed at first by Nazi leaders sworn to expand into eastern Europe, home of the bulk of European Jewry. In any event, the Nazis most certainly did not relish coming into possession of ever more Jews, especially now that they appreciated the difficulty of extruding them.

This difficulty was driven home by the seizure of Austria, the Sudetenland, Bohemia, and Moravia. The *Anschluss* alone added to Germany's population close to 190,000 Jews, over 90 percent of them in Vienna, or about 55,000 more Jews than had left Germany since 1933. The former Czech lands brought the Reich almost as many Jews. By themselves the twin provinces of Bohemia and Moravia counted over 120,000 Jews, including recent refugees from Germany, Austria, and the Sudeten territories. There were an additional 130,000 Jews in Slovakia and 100,000 in Ruthenia, but most of them fell not to Germany but to satellite regimes.

It took German officials and local Nazis only a few weeks to subject the Jews of incorporated Austria to the anti-Semitic decrees that had been inflicted on German Jewry over a period of five years. Along with suspected anti-Nazi Christians, several Jewish notables were arrested and sent to Dachau. Although they were soon released and returned to Vienna, their ordeal, combined with a rash of wild anti-Semitic incidents, created an atmosphere of fear which escalated toward panic with the temporary internment of 2,000 Austrian Jews in Dachau in May 1938. During the summer thousands of Austrian Jews fled to neighboring countries, 4,000 to Switzerland alone. At the same time, there was a marked rise in suicides in the Jewish community.

Presently, Himmler and Heydrich sent Adolf Eichmann to Vienna with orders to expedite the emigration of this unwanted legacy of Austrian Jews which threatened to expose the inefficacy, not to say bankruptcy, of the regime's efforts to make Germany judenfrei by pressured exile. Eichmann opened a Central Office for Jewish Emigration in the Rothschild mansion on Prinz Eugen Strasse in August 1938, when well over 10,000 Jews had already left Austria. Eichmann speeded up this exodus by streamlining the legal, administrative, and financial procedures for the issuance of exit permits. In particular, he implemented the idea of allocating 5 percent of the assets confiscated from wealthy Jews to pay for the emigration of poorer ones. About 50,000 Jews had left Austria by November, some 90,000 by March 1939, and close to 120,000 by September 1, 1939, when the war began. Eichmann supervised a similar effort in Prague, with 30,000 Jews leaving Bohemia and Moravia before the end of the year.

The "Aryanization" and extortion of Jewish property and wealth to help state finances as well as to force the pace of the banishment of Jews abroad was not limited to Austria. In Germany proper, as in Vienna, Göring pressed this new policy, while at the same time the Jews of the Greater Reich were being subjected to additional controls, restrictions, and limitations. In April 1938 Jews were required to report and register all assets in excess of 5,000 marks. Between July and October Jewish physicians, attorneys, and patent lawyers were forced to confine their practice to Jewish clients. On August 17 Jewish men were obliged to change their first name to Israel; Jewish women, to Sarah. Two months later Jews had to have a large red J stamped on the upper left of the front page of their passport. Incidentally, Swiss officials were the ones to suggest some such measure to the Germans in their effort to stop the flow of Austro-Jewish refugees into their country.

These official curbs were instituted against the backdrop of a rash of random anti-Semitic outrages, most of which went unpunished and were celebrated in *Der Stürmer*. Intermittently, individual Jews were harassed in the streets of Berlin as well as in several Bavarian towns. The summer of 1938 also saw the first desecrations of Jewish temples: on June 9 the main synagogue of Munich was demolished and its grounds turned into a parking lot; on August 10 the main synagogue of Nuremberg was leveled in time to impress and incite the next party congress; and later that same month the synagogue of Dortmund went up in flames.

Notwithstanding this unrelenting pressure, there was no significant increase in emigration from Germany. The condition of the Jews still appeared to be short of catastrophic. The old-established Jewish middle classes in particular remained confident that with time and mounting foreign pressure bureaucratic and economic rationality would temper the Nazi regime and cure it of its anti-Semitic mania. Their belief was partly sustained by their reluctance to pay the ever steeper emigration tax and their apprehension about their economic and social prospects in exile.

Until late 1938 fewer than 150,000, or 30 percent, of Germany's Jews had either emigrated or gone into exile. Over 20 percent of these went to Palestine, but fully half of the German-Jewish émigrés preferred to seek asylum in western Europe. Almost one-third of these opted for France, the historical pioneer of emancipation and current spearhead of the popular front against fascism. But western Europe was favored, above all, as closest to Germany both culturally and geographically, and therefore least alienating and most convenient for an early return home, which was widely anticipated. This may explain why relatively few German Jews set forth for the United States. During the first five years only 27,000 of them crossed to America, though under the quota for native Germans nearly that many could have sailed every year.

The sudden flood of émigrés from Austria nevertheless prompted a wary President Roosevelt to initiate a call for an international conference to discuss the problem of Jewish refugees. Delegates from twenty-nine nations deliberated in Évian on the French side of Lake Geneva from July 6 to 15, 1938. With the sole exception of the representative of the Dominican Republic, the delegates, after expressing their compassion, declared the disinclination of their governments to relax their quotas or visa requirements. The reasons for this inflexibility were altogether unexceptional by the standards of those times: their own countries were racked by unemployment and could not provide jobs; the influx of refugees would exacerbate xenophobia, notably against Jews; and the national treasuries were overdrawn and could assume no additional public charges. The problem was less with the well-to-do Jews, who could be expected to look after themselves, than the mass of poor Jews, who would rapidly exhaust the funds of Jewish welfare agencies. This preoccupation was the greater because at Évian the spokesmen for Poland, Rumania, and Hungary specifically called on other nations to take in some of their own sizable and impoverished Jewish populations.

Judging by the abortive Évian conference and its sequel, the outside world was not about to help Hitler get rid of "his" Jews. Although the Nazi leaders relished mocking the spurious humanitarianism of the democratic governments, they were also increasingly bewildered, if not infuriated, by the unanticipated and stubborn obstacles to what now became forced mass emigration.

Berlin was nettled by Warsaw's decree of October 15, 1938, barring Polish citizens who had lived abroad for more than five years from reentering Poland unless their passports were first revalidated at a Polish consulate. German officials construed this decree, which was to go into effect on October 29, as an attempt to foreclose any possibility of the Third Reich, including Austria, deporting over 50,000 Jews of Polish nationality. They rightly assumed that, notwithstanding their wretched plight in Germany, these Jews would not rush to the nearest consulate, let alone to Poland, whose anti-Semitism many of them continued to perceive as unequaled. This unwillingness was the more vexing because, being impoverished and unconforming, these Polish Jews, along with 100,000 other Ostjuden, were least apt to find havens abroad.

On October 26 the German ambassador in Warsaw warned that if the decree were not rescinded within forty-eight hours all Jews of Polish nationality would be expelled from Germany before the stipulated deadline. But Colonel Józef Beck, the Polish foreign minister, stood his ground. He even threatened to expel German citizens in retaliation. With time running out, and at the request of the Wilhelmstrasse (the Foreign Ministry), the Gestapo directed the arrest and concentration of 17,000 of Germany's Jews of Polish nationality for shipment to Polish border stations. Although under protest, the Polish authorities admitted approximately 10,000 Jews before finally closing their borders during the night of October 28. Berlin did not press the issue any further after agreeing to a face-saving arrangement with Warsaw.

However, early in the morning of October 29 about a thousand

Polish Jews had arrived at a border crossing near Zbąanszyń, on the main rail line from Berlin to Warsaw. Not too surprisingly, they were mercilessly shunted back and forth between the Scylla of Nazi Germany and the Charybdis of protofascist Poland. The Polish officials finally relented. The poor unfortunates were allowed to proceed to the village of Zbąanszyń on the Polish side of a muddy no-man's-land, where along with a swarm of previously arrived deportees they suffered severe hardships.

Among these ill-starred people there was a tailor from Hanover named Sendel Siegmund Grynszpan (or Grünspan). Born in Polish Russia, he and his wife had settled in Germany in 1911 and after 1918 had chosen Polish over Soviet citizenship. Berta, their daughter, was deported with them, and she wrote a post-card about their harrowing odyssey to her younger brother Herschel in Paris. At age fifteen, holding a Polish passport, Herschel had made his way from Hanover to Paris, where he had arrived in September 1936, after illegally crossing into France. His failure to secure a residence permit merely compounded his insecurity and anguish. Herschel had already read newspaper accounts of the torment at Zbąanszyń when, on November 3, he received his sister's lament, which heightened his own distress. He spent the weekend brooding over his family's ordeal. Then, on the morning of November 7, he bought a handgun and went to the German embassy, where he fatally shot Ernst vom Rath, the third secretary.

Hitler instantly dispatched his private physician to attend to vom Rath, whom he also hastened to promote to embassy counselor first-class just before he died two days later. Goebbels disingenuously hailed the old-school diplomat as a devoted party member and mounted a spectacular funeral to exalt vom Rath in the manner of Horst Wessel. But above all, restless zealots urged that Germany's Jews be held responsible for this latest outrage. As in March and April 1933, when the anti-Nazi rally in Madison Square Garden was made the pretext for the first massive anti-Jewish boycott, so now the ingenuous murder by the adolescent Grynszpan became the occasion for the second major nationwide eruption against the Jews.

At this juncture Hitler had his own reasons for turning a blind eye toward his fiery fundamentalists. After the Röhm purge they had ceased to be an independent force, and he was confident that he could unleash and bridle them at will. This being the case, and since he valued the true believers' contagious fervor and enthusiasm, Hitler made sure to cajole them periodically. Besides, the führer was in a quandary: on the one hand, he valued the Jews as an object of cathexis; on the other hand, he wanted the Jews hunted out of Germany, especially now that foreign expansion was saddling the Greater Reich with ever more of them. More than likely, the continuing pusillanimity of the major powers encouraged Hitler to try to browbeat them into accepting the Reich's Jews themselves or finding other dumping grounds for them.

The infamous Crystal Night of November 9–10, 1938—the twentieth anniversary of the revolution of 1918 and the fifteenth anniversary of the Munich Putsch of 1923—was no more spontaneous than the great boycott of five and a half years before. At about midnight Gestapo locals were notified by phone and telegraph that at the "earliest possible moment you are to take actions against Jews, in particular against their synagogues," whose archives were to be spared. They were also to arrest "between 20,000 and 30,000 Jews," preferably "wealthy Jews." A subsequent order specified that the Jews to be interned in concentration camps should be healthy adult males of under sixty years of age, and that they should not be roughed up. While Heydrich put the security police in overall charge of "wreckage and incendiary operations," he indicated that general and special SS units would be standing by. The police operatives were instructed not to wear their uniforms. In order not to appear as "instigators of the demonstrations," party members were told to lie low.

The assaults started at 1 A.M. on November 10 and continued full-force until early that evening. The targets for attack were identical all over the Greater Reich. Synagogues were set on fire, while Torah scrolls, prayer books, and tallithim were thrown into the streets and burned. Firemen were summoned not to put out flames but to keep them from spreading to adjoining buildings. The licensed vandals also attacked Jewish-owned stores in commercial districts, breaking shopwindows and tossing merchandise into the street. Quite a few shops were either completely gutted or severely damaged. There were, of course, enormous local and regional variations. Much depended on the size of the Jewish population and, above all, on the militancy of local party leaders and activists. The worst ravages were perpetrated in Berlin, Leipzig, and Vienna, and naturally also in Streicher's Franconia, including Nuremberg.

At Göring's request, Heydrich hurriedly prepared a tentative estimate of damages, which was ready on November 11. According to this report, 191 synagogues were set on fire and 76 were completely razed; 11 community centers and cemetery chapels were set ablaze and another 3 burned to the ground; 815 retail businesses were destroyed; 29 department stores and 171 private houses were wrecked by fire or in other ways. All told, some 7,500 stores were damaged throughout the Greater Reich.

By portraying the pogrom of November 9–10, 1938, as "the night of broken glass," Nazi propagandists meant to fix attention on this material damage. They went out of their way to stress that Jews were neither looted nor physically harmed. This was a gross misrepresentation. There was considerable pillaging, most of it at night and in poorer neighborhoods. But above all, even by Heydrich's own reckoning, thirty-six Jews were killed and thirty-six seriously wounded. Parenthetically, to this day there is no independent and comprehensive assessment of the material destruction, physical injury, and loss of life, including suicides, caused by the pogrom.

The government and party soon ceased to pretend that Crystal Night had been a spontaneous reaction to the murder of vom Rath. Admittedly, no one acknowledged that the wave of violence had been authorized and directed from on high. But official and semiofficial statements sought to justify the turbulence and threatened more drastic action should the Jews outside Germany persist in their "murderous excesses and slanderous provocations." As for the massive arrests, they were intended to put additional pressure on the Jews to leave Germany and on the outside world to accept them. The SS distributed approximately 25,000 Jewish hostages nearly evenly between Dachau, Buchenwald, and Sachsenhausen. Some 6,500 Jews were arrested in Vienna, of whom over half were taken to Dachau, the rest to Mauthausen.

By all accounts, considerable crowds gathered to witness the desecration of synagogues, the sack of Jewish shops, and the arrest of Jewish neighbors. Most onlookers watched silently, many of them disturbed, if not shamed by this contrived *Walpurgisnacht.* This is not to say that they rose in protest or resistance, of which there was even less than on April 1, 1933, when Jewish businesses were boycotted. By now, five years later, the regime ruled political and civil society with an iron hand and a firm consensus, so that there were no political parties, trade unions, universities, or local assemblies to serve as shields or buffers as there had been during the pogroms in late tsarist Russia. Accordingly, the Jews were totally isolated and vulnerable. They were the victims of the passivity and tacit complicity of Christian friends and acquaintances. There were few, if any, intercessions by the non-Nazi elite of bureaucrats, professionals, industrialists, agrarians, intellectuals, and artists. The silence of Protestant and Catholic prelates was equally deafening. Not that the classes, any more than the masses, kept quiet primarily out of fear. For one thing, most had bought into anti-Semitism to some extent, rejecting only what they continued to deceive themselves into believing were its adventitious excesses and improprieties. For another, they withdrew, more and more, into their own personal and corporate concerns. In brief, the leaders of the party-state had a completely free hand: neither the general population nor the upper ten thousand either urged or opposed the persecution of the Jews. But one and all preferred what then still appeared as the orderly and bureaucratic coercion of Himmler and Heydrich to the reckless and random violence of Goebbels and Streicher.

As for Hitler, he could switch his support back and forth between these two factions, confident of their mutual compatibility, even interdependence. In November 1938, as in April 1933, he momentarily turned loose the pogromists, only to pull in the reins at the first sign of backfire at home and abroad. But Hitler must also have been the first to realize that with the growth of the war-oriented Behemoth the enthusiasts of brute force would be increasingly supplanted by the impassive engineers of systemic coercion and violence. Besides, Goebbels and Streicher were no match for Himmler and Heydrich, especially once Göring, for his own reasons, became impatient with spasms of indiscriminate vandalism.

On explicit and insistent instructions from Hitler, Marshal Göring called an urgent meeting for the morning of November 12 to assess Crystal Night. After discussing Heydrich's preliminary report on damages, the assembled officials considered ways of streamlining the pressures and procedures for casting out the Jews. Even the composition of this special conclave was revealing. Göring and Heydrich were the key figures, representing the high-priority second Four-Year Plan and the hydra-headed security apparatus. On the economic side, in addition to Göring, there was Walther Funk, the economics minister and Rudolf Brinkmann, his state secretary; Lutz Schwerin von Krosigk, the finance minister; and Karl Blessing of the Reichsbank. On the security side, besides Heydrich, there were Interior Minister Wilhelm Frick, Justice Minister Franz Gürtner, and SS General Kurt Daluege, the chief of police. The two top party leaders from Austria and the Sudeten territories also attended, further strengthening the voice of the SS and the Gestapo. However, the presence of Goebbels, a chief instigator of Crystal Night, meant that the ascendance of the systematizers did not spell the disgrace of the firebrands, who were once again being bridled.

Göring chaired the meeting. Invoking Hitler, he asserted that the time had come to make an end of frenzied outbreaks "which harm us, not the Jews," notably in economic terms. Valuable consumer goods had been destroyed, and major insurance companies would go under if they had to settle all the claims for damages. Following a discussion firmly steered by Göring, it was decided to fine the Jews 1 billion marks beyond the cost of repairing the material damages they had, so the Nazis said, brought on themselves, which were estimated at 250 million marks.

But Göring was eager to forget the past and concentrate on ways to tighten the vise on the Jews with a view to speeding their banishment. In his view, they should be forced to yield their assets to the state, partly in the interest of Aryanizing the economy. Although the worth of Jewish assets was estimated at between 5 and 10 billion marks, the idea would be to appraise them at a fraction of their real value. In addition, instead of being paid for them directly, the Jews would be given a yearly return of 3.5 percent on their equity. It was agreed that, in order to appease the *Mittelstand,* this ill-disguised expropriation should begin with Jewish retail and department stores. But the next and more lucrative step would be the takeover of large factories and corporations in which Jews were major shareholders and served as directors. Göring expected that with these bargain-basement acquisitions and the expiatory fine of 1 billion marks he could ease the fiscal strain caused by spiraling military spending.

Impatient with Göring's economism, Heydrich interjected that Jews should have to wear a badge of infamy. The field marshal countered with a proposal that Jews be concentrated in ghettos, which Heydrich rejected as impracticable. In Heydrich's view a more effective way to segregate the Jews would be to deny them access to public transport, theaters, movies, health resorts, and hospitals. Despite differences in method and style, Göring and Heydrich were pulling in the same direction. For them economic asphyxiation and social ostracism were not ends in themselves but ways of increasing the pressure on Jews to leave. With this objective in mind Heydrich urged that the new procedures Eichmann had instituted in Vienna, which included taxing rich Jews to subsidize the departure of needy ones, be adopted throughout the Reich. After von Krosigk made a similar point, Göring promised to set up an emigration office in Berlin modeled after the one in Vienna.

Immediately following this meeting, decrees fining the Jews and imposing punitive damages were issued. That same day, November 12, the government also promulgated a "decree excluding the Jews from the German economy." Hereafter, Jews were barred from retail trade, independent crafts, markets, fairs, expositions, professional associations, and middle management. By January 24, 1939, Göring created the promised Central Office for Jewish Emigration, with Heydrich in charge.

Almost certainly, it was Heydrich who had either originated or approved the idea of seizing 20,000 to 30,000 well-off Jews during and immediately after Crystal Night. Not a few of them were mistreated during their arrest and once they were interned in concentration camps. But Heydrich's purpose was not to torture or kill these Jews but to frighten them into emigrating and, no less important, to have them set an example for others to follow. Accordingly, within a few weeks they were released after promising to get out of Germany, soon. The number of Jewish emigrants nearly doubled, from 35,000 in 1938 to 68,000 in 1939. The largest number of these refugees managed to secure regular or temporary visas to France and the Low Countries. Of course, after the outbreak of war many of them were put in internment camps, especially in France, where they were given the same treatment as the over 300,000 Republican refugees from Franco's Spain.

It took nearly seven years, from January 30, 1933, to the outbreak of war on September 1, 1939, for about 230,000 Jews, or nearly half of Germany's Jewish population, to leave their homeland. As we saw, starting in 1938, Austrian Jews left at a much faster pace, and so did Czech Jews. As for the Jews who stayed behind by either choice or necessity, they were confined to a steadily contracting ghetto without walls. All but barred from exercising any trade or profession, more and more were forced to live either on their savings or on aid provided by Jewish welfare organizations.

What would have been the fate of these straitened Jews if they had not been hostage to a regime bent and dependent on foreign war? Would the Nazis have continued to force the remaining Jews to emigrate, especially if a world economic recovery and political restabilization had facilitated their finding refuge abroad? Alternatively, with foreign doors well-nigh closed, notably to indigent Jews, would they have turned from radical deemancipation and reghettoization to physical extermination? To ask these questions is to gain the conviction that the transition from crippling restrictions at home to genocidal murder beyond the borders of Germany was closely correlated with the compulsions and vicissitudes of unrestrained war.

There were several hints of this linkage as early as 1938–39. At a meeting on November 12, 1938, Göring noted that should the Reich "become involved in an external conflict in the foreseeable future" Germany would have to consider giving first priority "to settling accounts with its [remaining] Jews." He also indicated that on November 9 Hitler had assured him that in these circumstances he would approach those foreign powers preoccupied with the "Jewish question" to explore the establishment of a Jewish settlement in Madagascar. Needless to say, short of defeat in war France was not about to yield this island off southeastern Africa for this purpose. Then, on January 30, 1939, while addressing the counterfeit Reichstag, the führer himself made the connection between foreign war and the persecution of the Jews. He recalled that "during the struggle for power the Jews never ceased to scoff at my prophecy that some day I would lead the German government and people and solve the Jewish problem along with many others." After gleefully noting that by now Germany's Jews were "choking on their once noisy mockery," Hitler took up his prophecy of the recent Nuremberg rally, giving it a new twist: "Should Jewish international finance in Europe and beyond succeed in pushing the peoples [of Europe] into another world war, the consequence would not be the Bolshevization of the world and hence the triumph of the Jews, but the destruction of the Jewish race in Europe." Nazi Germany and fascist Italy knew how to enlighten the masses about these Jewish machinations to send people to fight "totally senseless battles" on battlefields "on which they no longer wanted to die." They would tell them that only the Jews, "this rootless international race," would benefit from "the business of such a war" while at the same time "satisfying their biblical thirst for vengeance." Hitler proclaimed that "the Jewish rallying cry for 'the proletarians of all countries to unite their forces' " would be defeated by a "higher understanding" revealed in the injunction to "the toilers of all nations to recognize their common enemy." Although these statements by Göring and Hitler were decidedly threatening, they were made at the very time that Berlin began to float the idea of settling Jews in Madagascar. Moreover, Hitler did not give the "Jewish problem" first priority and urgency but continued to consider it as one among many others.

As of the spring of 1939, the führer more than ever concentrated on foreign policy. He strained to keep alive the predisposition of England and France to continue acquiescing to Germany's piecemeal revisions of the map of Europe, notably in the east. In this regard Crystal Night had been counterproductive, in that it had shocked the sensibilities of many Allied conservatives who were the mainstay of the diplomacy of appeasement. As if to recover lost ground, Hitler and Goebbels intensified their anti-Bolshevik rhetoric, pared of its anti-Semitic inflection. They did so with a view to stoking the obsessive fear of communism and distrust of Soviet Russia endemic in Europe's ruling and governing classes. Chamberlain and Daladier were under mounting pressure to shift from appeasing to containing Nazi Germany, possibly with Stalin's help, so it was more important than ever for Hitler to appeal to conservatives who wanted to stay the old course, convinced that fascism and the Axis were the best, or indeed the only antidote to the *Gesamtbolschewismus* which they felt more than ever was stalking Europe and the world. To this end, Nazi propagandists kept overstating Moscow's military power and insisting on its implacable resolve to take over the Continent, which Berlin and Rome claimed to have narrowly and momentarily checked in Spain.

Although publicly Hitler railed against the growing might and aggressiveness of the Soviet Union, privately he had nothing but scorn for the stamina of the Bolshevik regime and the strength of the Red Army. Obviously, he did not consider Moscow a danger in and of itself. But allied with London and Paris the Soviets would become the other jaw of a vise that could gradually close to reduce Berlin's room to maneuver. Not that either the Soviet Union and world bolshevism or the Western Powers were threatening Germany. The improving military preparedness and heightened diplomatic vigilance of the other powers, however, left little doubt that Germany's time and room for continuing and unopposed expansion was limited.

This narrowing of Nazi Germany's margin for maneuvering in the international arena coincided with ever more pressing but irreducible domestic pressures for war. Predictably, the forced-draft remilitarization was putting ever greater strains on the nation's limited supplies of raw materials, foreign exchange, and labor. As of 1938–39, the economy was overheating and it looked as if the ongoing military buildup would require wage controls and tax increases, as well as import restrictions on consumer goods. The Nazi leaders were loath to adopt measures contrary to their nostrum of guns *and* butter for the masses, which gave them their plebiscitary legitimacy. This is not to say that Hitler proceeded to precipitate international tensions and war in order to defuse labor discontent or to avoid taxing the wealthy. He certainly never even considered limiting his arms program and international objectives to fit the resource base of a *Kleindeutschland* with borders approximating those of 1914 or 1938. With the old elites as his docile collaborators, the führer conceived the Nazi Behemoth with a clear social-imperialist intention: to expand and regenerate Germany by iron and blood, notably in the east, without significantly reordering class and status relations. Hitler proposed to achieve this purpose with a succession of lightning strokes, which would avoid the stress and strain of protracted war as well as of all-out economic mobilization. To hedge against popular disquiet about wartime privations, he meant to steer clear of reducing consumption in order to produce the planes, tanks, and other matériel essential for successive blitz campaigns. There were bound to be bottlenecks and shortages along the way, but these would be offset by the material and spiritual benefits of foreign conquests.

After the annexation of Bohemia and Moravia on March 15, 1939, Hitler fixed his attention on Poland. If he considered Czechoslovakia the first stepping-stone to the east, he considered Poland the essential strategic gateway to the Urals. By April 3 he directed the armed forces to be ready to execute Operation White, the invasion of Poland, as of September 1. He gave this order just four days after Chamberlain and Daladier had issued their unilateral guarantee to come to the defense of Poland and Rumania. Hitler would try to isolate and cow Poland. But should all else fail, he would deliver a devastating military blow, convinced that England and France were not prepared to come to Warsaw's rescue. Should it nevertheless come to war with the Western Powers, this risk would be worth taking, on condition that the Allies remained estranged from the Soviet Union.

Hitler had good reason to assume that London and Paris would fail to come to an agreement with Moscow. London in particular kept temporizing. Nearly the entire conservative ruling and governing class of England shared Chamberlain's position: his visceral anticommunism and distrust of Stalin; his underestimation of Soviet military and economic capabilities, notably after the purges; and his overvaluation of the Polish army. Even so, on March 17, 1939, Chamberlain, increasingly wary of Hitler, and under pressure from his own back-benchers and Daladier, instructed the Foreign Office to join the Quai d'Orsay in exploring a comprehensive rapprochement with the Soviets. But having taken this first step, British officials kept stalling for time in the diplomatic and military negotiations of the summer of 1939. Even after mid-August, when they learned that Vyacheslav Molotov, the former Soviet foreign commissar, and von Ribbentrop were exchanging feelers, they remained unwilling to enter into a treaty that would be fully reciprocal and automatic.

Stalin, for his part, would settle for nothing less. He was as suspicious of Chamberlain as the latter was of him. He disparaged London's one-sided guarantee to Warsaw two weeks after the start of Anglo-Soviet negotiations, taking it to mean that the Western Powers continued to encourage Hitler to turn eastward.

Of course, Stalin had his own objectives. Like Chamberlain and Daladier, he needed time to improve military preparedness. But unlike them, Stalin also claimed to need space. Some of his generals wanted Russia's strategic perimeter to be moved farther west in order to allow more room for a defense in depth. Accordingly, on April 18, 1939, Stalin offered England and France a mutual collective security agreement providing automatic and instant military assistance to all eastern European countries between the Gulf of Riga and the Black Sea in the event of a German invasion. The British—less so the French—balked at any such all-encompassing and binding treaty, especially since Poland adamantly refused to be party to it. With London and Paris reluctant and slow to press Warsaw, Colonel Beck stuck to his position that there would be ample time to call in the Red Army *after* the start of a German attack. But Stalin doubted the ability of the Polish army to hold back the Wehrmacht for any appreciable length of time. He was no less skeptical of the capability of the Allies to storm the West Wall of German defenses and rush aid to Poland in time to prevent the strategic Polish gateway from falling to Hitler.

Stalin, Molotov, and Kliment Voroshilov, the People's Commissar for Defense, may well have been excessively rigid in their insistence that they would settle for nothing less than an absolutely explicit, reciprocal, and automatic arrangement. But their grounds for being so cautious were not trivial. They were still bitter about the Allied and Polish intervention after 1918, followed by the quarantine of the twenties. They had not forgotten the abortive Franco-Soviet agreement of 1936, the sham Allied nonintervention in Spain, and the warped appeasement of Tokyo, Rome, and Berlin. Nor could they ignore the blatant anti-Soviet hostility of the protofascist regimes of Poland, Rumania, and Hungary. Admittedly, Nazi Germany was by far the most formidable and imminent threat. All the more reason to exploit the conflicts of interest and contingent diplomatic opportunities in the tottering European system for Russia's short-term advantage.

Such was undoubtedly the logic behind Stalin's rapprochement with Nazi Germany. Once before, in 1922, in a less critical moment, the Soviet government had taken a similar step, signing an agreement of technical cooperation between the Red Army and the Reichswehr. Confident that the military purges had eliminated potentially disloyal and pro-German officers from his high command, Stalin was prepared to risk dealing with his archenemy in exchange for prompt and urgent, even if temporary, concessions that London and Paris would or could not grant him.

It is unclear how much Stalin knew about Hitler's general impatience and specifically about the projected timing of Operation White, scheduled to start September 1, 1939. In any event, following guarded diplomatic soundings about improved commercial relations, Stalin sent a direct signal of his readiness to go beyond a trade agreement. Von Ribbentrop flew to Moscow, where he and Molotov signed a five-year pact of mutual nonaggression on August 23, one week before the invasion of Poland was to begin. Stalin correctly assumed that Hitler would compensate him generously for not interfering with his march into Poland. In a secret protocol, supplemented by a rider signed on August 28, the Third Reich and the Soviet Union fixed the borders between their respective spheres of influence in the event of a territorial or political rearrangement in the east. Hitler was in such a hurry that he gave Stalin not only his respite but also the spacious strategic glacis he wanted so desperately. With two strokes of the pen the treaties of Brest-Litovsk and of Riga were nullified. As heirs of the Russian Empire, the Soviets reclaimed ascendancy over Finland, Estonia, Latvia, Lithuania, Bessarabia, and eastern Poland. In order to complete his liquidation of the Versailles *Diktat*, which was only the first step in his plans for expansion, Hitler allowed Stalin to move his borders westward, confident of keeping the upper hand. Immediately before sending Ribbentrop on his mission to Moscow, Hitler is said to have claimed that "everything . . . [he was] doing is directed against Russia." Should the West be "too stupid and too blind to grasp this, [he would] be forced to come to an understanding with the Russians, attack the West, and then, following its defeat, turn [his] assembled forces against the Soviet Union." He allegedly also stated that he "need[ed] the Ukraine" in order to make sure that Germany would "never again" be starved out, as it had been "in the last war."

In order not to lose precious time Hitler summoned his top military commanders to the Berghof, his Alpine home and headquarters on the Obersalzberg for a meeting on August 22. He was eager to tell them about the impending agreement with Moscow and reaffirm his resolve to go to war. As he put it, "now that I have completed the political groundwork, the road is clear for the soldiers." With Stalin neutralized, he expected Chamberlain and Daladier to cave in, as they had at Munich. But even failing that, there was every reason to keep to his schedule for Operation White. Germany was in a race against time. Hitler maintained that "a protracted period of peace will not benefit us," invoking Marshal Göring's estimate that the German economy could support the necessary military buildup for only a few more years. Fortunately, the arrangement with Russia would make it possible to move east without fear of blockade, since the supply of critical foods and raw materials would now be assured. Likewise, the führer asserted that the overall diplomatic and military situation was more favorable now than it would be in two or three years. England and France were still internally shaky, militarily unprepared, and without bold leadership. This being the case, they were "not very likely to intervene." Since these arguments for preventive war were reminiscent of those advanced by many leaders of the Central Powers in July 1914, a few generals, remembering Field Marshal Helmuth Count von Moltke's fatal miscalculations of that time, ventured to recommend caution.

But Hitler was determined. The invasion of Poland began as planned on September 1, 1939. The Wehrmacht moved swiftly. The Luftwaffe indiscriminately bombed and strafed open roads as well as cities. Warsaw was savagely battered, and capitulated on September 27. A few days later the fighting stopped, with nearly 200,000 Poles having been killed and wounded and about 400,000 taken prisoner. Although the Allies declared war on September 3, they did not order their battle-ready troops to march against the twenty-five German divisions deployed on the western front. The Third Reich conquered about 75,000 square miles, or slightly over half of Poland's territory, with a population of nearly 22 million people, of whom about 2 million were Jews. In turn, the Red Army crossed into eastern Poland on September 17 and advanced as agreed in the Nazi-Soviet protocol of August 28 to a line demarcated by the Bug and San rivers, or roughly the Curzon Line. This fifth partition of Poland denied the western Ukraine and western Belorussia to Germany. Moscow seized nearly as much territory as Berlin, but with a population of only about 13 million, including 1.2 to 1.5 million Jews.

Although the "Jewish question" was never on the agenda of the momentous diplomatic negotiations of 1939, it was centrally affected by them. The "lame and impotent conclusion" of the talks between the Western Powers and the Soviet Union was a calamity for much of the world, and for the Jews in particular. The Grand Alliance that miscarried in 1939 was the last chance to forestall Nazi Germany's barbarous drive for European hegemony and its built-in anti-Jewish fury. To be sure, desperate at being walled in and at having to settle for a stunted Behemoth, the führer might have vented his rage on the 400,000 Jews trapped in the Third Reich, including Austria, Bohemia, and Moravia. But would he have carried the torment of these Jews beyond forced exile or expulsion in the face of an ignominious diplomatic checkmate that would probably have sapped his position at home?

Paradoxically, for the Jews the secret protocols of the Nazi-Soviet Pact were in the nature of a partial and disguised blessing. At least one-third of the Jews of Poland were kept out of German hands, along with such great Jewish communities as Przemyśl, Lvov, Pinsk, Białystok, Grodno, and Vilna. This favorable corollary of Russo-German collusion was certainly unintended. Just as Berlin did not renounce any Polish provinces or districts in order to avoid acquiring additional Jews, Moscow did not claim any districts in order to prevent Jews from falling under the Nazi boot. In fact, Soviet propaganda stopped denouncing Nazi anti-Semitism at the same time that it ceased excoriating fascism, including nazism. And the Kremlin did abandon over 2 million Jews to Hitler, although in doing so it did not show itself any more indifferent to the fate of the Jews than the Western nations, which were hardly innocent bystanders. Still, as we shall see, by temporarily repossessing a broad band of the east-central European marchlands, Stalin inadvertently saved large numbers of not only Polish but also, later, Soviet Jews.

The Nazis also changed their propaganda. While they muted their attacks on the Soviet government and on Stalin, they persisted in preaching the anticommunism of an earlier vintage. Between September 1939 and June 1941 Goebbels simply ignored the ideological incompatibility of the two regimes while stressing the nonaggression pact and the economic complementarity between Germany and Russia.

Although in the 1930s Soviet Russia and Nazi Germany had intrinsically similar systems of domestic control and oppression, there was little if any likeness in the basic character of their international politics. Stalin was essentially defensive in foreign and military policy. His posture was a function not only of his personal disposition but also of the immanent tendencies of the Soviet regime, of the geopolitical endowment of Russia, and of sheer necessity. Hitler, for his part, was intrinsically bellicose and aggressive in external affairs. By virtue of its stringent social compromise and relentless ideological drive, the Nazi regime generated and required constant international tension and foreign expansion. With the conquest of Poland Hitler crossed the Rubicon of unlimited war. He did not set upon Poland in order to correct unjust borders and redeem German irredentas. Although Poland was targeted for inclusion in the Third Reich, it was valued less in and for itself than as an antechamber or passageway to the vast spaces lying beyond the Soviet zone, deep in European Russia. Eventually, Nazi Germany turned this antechamber into the principal staging area for the march farther east. But first Poland became the proving ground for the Wehrmacht's new style of wantonly violent blitz warfare as well as for the implantation of the SS reign of terror in conquered territories, particularly in the east.

During the fortnight preceding the attack Hitler repeatedly told his top military commanders that their assignment went beyond defeating the Polish army and occupying Polish territories up to a certain demarcation line. He made it clear that he conceived the crushing of the enemy forces as merely the first step in the subjugation of Poland's civil and political society. But Hitler said nothing about the Third Reich breaking Poland's ruling and governing class, smothering its culture, or enslaving its working population. Nor did he specify that some of the conquered territories might be colonized by ethnic Germans, which would require the prior forcible resettlement of indigenous populations farther east.

Although the generals were not given all the facts, they were hardly unaware or unsuspecting of the general drift of Hitler's plans. To be sure, for the most part their mission was military: in September 1939 they smashed the Polish army, and also tested the new strategy and tactics of blitz warfare conceived by General Heinz Guderian. But they knew that this military mission was politically and ideologically freighted. Before moving into Poland, the quartermaster general of the Wehrmacht, Brigadier General Eduard Wagner, and the deputy chief of the security apparatus, Reinhard Heydrich, agreed that special commandos would follow close upon the regular army to combat all politically hostile and dangerous elements in the rear of the fighting forces. The military had seen these security forces at work first in Austria and then in Bohemia-Moravia. Since then Himmler, Heydrich, and Eicke had improved the effectiveness of these embryonic Einsatzgruppen by giving them military training and equipping them with motorized transport. Himmler committed fourteen to sixteen SS units of 120 to 150 men each to the Polish campaign. In addition to deploying these 2,500 political shock troops, on September 7 Himmler ordered Eicke to send his three major Death's Head units into Upper Silesia. Recruited to run the concentration camps with an iron fist, the volunteers of these guard regiments had recently received military training in preparation for service abroad. Presently, the Oberbayern and Thüringen regiments were attached to the Tenth Army and the Brandenburg regiment to the Eighth Army. Older and less robust SS men were sent to garrison the major concentration camps.

These political soldiers went into Poland with general instructions to seize recent political refugees and to hunt for hostile elements among Freemasons, Jews, Communists, the intelligentsia, the clergy, and the aristocracy. The roaming SS interned their prey in five hastily improvised detention centers, of which Stutthof, twenty miles east of Danzig, was turned into a permanent concentration camp.

But these early searches and arrests were mild compared to the reckless nonmilitary violence which accompanied and followed the Wehrmacht's advance into formerly German western Prussia and Posen (Poznań). Facing overwhelming military odds and fearing a local fifth column, the Polish authorities hurriedly arrested 50,000 ethnic Germans for evacuation inland. In the course of this operation Polish civilians, incensed by the invasion as well as by the invaders' real and suspected local accomplices, massacred 4,000 to 5,000 German-Poles and plundered many homes and shops. The worst outburst took place on Sunday, September 3, in the Pomeranian city of Bromberg, or Bydgoszcz, where about 1,000 Germans were killed. German military and security officials instantly portrayed this explosion of murderous but spontaneous popular rage as an act of deliberate and gratuitous Polish terrorism.

During the next six weeks the field army, the SS, and their local collaborators used the "Bloody Sunday" of Bromberg to justify their own campaign of systematic murder, persecution, and deportation aimed at cowing the conquered population into submission. The Wehrmacht was in control of Poland until October 25, 1939, when civil and party authorities took over. During these eight weeks of military operations and administration, the German security forces, including the Einsatzgruppen, are estimated to have killed well over 10,000 people, most of them Polish Christians. In addition to carrying out individual and mass executions, the German invaders, fired by a sense of cultural and racial superiority, burned scores of villages and sacked scores of towns in the provinces of Łódź and Warsaw. Although the SS and their German-Polish supporters set the pace and tone for these so-called security and pacification operations, the armed forces both passively condoned and actively participated in them.

The first wave of anti-Jewish outrages and atrocities took place in this general atmosphere of intense military and civil violence, with the result that they appeared to be less exceptional or anomalous than they might have otherwise. Neither the Wehrmacht nor the Einsatzgruppen had moved into Poland with the specific or primary objective of persecuting and savaging the Jews, or of trapping them for destruction at a later time. But incited by Nazi anti-Semitism, they carried out scores of pogroms as part of the uncommon terror and violence that accompanied the military conquest and early occupation of Poland. In spirit and manner these pogroms were an expression less of the organized bureaucratic anti-Semitism of the SS than of the Judeophobia of old-fashioned Jew-baiters and street-fighters. Estimates of the number of Jews murdered in September and October 1939, while Poland was under German military government, range as high as 5,000. There were indiscriminate killings of Jews in Bromberg, Wieruszow, Częstochowa, Piotrków, Będzin, Łódź, Cracow, Kielce, Warsaw, Mielec, and Chełm. Some Jews were shot individually. Others were herded together to be executed as a group. Still others were burned alive in synagogues or other buildings that were set on fire, or else were shot trying to escape from them. Before or during these massacres, and at other times as well, Jews were publicly abused, reviled, and flogged. Many synagogues were burned or desecrated, along with holy scrolls, prayer shawls, and prayer books. In many villages and towns Jews were impressed for forced labor. And thousands of Jews were forcibly driven across the Bug and San rivers, into the Soviet zone.

The Germans justified striking out against Polish Jews, as they did against Polish Christians, by claiming they were retaliating for assaults on their own forces, or trying to prevent or discourage such assaults. Jews certainly contributed their proportion of soldiers to the defense of Poland as well as their quota of casualties and prisoners of war. They also engaged in nonmilitary resistance, and especially in the major cities the Jews were disproportionately represented in the political and syndical left, a natural locus of active antifascism. But none of this actual and potential Jewish resistance justifies or explains the scale and intensity of the victimization of Jews and the profanation of their religious and cultural life. Not that the Germans spared the core values and symbols of Polish Christians. But even if refractory priests were executed or deported to Dachau, the Catholic churches and sacraments were not desecrated. Characteristically, on November 11, 1939, Poland's chief national holiday, the Nazis razed the monument of Tadeusz Kościuszko, the nation's most revered hero, in Freedom Square in Łódź, and changed the name of the square to Deutschlandplatz. The Nazis chose that same day to burn several synagogues in this same city. Tragically, the laceration of Christian Poland, much of which was infected with the poison of anti-Judaism, reduced the sensitivity of Gentile Poles to the peculiarly brutal torments inflicted on Polish Jews.

The outrageous excesses of the so-called drive for security and pacification shocked the sensibility of some of the top Wehrmacht generals. As advocates of expansion, they were not about to criticize the violence against civilians inherent in the forcible acquisition of *Lebensraum.* But while they tended to overlook the crimes of their own soldiers and officers, they decried those of the SS and the Security Police. On September 12 Admiral Wilhelm Canaris, chief of the Abwehr (military intelligence) of the High Command of the Armed Forces, sent a first report about the mistreatment of innocent civilians—notably of Polish nobles, intellectuals, and priests—to General Karl Heinrich von Stülpnagel, quartermaster general on the Army General Staff, and General Wilhelm Keitel, chief of staff of the High Command of the Armed Forces. At about the same time, Lieutenant General Hans Boehm-Tettelbach, commanding units of the Eighth Army around Włocławek, took exception to the savageries being committed by members of the Brandenburg regiment in his sector. Similarly, his superior, General Johannes Blaskowitz, commander in chief of the Eighth Army and then of all the occupation forces, soon voiced his scruples about brutal offenses of the Einsatz units against Jews and prominent Poles to General Walther von Brauchitsch, commander in chief of the Wehrmacht. Georg von Küchler, commanding general of the Third Army, also demurred. None of these remonstrances had any effect. Though Hitler was irritated, he did not dismiss any of his protesting generals. Nor did any of them resign. Instead, they continued to fight the führer's wars of aggression, relieved that in the future the SS and the police rather than regular troops would sully their hands with the blood of innocent civilians.

Germany's churches eased many a troubled conscience. The Protestant and Catholic clergy, both high and low, legitimated the assault on Poland from the very outset, enjoining loyalty to führer and Reich. On September 2 the Evangelical Church issued an official appeal to soldiers and civilians to support this struggle to "recover German blood" for the fatherland. Similarly, the Catholic hierarchy "encourages and admonishes Catholic soldiers, in obedience to the führer, to do their duty and to be ready to sacrifice their lives." Some diocesan papers asserted that they were fighting "not just for self-preservation but for an equitable distribution of essential *Lebensraum.*" Protestant and Catholic army chaplains preached this message to the troops. After the fall of Warsaw, for a full week the bells of all German churches tolled at noon to celebrate the regime's first major feat of arms. Notwithstanding the execution and imprisonment of several Polish priests during and immediately after the conquest, no German churchmen dissented, publicly.

Several army officers continued to complain about the activities of the inchoate SS and police units, claiming that these interfered with regular military operations and governance. In late September, pressed by the High Command, Himmler even seemed to restrain his overzealous units. By October 5, however, Albert Forster, the fiery and impatient gauleiter, or party district leader, of Danzig and West Prussia, saw Hitler to protest the Wehrmacht's lack of understanding for the Third Reich's political mission in the east. The führer instantly ordered the military commanders of these two provinces to defer to Forster. Two days later, on October 7, Hitler appointed Himmler "Reichskommissar für die Festigung des Deutschen Volkstums," or Reich commissar for the consolidation of Germandom. Himmler now occupied an all-powerful position in the conquered lands: he was commissioner for resettlement as well as commander of the Political Police and Security Police. In addition, he reported directly to Hitler, without passing through any other authority. A week later, in mid-October, the führer decided to end military government in the occupied eastern territories effective October 25. The generals, eager to free manpower and resources for service in northern and western Europe, yielded control to the "civil" administration.

By this time plans were afoot to make the SS the nerve center of this civil administration. Heydrich, after conferring with Hitler, Himmler, and Forster, called a meeting of his top assistants and the chiefs of the five Einsatzgruppen in Poland for September 21 in Berlin. The assembled officials discussed the future of Poland, including Polish Jewry. Heydrich indicated that more than likely the old border provinces would be formed into German *Gaue*, or districts, to be incorporated into the Reich. Berlin would probably forge the territories lying farther east into a single foreign-speaking *Gau*, with Cracow, which had a population of over 300,000, including 60,000 to 70,000 Jews, as its capital. In both zones German authorities would continue to cow the ruling and governing elites. Although most of Poland's political leaders had either fled abroad or been arrested, those still at large, along with suspect members of the intelligentsia, were to be hunted down and sent to concentration camps. Heydrich assured the leaders of the Einsatzgruppen that their units would be reinforced so as to enable them to carry out their difficult assignment.

On October 8, 1939, the day after he ordered Himmler to take charge of Germanization, Hitler decreed the outright annexation of about half of the conquered area and population. The Third Reich annexed not only Pomerania, Posen (Poznań), and Upper Silesia, but also parts of the provinces of Cracow, Warsaw, Białystok, and Łódź, including the city of Łódź. All these territories were joined into two provinces of the Reich, which were subsequently consolidated into a single province, called the Warthegau. This appendage was to be settled by ethnic Germans following the forced relocation or resettlement of Poles and Jews farther east. On October 12 Hitler ordered the other half of German-conquered Poland to be treated as an occupied territory. Although the area was divided into four districts (to which a fifth province, Eastern Galicia, was added after the invasion of Russia in 1941), it was to be ruled as a single province by a "General Government" headed by Dr. Hans Frank. This zone, the heartland of Poland—and of the future extermination universe—was to become a ghetto, half of it open, the other half closed, in which to oppress, exploit, and debase Poles, Jews, and Gypsies.

High officials of the conjoint SS and police not only proceeded to design and staff the civil administration for captive Poland but also set about formulating the Third Reich's occupation policy. The spirit of this policy was foreshadowed in the violence against Christian and Jewish civilians during and immediately after the military campaign, while the Wehrmacht was still in control. On September 7 Heydrich instructed his operatives to break the back of the Polish elite and isolate it from the rest of the population. Two weeks later he told them to look for enemies of the Reich among Jews, intellectuals, clergymen, and aristocrats. The boundaries of the elite to be decimated and terrorized were constantly enlarged. In November Himmler decided to discourage Polish resistance by ordering exemplary killings as well as preventive deportations of members of the professions, the clergy, the bureaucracy, the intelligentsia, and the landed gentry.

The SS and the police carried out at least 10,000 allegedly retaliatory executions in the Warthegau by the end of 1939. There were a good many priests among the victims, and a large percentage of the clergy was deported. During this same period Hans Frank mounted a pacification drive in the General Government, notably in and around Cracow, Częstochowa, and Warsaw. No less than 3,500 members of the Polish elite were either executed or sent to concentration camps. Nearly the entire faculty of Cracow's Jagiellonian University was deported to Sachsenhausen.

In both halves of German-occupied Poland wholesale arrests were carried out. Local jails and detention centers were packed, and within a year about 20,000 Poles were taken to concentration camps in Germany. During the last four months of 1939 it was these Polish internees who accounted for most of the increase in the number of inmates from 6,500 to 12,150 in Sachsenhausen and from 5,300 to 11,800 in Buchenwald. Clearly, foreign conquest began to fuel the expansion of concentration camps in Greater Germany. Much the same was true, of course, of the growing pool of foreign laborers. Not counting Polish prisoners of war, by mid-1941 at least 900,000 Poles were working in the Old Reich, most of them impressed by force. This large-scale removal of labor together with the levy of high occupation costs led to a drastic deterioration of the Polish economy and standard of living.

Equally traumatic was the forcible resettlement to the General Government of Poles from the territories annexed to the Third Reich. The primary purpose was to consolidate Berlin's hold on the new salient of eastern *Lebensraum:* Poles were expelled to make room for the settlement of ethnic Germans from the Baltic and Volhynia. By late November 1939 well over 100,000 Poles were ruthlessly relocated to the General Government, a figure that rose to at least 400,000 by June 1941. Himmler meant to deport at least double that number, and at an accelerated pace. But Hans Frank balked at the overcrowding of his province with indigent deportees. In turn, Göring objected to the disruption of agriculture and manufacture in the Warthegau at a time when he was straining to gear the economy for war without imposing hardships on German workers and consumers. With the help of the Wehrmacht, which soon monopolized all transport for the preparation of the invasion of Russia, Frank and Göring managed to have the deportations all but stopped or suspended.

Of course, the Jews were to be cleared out of the Warthegau, along with Christian Poles and Gypsies. But it must be emphasized that their removal was not the crux of the racially motivated and untried population policy in Nazi Germany's newly conquered eastern living space. Until mid-1941 only about 10 percent of all Poles deported to the General Government were Jewish. To be sure, the bulk of Polish Jews were not concentrated in the Warthegau. Although there was a large Jewish population in and around Łódź, it was spared deportation because of its strategic economic importance for both Poland and Germany. Between September 1939 and June 1941, however, aside from this relative immunity from deportation to the General Government and total immunity from conscription into forced labor in the Reich, Jewish Poles were subjected to infinitely worse treatment than Christian Poles throughout German-occupied Poland.

The conquest of Poland suddenly and unexpectedly enlarged and complicated the tangled "Jewish question." All at once, Nazi Germany acquired Europe's second-largest Jewish population, after that under Soviet control. In 1939 undivided Poland had a population of 35 million, of whom about 3.2 million, or close to 10 percent, were Jewish. The Nazi-Soviet Pact left about 2.1 million Jews in the German zone, 1.1 million Jews in the Soviet zone. Since the Russo-German border remained accessible and open for two months after the conquest, 300,000 to 350,000 Jews fled to the Soviet side, leaving the Reich with about 1.8 million Polish Jews. Slightly over 500,000 of these Jews lived in what became the Warthegau. The districts of Posen, Pomerania, and Silesia had relatively small Jewish populations. In the Warthegau the area in and around Łódź had by far the largest concentration of Jews. The city of Łódź alone counted about 180,000 Jews, making it one-third Jewish and Poland's second-largest Jewish community after Warsaw. As for the General Government, at the outset it had a Jewish population of about 1.3 million. Heavily urban, Jews accounted for between 25 and 40 percent of the population of Cracow, Warsaw, Lvov, Kielce, Radom, and Lublin. The small towns and villages surrounding these cities were less than 10 percent Jewish.

The officers and men of the invading Wehrmacht and Einsatzgruppen were probably startled by the magnitude, density, and sheer foreignness of the Jewish population of Poland. *Der Jude an der Ostgrenze*, a party handbook published in 1940, reported that in each town and city German soldiers came upon a Jewish quarter which struck them as "repulsive." These crowded ghettos were a mixture of "stupidity and shrewdness," of "idiocy and intelligence," and of "*Ostjuden* with caftan and sidelock and westernized Jews." Since, it said, there were too many Jews for all of them to be "parasites," many of them were artisans, even if they worked "reluctantly and ploddingly." The vast majority were "downright poor or impoverished," the eastern marches having the largest concentration of "the world's poorest Jews." Even though this eastern Jewry had "the typical appearance of a degenerate race with little vital energy," it was the "wellspring for the regeneration of world Jewry," the fittest elements making every effort to leave the ghettos. Overall, the ghettos of the major cities "in no way made an unhappy impression." Even so, they could not help but strike "every wholesome human being as exceedingly unpleasant, to the point of stimulating physical disgust." No doubt some of the German conquerors were impassive, others recoiled, and still others, notably the political soldiers, gave free rein to their intense hatred of the Jews.

Heydrich convened his meeting of September 21 in Berlin against the background of the ongoing violence against the Jews in Poland. After outlining the overall regimen for conquered Poland, he laid out his battle plan for attacking the "Jewish question." Broadly speaking, he proposed to deport all Jews under German control, including the Jews remaining in the Old Reich, to a Polish province, the deportations to be spread over one year. In the first phase the Polish Jews would be concentrated in ghettos. This concentration would begin with the relocation of communities with less than five hundred Jews from small towns and villages to cities with large Jewish populations. But all transfers, regardless of size, should be directed to cities with or near major railway junctions, with a view to possible future moves. As a start, the Jews of the incorporated territories of the Warthegau should be clustered and resettled, but this same process should not be put off too long in the occupied zone of the General Government.

Heydrich confirmed these "projected general measures" in a directive sent not only to the commanders of the Einsatzgruppen but also to the High Command of the Armed Forces, to the state secretaries of three key ministries, and to the chiefs of the civil administration in the occupied territories. He wanted it known that his security and police officials were under orders to cooperate with local military and civil authorities, that they did not intend to interfere with the pacification, garrisoning, and feeding of the occupied territories. In this connection, Heydrich urged the preservation of Jewish industrial and commercial enterprises that were vital for civilian and military production.

This, then, was the first comprehensive plan by a Nazi official for the treatment of the "Jewish question." Although Heydrich focused on the over 2 million Jews unexpectedly acquired with the conquest of Poland, he clearly contemplated the removal of all Jews from the expanded core of the Third Reich, including the annexed Polish territories, to its outermost eastern marches. In his directive Heydrich marked out two distinct stages. The first stage of temporary concentration would be followed by or lead to a second stage that Heydrich himself called the *Endziel,* or end purpose. This *Endziel* was the resettlement of all Jews in a vast reservation to be established between the Vistula and the Bug, close to the demarcation line with the Soviet Union.

The deportation of the Jews from the Warthegau, which was to be the initial step in the forcible relocation of European Jewry, was delayed for the same reasons that Himmler agreed to postpone the all-out enslavement of Poland generally. On October 1, 1939, the High Command of the Army (OKH) notified its field commanders of this postponement, and Himmler sent a similar message to his men in Poland.

But with the end of military government on October 25, the civil administration, pervaded by the SS, fell upon the Jews. Most of the anti-Semitic measures of Old Germany were now applied to both the annexed and the occupied zones of Poland. Almost overnight the Jews were totally deemancipated. In addition, on October 26 Hans Frank issued a ukase making the Jews of the General Government subject to forced labor. Before long, Jews were impressed to clear swamps, build roads, and quarry stones. To avoid arbitrary abductions or dragnets, several Jewish leaders suggested the establishment of quasi-autonomous Jewish councils to fill the quotas of workers fixed by the Germans, thereby unwittingly adumbrating tomorrow's *Judenräte*. On November 28 Frank ordered all Jewish communities to form such councils, confident that he could force them to do his bidding. By the end of 1939 thousands of Jewish men were laboring in scores of forced-labor camps throughout the General Government. As of the fall of 1940 Jews were also sent to help construct military emplacements opposite the Soviet demarcation line. The working and living conditions of these forced laborers were wretched, causing much loss of life, sickness, and mental anguish.

Another infamous anti-Semitic measure must be attributed to Hans Frank. On November 23, 1939, he decreed that as of December 1 all Jews of both sexes over nine years of age must wear "on their right outer sleeve a white armlet at least ten centimeters wide emblazoned with the blue star of Zion."

In the meantime, Himmler, as newly appointed Reich commissioner for the consolidation of Germandom, began to press again for an immediate start on the re-Germanization of greater Prussia and Silesia as well as of the Warthegau. To make room for ethnic Germans from all over eastern Europe, he proposed to expel both Christian and Jewish Poles, as well as Gypsies. While Polish Gentiles were to be relocated throughout the General Government, Polish Jews would be deported to the remotest corner of Hans Frank's ironbound realm. Dispossessed and stateless, the Jews were to be concentrated and isolated in a reservation or settlement area in and around Lublin, a region fronting the central sector of the border with the Soviet zone.

On October 30 Himmler issued instructions to remove all Jews as well as potentially dangerous Poles from the annexed territories and also all Poles from West Prussia. The objective was to resettle a total of about 1 million people, including 30,000 Gypsies, within four months.

The security and police forces promptly cleared Danzig and Bromberg of all Jews. But elsewhere the deportations were fitful, slow, and chaotic, perhaps because the machinery and personnel for mass banishment were inadequate and untried. In any case, on November 28

Heydrich reduced the scale and pace of Himmler's design, ordering 80,000 "Poles and Jews" to be cleared out of the Warthegau by mid-December so as to vacate housing for ethnic Germans. This order was carried out instantly, the deportees being loaded into railway transports to be dumped, totally destitute, at several points in the General Government. Hereafter, Hans Frank faced the grim prospect of a deluge of indigents draining his zone's economy.

The proportions of Jewish and Christian Poles in these early transports remains uncertain. But it is likely that 40,000 were Jews, and by March 1940 probably twice that number of Jews had been relocated to Lublinland, where the SS and police were under the command of SS Brigadier General Odilo Globocnik, an archetypal Nazi thug and freebooter.

With voluntary emigration from Germany at a complete standstill, Himmler and Heydrich also looked eagerly upon the eastern marches as a place to disgorge the Jews remaining in the German heartland. Allegedly to free dwellings for Nazi officials, several thousand Austrian, Moravian, and Bohemian Jews were deported to the Lublin district, and so were about 1,200 Jews from Stettin. More than likely, these resettlements prefigured the deportation of the Jews from the whole of Greater Germany, and not just from the Warthegau, to the easternmost periphery of the Third Reich.

Without prior preparations Lublinland, a mediocre farming region, was unable to support a large and rapid influx of penniless Jews, few of them suited for rugged agricultural work. Certainly, Governor-General Frank was not disposed to facilitate their absorption. Not that he was averse to tormenting the Jews. Far from it. But he feared that mounting scarcities of food, fuel, and housing would result in famine, disease, and epidemic fraught with danger not so much for the Jews as for the population at large. Besides, he frowned at the prospect of his province becoming the site for the main reservation for European Jewry. At any rate, when he learned that there was some question of transplanting the Jews of Łódź to Lublin, he began to remonstrate and sought out Göring to help him challenge Himmler and Heydrich. As head of the Four-Year Plan intended to increase dramatically the Reich's war-making capabilities, Göring had his own reasons for wishing to preserve important economic centers like Łódź. Eventually, on March 23, 1940, Göring issued an order making future deportations into the General Government contingent on Frank's prior approval, which amounted to stopping them altogether. Himmler yielded, ever sensitive to military dictates as well as to Göring's superior power and cunning.

Like the drive to force German Jews to leave the Third Reich, the drive to relocate Polish Jews along the far borders of the empire promised to be difficult and slow. While the tentative end goal, eastern resettlement, was put off, the SS and police authorities pressed ahead with ghettoization. In many Polish cities the Jews already lived in crowded and poor districts, sometimes slums, but which were segregated as much by choice as by constraint. The occupation combined with the Nazi reign of terror aggravated conditions, the forced inrush of Jews from rural areas intensifying the overcrowding and immiserization of the large urban Jewish communities.

With their deportation canceled, in the spring of 1940 the 160,000 to 180,000 Jews of Łódź—now renamed Litzmannstadt—were among the first to be quarantined in a compact ghetto. To achieve this compression the German authorities moved about 100,000 Jews into two of the most rundown sections of the city. Between mid-February and late April 1940 this massive relocation was carried out in great haste and confusion, as well as without mercy. The Jews were forced to leave behind most of their worldly possessions and to scramble for scant and substandard housing in an area of less than two square miles. Notwithstanding the enormous strains and stresses of the social dislocation involved, for the time being the economy of Łódź remained largely intact, its skilled workers—especially in textile plants—being marked for hyperexploitation in the service of the German war economy. The wages and rations of the Jewish workers inside the only closed ghetto in the Warthegau were reduced to a level of dehumanizing and mortal destitution, as compared to those of their Christian counterparts in the world outside, which were fixed at the poverty line. On April 30, 1941, SS Brigadier General Johannes Schäfer, the police chief of Łódź, ordered the Jewish quarter hermetically closed.

The Jews of Warsaw were immured a half year later. On October 3, 1940, Ludwig Fischer, the German governor of the city, decreed that all Jews living outside the main and predominantly Jewish quarter would have to move there as part of a design to divide Warsaw into three distinct sections, the other two to be for Christian Poles and Germans. This meant relocating about 150,000 Jews living in different parts of the city. About 100,000 Christian Poles were forcibly moved out of the designated area to make room for Jews. As in Łódź, both Jews and Gentiles were given only a few weeks to relocate. The result was a frantic scramble for shelter, as well as a radical impoverishment, the evicted Jews being dispossessed of all property, both private and business, that could not readily be moved by hand and cart. The poor Jews of the suburb of Praga were woefully disadvantaged in this stampede.

Because Jews throughout Poland had sought refuge in Warsaw since the German conquest, the ghetto held a captive population of over 400,000, surrounded by a wall nine feet high with only thirteen closely guarded gates. The tenements were bursting at the seams, with between six and nine people per room. In addition, food and fuel were scarce, sickness rampant. Compared to the ghetto in Łódź, the Warsaw ghetto was considerably less resilient, for its economy was altogether less sound and less valuable to the Third Reich's warfare state. Large numbers of Jews, including some women, were impressed for compulsory labor. With the rigors of the winter of 1940–41 conditions went from bad to worse, with the result that a few thousand Jews died of starvation and disease. Through the first half of 1941, and until the invasion of Russia, the Jews were similarly quarantined and wracked in ghettos in Cracow, Radom, Lublin, and numerous smaller cities in the General Government.

With emigration out of Greater Germany at a standstill and with resettlement to its eastern perimeter stymied, ghettoization *in situ* was in the nature of a makeshift holding operation. Hitler came face to face with a stubborn reality: Allied appeasement was at an end and there were five times as many Jews in the Third Reich as there had been seven years ago when he took over the chancellorship. Even if acquired as an unwanted by-product of the expansionist drive of the Nazi Behemoth, this rich but unwanted harvest of Jews could only embarrass and incense Hitler. Having failed to frighten off Poland's allies with his brazen aggression, the führer needed first to overrun France and then, he hoped, to unnerve the British Cabinet before resuming his march to the east. The solution of his enlarged and increasingly complex "Jewish problem," a solution which became progressively more sinister, remained contingent on the character and success of Hitler's grand strategy and struggle for European hegemony, which required *Lebensraum* east of Poland.

Unlike Operation White against Poland, Operation Yellow against France and the Low Countries was not designed as a campaign to prepare the ground for the total subjugation of these nations. The troops that staged the invasion on May 10, 1940, were not instructed to crush the enemy forces, nor were they accompanied by Einsatzgruppen charged with pacifying and "purifying" the occupied territories. Not that the Wehrmacht was restrained and benevolent. Rotterdam, for example, suffered air attacks comparable to those of

Warsaw. The German command made expert use of mobile warfare, precision bombing, and terror strafing, having tested and refined these tactics in the Polish campaign. Hitler's armies struck with such lightning force, speed, and precision that the battle of France was over in six weeks, even ahead of the German High Command's most optimistic estimates.

Notwithstanding its speed and intensity, the western campaign was in the nature of a limited conflict within an absolute war. To be sure, in late May a unit of the Waffen-SS mowed down roughly a hundred English prisoners near Le Paradis, and between June 19 and 21 German soldiers killed a few score Moroccan and other African prisoners. But in the west such massacres were rare. All in all, the battle of France was relatively free of military atrocities and of wild excesses against civilians. Rather than press for unconditional surrender, Hitler settled for an armistice on June 22, 1940. Certainly, northern France, including Paris, became occupied territory. But even though the Germans fastened their direct military and civilian rule on this half of the country, they did not enslave it. In neither reannexed nor occupied France did the Germans turn to arresting notables for local imprisonment or deportation to concentration camps in the Reich, as they had on the morrow of victory in Poland. Nor did they mistreat the Jews. There were no wild pogroms and no Jewish communities were ghettoized.

Of course, there were expulsions, but even these had anything but a wracking or murderous intention. After barring French Jews from returning from unoccupied to occupied France, the German authorities prepared to rid themselves of the Jews remaining under their control. They began by trying to make the newly annexed territories and their hinterland *judenfrei*. To this end, in October 1940 they forcibly transported some 20,000 Jews from Alsace and a much smaller number from Lorraine into the unoccupied zone, which was left to be ruled by Marshal Henri Philippe Pétain. That same month they also deported nearly 7,500 Jews from Baden and the Pfalz (Palatinate) across that same demarcation line. Certainly, and not unexpectedly, Pétain's Vichy government interned the foreign or stateless Jews among these deportees in refugee camps, notably in Gurs, but also in Les Milles and Rivesaltes. Just the same, with these expulsions the Nazis did nothing other than continue their foundering policy of forced emigration by other means: they transported Jews beyond the borders of the expanding heartland of the Third Reich to its outlying provinces. They did so despite the fact that these deported Jews would fare considerably better in Vichy France than in either Germany or the General Government, in part because of greater opportunities for fleeing abroad and emigrating overseas, particularly for wealthier Jews.

Despite certain ideological affinities between Vichy and Berlin, their collaboration was rooted in mutual interest and power politics. Always racing against time, Hitler was eager to avoid a protracted battle and an overextended occupation. He was equally intent on impressing London with his diplomatic reasonableness while maintaining enough military pressure to gain ascendancy over another pliable satellite on the model of protofascist Rumania and Hungary. With the main body of France's army in captivity as well as its strategic territories, coastlines, and industries safely in German hands, Hitler looked to Vichy to provide not military assistance but economic and financial fuel for his Behemoth.

Pétain and his ministers, for their part, proposed to use their control of truncated and overseas France, and of the French fleet, to salvage a kernel of sovereignty as well as to press their bid to become Hitler's preeminent satellite in what they were certain would be a German-dominated Europe. In pursuit of this optimum goal, and susceptible to the fascist temptation, Pétain and his vice-premier Pierre Laval readily handed over, and hence sent to certain death, several left-wing political refugees from Germany who had received asylum in France. Hereafter, for reasons of both ideological inclination and rank opportunism, the Vichy leaders, having set up an authoritarian state, consistently displayed their anti-Semitism. Between late July and early October 1940 they chartered a commission to review recent naturalizations, they abrogated a law prohibiting anti-Semitic propaganda, they adopted a racist statute barring Jews from government service and the professions, and they authorized prefects to intern foreign Jews in special camps.

But even with all these unforced and infamous measures, Vichy France was neither Nazi Germany, nor the General Government of Poland, nor occupied France. There is no minimizing or excusing the wretched and scandalous conditions in Gurs, Les Milles, and the other camps of the southern zone and North Africa, which caused the death of a few thousand Jewish internees. Even so, the regimen of these camps was far less horrible than that of Dachau in Germany or the closed ghettos in Poland. In addition, thousands of the internees were released upon receiving visas which enabled them to leave France for other countries in Europe and overseas. What is clear is that Hitler neither expected nor compelled Vichy to persecute its own Jews or to become a major reservation for Jews from other parts of Europe. To the extent that prostrate France might help to meet the end goal of Jewish resettlement, it would do so by making available not a metropolitan region but an overseas territory, specifically Madagascar.

The victory over France and the Low Countries left Germany with at least 300,000 additional Jews, not counting the Jews who fled from the newly annexed or occupied territories to unoccupied France and elsewhere. A total of about 3.5 million Jews were now under German control. With emigration more than ever foreclosed and the Lublin project shelved or discarded, the Nazis were at a loss as to where to direct the Jewish exodus when the fall of France seemed to open a new possibility.

Actually, it was the Polish government which as early as 1937 had directed attention to Madagascar as a conceivable land for Jewish settlement, and sent an investigating commission to the island. In December of the following year Georges Bonnet, the French foreign minister, had spoken of settling 10,000 Jewish refugees in Madagascar in a conversation with von Ribbentrop. At about that same time, in the wake of Crystal Night, Göring had alluded to Madagascar in an in-house discussion, apparently with Hitler's approval. In 1939 Nazi officials had considered Madagascar along with British Guiana and former German East Africa as likely reservations for Jews outside Europe, in the colonial world.

But neither France nor Britain was about to offer up an overseas territory for so unseemly a project without being forced to do so or without its being part of a comprehensive diplomatic transaction. As for those Jews who in this emergency looked beyond Europe and America for a land to settle in, their eyes were fixed on Palestine. But in May 1935 the British, mindful of Arab sensibilities, had frozen the number of Jewish immigrants at 75,000 over the next five years. Likewise, although there was no organized local resistance to contend with, the French had never really considered ceding Madagascar. Their colony since 1896, this African island of 228,000 square miles had an indigenous population of 3.8 million and 36,000 European settlers, two-thirds of them French. But with the disastrous defeat in 1940 the leaders of France might opt or need to barter an overseas territory to safeguard interests closer to home.

In mid-May, after German tanks broke through the Ardennes and began their race to the Atlantic coast, the prospect of victory prompted Himmler to draft a memorandum outlining his thoughts "about the treatment of foreign peoples in the east." As part of a wide-ranging discussion of the enslavement of Ukrainians, White Russians, and Poles, Himmler recorded his hope "to see the concept

Jew totally extinguished [in Europe] by virtue of the possibility of a great migration of all the Jews to Africa or to some other colony." He stressed that "no matter how cruel and tragic" such a course would be "for the individuals involved," it would be "the mildest and the best if out of inner conviction one ruled out as both un-German and impossible the Bolshevik method of the physical extermination [*Ausrottung*] of a people." Two weeks later, on May 28, 1940, Himmler recorded that when he showed his memorandum to the führer on May 25, he expressed his agreement with it. By then Leopold II, the king of Belgium, had capitulated, General Erwin Rommel's panzers were drawing near the Channel, and the evacuation of the British from Dunkirk was about to begin.

On June 3, anticipating the defeat of France and probably also an early surrender of England, Franz Rademacher, specialist for Jewish affairs in the Foreign Office, submitted a position paper to von Ribbentrop in which Madagascar figured as a reservation for western and central European Jews. A month later, on July 3, 1940, Rademacher expressed his conviction that the impending victory gave Germany "not only the possibility but also the duty to solve Europe's Jewish question." He urged that France be forced to "make available the island of Madagascar" for this purpose. All French settlers should be "relocated and compensated" as Germany assumed the mandate for the island. In the meantime, on June 24, forty-eight hours after the Franco-German armistice, Heydrich wrote to Ribbentrop to ask to be associated with any diplomatic initiative for an overseas solution. Lamenting that only 200,000 Jews had gone abroad since January 1, 1939, leaving Greater Germany with over 3 million Jews, Heydrich insisted that since the "overall problem [*Gesamtproblem*]" was insoluble by emigration it now required a "territorial final solution [*Endlösung*]." Governor General Frank especially was overjoyed at the prospect of an overseas solution.

Clearly, the defeat of France was the essential precondition for the Madagascar project's becoming a serious historical possibility. Not only France but also England was expected to consent to Germany's assuming the mandate for the island. The transport of some 4 million European Jews to Madagascar over a period of four years was to be a multinational enterprise. But the Third Reich would exercise sole political control over the island, bolstered by naval and air bases. The Jews would enjoy limited self-rule, and would themselves have to bear the financial cost of their forced deportation and colonization. In Rademacher's words, "this solution avoids the Jews founding their own Vatican State in Palestine, which would enable them to exploit for their own purposes the symbolic meaning that Jerusalem has for the Christian and Moslem parts of the world."

Since the British controlled the sea-lanes to the Indian Ocean, they needed to be coerced into giving Germany a free hand on the Continent and an extended reach overseas. For Himmler and Heydrich, as well as other high officials, Madagascar remained a live option until it became clear that England would hold out despite the blitz. On October 12, 1940, Hitler indefinitely postponed the invasion of England, having in the meantime, on September 28, ordered the Wehrmacht to prepare for the invasion of Russia, to begin in the spring of 1941. By now Hitler realized that although Winston Churchill, at a critical moment, had withheld additional support from France in order to save Britain, he would not countenance German hegemony on the Continent. Notwithstanding his visceral anticommunism, and confident of American support, Churchill was not about to connive in Hitler's designs on Soviet Russia.

In keeping with the logic of the Nazi-Soviet Pact, Stalin did not stand by idly while Germany crushed France and the Low Countries. After occupying eastern Poland in late September 1939, the Soviet Union extended its military perimeter in the north. Moscow forced forward bases on Estonia and Latvia and made war on Finland with a view to improving Russia's strategic position northeast of Leningrad. But then the Kremlin was jolted by the lightning speed with which the Wehrmacht won the battle of France. Even before the French surrender, on June 17, 1940, Stalin ordered the occupation of Estonia and Latvia, as well as the occupation of Lithuania, which the secret rider to the Nazi-Soviet Pact had assigned to the German sphere of influence. In August 1940 the three Baltic republics were annexed or reincorporated into the Soviet Union. With these territories Moscow broadened and solidified its access to the Baltic. It also recovered about 250,000 Jews concentrated in such cities as Vilna, Kovno, Riga, and Revel (now Tallinn). Vilna, the new capital of Lithuania, was one of Europe's great centers of Jewish culture.

After Molotov issued two ultimatums to Bucharest, on June 28, 1940, the Red Army also crossed the Soviet-Rumanian border to occupy Bessarabia and northern Bukovina, which likewise were incorporated into the Soviet Union. Bessarabia counted about 200,000 Jews, with the largest Jewish community in Kishinev. Northern Bukovina had nearly 95,000 Jews, with Czernowitz as their vital center.

Except in northern Bukovina, where they overstepped the agreed-to bounds, the Soviets acted in keeping with the Molotov-Ribbentrop protocol. With their peremptory seizures they both closed and expanded the Soviet Union's security belt running from the Baltic Sea in the North to the Black Sea in the South. In the process they also added between 500,000 and 600,000 Jews to the 1.2 million Jews who had been included in the Soviet sphere with the annexation of eastern Poland. Meanwhile, from late September to mid-November 1939, from 300,000 to 350,000 Jews had either fled from German-occupied Poland into the Soviet zone, or else been forcibly expelled across the demarcation line. Accordingly, by mid-1941 the Soviet Union had a Jewish population totaling close to 5 million.

The refugees and expellees from the German half of Poland, most of them males, at first settled not too far beyond the border. As of mid-1940, however, the Soviets began to move many of them inland, along with native-born Jews from the newly annexed territories. This forced relocation of Jews was part of the large-scale deportation carried out by the Soviets from 1939 to mid-1941, forcibly removing real and imagined political enemies from all the territories seized in accordance with the Nazi-Soviet Pact. The number of people deported for compulsory labor or political exile remains unclear, but estimates run to over 1 million. There is the same uncertainty about the number who perished.

By mid-1941 about 400,000 Jews are estimated to have been moved to labor camps, towns, and villages in the remote Russian interior—in the Komi Republic, Kazakhstan, and eastern Siberia. Some of these Jews were deported because they wanted to return to Nazi-occupied Poland to rejoin their families, others because they were considered politically unreliable. But apparently the largest number were resettled in the interest of war production in remote parts of Russia. The resettlements and, above all, the deportations must have taken a terrible toll, but the extent of suffering is as yet undetermined.

Whatever the number of Jews deported and resettled, and whatever the number killed in the process, the Kremlin's purpose in maltreating Jews was political control and economic mobilization, not religious discrimination, let alone racial persecution. Likewise, when the Soviets sealed their borders in late November 1939, they did so not out of anti-Semitism but in order to stop the Germans from continuing to drive Polish Jews over the Bug and the San. Significantly, the Jews who wound up on the Soviet side of the border were permitted to stay and were offered Soviet citizenship, this at a time when elsewhere such refugees were driven back or interned for being either enemy aliens, stateless, or without visas. Of course, the Soviets applied their customary policy of suppressing the distinct religious and cultural life of Russian Jewry in the Jewish communities throughout the annexed territories. But as we saw, though highly repressive, this policy was not specifically anti-Semitic and did not preclude assimilated and secularized Jews from continuing to secure important positions in civil and political society. In any event, during the life of the Nazi-Soviet Pact, Stalin's Jewish policy remained essentially untouched by the lethal anti-Semitism of Nazi Germany and its satellites.

CHAPTER VII

CONCEIVING OPERATION BARBAROSSA

CONQUEST AND CRUSADE

Compared to the invasion first of Poland and then of France and the Low Countries, Nazi Germany's assault on Soviet Russia was *sui generis*. The eastern campaign exploded as an absolute or total war, to be fought without restraint in pursuit of unlimited secular as well as doctrinal objectives. From the outset it was conceived and planned not only as a blitzkrieg to smash the Red Army and conquer eastern *Lebensraum* but also as a crusade to extirpate "Judeobolshevism."

Not that the limited wars of 1939 to 1940 were old-fashioned and benign. The Wehrmacht struck Poland and France with the full force of blitz warfare, defeating both with uncommon speed and without causing excessive casualties and material destruction. By contrast, the blitzkrieg against the Soviet Union stalled and miscarried. This unanticipated failure aggravated the built-in brutality of Nazi Germany's military campaign on the eastern front and enormously intensified the violence of its "holy war" against "Judeobolshevism." Whatever the ideologically grounded ruthlessness of the Third Reich's conquest and enslavement of Poland from September 1939 through June 1941, it was surpassed by the savagery and crusading zeal of the assault on the Soviet Union. For Hitler the eastern war became a struggle for *Sein oder Nichtsein,* for life or death. The Judeocide was destined to be closely bound up with this monstrous fight to the finish.

The death and destruction resulting from the General Crisis and Thirty Years War of the twentieth century were unprecedented in the annals of European history. The Great War of 1914–18, the first major phase of this manmade cataclysm, claimed 12 million military and civilian casualties outside Russia. Russia endured 16 million deaths, including the lives lost in the civil war of 1918 to 1921. For all the belligerents the number of permanently disabled and seriously wounded was even greater. Of course, the warring nations suffered unequally. In some respects France and Germany were hardest hit, in that the number of their dead amounted to about 3.5 percent of their total populations, or about 10 percent of their male work force. Among men between the ages of twenty and forty-four, in France 20 percent were killed, in Germany 15 percent, and in England 10 percent. These casualties went hand in hand with great economic expenditures, national indebtedness, and inflation.

In every respect, the World War of 1939–45, the second major phase of this century's General Crisis and Thirty Years War, was even more destructive. There were more than three times as many dead and wounded as in 1914–18. Of a total of 42 million killed, 16 million were military casualties, 26 million were civilians. Indeed, the proportion of civilian victims was vastly higher than during the First World War. Once again, Russia suffered inordinately, incurring well over 50 percent of all dead and wounded. The Soviet Union lost about 20 million lives, or close to 10 percent of its population. Certain western European countries, however, were much less severely wracked by the war of 1939–45 than the war of 1914–18. The contrast between the principal western and eastern campaigns was particularly stark. The Third Reich lost fewer than 30,000 lives in its astonishing victory on the western front, and the Allies lost only 135,000 men in their ignominious defeat. To be sure, by the time the war was over Germany herself counted close to 7 million dead, but most of these lives were sacrificed in Hitler's premeditated and ultimately disastrous war of conquest and annihilation against Soviet Russia.

If Hitler had any fixed, overt, and long-range objectives, his demand for eastern *Lebensraum* ranked first among them. This commitment to foreign conquest and domination may be said to have had precedence even over his resolve to make the Third Reich *judenfrei*. Indeed, until the fall of 1941 the Nazi drive against the Jews remained indeterminate and erratic. Of course, the road to the Urals was as twisted and contingent as the road to the extermination sites. Paradoxically, while the unexpected impasse of the assault on Russia, beginning with the forced halt in front of Moscow in late 1941, fomented and hastened the Judeocide, the systematic persecution of the Jews actually hindered military operations on the eastern front. This is not to say that Nazi Germany ever gave the war against the Jews priority over the life-or-death struggle with Soviet Russia. The resources "wasted" on the "Final Solution" were probably not militarily decisive. But be that as it may, once Hitler and Himmler realized that the allegedly bestial soldiers and callous Bolshevik commissars of the Red Army were thwarting the peerless Wehrmacht, they increasingly vented their rage on the Jews.

· · ·

Even after the fall of France Hitler never really considered abandoning the quest for eastern *Lebensraum* begun with the seizure of Czechoslovakia and Poland. In addition to providing instantly needed economic resources and land for future settlement, Poland was the essential corridor and staging area for any future assault on Soviet Russia. Hitler continued to face the same strategic problem, not to say peril, of a two-front war which had prompted his accommodation with Stalin in August 1939 and his attack on France in May 1940. Germany was more than ever the *Land der Mitte,* flanked by the land-based Russian colossus and the sea-based British leviathan. It is clear that neither Stalin nor Churchill had any designs on Germany, nor was either of them bent on aggression or expansion elsewhere. But both were determined to contain Hitler, who showed no sign of relaxing his expansionist reach. Terrified by the rapid defeat of France, the Soviet leaders hastened not only to deepen and close Russia's forward defensive ramparts but also to improve its overall military preparedness. They hoped against hope that they might have until 1942 to get ready to parry the expected blow, which they knew would be devastating. As for Hitler and his generals, while they were agreed that the Red Army was not about to attack just then, they were concerned that by mid-1942 the buildup of the Red Army would be sufficiently advanced to commend Soviet Russia as a worthy ally to England and to increase dangerously the costs and risks of Berlin's projected *Drang nach Osten.* Just as in 1914 the leaders of the Second German Empire—and of the Austro-Hungarian Empire—had opted for preventive war in order to cut short the modernization of tsarist Russia's armies, so in 1940–41 the leaders of the Third German Empire decided to foil Soviet Russia's drive for military preparedness. Both times German politicians and generals used specious arguments about Russia's growing military menace to justify a bellicose course, and both times only the prospect of having to fight the Russians and the British simultaneously gave them momentary pause.

Whereas in July 1914 British policy had remained one of studied ambiguity, after June 1940 there could be no doubt where England stood. London spurned Berlin's repeated feelers proposing a trade-off between German hegemony on the Continent, including direct domination of eastern and Russian Europe, in exchange for British rule of the maritime and colonial world. Lacking the air and naval power to force London's acquiescence, but determined not to forswear eastern living space, Hitler had to decide when and how to attack Soviet Russia. The führer proposed once again to deal a lightning blow in the east before turning west and south to confront Great Britain.

As always, Hitler was driven by a sense of extreme haste and urgency. To be sure, he was at the height of his military power, with most of the Continent under German domination or influence. Even so, Hitler knew that if he was to tempt fortune with his bid for hegemony he would have to race against time. After the battle of France, when they began planning an eastern campaign, Hitler's generals agreed that by 1942 not only would the Soviet Union be in an advanced state of readiness but England would very likely be strengthened by American aid. Several military leaders actually urged an all-out attack on Russia for the fall of 1940. But before long the Reich's leading military men settled on striking in the spring of the following year. Despite residual qualms about defying England and risking a two-front war, not a single German general took exception to the proposed invasion and conquest of Russia. Although there were disagreements within the military, these were over tactics and logistics, not over the basic decision to invade the Soviet Union and to go to any length to dominate Europe.

The generals were not the only segment of Germany's non-Nazi elite to fall in with, if not encourage, the conquest state. Awed by the Nazi regime's stunning achievements at home and abroad, leading figures in business, the civil service, the churches, and the intelligentsia had become Hitler's unconditional collaborators. With time Hitler relied more and more on military glory and foreign spoils to bolster his legitimacy. Far more coherent and less controversial than his domestic program, his foreign and military policy was ideally suited to help him sustain popular support and cement elite collaboration. This was especially true once Hitler turned to securing additional eastern *Lebensraum*, whose appeals were manifold: military security, autarky, immunity to blockade, land for colonization, economic gain. Many traditional conservatives and reactionaries approved of his *Drang nach Osten*, which was one of their own perennial foreign-policy prepossessions. They were the more enthusiastic about this renewed drive to the east now that the renascent Reich could realize it at the expense of the Soviet regime and of world bolshevism, which they execrated. In fact, after mid-1940 it was a shared antibolshevism that moved critical sectors of the old elite to work together with the Nazi leadership to actualize what was an archaic as well as a preposterous presumption. Both wanted communism smashed in Russia as it had recently been smashed in Germany. Ideological blindness led Hitler and his coadjutors to grossly underestimate the political resilience, military capability, and economic endurance of the Soviet regime. The hubris inspired by the Wehrmacht's recent triumphs also contributed to this faulty assessment.

In any event, by July 2, 1940, less than two weeks after the French surrender and while increasing the pressure on England, General von Brauchitsch, chief of the Army High Command, ordered General Franz Halder, chief of the Army General Staff, to draw up plans for a strike at Russia. Within less than three weeks, on July 21, Hitler met with his three service chiefs as well as with the heads of the High Command and the General Staff of the Armed Forces. He told his top military commanders of his resolve not to squander Germany's newly gained international momentum. He meant to knock out England by mid-September, before turning east. Basing his assertion on General Halder's preliminary projections, the führer estimated that it should take only about four to six weeks to deploy the eighty to a hundred divisions needed to crush the Red Army, which at first was expected to be able to raise no more than fifty to seventy-five battle-worthy divisions. The immediate objective would be to defeat the enemy forces quickly, or failing that, to penetrate Soviet territory in sufficient depth to put its vital centers within the Luftwaffe's range while keeping those of the Third Reich beyond the reach of the Soviet air force.

But within a week, on July 29, 1940, Generals Keitel and Jodl convinced Hitler of the impossibility of moving in time to defeat the Red Army before the onset of winter. Meanwhile, they had instructed their staff officers to make preparations for the deployment and quartering of army and air force units in the General Government of Poland. Two days later, on July 31, Hitler conferred with Keitel, Jodl, Brauchitsch, and Halder at the Berghof. Confounded by Churchill's intransigence and increasingly doubtful that an aerial blitz could clear the way for a Channel-crossing, the führer proposed to break England's will to resist and frighten off the United States by overrunning the Soviet Union. He now fixed May 1941 as the target date and ordered the army's effectives raised to 180 divisions, of which 120 divisions, spearheaded by armored and motorized units, would be launched against Russia. Hitler was not about to settle for the mere seizure of large expanses of territory, partly because of the hazards of quartering German troops under winter conditions. His aim was to smash the Red Army as well as the Soviet state, and then to dismember Russia. To achieve this objective one army group would move on Kiev, another on Moscow. The entire operation was to take no longer than seventeen to twenty-two weeks, the brunt of the attack to be directed against the capital of the Ukraine. Without so much as a murmur, the four compliant generals issued orders to begin shifting the bulk of the Reich's military might to the east.

As of August 1940 an ever larger number of superior officers became involved in preparing and directing the deployment and redeployment of a vast fighting machine, as well as in directing war games to test operational plans. The fall of 1940 also marked the start of an internecine disagreement that continued through late 1941. Most army commanders urged giving first priority to taking Moscow, insisting that the capture of this nerve center of the Soviet regime would be the key to military success. Hitler, however, advocated battering the Soviets militarily while making every effort to capture vital economic zones to be exploited for Germany's war effort. Ever conscious of the Reich's economic vulnerabilities, the führer wanted to seize the agricultural resources of the Ukraine and the Don region, the industrial raw materials and plants of the Donets basin, and the ports of the Black Sea. While Hitler gave tactical and logistical reasons to forearm Germany for a possible war of attrition and blockade, he never lost sight of the importance of the Ukraine and Crimea for his prospective land empire. In any case, on December 18, 1940, he signed Directive No. 21, drafted by senior members of the High Command of the Armed Forces (OKW) and the Army High Command (OKH), and intended for the ranking generals of the armed forces. This directive ordered a two-pronged assault on the Soviet Union, to begin on May 15, 1941, and to be executed with the same lightning speed as the recent Polish and French campaigns. Because of the unexpected need to rush to the assistance of Mussolini in Yugoslavia and Greece in April, the starting date was postponed to June 22. In every other respect Directive No. 21 remained in force until October 1941, when the first serious setbacks of the invasion forced a revision.

Hitler and his generals spared no effort and expense in mounting this gigantic operation. They knew that to be effective it would have to be overpowering and overawing. Hitler himself boasted repeatedly that the onslaught on Russia would be so ferocious as to cause the world "to hold its breath." He also stressed that except for its speed, the eastern campaign would have nothing in common with the recent western campaign.

The military forces drawn up to invade Russia at 3:15 A.M. on June 22, 1941, were by far the largest and most power-packed fighting machine deployed on any one front for a single operation in the history of organized warfare. Some 17,000 trains were used to assemble 148 divisions, which were reinforced with an additional 5 divisions by late June. Of the 3.8 million men in the Third Reich's field army, 3.2 million were set against 4.5 million Soviet troops, while most of the remaining 600,000 were kept back for occupation duty in newly conquered lands. There were 112 infantry divisions along with 10 armored divisions, 12 mechanized infantry divisions, and 9 communications divisions. The *Ostheer,* or eastern army, crashed into Russia with 600,000 motorized vehicles, 600,000 horses, and 3,300 tanks, supported by 7,000 artillery pieces and 2,000 aircraft, among them 720 fighter planes and over 1,100 bombers. For the initial drive Finland contributed 17 divisions and 300 airplanes, and Rumania 12 divisions and 400 planes. Hungary and Slovakia each rushed 2 divisions into battle. Shortly thereafter, Mussolini sent 3 divisions, and Franco sent the Blue Division. Of course, German generals coordinated and directed the movements of all allied and satellite units.

The massed forces were divided into three legions. The northern group, under the command of Field Marshal Wilhelm Ritter von Leeb, consisted of two armies, one armored division, and one air fleet. Their mission was to destroy the enemy forces concentrated in the Baltic lands and to capture Leningrad, which would also be invested by the Finnish contingents to the north. The center group, under the command of Field Marshal Fedor von Bock, consisted of two armies, two armored divisions, one of them under General Heinz Guderian, and one air fleet of over a thousand planes under Field Marshal Albert Kesselring. Arrayed along 250 miles stretching from just south of the Memel River to just south of Brest-Litovsk, these units were not only the major pivot of the assault force but also its sharpest and fastest cutting edge. They were to envelop and destroy the core of the Red Army, including its most modernized formations, deployed in the Brest-Vilna-Smolensk triangle. Having taken Smolensk, the onrushing armored and mechanized corps were to either turn north or press on to Moscow. Lined up between the Pripet Marshes and the Carpathian Mountains, the southern group was composed of three armies, one armored division, one air fleet, and a conglomerate of satellite units. Commanded by Field Marshal Karl Rudolf Gerd von Rundstedt, it was to rout and trap the Soviet forces in the western Ukraine and Eastern Galicia, secure crossings over the Dnieper, and race to Kiev.

The deployment, movement, and supply of this enormous military force, as well as its lines of march and battle, corresponded closely to the geography of Jewish settlement in eastern and east-central Europe. As previously noted, the territories of the General Government in occupied Poland were the vital hub as well as the center of mass of this mighty army. While the rear of this key staging area was bounded by a line running from Warsaw in the north through Radom to Tarnów in the south, the area around Siedlce, Lublin, and Chełm was its forward sector. Just as the staging grounds were full of towns and cities with large Jewish populations, so were the chief transit and combat zones, first in the territories annexed by Russia in 1939–40 and then in western Belorussia and the western Ukraine. The attacking armies were bound to batter such large Jewish centers as Riga and Vilna in the Baltic states; Lida, Pinsk, and Kovel in eastern Poland; and Vitebsk, Minsk, Kiev, Berdichev, and Odessa inside the pre-1939 borders of Russia.

But the campaign against Soviet Russia was not an ordinary military operation. It was exceptionally destructive less because of the immense size, speed, and firepower of the invading fighting forces than by virtue of their built-in fury and the extremism of their non-military purposes. The Nazi conquest state originated in and was ultimately driven by domestic rather than international imperatives. Hitler looked, as we saw, to military preparedness, war, and expansion to solidify and legitimate his regime. This project called for an ever larger military-industrial complex which, with Germany's narrow resource base, was difficult to sustain, particularly given Hitler's reluctance to sacrifice butter for guns. The principal bottlenecks, both actual and potential, were shortages of labor, foods, especially fats, and raw materials, including fuel and rubber for mechanized warfare. Military campaigns were expected not only to provision the field and occupation armies but also to serve the urgent economic needs of the Reich. By the time of the invasion of Russia all of occupied and satellite Europe was working for the German war effort. Berlin acquired essential raw staples at cut-rate prices from east-central Europe. In addition, it pressed into service the industries of Austria, Czechoslovakia, Polish Silesia, and France. But with the war machine gearing up for Hitler's most ambitious campaign, worries about critical shortages resurfaced. Not surprisingly, Directive No. 21 made the procurement of foodstuffs and petroleum the principal economic objective of the drive into Russia, which meant seizing rather than destroying processing plants and stockpiles. On February 28, 1941, Göring created a general staff to prepare the mobilization of the economic resources of the east for the Four-Year Plan. He chartered public corporations and enlisted business firms to extract raw materials and take over important industries in the conquered territories, to be run by seasoned corporate executives from Germany's private sector.

Until March 1941 neither generals nor businessmen were told that the projected military and economic operations were designed as part of an ideological crusade. Of course, a growing number of high military and civilian leaders realized that the eastern campaign would be a war of all-out aggression and conquest. But they did not know what

Hitler and his inner circle knew all along but were careful not to divulge prematurely: that from the outset the attack on Soviet Russia would be ideologically charged and murderously destructive, if not exterminationist. The führer's vaulting ambition was concentrated on eastern *Lebensraum*, not only for reasons of military security, economic autarky, and German colonization but also because vast spaces would be conquered at the expense of the Soviet regime, the vital center of world bolshevism. Hitler was eager to resume giving free rein to his visceral and inveterate anticommunism, which he had had to repress for the duration of his pact with Stalin. In addition, by reviving the specter of bolshevism, he could focus anti-Semitism by portraying the Jews as the principal carriers and masterminds of the Bolshevik scourge. To dismember Russia and extend German control to the Urals would be to overthrow the Soviet regime, to root out the Bolshevik Party, and to destroy the hub of the "Judeobolshevik" world conspiracy.

Although present all along, this wild ideological purpose did not become decisive until March 1941, when it was implanted in the fully matured master plan for the attack on Russia. Hitler himself set the tone and general contours for the five steps which fixed the ideological thrust of the eastern campaign: the empowerment of the Einsatzgruppen; the relaxation of the code of military justice; the warranting of officers and men to mistreat Soviet commissars; the condoning of excesses committed by German soldiers in Russia; and the dissemination of fiercely intemperate battlefield propaganda.

On March 15, 1941, the führer told two officers of the armed forces' General Staff that the "most brutal violence" would have to be used to "liquidate" Stalin's intelligentsia and to "smash" bolshevism's governing apparatus. He predicted that since they lacked a general consensus, both the Soviet regime and the Russian nation would come apart with the elimination of the party cadre.

Within two weeks Hitler summoned well over two hundred of the highest officers of the armed services to the new Imperial Chancellery in Berlin. Like the meeting with his top-ranking generals a week before the invasion of Poland, this gathering of March 30, 1941, was intended to prime his commanders for the forthcoming attack on Russia. In a hortatory address of more than two hours—of which there is no verbatim record—Hitler seems to have been altogether forthright and blunt, except that he apparently never so much as mentioned the "Jewish question." According to notes written from memory, immediately after the speech, by one of those present, he stressed that the overarching objectives in the east would be to "crush" the Red Army and "dismember" Soviet Russia. The upcoming campaign would be a struggle not just between two countries but "between two ideologies." Hitler characterized bolshevism as nothing less than "social criminality," and communism as "an enormous danger for the future." This being the case, German soldiers would have to abjure the customary respect for the adversary: "The Communist can be no comrade, either before or after [battle]." In order to safeguard the future, the Reich was called upon to fight a "war of extermination" (Vernichtungskrieg), which precluded "sparing the enemy." In particular, the "Bolshevik commissars and Communist intelligentsia need to be annihilated," since they were the chief carriers of "the poison of subversion." Instead of being brought before military courts, such "criminals" would have to be dealt with by line officers "who have to be briefed about the stakes." Clearly, the recent fighting in the west was nothing like what the upcoming battle would be in the east, where even the lex talionis of an "eye for an eye" would be "too lenient."

Given these tenets, it is not surprising that the Einsatzgruppen were given an even freer hand in the Russian than in the Polish campaign. To avoid any repetition of the frictions between the Wehrmacht and the SS, their representatives agreed to a division of labor by March 5, to the advantage of the latter. In the occupied territories the army retained full jurisdiction over all intramural matters, but willingly, if not eagerly, agreed to the SS sharing responsibility for the maintenance of law and order and of internal security. Keitel and Jodl agreed that Himmler should have full authority to carry out special missions in the rear of the advancing armies. Indeed, the chief of the Reich's combined police and security apparatus was given or took charge of pacification in the coming Weltanschauungskrieg, or ideological war. Himmler's men were to destroy the Soviet system and implant Nazi Germany's iron heel by liquidating all Bolshevik leaders and commissars without regard for legal conventions. Following negotiations between Brigadier General Robert Heinrich Wagner, the quartermaster general of the Army General Staff, and Reinhard Heydrich, on April 23 von Brauchitsch directed his top officers to transport, provision, and billet the special units of the security police which would operate entirely independent of the combat and occupation forces.

At about this same time the legal specialists of the armed forces began drafting regulations intended to all but acquit, in advance, officers and soldiers for excesses committed while fighting against the "carriers of the Judeobolshevik Weltanschauung," either military or civilian. Keitel issued the final guidelines setting the terms and procedures of military justice for the theaters of war and occupied territories on May 13, 1941. In this rescript the OKW declared the problems of pacification too vast and complicated for regular courts martial. It authorized the troops to "take ruthless action themselves," directing them to "liquidate" guerrillas and to use the "most extreme methods" against hostile noncombatants. All officers were required to decide instantly whether or not to shoot individual suspects behind the lines, while commanders of battalion level were made responsible for seizing hostages for collective retaliation wherever individual terrorists could not be identified. In any case, the OKW categorically enjoined against holding suspects for trial by civil courts after the end of hostilities. As for the felonies and crimes of German soldiers against enemy civilians, they were not to be prosecuted unless they threatened to undermine military discipline. In sum, while Soviet civilians were to be executed on mere suspicion, German soldiers were to be guaranteed immunity even for proven excesses.

The OKH and the OKW also collaborated closely in drafting the "Guidelines for the Treatment of Political Commissars," or the "Commissar Order" (*Kommissarbefehl*), which was issued on June 6, 1941. In accordance with Hitler's directives, the generals required their men to be not only military combatants but political warriors as well. They forewarned their soldiers that "in the battle against bolshevism you cannot expect the enemy to abide by the ground rules of humanitarianism and international law." Germany's fighting men were told that the political commissars of the Red Army and of the Soviet system generally would be past masters of "barbaric, Asiatic" warfare, of fierce resistance to pacification, and of maltreatment of war prisoners. This being the case, instead of being granted prisoner status, these commissars were to be executed not only for committing hostile acts but for their official positions in the enemy power structure. The written text of this Commissar Order was transmitted to general officers with instructions to brief their field officers and men orally before battle.

In the meantime, starting February 21, 1941, the propaganda service of the armed forces, after consultation with the OKH, began drafting "Guidelines for the Conduct of Soldiers in Russia." Completed in mid-May 1941, they were not issued to the troops until immediately before the start of the invasion, along with Hitler's call to arms. The guidelines were in the nature of a summons to the soldiers not so much to defeat the Russian enemy as to fight an ideological crusade. As they were about to fall upon the Red Army, 3.2 million warriors were told that "bolshevism is the mortal enemy" of National Socialism and that Germany was determined to fight "this subversive *Weltanschauung* and its carriers." The upcoming battle "calls for a ruthless and energetic drive against Bolshevik agitators, guerrillas, saboteurs, and Jews, as well as for the thoroughgoing removal of all active and passive resistance." All combatants had to become aware of the "treachery" of the enemy, "in particular of the Asiatic soldiers of the Red Army who are inscrutable, unpredictable, devious, and heartless."

The same propaganda service also prepared leaflets, placards, and broadcasts addressed to Soviet soldiers and civilians. They were assured that the invading forces proposed to fight not the peoples of the Soviet Union but their "Judeo-Bolshevik government, its functionaries, and its Communist Party." The Wehrmacht was coming "to liberate" the Russian people from "the Soviet tyranny." Of course, in pursuit of this goal it would break any and all resistance.

This propaganda campaign was carried out on a large scale. Guided by a central office in Berlin with a large staff of researchers and writers, eleven propaganda companies of some 2,250 men served with the three army groups on the eastern front. During the first two weeks of the operation, the Germans rained a total of over 20 million copies of nine tracts on Soviet lines. Thereafter, the Luftwaffe joined the artillery in saturating the enemy with propaganda fliers, with the result that by early September over 140 million of them had been scattered about.

The first widely distributed flier charged Stalin's "Jewish-Communist" government with violating the treaties it had signed with Germany. It urged the soldiers and officers of the Red Army not to "spill their blood for the Third International . . . [and] for Stalin and his Jewish commissars," whose regime was "a hundred times worse" than that of the last tsars. The German troops were coming to put an end to the "criminal machinations of the Jewish clique . . . and will go after the commissars who are torturing and exploiting the peoples of the Soviet Union." Russians were summoned to follow the example of Hitler, who had "run the enemies of humanity [and] the parasites out of his own country." After cursing "all Jews and Communists," this leaflet also asked Russians to join in the "march on Moscow and Kiev" to help "liberate all the peoples of the Soviet Union from the Communist yoke and the cursed Jew, as well as all peasants and workers from their exploiters and torturers." Without the "decapitation of the Jewish Comintern" there could be "no peace in Europe." The ultimate exhortation was to do "away with Stalin and all Communists."

In late August the propaganda broadsides became much more sharply pointed against the commissars, in line with the Commissar Order of June 6. In words and caricatures, the commissars were portrayed as the incarnation of the Bolshevik evil and vilified as the chief agents of the insidious Soviet regime: murderers, barbarians, beasts, Jews, terrorists, revolutionaries. There were numerous variants on the same theme: "Down with commissars"; "Down with the Jewish commissars and their lackeys"; and "Down with Jews and commissars."

During the spring of 1941 most of the generals as well as many lower-grade officers of the Wehrmacht must have learned that the war against Soviet Russia would be an ideological crusade of enormous violence and brutality. Just as the top generals prepared, signed, and issued the orders for the planning and execution of the military attack on Russia, they also prepared, signed, and issued the directives for the "jihad" against the Soviet regime and "Judeobolshevism." These senior officers and their subordinates had few if any scruples about this monstrous enterprise. After their recent triumphs the commanders of the Wehrmacht were overconfident: they expected excesses of the sort witnessed in Poland to be momentary, and considered them a small price to pay for a double-quick victory over the Red Army. But above all, it was their broad agreement with the Nazi project which explains their readiness to serve as both military and political warriors. In addition to being profoundly antidemocratic and anti-Communist in their own right, they shared Hitler's zeal *for* territorial expansion and his rage *against* Stalin's regime. Furthermore, their own Judeophobia predisposed them to see the Jews as the chief cadres of the Bolshevik regime in Russia and the principal manipulators of "Jewish bolshevism" abroad. It was this unspoken ideological and programmatic consensus that impelled Germany's venerable generals to order the army not only to conquer living space from Russia but also to clear the way for the SS to massacre the "common enemy" at will. In fact, they were so convinced of the necessity and righteousness of their mission that they sacrificed their sense of limits and their military code for it.

Both the Wehrmacht and the SS marched against Soviet Russia and "Judeobolshevism," against Communist and Jew. Both considered Jews to be among the prime movers of bolshevism, Sovietism, and the commissar system. Even if regular officers and men did not set forth to hunt down commissars, Jews, and guerrillas themselves, they proposed to deliver them over to the coactive police and SS. Laid out before June 22, 1941, this policy of political warfare and Wehrmacht-SS collaboration could not have been a response to the call for partisan warfare that Stalin issued on July 3, although this defiance certainly intensified both.

In the meantime, the OKW and the OKH took it upon themselves to draft a special directive for the treatment of enemy prisoners of war. Although it dealt with a strictly military matter, it was infused with the same venom as all the other ideological commands issued since March 1941, thereby setting the stage for one of the greatest enormities of the Thirty Years War of this century, second only to the Judeocide, with which it was fatally entwined.

In its singular order of July 17, 1941, the High Command of the Armed Forces directed that all Bolshevik suspects among the Soviet prisoners of war be set apart and subjected to "special measures." Beyond its "purely military mission," the eastern campaign had "political objectives, which are to protect the German nation from Bolshevik agitators and to take quick and firm control of the occupied territories." By September 8, when over a million Soviet prisoners had been captured, both the justification and the license for their mistreatment was broadened. The OKW denounced bolshevism as the "mortal enemy of National Socialist Germany," and charged the Red Army with resorting to unlimited warfare, including "sabotage, subversive propaganda, arson, and murder." This being the case, "Bolshevik soldiers forfeit any claim to being treated as honorable soldiers and according to the Geneva conventions."

In preparation for the eastern campaign and without coercion or intimidation from Hitler and Himmler, the German officer corps made the Wehrmacht into a terror-inspiring instrument of absolute war. Indeed, the eminently respectable generals first fashioned and then unleashed such a mighty and ideologically conditioned military force that they threatened to steal much of the SS's thunder. Certainly, the Waffen-SS as well as the ordinary SS, including the concentration-camp guards, welcomed the regular army's belated conversion to the Nazi catechism. Himmler, Heydrich, and Eicke must have been heartened by the hatred of bolshevism, the Soviets, and the Jews which informed the directives to annihilate enemy soldiers, to massacre political commissars, and to brutalize Soviet war prisoners. But they also cast envious eyes on the old military establishment. The problem for Himmler was to secure a large and distinctive role for the SS in Hitler's war to conquer eastern *Lebensraum*, the moving frontier of nazism. Sharing the generals' confidence in a swift and spectacular victory, the SS leaders were fearful that the Wehrmacht would be credited and exalted for it. Accordingly, they strained to maximize their military contribution to the Russian campaign and to spearhead the policing and pacification of the conquered territories. And in March-April 1941 the senior military chiefs gave Himmler and Heydrich free rein for the Einsatzgruppen, no doubt because by then they not only approved of the ends and means of the assault on Soviet Russia but also were sanguine about enhancing the Wehrmacht's position within the power structure of the Third Reich.

By the start of the invasion Himmler had raised the strength of the Waffen-SS to about 160,000 men, of whom close to 100,000, or the equivalent of six divisions, were combat soldiers. To be sure, these SS troops made up at best 5 percent of the forces arrayed for the attack on Russia. But to some extent they compensated for their small numbers with the superior training and physical conditioning of their recruits and leaders, as well as with their fanatic dedication. Under the tactical command of the OKH, the divisions of the Waffen-SS were nearly evenly divided among the three army groups on the eastern front. For example, the crack SS Totenkopf (Death's Head) Division of General Theodor Eicke was transferred from France to East Prussia. On June 9, 1941, it was assigned to the northern sector, and attached to the Fourth Panzer Group, commanded by General Erich Höpner and pointed at Leningrad. Höpner was a firebrand in his own right. He saw himself as fighting to prevent Europe from being engulfed by Slavs, "Moscovite-Asianism," and "Jewish bolshevism." He went into battle determined "to exterminate the enemy mercilessly and totally" and resolved "not to spare any adherents of the present Russian-Bolshevik system." As for Eicke, during the week preceding the attack, he repeatedly briefed his top officers about the impending struggle between National Socialism and "Judeobolshevism," insisting that he expected his officers and men to fight without mercy. These briefings inspired his officers to incite their troops, which eventually became perhaps the most ruthless and tenacious German soldiers on the eastern front.

In addition to providing elite troops, the SS also contributed altogether unique brigades of political warriors. Modeled after the special-action groups improvised for the invasion of Czechoslovakia and Poland, the Einsatzgruppen for the Russian campaign were carefully primed for their murderous assignment. Their leaders were recruited from the Waffen-SS, the Gestapo, the Criminal Police, and the Security Service (SD). Although seasoned Nazi militants of proven loyalty to Himmler and Heydrich, most of them were not know-nothing thugs or street fighters. On the contrary, not a few of the officers of the action groups were wellborn and well educated. Scores of them were true believers with university degrees—lawyers, doctors, higher civil servants, teachers—eager to slay the "Judeobolshevik" dragon on their way to the promised land in cis–Ural Russia. As for the lower ranks of the Einsatzgruppen, they were drawn from the Waffen-SS and the different police forces.

Himmler and Heydrich marshaled a total of some 3,000 political soldiers to participate in the assault on Russia. They were organized into four Einsatzgruppen of battalion strength, each with 500 to 900 men. In turn, each action group was divided into four or five *Einsatz-kommandos,* or action commandos, special units of 70 to 100 men, many of them subdivided in turn into *Sonderkommandos,* or special commando squads of 20 to 30 men. Some units were to operate in the rear of the front lines, others alongside the advancing troops. All detachments were motorized for maximum mobility.

The four battalions were deployed as follows: Einsatzgruppe A, commanded by SS Brigadier General (Dr.) Franz Stahlecker, was assigned to the Northern Army Group headed for the Baltic lands and Leningrad; Einsatzgruppe B, under SS Brigadier General Arthur Nebe, to the Central Army Group aimed at Moscow; Einsatzgruppe C, under Brigadier General (Dr.) Otto Rasch, to the Southern Army Group pointed in the direction of Kiev; and Einsatzgruppe D, under Major General (Dr.) Otto Ohlendorf, to the sector of the 11th Army between Bessarabia and the Crimea.

In May 1941 Heydrich ordered 120 top leaders, most of them with prior experience in Poland, to report for instruction to a baroque castle that served as a training center for border guards in Pretzsch on the Elbe, in the easternmost corner of Saxony. By mid-June all the officers and men of the four Einsatzgruppen were concentrated near Düben on the Mulde River and near Bad Schmiedeberg, northeast of Leipzig.

As supreme head of the SS, Himmler appointed Heydrich commander in chief of the Einsatzgruppen. In March and April 1941 Heydrich had negotiated the pact of independence from the army with General Wagner, the quartermaster general. Either at Pretzsch or in the SS staging area, Heydrich personally briefed his officers and men about their mission immediately before they went into action. Presumably, he cited a direct command from Hitler as he exhorted and ordered them viva voce to set forth to kill Bolshevik officials and activists, Jews, Gypsies, and other "undesirables." Apparently, neither Heydrich, Hitler, nor Himmler ever issued a written command to liquidate these noncombatants. But no written warrant was needed, given the shared ideological predilection of the special SS commandos and the Wehrmacht, their indispensable host.

Since it was essentially political, not military, the mission of the mobile killing squads was indeterminate and boundless. Free of legal and ethical restraints, the SS zealots were certain to strike out viciously. But they literally ran wild once they encountered stiff and unanticipated military and partisan resistance, often in territories of heavy Jewish settlement for which they were equally unprepared. There was nothing exceptional about the three thousand men of the SS Einsatzgruppen conflating commissar, partisan, and Jew in their fanatic and callous minds, especially since the officers and men of the Wehrmacht not only gave them a free hand but became increasingly intemperate themselves.

No doubt Himmler and Heydrich, not unlike the army generals, expected pacification to be child's play. They presumed that the major task of the SS would be to extend their tyrannizing civil administration into the conquered territories. In actual fact, because the blitzkrieg foundered and partisan warfare erupted, the Einsatzgruppen along with other SS task forces were denied the opportunity to institutionalize their ruthless reign in Russia as they had done in Poland. Instead, they kept exterminating partisans and Jews, much as the army continued to take and decimate prisoners, in what was an inherently infinite ideological war.

By and large, Germany's Christian churches acted to consecrate Hitler's profane crusade in the east. To be sure, unlike the generals, who ceased their own polite criticism, several higher Catholic and Protestant clergymen continued to express dissent, particularly about the euthanasia program for the killing of the "incurably ill" (to be discussed in Chapter 12). But this opposition to one particularly heinous feature of the Nazi regime's domestic policy was not incompatible with indulgence or even praise for its foreign policy. Characteristically, on June 24–26, 1941, the Fulda Conference of Catholic Bishops at one and the same time protested the regime's interference with Catholic education and self-determination and summoned the faithful to do their patriotic duty, though without specific reference to the thundering assault on Soviet Russia, which had started a few days before. While the Protestant churches collectively thanked Hitler for taking up the sword to defend Germany and Christianity "against the murderous enemy of order," both the German Catholic hierarchy and the Vatican avoided any official consecration of the war against Russia. But this silence was far from innocent, and individual bishops hastened to break it. The bishop of Eichstätt hailed the eastern campaign as "a crusade, a holy war for homeland and people, for faith and church, for Christ and His most holy cross," while the bishop of Paderborn commended it as a struggle "for the protection of Christianity in our fatherland, for the rescue of the Church from the threat of anti-Christian bolshevism." Comparing the danger of bolshevism to that of the Turks in a somber past, the bishop of Augsburg publicly prayed for an "early, final victory over the enemies of our faith." Even Archbishop Count Clemens August von Galen of Münster, who had just publicly censured Hitler's euthanasia program, issued a pastoral letter praising him for breaking his mortifying pact with Stalin and for exposing the "deceit and faithlessness" of the Bolsheviks. Von Galen asked for divine intervention in support of the Reich's "valiant soldiers who are fighting against not only the [military] threat of bolshevism" but also "the heresies and errors" of communism which, as Germans knew from their own experience, were rooted in the spread of "naturalism and materialism." Well over a thousand Protestant and Catholic army chaplains preached variants of this same anti-Bolshevik gospel to the troops of the Ostheer, whom they glorified as crusaders not just for Christianity but for European culture and civilization as well.

Conceived and proclaimed as a "holy war," the campaign against Soviet Russia had all the earmarks of an absolute war, and clearly expressed the archaic side of the Nazi counterrevolution. The general idea of the crusade was anchored in a distant past in which Christians had marched to defend Europe against Moslem infidels or to liberate Jerusalem for the true faith. In the collective memory the crusades of the eleventh to thirteenth centuries were exalted as the apotheosis of righteous aggressiveness and violence. Usurping this memory, or legend, the Nazis mounted a "holy war" to protect Christian Europe from godless bolshevism and to capture Moscow, the center of this heresy. The original four crusades had of course been more authentically and importantly religious than their Nazi simulation, which was essentially secular. Still, the Christian crusades of the High Middle Ages—like the countercrusading jihad—had not been entirely or even essentially religious, any more than Hitler's profane "holy war" was altogether temporal. Although in roughly inverse proportions, both were an admixture of spiritual and ideological elements with social, political, and economic ingredients. Each had its share of true believers and opportunists, nobles and plebeians, warriors and murderers. The rallying cries of both the medieval and the twentieth-century crusades played on the emotions of individuals of conflicting and yet not irreconcilable beliefs, fears, and interests. And ultimately, their barbarous excesses were impelled by an authoritative and orchestrated fanaticism.

Hitler appropriated a vital strand in Europe's collective memory. He commended himself as prophet and crusader for a millenarian cause that justified or even enjoined the slaying of infidels. More than likely, it was not altogether fortuitous that the führer gave the campaign against Soviet Russia the code name of Barbarossa, which was heavy with symbolic significance.

Until the attack on Soviet Russia, Nazi Germany's war plans and operations had been given prosaic cryptonyms. As mentioned, the campaign against Czechoslovakia was called Operation Green, that against Poland Operation White. The two phases of the western campaign were designated Operation Yellow and Operation Red. The invasion of Denmark and Norway was labeled Operation Weserübung, that of Yugoslavia Directive No. 25, and that of Greece Operation Marita. The projected landing in England went by the name of Operation Sea Lion. The contingency plan for a preemptive move against Gibraltar was baptized Felix, that against Spain and Portugal, Isabella.

The earliest blueprints for the Russian campaign were known as "Aufbau Ost," or "Eastern Buildup." Perhaps even this first designation was not as neutral as it might appear since *Aufbau* was the name of a defunct association of early National Socialists and Russian émigrés sworn to antibolshevism and the deliverance of Russia from Soviet rule. On December 12, 1940, as preparations for the invasion gathered momentum, the chief military planners completed Directive No. 21, authorizing what was to be known as Operation Fritz. This directive, which set the basic strategy and the date of May 15, 1941, for the attack, was submitted to Hitler on December 17, 1940. The führer made only two changes in what became the final order for the invasion of Soviet Russia, issued to the General Staff on December 18, 1940. First, he gave the thrust against Kiev and Leningrad absolute priority over the drive on Moscow. Second, he changed the campaign's cover name from Fritz to Barbarossa.

"Fritz" probably stood for King Frederick II (Frederick the Great), celebrated as the father of Prussian Germany. Presumably, Hitler preferred Emperor Barbarossa to Frederick the Great because the former, in addition to uniting the German states, had championed eastern expansion and had taken up the cross. By late 1940 the führer was bent on combining his war of conquest for *Lebensraum* in the east with a crusade against the Soviet regime and bolshevism.

Frederick I of the Hohenstaufens, known by the name of Barbarossa, reigned from 1152 to 1190. In 1155, three years after he was elected king, he went to Rome to have himself crowned emperor by Pope Adrian IV. Thereafter, Barbarossa was almost constantly at odds with the sovereign pontiffs of the Church, whose reach he meant to reduce and whose excommunications he scorned and defied. Yet at the same time, he vigorously battled heresy and pressured

Pope Lucius III to issue rescripts of unsurpassed severity against Albigensians and other misbelievers.

Barbarossa was torn. On the one hand, guided by an expansive imperial ideal, he proposed to unite all German lands and to push southward to Italy and the Mediterranean. On the other, Barbarossa encouraged feudal devolution, hoping to free himself of administrative burdens in order to lead a holy crusade, which was his lifelong ambition. Although he bolstered his suzerainty over Bohemia and Poland, thereby signaling his retreat from the south, Barbarossa's imperial project was largely stillborn. His religious mission went equally unfulfilled: he eventually did take up the cross during the Third Crusade (1189–92), but only to drown in the Saleph River in Asia Minor before reaching the Holy Land. In the meantime, however, Barbarossa had become one of the first of Europe's great monarchs to pioneer in secularizing the idea of a holy war in defense of the royal realm.

In due course, German conservatives wove the saga of Frederick Barbarossa's enigmatic life and reign into their self-serving legends and rites of national redemption. Prophecies and parables about a future emperor completing Barbarossa's unrealized project began to circulate soon after his "glorious" death. By 1220 Frederick II, his grandson, seemed to incarnate this messianic yearning. Frederick was a grand emperor, and he also treated pope and Church with overweening insolence. No doubt this unseemly presumption eventually contributed to a transmutation of the persona in the myth, Frederick II being "gradually metamorphosed into the bearded Barbarossa, the immortal boy into the aged man." In what became a plastic myth Barbarossa ultimately replaced his grandson as the emperor who, resurrected, would return some day to lead Germany into another golden age. Pending this reappearance, Barbarossa was said to rest partly asleep and partly awake in the Pfalz, not far from Kaiserslautern, in the Untersberg near Salzburg, or in the Kyffhäuser mountain range in Thuringia.

Beginning in the early nineteenth century, during the aftermath of the French Revolution, the Barbarossa legend was used to promote nostalgia and hope for a heroic leader to restore Germany's national unity, imperial grandeur, territorial expanse, and social millennium. Even during the revolutionary era Hegel had pointed to Barbarossa as one of the ancient heroes who could serve as a reminder of the glorious imperial past that needed to be reclaimed. Certain poems of Friedrich Rückert and of the Brothers Grimm similarly enlisted the lasting fame of Barbarossa to extol the idea of reviving national unity along with imperial power and glory. During the *Vormärz*, the period of cultural and political ferment before 1848, Richard Wagner seized upon Barbarossa as a model in his quest for an imperial hero to exalt on a stage that for Wagner was at once dramatic and political. In October 1846, while working on *Lohengrin*, Wagner wrote a sketch for a five-act spoken tragedy with music, to be called *Friedrich I*, idealizing Barbarossa's reign. Two years later he abandoned this project for the opera *Siegfried*, in which the chief protagonist conveys Wagner's confused ideas, rooted in his vision of Barbarossa, about Germanic folk heroes and universal kingship. At Bayreuth, which soon after opening in 1876 became a shrine of imperial revivalism, *Siegfried* was believed to herald a Barbarossa redivivus, due for an imminent third coming.

In the meantime, the unification of 1870 began to be hailed as the fulfillment of the imperial dream or prophecy. In speeches, plays, and poems William I, now king of Prussia *and* emperor of all Germans, was celebrated for reembodying the spirit of Barbarossa, even to the point of being spoken of as Barbablanca. As part of the effort to create a conservative founding myth, the Hohenzollerns were portrayed as the heirs of the Hohenstaufens, whose line had culminated in Barbarossa, and the Second Empire as the restoration of the First Empire, over which he had presided.

In the late nineteenth century what had been an eschatological hope was turned into an ideologically freighted political program. By then the malleable legend fixed the Kyffhäuser mountains as Barbarossa's likeliest resting place, giving rise to a Kyffhäuser cult. Eight years after his death in 1888, William I was commemorated with an oversized equestrian statue of himself on top of the highest mountain in the Kyffhäuser range, "the most German of all mountains," which bore a life-sized likeness of the sleeping Barbarossa hewn into one of its slopes. The area surrounding this large *Kaiserdenkmal*, or emperor monument, became a sacred space for the performance of mass rituals of national self-assertion in an ultraconservative key. Hereafter the Second Empire was flooded with statues of William I and Bismarck, whose style and emplacement were designed to foster reverence and loyalty "for kaiser and Reich."

Even before 1914 the myth and cult of the heroic emperor and expansive Reich were acquiring an ever more stridently antidemocratic inflection. After 1918 they were turned against the Weimar Republic by the gravediggers of parliamentary democracy. Leading ultraconservatives and Nazis encouraged the conjuration of the imperial savior as dramatized in the secular sanctums of the Kyffhäuser and Bayreuth. The imperial pretense was emptied of its age-old Christian profession, to become an expression of contemporary Germany's self-assigned mission to act as the policeman for Western civilization, particularly against Bolshevik barbarism along the eastern marches.

Hitler was attuned to the nostrums of Kyffhäuser and Bayreuth. To be sure, he disdained and envied the wellborn conservatives who excelled at enlisting living atavisms in support of a restoration of the Hohenzollerns and the *ancien régime*. But he also knew that these old conservatives legitimated and amplified the longing for imperial grandeur and for a larger-than-life leader that was central to his prescription for radical renewal and that could redound to the benefit of the National Socialist movement and project.

After 1870 the Hohenzollerns and Bismarck glorified the First Reich as the keystone and prototype for the Second Reich, which now became an essential historic link for Hitler's Third Reich. The carefully choreographed ceremonies of Potsdam Day on March 21, 1933, were designed to celebrate and appropriate this legendary lineage. After embodying the irrepressible imperial pretension during much of the Weimar Republic, at Potsdam Marshal and President von Hindenburg mediated its integration into the self-representation of the nascent Nazi regime. In connection with Hitler's inauguration of the House of German Art in July 1937, Barbarossa was praised for having been the first to articulate and spread the Germanic idea of culture as part of his imperial mission. Hitler is said to have considered it a favorable augury that from his home and headquarters in Berchtesgaden he could see the Unterberg mountain range, one of Barbarossa's legendary though currently untended resting places.

Perhaps unwittingly, Hitler embraced ideas that were consonant with the Barbarossa reign and saga. In *Mein Kampf* he claimed to "take up again where things had been left 600 years ago"; he proposed to stop Germany's "external drive to southern and western Europe" in order to focus "on the lands in the east"; and he vowed "to put an end, once and for all, to the colonial and trade policies" of recent decades in favor of "the *Bodenpolitik* [land policy] of the future." Like Barbarossa, he had little patience for administrative routine, preferring to devote himself to imperial(ist) affairs, and he could identify with the Hohenstaufens, for whom "the crusade became their proudest ambition" once they "began to dream of world power."

By giving the code name Barbarossa to the drive against Soviet Russia, Hitler meant to invest it, even if only for himself, with a mythological aura anchored in a distant medieval past: as the returning savior he would not only restore the glory of imperial Germany by conquering the territories essential for the Thousand-Year Reich, but he would also reassume the crusading mission by taking up the twisted cross against "Judeobolshevism."

The crusading theme that permeated the military propaganda aimed at the soldiers of both the Wehrmacht and the Red Army also stood out in the propaganda directed to the home front and the rest of Europe. After two years of uncharacteristic tactical self-restraint, with the attack on Soviet Russia the Nazis resumed the thundering anti-Bolshevik rhetoric that had marked the growth and consolidation of their power. Once more true to themselves, they claimed to march not so much to protect the Third Reich or any other nation from imminent military attack as to save European culture and civilization from the perils of bolshevism. Berlin professed that "Germany's fight against Moscow was in the nature of a crusade of the European nations against bolshevism." Italian, Finnish, Rumanian, Hungarian, and Slovak soldiers were marching alongside German troops, and they were about to be joined by volunteers from all over the Continent. Goebbels portrayed Nazi Germany as holding high the banner of Western civilization rather than that of Christianity, for to claim the latter "would, after all, be too hypocritical." But he did not preclude urging "the bishops of both Christian persuasions to bless this war as being divinely approved."

Undoubtedly, the Nazi leaders were supremely confident of the support of the churches not only within Germany but abroad as well. Throughout the Continent, Catholic and Protestant primates and elders rushed to preach the anti-Bolshevik crusade and to bless its banners. In the process they sanctified both the *prophetae* and the armed zealots of their day. To be sure, neither the national churches nor the Vatican ever officially sanctified Hitler, the self-styled prophet of this latter-day, ungodly "holy war." But by conniving in his profanations they all but absolved and accredited him.

By June 30, 1941, Goebbels exulted that the Reich was "reaping the benefits of our earlier propaganda" and that the "whole of Europe is in motion." Abroad, the eastern campaign was seen as "a crusade, [and] this expression is being used for the benefit of the rest of the world, although it is less suitable for use at home."

All over Europe fascist leaders offered to raise volunteers for the German-led crusade against bolshevism and in defense of European culture and civilization. Hitler welcomed such volunteers with a view to giving his eastern campaign a Pan-European nimbus, but without compromising his overlordship. Of course, the governments of allied, satellite, and occupied nations had their own reasons for pressing their collaboration upon Berlin. With the Wehrmacht expected to crush the Red Army within a few weeks, they scrambled to extend military and material aid in the hope of impressing the führer and securing a favorable place in tomorrow's German-dominated Europe. While some governments sought to maximize territorial and diplomatic gains by actively participating in the monstrous eastern drive, others meant to avoid being put at a disadvantage, notably in relation to rival neighbors. But this is not to say that Marshal Mannerheim, Marshal Antonescu, Admiral Horthy, Monsignor Tiso, il Duce, General Franco, and even Marshal Pétain were moved by sheer opportunism, and that their crusading chants were mere siren songs intended to mask and ennoble their realpolitik. Fervently anti-Communist and anti-Bolshevik in their own right, they were not about to miss this opportunity to recharge and rechannel the ideological momentum of their regimes. Besides, these new caesars were pressed to join the crusade by the true believers in their own lands who reproved them for betraying the fascist counterrevolution with their conservative policies at home and calculating collaboration with the Third Reich abroad.

The governments of Finland, Rumania, and Hungary engaged their divisions alongside the Wehrmacht to conquer or reclaim territories from Soviet Russia. But even their interventions were fired by the anti-Communist fury. Antonescu and Horthy in particular had strong political and ideological reasons for taking up the cross against "Judeobolshevism." The result was that the Rumanian and Hungarian armies mass-murdered Jews independently of Hitler and the SS. Their own Judeophobia played a role, and so did their uneasy relationship with their anti-Semitically charged fascist opposition, which had close ties with the established churches. Although Mussolini's Expeditionary Corps and Franco's Blue Division were unsullied by political anti-Semitism, by fighting on the eastern front they quickened the anti-Bolshevik and anti-Soviet frenzy without which the Jewish persecution could not have run wild.

Much of the same is true of the over forty thousand Europeans who by late 1941 had signed up to go fight the Soviets. While volunteers of "Germanic" stock from the Scandinavian and Low Countries formed separate units which were incorporated into the Waffen-SS, the brigades of "non-Germanic" volunteers from Slovakia, Croatia, southern Belgium, and France were attached to the Wehrmacht. Not unlike the common milites Christi, or knights of Christ, of the Middle Ages, these latter-day crusaders had mixed motives for signing up, ideology being only one of many. While some of them were in search of adventure and material benefit, others sought status and glory. Among the commissioned and noncommissioned officers the prospect of rapid promotion played a role. As for the ideological drummers, many were seeking to improve their political leverage at home. Virtually all presumed that their soldiering would involve little risk and that they would be home by Christmas.

But even if the ideological impulse was not primary, it was far from negligible or hidden. The unpolitical soldiers of fortune among the volunteers were indoctrinated while being trained, before going into action, and in the front lines. Besides, all the volunteers, whatever their personal motives, became part of a vast collective enterprise whose chief bond, along with the German command structure, was the anti-Bolshevik demonology. Although the different foreign legions preserved the essentials of their national identity within the Waffen-SS and the Wehrmacht, most legionnaires swore unconditional obedience to Hitler, the moving spirit of the crusade against bolshevism.

The Legion of French Volunteers Against Bolshevism was characteristic of the many national detachments which went to battle bolshevism in the east and which were important by virtue of their makeup rather than their numbers or effectiveness. Apparently, Jacques Doriot, the leader of the Parti Populaire Français, was the first to call for the instant establishment of a volunteer corps to join the anti-Bolshevik crusade, hoping that such a step would radicalize French collaboration along fascist lines. His call was immediately echoed by such fellow fascists as Marcel Déat, Eugène Deloncle, Marcel Bucard, and Pierre Costantini. Although the German authorities in both Berlin and Paris favored the idea, they were wary that the Vichy government might seize upon it to strengthen its own hand. Accordingly, they insisted that the collaborationists of occupied France take the lead, that the number of volunteers not exceed ten thousand, that French prisoners of war in Germany be ineligible, that the legion be integrated into the Wehrmacht, that its members wear the German uniform, and that all officers and men take an oath to Hitler. During the first five months of Operation Barbarossa, until November 1941, only about 3,500 men signed up. At that time Berlin, rather than clamor for additional soldiers, was interested in the political and symbolic benefits of a French presence in the anti-Soviet host.

After abruptly breaking diplomatic relations with Moscow, the Vichy regime rescinded the law prohibiting French citizens from fighting under foreign colors. By July 8, 1941, Doriot and the other fascist leaders announced that "with the consent of Marshal Pétain, and the acquiescence of the führer," they would "participate in the crusade against bolshevism . . . and the defense of European civilization" by organizing a legion of volunteers "to represent France on the Russian front." In his own name Doriot stressed the "profound historical significance of the pact of faith against bolshevism" between Pétain and Hitler. Along with other European nations France was joining in the "crusade against communism, [which] revealed the real meaning of the present war." By fighting in the east, French volunteers would contribute not only to the defeat of "the most perverse force the world has known" but also to the "rebirth" of their own country, both at home and abroad.

Two contingents of French volunteers arrived at a training camp south of Warsaw during the first half of October. While swearing them into the crusade, the commander of the legion, Colonel Roger-Henri Labonne, hailed them as "the successors of Godfrey of Bouillon"—leader of the First Crusade and first king of Jerusalem—at the same time that he denounced the "Asiatic and bestial nature of the Red Army" and assailed Stalin as "Attila, the scourge of God." In early November, as his regiment moved forward to participate in the drive on Moscow, Labonne conspicuously offered thanks to "the great and venerated Marshal Pétain" for approving the "decision to take part in the anti-Bolshevik crusade, which was in harmony with the most cherished traditions of France." Though perhaps unwarily, Pétain gratefully acknowledged his vassal's obeisance. He openly assured Labonne that for assuming the "noble task . . . of participating in the anti-Bolshevik crusade, led by Germany," he would "earn the world's gratitude." But above all, he commended him for "defending part of our military honor, . . . [for] protecting your country from the Bolshevik peril, . . . [and for] keeping alive the hope of a reconciled Europe."

While Pétain endowed the legion with secular legitimacy, certain Catholic leaders gave it God's benediction. The most notable ecclesiastic voice was that of Cardinal Alfred Baudrillart, rector of the Catholic Institute of Paris. Convinced that the era of "a new crusade" had arrived, he prophesied that the "Sepulcher of Christ will be redeemed." In this spirit, and speaking as both "priest and Frenchman," Baudrillart praised the legionnaires for "actively embodying" the best of "both the old and the new France . . . and for doing their part in helping to prepare the great French renaissance." Characterizing the Legion of French Volunteers Against Bolshevism as a "new chivalry" and its warriors as the "Crusaders of the twentieth century," Cardinal Baudrillart prayed that "their weapons be blessed."

Operation Barbarossa was both a gigantic military drive against Soviet Russia and a fiery crusade against "Judeobolshevism." The Judeocide was deeply embedded in this eastern campaign. Ultimately, it was the crusade within the war that generated the destructive fury which became so singularly fatal for the Jews. Indeed, this crusade acquired a powerful momentum of its own, possibly to the point of suffusing the entire eastern campaign with its blind rage.

In essential respects Operation Barbarossa resembled the holy wars of the past, notably the archetypal Christian crusades. Just as the first mass murder of Jews since antiquity had been closely tied to the First Crusade of the late eleventh century, so the epochal Judeocide of the twentieth century was closely interwoven with the Nazi-led crusade against bolshevism from 1941 to 1945. Of course, there were important differences between these two massive and violent anti-Jewish eruptions. Above all, during the outbreaks of 1096 Jews were occasionally given the choice of baptism or death, and in many cities local bishops and burghers made every effort to protect them, sometimes with success. Still, as we saw in the Prologue, there is no denying the striking homologies between the slaughter of Jews accompanying the original crusades and the extermination of Jews attendant on Operation Barbarossa. There are significant correspondences not only of causes and preconditions but also of agencies, objectives, and methods. Both times the mass murder of Jews was a concomitant of a socially grounded project of comprehensive retrogression. Moreover, the fanatic violence of this temporal design was sanctioned by lay and ecclesiastical authorities and was initially directed against another and more inclusive target than the Jews. Lastly, in the eleventh and twelfth centuries as in the twentieth, the carnage of helpless Jews was perpetrated primarily by depraved members of the lower orders. It should be stressed, however, that in medieval as in modern times incumbent elites either licensed or condoned the Jew-killers of their day.

In November 1095, at the Council of Clermont, when Pope Urban II issued his wondrously weird summons to take up the cross, the power and influence of both the papacy and the Church permeated all aspects of life. But the dawn of the time of the cathedrals was a time of strange contrasts: in addition to being marvelously pious and chivalrous, it was intensely obscurantist, superstitious, and cruel. In fact, much of the spirit of the Dark Ages persisted, and provided a natural breeding ground for xenophobia. Pope Urban must have known that by preaching the crusade against infidels he would feed the simmering fire of prejudice and magic throughout medieval society. But he was prepared to run this risk not just to regenerate Christendom and reclaim the Holy Land from Islam, but also to steady the social foundations of the Christian world. The increasing incidence of armed skirmishes among land-starved lesser nobles and knights suggest that there may have been a link between concern for civic peace and recourse to holy war, especially since Urban II and the bishops meant to raise legions of fully equipped and trained knights rather than hordes of unfitted indigents. Instead of fighting and plundering each other, Christian lords and knights were urged to go forth to defend the faith against infidels. Ideally, they were to free the city of Jerusalem, if need be by putting Moslems to the sword. Fighting and dying for the cross would be rewarded by indulgences, perhaps even by absolution.

But the call to take the cross reached not only the upper classes. Self-appointed prophets took the word to the have-nots in areas in which rapid population growth was forcing peasants to leave the land for towns and cities that were hard-pressed to absorb them. Beginning in the late eleventh century, this was the case in parts of the Rhine and Moselle valleys, of northern France, and of Flanders. It was in this vast zone between the Somme and the Rhine that the poor rushed forward to serve God in a holy war against misbelievers and for the redemption and repossession of Jerusalem. For them, too, the crusade became a safety valve, in that they left to vent their local frustrations in distant lands.

Clearly, in 1095–96 two distinct movements converged in the first of the four crusades that marked the apotheosis of Christendom's righteous resort to arms and brutality. Besides the formless crusade of the plebeians there was the official crusade of barons and knights-errant, led by great magnates. These lordly and chivalrous soldiers of the cross proceeded to rally attendants and to equip themselves for combat, some of them by means of loans from Jews, the foremost moneylenders of that era. Because of the time needed for these preparations, this armed and disciplined pilgrimage did not set out for the Holy Land until August 1096, and it did not reach its destination until three years later, following many adversities and detours.

Whatever their high-minded sentiments and motives for coming forward, by the time the members of this militia of Christ captured Jerusalem and Acre, they had long since forsworn the precepts of Christian mercy and charity. When entering these and other cities, nobles and their underlings carried out large-scale atrocities, systematically massacring Moslems and Jews. Christian knights and foot soldiers not only slaughtered anyone daring to fight back but also murdered women and children for the greater glory of God. They left corpses rotting in the streets until they were burned on open pyres in order to avoid epidemics. In the Holy City, as we saw in the Prologue, the Jews were driven into the main synagogue, where they were burned alive.

Besides participating in this wholesale carnage, individual zealots took it upon themselves to mutilate, decapitate, and impale infidels. In the meantime there were also several incidents of cannibalism. These were attributed to the Tafurs, the mendicant warriors, who followed in the wake of the First Crusade. Probably inspired by Peter the Hermit, who finally joined the official host, these fierce but devout paupers are said to have practiced anthrophagy not just to avoid starvation but also for cultic reasons.

But it was the mainline crusaders, not the marginal Tafurs, who were responsible for the saturnalia of blood and profanity, which was presumed to have divine sanction. Even if Pope Urban never explicitly enjoined the lynching of infidels, he did not forbid it. There being no Curia to formulate and enforce a rigorous definition of the enemy, bishops and preachers gave free rein to their phantasms, and so did Mr. Everyman. In no time the pope's imprecation, presumably aimed at the distant and abstract Moslem, was broadened to cover any presumed foe of Christianity and Christ, both far and near. Since until the crusades Judeophobia was more widespread among the classes than the masses, perhaps there was nothing surprising about their massacring Jews in far-off Palestine. What was new and unexpected was the outburst of violent Jew-hatred among the *populus* fired by the great cause.

In fact, this anti-Jewish frenzy became a distinctive feature of the social flotsam that took up the cross between the Somme and the Rhine starting in 1095. Inspired and enthralled by such humble wandering prophets as Peter the Hermit, these coarse and ragged soldiers of God were not only more mercurial and undisciplined but also more impatient than their high-born fellow pilgrims in the incipient official crusade. But whatever their important dissimilarities in social composition, collective mentality, and military organization, the "high" and the "low" legions of Christ were galvanized by the same authority and became tributaries of a single torrent of consecrated intolerance, persecution, and violence.

In any event, in 1095 it was the popular crusaders who in their impatience rallied to the idea of making local Jews tangible surrogates for the Moslem infidels, who were beyond their immediate reach.

According to Guibert of Nogent, while the crusaders of Rouen certainly "wanted to fight the enemies of God in the East," they favored starting with the Jews right "under their eyes, . . . the Jewish people [being] more hostile to God than any other." It is not clear whether this contemporary chronicler was recounting the comments of elite or popular crusaders. The impoverished pilgrims in particular were prone to pillage and slaughter Jews along the long line of march to the Holy Land. The staggering material difficulties they encountered along their circuitous route merely increased the ardor and ferocity with which they "did God's work" and "avenged His blood" by turning on the Jews.

The first massacre of Jews may have occurred in Rouen within two months of Pope Urban's sermon of November 27, 1095, at Clermont. In this and a number of other French towns, embryonic hordes allegedly compelled Jews to choose between conversion and death. Probably no lesser person than Godfrey of Bouillon, Duke of Lower Lorraine, had passed the word that the army he was raising would avenge the murder of Christ with Jewish blood. To be sure, subsequently he repeatedly spared the lives of Jews in exchange for money. But there was no mistaking the anti-Jewish venom even among those proposing to take the "high" road to Jerusalem.

The Jewish torment was much worse farther east. The Jewish communities of some of the principal cities on the Rhine and Moselle rivers were infamously savaged by the peoples' crusade. The trail of bloody assaults moved north along the Rhine to Speyer, Worms, and Mainz; from there southwest along the Moselle to Trier and Metz; and then again north along the Rhine to Cologne, Neuss, and Xanten. Obviously, the beggarly crusaders were not wending their way, even roundabout, in the direction of Jerusalem, although eventually contingents of them advanced toward and along the Danube to Hungary.

The people's crusade consisted of three major volunteer legions, each with leaders of knightly status. Picking up recruits along the way, the largest and best equipped of these peasant armies was headed by Count Emicho of Leiningen, a fierce true believer. It was Emicho's host that made the most destructive onslaughts on episcopal cities with large Jewish communities. Invariably, the assailants could count on elite and popular collaborators behind the city walls to help them carry out their atrocities.

Emicho staged his first attack on May 3, 1096, when with local confederates he set upon the Jews of Speyer, slaughtering eleven Jews. If this foray fell short of Emicho's intention, it was because of the timely intervention of Bishop Johannes, who arranged for most Jews to take refuge in his own palace and other public buildings.

Two weeks later Emicho and his followers reached the outskirts of Worms. Sensing the danger, Bishop Adalbert also sheltered several hundred Jews in his palace, thereby encouraging not a few of the city's burghers to promise to stand by those Jews who chose to stay and fight. With the help of local collaborators, the crusaders promptly fell upon these Jews in their own districts. A few hundred Jews who apparently refused conversion were slaughtered while their synagogue and homes were despoiled. Intoxicated by this saturnalia of blood, several days later, on May 25, the warlike pilgrims surrounded the episcopal palace, demanding additional sacrificial offerings. In an effort to save the lives of his Jewish wards, Bishop Adalbert pressed them to yield to forcible baptism, which was contrary to canon law, thereby sanctioning the zealots' blackmail. But most Jews refused, preferring to "sanctify his Name" by suicide or violent death, and this included wives, children, and the aged. Another few hundred Jews were slain within two days, raising the number of victims in Worms to between 500 and 800.

Even before the end of this massacre in Worms, Emicho marched about 12,000 foot soldiers to Mainz. With a population considerably smaller than this horde, Mainz was home to Europe's economically and spiritually most important and vital community of Ashkenazic Jews. Terrified by reports from Speyer and Worms, the Jews of Mainz prevailed on Archbishop Ruthard and the local burgrave to give them shelter. They also sought to save their lives by bribing their tormentors. But on May 27 disaffected burghers and the general populace started a pogrom within the city before opening the city gates in defiance of Ruthard and the burgrave. The crusaders rushed in with a raging fury and the Jews of Mainz experienced the same hell on earth as their coreligionists in Worms. Between 700 and 1,100 of them lost their lives.

Emicho himself now headed for Palestine. But his followers proceeded to visit the same ritual murder and plunder on a number of other cities, first along the Moselle and then again along the Rhine before breaking up, either to return home or finally to start on the road to the Holy Land. By this time Volkmar and Gottschalk, inspired by Peter the Hermit, were leading two large legions of people's crusaders in the direction of the Balkans. While Volkmar's followers attacked the Jews of Prague in June, Gottschalk's forced the Jews of Regensburg, in the Upper Palatinate, to submit to a mass baptism in the Danube.

This frenzied violence against Jews took place during the six months preceding the start of the official knightly crusade in the fall of 1096. The exact number of victims will never be known. The best estimates are that between 4,000 and 5,000 Jews perished, or about one quarter of the Jewish population in the affected areas. There is no way of calculating the number of forced conversions, the extent of material devastation, and the depth of psychological injury.

The linked ideological aggressions and physical massacres of the First Crusade are difficult to grasp both because of the deficiencies of the sources and the sensitivity of the issues. And yet the received scholarly and general wisdom tends to impute all the horrors to the common people while all but exonerating the elites. Ostensibly, the massacres were committed by uncontrolled mobs of uprooted and uneducated, not to say primitive or barbarian, *pauperes,* or paupers. Gullible and impetuous by nature, this rabble is portrayed as having been driven to a messianic and fanatic frenzy by self-anointed prophets with questionable beliefs and motives. Once incited, the lowly, mean hordes allegedly rampaged on their own or under the spell of overzealous but shrewd leaders. Ultimately, paupers, prophets, and leaders were swept up in movements such as Count Emicho's, whose militancy and savagery presumably were fired by anomalous collective delusions.

But what about the role of men from the higher religious and secular spheres of medieval Christendom who were ostensibly more levelheaded? There was, to begin with, the pope's call to arms and his warrant authorizing the drive against infidels, seemingly in defense of the faith. Certainly, the bloody massacres of Moslems and Jews in 1099 in the Holy Land, the terminus of the First Crusade, would have been inconceivable without Urban's writ for persecution and promise of redemption. And this writ was hardly less potent between 1095 and 1099, when popular fanaticism surged wide and far. At the same time that pseudoprophets disseminated variants of this message to revival meetings, sober bishops diffused it to rather more staid and steady congregations. Indeed, by propagating it locally the prelates and their clergy legitimated the incitements of wandering ascetics. By not disavowing the prophets' perversions of the credo—if perversion there was—they were responsible, however indirectly, for the rise of murderous fanaticism. In the Rhine and Moselle valleys the Jews became the victims of this invasive proselytism encouraged by the church establishment. Except in Speyer, the bishops failed in their efforts to protect the Jews not only because their intercessions were halting and dilatory, but also because they themselves were part of contested power structures. In most episcopal cities the ecclesiastic authorities were allied with or opposed by burghers and commoners whose religious zealotry was correlated with local struggles to advance or defend secular interests in which Jewish merchants and moneylenders were enmeshed, since they were considered agents of social change and corruption.

As for the leaders of the armies of popular crusaders or pilgrims, they were not simply blind fanatics of plebeian origin and without military skills. Peter the Hermit and Emicho were both zealots and men of the world, and apparently so were Volkmar and Gottschalk. In addition, they were surrounded or seconded by respectable and experienced knights. Peter the Hermit counted seasoned nobles from northern France and southern Germany among his field officers, and so did Emicho of Leiningen, who was a great noble in his own right.

There is no denying that established ecclesiastic and secular elites conceived, summoned, and directed Europe's first holy war. In addition to being paramount in the crusade of the lords, great magnates and lesser knights—the *principes*—were centrally involved in launching, legitimating, and heading the popular hordes of religious warriors. To be sure, just as Godfrey of Bouillon himself is not likely to have committed atrocities against Moslem and Jewish infidels in Jerusalem, Emicho of Leiningen is not likely to have massacred Jews in Worms. But the fact that they and others of their ilk did not sully their own hands with unchristian blood in no way absolves them of responsibility for the cruelties and profanations of the *exercitus Dei*. Probably the rank and file of both the knightly and indigent armies occasionally forced the pace of intemperance. But especially since the masters of medieval Europe ordinarily excelled at controlling the landless underclass, they could almost certainly have checked the orgies of pious bloodshed and defilement had they been disposed to do so. Although there was little innocence among the soldiers of Christ, perhaps the *maiores*, the men of power and prestige who led them and kept their own hands clean, were the least innocent of all.

This discussion of the First Crusade is intended to point up the historical circumstances and dynamics which gave rise to the first mass murder of Jews in the lands of western Christendom. The archetypal persecution of Jews in 1096 was inseparable from a much larger movement of extreme zealotry which was fueled by acute stresses in medieval society and was primarily directed against other infidels who were more numerous, less defenseless, and largely beyond reach. The Judeocide of the first half of the twentieth century burst forth in a similar historical setting. It was entwined with a great surge of fanaticism which was fired by a general crisis in European society and culminated in the triumph of nazism in Germany, before reaching its apogee in the Third Reich's crusading war against Soviet Russia and bolshevism.

CHAPTER VIII

THE MISCARRIAGE OF BARBAROSSA

FROM POGROM TO BABI YAR

The Judeocide was forged in the fires of a stupendous war to conquer unlimited *Lebensraum* from Russia, to crush the Soviet regime, and to liquidate international bolshevism. The regular Wehrmacht and the special Waffen-SS first blazed the trail for the Einsatzgruppen and then exercised the power of last resort over the territories and populations surrounding the extermination sites. Without Operation Barbarossa there would and could have been no Jewish catastrophe, no "Final Solution." Not that the Jews went unscathed in the period between the invasion of Poland on September 1, 1939, and the invasion of Russia on June 22, 1941. During this early phase of the Second World War, between 5,000 and 10,000 Jews, virtually all of them adult males, were murdered individually, and twice to three times that many Jews of both sexes died of malnutrition and disease, above all in the ghettos of Warsaw and Łódź. But this killing was neither systematic nor comprehensive: it affected a small percentage of several Jewish communities and it was confined to German-occupied Poland.

The invasion of the Soviet Union brought a quantum jump in the scale and intensity of the suffering inflicted on the Jews. It is certain that Barbarossa and the Judeocide were symbiotically linked, although the permutations of this interdependence were extremely complex and fluctuating. The mass murder of the Jews was not self-contained, nor did it have absolute primacy. Hitler cannot be said to have invaded Russia in order to capture the 5 million Jews under Soviet control. Nor can he be said to have done so with the intention of creating emergency conditions which could be used to camouflage the extermination of the Jews of the rest of the Continent. Certainly, from its very inception Barbarossa had a deadly anti-Jewish impetus. As we saw, Jews were designated as among the chief agents of "Judeo-bolshevism," and the Commissar Order called for the summary execution of all such agents. But this directive ordered only the killing of the Jewish members of the "common enemy" in the eastern theater of military operations and conquest. It was issued prior to and independent of the launching and implementation of the "Final Solution," which enjoined the torment and physical extermination of all the Jews of German-occupied and -satellized Europe.

The course of the war accounts for the radical transformation of the initial Commissar Order into the subsequent "Final Solution." While the unsettling slowdowns in the blitzkrieg between late July and late October 1941 intensified the anti-Jewish furor of the assault squads, the desperate but unsuccessful race to Moscow in November–December 1941 precipitated the rush to the "Final Solution." The gradual miscarriage of Barbarossa shook the hitherto unshakable defiance and presumption of the Nazi fundamentalists and their accomplices, with the result that they turned to venting their rage on the Jews. Accordingly, the escalation and systematization of the assault on the Jews was an expression not of soaring hubris on the eve of victory, but of bewilderment and fear in the face of possible defeat. Indeed, the decision to exterminate the Jews marked the incipient debacle of the Nazi Behemoth, not its imminent triumph.

This is not to suggest that the Judeocide was pure improvisation in the face of unexpected and disconcerting military reverses. As previously noted, Barbarossa was not an ordinary war. Rather, it was a crusade, rooted in and driven by the warped social compromise, party-state government, and millennial ideology of the Third Reich. When this crusading campaign began to stall, Hitler and his generals never really faltered. Instead, inherently incapable of contemplating and seeking a negotiated settlement, they intensified the built-in brutality of their military and ideological warfare. In the war against the Red Army and the Soviet partisans, the Wehrmacht increasingly resorted to terror, to spoliation, to scorched-earth practices, and to the decimation of Soviet war prisoners. Simultaneously, the SS shifted to helping force the pace of war production at the same time that they radicalized the war against the Jews. The widespread destruction in the occupied eastern territories and the mass murder of the Jews may have been counterproductive and irrational in strictly military terms, but this unsoldierly savagery and anti-Semitic fury were in keeping with the inner logic of Barbarossa and the Nazi project.

No written document containing or reporting an explicit command to exterminate the Jews has come to light thus far. This does not of course mean that such direct evidence will not appear in the future. In the meantime, the presumption must be that the order or informal injunction to mass-murder Jews was transmitted orally. More than likely, Hitler himself gave the general enabling signals, probably encouraged by members of his closest entourage, among whom none seems to have raised objections. Significantly, as of October 1941 the führer made more and more frequent and ominous threats against the Jews, and did so in public statements as well as in private. His coded signals were translated into concrete orders and diffused by leaders of the SS, notably Himmler and Heydrich, who had direct access to him. As a matter of course, the heads of the SS left their middle and lower echelons a relatively free hand, which is not to say that regional and local officials played a determining role, except as executors and executioners.

For lack of evidence, much remains conjectural about both the chain and the idiom of command which mandated the successive steps toward the mass murder of totally innocent and helpless Jewish civilians. All the more reason to pay close attention to the circumstances surrounding this final radicalization of Nazi anti-Semitism, particularly to the course of the crusading war in which it was so deeply implanted.

In the preceding chapter we examined the written directives which empowered the Wehrmacht and the SS to ferociously mistreat Soviet soldiers, commissars, politicians, intellectuals, partisans, and prisoners of war. The Jews were portrayed as an integral part of the Soviet dragon to be slain, especially since the principal battle zones included many strategically important towns and cities with disproportionately large Jewish populations. Early in the crusade against "Judeobolshevism" the Nazi legions made no hard and fast distinction between the different members of their "common enemy." Significantly, some of the first and for a time the worst outrages against the Jews were committed not by the new-model Einsatzgruppen but by latter-day local pogromists in the "liberated" territories—Lithuania, Latvia, Estonia, White Ruthenia, the Ukraine—and by units of the Rumanian army assigned to Barbarossa. No doubt the perpetrators of these old-style pogroms were steeped in traditional anti-Judaism. Be that as it may, for them the assaults on Jews were an integral part of their national or territorial conflict with Soviet Russia and their sectarian struggle with communism, both of which dated from the end-of-the-war crisis of 1917 to 1920. Of course, before long the trained action squads of the SS carried out much larger and more methodical mass slaughters of Jews than these wild cohorts. But these did not start until the fall of 1941, after the Red Army had slowed the German advance, forcing some of the heaviest and bloodiest fighting in the thick of the former Jewish Pale of Settlement. By then the commanders of both the Wehrmacht and the Einsatzgruppen were specifically denouncing the Jews for masterminding, joining, and assisting partisan activities behind German lines, and they used these charges to justify making the Jews pay for the stiffening Soviet resistance. Not only inveterate Nazis but traditional conservatives, in particular generals, made this spurious charge, as they came face-to-face with large Jewish communities along the line of march and in the deadliest battle theaters.

During the second phase of the Thirty Years War of the twentieth century, the first Jews to be mass-murdered—rather than deemancipated, ostracized, expelled, relocated, or ghettoized—were the Jews under Soviet jurisdiction, including the Jews who had wound up there during the life of the Hitler-Stalin pact. But this is not to say that the extermination of Soviet Jewry was an integral part of Hitler's grand design for a Thousand-Year Reich. After a brief, victorious campaign the Nazis expected to resettle the Jews of Europe, including the Russian Jews, in a Lublin-like reservation beyond the Volga or the Urals. And it was not until they woke up to the enormous difficulties of winning the war and "liberating" Moscow, this century's profane Jerusalem, that Nazi fanatics fastened upon the Jews as the most reachable and vulnerable incarnation of "Judeobolshevism." In particular, the SS, the archetypal crusaders of their day, made it their business to eradicate what they saw as the Jewish arm of this biform specter. Compared to their counterparts in the eleventh century, who had constituted a formless host of fervid zealots, the SS were a small corps of disciplined and unimpassioned true believers. But whatever their dissimilarities in makeup, the Christian and Nazi crusades shared fundamental correspondences in structure and properties which informed their cruel violence against the Jews. Ultimately, it may be inconsequential that in medieval times the violence against the Jews was primitive while in modern times it was rational-bureaucratic, for it was equally extreme and brutal both times.

Hitler brazenly but also rightly predicted that the stupendous and lightning irruption of Barbarossa would cause "the world to hold its breath." At the outset the eastern campaign also promised to bear out his conviction, fully shared by his generals, that the Wehrmacht merely needed "to kick in the [front] door" of the Soviet Union for "the entire rotten structure to come crashing down."

During the first forty-eight hours of the attack of June 22, the Luftwaffe claimed to have destroyed about 2,000 enemy planes, 20 percent of Russia's air force. It also laid waste scores of vital supply and transportation centers. At the same time, the ground armies easily broke through the front-line defenses of the Red Army. Within a week the Wehrmacht's armored and motorized divisions penetrated deeply into Stalin's recently secured forward salient, which nevertheless served its purpose of providing extra space and time. Under the command of General Erich Höpner the three panzer divisions of the Northern Army Group overran most of Lithuania and much of Latvia in their drive toward Leningrad. In the process they seized such major cities as Grodno, Vilna, Kovno, Riga, and Dvinsk. All of these cities had large Jewish communities, ranging from over 40 percent of the population of Grodno to 10 percent of Riga's. Simultaneously, the Second and Third Panzer Corps of the Central Army Group, commanded by General Hermann Hoth and General Heinz Guderian, easily took Białystok, Slonim, and Minsk, which were at least 40 percent Jewish. As they tore apart twenty Soviet divisions, these crack units, headed for Smolensk and Moscow, trapped over 300,000 prisoners and captured over 3,000 tanks and 1,500 guns. The defenses of the Red Army were strongest and most effective opposite Field Marshal Gerd von Rundstedt's Southern Army Group. Even so, his tank and mobile forces broke through to Kovel and Lvov, which were one-half and one-third Jewish respectively, in their two-pronged charge toward Kiev and Odessa, Soviet Russia's two largest Jewish centers.

These lightning advances continued until just past mid-July. On the southern front the panzers of General Ewald von Kleist pressed ahead in the direction of Vinnitsa and Uman. No less important, units of Field Marshal Fedor von Bock's Central Army Group breached the defensive perimeter of the vital Orsha-Vitebsk-Smolensk triangle which controlled the road to Moscow. After crossing the Dnieper, but in the face of stubborn Soviet resistance, one of Guderian's divisions stormed Smolensk on July 16, some of Hoth's armor having sealed the city on the north. All these towns and cities were strategically important transportation and economic centers and, except for Smolensk, they were between 35 and 55 percent Jewish.

The warlords of the Third Reich had good reason to be jubilant about their accomplishments during the first month of Operation Barbarossa. The Wehrmacht had seized Eastern Galicia; parts of the Ukraine, White Russia, and Latvia; and all of Lithuania. It had all but crushed about ninety enemy divisions, taken about 600,000 prisoners, destroyed half the Soviet air force, and captured large quantities of military hardware, notably tanks and field guns. On July 3 General Franz Halder, chief of the General Staff, self-confidently concluded that the German fighting machine had won the Russian campaign "within a fortnight." A day later, on July 4, Hitler exulted that the Soviets had "virtually lost" the war, convinced that they could not make good their losses of planes and tanks. To be sure, he still needed to make a vital and urgent decision: whether to let the panzers of the Central Army Group press ahead to Moscow, or whether to order General Hoth to turn north to help take Leningrad and General Guderian south to expedite the capture of the Ukraine and the Crimea. While pondering this decisive step, the führer confirmed his resolve to "raze Moscow and Leningrad to the ground." Unlike most generals, he stressed the political rather than the purely strategic importance of both cities. Hitler wanted Moscow bombed in order to break "the center of Bolshevik resistance" and to prevent the "orderly evacuation of Russia's government apparatus." As for Leningrad, it was the "citadel of bolshevism," replete with symbolic significance for both the regime and the people at large. Although by mid-July Hitler had become increasingly tense over the urgent decision before him, given the "overall situation," he continued to "count on an early Russian collapse," and so did all senior officers, including Halder.

Certain of victory, Hitler and the military began to think about the future "occupation and security of the Russian orbit" as well as "the reorganization of the army after the end of Barbarossa." On July 17 the führer appointed Alfred Rosenberg Reichminister for the occupied eastern territories, with his main office in Berlin. It was understood, however, that the real power of the civil administration of the conquered lands would be vested in Göring, head of the Four-Year Plan, and in Himmler, chief of the SS and the police. Himmler was put in charge of the "internal security of the newly occupied territories" and empowered to issue orders to all civil administrators, including Rosenberg. On July 22 Hitler turned over the districts around Vilna, Białystok, and Lvov to civilian rule, effective August 1, 1941.

By then, however, there were a number of danger signals. The Wehrmacht had paid a considerable and unexpected price for its spectacular advances: although its infantry divisions lost only 20 percent of their effectives, about 50 percent of the tanks and motor vehicles of the armored divisions were destroyed or disabled. Even more worrisome was the cunning with which battle groups of the Red Army kept slipping out of pincer movements designed to entrap them. To be sure, a staggering number of enemy soldiers and officers were killed, wounded, and captured. Nevertheless, many of them managed to retreat to positions farther inland, to continue the fight. In addition, within weeks the Soviet government raised over a hundred new divisions and proceeded to relocate important war industries to the far interior. Of course, having refused to heed warnings of the impending German assault, Stalin was momentarily disconcerted by it. But he quickly regained his composure and took charge. On July 3 Stalin called for guerrilla warfare, which was in keeping with Soviet military doctrine, thereby giving the armed conflict a new—a fourth—dimension.

As of the last week of July, it was clear to Hitler and his generals that their expectations about an easy and swift breakdown of the Red Army and the Bolshevik regime had been overly optimistic, if not wholly mistaken. The advance of the Wehrmacht became increasingly slow and costly in all three sectors. In the north the Soviets all but stayed Field Marshal Wilhelm von Leeb's Leningrad-bound forces in Estonia and prevented their linking up with the Finns. In the center General Semion Timoshenko's troops mounted a stubborn rearguard action, with the result that von Bock needed until August 5 to penetrate the strategically vital defense line east of Smolensk, only to become stalled around Jelna, 250 miles southwest of Moscow. In the south, Soviet divisions similarly delayed von Rundstedt's double thrust to the lower Dnieper and to Uman, aimed at Kiev.

Outward appearances notwithstanding, the eastern campaign, and hence the centerpiece of Hitler's bid for the mastery of Europe, was in serious difficulty. Barbarossa was designed to be completed within a maximum of five months. During the first three weeks the Wehrmacht was expected to reach the Dvina in the north, clear Smolensk in the center, and cross the Dnieper in the south. Having ripped apart the Red Army, and after consolidating their position and resupplying their forces, the German divisions were scheduled to start their second and final push no later than around August 1, 1941. They were to secure the advanced line of the Dvina-Volga-Don well before the end of autumn. It was assumed that if the Kremlin had not capitulated by then, there might at worst have to be an additional offensive toward the Urals in 1942. As it turned out, the first stage had taken at least twice as long as expected, with the result that the German forces could not afford to take time out to resupply and to rest if they were to stay ahead of the autumn rains and if they were to deny the Red Army a sorely needed breathing spell. As it was, quite apart from fighting tenaciously, the Soviet troops were better equipped and better led than anticipated. Enemy officers kept avoiding encirclements and yielding space to gain time, thereby contravening the fundamental premises of the Wehrmacht's blitz strategy.

All in all, not only Hitler but his general officers had miscalculated. The surprisingly quick and easy victory over France had forged a sudden and improbable consensus between them. Overconfident, and imbued with the Nazi presumption, the leaders of the Third Reich had systematically underestimated Soviet capabilities and overestimated their own. On August 11, 1941, five weeks after having claimed victory prematurely, General Halder conceded that it was becoming ever clearer that "we have underestimated the organizational and economic strength, the transportation system, and above all the purely military efficiency of the Russian colossus." While the General Staff originally had reckoned with "200 enemy divisions, by now there are an estimated 360 divisions." Although these divisions might not measure up to German standards of equipment and leadership, what mattered was that they existed and that "for every dozen divisions we smash, the Russians will raise another dozen."

Further, only incompetence or braggadocio can account for the German generals' misjudgment of the vastness of the Russian spaces and, above all, the conditions of transport for blitz warfare. Of some 850,000 miles of roads, only about 40,000 miles were paved, the rest being soft roadways difficult to clear, especially in bad weather. Because of unplanned-for distances and wear and tear, many of the Wehrmacht's mechanized units experienced shortages of fuel, spare parts, and tires. As for the railroad tracks, they were sparse and needed to be regauged if non-Russian rolling stock was to continue through to forward positions.

Four to five weeks into Barbarossa, Hitler's generals had good reason to worry that the Soviets might have won enough time to bolster their defenses, especially west of Moscow. For most of them the capital was not just the enemy's political headquarters but above all the nerve center of their military, industrial, transportation, and communications system. They expected Stalin to make every effort to force the Wehrmacht into a war of position and to halt its advance before the onset of winter, particularly in the approaches to Moscow. Should he succeed, Germany would be caught in the quicksands of a drawn-out two-front war, a situation to be avoided at all costs.

While Hitler shared this somber diagnosis, he disagreed with his military experts, who wanted to press on to surround and capture Moscow. Rather than risk the worn panzer units of the Central Army Group in another "wide-flung" enveloping maneuver, the führer argued for "tactical battles of extermination confined to small pockets, in which every last enemy soldier could be annihilated." Such engagements should be fought for regions with vital resources, to be denied to the Soviets and tapped for the Reich's own war economy. This would mean diverting Guderian's panzers for an all-out drive to conquer first the Ukraine and then the Donets Basin, the Crimea, and the Caucasus. Weather conditions also argued for such a course. While the High Command insisted that the momentous choice between charging Moscow or Kiev would have to be made by very early August, both General Hoth and General Guderian stressed that their armored columns needed thorough refitting before moving out, at the earliest in mid-August.

The die was all but cast in favor of Kiev, although the führer kept postponing his decision until August 21, 1941. By then another assault on Leningrad had failed and heavy fighting continued near Smolensk. Farther south the Soviets put up fierce resistance around Korosten and Zhitomir, which was over 40 percent Jewish. Both Hitler and his ranking generals now realized that Barbarossa had misfired, putting the outcome of the entire war and the Behemoth itself in grave jeopardy. Whatever their strategic differences over the eastern campaign, they still agreed that there was no alternative but to give absolute priority to crushing Russia before turning to face down England in the Atlantic and the Mediterranean. No effort should be spared to overpower Stalin before the onset of winter. In the event this effort failed, the eastern campaign would have to be resumed full force in the spring and summer of 1942. As the Wehrmacht was unable and unfit to mount more than one major drive, Hitler opted for a supreme effort in the south. After conferring with several top theater and field commanders, as well as with General Halder, Guderian flew to the Wolfsschanze (Wolf's Lair) to urge Hitler to reverse his decision and authorize a concerted drive on Moscow. He proposed to invest the Soviet capital after first forcing Stalin to draw in all his forces for its defense. But the führer stood his ground, stressing the importance of securing critical raw materials, foods, and fuels for continuing the war. Guderian dutifully turned south to help conquer the Ukraine and Kiev, after which he was expected to double back for a headlong assault on Moscow, ahead of subzero weather.

Even with this reinforcement, it took von Rundstedt until mid-September to close the ring around Kiev. With some 600,000 Soviet troops trapped and no reserves to send to their rescue, Stalin finally surrendered the capital of the Ukraine. On September 19, units of von Reichenau's Sixth Army entered the city and a week later the battle of Kiev, one of the most momentous in history, was finally over. The Wehrmacht had completely overpowered seven enemy armies, killing, wounding, or capturing 1 million men. Over 650,000 prisoners were taken, raising the total in German hands to over 1.3 million. Nazi propagandists loudly celebrated the capture of Kiev. They used photographs and newsreels to dramatize the surrender of bedraggled and dazed Soviet prisoners, who were portrayed as typical of the execrable Slavic *Untermenschen*, crying out for subjugation. Indeed, Berlin proclaimed *urbi et orbi* that the triumph at Kiev proved that except for a few minor battles, the war in the east was over and won.

In private, Hitler and his generals were not nearly so sanguine. They knew that it had taken the Wehrmacht three months to take Kiev, at least four weeks behind Barbarossa's exacting schedule. They also realized that their overextended and exhausted armies would be hard-pressed to capture Moscow and Leningrad in the few remaining weeks of passable weather. All three army groups, but in particular the divisions of the central front, including Guderian's armored units, were suffering increasingly serious shortages of munitions, spare parts, and fuel. Even assuming the necessary stores could be mustered, it would be difficult to transport them to where they were most urgently needed.

Even so, the führer and the generals readily agreed to press the attack on the Soviet capital, irrespective of costs and violations of the norms of combat. Their decision was a natural outgrowth of Barbarossa's built-in fury, which began to spiral. The generals, who considered themselves unpolitical, were quite prepared to wage an increasingly savage kind of warfare. In past weeks they had ordered or authorized the stepped-up mistreatment of enemy prisoners. They had also instituted massive and indiscriminate reprisals against civilian hostages for real or suspected partisan activities. In all of this the military collaborated closely with the SS. Because of the acute supply problem, the resolve to make a desperate rush for Moscow entailed a conscious and deliberate readiness to starve enemy prisoners and cities as well as to hyperexploit the occupied eastern territories. The necessities of total war increasingly were used to justify turning famine and disease into murderous military weapons, fatal for noncombatants.

On the last day of the battle of Kiev, racing against the clock, Hitler ordered Operation Typhoon, the drive on Moscow, to begin on October 2. He rushed to Borisov, the headquarters of the Central Army Group, to give last-minute instructions to Field Marshal von Bock. The führer wanted both Moscow and Leningrad to be completely leveled, without regard for civilians, let alone for soldiers.

On October 2, the appointed day, Hitler issued a ringing proclamation to his troops on the eastern front. He assured them that during these last "three and a half months" the Wehrmacht had prepared the ground for "this last powerful blow, intended to crush the enemy before the beginning of winter." The territories conquered thus far were "more than twice the size of Germany in 1933, and more than four times the size of the English home islands." These territories were bulging with raw materials and were the gateway to the Soviet Union's "three major industrial regions," to be captured tomorrow. As part of their triumphant advance the German armies had "smashed countless enemy divisions, taken over 2.4 million prisoners, destroyed or captured over 17,500 panzers and over 21,000 field guns, and shot down or destroyed 14,200 airplanes." Indeed, "the world had never seen anything like it." But as if to account for the Soviet Union's refusal to cave in and surrender, Hitler warned his troops that the enemy forces were "largely composed of beasts, not soldiers," conditioned to fight with animal-like ferocity. He apprised them that the extreme poverty in which Russians were nurtured was "the result of nearly twenty-five years of Jewish rule, with a Bolshevik system that is essentially similar to the capitalist system, the carriers of both systems being the same, namely Jews and only Jews." The Reich's legions stood more than six hundred miles deep in enemy territory, alongside Slovak, Hungarian, Italian, and Rumanian divisions. Spanish, Croatian, and Belgian units were about to arrive, and they would be followed by brigades from other nations. At the start of this "last great decisive battle" of 1941, the führer wanted to bolster the morale of his warriors with the claim that "perhaps for the first time all the nations of Europe are agreed that this war is a common struggle for the salvation of the Continent with the [world's] most precious cultural heritage."

At the start of Typhoon, the Wehrmacht's forward units were deployed along a 1,500-mile front. In the north they held most of the Baltic region, except Leningrad. In the south they occupied most of the Ukraine and were extending their hold on the Crimea and the Caucasus, while Rumanian forces at long last had managed to close in on Odessa. In the center, von Bock's divisions, which were to spearhead the charge on Moscow, were deployed along a line barely 200 miles west of the Soviet capital. With over 1 million men as well as 2,000 tanks, 14,000 artillery pieces, and 1,000 planes, von Bock was to tear through and encircle two Red Army groups of 1.2 million men, 850 tanks, 7,000 guns, and 500 to 600 planes.

During the first two weeks, the German forces gathered considerable momentum, covering thirty miles a day between October 2 and 10. By the third week of October they completed two pincer movements, capturing Bryansk, north of Kiev, and Vyazma, northeast of Smolensk, along with 650,000 prisoners, 1,200 tanks, and 5,000 field guns. At the same time General Guderian, racing up from the south, overran Orel. The total of Russian prisoners reached 2 million as von Bock's Fourth Panzer Group and Fourth Army advanced to within sixty-two miles of Moscow. With the city gravely imperiled, the Soviets proceeded to evacuate key government offices, and also the General Staff. At the same time, they bolstered their defenses some thirteen miles west of the city. Stalin ordered General I. S. Konev, who took command of the Kalinin Army Group, to hold the perimeter north of Moscow, and General G. K. Zhukov, chief of the Western Army Group, to block the southern approaches, which were threatened by Guderian's drive to Tula.

The Germans continued to forge ahead in the south, taking Kharkov and Rostov, which were about 15 percent Jewish, and drawing near to the Crimea. In the center, however, their advance slowed to less than five miles daily, and in early November they began to bog down about fifty-five miles west of Moscow, on the Kalinin–Tula axis. The rains had started and Soviet resistance was stiffening. Von Bock decided to consolidate and brace his forces while waiting for the early frosts to harden the roads, which would make it easier for mechanized units to make their final run, before the snows. The Soviets, for their part, used this respite to strengthen their forward lines as well as to improve Moscow's air defenses and to reinforce Zhukov's sector. At the same time they, unlike the Germans, fitted their soldiers and their equipment for the harsh winter. In the event, the German troops and their officers were not only unprepared for the bitter weather; they were, above all, tired, bedeviled by acute shortages, and dispirited about the slowness of the offensive and its rising toll of German lives.

Clearly, the margin for maneuver kept narrowing. The OKH summoned the chief field commanders to Orsha for November 13, to impress them with the urgency of racing to Moscow before it became too late. By now there was considerably less consensus among the generals, except for their agreement that Barbarossa could not be won in 1941. Daunted by the long odds and hazards, both von Leeb and von Rundstedt advised against continuing Typhoon. They urged breaking off battle and transforming the forward lines into defensive salients, pending a renewed drive in the spring of 1942. Although chastened by recent setbacks and conceding the high risks, only von Bock was ready, perhaps even eager, to go to any length to try to surround, if not storm, Moscow. Relying on von Bock, Hitler and the High Command ordered the perilous offensive resumed on November 15.

Once again, the drive got off to a good start. In the north the Ninth Army took Kalinin, cut the road and rail links between Moscow and Leningrad, and finally, at the end of November, crossed a bridge over the Moscow-Volga Canal to approach to within less than twenty miles of the capital. Simultaneously, General Hoth's Third Panzer Group advanced some forty miles to take Klin, which was about thirty-one miles from the Kremlin. On the other hand, Guderian's armor had difficulties flanking and capturing Tula. Besides running into bitter Soviet resistance, by late November he was confronted with bad weather as well. Temperatures fell to at least minus twenty degrees centigrade, disabling motors and automatic weapons. Worse still, without proper clothing, men succumbed to the elements in the lines and in hospitals. In fact, the weather began to exact a greater toll among German troops than combat. Replacements and supplies, including fuel, were slow in coming, and the fighting spirit began to flag.

Realizing that the great gamble had failed, Guderian decided to limit the damage. Instead of merely stopping his forward units, he pulled them back, and did so without Hitler's prior approval. Similarly, von Rundstedt, despairing of holding Rostov against a Soviet counterattack, defied his superiors by bringing to a halt the entire Southern Army Group. Ominously, when von Rundstedt tendered his resignation on December 1, 1941, the führer appointed Field Marshal von Reichenau, chief of the Sixth Army and ardent Nazi, to take over the southern command. Although von Reichenau promptly rescinded von Rundstedt's stop order, almost overnight he, too, decided to give up Rostov, presumably to better hold the Donets Basin. Finally, on December 3, the commands of the Northern and Central Army Groups also ordered their divisions to cease all offensive operations and to take up defensive positions. Evidently, the front lines of all three army groups reached their points of no return more or less simultaneously.

In turn, the Soviets went over to the offensive, General Konev on December 5 and General Zhukov on the following day. Neither subzero temperatures nor high accumulations of snow deterred properly equipped divisions of the Red Army, bolstered by fresh troops from Siberia, from pushing back the units of the Wehrmacht's Central Army Group nearest Moscow. Within a matter of days, von Bock's forward divisions were forced to begin their retreat, first to Kaluga, then to Vyazma. Eventually, in mid-January, the German commanders managed to stabilize their front along a jagged north-south line 62 to 150 miles west of Moscow, close to their starting positions of late September and early October. Their campaign had failed, conspicuously. In the meantime, on December 8 Hitler had issued Directive No. 39 confirming the suspension of all offensive operations. But with so many divisions reeling, if not foundering, on December 16 Hitler decided to issue a categorical *Halt Befehl,* ordering his troops to stand and fight. This command proscribing any further retreat, whether tactical or otherwise, may well have headed off a serious rout.

Von Brauchitsch asked to retire in early December, and the führer assumed the post of commander in chief himself. He did so on December 19, after dismissing Guderian and Hoepner, and after agreeing to relieve von Bock and von Leeb of their commands. While this housecleaning shifted the blame from the führer to the military, which was anything but blameless, it was not out of the ordinary, given the magnitude of the failure in both the planning and execution of Barbarossa. Having lost what little it had kept of its autonomy, the Wehrmacht was reduced to complete subservience.

Of course, the time had long since passed when only the Soviets were suffering heavy losses. When Operation Typhoon stalled before Moscow, the Central Army Group counted about 125,000 casualties. Taking Barbarossa as a whole, of the 3 million men who had originally invaded Russia, 750,000, or close to 25 percent, were dead, wounded, or missing, the dead alone running to 200,000. The Wehrmacht also reported over 3,000 tanks and over 5,000 airplanes destroyed or seriously damaged, as well as about 150,000 horses killed. By the end of January 1942 the Soviet counteroffensive had increased these and other losses by roughly 25 percent. Casualties rose to over 900,000, among them about 30,000 officers, not counting those of Germany's allies and satellites. In military terms the damage to tanks and mechanized vehicles was even more debilitating, since the Wehrmacht's overall mobility was severely impaired. These human and material losses undermined the morale of the troops and the self-confidence of their military and political leaders.

The miscarriage of Typhoon dispelled all remaining illusions that Hitler's generals and legions would be able to take and hold Moscow, Leningrad, and Rostov in the near future, if ever. Not that the Wehrmacht was done for. But clearly, the conquest of Soviet Russia was beyond its capabilities. By holding firm, the Red Army had forced Germany into a war of position and attrition. Hereafter, both time and the initiative would be with Germany's enemies, especially now that the United States was joining the Allies. In due course, the vitality of the Third Reich would be sapped by a host of shortages: manpower for army and industry, critical raw materials, food, and arms. Indeed, the failure of Typhoon in late 1941—not the defeat at Stalingrad a year later—marked the turning point of Nazi Germany's bid for continental hegemony. Hitler and his acolytes were certain to intensify the fighting savagery and crusading fervor of Barbarossa, but with little if any chance of reversing the Reich's declining military fortunes.

. . .

As previously noted, the greatest military ruthlessness and ideological intoxication of the war, even though deeply rooted in Barbarossa's very nature, did not explode until the eastern campaign began to run aground. The Wehrmacht needed no coaching from the SS to intensify the violence against civilians and prisoners of war, including the Jews among them. The eruption of the Judeocide was closely correlated with this relentless recourse to violence against noncombatants by the military. Far from being either duped or innocent, the army was a pacesetter of both war crimes and crimes against humanity: the savageries of the SS were altogether inconceivable apart from Barbarossa and without the help of the armed forces; the deadly misdeeds of the Wehrmacht were facilitated by the eager collaboration of both the regular Death's Head Division and the Waffen-SS. There was a symbiosis between Wehrmacht and SS, though the degree of closeness differed in different times and places.

On September 12 General Keitel issued a directive forbidding any and all dealings with Jews in the occupied Soviet territories. The chief of staff of the High Command of the Armed Forces proclaimed that "the struggle against bolshevism calls for ruthless and energetic measures, especially against the Jews, the chief carriers of bolshevism." Accordingly, the OKW barred army units from employing individual Jews, insisting that "Jews can only be used in special labor columns, under German supervision."

Four days later, on September 16, at the height of the difficult battle for Kiev, Keitel put out instructions for dealing with insurrectionary movements in all German-occupied territories, but especially in Russia. He charged that "nationalist and other elements" were tied to a "mass movement directed from Moscow" which engaged in a broad spectrum of activities ranging from mere propaganda, to individual assassinations, to "outright rioting and partisan warfare." Hereafter, the presumption would have to be that every attack on the German occupation forces was of "Communist origin." Keitel ordered that this partisan resistance be "nipped in the bud by draconian measures," mindful that "life is cheap in many of these countries" in which nothing short of "uncommon hardness" would be effective. In the east this meant massive reprisals, notably against civilians: "In expiation for the life of each German soldier between 50 and 100 Communists" would have to be shot, the summary executions to be carried out in public for maximum effect.

On October 12, after delayed-action Soviet bombs had killed scores of Germans in occupied Kiev, and at the height of Operation Typhoon, Keitel and von Brauchitsch, the commander in chief, notified the command of the Central Army Group that "the führer once again has decided to refuse the surrender of Moscow, should it be offered." They maintained that since Moscow and Leningrad, like Kiev, would almost certainly be mined, German soldiers should not be asked to risk their lives in storming these cities, which were also rife with epidemics. Before capture, both cities should be "leveled by artillery fire and air attacks," and their populations "put to flight." The two senior generals insisted that it was Hitler's will that Russian cities be destroyed, partly to avoid having to feed their populations "at the expense of the German *Heimat.*"

On October 10 Field Marshal von Reichenau, enraged by the difficulties and embarrassments of the eastern campaign, issued a particularly revealing and portentous directive for the "Conduct of Troops in the Eastern Theater." As commander of the Sixth Army, he had spearheaded the capture of Kiev. To make sure that his men should not flinch in the face of the increasing ordeals of total war, he proceeded to remind them that the end purpose of the eastern campaign was the "complete destruction of the instruments of power of the Judeobolshevik system and the extermination [*Ausrottung*] of Asiatic influences in the European cultural sphere." Given the nature of this mission, the assignment of the army went "beyond conventional combat . . . according to the rules of warfare." On the Russian front each soldier was also "the carrier of a ruthless national [*völkisch*] ideology and the avenger of all [past] bestialities inflicted on the German *Volkstum* and its kinsfolk." Von Reichenau made a special point of exhorting his soldiers to "have full understanding of the necessity to take hard but righteous reprisals against Jewish sub-humanity," not least because Jews were "the instigators of terrorism in the rear of the Wehrmacht."

Von Reichenau was particularly concerned with this "war against the enemy behind the front." There were no grounds to make prisoners of "brutal partisans and degenerate women, and to treat [civilian] snipers and loiterers as decent soldiers" to be spared. It was nothing less than "misguided humanitarianism . . . to feed enemy populations and prisoners of war in military kitchens . . . and to distribute cigarettes and bread to them." Even when taken from Germany's rightful booty, such handouts were inadmissible at a time that the *Heimat* and the eastern army faced scarcities. Nor was there any reason to preserve public buildings, except "when needed to billet soldiers." Some of these buildings were "symbols of the one-time Bolshevik regime," and in keeping "with the war of extermination [*Vernichtungskampf*]" they should be destroyed, regardless of their "historical or artistic" value.

But above all, there was a need for "draconian steps" against partisans behind the lines, including steps against "the male population" as a whole, which should be held responsible for not "preventing or forewarning of attacks." Von Reichenau stressed that in order to make Russia's passive "anti-Soviet elements" into "active collaborators against bolshevism" the German terror would have to become more daunting than that of roving Bolshevik bands.

In sum, each soldier had a dual assignment: first, "the total destruction [Vernichtung] of the Bolshevik heresy, the Soviet state, and the Red Army"; second, "the merciless extermination [Ausrottung] of alien treachery and cruelty to safeguard the security of the Wehrmacht in Russia." According to von Reichenau, there was no other way for the Wehrmacht "to discharge its historical mission of once and for all delivering the German people [Volk] from the Asiatic-Jewish peril."

Von Reichenau, who apparently acted on his own initiative, expressed more than his own thoughts and rancors. The führer himself was reported to consider Reichenau's rescript "excellent." It also struck a favorable chord with several top generals. Von Rundstedt, Reichenau's immediate superior, expressed "complete agreement" with the directive, which he distributed throughout the southern command. In a cover note he asked that his chief officers consider it a guideline for their own actions. On October 28 von Brauchitsch directed Major General Eduard Wagner to distribute copies to all the top commanders on the eastern front with the urging that they proceed in the "same spirit." General Hoth, commander of the Seventeenth Army, was inspired to spur his troops to take "hard measures against [those] elements of alien peoples and races . . . who are spiritual supporters of bolshevism, couriers for its murderous organizations, and accessories of partisans." General Hoth's order stressed that this same "Judaized class of humanity" (jüdische Menschenklasse), which had tried but failed to destroy Germany, was fostering "anti-German movements" the world over and calling for vengeance. By now their "extermination" (Ausrottung) was "a prerequisite for self-preservation."

General Erich von Manstein, commander of the Eleventh Army and one of the Wehrmacht's most respected generals, also issued his own version of von Reichenau's order. On November 20, from Simferopol in the Crimea, which had a large Jewish community, he proclaimed that "since June 22 the German people [Volk] have been locked in a life-and-death struggle with the Bolshevik system" that could not be fought "according to the customary conventions of European warfare." This struggle extended and continued to the rear, where snipers were assassinating German soldiers and partisans were trying to sabotage vital transports. Bolsheviks who had managed to stay behind in the occupied territories were "using terror to unsettle" the civilian population. They were also disrupting agricultural and factory production, thereby "recklessly fostering famine in cities." Von Manstein charged that by virtue of their pivotal position in Soviet society the Jews were the chief "conduits" between the partisans and the remnants of the Red Army. They also constituted "a nucleus for unrest and possible insurgency." Von Manstein repeated von Reichenau's injunction to wreak vengeance on the Jews as well as his clarion call to "exterminate [ausrotten] Judeobolshevism once and for all."

The senior commanders ordered or sanctioned this totalization of war, and the field officers implemented it. On November 23 the 290th Infantry Division ordered its battle zone "cleared of all civilians," with the warning that "any civilian (man, woman, or child) found in the security zone after December 11 will be considered a partisan, and summarily shot." On November 26, in the face of growing partisan activity, the XXX Army Corps ordered a massive arrest of hostages in all occupied localities: "all individuals related to partisans"; "all individuals suspected of being in contact with partisans"; "all members of the party and the Komsomol, as well as party caretakers"; "all former party members"; and "all individuals who occupied official positions before the arrival of German and Rumanian troops." These hostages were to be held "in concentration camps." For every German or Rumanian soldier killed by a partisan, ten of these hostages were to be executed, and for every German or Rumanian soldier wounded, one hostage was to be shot. The executions were to take place near the spot where the act of terrorism had been committed and the corpses of the hostages were to remain on public view for three days. On December 13, partisan attacks also prompted the II Army Corps to take merciless reprisals: entire communities were burned down and "their entire male populations between the ages of sixteen and fifty years" were shot.

With the failure of Operation Typhoon the Germans also set about systematic plunder and destruction. On December 29, before starting a strategic withdrawal, the men of the 7th Panzer Division were ordered to confiscate "the furs and lined boots of the civil population (to be deloused before distribution) and to seize all horses, sleds, and wagons." They were also to seize "all available cattle and other victuals." The rearguard was instructed to "level all villages . . . and to destroy all remaining vehicles, cattle and provisions, as well as all bridges, crossings, barriers, etc." By January 16, 1942, this division had special commandos (Sonderkommandos) to burn down villages and towns.

The spiraling mistreatment of Soviet prisoners of war was part of this rising fury. It was, of course, generated by the nonmilitary causes and end purposes of Barbarossa. When planning their campaign Hitler's generals had been too ideologically intoxicated and self-confident to make provisions to care for the masses of prisoners they meant and had to capture. This military malpractice was to have catastrophic consequences, especially once the blitzkrieg stalled. But even before then, during the heyday of Barbarossa, the generals took a step that was in keeping with the crusading character of the war. Following negotiations between Lieutenant General Hermann Reinecke, chief of the prisoner-of-war section in the OKW, and Heinrich Müller, chief of the Gestapo, the Wehrmacht licensed the security services to screen Soviet POWs. On July 17 Heydrich issued a directive setting up special commandos to comb prisoner camps for "political criminals and other disreputable elements . . . , for individuals who could be used for the reconstruction of occupied territories . . . , and for reliable elements to serve as informers in the camps . . . and eventually also in the occupied territories." Heydrich left no doubt, however, that his principal objective was to identify dangerous, subversive, and undesirable elements, as follows: "all important functionaries of the state and the party, in particular professional revolutionaries . . . ; all former political commissars in the Red Army [and] the leading personalities . . . of the state bureaucracy . . . ; and the Soviet intelligentsia, all Jews, [and] all persons proven to be agitators or fanatical Communists." These elements were to be subjected to "special treatment." Heydrich specified that "executions are not to be carried out in or near prison camps."

Before long, the effects of this politically charged "selection" (Aussonderung) of prisoners for special treatment, notably killing, was compounded by the brutalization of prisoners due to the German command's initial negligence and the quickening barbarization of the war at large. Hunger, cold, and disease became the biggest killers, especially since many of the Soviet prisoners were wasted or sick before their capture. In early August the minimum ration was fixed at an inadequate 2,000 calories, but even that standard was never really met. By October 21 it was lowered to 500 calories. In the meantime, on September 8 General Reinecke issued guidelines for the handling of Soviet prisoners of war. Insisting that they had no claim to being treated as "honorable soldiers," Reinecke prescribed that there be a "ruthless and energetic" reaction to "the slightest sign of contumacy, especially by Bolshevik instigators." He ordered that any such restiveness as well as "active or passive resistance be crushed *at once* and thoroughly by the use of weapons (bayonet, rifle butt, firearm)." As for prisoners trying to escape, they were "to be shot *instantly, without prior summons to halt.*"

Between June 22 and the end of the year the Wehrmacht took well over 3 million prisoners. Over half of these prisoners were dead by February 1942, the bulk of them having perished since September. By November 25, 1941, Molotov, the Soviet commissar of foreign affairs, had good reason to protest the "outrageous bestialities and mistreatments which the German military command and government are inflicting deliberately on the captured officers and men of the Red Army." No doubt he exaggerated when he charged that prisoners "are being tortured with hot irons; that their eyes are being gouged out; that their legs, arms, ears, and noses are being hacked off; and that their bellies are being slit open." But there was no exaggeration in Molotov's claim that "many prisoners are dying of exhaustion, . . . that the disabled are being shot on the spot, . . . and that for lack of medical treatment in German prison camps, the sick and wounded are condemned to die of typhus, dysentery, pneumonia, and other diseases."

While most Soviet prisoners died of "natural" or "nonviolent" causes, over 100,000 of them, possibly as many as 200,000, were deliberately maltreated and killed in captivity. Among the specially selected victims, there were many thousands of Jews, though their exact number remains unknown. Some of these victims were shot immediately or soon after capture; others were sent to concentration camps for detention or execution. In September and October 1941 about 10,000 Soviet prisoners were killed in Sachsenhausen, Buchenwald, Flossenbürg, Mauthausen, and Auschwitz.

Nazi Germany treated none of its other prisoners of war, be they French or Polish, with anything approaching the premeditated and pitiless cruelty it visited on its Russian captives. Admittedly, the Soviet government had never signed the Geneva conventions. Even so, as a signatory, Germany was bound by them. Besides, on July 17, 1941, the same day that Heydrich issued his screening order, the Soviet government, through the good offices of the Swedish government, assured Berlin that it would respect the generally recognized international principles for the treatment of war prisoners. And certainly, having captured few prisoners in 1941, the Red Army offered its enemy little if any excuse for retaliation. To be sure, there were excesses on the Soviet side, including scattered shootings after capture. But these atrocities were random. They were ordered by individual political commissars enraged by German brutalities and they were reproved, not sanctioned, by higher authorities.

Several high German officers were appalled and incensed by their own side's willful mistreatment of enemy prisoners, which violated their military ethos and was a blot on what remained of the Wehrmacht's honor. On September 15, Admiral Wilhelm Canaris, chief of counterintelligence at the OKW, questioned the wisdom of violating international norms and military traditions, as prescribed by the Reinecke-Heydrich directives. But General Keitel instantly and peremptorily dismissed his veiled remonstrance: whereas the "scruples [of Canaris] are in accordance with the soldierly concepts appropriate to a chivalrous war," they were out of season in this campaign "for the annihilation [*Vernichtung*] of a *Weltanschauung.*"

In this all-out war, fueled by the crusading fire, the Wehrmacht recognized fewer and fewer limits to warfare, except as regards the use of gas in military combat. The officers of the German army readily accepted, indeed solicited, the help of irregular political warriors to decimate prisoners of war and strike at real and imagined ideological enemies behind the lines. The SS, above all, seized upon the army's obsession with deterring sabotage and assassinations by Soviet guerrillas to press their own drive against Bolsheviks and Jews. As early as mid-July 1941 Hitler asserted that the partisan war declared by Stalin had "the advantage of offering us the opportunity to exterminate [*auszurotten*] whatever stands in our way." Before long, Himmler and Heydrich began to deflect the Einsatzgruppen and security forces from hunting down political and ideological enemies generally to persecuting and murdering Jews in particular. This redefinition and narrowing of the mission of the Third Reich's political warriors, including their non-German helpers, was contingent on the support of the Wehrmacht and the Waffen-SS.

The drive for eastern *Lebensraum* kept enlarging and complicating the Nazi regime's "Jewish question." With the conquest of Poland, close to 2 million Jews had fallen to Germany. For twenty months the German civil administration ruthlessly ghettoized and relocated Polish Jews, pending their removal as part of Berlin's iron resolve to make the heartland of the expanding Third Reich *judenfrei* by expulsion and resettlement. Meanwhile, however, the Nazis had many times more unwanted Jews on their hands than they had ever anticipated.

The conquest of Russia could only compound their conundrum. In June 1941 the Soviet Union had a Jewish population of about 5 million, or two and a half times the number of Jews acquired by

Germany with the conquest of the western part of Poland. Before 1939 Russia counted roughly 3 million Jews, of whom about 2 million were concentrated in Belorussia, the Ukraine, and the Crimea. The seizure of eastern Poland, ratified by the Nazi-Soviet Pact, brought Russia another 1.2 to 1.5 million Jews, to whom were added the 300,000 to 350,000 Jewish refugees from German-occupied Poland. In 1940, when Stalin extended his security perimeter still farther, Russia's Jewish population increased by another 550,000: there were about 250,000 Jews in Bessarabia, about 50,000 in northern Bukovina, and about 250,000 in the three Baltic states, three-fifths of them in Lithuania.

Inevitably, and fatally, about 4 million of Russia's 5 million Jews were concentrated in territories that were overrun by the Wehrmacht or became bloody theaters of war. Nearly 90 percent of them were urban, and they lived in cities and towns that became vital military objectives by virtue of their strategic importance as communication and economic centers.

The Germans may not have been any better prepared for this additional mass of Jews than they had been for the Polish Jews in 1939. To be sure, throughout the territories recently seized from the Soviets, the profile of the Jews was still essentially the same as that in German-occupied Poland, with which they were now familiar and which they imagined conformed with their scurrilous stereotype of the Ostjuden. But how much did the SS know about the transformation and integration of Soviet Jewry east of the pre-1939 borders? There, between 35 and 40 percent of working Jews were functionaries and employees, over 12 percent practiced the professions, and over 20 percent were factory workers. At most, 20 percent of the Jewish labor force were artisans, most of them organized in cooperatives, while over 70 percent were salary and wage earners. To the extent that the Nazis were aware of this new occupational structure of Russian Jewry, this awareness merely reinforced their extravagant notions about the sway of Jews in Soviet polity and society.

The Wehrmacht did not invade Russia, any more than it had invaded Poland, in order to enable the SS to implement a blueprint for the entrapment and murder of the maximum number of Jews. The mission of the Wehrmacht was infinitely wider in scope, even if less savage, than the "mere" extermination of the Jews, and so was the mission of the SS. Licensed to operate both in the fighting zones and to the rear, in the occupied territories the Einsatzgruppen were responsible for general pacification. This meant gathering political and economic intelligence, liquidating hostile and suspect elements, and preventing the organization of resistance behind the lines. On July 2,

1941, Heydrich ordered his commandos to concentrate on executing "all functionaries of the Comintern; the higher, middle, and radical lower functionaries of the party, the central committees, the provincial and territorial committees; people's commissars; Jews occupying party and state positions; other radical elements (saboteurs, propagandists, snipers, terrorists, agitators, etc.)." Two weeks later the SS was asked to prepare to take charge of all Soviet territories which the Wehrmacht was about to turn over to civil administration. These were to be subjugated and enslaved with the methods devised and tested in Poland. Himmler would be in full command as both chief of the protean security forces and Reich commissar for the consolidation of Germandom, responsible for all settlement and resettlement policies. But by and by, unlike in Poland, the setbacks of the blitzkrieg prompted the would-be civil administration of Himmler and Heydrich to give priority to the conjoined drive against partisans and war against the Jews, with the former being used as the principal pretext for the latter until the end of 1941.

The Wehrmacht captured Soviet-occupied eastern Poland without difficulty. Because of the speed of the German advance and the accompanying chaos, few Jews managed to escape. The Jews of all of Poland were now in German hands, except for about 450,000. As previously noted, before the invasion the Soviets had relocated or deported some 300,000 Polish Jews to the east. After the assault they evacuated perhaps another 150,000 inland, most of them functionaries and skilled workers. It is difficult to say how many Jews from eastern Poland were drafted into the Red Army, and their fate remains unknown. Since most of the Baltic region had been captured as swiftly as eastern Poland, nearly all Jews fell to Germany there as well.

In some other regions a certain number of Jews succeeded in leaving ahead of the Wehrmacht. Winning time and space were as critical for the flight and evacuation of Jews as for military defense. Although the German armies quickly overran most of the Baltic, eastern Poland, and parts of the western Ukraine, the Red Army forced them to reduce the pace of their advance beyond Smolensk, in the central and eastern Ukraine, and in parts of the southeast. It was not uncommon for 70 to 90 percent of the Jewish population of the cities and towns of these areas to get out in good time. Such was the case in Baranovichi, Minsk, and Mogilev; in Vinnitsa, Zhitomir, and Berdichev; and in Kiev, Kharkov, and Dnepropetrovsk.

The longer it took the Germans to encircle or capture an area or a city, the greater the number of Jews who fled on their own or were evacuated in the interest of the Soviet war effort. Of course, a great deal depended on the availability of transport and other services controlled by the Soviet civil and military authorities. Wherever there was industry, officials evacuated workers and cadres, among whom the number of Jews was disproportionately high. This organized removal of valuable manpower combined with the military draft radically shifted the balance in the remaining Jewish communities in favor of women, children, and the aged. The extent to which Moscow made special efforts to evacuate endangered Jews is still unclear. All in all, about 1.5 million Jews are estimated to have fled or been evacuated from the territories that were first captured by enemy forces and then scourged by local vigilantes, Einsatzgruppen, and commandos of the RSHA (Reich Central Security Office).

Although from its inception Barbarossa carried a lethal anti-Jewish charge, the assault on the Jews did not explode with the same immediate virulence as the attack on Soviet Russia. The start of Barbarossa did not mark the start of a further aggravation of the Jewish condition either in Old Germany or in any of the annexed and occupied territories. Nor were there any plans to massacre the Jews who were certain to be trapped by the lightning sweep into and through the territories that Moscow had seized since 1939. In various places there were savage pogroms immediately following the arrival of German troops. But these instant and unpremeditated pogroms, reminiscent of those attending the conquest of Poland in September 1939, were the work of local vigilantes, not of the Wehrmacht or the Einsatzgruppen.

Not that the Germans were innocent. Apart from the fact that their furious invasion created conditions of violence and lawlessness favorable to anti-Semitic excesses, here and there Nazi officers or security officials actively condoned or encouraged attacks on the Jews. Still, during the first four to five weeks, while Operation Barbarossa went like clockwork, there were no systematic, SS-directed massacres of Jews of the sort that were perpetrated once the German forces crossed into pre-1939 Russia and ran into stiff resistance. Except for northern Bukovina and Bessarabia, which reverted to Rumania, these forward territories were turned over to a rudimentary civil administration on the Polish model, Galicia actually being added to the General Government of Hans Frank. The latter's repressive regimen was to be applied to the Jews of the whole buffer zone until after the anticipated German victory, when they were to be deported, along with all Polish Jews, to the far interior of Russia, in accordance with the Third Reich's unfolding plans for the settlement and resettlement of populations in its eastern *Lebensraum*.

These early pogroms were well-nigh confined to the territories annexed by Russia under the Nazi-Soviet Pact. This rimland stretching from the Baltic in the north to the Black Sea in the south was destined to be one of the most contested and hapless terrains of the second Thirty Years War. Between 1917 and 1920 it had been ravaged by revolutionary conflicts and national rivalries related to the collapse of the Romanov and Habsburg empires and the temporary infirmity of Germany. Throughout the interwar years the lands and peoples of these eastern marches were ruled, as we saw, by regimes that were conservative or reactionary in domestic affairs and anti-Soviet in international politics. During the climacteric of Europe's general crisis in the 1930s, the political classes of these regimes yielded to the fascist temptation and refused to help to contain Nazi Germany at the expense of collaborating with Soviet Russia. In any event, in these borderlands little was done to exorcise the ancient demon of Judeophobia, and in the thirties far-rightists summoned up this evil spirit to fuel the fires of their politically motivated anti-Semitism.

When occupying these marchlands in 1939–40, the Soviets came up against civil and political societies that, to a large extent, were anti-Russian, anti-Communist, and anti-Semitic. Not surprisingly, there was a disproportionate number of Jews in the left-wing opposition between the wars as well as among local collaborators with the Soviets between 1939 and 1941. As it turned out, the Soviets had little time to create an environment less hostile to Jews as they rushed military preparations in the lands they had seized to provide their vulnerable borders of 1920 with a defensive buffer.

The hostility of large segments of the local populations to their self-appointed Soviet Russian protectors facilitated Nazi Germany's military conquest and the political subjugation of most of Stalin's forward bastion. Among them there were fewer pro-Germans and pro-Nazis—or pro-Rumanians—than there were anti-Russians, anti-Bolsheviks, and anti-Semites. Despite widespread apprehension about the Third Reich's *Drang nach Osten*, there was considerable sympathy and support for its drive against "Judeobolshevism" in general and the Jews in particular. In many cities and towns of Lithuania, far western Belorussia, and the far western Ukraine, local vigilantes and militias took advantage of their "liberation" by the Germans to attack known and suspected Bolsheviks as well as to massacre Jews, allegedly for collaborating with the Soviets. Contrary to common military practice, the Wehrmacht failed or refused to stop or restrain these atrocities.

As for the Einsatzgruppen, they applauded and encouraged these murderous assaults, even if they instigated or masterminded only a few of them. It is not clear whether the leaders of the SS action squads had planned beforehand to make use of native thugs. But once they saw them at work, they recruited them as auxiliaries, in part because they soon realized that their own personnel was unequal to their growing task. In due time in the north Einsatzgruppe A hired Lithuanians, Latvians, and Estonians as executioners, while in the center and the far south Einsatzgruppen C and D enlisted the services of Ukrainians and "ethnic" Germans. Although in Bessarabia and north Bukovina the Rumanians seem not to have resorted to native helpers, they were confident of their sympathy.

The first outbreak of large-scale violence against the Jews took place in Kovno. The capital of Lithuania after Poland annexed Vilna in 1920, Kovno had a population of about 110,000, of which over one-quarter was Jewish. On June 23, 1941, when evacuating the city, Soviet troops and political cadres were attacked by local partisans who were both ultranationalists and fascists. Led by Klimaitis, these partisans took advantage of the political vacuum to seize control of Kovno and avenge Moscow's reannexation of their country by setting upon local Communists and Jews. The assault on the Jews started on the night of June 25 and continued through the evening of June 29. During these four days and four nights some 3,800 Jews were murdered while synagogues and Jewish homes were set on fire. Hundreds of Jews were beaten to death in the streets and public squares of Kovno, but most of the others were taken to the Seventh Fort to be shot. Simultaneously, another 1,200 Jews were killed in nearby towns. Within about a week, between July 4 and 6, Lithuanian murder gangs slaughtered "2,930 Jews and 47 Jewesses."

On October 15 SS Brigadier General Dr. Franz Walther Stahlecker, commander in chief of Einsatzgruppe A, informed his superiors that he had persuaded reticent "local anti-Semitic elements to start [their initial] pogroms against the Jews." Likewise, at the end of the year SS Colonel Karl Jäger, chief of Einsatzkommando 3, reported that while in Kovno he had prevailed on Lithuanian partisans to undertake the massacre of July 4 to 6. Since by the time they drafted their reports the brutalization of war, including the mass killing of Jews, was official policy, probably both Stahlecker and Jäger claimed excessive credit for what the Lithuanians were inclined and able to do on their own, especially since there was neither army nor police to restrain them. Admittedly, on July 8 General Franz von Roques, commander of the forces to the rear of the advancing Northern Army Group, complained to Field Marshal von Leeb about "the massive executions of Jews in Kovno (thousands!) by Lithuanian partisan bands [Schutzverbände] at the instigation of German police authorities." When recording this remonstrance in his diary, von Leeb disingenuously remarked that "we [i.e., the Wehrmacht] have no influence on these measures and have no other choice but to keep our distance." Significantly he also noted that "Roques quite correctly believes that the Jewish question cannot be solved in this fashion and that the sterilization of all Jewish males would be the surest way to solve it." Obviously, German generals were not beyond conceiving and entertaining the idea of a "definitive" solution, albeit one less bloody and instantaneous than outright murder.

Whatever the license offered by the Wehrmacht and the encouragement given by the SS, the assaults on the Jews in and around Kovno, as well as those in Vilna, were essentially wild pogroms perpetrated by self-styled Lithuanian "freedom fighters." These early massacres were more in the nature of a resumption of the Civil War and foreign intervention in Russia after World War One than a calculated first step in Nazi Germany's willful and systematic liquidation of European Jewry. The Lithuanian partisans, like their Latvian counterparts in Riga, were traditional, not racial, anti-Semites. They killed Jews not to further any policy of systematic extermination, but as part of their unbroken battle against Communist and (Soviet) Russian encroachment. Apparently, their victims were primarily adult males.

After another deadly pogrom which claimed several hundred additional Jewish men, the German security forces herded Kovno's Jews into a ghetto in the outlying Viliampol district. All Jews were ordered to wear the Star of David, presumably to facilitate the identification of Jews seeking to slip back into the center of town. While the Wehrmacht and Einsatzgruppen charged ahead, the RSHA regulars ghettoized the Jews of Lithuania and Latvia, apparently without any thought of exterminating them after victory, which was believed to be close at hand. Of course, as of late October the Ninth Fort in Kovno and Rumbuli Forest near Riga became the sites of mass executions on the model and scale of Babi Yar outside Kiev. By then, however, the military drive against the Soviets had taken a disastrous turn, and with it the fate of the Jews.

The lot of the Jews was the same farther south, in Eastern Galicia. Lvov was the capital of this former Polish province. Not including the Jews who fled there from western Poland in September–October 1939, Lvov counted over 100,000 Jews in a population of 300,000, making it the third-largest Jewish center of interwar Poland, after Warsaw and Łódź. The Wehrmacht captured the city by the end of June, leaving little time for escape. Lvov also had a substantial Ukrainian minority which, not unlike the Polish majority, had spawned a movement of resistance to the Soviet occupation, some of whose activists were imprisoned and deported. Immediately after the German occupation local Ukrainians organized a militia to fight the "common enemy." Like the Jews of Kovno, Vilna, and Riga, the Jews of Lvov were traduced for having been, and continuing to be, among the major carriers of communism and collaborators of Soviet Russia. On July 2 and 3, apparently with considerable popular support, the Ukrainian vigilantes tortured and killed at least 7,000 Jews in an action that was part militia riot, part pogrom. While the German security forces probably did not foment this massacre—the action commandos of Einsatzgruppe C had not arrived as yet—neither they nor the military did anything to put a stop to it. But again, it is worth noting that in Lvov the Ukrainian bands acted in the spirit of Simon Petlura rather than Reinhard Heydrich, both in early July and in a second murderous action of July 25. Analogous pogroms occurred in Drogabych, Krzemieniec, and Tarnopol, three smaller East Galician towns, where Ukrainian ruffians slaughtered 200 Jews, allegedly to avenge their recent sufferings and defeats at the hands of Soviet Russians and Poles. Following these and many other atrocities, it was left to Hans Frank to ghettoize and brutally hyperexploit the Jews of Eastern Galicia, when this province became the fifth district of his General Government on August 1, 1941.

In the far south of the rimland and of Barbarossa's front line, Rumanian soldiers and paramilitary fascists massacred Jews without Nazi German encouragement or coaching. Rumania was territorially the most overextended and militarily the least endangered country of eastern and east-central Europe. Even so, it turned into a towering outpost of autocratic fascism. The growth of the Iron Guard and its brutal but circumspect domestication by Marshal Ion Antonescu were profoundly indigenous. At best, they benefited from Nazi Germany's éclat and Soviet Russia's seizure of Bessarabia and northern Bukovina. Antonescu, who prided himself on being a barbarian, resolved to collaborate with the Third Reich to reconquer the two provinces recently repossessed by Stalin and to use anti-Semitism to further his conservative national revival. But his barbarism and anti-Semitism were of an old-fashioned sort, certainly compared to Hitler's. Of all the satellites, Rumania made by far the largest military contribution to Barbarossa. In return, Antonescu and his inveterate collaborators counted on recovering the two lost provinces. But rather than have the expansion leave Rumania with an additional 400,000 Jews, Bucharest proposed to forcibly deport these Jews to other territories to be conquered from Russia.

The massacre of the Jews of Jassy, synchronous with the massacre in Kovno, was intimately connected with the invasion of Russia. The capital of Moldavia, Jassy was located twelve miles within the borders of Old Rumania. It had a population of 80,000, of which more than half was Jewish. From June 22 to 29, when Rumanian troops at last succeeded in crossing the Pruth into Bessarabia, the city suffered several air attacks. Local Iron Guardists lost no time accusing the Jews of Jassy of being active fifth columnists for the Red Army. In any case, on June 29 Rumanian soldiers and policemen proceeded to round up Jews indiscriminately and march them to assembly points at which they crammed them into sealed trains for deportation to the interior, away from the front lines. Apart from the scores of Jews maltreated and killed during the roundup, between 2,000 and 4,000 Jews—exclusively adult males—are estimated to have died from suffocation during their tortured passage.

Once the Rumanian army crossed the frontiers of the Regat, or the Old Kingdom, pogroms became a regular occurrence. During the first week of July there were pogroms in several towns and cities of Bukovina in which hundreds of Jews were killed. Starting on July 5, it was the turn of Czernowitz, the capital of Bukovina, whose population of 100,000 was about half Jewish. Within a few days about 2,000 Jews were murdered, and hundreds more were killed during the following weeks. By this time a special commando of Einsatzgruppe D had arrived on the scene, but it is unclear what role it actually played.

On Rumania's central front, east of the Prut River in Bessarabia, Jewish communities suffered the same fate. In the district and city of Belcy the Rumanian savagery became so brutal as to horrify several German officers, who feared for the morale of their troops. On July 17 a combined Rumano-German force captured Kishinev, the capital of Bessarabia, with a population of 130,000, 60 percent of it Jewish. It is not clear how many Jews left with the retreating Soviet forces, nor how many of these were recaptured later. In any case, still haunted by the memory of the pogrom of 1903—in which about forty-five Jews had been beaten to death and hundreds more wounded—the Jews of Kishinev feared the worst. During the weeks following the occupation the Rumanians killed thousands of Jews, probably in either connivance or collaboration with an action commando of Einsatzgruppe D.

At about this time the pogroms attendant on the reconquest of northern Bukovina and Bessarabia came to an end. Within a few weeks, beginning sometime in August, the Rumanians started to deport the Jews from both provinces to a territory carved out of the conquered Ukraine and bounded by the Dniester, the Bug, and the Black Sea. Hitler provisionally ceded this space, to be known as Transnistria, to Antonescu, to create a reserve for Jews, patterned after the abortive Lublin reserve. Conditions were execrable during the forced marches and transports beyond the Dniester as well as in the camps of Transnistria, and they grew progressively worse once the adversities of war increased.

The Magyar power elite was not to be outdone by its Rumanian counterpart. The leaders of Hungary rushed to take advantage of their junior partnership in Barbarossa to resettle their foreign and stateless Jews in another Ukrainian territory to be relinquished by the Germans. Many of these Jews were refugees from lands recently conquered by Nazi Germany. During the month of August, Budapest deported nearly 18,000 non-Hungarian Jews, primarily but not exclusively from annexed Carpathian Ruthenia, to Kőrösmező, near the Polish border. By prior agreement with Berlin they were to be taken from there to Kamenets-Podolsk, southwest of Tarnopol. The local German authorities balked, insisting that the deportation interfered with military operations, which precluded their making the necessary preparations. But except for diverting a few thousand Jews to forced labor battalions, the Hungarians stood their ground, with the result that over 10,000 Jews were handed over to an action commando of Einsatzgruppe C, which slaughtered them on August 27–28.

This massacre at Kamenets-Podolsk was clearly and unequivocally the work of German security forces and their Ukrainian helpers. It was the outcome of negotiations between Major General Eduard Wagner, the quartermaster general of the OKH, and SS General Friedrich Jeckeln, Higher SS and police chief for the Ukraine, at Vinnitsa on July 25, in the thick of the difficult and lagging drive for Kiev, and as such it was conditioned by the barbarization of the war. As for the determination of the Regent Miklós Horthy and Premier László Bárdossy to forcibly repatriate or resettle Hungary's alien and stateless Jews, at the time they could neither have known nor suspected that this reckless resettlement would or could result in the death of the deportees.

Unquestionably and infamously, during the first five weeks of the eastern campaign more Jews were killed or sent to their death than during the twenty-two months since the outbreak of war. But as we have seen, although the Wehrmacht and Einsatzgruppen created the enabling conditions for this bloodshed, they were neither its principal organizers nor its chief perpetrators. In the early, triumphant days of Barbarossa the Jewish massacres were the product of random pogroms rather than of an official plan or warrant for systematic genocide. The main malfeasants were refractory Latvians, Lithuanians, Estonians, Ukrainians, and Rumanians who took advantage of the crusading war against the Soviet Union and exploited the residues of age-old Judeophobia to advance a cause that was both ultranationalist and fascist. The killing of Jews was not their end purpose; it may not even have been one of their foremost objectives. Having allowed the pogroms to run their course, the German conquerors proceeded to ghettoize and torment the Jews of the Baltic countries and of Galicia. They also ceded part of their conquered *Lebensraum* to Antonescu to resettle the Jews of northern Bukovina and Bessarabia and to Horthy to resettle the Jews of Carpathian Ruthenia. It is highly unlikely that Hitler, Himmler, and Heydrich conceived of this ruthless quarantine as a cunning holding operation in a premeditated plan for the extermination of European Jewry, to be carried out after the approaching victory over the Soviet Union.

There was a marked escalation of anti-Jewish violence by the Germans themselves once their armies and security forces crossed into the territories east of Russia's pre-1939 borders. Soon after sweeping through the forward zone, their juggernaut met with stiffer resistance. The invaders came upon methodically deployed defensive positions manned by troops ready for battle. In addition, unlike in the buffer zone, where much of the local population was hostile to the Soviets or favored the Germans, farther east, in Russia proper, Soviet soldiers fought with the support of their own people in an atmosphere of resurgent patriotism. The Germans now entered territories in which the Bolsheviks had had twenty years to implant their regime, having fostered popular loyalties with a mixture of persuasion and coercion. As they advanced into Soviet Belorussia, the Russian Ukraine, and the Crimea, the invaders found ever fewer collaborators and ran into defiant populations and partisans. The Wehrmacht and the Einsatzgruppen did not really engage the Bolshevik enemy in all his manifestations until after they reached these territories beyond the pre-1939 borders. Here the Jews were an integral part of the political society to be destroyed and the civil society to be subjugated. Although a high percentage of Jews escaped or were evacuated, those staying on or left behind became the most visible and accessible civilian victims of the crusade against "Judeobolshevism," in particular once the military campaign slowed or faltered.

At the start of Barbarossa, von Bock's Central Army Group had what was considered to be the most important and urgent assignment along the 1,500-mile front: the capture of Moscow. With fifty divisions, nine panzer and six motorized divisions among them, it was the largest and most power-packed of the three major army groups. The first major objective was Smolensk, to be taken with a pincer movement that would also trap and destroy the large Soviet forces concentrated in this vital sector. Splitting his group in two, von Bock launched a northern force toward Vitebsk and a southern force in the direction of Minsk and Orsha. They got a running start by cutting through Soviet-occupied Poland, the northern force seizing Białystok and Grodno, the southern force Brest-Litovsk and, moving northeast to circumvent the Pripet Marshes, Baranovichi.

Even without the benefit of a Trojan horse, the Wehrmacht overran this center sector of the buffer zone quite as swiftly as it had the northern and southern sectors. German troops occupied Białystok, a city with about 50,000 Jews, on June 27. That same day, in two separate actions, a Wehrmacht unit and an action commando of Einsatzgruppe B massacred about 2,000 Jews. Manifestly, this early massacre was entirely a German affair, and as such runs counter to the argument that the Einsatzgruppen did not begin their mass killings of Jews until late summer 1941. What accounts for this premonitory wholesale murder of Jews in Białystok at purely German hands?

The panzers crossed the pre-1939 Russo-Polish border without difficulty, capturing Minsk, Bobruisk, and Mogilev. They encountered their first serious resistance at Vitebsk and Orsha, forming the base of a triangle ahead of Smolensk. It was to take until mid-July to capture these three cities, by which time at least half of their Jewish populations had left.

There were no random pogroms or controlled liquidations in these or any other Belorussian cities. Individual Jews, mostly adult men, were killed in many places. But these killings were not confined to Jews, and were in any case nothing like those farther north and south. Instead, the Jews were stigmatized, humiliated, and, above all, confined to ghettos. This confinement lasted about three to four months, until the military campaign was in serious difficulty. Then, around mid-October, special and action commandos of Einsatzgruppe B started decimating the Jewish communities of Soviet Belorussia by murdering not only men but women, children, and the aged as well. The ghetto of Minsk was among the few to be largely spared. By the end of the year a large percentage of the Belorussian Jews were dead, and those who remained alive were enclosed and tormented in ghettos.

While the Central Army Group had run into difficulties in its drive to Smolensk, these were negligible compared to those encountered by the Southern Army Group in its drive to Kiev. Perhaps the best divisions of the Red Army were deployed west of the Ukrainian capital along a line running due south from Korosten through Zhitomir and Berdichev to Vinnitsa. All at once, the German advance was seriously slowed down, the panzers having difficulties drawing closer to Kiev and encircling it. The Soviets refused to surrender Korosten and Zhitomir until late July. And although presently they also yielded

Vinnitsa, they succeeded in forcing the Germans to enlarge the radius of their encirclement of Kiev to Uman and Poltava, which took them further south and east than originally planned. The battle for Kiev was the first to cost the Wehrmacht dearly in men and equipment. But more important still was the loss of precious time and self-assurance.

The Jews of the Ukraine were fated to be engulfed and victimized by one of the truly momentous battles of the second Thirty Years War. Because the Germans were significantly slowed down, in the western Ukraine over three-quarters of the Jews managed to leave in good time. Further east an even higher percentage escaped. But those who stayed on or were left behind were trapped, for they were concentrated in cities and towns that were crossroads of vital strategic importance. Before the war, the embattled Ukrainian cities had been heavily Jewish: Poltava 28 percent, Vinnitsa 39 percent, Zhitomir 42 percent, Uman 57 percent, and Berdichev 65 percent. The last-minute exodus drastically cut these percentages, reducing each of these Jewish communities from between 20,000 and 28,000 to between 5,000 and 10,000. Their demographic balance was also greatly unsettled since there was probably a preponderance of adult males among those who were evacuated and escaped.

The hard-fought and delayed capture of these cities was soon followed by mass killings of Jews, because the Einsatzgruppen practically moved in with the army or Waffen-SS. These massacres were carried out by members of the action commandos of Einsatzgruppe C with the help of Ukrainian auxiliaries. Characteristically, the first large-scale massacre took place in Zhitomir, the first major strategic intersection at which the Wehrmacht was fought off more than momentarily. Within two weeks the Germans murdered about 3,000 Jews in Zhitomir, a much larger number than in the other cities about to be captured. But these massacres soon ended and the traumatized Jewish communities were enclosed in ghettos. Six weeks later, however, the killing resumed. The remaining Jews of Zhitomir were slaughtered on September 19, those of Uman on September 22, and those of Berdichev on October 5. By this time Barbarossa had run aground, most seriously in the theater of the Southern Army Group. Significantly, von Reichenau, the most prominent field general to press for the extreme brutalization of warfare, was in command of the overstrained Sixth Army fighting its way toward Kiev.

The pattern and scale of Jewish massacres was similar in Kiev. Before the war the capital of the Ukraine had a population of 600,000, of whom about 25 percent, over 150,000, were Jews. Of these, between

45,000 and 50,000 stayed on, many of them to contribute to the defense of their city. The Soviet forces held out for at least a full month after the enemy all but closed the ring around them. Despite heavy losses, Stalin refused to surrender Kiev until September 19. By then Hitler and his closest military and political associates were furious, for their timetable and battle plans had been thrown into extreme disarray by this prolonged and improbable resistance. Almost immediately, insult was added to injury: on September 24 the embarrassingly difficult and late capture of Kiev was followed by a chain of explosions in the heart of the city. The blasts were so powerful that entire city blocks were ravaged, including buildings housing offices of the German military command and security forces. Hundreds of German officers and men were killed, some of them while fighting the raging flames.

This additional defiance and humiliation came at the time when the Germans were intensifying their mistreatment of the "common enemy." It was on September 16 that General Keitel had issued the order to repress any act of real or suspected partisan resistance summarily and mercilessly, insisting that "life is cheap" in the east and that for the "life of each German soldier between 50 and 100 Communists" should be shot. Given their mission and disposition, the accompanying security forces needed no special warrant for reprisal.

Almost certainly, the explosions in central Kiev were set off by delayed-action mines planted by the Red Army or the KGB under buildings that had once served as their own headquarters. Although the German authorities, in particular the military command, knew better, they held the Jews responsible for this spectacular counterblow, which lashed them into a fury. True to form, the SS officials urged that the Jews be taken hostage and made the chosen victims for reprisal, thereby discouraging the resistance of the rest of the population, which was the larger target. This suggestion came all the more naturally to the SS since in many recently captured towns of the western Ukraine they were making Jews pay for the Red Army's tenacious military resistance. In addition, in their hot pursuit of dangerous "Judeobolsheviks," they found it easier to catch unarmed Jewish civilians than Bolsheviks. For one thing, Soviet officials generally either were evacuated or went underground. For another, the Wehrmacht was vigilant in its own right: it assiduously hunted down political commissars and with the help of the SS screened the enemy prisoners for dangerous elements. Besides, being under orders to carry out wholesale reprisals, the military command, which included officers of von Reichenau's Nazi bent, was hardly averse to a mass reckoning.

There is still considerable uncertainty not only about the role of the military in the decision to wreak vengeance on the Jews, but also about the complicity or collaboration of army personnel in the implementation of this decision. At any rate, the leaders of Einsatzkommando 4a of Einsatzgruppe C soon notified their superiors in Berlin that "in retaliation for the arson in Kiev all Jews were arrested and that on September 29 and 30 a total of 33,771 Jews were executed." This laconic report concealed the absolute horror of this quintessential but far-from-unique act of Nazi-German barbarity. The Jews of Kiev were given three days to report to an assembly point. From there they were marched in small groups to a ravine just beyond the city's outskirts. After undressing, the dazed victims were told to clamber, single file, to the mound above this ravine of Babi Yar. As they stepped onto a protruding platform, they were shot in the neck, to fall face down on the preceding row of now lifeless yet still warm corpses below. All but the very young suffered the agony of knowing their ineluctable fate. The dead included a disproportionately large number of children, women, and old people, as many of the young and middle-aged men were in the Red Army or in flight.

In the embattled Ukraine as well as farther east, the Kiev massacre was not out of the ordinary. The Jews suffered a similar fate in four other industrial cities: Dnepropetrovsk, Kharkov, Rostov, and Odessa. The Wehrmacht seized Dnepropetrovsk, halfway between Kiev and Rostov, in mid-September. Einsatzkommando 5 of Einsatzgruppe C was not unleashed until October 13 and 14, perhaps because it was slow in moving into the area. Within a few days a very large percentage of the over 15,000 Jews who had stayed behind were slaughtered. Located on a Donets tributary, Kharkov was occupied on October 24. In mid-December Einsatzkommando 4a moved the Jews of Kharkov to barracks just outside the city. The conditions there were deadly, but the actual massacre of these Jews in the adjoining Travitsk Valley did not begin until February 1942. As for Rostov, it fell to the Germans on November 21, only to be retaken by the Red Army within eight days. Apparently, Einsatzkommando 10a of Einsatzgruppe D murdered most of Rostov's greatly reduced Jewish community during this first occupation.

Odessa and Kiev had much in common. The two cities had the two largest Jewish communities in Russia, Odessa ranking first in absolute as well as relative numbers. Both were of immense strategic and symbolic significance. The Germans had entrusted their Rumanian associates with the capture of Odessa, which was not easy. After a protracted siege the troops of the Fourth Rumanian Army finally entered the city on October 16, by which time the bulk of the Soviet troops had evacuated Odessa by sea, in Dunkirk-like fashion. The result was that Antonescu and his generals were not able to bolster their sagging military reputation, already tarnished in Hitler's eyes, by flaunting a large haul of enemy prisoners. Their frustration was compounded by another instance of Soviet defiance of the sort that had recently exasperated their stalwart allies in Kiev. On October 22, a week after its capture, Odessa was shaken by a powerful explosion which destroyed the building housing Rumanian military headquarters. The mine set by retreating troops or by partisans killed the commanding general of the local Rumanian forces and a score of officers and men, some of them German. Within hours the dead general's deputy notified his superiors that he had taken steps "to hang Jews and Communists" in public. That same night Rumanian security men indiscriminately seized a large number of men and women, both Jews and non-Jews, and either hanged or shot them.

But this was but a first step. Inspired by the Wehrmacht's punitive practices, and probably also aware of the monstrous hecatomb at Babi Yar, Antonescu himself ordered that 200 hostages be executed for every officer killed, and 100 for every victim of lesser rank. Indeed, even before this order was received, it was open season on Communists and, especially, on Jews. On October 23 about 19,000 Jews were herded into an open space near the harbor front. After shooting their prey, the Rumanian blackguards burned them, having first doused them with gasoline. On October 24 and 25 at least the same number of Jews, but probably twice as many, were taken to Dalnic, a village not far beyond the city limits, where some of the victims were gunned down near open ditches and others were burned alive in storehouses.

The nature and degree of German complicity in this joint enormity is uncertain. Although Einsatzkommando 11b of Einsatzgruppe D was on hand, it seems not to have gone into action. The savagery of the Rumanian officers and soldiers was probably fueled less by racial anti-Semitism than by the vengeful fury built into and unleashed by Barbarossa. Their intense animus against bolshevism and Soviet Russia as well as their long-standing Judeophobia predisposed them to capitalize on the ambience and example of Nazi depravity to give free rein to their own hatred. In any event, the Rumanians carried out a massacre that was no less depraved and methodical than the one that the SS operatives had perpetrated at Babi Yar a month earlier. At the same time, Antonescu continued to relocate the Jews of Bessarabia and northern Bukovina to Transnistria despite firsthand knowledge of the worsening conditions throughout the occupied Ukraine.

· · ·

Ab origine and in the first place, the Wehrmacht and its associated armies were fighting to defeat the Red Army, to conquer Russian territories, to destroy the Soviet regime, and to extirpate bolshevism. The Jews became the chosen civilian victims of this furious total war. Political and politicized soldiers of Barbarossa fell upon them because they considered the Jews the primary carriers of the Bolshevik system and ideology—and because they were more vulnerable than other real or imagined carriers. This crusade within the war became ever more vicious and systematic with the unanticipated blockage and soaring ferocity of the military campaign.

Even so, and notwithstanding the unparalleled magnitude of the Jewish suffering, the extermination of eastern Jewry never became the chief objective of Barbarossa. The fight for *Lebensraum* and against bolshevism was neither a pretext nor an expedient for the killing of Jews. Nor was it a mere smoke screen to disguise the Jewish massacres as reprisals against partisans. The assault on the Jews was unquestionably intertwined with the assault on bolshevism from the very outset. But this is not to say that it was the dominant strand in the hybrid "Judeobolshevism" that Barbarossa targeted for destruction. In fact, the war against the Jews was a graft onto or a parasite upon the eastern campaign, which always remained its host, even or especially once it became mired deep in Russia.

When they set forth on their mission, the Einsatzgruppen and the RSHA were not given the extermination of Jews as their principal, let alone their only, assignment. Of course, there was the pre-June agreement in which the Wehrmacht gave Himmler's security forces all but a free hand, notably in the combat zones. But did Himmler and Heydrich press for the motorized action groups to follow close upon the advancing armies primarily to deny the Jews the time and opportunity to escape? True enough, the SS and RSHA commandos rushed into all the captured towns and cities with large Jewish communities. But there were few if any strategically important urban centers without sizable concentrations of Jews. The Einsatzgruppen's entrapment of Jews was in a sense a correlate of their fearfully efficient security sweeps. They killed few Jews in the buffer zone, and even once they penetrated beyond Russia's pre-1939 borders, they initiated their infamous butchery only upon reaching towns and cities captured after heavy fighting. It is not surprising that this costly obstruction infuriated the brazen commanders of both the Wehrmacht and the SS: since January 1933 this was their first encounter with organized, defiant, and deadly resistance. Worse still, this resistance came from ostensibly inferior Slavs and accursed Bolsheviks whom they presumed unfit for survival.

The SS may have had other reasons for waiting so many weeks and putting so many miles behind them before unleashing their cold-blooded wrath. Being few in number, they might be said to have concentrated on rushing forward with the troops to seize the maximum number of Jews, confident that they could soon double back to liquidate all the Jews they had bypassed. In other words, without prior agreement, the Wehrmacht and the SS might be presumed to have practiced the same envelopment strategy: the army seeking to trap the bulk of Soviet troops, cutting off their retreat and devitalizing them in captivity, pending future disposition; the security forces seeking to trap the main body of Soviet Jews with a view to ghettoizing the most accessible among them and liquidating those farther east. In this interpretive construct, ghettoization was a preprogrammed intermediate stage between capture and extermination. But just as the Wehrmacht did not plan the mass murder of Soviet prisoners of war, the SS did not predetermine the genocidal murder of Jews. In the fall and early winter of 1941 the field armies and Einsatzgruppen were driven to their respective but inseparable crimes by the intrinsic enormity and savagery of Barbarossa, compounded by its contingent derailment. Regardless of cost, the socially conservative compact between Hitler and the old elites, dating from 1933, held fast and tempered the Nazi regime's compulsion for absolute war and unlimited conquest.

The Einsatzgruppen and the RSHA were sent into Russia to serve this immutable exigency. Himmler eagerly assumed responsibility for internal security close to the front lines as well as in the rear. This meant that initially the SS proceeded to crush political resisters and their fellow travelers as well as partisans and their helpers. Needless to say, in the newly conquered territories, as in German-conquered western Poland, this repression was bound to be incomparably more ruthless than any such measures had been at home in the Reich. The second step would have been to set up control organs of a more permanent nature, on the model of those devised and established in the General Government.

There was relatively little anti-German political hostility to contend with in the buffer zone. But deeper into Russia and with the Red Army making an ever more resolute stand, the reality and fear of organized resistance and subversion became ever greater. With their stringent friend-enemy mentality, their all-or-nothing temperament, and their belief in Germany's eastern mission, the leaders of the security forces were predisposed to be merciless in their persecution of Bolshevik infidels and their imposition of a new order. As noted above, Stalin's call for partisan warfare behind enemy lines came as a welcome justification for this predetermined policy of extreme violence, and Hitler as much as said so. In sum, just as the war for *Lebensraum* was not a screen for the capture of Soviet Jewry, so the relentless pursuit of Bolsheviks and the implantation of the SS state were not subterfuges designed to facilitate the mass murder of Jews. But as is so often the case in history, origin and intent were not the only or the principal keys to process and outcome.

Given their disproportionate numerical, political, and economic importance in the urban areas of the conquered eastern territories, the Jews were particularly vulnerable. A deeply ingrained hatred of Jews and "Judeobolshevism" inclined the SS commanders to focus their fearsome search-and-kill operations on the Jewish communities in the cities they were charged with pacifying and enslaving. The reversal of military fortunes accentuated this predilection, especially once real Bolsheviks became increasingly difficult to find.

Some security officials realized that it was unrealistic to expect to root out bolshevism and to pacify the occupied territories by murdering the Jews. In mid-September a report from Einsatzgruppe C, operating in the Ukraine, stressed that "even if it were possible to shut out Jewry 100 percent, the center of political danger would not be eliminated." Not only Jews, but "Russians, Georgians, Armenians, Poles, Latvians, [and] Ukrainians" were carriers of bolshevism. Indeed, the report said, "the Bolshevik apparatus is by no means identical with the Jewish population." Such being the case, "the goal of political security" could not be reached "by replacing the main task of destroying the Communist machine with the relatively easier one of eliminating the Jews." This same note stressed that since "in the western and central Ukraine nearly all urban workers, skilled mechanics, and traders are Jews" it would be impossible to "rebuild Ukrainian industry and build up the urban administrative centers" without the full use of this labor. The only alternative, for conquered Soviet territories and the General Government in Poland, would be to pursue the "final solution of the Jewish question through complete labor utilization of the Jews," which, in turn, "would result in a gradual liquidation of Jewry." In mid-December an official of the Armament Inspectorate in the Ukraine similarly questioned the wisdom of a policy of wholesale violence: who would look after production "if we shoot the Jews, let the prisoners of war perish, condemn considerable parts of the urban population to death by starvation, and also lose part of the farming population by hunger next year"?

The massacre of Soviet Jews was closely interrelated not only with the increasing brutality of the military campaign but also with the intensifying mistreatment of the civilian populations. If the mass murder of Jews aroused little indignation, let alone resistance, it was not because it was carefully hidden but because its unique and absolute horror was submerged in an atmosphere of rampant naked violence. The local populations became indifferent to the torment of the Jews less because of any residual Judeophobia than because they, too, were being terrorized and brutalized, even if to a lesser extent. The torture and killing of Jews, allegedly in reprisal for resistance, contributed to this general reign of terror, as did the fearsome presence of the Wehrmacht.

Under the circumstances, it was relatively easy for the numerically insignificant Einsatzgruppen to carry out their assigned task. Their would-be victims were completely at their mercy, and there was no one to restrain them. As we saw, the four action groups combined counted no more than 3,000 men amid an army of over 3 million. To keep up with the panzers, the action commandos had to be mechanized, but their weapons and methods of killing were conventional. Recruited from the SS, the Gestapo, the Security Police, the Criminal Police, and the Waffen-SS, most of the time the executioners used firearms to slaughter their victims. Their commanders regularly enlisted native auxiliaries to help with the *basse besogne*. They also commandeered Russian prisoners of war to dig and cover mass graves, while it was not uncommon for Jews to be forced to dig graves for their fellow Jews.

More than likely, the social and psychological profile of the triggermen, whether Nazi-German or other, was no different from that of the executioners of other times and places. But what about their superiors in the field, and at regional and national headquarters? The real true believers were to be found at these higher echelons. Even if the rank and file of the killing squads came from the lowest classes, most of the officers were well educated and many of them were also wellborn. Socially respectable and psychologically "sound," they served in the Einsatzgruppen out of a sense of mission and for reasons of advancement in the vanguard of nazism. The officers of the SS— from the Untersturmführer, or second lieutenants, to the Gruppenführer, or major generals—were inveterate champions of the Nazi dogma and operational code. Given their shared unspoken assumptions, no written command from Hitler or Himmler was needed for them to issue their own orders to kill political enemies and to stretch these orders to cover the indiscriminate massacre of Jews. This small band of officers was held together by faith, zeal, and complicity. They were moved to action as much by magic formulas and conjurations as by formal orders. Theirs was not just an army with a chain of command, but a sectarian order fired by fanaticism hardened with impenitence.

It is impossible to give an accurate count of the total number of victims of the SS during the first six to seven months of Barbarossa, down to the early winter of 1941–42—to the debacle of Moscow and the Wannsee Conference. To date, all estimates are based, essentially, on the daily and monthly reports to higher headquarters from the field offices of the mobile Einsatzgruppen and of the back-up and rearguard security forces. No doubt these reports contain inaccuracies of time, place, and numbers. But whatever their deficiencies and defects, the general magnitude of the slayings is beyond dispute. The mobile action units took about 500,000 lives. At least nine-tenths of these victims are estimated to have been Jewish, with, over time, a rising proportion of women, children, and the aged among them. Close to half of the victims were murdered by the commandos of Einsatzgruppe A in the Baltic countries and Belorussia; between 45,000 and 60,000 by the commandos of Einsatzgruppe B in the center; about 95,000 by the commandos of Einsatzgruppe C in the Ukraine; and between 55,000 and 80,000 by commandos of Einsatzgruppe D in the far south. In addition, about 200,000 Jews were killed by "regular" security forces and in pogroms.

The vast majority of the Jews killed were massacred after the military campaign began to falter. Such was certainly the case in the difficult forward theaters of the central and eastern Ukraine, the Crimea, and the Caucasus. But the sequence of events was not really different farther to the rear, in the buffer zone as well as in western Belorussia and the western Ukraine. In these territories the German armies had met practically no resistance, and the Einsatzgruppen, instructed to keep pace with them, had all but bypassed vast numbers of Jews. It was left to the "civil" administration of the SS, which took over on August 1, to ghettoize, hyperexploit, and break them. Was this a temporary expedient pending some overall resolution of the intractable "Jewish question" or was it designed to facilitate the predetermined liquidation of the eastern Jews, primarily by concentrating them for easy slaughter? Whatever the answer, the mass shootings in the rear of the battle zones did not really begin until the late fall.

The largest massacres were carried out in the Baltic lands, which had long since been occupied by von Leeb's forces in their relentless effort to reach Leningrad. Also, Einsatzgruppe A, the largest of the four action groups, had moved up, to be present to share in the prestige and control attending the capture of Soviet Russia's second city. But even with Finnish divisions pressing down from the north, the Wehrmacht was stymied. With winter closing in, both the military and the security forces ran aground throughout the northern sector, and not just in the forward lines. The leaders of Einsatzgruppe A as well as those of the regular SS and police at RSHA headquarters in Riga chafed at this humiliating impasse, which ran counter to their ideological and political temperament and presumption. Besides, their forces were highly concentrated and they had ample native helpers. In any event, from October to December the Baltic cities which had been overrun in June and whose Jews had been spared but ghettoized became the scene of infamous massacres. In Latvia the Jewish community of Riga was struck at the end of November and again on December 8. Each action claimed about 10,000 victims, leaving only between 2,500 and 4,500 survivors. At about the same time, the Jewish communities of Libau and Dvinsk endured a similar fate. In Lithuania the Jews of Kovno and Vilna suffered an even greater calvary than the pogroms of June and July: 10,000 Jews were slaughtered in Kovno and 25,000 in Vilna, reducing the Jewish community of each city to between 15,000 and 20,000. The mass executions in the Rumbuli Forest outside Riga, in the Ponary woods near Vilna, and in the Ninth Fort of Kovno corresponded in both spirit and modus operandi to the monstrous slaughter at the ravine of Babi Yar outside Kiev.

The season of latter-day pogroms was over. There was now something irreversible about the Jews being the chosen hostages for Nazi Germany's desperate all-or-nothing war as well as the chosen martyrs of its fiery crusade against bolshevism. Hitler himself kept prophesying that not Germany but the Jews would perish in the cataclysm of the Second World War.

PART THREE

CHAPTER IX

WANNSEE

TOWARD THE "FINAL SOLUTION"

The German defeat at Moscow, including the difficult retreat which continued through mid-February 1942, was a major turning point in the history of both the Third Reich and the Second World War. It ended an unbroken string of stunning political, diplomatic, and military victories for the führer and his acolytes. The fiasco of Typhoon robbed them of their overconfidence. As charismatic leader of the predatory Behemoth, Hitler needed success abroad to keep refueling the legitimacy of his office and regime at home. Certain that a no-win war would spell the end of the Nazi project, he was not about to seek a negotiated settlement. Not too surprisingly, no one inside Germany pressed him to do so. The generals in particular were quiescent, largely because they were awed by the effectiveness of Hitler's peremptory order to stand and fight, which was thought to have prevented a strategic withdrawal from turning into a headlong rout. Besides, not only was Hitler incapable of contemplating a face-saving compromise, but the state of international politics was such as to preclude it.

As of the winter of 1941–42, the führer was entrapped in a war that could neither be won militarily nor terminated politically. Of course, he and his associates hoped against hope that Germany might still be able to seize back the initiative in 1942 by attacking in the direction of Stalingrad and capturing the Caucasus, rich in desperately needed oil. At the same time, Hitler feared that the military situation might have become irreversible and that Barbarossa, the pivot of his overall project, had miscarried, and for good. His despondency became so intense that it began to color both his private and public discourse. After repeatedly invoking the help of God, Hitler even lashed out at the German people, insisting that it deserved to "disappear" if it could not "preserve" itself. But above all he stepped up his malediction of the Jews.

Whereas in the fall Hitler and his generals had taken the great gamble of trying to storm Moscow in a supreme effort to salvage Barbarossa, so now they set about steeling Germany for a drawn-out war that they suspected could not be won. Once again, the Nazi elite and its faithful collaborators took a fatal turn, this time less by free choice than out of dire necessity. With their overweening presumption exacerbated by rage, their bipolar view of the world became more frenzied. Hitler caught and expressed the incipient apocalyptic mood when in late 1941 he twice declared the issue to have become one of *"Sein oder Nichtsein."*

Hitler had no intention of seeking a strategic surrender to cut Germany's losses and Europe's suffering. Instead, he meant to fight it out to the bitter end, if need be by pulling much of Europe down with the Third Reich. As always, Hitler had no difficulty persuading the best of Germany's power elite to back this preposterous military stand. Meanwhile, he gave the SS free rein to intensify their ideological crusade and to vent their spleen for the affront to their self-esteem. The mix of rational-bureaucratic and fanatical impulses, so characteristic of the Nazi project, was certain to become ever more lethal and insidious.

To fortify the Behemoth for a reckless all-or-nothing struggle meant taking a series of interrelated steps, all of which exacerbated the totalization and increasing brutality of war. The shift from blitz warfare to a war of endurance called for full economic mobilization. Given the Reich's grave deficiency in critical foods, raw materials, and manpower, this called for the intensified exploitation of all conquered and German-dominated territories. The occupied east was in double jeopardy, since vast German armies there would also have to live off the land. The extraction of economic surplus called for ever tougher occupation policies, partly in order to contain growing resistance to conscription for forced labor at either local work sites or within the Reich.

This hardening of the German war effort would have the most catastrophic consequences in the east, where it would feed the fury of the Wehrmacht and the SS, already intensified by the stubborn and unexpected resistance of the Red Army. Unlike the political class of France's Third Republic, which Berlin proposed to break without utterly destroying it and its homeland, the Soviet elite was marked for extinction and its country for conquest and dismemberment. Not torn by internecine power struggles, Russia's political class meant to hold fast against overwhelming odds and at any cost. By yielding space and sacrificing men, Stalin and his inner circle sought to gain the time needed to raise new divisions, to relocate industries and skilled workers inland, to fortify major cities, to organize a *levée en masse,* and to unleash partisan warfare. No less resolute than Hitler, by November 6, 1941, Stalin had proclaimed that "if the German invaders, . . . these people without honor and conscience, [and] with the morality of animals, . . . want a war of extermination, . . . they shall have it."

In Nazi eyes this determination to fight to the last was the crowning crime of the Soviets and of bolshevism. As Himmler is reported to have told his SS leaders in mid-1942, in all previous campaigns Germany's enemies had had the good sense and decency to yield to superior force, largely because of their "age-old and civilized . . . west European refinement." In the battle of France, enemy units surrendered as soon as they were forewarned "that all further resistance would be senseless." Of course, "we SS men" moved into Russia without delusions. But until this last winter too many Germans had failed to realize that "Russian commissars and unconditional Bolsheviks are thoroughly permeated with a brutal will power, a beastlike tenacity which makes them fight to the finish and which has nothing to do with human logic or duty but . . . is a drive common to all animals." Indeed, the Bolsheviks were such "dehumanized beasts" that when "encircled and without food they resort to slaughtering some of their own comrades in order to hold out longer," a behavior bordering on "cannibalism." In what was a "war of annihilation [*Vernichtungskampf*]," two "races and peoples" were locked in "unconditional" combat: on the one side "this brute matter, this mass, these primeval men, or better these subhumans [*Untermenschen*], led by commissars"; on the other, "we Germans, still saddled with a Christian mentality which, however, no longer tolerates the suffering of Christian martyrs or fanatics." Naturally, the SS leaders elected to be "the [principal] carriers of this fight against the commissars." Following the "brutal struggle of this last winter . . . there can be no capitulation, no peace or armistice, but only either Russia's destruction [*Vernichtung*] or our own."

The first step in bracing the Behemoth for all-out war, which Napoleon had once called "the business of barbarians," was a change in military leadership. As noted above, when von Brauchitsch stepped down, Hitler became his own commander in chief. This was an essentially symbolic but telling act, since the führer had long since taken charge. As if to remove any vestige of vacillation, he replaced the three principal field commanders in the east with generals of proven Nazi sympathies: Field Marshal Walter von Reichenau replaced von Rundstedt, Field Marshal Günther von Kluge replaced von Bock, and General George von Küchler replaced von Leeb. Quite a few divisional officers were displaced as well. But since the old team had not exactly opposed the dehumanization of warfare, these personnel changes were more in the nature of a mutation than a purge. With one exception, the officers who were imputed to have bungled Operation Typhoon were cashiered or resigned. They were neither arrested and tried, nor executed. Characteristically, von Rundstedt and Guderian were relieved of their commands without being dishonored, and their eclipse was temporary.

Germany's military caste eagerly faced the challenges presented by the disastrous conditions and enormous obstacles on the eastern front. If senior generals were fiercely determined to persevere, middle and lower level officers were even more so. Up and down the command hierarchy there was an iron resolve to keep the troops fighting regardless of casualties, physical hardships, and mental strains. As a privileged collaborator and beneficiary of the regime, the officer corps almost naturally slipped into preaching the Nazi decalogue to justify the worst excesses to themselves and to others. True, from 1914 to 1918, during the first major phase of the Thirty Years War of the twentieth century, German officers also had used defamatory slogans to incite their men to lay down their lives for what was proclaimed to be a noble cause. But at the time they had not portrayed the soldiers in the opposing trenches as subhumans, nor had they traduced their leaders as infidels to be slain. As of the winter of 1941–42, the worsening battle conditions and the execration of "Judeobolshevism" fomented a peculiar soldierly callousness coupled with a distinct indifference to the torment of civilians, especially of Jews. Fitting the Wehrmacht to fight an increasingly reckless and futile war, its officers made it a shield for the rampant expansion of the fatal SS state within the Behemoth, and also used its needs to justify that expansion. For in order to muster the resources and command the obedience for this barbarous conflict, there was need for ever more coercion throughout German-occupied Europe.

The forced shift from blitz warfare to a protracted and grinding war of position necessitated a radical reorganization of the Reich's economy. The logic of the blitzkrieg had never been purely military and strategic. In addition to conforming with nazism's pretense of dynamic energy, the idea of lightning campaigns had suited Hitler's diplomatic and political strategem. Although he had speeded rearmament during the 1930s, stealing a march on the other major powers, he had done so without converting to a full war economy. After achieving a comparative advantage in arms output, both quantitative and qualitative, the führer set out to defeat his foreign enemies, one by one, in a succession of quick campaigns. All along, he sought and raced to avoid a war of endurance, because he knew that even with all-out mobilization—a prospect he abhorred—Germany would be at a disadvantage. Barbarossa was conceived and launched in this same spirit. The conquering armies, apart from living off the land, were instructed to exploit instantly and maximally the occupied territories with a view to making possible the continuation of the war without a full-scale conversion of the German economy. From the outset the stress was on despoiling Russia of cereals, oil seeds, and industrial raw materials, notably petroleum, for shipment back home.

On July 27, 1941, Göring issued orders for the management and ruthless despoliation of "the newly occupied eastern territories." For the time being, collective farms were to be maintained to guarantee "maximum production . . . in the interest of the German war economy." As for Soviet Russia's oil industry, because of "its supreme importance for the German Wehrmacht and economy," it would be taken over and operated by German firms, following guidelines set by the Kontinentale Öl A. G., the oil consortium of the Four-Year Plan. In the long run, not Bolshevik collectivism but government-directed private enterprise would guarantee maximum efficiency in territories to be exploited along colonial lines. In the short run, however, since production for war had "absolute priority," there would be no "abrupt changes in the economic system" in the Russian territories. During this transitional period the "most important industrial and commercial establishments will be run by German entrepreneurs, acting as individual trustees." But Göring made a point of stressing that "this trustee system, under strict state supervision, does not constitute the final solution [Endlösung]."

Four days later, on July 31, General Georg Thomas, chief of the Economic and Armament Bureau of the Supreme Command, presided over a conference of his senior staff concerned with the eastern territories. Having made overly optimistic assumptions about the speed of military operations, the bureau had thought rather too much in terms of "political economy." Under present circumstances, however, its "principal assignment" was to solve "short-term problems." In the east, while Alfred Rosenberg was charged with working "for the future," for the time being Göring was "exclusively interested in oil and cereals." General Thomas stressed that the primary task was "to provision the field armies and Germany," which might entail starvation in certain territories, especially since the local "intelligentsia has been slain" and Berlin would be in "no position" to administer all of them. Unless "Russia runs out of reserves and the Russian state breaks down," it might take a long time to capture the Caucasus and the lower Volga. In the meantime, the staff earmarked

for regions whose seizure was delayed should be given other assignments. Long-term political considerations, Thomas insisted, would
have to give way to pressing economic needs. Accordingly, there
would be "no restoration of private enterprise," except in the territories taken by Russia under the Nazi-Soviet Pact. The assembled officials agreed that petroleum would be used "in the first instance to
cover German needs"; that "raw materials will be carried off ruthlessly" and that "Jews will be lodged in barracks [kaserniert] and put
to work in closed labor columns."

Mounting tensions soon developed between supplying, on the one
hand, the field armies and local populations and, on the other, the
home front. On November 6 the southern military command, in
agreement with the Economic Inspectorate, insisted that "provisioning of the troops should take precedence over provisioning of the
Heimat." There were economic and security reasons for feeding the
native work force, but the rest of the population might have to be
starved in order to extract surpluses for shipment to the fatherland.
Two days later, on November 8, Göring presided over a high-level
conference to set "the general principles of economic policy for the
newly occupied eastern territories." By now the chief injunction was
unequivocal: "For the duration the needs of the war economy will be
the supreme law of all economic activity, . . . with emphasis on the
production of food and raw materials." The local standard of living
must be kept to a minimum in order to extract low-cost surpluses for
"the Reich and other European countries," and also for reasons of
war financing. While stockpiles of cereals should be secured, no effort
should be spared to procure "maximum grain surpluses" for 1943,
which meant concentrating on the harvest of 1942. Equally vigorous
measures were called for to relieve the meat shortage in the Reich. As
for the provisioning of the local urban populations, it could be no
more than minimal. For the time being, "nothing at all can be done
for the big cities (Moscow, Leningrad, and Kiev), the resulting consequences being hard but unavoidable." In the nonagrarian sector the
emphasis should be on obtaining first oil, then manganese, followed
by coal, iron, and timber.

Meanwhile, Göring had issued instructions for the exploitation of
Soviet labor. In the operational zones it was to be used "in the
construction of roads, rail lines, and airports; in the removal of
rubble; and in the clearance of mines." Most "construction battalions" of the Wehrmacht should be dissolved and their skilled labor
sent to work in armaments plants, since there were enough Russians
"to dig ditches and crush stones." Use should also be made of Soviet
prisoners of war, to be selected with an eye to their reliability. Some

of them, together with "free Russian workers," could be sent to work in the Reich.

Even before the start of Barbarossa, General Thomas as well as Fritz Todt, Reich minister of arms and ammunition, had questioned the wisdom of not converting to full war production. As of the early fall of 1941, the economy was hard-pressed to make good the unanticipated material needs and losses on the eastern front, the principal impediment being the shortage of manpower and raw materials. Even so, Hitler continued to resist a changeover. He still preferred to strain the limited war economy, to use up existing stocks, and to cling to the hope of relieving shortages by despoiling the rest of the Continent, in particular eastern Europe and most especially the Soviet Union.

But immediately following the halt before Moscow and the American entry into the war, the führer conceded the need for at least some changes in the Reich's economy. Finally, on January 10, 1942, he signed the directive "Armament 1942," which called for a switch to an all-out war economy. It prescribed a radical reordering of priorities, involving the sharp cutback of consumer production in the interest of rapid and massive increases in the output of weapons, munitions, and other military essentials. Against the somber background of continuing reverses on the eastern front, the appropriate officials and agencies rushed to reorganize the economy for a protracted, grueling, and draining war. The new exigencies and priorities called for a review of the proper place and relationship not only of the armed forces and the private sector, but also of the SS, which was about to play an expanding economic role of its own.

On January 20 and 21, 1942, leading armaments officials met in Berlin to set the new guidelines for the rationalization of the war economy. Significantly, this meeting took place the same day and in the same city as the Wannsee Conference, summoned to expedite the solution of the "Jewish problem." Even though these two conclaves proceeded independent of each other, their participants moved in the same political and bureaucratic circles and they acted from shared premises and in response to similar circumstances.

At the armaments conference, General Thomas set forth the context and rationale for converting to a full-scale mobilization for war. He assured the assembled officials that although he fully understood their being "weighed down with worry" he was also certain that they would do their utmost to "serve the fatherland in this critical moment." The conflict had entered a new phase, and "the longer it lasts, the more taxing the war effort and its attendant complications will become." While the Wehrmacht was equal to any task on the military front, there was need for "comprehensive measures on the economic front to keep up with Anglo-American economic and arms production." General Thomas conceded that until recently, in anticipation of a swift victory over the Soviets, the stress had been on bolstering the air force and navy. But this expectation had been defeated by "the early winter in Russia, the tenacity of the Russian soldier, and the surprising performance of Russia's armaments industry," with the result that the Wehrmacht had suffered "unexpectedly high material losses." As things stood, it would take "another campaign to completely smash and once for all dispose of the Bolshevik army." General Thomas announced the führer's decision to give first priority to the needs of the army, ahead of the other two services, along with the production of oil and coal.

Both General Thomas and Fritz Todt took it for granted that big industry and agriculture would remain the essential motor of the new war economy. Indeed, there was every reason to continue trusting the stewardship of the economy to the established industrial and agrarian magnates and managers, who with rare exceptions eagerly served and abetted what might be called the Nazi warfare and conquest state. In this critical moment the economic elites were no less ready and willing to go to unconscionable extremes than the military and civil-service elites. In fact, among industrialists and agrarians there were no dissidents comparable to von Rundstedt and Guderian, perhaps because their economic autonomy was unimpaired and their businesses continued to prosper. Disinclined to dispute their expertise, Hitler was loath to cashier any of the field marshals of organized capitalism. Just as the generals of the army readily went along with the barbarization of warfare, so the captains of industry and agriculture agreed that slave and prisoner labor be harnessed for war production.

There is no denying the Third Reich's escalating shortage of labor. Germany simply lacked the manpower to sustain a protracted war for European hegemony. In the winter of 1941–42 Berlin faced a rising demand for both soldiers and workers. The Wehrmacht had to make good its losses in the east while preparing for a two-front war. Additional conscripts could only be drawn from the workforce, notably from the ranks of industrial labor essential for war production, in large part because the regime was ideologically predisposed against mobilizing women to work in factories. Faced with this dilemma, the Nazi authorities increasingly pressed into service non-German labor to man their hard-pressed war economy.

There were three principal sources of alternate labor: prisoners of war, foreign civilian workers, and the working slaves in concentration camps and ghettos. Following Marshal Pétain's strategic surrender, Germany held over 1 million French POWs. At first, of those who were put to work, most were employed in agriculture. Over time, however, ever larger numbers were shifted into industry to meet the urgent need for skilled manpower. Even though the Soviet Union was never defeated, no less than 5 million of its citizens were taken captive by the Germans. Unlike the French prisoners, they were mistreated mercilessly: well over 50 percent of them were murdered or left to die of starvation, disease, and exhaustion. In addition, to relieve their acute labor shortage, the Germans began to impress Soviet prisoners for hard labor. During the first half of 1942, which saw a considerable leap in armaments production, 200,000 skilled hands were selected from among them for work in the Reich, principally in mines. This captive Soviet work force almost doubled within a year and reached close to 750,000 in mid-1944.

As for foreign civilian workers, Berlin recruited them throughout occupied Europe. At first, scores of them rushed to the Reich voluntarily, driven there by unemployment in their own countries. Some 100,000 Poles went to Germany before the end of 1939. Between May 1940 and October 1941 another 300,000 foreigners came to work in German industry, most of them from western Europe. Soon it became clear, however, that voluntary foreign labor and the use of prisoners of war would be insufficient. Under mounting coercion 1.6 million foreign workers came to the Reich during the next six months, and their total rose to 3 million before the end of 1942. This transfusion of cheap foreign labor was far from negligible, since in 1942 it accounted for most of the expansion of the German work force and replaced the workers conscripted into the Wehrmacht. By mid-1943 an additional 800,000 foreigners were working in Germany, most of them having been taken there against their will. All told, and as we shall see in the next chapter, between 1940 and 1945 over 7 million foreign workers toiled in Germany. In 1944 they made up over 25 percent of the work force in the armaments industry, which meant that every fourth tank, truck, or case of munitions was produced by them.

Throughout these years the proportion of *Ostarbeiter*, or workers from eastern Europe, in the foreign labor force kept rising. At Albert Speer's suggestion, on March 21, 1942, Hitler appointed the gauleiter of Thuringia, Fritz Sauckel, general plenipotentiary for labor, responsible to Göring. Within a month Sauckel circulated a statement insisting that "the occupied eastern territories are [Europe's] greatest reservoir" for foreign labor. In particular, labor would have to be procured from the "conquered Soviet territories . . . if need be by impressment." Sauckel estimated that the occupied countries of western Europe could provide only "one-quarter of the total requirement of foreign workmen." Eventually, at least 75 percent of all foreign workers in Germany, not counting working prisoners of war, were levied in the eastern occupied territories, among them well over 1 million Poles.

The concentration camps and ghettos became the third source of forced labor, and will also be discussed in greater detail in the next chapter. Meanwhile, it is worth noting that the camps were of practically no economic importance until well after the outbreak of war, when the inmate population increased rapidly. But almost from the start top leaders of the SS contemplated exploiting the labor of their victims to expand their own political and economic reach. Himmler in particular proposed to gear the camps to help supply and provision the expanding Waffen-SS, his other lever of influence and power. To this end the SS set up the German Equipment Works. But since Himmler and his associates expected the wars of conquest to be won in no time, they envisaged using camp labor above all to expedite the architectural exaltation of the Thousand-Year Reich. With this in mind, and with a view to fostering their financial autonomy, they chartered the German Earth and Stone Works to produce granite for the construction of monumental public buildings as well as of stately SS headquarters and German outposts in the east. The inmates of concentration camps were to serve as forced miners and masons for this brazen project. By late 1941 the SS had contributed over 10,000 forced laborers to the Reich's work force, having abandoned their own construction program in July.

With the changeover to concerted industrial mobilization in early 1942, the SS resolved to enlarge their slave-labor force with a view to serving the war effort. As the Third Reich braced for a long war, the SS had two alternatives: they could continue to use this manpower to build and run their own factories or they could hire it out to firms in the private sector. The SS and big business soon agreed on the expediency and profitability of locating private plants near or inside concentration camps, to be enlarged or set up for this purpose. The reservoir of camp labor could also be tapped for mining and construction workers.

Shortly after Sauckel became labor boss of the war economy, SS General Oswald Pohl was appointed to head the newly created Central Economic and Administrative Office (WVHA) within the SS, which was to rival Reinhard Heydrich's Reich Central Security Office (RSHA) in importance. He was charged with coordinating the use and deployment of concentration-camp labor. In agreement with Himmler, in a charter memorandum parallel to Sauckel's, on April 30, 1942, Pohl stressed that the war had "radically changed" the purpose of the camps: whereas heretofore their principal mission had been political, with emphasis on "security, [re]education, and prevention," hereafter it would be economic. He vowed to "give first priority to mobilizing the full working capacity of the inmates for war—for the increase of armaments—until later, when it will be used for peacetime undertakings." In time, Pohl became the economic tsar of the sprawling SS establishment and, as such, a powerful force in the German economy.

Of course, there was an intense contradiction between exploiting captive labor "rationally" and optimally for war production and hyperexploiting and scourging it for political reasons. In this regard Pohl and Heydrich worked at cross-purposes, with Himmler supporting both simultaneously. The two pursued clashing objectives, and their cooperation was marred by personal rivalries and bureaucratic squabbles. But whatever their differences, both Pohl and Heydrich considered their captives in instrumental terms dictated by the conflicting exigencies of simultaneously maximizing war production and implementing the Nazi warrant for destruction. This same antithesis informed Nazi Germany's deadly practices in the Jewish ghettos.

The intense radicalization of Jewish policy coincided with and was fueled by the breakdown of the eastern campaign and of the sense of invulnerability of the Nazi regime, now embarked on a reckless struggle for *Sein oder Nichtsein*. As we saw, even the military shortfalls of the late summer and fall of 1941, which preceded this radical turn, conditioned and fired the transgressions of the Wehrmacht and the savageries of the Einsatzgruppen. Now that their military undertaking had come to a perilous impasse, the Nazi leaders not only steeled their armed forces, economy, and party state for a war to the finish; they also intensified their murderous crusade against "Judeobolshevism," and increasingly directed it against the Jews. Since the key cities and cadres of bolshevism remained out of reach, the political soldiers of the Third Reich increasingly struck out at a purported member of the "common enemy" who was close at hand and defenseless—the Jew. Throughout, however, the Nazi leaders continued to portray their battle on the eastern front as a death struggle against the protean Bolshevik peril, not least because they felt that the appeals of antibolshevism were much more effective than the appeals of anti-Semitism, both at home and especially abroad. Until the inglorious defeat at

Stalingrad, Nazi propaganda also execrated the twin evil of "Judeo-bolshevism," but thereafter it increasingly anathematized bolshevism *tout court.*

The Wannsee Conference, which met to work out a comprehensive and definitive solution of the "Jewish problem," was held on January 20, 1942, when the Nazi leaders were facing up to their bitter predicament in the eastern theater of war. The resolve to systematize and coordinate the treatment of the "Jewish question" thus coincided with the resolve to steel the Behemoth for an unanticipated and grueling *guerre à mort.* But not surprisingly, the origins and objectives of this Wannsee meeting were singularly complicated and circuitous.

The first step toward the Wannsee Conference was taken by neither Hitler nor Himmler, but by Göring and Heydrich, under very different circumstances and with very different intentions than those which eventually prevailed during the conference itself. While apparently Heydrich instructed Eichmann to draft the letter of July 31, 1941, which was addressed to Heydrich and eventually warranted the conference, it was initiated and signed by Göring. By this time Hitler's respect for Göring had cooled. But by making him Germany's only Reich marshal the führer had validated his unique standing in the Nazi hierarchy and indulged his boundless vanity. Despite his executive failings, Göring wielded great power as head of the Four-Year Plan, go-between with the business establishment, and nominal commander in chief of the Luftwaffe. Once before, he had taken a hand in the "Jewish question." At Hitler's behest and with Heydrich's assistance, in late 1938 Göring had seized on the unintended aftereffects of Crystal Night to force the Aryanization of the economy and the flight of Jews from Germany. On January 24, 1939, he had instructed Heydrich to set up a Reich Bureau for Jewish Emigration within the Interior Ministry. With delegates from all interested government departments, this agency was empowered to take financial and diplomatic measures to speed the Jewish exodus. Within four months Heydrich's office expedited the departure of 34,040 Jews from the Old Reich and 34,320 Jews from Austria. By October 1941 the number of Jews remaining within the boundaries of pre-1938 Germany was down to 163,692, most of them concentrated in big cities.

The Göring-Heydrich letter of July 31, 1941, explicitly referred back to the letter of two and a half years ago ordering the establishment of the special emigration office. In the meantime, the situation had changed radically. By the beginning of the war, Germany's Jewish population had been greatly reduced by emigration and expulsion, but since then the outside world had all but blocked the exodus and the Third Reich had acquired millions of Jews through foreign expansion. Under the circumstances, with voluntary and forced emigration foreclosed, between September 1939 and June 1941 the Nazis put into effect a policy of forced evacuation and resettlement. Determined to make Germany and its newly incorporated territories *judenfrei*, they began to relocate and confine their millions of unwanted Jews to a large reserve and to ghettos in conquered eastern territories, notably in the General Government of Poland—pending their wholesale transport to Madagascar. But with England set against Germany's continental hegemony and in control of the seas, Madagascar or other overseas reservations, including Palestine, were out of reach.

The invasion of the Soviet Union gave the idea of a territorial solution a new lease on life. After conquering the eastern *Lebensraum* along with additional Jews, the Reich would banish European Jewry to vast lands deep in Russia, east of the Urals. At the time that Göring instructed Heydrich to draft the letter signed on July 31, 1941, a quick and decisive defeat of Soviet Russia was still taken for granted. To be sure, by late that month the Einsatzgruppen were already launched on their politically inspired massacres. But as we saw, these killings were at first an expression of the general fury of Barbarossa rather than part of a systematic drive against the Jews. Besides, in the second half of July Hitler and his closest associates were making plans to place the Soviet territories conquered by the Wehrmacht under civil administration. To the extent that the Göring-Heydrich initiative was part of this project for imperial domination and exploitation, it was in line with the führer's will and a reflection of Nazi hubris.

What, then, did Göring write to Heydrich? The full text of the letter of July 31, 1941, must be quoted.

> This is to supplement the assignment given to you in the decree of January 24, 1939, to solve the Jewish question by emigration or evacuation under the most favorable conditions possible given present circumstances. I hereby charge you to make all the necessary administrative, practical, and financial preparations for a *Gesamtlösung* [total/complete/comprehensive solution] of the Jewish question throughout Germany's European sphere of influence.
>
> Insofar as these preparations will touch on the jurisdiction of other government agencies, these are to be asked to collaborate.
>
> I further commission you to submit to me, before long, a master plan of the administrative, practical, and financial measures that need to be taken *zur Durchführung* [to carry out] the sought-after *Endlösung* [final/definitive solution] of the Jewish question.

There is nothing in these instructions, either explicit or implicit, to indicate that by directing Heydrich to prepare an overall and definitive solution—a final solution—of the "Jewish problem," Göring was asking him to prepare for the immediate or eventual mass murder of Jews. Both text and context suggest that he was ordering Heydrich to reactivate and reorganize the special bureau established in January 1939 so that it could handle a vastly enlarged "Jewish problem" under vastly changed circumstances. Of course, as chief of the regular and SS Security Police, SS Gruppenführer (Major General) Heydrich was in command of the Einsatzgruppen. But with the end of military operations he would also and above all become Himmler's commissioner plenipotentiary for the establishment and operation of the SS state throughout the newly acquired eastern *Lebensraum*. Göring addressed Heydrich not so much as commander of the provisional action commandos but as a leading political official in the nascent imperial administration of the would-be Thousand-Year Reich, in which the place of the Jews remained to be determined. Needless to say, the reverses of Barbarossa radically changed the context in which Göring's orders would be discussed, elaborated, and implemented.

Starting in the fall of 1941, the conditions of the Jews in German Germany went from bad to worse. Thus far, the wearing of the Jewish badge had been introduced only in the conquered eastern territories: in the Warthegau and the General Government in late 1939, and in the Baltic states in early July 1941. Now, as of September 21, 1941, all Jews over six years of age in Germany—including Austria and the Protectorate of Bohemia and Moravia—were required to display on the left upper front of their outer garment a six-pointed yellow star bordered in black with *Jude* inscribed in black in its center. Hereafter, Jews needed special permission to leave their neighborhood and to use public transport. They were also deprived of telephones and forbidden to buy newspapers. Their rations were cut as well. These additional restrictions were followed by a decree formalizing a policy that may be said to have come into effect with the start of Barbarossa: on October 23, 1941, in the name of Himmler, the Gestapo chief Heinrich Müller prohibited Jews from leaving Germany.

As if to compensate for this ban on emigration, which marked a major watershed in policy, the police and security offices made plans for the forced removal of Jews from the Greater Reich to the east. Admittedly, the Nazis were not novices at expulsion, deportation, or evacuation. Between 1938 and mid-1941 they had herded Polish Jews resident in Germany across the Polish border; they had driven Polish Jews from the General Government over the Nazi-Soviet demarcation line; they had deported Jews from Vienna and Stettin to Lublin; they had evicted Jews from Baden and the Rhineland to unoccupied

France; and they had expelled Jews from Luxembourg to both parts of France as well as to Portugal and Spain. But these ejections had had no murderous intent, either direct or indirect. They were part of a deliberate campaign to hound or simply throw the Jews out of Germany at a time when throughout Europe material conditions were still tolerable. All this changed with the refusal of the British Empire and the Soviet Union to capitulate: emigration was all but foreclosed and the scourge of war began to ravage eastern Europe, the designated dumping ground for the Jews from Greater Germany. In addition and almost simultaneously, for both economic and punitive reasons the Nazis began to consider the Jews as a pool of expendable labor.

On September 18, 1941, Himmler notified SS General Artur Greiser, gauleiter and Reich governor of the Warthegau, that "the führer wanted the Old Reich and the Protectorate emptied and disencumbered of Jews" and that this should be done by "moving them from west to east as soon as possible." Himmler promised to try his best to "transport . . . [these Jews] before the end of this year." At first, they would be taken to "the eastern territories that two years ago were newly incorporated into the Reich, only to be banished farther east next spring." Himmler intended to "send about 60,000 [of these] Jews . . . into the ghetto of Litzmannstadt [Łódź] . . . which [could] barely accommodate them." He also proposed to deport Jews from Greater Germany to ghettos in cities in Belorussia, Latvia, and Lithuania. SS General Kurt Daluege, chief of the regular police under Himmler, issued the necessary deportation orders on October 14 and 24, 1941. No doubt Heydrich was closely associated with these moves, since security and police agents organized the convoys and rounded up the deportees.

Between mid-October and mid-November, twenty-one transports left Greater Germany for Łódź. This city's by now overcrowded and starving ghetto was thus burdened with 20,000 additional charges, 331 of them from Luxembourg. Another 50,000 Jews were scheduled for removal to Minsk, Riga, and Kovno. But because of transport problems occasioned by the difficult military situation in the east, no more than 30,000 of these were actually sent, all but 6,000 or 7,000 of them to Riga.

Most of these deportees came from big cities, which also served as collection centers: Berlin, Vienna, and Prague, as well as Cologne, Frankfort, Munich, Nuremberg, Hamburg, Düsseldorf, Würzburg, and Dortmund. Many of them were wellborn, university-educated, ultra-assimilated, and unreligious, which compounded the difficulties of their adjustment to the unfamiliar and impoverished world of the eastern ghettos. By the time they got out of the train, they were shaken by the physical and mental torment of their roundup and journey. In the ghettos material conditions—housing, food, fuel, health services—became worse and worse, with particularly dire consequences for the aged and infirm, whose mortality rate soared. Over half of the newcomers to Łódź were over fifty years old, 1,400 of them seventy or over.

Back in the Reich the authorities made no effort to conceal this newest escalation in the persecution of the ever shrinking Jewish minority. German citizens were as unconcerned about the Jew next door being branded with the yellow star as they were indifferent to 50,000 Jews being deported or disappearing from their neighborhoods. Indeed, the vast majority of Germans remained apathetic and passive not out of blindness or fear but because of more pressing and private concerns. By the late fall and early winter of 1941, there were mounting apprehensions about the troubles on the eastern front and their likely impact on the homeland. The growing losses and privations of war prompted absorption with personal and family affairs and certain excesses on both the battlefield and the home front doubtless seemed a necessary but small price to pay for a righteous cause.

But over and above the indifference of the masses, there was still and always that of the classes. Rather than remonstrate, the elites and notables of the civil service, the armed forces, the churches, the academies, and the business world continued to acquiesce with their silence. Neither the masses nor the classes actively urged or supported these latest anti-Semitic indignities and outrages. Instead, desensitized by latent Judeophobia and inured by the rigors and imperatives of total war, they simply ignored them. Besides, to the extent that Germans were troubled by the Jewish persecution, they may have been relieved by its being removed from their backyard to be eclipsed and absorbed by Barbarossa. Not that they knew it, but the first German Jews to be massacred were slaughtered in the genocidal murders of Kovno and Riga in late November. In any event, in forging their total solution of the "Jewish problem," Hitler and his inner circle had a free hand, except for the internecine feuds of the regime and the constraints of an irretrievable absolute war.

The führer's anti-Semitism was dangerous less because it was comprehensive and unchanging than because it was singularly malleable and protean. Tirades against the Jews bolstered his credibility with the faithful by papering over the incoherence not only of his diagnosis of Europe's general crisis but also of his self-assigned mission to resolve it in Germany's favor. Characteristically, in his prophetic discourse Hitler struck distinctly apocalyptic notes whenever he ran into imagined or real obstacles. As of the late fall of 1941, this tone became more pronounced and consistent. At the same time, there was a metastasis in his execration of the ever diabolical Jew, which went hand in hand with a doctrinal mutation. Whereas heretofore Hitler had fulminated against "the Jew" as the all-powerful and insidious core of the "common enemy," he now reviled him for his wretchedness and fixed on him as the chosen expiatory victim.

As we saw, it was on January 30, 1939, that the führer had first prophesied that another world conflict would "result not in the Bolshevization of the world and with it the victory of the Jews, but in the annihilation of the Jewish race in Europe." At the time, in what was an open address to the new Reichstag, he had still invoked the vast reach of the supposed Jewish world conspiracy as he sought to cow the Western Powers into helping him expatriate German Jews and into continuing their diplomacy of appeasement. He did not repeat this prophecy until January 30, 1941, exactly two years later, when he again spoke to the Reichstag. On this occasion, Hitler used it not only to stir the faithful, but also once more to pressure England to yield Europe to the Reich. He warned Germany's enemies not to make light of his prophecy of the dire consequences for the Jews should they be allowed once again to drive the world into a general war. By now even the Allies should "recognize that they have a greater enemy at home . . . and join us in a common front . . . against the Jewish international bent on exploiting and corrupting the nations."

Once Hitler was locked into the two-front war and bogged down in Russia, his verbal attacks on the Jews became more categorical and frequent. On October 25, 1941, with Himmler and Heydrich at his dinner table, he asserted sententiously:

At the Reichstag I prophesied to Jewry that if war were not avoided the Jew would disappear from Europe. This race of criminals has on its conscience the two million dead of the Great War, and by now hundreds of thousands of additional ones. Let no one tell me: for all that we cannot drive them into the [eastern] marshlands! Who worries about our people? Actually, it helps us to have the horror of our exterminating Jewry precede us [into the east(?)]. The attempt to found a Jewish state will fail.

In this same monologue the führer ranted about bolshevism wading deeper in blood than tsarism, presumably to justify liquidating the former.

Within two weeks, on November 9, 1941, in his yearly speech to the party old guard in Munich's Löwenbräukeller, Hitler stressed that even the previous year, when he had spoken to them in "the glow of recent victories," he had been weighed down by the certainty that ultimately the "international Jew" had instigated this war. Having prevented this enemy from realizing his "Jewish-Marxist objectives" in Germany, the Nazis now faced him abroad. At first, the Jews had managed to make Poland, France, Belgium, Holland, Norway, and, chiefly, England their pawn. With time, however, "nothing was more natural" than for the Reich to confront the Soviet Union, "which was most clearly dominated by the Jewish spirit . . . and certainly was the greatest servant of Jewry." Hitler credited the Nazis with having been the first to grasp that after the "liquidation of the entire national intelligentsia" all that remained in Russia was "a mindless, forcibly proletarianized subhumanity, . . . kept down by a huge organization of Jewish commissars." Even Stalin was an "instrument in the hands of this ascendant Jewry." To be sure, he appeared "on stage, in front of the curtain, but Koganovich stood immediately behind him."

Only after he had once again conflated Judaism and bolshevism did Hitler turn to the difficult eastern campaign, which he now portrayed as "a struggle for *Sein oder Nichtsein* not just for Germany but for all of Europe." The Third Reich and its many allies shared a "common European consciousness" in their joint battle against "the Mongolian state of a second Genghis Khan." But these were so many diversionary rhetorical flights before the führer finally broached the painful subject of Leningrad. At first sight, he said, the Wehrmacht appeared to be on the defensive. In actual fact, it held the original capital of bolshevism in its grip. Being trapped and surrounded, the enemy "will starve . . . and Leningrad . . . [will] fall into our hands." Putting a bold face on things, Hitler disclaimed any interest in the city or in the prestige attaching to its capture. What mattered was "the annihilation of Leningrad's industrial center," and should the Soviets really "enjoy blowing up their own cities," they would save the Wehrmacht "quite a bit of work." At any rate, even with the Red Army driven by "fear and insane animalistic fanaticism," it could not recover from the loss of 3.6 million prisoners and 8-to-10 million killed and wounded.

While on this occasion Hitler did not repeat his dark prophecy about the annihilation of the Jews, within a week, in the November 16 issue of the official weekly *Das Reich*, Goebbels referred to it, maintaining that it was being "fulfilled . . . at this very moment." In this same spirit, in *Der Stürmer* of December 25 Streicher declared that he saw no solution other than the "extermination" (*Ausrottung*) of the "[Jewish] people, whose father is the devil," if the "curse of God, lodged in its blood" was to be exorcised. Three days later, at his headquarters, the führer defended Streicher against some of his detractors, insisting that he was irreplaceable. Although he conceded that "in some respects Streicher is mad," Hitler asserted that "the Jew is much meaner, bloodthirstier, and more satanic" even than Streicher portrayed him in Der Stürmer.

In his New Year's message of January 1, 1942, Hitler once again invoked his prophecy about the perdition of the Jews. Significantly, this time it was embedded in a furious tirade against Churchill and Roosevelt for selling out to Stalin and bolshevism.

> [It] is difficult to imagine the horrible calamity that would sweep over Germany and all of Europe in the event of a victory of Jewish bolshevism in alliance with Churchill and Roosevelt. Because: Churchill and Roosevelt [plan to] hand over Europe to Stalin! . . . The Bolshevik monster to which they want to surrender the European nations in turn will subvert them and their peoples. *In any event, the Jew will not exterminate the peoples of Europe, but will be the victim of his own plot.* Great Britain and the U.S.A. cannot use bolshevism to destroy Europe, in as much as their own people will sooner or later fall victim to this pest. [Italics mine]

The fact that the sinister malediction of the Jews was inserted in such an implausible denunciation of the Allies meant that few serious people in or out of Germany would pay much attention to it. Hitler was hardly in an exultant mood and closed his message on a decidedly somber note. After conceding that the eastern campaign was stalled, he declared that "the coming year will make enormous demands" on combatants and civilians alike. As if to stress the gravity of the moment, he implored the "Almighty to give Germany and her soldiers the strength" to persevere and to make 1942 the year of decision "for the salvation of our people and the nations allied with us."

Hitler sounded no less embattled in his New Year's proclamation to the armed forces. Of course, he made a particular point of commending the men of the Wehrmacht and the Waffen-SS for having driven back the allegedly aggressive Soviets "over 1,000 kilometers beyond their own borders." But then, in the same breath, the führer had to summon his troops to continue giving their best in an eastern campaign that was far from won.

> During the winter of 1941–42 the [enemy's] effort to turn the tide and advance against us must and will fail! On the contrary, once all

the preparations are completed, in 1942 we will again seize and pound the Jewish-capitalist and Bolshevik enemy of humanity until his will to destroy the world is broken.

Hitler called for a lasting victory so as to prevent "a bunch of self-seeking Anglo-Saxon and Jewish conspirators" from throwing Germany into a "war for *Sein oder Nichtsein*" every twenty-five years.

On January 6, 1942, over lunch, the führer once again held forth on the responsibility of the Jews for the crisis.

> This war will bring about the greatest world upheaval, even if not entirely in line with our wishes. The Jews have been all-influential; they do not care a damn for Britain's fate either. A man like Hore-Belisha [England's secretary of war, 1937–40], who grew up in a ghetto, cannot become attached to English history!

At this point Hitler is reported to have expressed a train of thought full of grave implications:

> Experience shows that following every catastrophe there is a search for a scapegoat. Probably the Jew will also be set upon in England. But let us hope that we will not end up as the international executioner!

Within a week, during the night of January 12–13, Hitler renewed his off-the-record diatribe against the British and their supposed manipulation by Jews. Clutching at straws, he voiced his "holy conviction" that the fall of Singapore presaged the downfall of Churchill.

> The Jews alone are interested in the [continuation of the war]. But the longer the war lasts, the more hardened people will become. The Jews are the dumbest of chosen people: for God's sake, they should never have instigated this war. *They will disappear from Europe.* All that because of a few fools. Imagine, a Moroccan Jew becoming minister of war in England! [Italics mine]

With his retaliatory venom at a boil, Hitler became increasingly contemptuous of the Jews he had hitherto seen as awesome, if accursed.

The Wannsee Conference finally convened under circumstances radically different from those that had conditioned the formulation of the original Göring-Heydrich letter. At the time it was written, in late July 1941, the Nazi leaders still felt assured of a quick and easy victory over the Soviet Union. As we saw, it was not until mid-September that wounded pride replaced overweening confidence as the primary fuel of the Nazis' fury. Militarily stymied, and with a diplomatic compromise unthinkable, those who governed the Reich resolved to stay the course, regardless of consequences and costs. In the east both the military campaign and the ungodly crusade became even more savage than originally planned, while throughout German-occupied Europe the Nazis kept tightening their barbarous shackles. At the same time, forced into a war of position and faced with an ineluctable shortage of men and raw materials, they switched to a war economy programmed to commandeer resources from all over the German-dominated Continent. Recourse to deported and forced labor was intended not only to benefit the economy of the Old Reich but also to tighten the hold of the SS over the conquered and occupied territories.

This extreme hypertrophy of the Nazi warfare and conquest state was the essential precondition for the radicalization of the torment of the Jews. As we have seen, as long as the military drive fared well, except for the pogromlike assaults of the first weeks, the violence wreaked on Jews was part of the general, ideologically driven violence of Barbarossa, which was also directed against Bolsheviks, commissars, and partisans. It did not take on a unique character until the military frustrations of the late summer and fall, when the Einsatzgruppen systematized the victimization of Soviet Jews and the RSHA rushed the ghettoization of Polish Jews. That was also the time of the stepped-up drive against the Jews of Greater Germany in the form of the introduction of the yellow star, the ban on emigration, and the deportations to eastern ghettos.

Of course, the impasse of Barbarossa was neither the only nor a sufficient cause for this hypertrophy of the Behemoth and of its anti-Semitic rage. There is no denying the relative autonomy and irrepressible force of the Nazi *Weltanschauung,* which had a fixed canon and ritual. But except for the old fighters and true believers, anti-Semitism occupied neither a prominent nor an unchanging place in this ideological constellation. It could recede or drop from view, only to resurface under new conditions, with different emphases, and for different purposes. Beginning with the boycott of April 1933, vast dissimilarities had marked each of the major attacks on the Jews. In any case, with the invasion of Russia Hitler forgot about using dramatic anti-Semitic outbursts at home to momentarily pacify his zealots and to periodically redynamize his regime. While the drive against the Jews moved abroad with the conquest of Poland, it did not take an irreversible turn toward systematic mass killing until the breakdown of Barbarossa in the fall of 1941. This development marked a fundamental change not only in the precept of Nazi anti-Semitism but also in the practice of Nazi Germany's "holy war." No doubt the ideologically grounded cathexis of Jew-hatred contributed to this fatal change. But the Nazis' rising fury against the Jews sprang from the mediated encounter between an enduring *ideological* impulse, itself highly tractable, and a totally unanticipated and intractable historical conjunction of events. Hereafter, Hitler and his closest political accomplices shaped and used anti-Semitism as part of their response to the grave imperilment of the Nazi project, abroad as well as at home. They licensed, perhaps even ordered, the vengeful torment of the Jews, which was put into effect by a combination of commands from on high and local initiatives.

This, then, was the historical context in which Heydrich set about implementing the order that had been conceived under such radically different conditions. Ever since the start of Barbarossa, of course, Heydrich had been in charge of the Einsatzgruppen on the eastern front. He also helped expedite the deportation of Jews from Old Germany. Finally, on November 29, 1941, Heydrich sent invitations to a number of government and SS officials for a meeting to work out a coordinated plan for the solution of the "Jewish problem," now that Jews from the Reich were being banished to the east, where conditions were tempestuous and chaotic. If Heydrich spoke of a "total" or "final" solution in this summons, he certainly did not spell out what he or his superiors understood by this term. The conference was to be held on December 9 in Berlin, at the headquarters of the International Criminal Police Commission at Grosser Wannsee 56-8.

At the last moment this meeting was put off for six weeks, until January 20, 1942. The reasons for this rescheduling remain unclear. Heydrich claimed that on the original date at least one of the invited officials, SS Major Dr. Rudolf Lange, was unable to attend because as security chief for Latvia he was busy supervising the execution of Jews in Riga. By itself, however, this explanation seems insufficient and implausible, especially since the press of business of a subaltern in the field, always eager to consult with superiors in the imperial capital, would not justify such a long postponement. More likely, Heydrich temporized, or was ordered to do so, because the weeks from early December through mid-January marked Nazi Germany's most critical and ill-fated juncture: the defeat west of Moscow and the Soviet counteroffensive; Pearl Harbor and America's entry into the war; the shift to a war of position and full war mobilization; the loss of initiative, of surprise, and of the appearance of invulnerability.

It is most unlikely that once they did convene in Wannsee the assembled state and party functionaries were unaware that Germany and the Nazi regime had reached a dangerous turning point, with hard times ahead. This is not to say that they understood the full gravity of the situation, as did many of the highest civil and military leaders, none of whom were present. With Himmler absent, Heydrich chaired the meeting. The other fourteen participants were officials of Heydrich's subordinate rank, or lower. As the objective was to coordinate the solution of the "Jewish problem," there were delegates from both spheres of the dual state. There were three functionaries from traditional ministries, all of them party members or declared Nazi sympathizers: Dr. Wilhelm Stuckart, state secretary for legal affairs in the Interior Ministry; Dr. Roland Freisler, state secretary and second-ranking official in the Justice Ministry; and Martin Luther, deputy state secretary and close associate of von Ribbentrop in the Foreign Office. An additional four participants came from Nazi-created state administrations: Gauleiter Dr. Alfred Meyer and Dr. Georg Leibbrandt, state secretaries in the Ministry for the Occupied Eastern Territories; Dr. Josef Bühler, state secretary and first adjunct to Dr. Hans Frank in the General Government; and Erich Neumann, state secretary in the Office of the Four-Year Plan. One delegate may be said to have come from the nerve center of the dual state: Ministerial Director Wilhelm Kritzinger, sitting in for Dr. Hans Heinrich Lammers, chief of the Reich Chancellery, who had frequent access to Hitler.

The remaining six delegates, all of them SS officers, spoke for the party side of the state: SS Colonel Dr. Gerhard Klopfer, chief of the Third (political) Division of the Party Chancellery, headed by Martin Bormann; SS General Otto Hofmann, director of the Bureau of Race and Resettlement in the Reich Central Security Office (RSHA); SS Major General Heinrich Müller, head of Section IV (Gestapo) of RSHA; SS Lieutenant Colonel Adolf Eichmann, chief of Division B-4 (Evacuation and Jews), also Section IV; SS Colonel Dr. Karl Schöngarth, commander of the Security Police and Security Service in the General Government; and SS Major Dr. Rudolf Lange, commander of the Security Police and Security Service in Latvia, who also represented his superior, the security chief of Reichkommissariat Ostland.

Eight of the fifteen participants at Wannsee, including three of the SS leaders, were university graduates. Without exception, all fifteen were versed in the "Jewish question," each from his own specialized perspective. Moreover, all must have known about the worsening plight of the Jews throughout the eastern territories, including Poland. How many of them were informed about the anti-Jewish ravages of the Einsatzgruppen and the regular SS is unclear. But at the very least, Heydrich, Lange, Bühler, and more than likely Stuckart, had

firsthand information which they had no reason to keep to themselves. This is not to say that for any of these officials, even Heydrich,
the massacres outside Kiev and Riga were necessarily rehearsals for
a "final solution" of liquidation to be systematized and streamlined
at Wannsee. Even so, there could be no doubt for any of them that
they were assembled to increase, not alleviate, the torment of the
Jews.

Hans Frank had assigned Bühler to represent the General Government at Wannsee, and apparently had sent him to Berlin for a preliminary briefing. On December 16, 1941, while the conference was on
hold, Frank addressed the top members of his administration in
Cracow. On this occasion he expressed ideas which were probably
widespread in the higher political echelons in the east and reflected
his deputy's report on the temper in the capital. Frank's own words
must be quoted *in extenso*.

> Let me tell you quite frankly: in one way or another we will have
> to finish with the Jews. The führer once expressed it as follows: should
> Jewry once again succeed in inciting a world war, the bloodletting
> could not be limited to the peoples they drove to war but the Jews
> [themselves] would be done for in Europe. . . . As an old-time National
> Socialist I must say that if the Jewish tribe survives the war in Europe
> while we sacrifice our blood for the preservation of Europe, this war
> will be but a partial success. Basically, I must presume, therefore, that
> the Jews will disappear. They must go away. To that end I have started
> negotiations to expel them to the east. In January this issue will be
> discussed at a major conference in Berlin, to which I am sending State
> Secretary Dr. Bühler. . . . In any case, there will be a great Jewish
> migration.
>
> But what is to become of the Jews? Do you think that they will be
> settled in villages in the conquered eastern territories? In Berlin we
> have been told not to complicate matters: since neither these territo-
> ries [nor our own] have any use for them [i.e., the Jews], we should
> liquidate them ourselves! Gentlemen, I must ask you to remain un-
> moved by pleas for pity. We must annihilate the Jews wherever we
> encounter them and wherever possible, in order to maintain the over-
> all mastery of the Reich here. . . . Anyhow, we must find a way [other
> than a legal one] to achieve this goal, and I am perplexed as to how
> to proceed.
>
> For us the Jews are also exceptionally damaging because they are
> being such gluttons. There are an estimated 2.5 million Jews in the
> General Government, perhaps . . . [even as many] as 3.5 million. These
> 3.5 million Jews, we cannot shoot them, nor can we poison them. Even
> so, we can take steps which in some way or other will pave the way

for [their] destruction, notably in connection with the grand measures to be discussed in the Reich. The General Government must become just as *judenfrei* as the Reich.

Unlike before, Governor-General Frank was no longer satisfied with keeping his captive province from becoming the main dumping ground for unwanted Jews from farther west. He now saw an opportunity to rid it of its own Jews—whose numbers he exaggerated greatly—by either expelling them eastward or doing away with them in other ways. Incidentally, if Frank knew about the setbacks in Russia, as he must have, he did not mention them. Instead, he spoke of exploiting both the Ukrainians and the Poles, and playing them off against each other, in the interest of making the General Government the essential bridgehead for the control of the vast spaces being conquered in the east.

Apparently, Eichmann, the lowest-ranking official at Wannsee, took the minutes which, after review by Heydrich, became the official "protocol" of the proceedings. Naturally, this text reveals nothing about the private conversations of the participants before and after the meeting. It also makes it appear as if during the deliberations they never so much as mentioned the serious military crisis which just then preoccupied the top leadership. Even so, this crisis must have cast a wide shadow over the conference.

On January 20, 1942, in his opening statement at Wannsee, Heydrich noted that Reichsmarschall Göring had charged him "with preparing the *Endlösung* [final/definitive solution] of the Jewish question in Europe," and that he had summoned this meeting to "clarify some of the fundamental issues." Göring's request for a draft proposal for the necessary "administrative, practical, and financial" arrangements called for prior consultation with all interested government agencies. Having established the source of his authority, Heydrich went on to claim that "without regard for geographic boundaries" in the main Himmler and he himself were responsible for the "implementation of the final solution."

Before turning to what needed to be done, Heydrich reviewed what had been achieved since 1933. After being deemancipated and subjected to restrictions within Germany, the Jews had been urged and pushed to emigrate. Eventually, in January 1939, Göring had ordered him, Heydrich, to set up and direct a special emigration office to speed and organize the extrusion of Jews "by legal means." There being no other solution, this office proceeded to force emigration in the face of both domestic and foreign obstacles. All told, and despite numerous stumbling blocks, between January 30, 1933, and October 31, 1941, some 537,000 Jews had left the Old Reich, Austria, and the Protectorate. In the meantime, however, "in view of the risks of emigration in wartime and considering the [new] possibilities in the east," Himmler had forbidden all further emigration. Then Heydrich came to the core of the agenda.

> To take the place of emigration, and with the prior approval of the führer, the evacuation of the Jews to the East has become another possible solution.
>
> Although both courses of action [emigration and evacuation] must, of course, be considered as nothing more than [so many] temporary expedients, they do help to provide practical experience which should be of great importance in view of the coming *Endlösung* of the Jewish question.

Needless to say, as it stands, and considering later developments, this statement was full of "warnings, and portents and evils imminent." But from the protocol it is not clear whether or not Heydrich amplified his proposition by discussing the disastrous plight of eastern ghettos like Riga and Łódź, which was being aggravated by the arrival of Jewish deportees from Germany. Did he himself have a clear idea of what he meant by *Endlösung*? Did he use coded language, confident of being understood by the assembled initiates?

Heydrich was, in any case, breaking altogether new ground. Until this day, the Nazi persecution of the Jews had been confined to the Jews of Germany, Austria, and the Protectorate, as well as of the territories conquered—and still to be conquered—in the east. Now, however, Heydrich broadened the range, in that he meant his projected *Endlösung* to apply to all of Europe. He circulated a table listing the Jewish populations of the entire Continent as well as of England and Ireland, for a total of over 11 million Jews. He claimed that this figure was on the low side, the count of Jews being based on confessional rather than "racial" criteria in many countries. To implement the *Endlösung*, Heydrich proposed "to comb Europe from west to east," beginning with German lands.

Heydrich envisaged that "under proper direction . . . and in an appropriate manner" the Jews would be put to work in the east. His idea was to form the Jews who were fit to work into "large labor columns, separated by sex," to be marched to the eastern territories, where they would build roads. Doubtless a great many Jews "will fall by the wayside from natural exhaustion." In turn, however, the "surviving remnant" would certainly consist of the "toughest" elements.

In as much as the members of this residue would be the product of "natural selection," they would have "to be dealt with appropriately, [for] upon being freed they will constitute the embryo for the reconstruction of Jewish life (see the lessons of history)."

The idea was to make a clear distinction between Jews fit for hard labor and those unfit for it, with the expectation that many of those declared fit would be marked for early death by virtue of being unsuited for backbreaking work. It may well be that not only the vengeful fury against the Jews but also the straitened logistics of Barbarossa prompted Heydrich to propose the use of expendable slave labor for road and railway construction in the east. In any case, here was a program of extermination through forced labor, with an ominous but generic reference to an "appropriate" treatment for those managing to bear up.

Apparently, the unfit—children, many women, the infirm, the elderly—were to be evacuated "to so-called transit ghettos, for transportation further east from there." Heydrich saw a need to divide all potential evacuees into different categories and allow for exceptions. The Nuremberg Laws would be the basis of this projected operation. Certain half-Jews would be given a choice between, on the one hand, sterilization and staying in Germany, and, on the other, deportation. Jews over sixty-five years of age "would not be evacuated but sent to a ghetto for the aged," most likely to Theresienstadt, along with badly wounded and heavily decorated Jewish war veterans. As for the timing of each major evacuation, "it will largely depend on military developments."

According to the protocol, not a single voice was raised to protest even the most egregious and unconscionable provisions of Heydrich's proposal. Almost certainly moved by a shared outlook rather than a common fear, those officials who did speak out did so in the treacherous spirit of bureaucratic rationality. Martin Luther of the Foreign Office noted that while there might be difficulties in removing Jews from the "northern [Scandinavian] countries," where they were rare in any case, he foresaw none for "southeastern and western Europe." To avoid "endless red tape," Wilhelm Stuckart of the Interior Ministry recommended that the sterilization of half-Jews be made not voluntary but compulsory. Erich Neumann of the Four-Year Plan urged that Jews "working in vital war industries not be evacuated until replacements were found," to which Heydrich agreed. For his part, Josef Bühler, Hans Frank's emissary, asked that "the final solution of this question" begin in the General Government, which could guarantee that there would be no local transportation and economic difficulties.

Jews should be removed as rapidly as possible from the territories of the General Government, in particular because as carriers of disease they are a great danger to society at large and as incorrigible black marketeers they are undermining the economy of the country. Besides, of the 2.5 million Jews, the majority was unfit for work.

Bühler concluded with the plea "that in this territory the Jewish question be solved as quickly as possible." Apparently, Bühler, along with Alfred Meyer of the Ministry for the Occupied Eastern Territories, took the lead in the closing discussion of "different types of possible solutions" (die verschiedenen Arten der Lösungsmöglichkeiten). Both advocated "the immediate implementation of certain preparatory measures in the affected territories, care being taken not to disquiet the [local] populations." Given their responsibilities, Bühler and Meyer were mainly concerned with the eastern territories.

There was nothing definitive about the Wannsee Conference, nor could there be. Whatever its origin, it was held at an unexpectedly trying moment in the history of the Third Reich. War policy was in extreme flux, and so was Jewish policy. At the same time that Nazi Germany's leaders decided to go to any length in pursuit of the war against the Soviets, they resolved to step up the war against the Jews. With emigration to European countries and Madagascar foreclosed, they fixed upon the east as holding the key to victory over not only their military enemies but also the Jews. For them, the two campaigns were closely and fatally intertwined. For a while some Nazis continued to look to the defeat of the Soviet Union to provide space for the resettlement of Jews deep in the interior of Russia. Paradoxically, in this perspective military victory was the precondition for Jewish survival. To be sure, the Jews would in that case have suffered cruelly and disproportionately while the war lasted. Still, victory would have kept open the historical possibility of a significant remnant of Jews enduring, if only to be ghettoized in a distant reserve, or to be used as a pawn in bargaining for a negotiated settlement with the Western Powers. In fact, the faster and easier the victory, the larger this remnant and the better the chances for contingent survival would doubtless have been. Conversely, the longer and harder the fighting and the more ineluctable the defeat, the more catastrophic the consequences for the Jews. Such was, after all, Hitler's grimly insistent private and public prophecy.

On January 25, 1942, five days after the Wannsee Conference, Hitler held forth bluntly in the presence of Himmler and Lammers.

The Jew must get out of Europe. Otherwise we will get no European understanding. The world over he is the chief agitator against us. ... All I say is that he must go away. If, in the process, he is bruised, I can't help it. If he does not leave voluntarily, I see no solution other than extermination.

Of course, by this time emigration had long since come to a halt. Besides, the issue was no longer simply to make Old Germany *judenfrei* but to settle accounts with the Jews of all German-occupied and controlled territories. In this same diatribe Hitler wondered "why I should see a Jew in a different light than a Russian prisoner [of war]." He declined all responsibility for "the many [Russians] who are dying in prison camps." Instead, he blamed the Jews for "having driven us into this situation," and once again asked, rhetorically, "why the Jews incited this war."

Two days later, on January 27, in another monologue at his Wolf's Lair headquarters in East Prussia, Hitler reiterated that "the Jew has to disappear from Europe," including from Switzerland and Sweden. On this occasion he said nothing about extermination, limiting himself to declaring that "it would be best if [the Jews] went to Russia." At any rate, he had "no pity" for them.

The führer's ferociously destructive posture must have become known to ever larger circles of senior officials. A considerable number of party, government, and military leaders themselves heard Hitler soliloquize in the dining hall or sitting room of his headquarters. In turn, they must have shared their privileged information and impressions with many of their associates, as well as with connections in the business, social, and cultural world. Besides, Hitler made no secret of his anti-Jewish fury, since he spoke his mind in public.

On January 30, 1942, he addressed a rally in Berlin's Palace of Sports. The führer made a special point of berating the British for rejecting his efforts to reach an accommodation. He maintained that if not for this English bullheadedness, it would take little additional effort and time to finish off the Soviets. With his back to the wall, Hitler struck out at the Jews.

We fully realize that the war can only end either with the extermination of the Aryan peoples or the disappearance of the Jews from Europe. While I guard myself against making rash prophecies, on September 1, 1939, I declared in the German Reichstag that this war would not end, as the Jews suppose, with the extermination of the European-Aryan peoples, but with the destruction of Jewry. For the

first time the ancient Jewish maxim will be put in practice: "an eye for
an eye, a tooth for a tooth."

Certain that anti-Semitism would spread with the protraction of the
war, Hitler predicted that "the hour would come when the most evil
world enemy of all time will be put out of action for at least a
thousand years."

In less than a month, on February 24, 1942, he returned to this
same theme in his yearly message marking the foundation of the Nazi
Party in Munich. Hitler told the *alte Kämpfer* that now, unlike at the
start of their struggle, they were "no longer alone in fighting the
[unholy] alliance of Jewish capitalism and communism, . . . the ideas
of the National Socialist and Fascist revolutions [having] conquered
great and powerful states." It was in keeping with the nature of the
audience and setting in Munich for the führer to slight the military
aspects of the war, which just then consumed him, in order to stress
its messianic side.

> . . . my prophecy will be fulfilled: this war will not destroy Aryan
> humanity, but will exterminate the Jew. Such will be the ultimate
> outcome of this conflict, whatever its repercussions and no matter how
> long it lasts.

The world simply could not be at peace until after "the liquidation
of this parasite."

In the meantime, Hitler kept reiterating his animus in private.
During the night of February 3–4 he asserted that after many false
starts in the persecution of Jews through the centuries, "this time they
will disappear from Europe." On February 17, in the presence of
Himmler, the führer charged that just as the Jews had once used
Christianity to subvert the natural order of things, in which "the
fittest rule," not the meek, so now they had recourse to bolshevism
to advance their world conspiracy. Clearly, "the more thoroughly the
Jews are thrown out, the faster this danger will be removed." According to Goebbels, in mid-February Hitler also spoke to him about the
need to be unsparing with the Jews.

> There is no room for sentimentality. The Jews deserve the catastro-
> phe in which they are caught up today. They will experience their own
> destruction along with the destruction of our [other] enemies. We
> must hasten this process impassively, and in so doing render an inesti-
> mable service to humanity, which has suffered at the hands of Jewry
> for thousands of years.

If the propaganda minister is to be believed, Hitler told him that "this unequivocal hostility to the Jews will also have to be beaten into the heads of the recalcitrants among our own people."

At about this same time, on February 22, Hitler credited Streicher for conspicuously branding the Jews, making it impossible for them to hide. In the presence of Himmler, he said that this identification and isolation of the Jew would result in "one of the greatest revolutions in world history." Not unlike "Pasteur and Koch," Nazi Germany would have to fight a "bacillus," the Jew being "the cause of innumerable diseases which . . . would also have ravaged Japan if it had continued to be open to him." At any rate, Germany "will pull through if we eliminate the Jew."

His public vilification of the Jews continued. On March 15, 1942, which was Martyrs' Day, Hitler traduced the "Jewish wire-pullers for their worldwide conspiracy to unite democracy and bolshevism in a common drive for the destruction of Europe." Six weeks later, on April 26, in a speech to the Reichstag, the führer castigated the Jews for having been the "hidden force that goaded" the British into both world wars. The Jews, he said, had masterminded the defeat, revolution, and diplomatic calamity of 1918–19. Between the wars it was they who had become the chief "carriers of the Bolshevik infection . . . and the warmongers in the plutocracies." At present, Germany's soldiers were "suffering the most palpable consequences of this warmongering" in Russia, whose "dictatorship is purely Jewish."

In the Reichstag Hitler claimed to speak with "the feelings of a man who had just won the most difficult battle of his life in the service of a holy cause." The battle of this past winter had been won not in some "ordinary war" but in the struggle against bolshevism. National Socialists were particularly well placed to "understand the theoretical principles and gruesome . . . objectives of this world pest." Bolshevism was not a proletarian regime but a Jewish dictatorship bent on "exterminating the national leadership and intelligentsia" of peoples the world over. While in Russia bolshevism was the "pliable product of this Jewish infection" elsewhere the preconditions for this same subversion were being created by "democratic capitalism," which the Jews were pushing toward the same abyss. At any rate, the world was now divided into two camps. The enemy side had two major constituents: "the men of democracy, the heart of Jewish capitalism, with their ballast of tarnished political theories, parliamentary corruption, antiquated civil societies, Jewish brain trusts, newspapers, stock markets, and banks . . . ; and allied with them the Bolshevik state, that is to say that mass of animalized (*vertiert*) humanity over which the

Jews are cracking their bloody whip." As for the Axis side, it consisted of "the peoples fighting for their freedom and independence, as well as the daily bread of humanity." In conclusion Hitler affirmed that the world conflict between these two camps "will be decided on the battlefields of eastern Europe."

At the Wannsee Conference the switches were set for the deportation of Jews from German-occupied Europe west of the Warthegau to the ghettos and transit camps east of that line. The result would be not only the overcrowding of ghettos but also the concentration of all Jews in the most ill-starred lands of the Continent. Europe's Jews risked being trapped in the most politically tyrannized, economically wasted, and militarily vulnerable zone of German-occupied Europe. The Jews would have been gravely imperiled in this precarious region even without having violence deliberately done to them during and after their roundup and deportation in overcrowded railway cars. The idea was to use their evacuation and resettlement to decimate them, but not without concurrently exploiting their labor for the war effort. The result was a chronic but not irreconcilable tension between liquidation and productivity. Although Heydrich proposed to impress Jews for road-building, he put decimation through forced labor ahead of economic output. Although he had received his original charge from the head of the Four-Year Plan, Heydrich was a fanatic Nazi executioner, and was not about to give first or high priority to channeling workers into the concentration-camp economy.

But Himmler, his immediate superior and overall head of the incipient "Final Solution," had a more far-reaching view of the function and place of the security services in the regime. He had long since resolved to make the SS into the principal political shield of the Nazi regime, hopefully to become one of the two supporting pillars, along with the Wehrmacht, of the Third Reich's dual state. To that end, just as in 1938 with the war in the offing he had conceived and founded the Waffen-SS with a view to enlarging and securing the place of the general SS, he now proposed to harness the labor of an expanding concentration-camp system for the war economy of the embattled Behemoth. To be sure, Himmler was not at Wannsee and he seems not to have alerted Heydrich to this new turn before January 20. But within less than a week after Wannsee, on January 26, 1942, he sent a wire to SS Major General Richard Glücks, chief inspector of concentration camps, prefiguring a radical change in the population as well as the purpose of the camps.

Since no Russian prisoners of war can be expected in the near future, I will send many of the Jews and Jewesses to be evacuated from Germany to the camps. Prepare the concentration camps to take in 100,000 Jewish men and 50,000 Jewish women next month. In the coming weeks the concentration camps will receive great economic contracts and assignments. SS Major General Pohl will provide you with necessary details.

By instructing Glücks to follow Pohl's orders, Himmler signaled the rising importance of the newly chartered Central Economic and Administrative Office (WVHA) within the SS. Paradoxically, Himmler's telegram did not distinguish between Jews fit and unfit for work, nor did it hint at any hoped-for decimation. There was either a hidden agenda or, more likely, the process of "selection" was to grow out of the iron exigencies of concentration camps and ghettos, which became total institutions of forced dehumanization, exploitation, and liquidation.

Hereafter, Himmler directed a twofold policy through the WVHA and the RSHA. Pohl's WVHA was charged with raising the largest possible Jewish labor force for hyperexploitation, either within concentration camps and ghettos or in private industry outside. Of course, Jewish workers would be mercilessly expended by deliberate mistreatment, which included overexposing them to the vicissitudes of wartime shortages. Notwithstanding its built-in deadliness, Pohl's massing of Jewish labor—along with non-Jewish workers from all over Europe—was grounded in the logic and purpose of expediting the forced-draft industrial production necessitated by the failure of Barbarossa and its military sequels.

Simultaneously, Heydrich's RSHA undertook to make all but Slavic Europe *judenfrei* "by combing it [of Jews] from west to east." For the moment these Jews, many of them highly assimilated and acculturated, were to be sent to the occupied eastern territories to be crammed into ghettos as well as concentration, labor, and transit camps, pending resettlement farther east. Although Heydrich meant to use some of these Jews to build roads, perhaps even strategic ones, he did not consider such makeshift construction work a significant contribution to systematic economic mobilization for a protracted all-out war. For him, the ideological warrior and policeman, the economic imperative counted for little. Heydrich saw above all the punitive side of forced and slave labor.

After Wannsee, Pohl and Heydrich were pulling the emerging "Final Solution" in opposite directions, or at any rate pressing it ahead along different roads and at different speeds. But since Himmler kept a tight rein on both of them, they were not about to pull apart. Though fired by a shared anti-Semitic fury, the drive against the Jews was not uniformly exterminationist. It was an admixture of the hyperexploitation of Jewish labor for the war effort and the fixed determination to remove the Jews from Europe, if need be by rank liquidation. At first, the blend of hyperexploitation and annihilation varied according to time, place, and circumstance. But with the irretrievable impasse and defeat of the eastern campaign, this blend became ever more lethal. Meanwhile, it is highly revealing that by March 27, 1942, Goebbels noted that Hitler's prophecy concerning the punishment of the Jews "for having instigated a new world war is beginning to be fulfilled in a most ghastly fashion," insisting that "once again the führer is the dauntless advocate of a radical course."

CHAPTER X

WAGING WAR
TO THE DEATH

THE RAPE OF EUROPE

As of the winter of 1941–42, the unique torment of the Jews was correlated with and facilitated by the savageries and miseries of war which increasingly scourged most of Europe. While this ideologically conditioned physical and mental wrack of civilians and soldiers had its epicenter in conquered Poland and Russia, eventually its shock waves traveled even to the farthest corners of the German-controlled Continent. The frustrations of the eastern campaign and the insatiable demands of unlimited war drove the Third Reich to continue tightening its vise not only on its conquered and embattled eastern provinces but also on most of the other territories within its overextended sphere of domination and influence. In the interest of the war effort not only the SS but all the principal military and civilian agencies of the raging Behemoth set about impressing foreign labor, commandeering foreign resources, and cutting foreign rations. This relentless despoliation, pillage, and hyperexploitation incited first passive and then active resistance. Since the Germans systematically overestimated it, particularly in its early stages, this resistance lashed them into an ever-greater frenzy of coercion and retribution. This Nazi fury, incited by the frustrations attendant on controlling and exploiting a complex empire, increasingly found a target in the Jews. The murderous persecution of the Jews was not so much a separate policy as part of the desperate political hubris of political leaders who more than half-realized that their dreams of power were unrealizable but were incapable of surrendering them. These blighted dreams led the Nazi regime to violate most traditional political, moral, and religious norms and, more importantly, the notions of humanity defined by them, so that naked power now normalized brutality as its response to its own irreversible loss of control. There were, of course, momentary and local remissions in this spiral of general and anti-

Jewish ferocity. But these were due, essentially, to the intermittently neutralizing contradictions in the parallel but discordant exercise of functional and nihilistic violence. All in all, the "Final Solution" may be said to have been forged and consummated in the crucible of the abortive crusading war against Soviet Russia and "Judeobolshevism," which in eastern Europe created the context of extreme cruelty and destruction apart from which the Judeocide would have been unthinkable and impracticable.

From the start of Barbarossa the war was a burning preoccupation for the Jews trapped in eastern Europe, conscious that their own fate depended on its course and outcome. Perhaps Emmanuel Ringelblum's authentic and heart-wrenching *Notes from the Warsaw Ghetto* best testify to this intense awareness. On July 12, 1941, he recorded that since Kiev had not "fallen by the 5th of July" and the Russians had managed to "hold out for seven weeks," the populace of the Warsaw ghetto was "confident of the eventual Soviet triumph, as of the triumph of the Allies in general." By October 19, however, the German advance toward Moscow "called forth a huge wave of pessimism among the Jews" who, looking to the Red Army for liberation, asked themselves "whence shall our help come?" Soon thereafter, once the Wehrmacht was stopped and thrown back, Ringelblum again took heart. But in June 1942, in view of the stepped-up campaign against Polish Jewry, Ringelblum postulated that because the Germans "are being defeated [and] their cities are being destroyed, . . . they are taking their revenge on the Jews. . . ." By then he saw their "extermination being executed according to a plan and schedule prepared in advance." This being the case, "only a miracle can save us: the sudden end of the war, [for] otherwise, we are lost." Ringelblum recorded that "the more sober among us . . . [are warning] against having any illusions [and against expecting any] compassion from the Germans." In this view, "whether we live or die depends on how much time they have." Ringelblum's insight was terrifyingly realistic: "If [the Germans] have enough time, we are lost. If salvation comes soon, we are saved."

In his search for historical signposts to help them understand the present tragedy, Ringelblum and his companions turned to reading about previous wars, notably about the First World War and the Napoleonic Wars. Ringelblum himself thought that "every stage of [Germany's] occupation of . . . France and Belgium [in 1914–18] . . . simply begged for comparison with the present, far crueler war." Having read Maxence Van der Meersch's *Invasion: 1914,* he saw "cold, merciless pillage" as common to both world wars, "the occu-

pied countries [being] completely devastated, their population enslaved and forced to work for the Germans."

But there were also people who "relished reading about Napoleon," only to "draw parallels between the Cursed One [Hitler] and
Napoleon—always to the latter's benefit." While the French emperor
certainly had "rivers of blood" on his conscience, he did have the
merit of having "overturned the feudal world and introduced a new,
revolutionary order." By way of contrast, "after the Cursed One,
nothing will remain but tens of millions of victims in every country
of the world, and a Europe that, leveled and ravaged, will be thrown
back centuries by the war." Meanwhile, Napoleon's "march on Moscow," which marked "the beginning of [his] end," provided some
comfort: "Reading in the winter here about the severities of the
Russian winter, we hope that history will again repeat itself and the
end will be the downfall of the Cursed One." To be sure, this last
winter "did not conclude, as the winter of 1812 did, with the catastrophic defeat of a tyrant." Even so, Ringelblum was convinced "that
H[itler], like Napoleon, has committed the mortal blunder of tangling
with the Russian colossus, with its enormous reserves of manpower
and material."

But though he probed the past for glimmers of hope, Ringelblum
ultimately concluded that "all this search for historical analogy is
beside the point." To his mind, "history *does not* repeat itself, especially . . . now that we stand at the crossroads, witnessing the death
pangs of an old world and the birth pangs of a new." There simply
was no comparing "the White Terror of the feudal world and the
slaughter of Kiev, or Rostov, where hundreds of thousands of civilians were murdered." Still and always the humanistic scholar, Ringelblum charged posterity with undertaking "a special research project
to investigate the similarities and differences between the wars at the
end of the feudal world and the end of the capitalist one." But from
his vantage point in the eye of the hurricane he was certain that "a
simple comparison . . . is impossible," the two periods being "completely different, with other concepts entirely."

By this time Ringelblum had long since witnessed, firsthand, some
of the horrors and the attendant dehumanization particular to his
age. On August 26, 1941, he noted "a marked, remarkable indifference to death" which, given its omnipresence in the ghetto, "no
longer impresses." People were "walking past corpses with indifference" and it was "rare for anyone to visit the hospital to inquire after
a relative." For the Jews of Warsaw, "next to hunger, typhus . . . has
become the burning question of the hour." A month later, Ringel-

blum registered the rumor that the Germans were "about to liquidate the Small Ghetto," reducing the ghetto as a whole by "40 percent." The authorities either claimed to need the space for "1.5 mil. soldiers who are supposedly coming to Warsaw" or considered it to be located "on the route taken by the German army," along which they wanted no Jews. This was also the time when doctors were "fearful that next winter every fifth person—and some maintain that the figure will be as high as every other person—will be sick with typhus." On May 8, 1942, in the wake of the mass murder of Jews in many cities of the General Government, Ringelblum speculated that Himmler had ordered these massacres "in order to terrorize the Jewish populace, probably . . . in connection with the spring campaign, [for which the Germans] want their rear to be secure."

But in late April and early May 1942, the Jews of the Warsaw ghetto above all "lived in terror of deportation," notably of the deportation of all " 'nonproductive' elements." The rumors turned out to be a false alarm, "thanks to the presence of factories in the ghetto that are supplying the needs of the German Army." Here, then, was the "tragic paradox" which Ringelblum considered central to the uniqueness of the present Jewish catastrophe.

[In Warsaw] only those Jews have the right to live who work to supply the German Army. The same was true in Vilna, Rovno, and dozens of other cities where there were mass slaughters of Jews. The only Jews left alive were those who directly or indirectly worked for the Germans. Never in history has there been a national tragedy of these dimensions. A people that hates the Germans with every fiber of its being can purchase its life only at the price of helping its foe to victory—the very victory that means the complete annihilation of Jewry from the face of Europe, if not of the whole world.

As of mid-June 1942, Ringelblum knew that the trains that were transporting "children up to the age of ten and old people over sixty" in the direction of Bełżec were taking them there to be killed. He also knew that there was "no camp involved," but some other installation for annihilation which had no facilities for resettlement. Although he noted that "the very young and the very old" were only "the first to be exterminated," Ringelblum, in his awareness of the uniqueness of the current Jewish suffering, stressed that except during Israel's bondage in Egypt, the slaughter of children was "unprecedented in Jewish history." Indeed, "even in the most barbaric times, a human spark glowed in the rudest heart, and children were spared." If only in this regard, "the Hitlerian beast was quite different, [in that] it would

devour the dearest of us, those who arouse the greatest compassion—
our innocent children."

After the Wannsee Conference the imperatives of total war became
ever more relentless. In late February 1942 the Soviet counteroffensive finally slowed and was halted along an uneven line running
north-south sixty to a hundred miles west of Moscow. During March,
Hitler and his generals completed their plans for a second summer
offensive, to be known as Operation Blue. Considerably chastened by
the failure of Barbarossa and Typhoon, they set themselves not just
a maximum objective, but a minimum one as well: either the total
defeat of the Soviet Union or (more likely?) the establishment of a
stable and fortified front deep in Russia behind which to gear up for
subsequent campaigns against not only the Red Army but the armies
of the Western allies as well. In any case, they now bent all their efforts
to an all-out resumption of the eastern drive.

The most obvious and urgent requirement was to make good the
Wehrmacht's losses in manpower. These ran to about 1 million, or
about a third of the eastern army, including close to 200,000 dead and
over 700,000 wounded. Numerous regiments, battalions, and divisions of the Wehrmacht as well as of the Waffen-SS were down to a
fraction of their original strength, and several of them were depleted.
The armed forces asked for an additional 800,000 men. Many of the
new recruits would have to come from industrial sectors which, now
that they were shifting to full war production, faced acute labor
shortages of their own. Albert Speer, the newly appointed armaments
chief, warned of the disastrous economic consequences of such a
draft. There seemed only one way out of this critical crunch: to
impress foreign workers in order to free German workers for military
service and to expand the Third Reich's relatively inelastic labor force
for full-scale war production.

It would, however, take time to do so. Accordingly, Hitler, Keitel,
and von Ribbentrop pressed both Rumania and Hungary, but also
Italy, to make available additional troops for the forthcoming offensive. Marshal Antonescu sent two new field armies, or 21 divisions,
to the southern front, and Admiral Horthy dispatched another 9
divisions. Desperate for manpower, the German command ordered
a total of 42 Rumanian, Hungarian, and Italian divisions to take an
active part in Operation Blue. Admittedly, because of their insufficient equipment and training, these troops were assigned to the rear
guard, which freed German contingents for offensive operations.
Still, by September 1942 the 2.5 million men in the 163 German
divisions on the eastern front were reinforced by some 65 non-Ger-

man divisions, including 17 Finnish divisions. There were, in addition, close to 25,000 volunteers from France, Spain, Walloonian Belgium, and Croatia, although few of them were trained soldiers. As noted previously, these anti-Bolshevik crusaders were originally meant to give Barbarossa a Pan-European aura. By now, however, foreign recruits were a sheer military necessity as well.

Having suffered disproportionately heavy losses since June 22, 1941, the Waffen-SS started a major new recruiting drive at the same time as the Wehrmacht. The Waffen-SS had grown from 18,000 men at the start of the Polish campaign to 160,000 at the start of Barbarossa, to reach a total of 220,000 in late 1941. In the middle of that year it had sent five divisions into battle: the Leibstandarte Adolf Hitler and the Viking divisions on the southern front; the Das Reich Division on the central front; and the Death's Head and Police divisions on the northern front. By early November the Waffen-SS had lost over 35,000 men and 1,200 officers, among them 13,000 dead. These casualties rose significantly in the first retreat from Moscow, during which select units of the Waffen-SS, fighting to the last ditch, were almost completely wiped out. By the end of the winter of 1942–43 one-third of all SS soldiers were dead, seriously wounded, or missing. No doubt Hitler was impressed by the exceptional performance and fighting spirit of the Waffen-SS, and ordered Himmler to double his military corps. At the same time, he decided, however, that the regular army should have first call on whatever additional German manpower could be mustered for military duty.

Consequently, Himmler looked beyond Germany's borders to supplement his domestic allocations. Through 1942 the Waffen-SS was still able to tap a considerable reservoir of volunteers both at home and abroad. But thereafter, and particularly once it was clear that the tide was turning, it had to resort to pressure and compulsion to fill its rank. In any case, the effectives of the Waffen-SS were raised to 330,000 by the end of 1942, to 540,000 by the end of 1943, and to over 900,000 by the end of 1944. About 500,000 of these recruits, or over one-half, were foreigners, and during the last year of war there were more foreigners than Germans in the Waffen-SS.

About 125,000 of these foreigners were volunteers from western and northern Europe, notably from France, Flemish Belgium, Holland, Norway, and Denmark. Among them about one-third were true believers, the rest adventurers or careerists. But the two largest pools from which recruits were drawn were the so called *Volksdeutsche* and *Osteuropäer*. The former were Germans resident in the Baltic countries, Rumania, Hungary, Croatia, and Slovakia. Certainly, until the winter of 1942–43 most of these *Volksdeutsche* had the same motives for enlisting in the anti-Bolshevik crusade as volunteers from the different west European countries. After Stalingrad and until late 1944, *in extremis*, the Waffen-SS stepped up its recruitment among east Europeans, notably Estonians, Latvians, Ukrainians, Tartars, Georgians, and so forth. Many of these *Osteuropäer* rallied to the anti-Soviet and anti-Bolshevik banners chiefly in pursuit of national independence or autonomy. All told, the Waffen-SS raised twenty-two divisions of foreigners, of which eight divisions were never moved to the front and four did not go into action until early 1945.

As of the spring of 1942, and particularly in the fall of that year, Hitler not only encouraged the growth of the Waffen-SS but also ordered that its star divisions be turned into crack panzer units. The führer increasingly considered the Waffen-SS the cream of his armed forces. He was confident that the professional cadres and true believers of nazism's military vanguard would forge their motley recruits into effective and worthy auxiliaries.

Notwithstanding the large foreign phalanges in its oversized ranks, the Waffen-SS remained the military arm of the *Allgemeine*, or General SS, which more than ever embodied the inner nature of the Nazi regime and project. Although Himmler had no influence over combat operations, he continued to exercise ultimate control over the Waffen SS. He played an essential role in procuring and allocating personnel, equipment, and supplies. Himmler also set the tone for the ideological indoctrination so essential for shaping the morale, ethic, and effectiveness of an increasingly heterogeneous fighting force. Even before the assault on Russia he had decreed that the concentration-camp guards and the Waffen-SS belonged to the same corps: they wore the same black uniform; they carried the same pay book; and they were rotated back and forth between the two branches. Just as officers and men of the general SS who were guarding the concentration camps were detached for service in the Einsatzgruppen, so members of the Waffen-SS were detached for service in camps and in units charged with carrying out punitive security raids. By dint of his pivotal and overlapping positions—chief of the police, chief of the security services, chief of Germanization and resettlement—Himmler was a centripetal force, calibrating the sprawling operations of the SS state, particularly in the east, which was its principal habitat.

On June 9, 1942, immediately after two Free Czech agents had assassinated Heydrich near Prague, Himmler spoke to the top leaders of the SS in starkly realistic terms about the war-induced mutations in their sacred order. He proudly claimed that this past winter the Waffen-SS had helped the führer stave off an "absolute catastrophe" on the eastern front. But he readily conceded that it had done so at a considerable price, the loss of a large number of tried and true SS leaders. Himmler even went so far as to say that he did not think that the war could be won in 1942. He expected the struggle to continue many more years and victory to go to the side that would go to any length to win and would field every last man. Hereafter the SS could no longer be as selective in its recruitment as it had during the 1930s, when candidates had had to meet exceptional standards. This meant that the battalions of the future would be radically different from those of "June 1941." If need be, the SS would throw into battle sixteen-year-old boys and men between the ages of fifty and fifty-five. Only SS men with one leg or one eye should staff the offices to the rear of the front. Because of the large intake of raw recruits, leadership was more important than ever, and it would have to be provided by experienced hands. The old fighters and their disciples alone understood that henceforth no means would be too foul and no sacrifices too great to win through.

Himmler reiterated that this was a contest between Russian commissars and German officers, or rather between two strata of leaders. On the enemy side, the leaders of the *Untermenschen:* "Jews, commissars, and party cadres, ideologically sworn and fanatically dedicated to their gospel of destruction, . . . [and] ready to use the most brutal methods." On this side, "Germany with its officer corps and our [i.e., the SS's] corps of leaders." According to Himmler, if a catastrophe was avoided in the winter of 1941–42, it was only thanks to the staunch political beliefs of the fighting men and especially the leaders of the Reich. Without this deep-rooted faith, in which there was no room for pessimism, this *Weltanschauungskampf* simply could not be won.

Even more than the Wehrmacht, the Waffen-SS was permeated with a sense of Nazi mission, a cult of the führer, and an ethos of daring and steadfastness. The heavy setbacks and casualties suffered on the eastern front gave these attributes a particularly deadly bent, and the Waffen-SS became a pacesetter of the brutalization of warfare and in self-immolating zeal. By late 1943 well over a quarter of the authentic volunteers had sacrificed their lives, and the proportion of officers killed continued to be particularly high. This loss of qualified leaders was the more serious at a time when officers were needed to train and discipline the influx of ideologically and militarily unprimed recruits who were diluting the ethos and dynamism of the Blackshirts. Younger and less qualified officers probably fostered a raw or wild fanaticism as a substitute for in-service training, for which there was little time. In any case, the bulk of the Waffen-SS fought on the eastern front, and it was there that it regularly committed military and political atrocities. Germany's armed forces perpetrated relatively few war crimes and crimes against humanity on the western front, which was all but spared the fury of the anti-Bolshevik crusade. Indeed, outside the eastern theater the massacres of Le Paradis, Tulle, Oradour-sur-Glane, and Malmédy were the exception, not the rule. But even those outrages must be attributed to some of the few Waffen-SS contingents which were deployed in the west.

Before discussing the impressment of foreign labor and the recasting of the concentration-camp system, both of which were designed to gear the Behemoth for a protracted war, we must deal with the course of the second summer offensive. Clearly, it would be difficult to muster not only sufficient men but also tanks and planes for another blitzlike drive. In 1941 Hitler had paid heavily for allowing his Balkan expedition to delay Barbarossa until June 22. A year later, time would again be of the essence. But because of the need to refurbish the Wehrmacht, Hitler had to postpone the start of his second major attack to the end of June. Notwithstanding warnings against a premature and overambitious operation, the führer was determined once more to go to any length to crush the Red Army and liquidate the Soviet regime. He was more than ever psychologically fixated upon Russia as the key to Germany's bid for European hegemony and to the success of the Nazi project. After the recent shake-up in the command of the eastern field armies, Hitler had even fuller control of the army than heretofore. Of course, neither he nor his generals looked on the dark side or despaired. But this time they were sober, without braggadocio. No one proclaimed that the upcoming assault would stun the world, smash the Bolshevik regime, and overwhelm the Red Army. From the outset of this second offensive the risks were clear. In addition to facing a vigilant, reinforced, and battle-tried Red Army, the German command had to reckon with overextended supply lines, sparse reserves, and the haunting prospect of becoming ensnared in a second eastern winter.

Because the Wehrmacht's eastern armies were seriously impaired, it seemed inadvisable to attack along the entire front. Except for the Eleventh Army, which was to move north to participate in yet another thrust to take Leningrad and cut the Murmansk railroad, the entire drive was to be concentrated in the south. A year earlier the prospect of self-sufficiency in strategic materials, particularly grain, had inclined Hitler to make his main push for Kiev. Now the prospect of securing oil for the Wehrmacht and denying it to the Red Army decided the führer to give first priority to conquering the Caucasus. After smashing through a corridor between the Don and the Donets rivers, the main attacking force was to head south toward the Black Sea and into Transcaucasia. While the generals agreed that this strategy was feasible despite overstretched supply routes, they warned against dividing the southern forces for a simultaneous rush to Stalingrad. But Hitler, marginally more confident than they, insisted that a lesser force should charge in that direction after the initial breakthrough. Accordingly, the Southern Army Group was divided in two: under the command of Field Marshal von Bock, Army Group B would eventually turn toward Stalingrad, while Army Group A, led by Field Marshal Wilhelm List, would carry the main drive to the south. As for the armies of Berlin's allies, as we saw, they were assigned to cover the flanks and the rear of the quick-moving German armor and infantry.

Operation Blue started on June 28, 1942. At first, and as once before, everything proceeded according to plan. Von Bock's Fourth Panzer Army, under the command of General Hermann Hoth, forced its way past the enemy defenses between Kursk and Belgorod and rushed ahead 100 miles to reach the Don near Voronezh on July 6, threatening Stalingrad from the north. Simultaneously, List's First Panzer Army, headed by General Ewald von Kleist, broke into the Don-Donets corridor south of Izyum. Near Chertkovo Kleist's tanks took a sharp right to start their sweep through the south. By July 23 they had captured Rostov, having covered 240 miles in three weeks. Even so, since the Germans had moved slower than expected, most Soviet officers managed to avoid capture and took the bulk of their troops to Stalingrad.

This was the moment when Hitler confirmed his order for von Bock to head for Stalingrad, while List stayed on course. His crack armored division, under von Kleist, raced 200 miles to take Maykop on August 9. Kleist was expected to continue covering hundreds of miles first to Grozny and Tiflis, and then to Batum and Baku.

But at this point Kleist's units were vastly overextended. Above all, they ran short of fuel, in part because, before retreating, the Red Army had destroyed the important oil fields and refineries of Maykop. Furthermore, the infantry trailed too far behind, largely on account of the difference in rail gauge, which meant that it could not be moved forward by fall. Worse still, the Caucasus Mountains would not be easy to cross, the rains were fast approaching, and the incipient battle at Stalingrad began to draw off essential manpower and air cover.

Like Moscow the year before, Stalingrad was at first a distinctly secondary objective. General Friedrich von Paulus, commander of the Sixth Army, was ordered to exploit the breach made by his own panzer corps to advance in a straight line toward Stalingrad, where he was to cover the flank of Army Group A. Although he lacked armor, within four weeks von Paulus forged ahead four hundred miles to the Volga, at a point fifty miles north of the city. From there, however, it took his advance units another four weeks, until August 23, to reach the outskirts of Stalingrad. The closer the Germans came, the tougher were the Soviet defenses. As of late July General Maximilian von Weichs, who now replaced von Bock as head of Army Group B, was under strong pressure to capture the city before the end of the summer, the more so since none of the campaign's other objectives were within reach.

Hitler and Stalin were equally determined to prevail, whatever the cost. The fighting became increasingly bitter and unyielding. On July 28 Stalin issued a special order enjoining his officers and men to stand fast and threatening "cowards and panic-mongers" with instant execution, insisting that "iron discipline" alone could secure victory. Incensed by Stalin's tenacity, Hitler resolved to level and capture Stalingrad, if need be at the expense of the southern drive. In terms of the massive and heroic bloodletting concentrated in a small area and in a short time, Stalingrad became the Verdun of World War II. But in other respects this analogy is inapt. Whereas between February and December 1916 the opposing forces had been evenly matched, not only in numbers but also in the amount of time and supplies available, this was not the case from late August 1942 through early February 1943, when the Wehrmacht was recklessly overextended and undersupplied.

As of late August or early September, Hitler and his generals were in the same plight as the year before. Running dangerously late in both major operational sectors and with inclement weather fast approaching, several officers once again urged a timely strategic halt and withdrawal. But Hitler would not consider falling back, particularly now that American aid to Russia was beginning to tell and time more than ever turned against the Third Reich, and against him. Enraged by the defiance of Leningrad, Moscow, and Stalingrad, the three holy places and citadels of bolshevism, he was more determined than ever to storm and raze them.

Shortly after the start of the offensive the führer had moved his headquarters to a forest a few miles northeast of Vinnitsa in the Ukraine, thereby marking his total absorption in the eastern campaign. Vinnitsa was a town southwest of Kiev which, as we saw, had seen heavy fighting in August 1941. Its population had been close to 40 percent Jewish until a considerable number of Jews fled before the Wehrmacht and most of those remaining were massacred by Einsatzgruppe C. It was at his Vinnitsa headquarters, the "Werwolf," that Hitler—increasingly reclusive, frenzied, and rancorous—rejected pressing advice not to risk having his troops frozen into another Russian winter and decided to persist in his resolve to stay the course both in the Caucasus and at Stalingrad. On September 9 he dismissed Field Marshal List for being overly cautious on the southern front, and himself assumed the command of Army Group A. Two weeks later he cashiered General Halder, the chief of staff, replacing him with General Kurt Zeitzler, who apparently concurred with the führer's resolve not to give way.

Not that all was yet lost, notably at Stalingrad, where German troops penetrated far into the city. Fighting street-to-street, even house-to-house, they seized control of well over half of the city by late October, reducing it to rubble. Even so, with their backs to the Volga, bolstered by popular support, and hardened to the snow, the Red soldiers continued to give battle. Finally, on November 19, the Soviets launched a massive counteroffensive which quickly and radically reversed the situation. Having learned from the Wehrmacht, with a sweeping pincers movement they encircled some twenty enemy divisions near Kalach on the Don within four days. These first rushes, as well as later ones, were so successful largely because the Wehrmacht's rear guard was surprisingly thin and ineffective, most of it consisting of Italian, Rumanian, and Hungarian divisions. In mid-December General Erich von Manstein struck back unsuccessfully, with the result that the Germans were driven out of the Don-Donets corridor by the end of the year, leaving behind about 60,000 prisoners. In the meantime, trapped in the Stalingrad salient, the Sixth Army fought on despite acute shortages of fuel, ammunition, food, and warm clothing.

On January 8 Stalin offered von Paulus the opportunity to lay down his arms. As soon as he refused, the Soviets tightened their net still further. On January 22, von Paulus, fearing total disaster, asked Hitler for permission to surrender, insisting that he lacked supplies, that thousands of wounded were unattended, and that the encircling forces were too strong to be resisted any longer. But he was ordered to fight on to the last man. Relentlessly battered, von Paulus surrendered between January 31 and February 2, exactly ten years after Hitler's accession to power.

The battle of Stalingrad had cost over 130,000 German lives and nearly 300,000 wounded. As for von Paulus, he himself led some 90,000 of his men into captivity. After Stalingrad the Allies were able to show newsreels of bedraggled prisoners—would-be supermen—comparable to those the Nazis had shown after Kiev.

The situation was no better in the Caucasus, except that von Kleist's First Panzer Army managed to avoid encirclement. Still, having started their southern offensive in late December, the Soviets drove the Germans out of most of the Caucasus with disconcerting speed.

Of course, the war was far from over. It continued for another two years even after the Red Army recaptured Kharkov and Rostov and then, in the spring of 1943, broke the siege of Leningrad. The worst of the fighting and despoliation ravaged the ill-fated eastern territories in which the Jews became the lightning rod for the raging Nazi fury, which defeat and mortification kept at a fever pitch.

What needs special emphasis is that after the failure of Operation Typhoon the Wehrmacht never managed to recover the initiative and momentum indispensable for the survival of the Nazi regime and presumption. The decisive turning point of the war was in fact Moscow in late 1941, not Stalingrad in late 1942. To be sure, during the summer of 1942 the Reich's leaders were heartened by the seizure of the Crimea, the advance into the Caucasus, the march to Stalingrad, and the approach to Alexandria. But they were almost immediately discomfited again by a string of serious reversals. The inglorious defeat of Operation Blue aggravated the impasse in the east, confirming the impossibility of military success prefigured the year before. As if by itself this second major fiasco on the eastern front was not disconcerting enough, it coincided with two other portentous setbacks. On November 2 General Bernard Montgomery breached the lines of General Erwin Rommel at El Alamein despite one of Hitler's peremptory "victory or death" orders. A week later British and American troops went ashore in French North Africa.

Equally troublesome for the leaders of the Third Reich, the Western Allies had long since started to demonstrate their capacity and will to carry the air war to the German homefront. Several major German cities were struck during the spring of 1942: Lübeck, Rostock, Essen, Cologne, and Bremen. Although for tactical reasons the British slowed the pace of bombing during the second half of 1942, by the end of the year they had dropped a total of 50,000 tons of explosives. While there was little industrial damage, the pounding of civilians and residential districts caused considerable psychological fallout. It became increasingly difficult to dissemble the perils of the war and to proclaim the invulnerability of the Reich. Instead, Nazi propaganda seized upon the death and destruction wrought by the

Royal Air Force to revile the Allies for their ruthlessness, without ever mentioning Germany's prior terror bombing of Warsaw, Rotterdam, and Coventry, not to mention Guernica. In any case, hereafter the reality and the dread of punishment from the air undercut Hitler's efforts to spare the German homefront the miseries of war, which he feared would spark popular discontent, much as they had in 1917–18. German civilians now began to experience firsthand the horrors of war over and above the numbing reports of rapidly rising casualties on the eastern front. Paradoxically, this turn of events exacerbated the spiraling Nazi fury, for it desensitized the population of the Third Reich to the sufferings inflicted in their own midst on deported foreign workers, concentration-camp inmates and, above all, Jews.

Throughout 1942 the dual state intensified economic mobilization as well as security controls, especially in the occupied territories. There was no letup in this hardening of the Behemoth during the expectant summer of the second eastern offensive, for even in the event Soviet Russia were defeated, Nazi Germany would still have to bring the British and the Americans to terms. The ideologically grounded decision to persist in an impossible and devastating war went hand in hand with a policy of rising exploitation, terror, and savagery, primarily beyond the borders of Germany, but also within. The crusading war was as irreversible as the spiraling barbarity. Their logic was inherent in the Nazi system. The decision to persist was also prior as well as unrelated to the Allied demand for unconditional surrender of January 14, 1943, which precluded a negotiated end to the war.

It was in the perspective of this life-and-death struggle that in the spring of 1942 Sauckel launched the drive to recruit foreign workers to help cover the needs and losses of the armed services as well as to man the expanding war economy. Between September 1939 and March 1942 over 7 million males left industry for military service. As we have seen, within the next three years Sauckel raised over 5 million new men for the Reich from occupied territories. By late 1944 every fifth worker in the Reich was non-German, although there had of course been foreign workers in the German labor force before Sauckel's appointment. Needless to say, to accomplish this feat Sauckel's recruiters had to have the collaboration of the Wehrmacht and the security services, especially since they had to rely more and more on coercion. On the average, the productivity of the Reich's foreign workers was about 75 to 80 percent that of German workers. From the very outset, by far the largest contingents of foreign workers were brought in from the east, notably Poland and Russia, and their numbers kept growing. Poland alone provided close to 1.8 million forced laborers, not counting the 300,000 Polish POWs put to work in the Reich. But since most of the eastern workers were unskilled or semiskilled, Sauckel increasingly looked to western Europe to supply skilled hands, if necessary by impressment.

Between April and July 1942 Sauckel recruited well over 1 million foreign workers, and over a million more by the end of the year, easily half of them from occupied Soviet territories. In the meantime, realizing that he had been forced into a protracted struggle of attrition, Hitler had put his full weight behind the recruitment of foreign labor for the war economy. Even before the debacle at Stalingrad the führer expanded Sauckel's powers. He authorized him to issue direct orders to military and civil authorities throughout German-occupied Europe, including orders to use compulsion to meet the labor quotas set in Berlin.

After the second winter of calamity the conscription of foreign workers assumed still greater urgency. Speer asked for an additional 400,000 men by the end of March 1943, stressing the need for skilled workers. Of the 250,000 men he demanded from France, Sauckel asked that 150,000 be skilled. He also pressed Holland and Belgium for qualified workers. At the same time, the drive for unskilled manpower was stepped up. In mid-March Sauckel notified Rosenberg that during the next four months another 1 million men would have to be mustered in the east, at a rate of 5,000 a day until April 1, and at double that rate thereafter.

By now more and more prisoners of war, including Soviet captives, were being put to work in Germany. The eastern command was ordered to "hand over the mass of war prisoners to the *Heimat*" and to meet the labor requirements of the field armies with local civilians, mostly women, the "Reds having evacuated all men between 17 and 50 years of age." To the rear there remained more males to be put to work, and both they and the women became liable to compulsory labor. At first the danger of resistance was expected to be minimal, since "Russians are used to obeying . . . and living in fear of their masters," and there were few "convinced Bolsheviks in the countryside." And yet, as early as the fall of 1942, when relatively uncoerced levies all but ended, army authorities cautioned that the forced recruitment and deportation of labor were playing into the hands of the partisans. In some areas the military was hard put to satisfy its own local labor needs, let alone help to meet those of the homefront. Increasingly, prisoners were put to work building essential military emplacements and roads, while men and women between the ages of sixteen and sixty were pressed into labor columns, with orders to report with their own trenching tools. In January 1943 the XXIX

Army Corps directed that the "minimum work time will be 9 hours, not counting rest periods, and that whoever resists or interferes with labor shall be hanged," the order for such executions to be issued by the "first officer within reach." In early February General Kurt Zeitzler, the new chief of staff, ordered that to "meet the military and economic needs in the [eastern] operational theater . . . all residents between the ages of 14 and 65 are liable to labor in accordance with their fitness for work." The work week should be fifty-four hours, to be supplemented by additional hours at night, Sundays, or holidays. Zeitzler stressed that "special regulations will be issued concerning the Jews."

On March 10, at a meeting of the chief representatives of the army's economic staff in the east, Staatsrat Peuckert, who was both a high official on this staff and Sauckel's representative, announced that "the labor needs of German agriculture and the armaments program set by the führer require the quickest possible procurement of an additional million hands from the eastern territories." He stressed that "recourse to compulsory labor in all the European territories occupied by German troops is in keeping with the explicit will of the führer." In the Reich Commissariat of the Ukraine this search for workers would entail "a drive against partisans, in the first instance in a strip 50 kilometers wide along the rail line Brest-Pinsk-Gomel." Special police contingents would carry out this operation, to be "discussed next week by Sauckel, Rosenberg, and Himmler." Another strip would have to be cleared west of Cernigov, halfway between Kiev and Gomel. In this general area of the Ukraine, Peuckert expected to levy between 200,000 and 250,000 workers for the Reich. Major General Hans Nagel, speaking for the southern sector, was altogether more optimistic about meeting new quotas: "Thus far close to 700,000 workmen have been transported to the Reich, and I will not flinch at large figures in the future." Not that it would be easy to meet the new quotas for Germany in the specified time. There were transport problems and, above all, workers were needed locally for the troops, for agriculture, for industry, and possibly also "to build fortifications, notably an eastern wall."

On April 10, 1943, the Sixth Army began to register local women born in 1924 and 1925 for forced labor in Germany. But even in this instance the local military retained first claim. Ten days later the OKH ordered the instant conscription, throughout the conquered Soviet territories, of all men between eighteen and twenty-one years of age "for labor service" in the Reich or locally, excepting those men "suitable or likely to join the Hilfswilligen or to volunteer as legionaries." All men between twenty-two and forty-six fit for work were also liable to conscription, while women were to be called up for local chores. The field armies were directed to extend "all necessary help" to facilitate this mass impressment.

In mid-April 1943 Sauckel promised Hitler that by the year's end he would recruit an additional 1 million workers from Russia, 150,000 from Poland, and 450,000 from western Europe, or a total of 1.6 million. However, with the Axis on the defensive and the Red Army advancing, evasion and resistance kept mounting, with the result that levies became more difficult and smaller, despite coercion. Even so, keeping faith with Hitler's and the Nazi regime's unshakable precept of *Sein oder Nichtsein*, Speer and Sauckel kept at it, though the former sought to temper labor recruitment and utilization in the west in the interest of raising war production locally. For 1944 Sauckel proposed to provide Germany with an additional 3.5 million foreign workers, mostly from western Europe, primarily Italy and France. This plan turned out to be stillborn, unlike the other murderous strategems conceived in nazism's terminal desperation. In the meantime, it is worth stressing that on the whole and throughout the war the lot of the impressed foreign workers in the Reich was bearable compared to that of the foreigners condemned to toil in the economy of Nazi Germany's concentration-camp universe. This was true even for most eastern workers, whose ill-treatment and exploitation were softened beginning in 1943, in the interest of productivity. Still, all things considered, Nazi Germany's vast and violent impressment of labor all over Europe significantly contributed to conditioning Gentiles and Jews to accept as normal the forced deportations and resettlements of civilians which became the visible and commonplace sides of the Judeocide. Auschwitz and Majdanek, in particular, became living proof of the conjunction, nay inseparability, of labor exploitation and extermination.

The sweeping transformation and expansion of the concentration-camp system became the most outrageous and characteristic expression of the Nazi regime's resolve to hold Europe hostage for the victory it could not win and the strategic surrender it could neither consider nor survive. As we saw, the first concentration camps were set up in the time of Hitler's official enthronement. In 1933 over 30,000 men were incarcerated for political reasons, most of them after the Reichstag fire. There was something frenzied and improvised about these arrests, which were intended to intimidate, if not terrorize, the residual opposition and resistance. By early 1934 the number of inmates was down to between 7,000 and 8,000, the others having been released. Until 1938 the camp population hovered around this figure. Judging by the regulations and conditions that Eicke fixed at Dachau and that were reproduced in the other camps, the inmates were to be broken psychologically, morally, and physically. At this point they were forced to work for their own upkeep. But they were not subjected to hard labor, except as part of the discipline of subjection and "reeducation." This labor was Sisyphean, not productive.

There was a sharp increase in the number of prisoners in 1938, partly due to the arrest of anti-Nazis in Austria and the Sudetenland. With the internment of about 30,000 Jews following Crystal Night, the total reached 60,000. Since these Jews were soon released, the number of inmates stood at about 20,000 when Germany invaded Poland on September 1, 1939. Among them there were a good many recidivist criminals and so-called "asocials," but just how many is unclear. The three camps holding the bulk of prisoners were Dachau, Buchenwald, and Sachsenhausen. They were the inner core of the incipient concentration-camp universe, headed by Himmler. First the personnel training center and general inspectorate, and then, as of 1939, the administrative headquarters for the expanding system were located near Sachsenhausen in Oranienburg, less than twenty miles north of Berlin.

We also noted that from the very start the war fueled the growth of the camps. With the attack on Poland, numerous suspected security risks were arrested or rearrested in Germany, and hereafter few inmates were ever released. But above all, Poles from both the Warthegau and the General Government began to be interned in large numbers, to become the vanguard of the swelling number of foreign nationals in the Third Reich's camps. Until the invasion of Russia, however, none of the other conquests or occupations were followed by large-scale arrests of political opponents for imprisonment in Germany.

Without doubt Barbarossa marked an important turn. Beginning with the military difficulties of the fall of 1941, significant numbers of Soviet prisoners were sent to concentration camps in the Reich. Together with the Poles, these POWs probably accounted for most of the increase from about 20,000 internees at the outbreak of the war to about 100,000 by the end of the winter of 1941–42.

Until this moment there were still relatively few camps and the number of their inmates rose only slowly. Even this slow growth was, however, a concomitant of the Third Reich's territorial expansion and foreign wars. The annexation of Austria occasioned the establishment of Mauthausen near Linz, and the conquest of Poland led to the founding of Stutthof near Danzig and Auschwitz in the Warthegau. Similarly, in May 1941, a year after the defeat of France, the SS set up Natzweiler, about thirty miles from Strasbourg. The inmates of all these camps, as well as of those in Old Germany, by this time were mostly foreign resisters and war prisoners. In addition, the stresses and strains of war quickened the deterioration of material conditions in the camps, which the Nazis used to justify gratuitous but as yet limited excesses.

But this war-related expansion and hardening of the camps did not entail a change in their mission, which was to detain and bend political enemies and military prisoners, as well as "asocials." Admittedly, under the direction of Oswald Pohl, the SS began to develop its own mining and construction enterprises in and near various camps. But these undertakings were of distinctly secondary importance and were designed to serve the new order after the war. Even when Pohl established a separate economic bureau within the SS administration in 1940, the idea of exploiting camp inmates for economically productive purposes remained embryonic.

All this changed radically in the late winter and early spring of 1942, in the face of the first major reversal of the eastern campaign. Long-range projects were shelved in favor of harnessing the economic resources of the concentration camps for the war effort, primarily by enlarging and putting to use their reservoir of captive labor. To this end the Reich's military, police, and security forces were ordered to seize and deliver a steady supply of potential forced laborers from all over Europe. In their bid to bolster the economic base of their power, Himmler and Pohl even entertained the idea of committing all foreign workers already in Germany to the camps.

There is no question that the metastasis of the concentration-camp system was intimately correlated with Berlin's forced shift from a lightning war and limited war economy to a war of endurance requiring all-out economic mobilization. Henceforth, the camps proliferated, the number of inmates swelled, and conditions went from bad to worse. However, the growing abuse and mortality rate of the worker-inmates in the camps of German-controlled Europe were due not only to the material adversities of a taxing and unsuccessful war but also to the ideologically informed brutality of their guards. In this sense there was a built-in tension between economically "rational" exploitation and politically obsessive persecution.

We have seen that appointments to three newly created posts high in the Nazi leadership signaled a crucial turn in policy: in February 1942 Albert Speer was appointed Reich minister for the production of arms and munitions; in March Gauleiter Fritz Sauckel became general plenipotentiary for the deployment of labor; and in April SS General Oswald Pohl was confirmed as chief of the Central Economic and Administrative Office of the SS (the WVHA), which now subsumed the Inspectorate of Concentration Camps. Of these three, Speer best personified the changeover. Originally, Hitler had charged him with choreographing the mass rituals of the Nazi regime and with monumentalizing its project, with license to use concentration-camp labor in carrying out these grandiose endeavors. Now Speer ceased to be the aesthetician and cosmetician of the Third Reich and became instead the supreme coordinator of its military-industrial complex. Thereafter, he relentlessly pushed both Sauckel and Pohl to increase the supply of captive foreign workers and to systematically exploit them in the hope of overcoming Germany's refractory labor shortage.

Five days after the Wannsee Conference, Himmler had, as we saw, ordered the concentration camps to prepare to receive 150,000 Jews as potential war workers at the same time that he had started to broaden Pohl's powers. During the following weeks Himmler and Pohl agreed that henceforth they would give absolute priority to using the labor of a fast-growing camp population to advance the war effort. On March 3 Himmler directed Pohl to make all necessary plans and arrangements. Within two weeks, on March 16, there was a conference at Speer's ministry to discuss the new role of concentration camps. After invoking orders from the führer's headquarters, SS Major General Richard Glücks, who had worked with Eicke before becoming one of Pohl's key subordinates, held out roughly the following prospects: 5,000 workers at Buchenwald, 6,000 at Sachsenhausen, 2,000 at Neuengamme, 6,000 at Auschwitz, and 6,000 (women) at Ravensbrück. He also noted that once "filled up," the camp near Lublin, the future Majdanek, could make a contribution as well. With a considerable influx of internees expected for late March, Glücks declared that "all craftsmen and skilled workers will be sorted out and assigned to camps turning energetically to the production of arms." At this stage Glücks still insisted that Himmler wanted all production to be carried on inside the camps, where interested firms would have to "make available engineers and foremen for the training of inmates."

By April 30, 1942, Pohl submitted a working plan to Himmler outlining the main locations and pressing assignments of the concentration-camp system. By his accounting, since September 1939 the population of the six major camps had grown by 23,300: Dachau from 4,000 to 8,000; Sachsenhausen from 6,500 to 10,000; Buchenwald from 5,300 to 9,000; Mauthausen from 1,500 to 5,500; Flossenbürg from 1,600 to 4,700; and Ravensbrück from 2,500 to 7,500. According to Pohl, nine additional camps had been set up in 1940–42, though he did not specify the number of their prisoners: Auschwitz, Neuengamme, Gusen (near Mauthausen), Natzweiler, Gross-Rosen, Lublin, Niederhagen, Stutthof, and Arbeitsdorf. Pohl also indicated that in recent weeks the high command of the RSHA and the Waffen-SS had requested SS personnel to staff camps to be located in Riga, Kiev, and Bobruisk. He quite agreed that hereafter his office should coordinate the activities of the SS and the police in the planning and implementation of all such projects.

In the second part of his plan Pohl stressed the fundamental recasting of the camp system to justify the centralization of power in the WVHA.

> The war has brought a manifest change in the structure of the concentration camps along with a fundamental change in their mission concerning the utilization of their inmates.
>
> The detention of prisoners for reasons of security, correction, and prevention is no longer the first priority. The center of gravity has shifted to the economic side. The mobilization of the labor power of all internees primarily for war tasks (increase of armaments) must take absolute precedence, until such time as it can be used for peacetime assignments.
>
> Such being the case, all necessary measures must be taken to transform the concentration camp from an exclusively political organization into one fitted for its economic mission.

Pohl assured Himmler that the leaders of the former camp inspectorate as well as the commanders of all camps and the chiefs of eleven camp enterprises were fully briefed about this radically new course.

The same day that Pohl submitted his report to Himmler, he directed these same SS officials to see to it that production for war begin no later than May 1. The camp commanders were ordered to force the pace of work in all enterprises under their jurisdiction. Pohl made them and them alone "responsible for the use of [their] labor forces," insisting that this use would have to "be exhausting in the true sense of the word, in order to achieve maximum productivity." Camp commanders should not feel bound by limits on the workday or work week, and time spent on meals and roll-calls should be kept to a minimum. On June 3, in a follow-up directive, SS Colonel Gerhardt Maurer, director of labor allocation in WVHA's concentration-camp division, invoked "today's war situation [to] demand that the labor power of all internees be taxed to the limit, [which required] their working a full day on Saturdays and half a day on Sundays."

As for security at the camps, Pohl urged that it be reinforced with "mounted outposts, watchdogs, mobile watchtowers, and movable obstacles."

This recasting of the camp system coincided with the preparation of the second summer offensive on the eastern front. On May 29 Himmler wrote to Pohl to express his general approval of the new course. He had only one reservation: the camps should continue to be portrayed as serving to rehabilitate the "educable" internees; otherwise the idea might spread that people were being put and kept in camps for the sole purpose of creating a pool of chained workers. In other words, although he agreed with giving "out-and-out priority to labor," Himmler wanted to preserve the old image. In the wake of Heydrich's assassination he meant to reassure the RSHA that, notwithstanding the turn to productivism and the transfer of the Inspectorate of Concentration Camps to Pohl, the political police would continue to have a strong voice in the running of the camps. Clearly, Himmler wanted it understood that the SS was not about to become a mere handmaiden of economic and military necessity and that he, its chief, remained the ideological watchdog—the "Loyola"—of the Nazi regime. Accordingly, both Müller, head of the Gestapo, and Glücks, now chief of the division of concentration camps in the WVHA, notified their respective staffs that the RSHA retained full control of the detention, reeducation, and eventual release of all internees.

Not surprisingly, the severe setbacks on the eastern front in the early fall of 1942 exacerbated the chronic tension between two SS factions within the concentration-camp universe: on the one hand, the expediency-mongers who were determined to harness the labor of captive workers for the uphill if not impossible war, if need be by improving their condition; on the other, the ironbound zealots who put destruction through premeditated overexertion ahead of productivity. Of course, in his hydra-headed security organization, including inside the camps, Himmler kept both factions going, favoring the one over the other in accordance with changing military conditions and political stratagems. With the Wehrmacht reeling under the hammer blows of the Soviet counteroffensive, he could not afford to ignore the urgent need for forced-draft arms production, even if his own penchant was for a distinctly less constructive and more nihilistic response. Himmler must have endorsed the WVHA's latest manpower requests, for on December 16, 1942, Müller assured him that the Gestapo would be able to provide the concentration camps with 35,000 to 40,000 additional forced laborers within six weeks. The following day Müller advised his agents that "because of war exigencies not to be discussed here and now, on December 14, 1942, [Himmler] has ordered [that] at least 35,000 able-bodied internees be turned over to concentration camps before the end of January 1943." The Gestapo chief instructed his men to search at once for workers in all prisons and detention centers not part of the concentration-camp system, insisting that at this time "every last laborer counted." Orders were also issued to round up suspected partisans throughout the eastern territories for internment and forced labor in Auschwitz and Majdanek.

By this time Pohl had all but given up on the idea of developing a separate industrial empire for the SS. Instead, he proposed to step up the practice of hiring out the elastic supply of forced labor under the control of the WVHA to large private firms operating either inside or near the expanding camps. It was in this perspective and with breathless impatience that Speer and Göring spurred on Himmler and Pohl. Although they now and then complained about the inefficiency of working inmates to the point of utter exhaustion, Speer and Göring never questioned the camp system as such. Quite the contrary: like many if not most of Germany's big industrialists, they kept clamoring for scarce laborers, no matter how they were rounded up or how badly they were mistreated.

Pressed and eager to serve the war effort, large-scale industry became particularly desperate for workers. To be sure, the need eventually became equally acute in medium-sized agriculture and manufacture. But compared to big business, the core of the war economy, other sectors not only used less foreign contractual, forced, and prisoner workers but also extracted less surplus profit from them. The giant concerns, including those of the public sector—notably the Hermann Göring Works and the Todt Organization—were the principal "war profiteers," thanks in large part to their plunder of the economic resources and enslavement of the workers of the occupied territories.

The list of companies competing for and using concentration-camp labor reads like a who's who of German big industry. To take advantage of a concentrated labor supply, some firms located plants inside or right next to camps. I. G. Farben, Krupp, and Siemens put plants in Auschwitz, and Siemens put a plant in Ravensbrück as well. Walther Zella-Mehlis situated one factory near Buchenwald and another near Neuengamme. Other large corporations took advantage of some of their existing plants' proximity to camps to "hire" forced labor. The Gustloff Works and Siemens secured workhands from Buchenwald, Zeppelin from Sachsenhausen. Indeed, the giants of most branches of German industry contracted for camp labor: in the aeronautics industry Messerschmitt, Junkers, and Heinkel; in the automobile industry the Bavarian Motor Works (BMW) and Daimler-Benz; in the electrical industry AEG and Telefunken; and in the munitions industry Nobel Dynamite and Rheinmetall. Mining and construction companies similarly turned to the camps—to Himmler and Pohl—for cut-rate labor.

All things considered, the camp authorities preferred to deal with big rather than small firms, for they could hire and, if need be, billet large contingents of inmates. Since few of the captives qualified as skilled or even semiskilled workers, the bulk of them were rented out as unskilled workers particularly liable to being driven to exhaustion by hard physical labor. Outside the camps the hours and conditions of work were only marginally better than within. The paltry "wages" paid for the laborers were divided unevenly between the SS and the firms that contracted to exploit, house, and feed them.

In time and by stages, most of the Third Reich's detention, penal, and labor compounds were forged into a network of twenty-three concentration camps with about a thousand satellite compounds and external work commandos (Arbeitskommandos). Whatever their initial and early objectives, with the war emergency all camps came to be geared primarily to serve the war effort, key to the survival of the Nazi regime. This is not to say that the contradiction between the calculated overwork and the maximum efficiency of forced human labor was dissolved or significantly lessened for the sake of productivity. To the extent that such may have been the intention of the WVHA, it was counteracted not only by the deep-seated contempt for enemy lives throughout the SS but also by the baneful shortages of bare necessities, which were particularly fatal for life in the camps. Even so, with few exceptions the camps were continually expanded and overcongested. However warped and misguided, the idea was to serve the war economy, less to finance the SS or to exterminate through grueling Sisyphean labor.

The camp population kept growing. There were about 100,000 registered inmates in late 1942, 220,000 in August 1943, 520,000 in August 1944, and 710,000 in January 1945, some 200,000 of them women. Thus from 1943 to 1944 the jump was 300,000; from 1944 to early 1945 it was 190,000. Dachau rose from 17,000 in August 1943 to 47,000 in December 1944, to 67,000 in April 1945. In late 1944 Buchenwald (including Dora) stood at 63,000, Sachsenhausen at 47,000, Mauthausen-Gusen at 72,000, Ravensbrück at 42,000, and Auschwitz at over 100,000. These figures of registered inmates do not include the 700,000 to 800,000 inmates who died or were killed, bringing the total number of wretched souls to have passed through the infernal camp system to 1.5 million. In some camps—notably in Stutthof, Auschwitz, Mauthausen, and Neuengamme—the death rate is estimated to have exceeded 50 percent.

Although the concentration camps were first designed and used to break the opposition within Germany, in time German citizens became but a small minority among the internees, and easily over half of these German inmates were "asocials," homosexuals, and common-law criminals. After the fall of 1941 few if any real or imagined political and religious opponents remained at large. In the Old Reich the Gestapo was all but reduced to arresting so-called shirkers among German and foreign workers for consignment to concentration camps.

Foreigners made up the lion's share of the camp population. In absolute numbers Russians and Poles came first, along with Jews (many of them of Russian and Polish nationality), to be discussed below. But there was a significant representation from all the conquered and occupied lands. Again, the war was decisive, especially after the winter of 1942–43. In the east the Wehrmacht and the SS seized ever more Russian and Polish civilians on suspicion of resistance, for forced labor in the camps. As of early 1943, the retreating armies and security forces not only scorched the earth but also forcibly evacuated all potential laborers by forced marches, some of them to be used in the war theater, some of them in the Reich. In the rest of Europe the reality and fear of conscription for labor in Germany prompted young men to slip away, some of them into the resistance. The Gestapo responded by arresting proven and suspected members of the underground for deportation to concentration camps, for labor.

The Germans, of course, began to hunt down the resistance well before this turn of events. As early as December 7, 1941, under the impact of the defeat at Moscow, General Keitel issued guidelines for the unsparing punishment of "attacks on the Reich or the occupation forces in the occupied territories." He claimed that since the start of the eastern campaign "Communist and other anti-German circles" had stepped up their activities throughout Europe. Referring to express orders from the führer, the chief of the High Command insisted that "effective and lasting deterrence calls for the death penalty or for measures which leave relatives and the population at large uncertain about the fate of offenders." In this ruthless *Nacht und Nebel* (Night and Fog) Decree Keitel specified that "culprits, or at least the leaders among them" should be either charged and executed on the spot, or else "deported to Germany" without explanation to their kin. In early February 1942 Himmler communicated Keitel's directive to key SS stations. Six months later Glücks, speaking for Pohl, sent this same order to the commanders of all concentration camps. Hereafter, political deportees from occupied lands became a separate category of inmates inside the camps.

The bombing attack on Heydrich in Prague on May 27, 1942, followed by his death on June 4, not only incensed the Nazi leaders but also drove them to tighten their repressive system throughout occupied Europe. In their view Heydrich was assassinated less for serving as deputy Reich protector of Bohemia and Moravia than for heading the Reich's awesome security apparatus. Predictably, not a few Nazi fanatics denounced the Jews for masterminding or carrying out this spectacular assassination. Goebbels and others seized upon this affront to once again urge holding the Jews hostage for the Reich's misfortunes and to advocate intensifying reprisals against them. Apparently, Goebbels was instrumental in having about 500 Jews arrested in Berlin, of whom between 100 and 150 were shot. Several Jews also seem to have been executed in Sachsenhausen. The murder of Heydrich may also have moved Eichmann to advance the date of the deportation of some 90,000 Jews from occupied France, Holland, and Belgium to eastern Europe.

Although severe and totally gratuitous, this action against the Jews went unnoticed, compared to the reprisals visited on the Czechs, particularly at Lidice. Apart from being unprecedented, the punishment of the Czechs was widely publicized and intentionally monstrous. It was held up to view in order to daunt and terrify active resisters and above all their potential helpers and sympathizers not only in Czechoslovakia but throughout the Continent.

In his funeral oration in the central hall of the Reich Chancellery in Berlin, Hitler hailed Heydrich as "one of the greatest of all Nazis, . . . one of the toughest opponents of the enemies of the Reich, . . . [and] the man with the iron heart." Himmler, for his part, adjured the leaders of the SS to carry themselves as worthy champions of Heydrich's creed. To mark the gravity and urgency of the situation, Himmler decided to run the RSHA himself rather than appoint an untried successor, and continued to do so for a full half year. More than likely, he personally authorized or ordered an exemplary reprisal for the political murder of his premier henchman. Immediately following the shooting of Heydrich the SS arbitrarily arrested over a thousand hostages in Prague, of whom one hundred were summarily executed. But the most savage retribution did not take place until June 9, at Lidice, a village some twenty miles northwest of the Czech capital. The Germans claimed that after training abroad, four Czech assassins had been parachuted by the British into Lidice, whose citizens were accused of having harbored and assisted them. In actual fact, the Czech agents had landed a considerable distance to the east of Lidice, in Lezhaky, near the Polish border. Even so, and with cold indifference, Heydrich's heirs vented their rage on the innocent villagers of Lidice: over 170 adult males and boys were either shot or burned alive, with their families watching; nearly 200 women were deported to Ravensbrück; and about 100 children were taken off to Germany, where most of them perished. Before leaving, to show that their vengeance knew no bounds, the SS razed the village to the ground. What needs special emphasis is that while Berlin kept quiet about the concurrent mass murder of Jews throughout the east, it widely publicized the massacre at Lidice. The Allies, in turn, denounced it as characteristic of Nazi inhumanity, not least because this was the first large-scale atrocity so far to the west.

It is no less significant that the Germans decided to be so merciless and ostentatious in their reprisal on the eve of their new summer offensive. Perhaps the leadership was not as confident as it pretended. As of the early spring, the Wehrmacht and the SS were intensely preoccupied with the growth of the partisan movement behind German lines in Russia. Soviet guerrillas were becoming increasingly adept at disrupting rail and road traffic. All German army groups created special mobile units to battle this "invisible army," with orders to kill partisans, not capture them. The security forces cooperated closely with the armed forces, including the air force. Attacks on "German property or blood" were being answered swiftly and ruthlessly, in accordance with "the führer's order that for every German who is murdered a large number of enemies will have to pay with their lives."

Of course, with the new German offensive the partisans stepped up their raids on transport lines and food stores. The invisible enemy rendered entire regions, particularly in Belorussia and the Ukraine, unsafe for the Wehrmacht. By July 23, 1942, less than a month after the start of Operation Blue, Keitel informed all the eastern commands that "the führer has decided that the police have primary responsibility for the fight against the partisans." Accordingly, the High Command had contacted Himmler "with the request that he set up a single command" for this purpose. Needless to say, the Wehrmacht would cooperate in every possible way. As a first step, "to increase security, on each side of the main transportation arteries [railway tracks and roads] in the rearward military zones a strip of 300 meters is to be cleared of all brush, except for hedges that offer protection against snowdrifts."

Although the partisan bands were still far from a serious military threat, they became a burning obsession with Nazi Germany's political and military leadership. On August 18, 1942, as the new offensive began to founder, the High Command issued Directive No. 46 over Hitler's signature, fixing guidelines for the intensified battle against the "partisan disorder in the east." The führer claimed that "during the last months" this disorder had reached such "intolerable proportions" as to "seriously threaten the provisioning of the front and the economic exploitation of the [occupied] territories." Accordingly, "the [partisan] bands should be virtually exterminated [*ausgerottet*] before the winter" so as to pacify the rear and forestall interference with the winter campaign. Of course, for tactical reasons the local population should be guaranteed "minimum subsistence" and local collaborators should be generously rewarded.

Hitler put Himmler in charge of "collecting, evaluating, and using the experience gained in fighting partisans" and gave him "sole responsibility for antipartisan operations" in all the territories under civil administration. The military commands were under instructions to provide all necessary assistance. In fact, the closest possible cooperation between the leaders of the SS and the Wehrmacht would be "the key to success."

Two months later Hitler repeated his order to liquidate all partisans throughout the occupied eastern territories. On December 16, 1942, Keitel informed his commanders that the führer had ordered that no "German be subjected to disciplinary or legal punishment for [any of] his actions in the battle against the [partisan] bands and their fellow travelers." Hitler reminded his officers that the issue was "more than ever one of *Sein oder Nichtsein*," and the fight against the "fanatic and Communist-indoctrinated partisans . . . has nothing to do with soldierly chivalry or the Geneva conventions." Unless the "most brutal methods" were promptly used in the East and in the Balkans, it might be too late "to crush this pest." Under the circumstances in this "unlimited war [against partisans], soldiers have the right and duty to use any means, even against women and children, so long as they are effective."

Of course, the civil and military authorities adjusted their propaganda to reflect the Behemoth's new and difficult situation. With the breakdown and failure of the second offensive, whatever there remained of yesterday's optimism disappeared from the official rhetoric. Hereafter, rather than fighting to establish a Thousand-Year Reich and create a *new* Europe, Germany was fighting for survival and for the salvation of the *old* Europe. Not surprisingly, Goebbels delayed informing the public about the plight of von Paulus at Stalingrad. Once he acknowledged the defeat, he made no mention of the humiliating surrender. The official line was that the soldiers of the Sixth Army had fought to the last man, sacrificing their lives to save not just Germany but all of Western civilization from bolshevism.

January 30, 1943, was the tenth anniversary of Hitler's assumption of power. As a major date on the regime's ceremonial calendar, the projected celebration could not be cancelled. But neither could Stalingrad be passed over in silence. Hitler himself set the tone in his customary proclamation. After extolling the Reich's crusaders for their bravery, he called for additional sacrifices for the momentous battles ahead.

> Either Germany, its armed forces, and its allies, that is to say Europe, will prevail, or the tide of Asiatic bolshevism, coming from the east, will sweep over the Continent. . . . [Should bolshevism triumph], it will destroy and annihilate the oldest of all civilizations much as it has in Russia, . . . leaving the world's most flourishing Continent in chaos.

That same day Göring invoked the timeliness of the "heroic song . . . of the Battle of the Niebelungen" and compared the stand of the Reich's heroes on the distant Volga with that of Sparta's warriors at Thermopylae. In the afternoon, at a military rally in Berlin, Göring intoned the new refrain that Germany would long since have defeated Bolshevik Russia but for its barbarian ways of fighting, which represented a danger for all humanity. At night Goebbels addressed a mass rally in the Sports Palace. After characterizing the war as one against "Jewish bolshevism," he admonished London not to make light of the danger of the Continent falling to bolshevism, since "ideas do not need convoys to cross the Channel [but can do so] through the atmosphere." In the *Völkische Beobachter,* the chief daily of the National Socialist Party, Alfred Rosenberg spoke in the same key as the other leaders of the regime.

Hereafter, and until the end of the war, the defense against bolshevism remained the central theme of the propaganda addressed to the homefront, the eastern armies, and the rest of Europe, including England. Germany was said to be fighting, unselfishly, for a gravely imperiled Western civilization, the stark alternative being the "victory of Bolshevik chaos." Goebbels revived the scare tactics which originally had assured the success not only of German nazism but of

European fascism in general. He claimed that the Wehrmacht had captured lists of the Soviet secret police designating leaders in all walks of life "to be liquidated" by the Red Army should it penetrate into Germany and other countries, and that these lists were so extensive that "nothing but a leaderless mass would remain." Goebbels instructed his staff to avoid using the term "communism" in favor of the more frightening-sounding "bolshevism." Especially when addressing eastern European publics, propagandists were to stress *Jewish* bolshevism. Furthermore, from now on they were to "attack the beast that was Stalin and the bestiality of the Bolshevik system, and not the peoples they had subjected."

Goebbels set the new tone on February 18, 1943, at another mass meeting of 15,000 people in Berlin's Sports Palace. He claimed that not unlike the prewar Nuremberg rallies, this rally stood under the sign of "the battle against bolshevism." Both then and now not only the German Reich but the entire world needed to be warned of the "gruesome danger" of eastern bolshevism which had made "a people of nearly 200 million into an instrument of Jewish terror" primed to sweep over the Continent. From its very inception the Nazi Party clearly realized that "bolshevism was not just a terrorist *doctrine,* but also a terrorist *praxis,*" whose ultimate aim was "the world revolution of the Jews."

Goebbels put forth three theses concerning the present stage of the struggle against bolshevism: that without the heroic battle put up by the Wehrmacht in the east, "first the Reich and then *all* of Europe would have fallen to bolshevism"; that "*only* the German Wehrmacht and German people, together with their allies, have the power to save Europe from this threat"; and that this danger being imminent, "there is need for *rapid* and thorough action, *lest it be too late.*"

The danger facing Germany was in the nature of a single "infernal political deviltry" which had, however, two faces: "in the Soviet Union Jewry wears the mask of bolshevism, whereas in the Anglo-Saxon nations it wears the mask of plutocratic capitalism." But the danger threatened above all, in the east, where "Jewish liquidation commandos" would accompany the advancing Soviet armies, to be followed by "terror, the specter of starvation, and total European anarchy." Goebbels proudly proclaimed that the Nazis "have never been afraid of the Jews" in the past and were even "less so today," when international Jewry had made bolshevism into a formidable "terrorist military power." Even though there was a "pressing Jewish danger" in every country, Germany left it to the "*others*" to handle it in their own ways. In turn, "how *we* go about defending ourselves . . . against Jewry, which is an infectious phenomenon, . . . is our own business, and we will *brook no outside interference.*" Germany would not hesitate to take "all necessary measures," even if these provoked the "self-righteous protests . . . and hypocritical crocodile tears" of the enemy world. Unwilling to "bend to the Jewish threat," Germany proposed to confront it *"in the nick of time,* if necessary by resorting to the *complete* and *radical Ausrott-, -schaltung* [exterm-, elim-ination] of Jewry."

This, he maintained, was the proper context in which to view the "military burden in the east," where the Axis powers were "carrying out what was in the truest sense of the term a European mission." Rather than deny or minimize the debacle on the Volga, Goebbels exploited it to create a mood of national pride and sacrifice, in the manner of a *levée en masse.* He made the battle of Stalingrad "into a symbol of the . . . military and spiritual resistance against the assault coming out of the steppes," which simply had to be stopped. In the past, at home, National Socialists had "fought the Communist Party with different methods than the bourgeois parties." In like manner today, in the east, the surging "terror could only be broken with counterterror, not with spiritual arguments." The battle against bolshevism called for "total war" without limits. The time had come to discard "bourgeois squeamishness, . . . take off the *kid gloves,* and mail the fist." The issue was not whether "the methods we use [to destroy bolshevism] are more or less pretty, but whether they are effective." With the German people sacrificing its blood, the "least Europe can do is to make available its labor," since its "own future depends on the outcome of *our* struggle in the east." The stakes being what they were, Goebbels insisted that Germany would not even take offense at its enemies charging that the measures it was taking to "totalize the war" were not unlike those used by the Bolsheviks themselves. The point was that "the most total and radical war would also be the shortest," and the primary task was "to regain the offensive in the east."

Goebbels instructed the media and party spokesmen "to give special emphasis . . . to the themes of antibolshevism . . . and the total mobilization for war" in commenting on this, his latest speech. He also enjoined them to deny that "Germany had any selfish goals in the east" and to evoke "the holy crusade of the twentieth century against bolshevism." These same guidelines were circulated to information officers in the armed forces.

This orchestration of the rolling drumbeat of antibolshevism to whip up support for total war was accompanied by orders to temper the expression of disdain and hostility for the Slavs. No doubt the all-out drive for voluntary as well as involuntary labor recruits for the war against the Soviets made it counterproductive to "humiliate the peoples of the east [by reviling them] as beasts and barbarians . . . notably in public speeches and articles." There was to be no further talk either of exploiting eastern territories and populations for the benefit of the Reich or of resettling local inhabitants to make room for ethnic Germans.

Significantly, the Nazis' verbal assaults on the Jews, which had eased off in the spring and summer of 1942, were not similarly tempered. Quite the contrary. Hitler chose the start of the fourth year of war and of the campaign for *winterhilfswerk*, or winter relief, to appeal for support of those fighting against "Bolshevik barbarism and Jewish–Anglo-Saxon–capitalist exploitation." He made a point of denouncing "world Jewry for leading both bolshevism and plutocracy" in a campaign "to destroy the culture-bearing states of Europe and above all to exterminate all upholders of genuine [national] independence."

By September 30, 1942, when Operation Blue was running aground, Hitler's discourse again became explicitly threatening. In a speech to a mass audience in Berlin, he harked back to his prophecy of 1939 that "should Jewry instigate another international world war for the extermination of the Aryan peoples of Europe, not the Aryan peoples but Jewry would be exterminated." Since then, he said, "the Jewish wire-pullers have maneuvered one people after another into the war" and to this day they were manipulating Germany's enemies, including "that psychopath in the White House." Following these ravings, Hitler uttered particularly dark words.

> . . . There was a time when the Jews in Germany also laughed at my prophecies. I do not know whether they are still laughing today, or whether they have been cured of laughter. But take my word for it: they will stop laughing everywhere.

Hitler added that, like his other prophecies, "this one will be fulfilled as well."

The situation on the eastern front was considerably worse on November 8, when the führer sent a message to a gathering of "Old Fighters" of the *Kampfzeit,* or "time of struggle," in Munich. After vowing to fight to the finish, he warned the world "that National Socialist prophecies are not empty phrases." Once again, he reminded his audience of his original admonition that should the Jews precipitate "an international world war for the extermination of the European races" they would have to pay for it with their own extermination.

. . . People always laughed at me as a prophet. Of those who once laughed, many are no longer laughing today, and perhaps whoever is still laughing today will stop laughing before too long.

Hitler added that National Socialists would see to it that the rest of Europe would recognize the "full extent of international Jewry's demonic danger."

After Stalingrad bolshevism and Judaism were subjected to equally ferocious excoriation. On February 5, 1943, Otto Dietrich, press secretary of both the party and the government, as well as state secretary in the Propaganda Ministry, issued particularly revealing instructions to the daily and periodical papers:

Anti-Jewish propaganda is on the same level as anti-Bolshevik propaganda. The treatment of this [former] theme is part of an essential campaign to stimulate feelings of hatred.

Dietrich, who was close to Hitler, stressed that since all of Judaism had "criminal roots [and] . . . criminal tendencies, [its] *Vernichtung* [destruction/annihilation] will not be a loss for humanity."

On February 24, 1943, a week after Goebbels' "total war" speech, with its dire threat to the Jews, Hitler sent a message to be read by Hermann Esser, one of his oldest and most loyal lieutenants, to the yearly celebration of the founding of the Nazi Party in Munich. He told the party veterans that just as in the twenties and thirties they had been in the vanguard of Germany's national renewal and revolution, so "in the coming months and perhaps years" they would "carry out their second historical mission: to alert Germany . . . to the gravity of the [present] dangers, to bolster the nation's holy faith in overcoming these perils, and to hearten all weak souls." Hitler called on his tried-and-true followers "to fight terror with a tenfold greater terror, and to exterminate traitors, whoever they may be and no matter how they might try to dissemble their subversive purposes." While he hailed party members generally for being exemplary soldiers on the battlefield, he gave special praise to "the old [political] warriors" for remaining "the most fanatic champions of Germany's will to prevail" in the face of all enemies.

Thank God the Jews in London and New York, as well as in Moscow, have unequivocally spelled out the destiny that would be in store for the German people in particular [should they prevail]. But we give them an equally clear answer: contrary to their intentions, this struggle will not result in the destruction of Aryan humanity but in the extermination of Jewry in Europe. . . . Above all, this war will demonstrate the complete similarity of plutocracy and bolshevism, as well as the unchanging goal of Jews to plunder all peoples and make all peoples slaves of their international guild of criminals. . . . Just as on the strength of this insight the German people successfully fought this Jewish enemy within the Reich and is about to finish him off [erledigen] once and for all, so in the course of this war, the other peoples will come to see the light and finally make a common front against a race that means to destroy all of them.

Both the tone and content of Hitler's rantings clearly betrayed his mounting fury, despair, and disconcertion, all increasingly fixed on the Jews.

On March 20, 1943, Goebbels recorded in his diary that Hitler was "happy" about the "evacuation" of most remaining Jews from Berlin, adding that "in any case, the Jews will be the great losers of this war, whatever the outcome." The following day, March 21, the führer repeated his by now standard prophecy, burying it in a long and fierce tirade against Asiatic bolshevism. Hitler claimed credit for his timely restabilization and rearmament of Germany, without which, he said, all of Europe would have been at the mercy of the Red Army.

> By now it is clear that [this] conflict has . . . gradually assumed the characteristics of a struggle that can only be compared to the greatest historical events of the past. The pitiless and merciless war that has been forced upon us by external Jewry will lay the entire Continent in ruins unless the forces of [eastern] destruction can be stopped before reaching Europe's borders. [Should they break through], the worst consequence would be not burned cities and wrecked cultural monuments but the bestial massacres of masses of human beings comparable to those that followed the invasions of the Huns and Mongols out of inner Asia.

Posing as the great protector of Western culture and civilization, Hitler proclaimed that the "so-called West" was allied with "the sinister world of eastern barbarism supercharged with a furor of satanic destruction."

On May 6, 1943, Goebbels spoke again at the Berlin Sports Palace. He now predicted that there would soon be a universal clamor to identify "the culprit" in the present war, which was a "horrible human catastrophe." Germany would see to it that the Jew was held responsible, which would be easy, now that all countries understood the extent of his "nefarious influence." On this occasion Goebbels fell back on the Protocols of the Elders of Zion, claiming that they specified that "when the King of the Jews will don the crown, which Europe must offer him, he will be the ancestor and patriarch of the whole world." In the past the Jews had many times come close to "achieving their goal," only to be defeated in the last moment. This time their fate would also be to be knocked from "their greatest height to the lowest depth," since Europe would present them "with a mailed fist, not a crown." Hereafter, the Jew would be not the ruler but "the leper, the scum, the victim of his own criminal ambitions."

Goebbels stressed that there was no room for "sentimentality" and "morality" in the drive to "eliminate Jewry from Europe." Since the Jews threatened the security of all nations, they had to be "radically removed," like "the Colorado beetles which ravage potato fields." The Jews were omnipresent. They were "around Roosevelt as his brain trust and Churchill as his prompters." Jews were also the "agitators and masterminds of the entire Anglo-American–Soviet press, and . . . the real carriers of bolshevism in the dark corridors of the Kremlin." Furthermore, by virtue of their worldwide network the Jews "built the bridges between Moscow, London, and Washington." Ultimately, the Jew was "at the origin of this war, and he was directing it from behind the scenes." But just as National Socialism had "brought him down" within Germany, so it would know how to "smash his power, which threatens us from abroad."

Manifestly, the spiraling public vilification of the Jews was part of a discourse that became ever more violent and incoherent. Judging by the audiences to whom Hitler and Goebbels addressed their harangues and messages, these were aimed first and foremost at faithful party members, which may explain why they were ignored or dismissed, especially by the outside world. Not unlike Hitler himself, these zealots were profoundly shaken by the turn of events in the east and the gloomy prospects for the Nazi project as a whole, to which their own personal futures were tied. For most true believers, the führer's words reinforced and legitimated their own seething and exploding rage. Through them they could relive the ideological intoxication of their early days of glory. Through them they could find a way to justify making the Jews the convenient and defenseless scapegoat for their mortifying failure to lay hold of and prevail over the infinitely vaster and more powerful—but also chimerical—"common enemy."

CHAPTER XI

AUSCHWITZ

It is neither to justify nor to minimize the indelible infamy of the extermination camps to insist that though they were the ultimate scourge of the Thirty Years War of the twentieth century, they had not been planned by the Nazis from the very first. To be sure, without the peculiar ideology and mentality of National Socialism the purposes, structures, and methods of these killing centers could not have been conceived, let alone put into practice. But it is equally certain that had it not been for the absolute war in eastern Europe, the Nazis could not have created what became an unprecedented kingdom of death. The growth of the six centers of mass killing coincided with the refounding and expansion of the concentration-camp system, which was part of the Nazi regime's rush to fight its crusading war to the death. By themselves such hackneyed phrases as "all-out war" and "total mobilization"—current in both the Axis and Allied countries during the war—fail to convey the unique ferocity and inhumanity built into the Third Reich's struggle for *Sein oder Nichtsein*. To examine the camps apart from the context of the colossal horrors and miseries of war engulfing large parts of the European Continent is to fail to understand the camps, for this context contributed to the environment of rampant general violence in which the Nazis were able to execute the Judeocide.

As we have seen, the Nazis did not generate this atmosphere of pervasive brute force as a cover for their merciless war against the Jews. Nor did they force the growth of their stockades of slave labor with a view to creating a combined camouflage, pretext, and catalyst for the wholesale murder of innocent noncombatants.

The very origins of the centers of mass killing reflect the existence of an iron nexus between absolute war and large-scale political murder in eastern Europe. Of the six such centers—Auschwitz, Majdanek, Chełmno, Bełżec, Sobibór, and Treblinka—Auschwitz and Majdanek were started as stalags for prisoners of war and concentration camps for political prisoners. At the outset Auschwitz and Majdanek were also meant to serve as outposts for the implantation of the Thousand-Year Reich in occupied Poland and Russia.

This nexus of absolute war and deliberate mass murder remained all-pervasive. At Auschwitz and Majdanek, which were at one and the same time concentration camps and annihilation centers, the hyperexploitation of inmates for war production was anything but spurious. Of course, at both camps, in the face of irreversible military setbacks and material shortages, the line between egregious exploitation and outright exterminism kept wearing thin. Indeed, ultimately the execrable living, sanitary, and working conditions in the concentration camps and ghettos took a greater toll of life than the willful executions and gassings in the extermination centers.

Admittedly, at the other four "camps," which were purely extermination sites—Chełmno, Bełżec, Sobibór, and Treblinka—the victims' labor was not harnessed, except to service the death machines themselves. But as we shall see, the eastern campaign provided the indispensable context for their operation as well. It is no less revealing that although Jews were the preeminent victims of premeditated mass murder, in Auschwitz and Chełmno, Soviet prisoners of war were the first, or among the first, to be deliberately killed by lethal injections and gassing.

But perhaps most important, as of late 1941 the drive for full economic mobilization provided a universally plausible justification for deportation, resettlement, and hyperexploitation. Throughout German-occupied and -controlled Europe, including in the ghettos and camps, the belief took root and persisted that self-interest and the rational imperatives of the war effort would keep the Nazi fury within bounds. Especially in the antechambers of hell it was difficult, if not impossible, to fathom the intrinsic coexistence of the calculated utilization of labor and outright murder.

The close link between *guerre à mort* and mass murder must be kept in view if there is to be no distortion of the complex sources of responsibility for both, but in particular for the latter. Of course, the SS masterminded and carried out Nazi Germany's murderous hyperexploitation and large-scale slaughter of civilians. But at all times the SS functioned as as integral part of a comprehensive project and strategy for European primacy, key to the survival of the conjoined old and new order inside the Third Reich. The SS leaders were in the first instance auxiliaries in the war of conquest and ideology against the Soviet Union, whose premises continued to be shared by the entire German establishment well past the defeat of not only Moscow but also Stalingrad. They were no more than accessories to the decision first to mount and launch Operation Barbarossa and then to persevere, at any cost, in the face of impossible odds. Naturally, Himmler and Heydrich eagerly organized the Waffen-SS and the Einsatzgruppen to participate in the eastern campaign and to intensify its ideological furor. But it is worth repeating that by and large their contributions were welcomed, and that not even their worst excesses were disavowed or criticized by Germany's upper ten thousand, except perhaps sotto voce. Well before the climacteric of the winter of 1941–42, the SS had become a vital agency of the Third Reich's deadly war machine for unlimited expansion and against bolshevism in the east. Thereafter, the SS merely consolidated and reinforced its position by taking advantage of opportunities created by the unexpected military impasse. As trusted and experienced operatives of the party-state geared to foreign conquest, Himmler and his henchmen sought to occupy and expand unattended interstices of the economic, military, and political power structure. Rather than wrest contested terrain from rival state or party agencies, they rushed forward to handle Augean tasks that others were unable or reluctant to take on themselves.

Could this totalization of war and violence have occasioned the second and final recasting of the Nazi regime? In 1932–33 a self-appointed oligarchy of traditional conservatives and reactionaries had prevailed on Hitler to assume power and, under their aegis, to put through a reordering of German political and civil society for which they themselves lacked the necessary unity and popular support. As it turned out, the unlikely chancellor pushed this internal reordering considerably further than his principals had envisaged. Of course, they had approved of the forcible dismantling of the political and syndical left, the perversion of parliament, and the establishment of concentration camps. They had also condoned the emasculation of the Rechtsstaat and the purge of high culture. But the old elites were caught short by the efficacy, speed, and thoroughness of the Nazi reaction, and unnerved and disoriented by its revolutionary nihilism. At any rate, there was a first recasting of the regime in mid-1934: Hitler maneuvered his original sponsors into accepting their position as his subordinate collaborators at the same time that he made the SS the praetorian guard, the security organ, and the Inquisition of the Third Reich. Having fallen in line, the old elites kept reaffirming their loyalty despite continuing violations of their traditional ethos and prerogatives in domestic affairs as well as of their seasoned judgment in foreign policy.

It is an open question whether Operation Barbarossa or, more likely, its stalemate and the attendant steeling of the Behemoth led to the final recasting of the Nazi regime. In some respects, by knowingly and eagerly endorsing Barbarossa, Germany's old elites merely capped their collaboration, which was essentially unforced. They had continued to condone, not to say approve, all the outrages perpetrated by their senior partners since January 1933, with the exception of euthanasia, to be discussed in the next chapter. Their acceptance of the Einsatzgruppen and the Commissar Order was entirely in keeping with this compliance. In fact, the war for eastern *Lebensraum* and against "Judeobolshevism" probably marked the culmination of the unforced collaboration between the Nazi leadership and the traditional elite. Of course, in the beginning only a few members of Germany's upper ten thousand knew about the uncommon fury built into Barbarossa. In the late fall of 1941, however, most of them must have learned about the ferocity of the campaign. But by then they easily persuaded themselves that the barbarian Soviets provoked the German forces to commit certain excesses, and that in any case these were a necessary but minor blight on a noble cause that they considered their own. It was natural for them, therefore, to close ranks when the stalling of the eastern campaign led to the further brutalization of warfare along with the stepped-up impressment and exploitation of peoples of the occupied countries and territories.

As Jews became the primary but largely unknown victims of this rape of Europe, they could not expect either interposition or compassion from the non-Nazi ruling and governing elements of the Third Reich. Even in peacetime, after helping to revile and overthrow the Weimar regime for being a *Judenrepublik*, Germany's notables had closed their eyes to the Nuremberg Laws and Crystal Night. They had similarly condoned the relocation and ghettoization of Polish Jews as well as the laceration of Soviet Jews during the heyday of Barbarossa. As sworn imperialists, the inveterate elites were not about to censure the wrack of German and foreign Jews in a moment of extreme national emergency, especially since the SS "merely" proposed to marshal them for war work, even if in questionable ways. When in the wake of the winter of 1941–42 the non-Nazi generals, industrialists, and bureaucrats solicited the help of Pohl, Heydrich, and Sauckel, and hence of Himmler, they could not have been unaware of the moral and political implications of the request. Whatever their presumed innocence in January 1933 and their know-nothing stance until the start of the war, by this time they must or should have been thoroughly disabused. Yet, significantly, only a few of the notables in the latent anti-Nazi opposition objected to the enslavement of eastern peoples, let alone to the persecution of the Jews. As we shall see, when this *fronde* finally staged its abortive plot against Hitler in July 1944, it did so first and foremost, if not exclusively, to protest his by then disastrous military and foreign policy and to restore a variant of the old pre-1914 regime. But big business, which was best placed to know about the horrors of the concentration-camp universe, was all but absent even from this eleventh-hour defection.

The willful mass killing of the Jews was part of the tightening vise of oppression that the Third Reich clamped on the Continent beginning with the critical winter of 1941–42. The Jewish deportations were closely tied in with the resolve to speed and increase war production by recruiting foreign workers and filling the concentration camps with captive labor. The torment of the Jews was also inseparable from the intensified security drive against the resistance. Throughout Europe, Nazi Germany incited active opposition by its relentless conscription of labor and political terror. By pressing this levy of forced labor and this drive for security, which were mutually antithetical, Berlin aggravated the general chaos and desolation of war, which became the crushing backdrop for the Judeocide.

The confinement of Jews to closed ghettos and their deportation to concentration camps were part of the political economy of forced war production. Given the acute manpower shortage, not only the SS but above all Speer, Göring, and key industrialists were determined to put the allegedly parasitic Jews to work. Moreover, the Nazis set out to exploit and drive the Jews harder than any of their other slaves. Even so, they were not simply bent on decimating the Jews through systematic and economically wasteful overwork. Although the Nazis willfully sapped their productivity, in some measure the labor of Jews contributed to the war effort. This is not to deny or minimize the fact that the Jews were despoiled and massacred with total disregard for their economic usefulness, most notably in the four specialized killing centers. But it is to insist, nevertheless, that until late 1944 the Judeocide was closely tied to a desperate economic and political effort in support of a war to the death. This dual but internally incompatible drive *against* the Jews and *for* war production acquired its own momentum and relative autonomy.

As previously noted, the link between the "Final Solution" and the pressing need for production was barely touched upon at the Wannsee Conference of January 22, 1941. During the following weeks, however, Himmler gave it his full attention. In close cooperation with Pohl he reorganized the command structure of the concentration-camp system in the light of its new economic functions. The RSHA was charged with procuring, disciplining, and guarding the rapidly expanding reserve army of camp labor; the WVHA became responsible for allocating and deploying it for war production. Although this reorganization did not dissolve the endemic contradictions between the RSHA and the WVHA, both bureaus were now under strict orders to give unequivocal priority to gearing the camps to serve the total war effort.

The Gestapo as well as the other police and security forces of the Third Reich quickly rose to this unexpected occasion. By mid-1942 they began to herd and channel what soon turned into a flood of deportees into the rapidly overcrowding main camps and their proliferating external work commandos. Transports arrived in ever growing numbers from all the German-annexed and -occupied territories.

By far the largest number of captive workers were deported from the Polish and Soviet territories, with the result that Polish and Soviet citizens became the two largest national groups in Nazi Germany's concentration-camp universe. Of course, most but far from all deported Jews came from these same eastern territories, and it is difficult to determine the proportion of Jews among Soviet and Polish deportees. Including the Jews shipped from outside eastern Europe, but not those killed before being entered in the camp registers, there were as many Jews as there were non-Jewish Poles and Russians in the camps, not counting Polish and Russian prisoners of war. Overall, and at all times, there were, however, more Gentile than Jewish inmates.

There were relatively few Jews left in Old Germany, since many of those still trapped there in mid-1941 had been deported to eastern ghettos and work camps beginning later that year. Those Jews who remained in Germany, including Austria and the Protectorate, and who were interned in local concentration camps, were ordered transferred to Auschwitz and Majdanek in November 1942. By then the first mass transports of Jews from western Europe had long since started to arrive in Auschwitz. Most of these were not citizens of France, Belgium, Holland and Luxembourg, but foreign-born Jews—many of them *Ostjuden*—who were either long-time residents or recent refugees in these countries. Confronted with orders to turn over Jews for shipment to labor in the east, the Jewish consistories, which reluctantly collaborated with local officials, at first arranged to spare native and nationalized Jews by urging or consenting to the deportation primarily of foreign and stateless ones. Besides, a considerable number of native-born western and central European Jews had been and still were being transported to Theresienstadt, which initially was a relatively privileged detention center. Thus many of the Jews deported to eastern concentration camps from western and central

Europe were *Ostjuden,* most of them émigrés or refugees from tsarist Russia and post-1918 Poland. In any event, by far the greatest number of both Gentile and Jewish inmates and victims of Nazi concentration camps were natives of eastern and southeastern Europe, the main vortex of the climactic phase of the second Thirty Years War.

The torment of the Jews at Auschwitz—and throughout occupied Europe—was at one and the same time *sui generis* and yet similar to that of other victims of the Nazis. It was fueled by the same conditions, served the same purposes, and was perpetrated by the same agencies as the wrack of the other peoples of the occupied Continent, most particularly of eastern Europe. Total war was omnipresent and inexorably intensified the suffering of Jews and non-Jews alike. It impregnated nearly every aspect of the impressment and brutalization of Europe.

Originally, Auschwitz was conceived, built, and operated in the confident spirit of September 1939. Following the conquest of Poland, and in the expectation of further easy conquests, the Nazis transformed their concentration-camp system from an instrument for the repression of domestic enemies and dissidents into an instrument of state terror that could also or primarily be used to subjugate the peoples of annexed and occupied territories. At first, and until the incipient impasse of Barbarossa, Auschwitz was charged with holding and putting to work first Polish and then also Soviet prisoners of war and political enemies while at the same time, as we shall see, advancing the cause of eastern colonization. As of late 1941 this mission was radically redefined. Like all the other concentration camps, Auschwitz was geared to serve an uphill and desperate war effort by hyperexploiting an inexhaustible reservoir of "expendable" foreign slave labor. Before long it was also turned into a center for the willful and outright extermination of "unproductive" Jews and Gypsies.

The innumerable Jews who were selected to work, die, and be murdered at Auschwitz and Majdanek were deported there as part of the vast impressment of all of Europe for the benefit of Nazi Germany's overstrained war machine. Any attempt to explicate Auschwitz requires facing up to this diabolic fusion between, on the one hand, the ideological and institutional press for extermination and, on the other hand, the contingent exigencies of an intractable and failing total war. Auschwitz was a microcosm not only of the systematic license of the Nazi regime's destructive impulses but also of its rising entropy. No doubt, Auschwitz was conceived and run by the SS, which eventually turned it into a hell on earth. But this hell was located in a space conquered by the regular army; it was capitalized and exploited by big industry; and it was used for sinister medical experiments by licensed physicians. As for the inmates and victims of Auschwitz, they included a cross section of the Third Reich's designated archenemies, both domestic and foreign. Auschwitz was the quintessential total institution, with no exit: of the over 400,000 registered and countless unregistered prisoners, only several score ever escaped without being recaptured and killed. It encapsulated the singularities of the miseries of Europe's second Thirty Years War, of which the Judeocide was the most execrable.

Auschwitz started as a concentration camp modeled after Dachau in Germany and Mauthausen in annexed Austria. The city of Oświęcim, renamed Auschwitz, is located in eastern Upper Silesia, which was part of the conquered Polish territories incorporated into the Third Reich as the province of the Warthegau. The initial idea was to set up a camp to hold Polish prisoners of war and a rapidly growing number of Polish political prisoners. By the end of 1939 Stutthof, the detention camp twenty-one miles east of Danzig, held about 3,500 prisoners. Because of bureaucratic infighting it was not expanded until February 1942, when Pohl decreed that the capacity of Stutthof had to be increased to 25,000 as part of the transformation of the camp system. In the meantime, the failure to find another satisfactory location in the north, in eastern Prussia, prompted Lieutenant General Erich von dem Bach-Zelewski, a high SS official in Silesia, to press the search for an appropriate site in the south. He commissioned one of his chief deputies to head this search, which soon centered on Auschwitz. Following a feasibility study and two reviews in the home office of the concentration-camp inspectorate, Auschwitz was chosen for the establishment of a transit camp to hold 10,000 Poles. On May 4, 1940, Glücks appointed Rudolf Höss, the deputy chief of Sachsenhausen, to take charge. At the time, it was still uncertain whether the Polish prisoners sent to Auschwitz would be put to use locally or would be sent on to work for the nascent SS economy in camps in Germany.

The town of Auschwitz had a population of about 10,000, of whom about 4,000 were Jewish. It was situated on the main rail line between Katowice and Cracow, at the confluence of the Vistula and Sona rivers. In addition to being easily accessible from the rest of Poland and points further west, Auschwitz was surrounded by large expanses of unused land. Moreover, the city could provide several military barracks and a large building of Poland's defunct tobacco monopoly to house the Polish prisoners and forced laborers who were to rapidly construct the camp.

Höss promptly ordered the evacuation of the people living in the barracks, the impressment of suitable local Jews to help with the construction work, and the importation of a labor detail from Dachau. In addition, he asked that a squad of hardened criminals be brought in from Sachsenhausen to help with the policing. While the first thirty serial numbers of Auschwitz were assigned to these German "asocials," the next 728 numbers were given to Polish political prisoners, who began to arrive in mid-June.

By then Himmler had reformulated the mission of Auschwitz. As Reich commissar for the Germanization of the east, he proposed to have it serve as an outpost for the implantation of German colonizers. In addition to operating an agricultural experiment station, the inmate labor was to be used to clear land for cultivation and settlement.

This same colonizing thrust almost immediately assumed an industrial inflection as well. During the second half of 1940 officials of the Four-Year Plan and the Economics Ministry pressed I. G. Farben, the giant chemical combine, to put a plant for the production of synthetic rubber and fuel into annexed Polish territory, along the eastern marches of the Third Reich. They kept stressing the importance of increasing Germany's self-sufficiency in these critical materials and of bolstering Germany's industrial presence in Upper Silesia. Once the government spokesmen put forward Auschwitz, the board of directors of Farben delegated Dr. Otto Ambros, probably its leading synthetic rubber, or Buna, expert to survey the proposed site. Ambros soon judged it very suitable: there were rich coal deposits nearby; the local rivers provided ample water; and the railway and road links were excellent. The only drawback was the absence of an adequate work force, but the local concentration camp could partly compensate for this deficiency.

By early 1941 plans were well advanced for what would be a Buna installation producing 30,000 tons of rubber per year and a hydrogenation plant to convert coal into oil at the rate of 700,000 tons per month. With Great Britain determined to fight on, urgent military needs now came into play in addition to the long-term objectives of the government and I. G. Farben respectively. General Keitel gave the project top priority, and so did Göring, who agreed to provide the necessary pool of skilled German workers. On February 18, 1941, Carl Krauch, chairman of the board of I. G. Farben, urged Göring to ask Himmler to make available construction workers from the Auschwitz camp. Two weeks later, on March 4, Krauch informed Ambros, who was also a director of Farben, that on February 26, on Göring's "instructions," Himmler had ordered that the Jews still remaining in the town of Auschwitz be "resettled as rapidly as possible" so as to "liberate their dwellings" for use by "the [incoming,

skilled] construction workers for the Buna plant." Himmler also ordered that local Poles suitable for construction work not be deported.
In addition to instructing Glücks and Pohl to contact the chief of
construction of the Buna plant in order "to help to the utmost by
making available the prisoners from the concentration camp,"
Himmler made SS Lieutenant General Karl Wolff, chief of his personal staff, his "liaison officer" with IG-Auschwitz. In turn, Farben
made Dr. Heinrich Bütefisch, its chief expert for synthetic fuel and
a member of the SS, its contact with Wolff.

Meanwhile, on March 1 Himmler and Glücks visited Auschwitz.
They were accompanied by senior government, party, and security
officials of Upper Silesia, as well as by high I. G. Farben executives.
After inspecting the site, including the camp, which then counted
8,000 inmates, Himmler issued three orders: to triple the capacity of
the original camp to 30,000; to build a second camp in the adjoining
village of Brzezinka, renamed Birkenau, for an additional 100,000
prisoners of war; and to supply I. G. Farben with 10,000 inmates for
the construction and operation of its large industrial facilities at
Dwory, five miles east of Auschwitz.

Two facets of policy now merged. On April 7 Dr. Ambros told the
board of Farben that with "project Auschwitz" the firm was "fulfilling
its highest duty": by giving its best to the establishment of a major
industrial installation, it was contributing a "solid cornerstone" to
the development of a "strong and healthy Germanic presence
[Deutschtum] in the east." On this same occasion, the board also
learned that Himmler intended to make the Auschwitz area into "a
model of eastern settlement," which entailed both "the resettlement
of all Poles" and the "settlement of highly qualified Germans."

By now both Poles and Jews were being forced out of their homes
in Auschwitz and nearby villages to make room for German personnel. While the Poles not used for local labor were being deported to
the General Government, the Jews were resettled not too far to the
north of the town. An area of about fifteen square miles was being
cleared for the expansion and seclusion of the nascent Auschwitz
complex.

As of the spring of 1941, besides being readied to serve Germany's
projected colonization in the east, Auschwitz was also being geared
to help the forthcoming campaign against the Soviet Union. Not that
any of the Farben executives necessarily knew about Barbarossa. But
when Himmler ordered Höss to build a camp for an additional
100,000 prisoners of war at Birkenau, he must have done so with
an eye to future Soviet prisoners. Since it took time to make plans
and preparations, construction at Birkenau and Dwory did not really

begin until the fall of 1941. By then the Wehrmacht was deep in Russia and was capturing millions of prisoners, of whom about 100,000 apparently had been promised to Himmler to build Birkenau and work for Farben. During October some 10,000 emaciated Soviet prisoners were checked into the main camp—Auschwitz I. Because of overcrowding and overwork, most of these prisoners who were not killed outright died of exposure, hunger, and disease. On the whole, their fate, not unlike that of the many thousands of Soviet prisoners who followed them at Auschwitz, was identical to that of other Soviet prisoners during the climacteric of Operation Barbarossa. It must be stressed that this was the moment, six days after the Wannsee Conference, that Himmler, concluding that "no [further] Russian prisoners can be expected in the near future," ordered Glücks to prepare the concentration camps "to take in 100,000 Jewish men and 50,000 Jewish women from Germany next month."

Beginning with the winter of 1941–42, Auschwitz assumed an ever greater but also unforeseen importance and incoherence. As the largest concentration-camp complex of the Third Reich, it was to hold prisoners of war and political prisoners; it was to become a vast reservoir of forced labor for work within and in the vicinity of the camp; and it was to establish and manage branch camps near external industrial plants. With the failure to seize Russia's oil fields, the Farben project took on exceptional urgency, especially because by virtue of its location Auschwitz seemed safe from air attacks. Eventually, the lure of available and cheap labor as well as of relative safety prompted a number of other large firms to locate in or near Auschwitz.

Auschwitz was conceived and started in the euphoria of a triumphant *Drang nach Osten,* which it was to help foster and consolidate. But once this overambitious drive faltered and euphoria gave way to vindictive rancor, it became a redoubt for the internment, exploitation, and decimation of prisoners of war and political hostages, as well as of racial or ethnic "inferiors," notably Jews and Gypsies.

The population of Auschwitz grew very rapidly, in spite of the vast number of inmates who were killed intentionally or left to die from malnutrition, exhaustion, sickness, or disease. It is impossible to give exact figures about the total number of prisoners and the number of Jews among them from the fall of 1941 to the liberation of the camp complex in January 27, 1945. Nor is it possible to reconstruct the inmate population of Auschwitz for any particular day during those forty terrible months. Because of the highly variable mortality rate, which defies close scrutiny, there were constant and wide fluctuations in the number of captives. The rise and fall of Auschwitz's population was also affected by the erratic arrival of transports. It seems clear, however, that whatever the rate of death before or after registration, the number of living prisoners rose steadily from early 1942 through late 1944. During 1942 the number rose from over 11,000 to over 30,000, during 1943 to over 75,000, and during 1944 to over 135,000. The camp authorities tapped this enormous and perpetually replenished reserve of captive labor to slave for over four hundred public and private war-related industries in Auschwitz proper as well as in scores of branch camps. By the fall of 1943 the SS command concluded that the camp complex had become so vast and multiform as to be unwieldy. To ensure greater efficiency Pohl proposed consolidating the camp at Monowice, which serviced the Farben operations, and nine lesser external camps, into an autonomous administrative unit. Himmler agreed, so that starting on November 10, 1943, the complex consisted of three branches: Auschwitz I, the original and main camp, which included the overall command center; Auschwitz II, or Birkenau; and Auschwitz III, the external branch camps.

I. G. Farben was the vital economic pivot of Auschwitz, and it was prototypical of the unflinching complicity of big business, including its professional cadres, with the worst excesses of the Third Reich. By the end of the war Farben accounted for at least 50 percent of Germany's chemical production, most of it essential for the war effort. Between 1939 and 1944 its work force rose by close to 50 percent, and so did its gross profits. During these same years, as new plants were built, Farben shifted the weight of its operations from the Rhineland to points farther east. The chemical and pharmaceutical colossus became a leading employer of prisoners of war, forced laborers from all over the Continent, and concentration-camp inmates. Most of the foreign recruits were used for construction work and other unskilled jobs. Just as Farben's overall work force doubled during the war, so the proportion of foreign workers nearly doubled, to reach well over 80,000. Prisoners of war were only half as productive as German workers, and camp inmates even less so. But Farben also paid considerably less for their services, with the result that it continued to profit substantially from the use of forced labor.

IG-Auschwitz reflected all these trends. It became the largest of Farben's eastern production centers. By the spring of 1944 it "employed" between 27,000 and 30,000 workers. Only between 3,000 and 6,000 of them were ethnic Germans employed there of their own free will. The rest of the labor force consisted of 12,000 to 15,000 foreign workers and 8,000 to 9,000 camp inmates. As of 1943, when forced Polish workers were being sent to labor in Germany in ever-greater numbers, the Jews occupied an ever more important place in this pool of concentration-camp labor, which was quartered in Mono-wice (called Monowitz by the Germans). These Jewish workers suf-fered the ultimate in exploitation, deprivation, and degradation. They were constrained to perform heavy menial labor without the benefit of the most elementary tools and equipment. In addition, because of radical undernourishment and scandalous housing, their physical stamina declined rapidly. On the average, the life expectancy of the able-bodied Jewish inmates who were assigned to the constantly replenished pool of unskilled, heavy labor at Monowitz was between three and four months. They either collapsed and died at Monowitz, or were returned as "unfit" to the SS for disposal at Birkenau. In 1943–44 some 35,000 concentration-camp inmates worked in Mono-witz, of whom 23,000 are known to have died or been killed. In some of IG-Auschwitz's nearby mining operations, conditions were even worse, and the life expectancy lower.

The directors, executives, and managers of I. G. Farben could not *not* have known about these infamous labor conditions in one of their largest production facilities, whose Buna plant, though never com-pleted, remained their chief wager on the future. They must also have had a general idea of the nature of the objectives and methods of the SS, the masters of Auschwitz's main camps, with whom they con-tracted for their cut-rate labor. The same holds true for the other business leaders whose corporations similarly exploited the wretched of Auschwitz.

In March 1944, shaken by the military debacle in the east, Himmler cautioned Pohl about the danger of unrest among the vast concentra-tion of inmates in Auschwitz. On April 8 Pohl sought to reassure his chief with a report that also contained a profile of the "damned" of Auschwitz, valid for that moment. The compound of the main camp held about 16,000 men. Birkenau, which was about 1.8 miles due west, held roughly 15,000 males and 21,000 female inmates, or a total of 36,000, of whom about 15,000 were *"nicht einsatzfähig,"* or unfit for work. As for Auschwitz III, "it comprised all the external camps in Upper Silesia that were located near industrial plants and were geographically far removed from each other." These camps had a total of about 15,000 male inmates, by far the largest compound being the one "in Auschwitz near I. G. Farben," which held about 7,000 men. The three camps combined detained 46,000 men and 21,000 women, or 67,000 inmates, of whom 18,000 were infirm or handi-capped.

With regard to security Pohl told Himmler that since there was no need to worry about the 18,000 infirm and the 15,000 men in the external camps, there were only 34,000 inmates to be watched over. In any case, all the camps, including the external ones, were enclosed by electrically charged wire fences, and overlooked by watchtowers. Some 2,300 SS guards were on hand for Auschwitz I and II and, in an emergency, they could be reinforced by police and military units stationed in the surrounding area. Pohl's confidence in the sufficiency of the local security forces was borne out in early October 1944 when a mutiny by the prisoners of a special commando working at Crematorium IV was easily and brutally quelled.

In the meantime, the number of inmates and subsidiaries kept growing. Auschwitz probably reached its ghastly peak in August 1944, with some forty branches and a total of over 105,000 registered inmates—not counting many thousands of unregistered Jews locked into transit and quarantine enclaves within Birkenau. But soon thereafter, as the Red Army liberated Majdanek and moved closer, the SS began to dismantle the camp and cover up their tracks without, however, relenting in their brutality. By early 1945, having exterminated the "unemployable" wretches concentrated, above all, in Birkenau, they destroyed all gassing and cremation facilities. Under the whip of the SS pragmatists many thousands of still "employable" inmates were shipped to Dachau, Sachsenhausen, and Buchenwald for work, while others were marched to work locations closer by. Monowitz, in fact, continued to expand to a complement of about 35,000 inmates in mid-January 1945, by which time Birkenau had been reduced to less than 32,000. When the troops of Marshal Konev's First Ukrainian Army reached Auschwitz on January 27, they found about 1,200 men in the main camp, 4,000 women and 1,800 men in Birkenau, and 1,800 men at Monowitz. All the other able-bodied internees had been hastily evacuated by forced marches. The most fit among them were shipped to the Reich from the rail junction of Wodzislaw Śląski, southwest of Katowice. Needless to say, all the forced marches took a monstrous toll of life and suffering.

From the outset Auschwitz was overcrowded, and it became ever more so. The physical facilities were designed for subhumans. The barracks were woefully inadequate, and unsuitable for the local climate and terrain. Sanitary conditions were worse still, and clean water was in short supply. Food and clothing were notoriously deficient, and so were medical services.

To a degree, war scarcities might be said to have contributed to the material deprivations inflicted on the inmates. But these shortages cannot be invoked to justify or explain the psychological and physical torture which the SS guards and their auxiliaries were ordered or licensed to exercise on their wards. Nor can the abuse of inmate labor be attributed, not to say imputed, to the practical exigencies of war. This lethal mixture of deliberate deprivation, overwork, and mistreatment fueled the appalling rate of sickness and "natural" death at Auschwitz. It also worsened the epidemic which ravaged Auschwitz, especially Birkenau, in the summer of 1942 and again during the winter of 1942–43. In time, Auschwitz became a camp for the confinement, overexploitation, degradation, and decimation of inmates, regardless of nationality, religion, and ethnicity.

But it was something more and even worse for the Jews, and also for the Gypsies. Jews and Gypsies were taken to Auschwitz because they were Jews and Gypsies, which meant that the Jewish and Gypsy inmates, unlike all the others, were men and women of all ages, including infants, children, and the aged, as well as "the poor, the maimed, the lame, the blind." While Auschwitz was altogether harrowing and unendurable for adults of both sexes in the prime of life and health, it was even more so for the very young, the elderly, and the sick. By forcing unfit Jews to accompany Jewish men and women who were impressed for forced labor, the Nazis condemned the former to a quick "natural" death. In sum, selection for almost certain and instant death was implicit in the very decision to send Jews, regardless of age and physical condition, to Auschwitz and other camps. Selection upon or after arrival was merely the logical consequence and implementation of this prior warrant for destruction.

This is not the same as saying that the "preselected" Jews and Gypsies were sent to Auschwitz, especially to Birkenau, to be gassed. At Auschwitz—and Majdanek—the idea and practice of gassing only developed gradually. But for the Jews Auschwitz was an unqualified inferno even without gas chambers. Indeed, the killing by asphyxiation may be said to have intensified the torment of the camp's Jews in degree, not in kind.

Sources for the study of the gas chambers are at once rare and unreliable. Even though Hitler and the Nazis made no secret of their war on the Jews, the SS operatives dutifully eliminated all traces of their murderous activities and instruments. No written orders for gassing have turned up thus far. The SS not only destroyed most camp records, which were in any case incomplete, but also razed nearly all killing and cremating installations well before the arrival of Soviet troops. Likewise, care was taken to dispose of the bones and ashes of the victims. Most of what is known is based on the depositions of Nazi officials and executioners at postwar trials and on the memory of survivors and bystanders. This testimony must be screened carefully, since it can be influenced by subjective factors of great complexity. Diaries are rare, and so are authentic documents about the making, transmission, and implementation of the extermination policy. But additional evidence may still come to light. Private journals and official papers are likely to surface. Since Auschwitz and Majdanek, as well as the four out-and-out killing centers, were liberated by the Red Army, the Soviet archives may well yield significant clues and evidence when they are opened. In addition, excavations at the killing sites and in their immediate environs may also bring forth new information.

In the meantime, there is no denying the many contradictions, ambiguities, and errors in the existing sources. These cannot be ignored, although it must be emphasized strongly that such defects are altogether insufficient to put in question the use of gas chambers in the mass murder of Jews at Auschwitz. Much the same is true for the conflicting estimates and extrapolations of the number of victims, since there are no reliable statistics to work with. Just as the fact of the Jewish ordeal at Auschwitz is not contingent on the use of gas chambers, so the crime of gassing does not turn upon the exact number of Jews gassed. The want of precise and verifiable information about the method and extent of the mass murder of Jews by the crusaders in the Rhine Valley in 1096 does not in any way put into question the reality and general magnitude of this prototypical Judeocide of the Middle Ages. Both radical skepticism and rigid dogmatism about the exact processes of extermination and the exact number of victims are the bane of sound historical interpretation. Neither new documents nor flawless statistics are essential to the urgent task of thinking, critically, about the unthinkable. Judging by the debates concerning other major historical problems, the explication of the Nazi gas chambers will be advanced chiefly by changing historical perspectives as well as by the formulation of new interpretive questions, contextual definitions, and conceptual constructs.

To date there is no certainty about who gave the order, and when, to install the gas chambers used for the murder of Jews at Auschwitz. As no written command has been located, there is a strong presumption that the order was issued and received orally. Whether Hitler himself ever *formally* issued or approved the writ to exterminate the Jews remains uncertain, though it is well-nigh inconceivable that it could have been given and executed *without* his approval or *against* his will. Meanwhile, this much is beyond dispute: the locus of decision and execution was within the SS, both at headquarters and in the field. Without exception, the principal architects, directors, and pace-setters of the Judeocide were the overlords of the SS: Himmler, Heydrich, Pohl, Glücks, and Maurer. No doubt there was considerable scope for local initiative, as was the case with Höss in Auschwitz, but probably only within a framework of general directives or of following prior clearance from higher up. At the apex the complicity of Hitler and Himmler was decisive, with Himmler in frequent personal contact with the führer.

The question of the identity of the prime mover or movers of the order to exterminate the Jews systematically at Auschwitz is closely linked to the question of when this order was issued and acted upon. All things considered, the command seems to have been given in the late winter of 1941–42 or the very early spring of 1942, in conjunction with the recasting of the concentration-camp system for war production. If such was the case, then the decision and warrant were framed at the same time that Himmler upgraded the WVHA to be coequal with the RSHA, placing the former under the direction of Pohl, Glücks, and Maurer. Hereafter, Heydrich—and following Heydrich's assassination Himmler himself along with Heinrich Müller and Ernst Kaltenbrunner—worked closely with Pohl and his associates. There were, of course, constant strains between the symbiotically linked RSHA and WVHA. But these strains were due to normal bureaucratic competition rather than extraordinary personal rivalries, and not too much should be made of them. The chiefs of the security and police apparatus fixed the quotas and timetables for the deportation of Jews to Auschwitz in consultation with the chiefs of the economic department of the SS.

Probably Höss was the last to be consulted. An ultra-Nazi, he was charged with building and running his combined production and death center at a pace that was set for him by others but that compelled and encouraged him to exercise enormous discretion. It was within this framework of both extreme urgency and latitude that Höss transmuted the ordinary practice of screening the transports arriving in Auschwitz for housing and work assignments into an execrable system of selection for either slow or instant death, for consignment to the perils of life in the camps or to the gas chambers. In any case, as previously noted, given the local conditions and needs, selection for death was already implied, even if not prescribed or specified, by the order to deport Jews unselectively from their points of departure. It is unclear what percentage of the incoming Jews was selected on arrival as "unfit for hard labor"; estimates range between 60 and 80 percent. It is also uncertain how many of these "unfit"—the sick and infirm as well as healthy women, infants, children, and old people—

were sent to the gas chambers immediately upon arrival or shortly thereafter, how many were sent sometime later, and how many ultimately died a "natural" death.

At Auschwitz the assembly-line selection did not really begin until the arrival of the first transports of *un*selected Jews from western Europe during the summer of 1942. By then the construction of Birkenau was well advanced. Unlike the main camp, which was and remained an all-male camp for about 15,000 slave workers, Birkenau was to become the major compound not only for forced laborers of both sexes but also for the nonworking inmates of the entire complex. Accordingly, upon their arrival after a grueling and dehumanizing journey in freight cars, all temporarily and permanently "unemployable" Jews were summarily assigned to Birkenau, where housing and sanitation were disastrous, as they were throughout the Auschwitz complex. Half-starved and practically without medical care, the frail and the sick were particularly imperiled, the more so since at the journey's end the whole of Auschwitz was intermittently in the grip of a devastating typhus epidemic. The result was an unspeakable death rate, partly because the ailing and the dying were brought to Birkenau from both the main camp and from Monowitz. In addition to being the wretched and miasmic habitat for the least fit, Birkenau was the site of Auschwitz's main medical facility and quarantine center, as well as of most of its crematoriums and gas chambers.

There is a distinction between dying from "natural" or "normal" causes and being killed by shooting, hanging, phenol injection, or gassing. But quite apart from the vital importance of not allowing this distinction to be used to extenuate and normalize the mass murder at Auschwitz, it should not be pressed too far. The Nazi leaders decided to transport frail and sick Jews, and Gypsies, to Auschwitz in full awareness of the perils they would face, and they continued to do so once there was no ignoring and denying the deadly conditions there, including the endemic danger of epidemics. Besides, from 1942 to 1945, certainly at Auschwitz, but probably overall, more Jews were killed by so-called "natural" causes than by "unnatural" ones.

Given the high death rate at Auschwitz, the corpses had to be disposed of quickly and without creating further health hazards. After burying the dead in pits for some time, the SS shifted to burning them, first on open pyres and then, above all, in crematoriums. Except for one crematory installed in the main camp, all the cremating facilities were clustered in Birkenau. The decision to order four modern crematoriums with multiple ovens for emplacement in Birkenau was made late in the winter of 1941–42—in other words, well before the arrival of the Jewish transports from western Europe. SS specialists worked closely with representatives of the two private firms that were commissioned to manufacture and install the new equipment, a task which was to take a full year. The four crematoriums, numbered II through V, began to operate at different dates between March 23 and June 25, 1943. Crematoriums II and III were built partly underground, each complex consisting of fifteen ovens and a daily capacity of 1,440 bodies. Crematoriums IV and V were entirely aboveground, each installation consisting of eight ovens for a daily capacity of 768 corpses. Located along the western fringes of Birkenau, the four crematoriums combined could dispose of 4,416 bodies every day. Taking account of the 340 bodies that could be burned in the crematorium of the main camp, which also operated off and on until the fall of 1944, Auschwitz's daily crematory capacity reached 4,756. In sum, from the summer of 1943 through the fall of 1944, provided they operated at full capacity and around the clock, the five crematoriums could incinerate 33,292 bodies per week, 142,680 per month, and 1,712,160 per year.

But many questions remain open. To begin with, to what extent did the resolve to impress and decimate or exterminate the Jews influence the decision to equip Birkenau with four immense crematoriums? All in all, how many bodies were cremated in Auschwitz? How many died there all told? What was the national, religious, and ethnic breakdown in this commonwealth of victims? How many of them were condemned to die a "natural" death and how many were deliberately slaughtered? And what was the proportion of Jews among those murdered in cold blood—among these gassed? We have simply no answers to these questions at this time.

The outright killings began in July or August 1941. Judging by their victims and the methods used, these early slayings were characteristic of the original mission of Auschwitz. The first to be killed were Polish and Soviet prisoners who were selected for being sick, unfit, or unruly. They were taken from Auschwitz to a half-dormant euthanasia establishment at Sonnenstein to be dispatched, individually, by phenol injection or gassing. Much like the SS after the outbreak of war in 1939, the cadres and operatives of the euthanasia program, stymied at home as we shall see, were eager to serve the Third Reich in eastern Europe. The next chapter will show how starting in mid-March 1942, these miscreants played a considerable role in Operation Reinhard at Bełżec, Sobibór, and Treblinka. But even before then, several of them apparently went first to Poland and then as far east as Smolensk and Kiev in Russia to act as observers, consultants, and experimenters in the wake of special SS commandos. Though few in number and without clear authority, they proffered their know-how through informal connections that eventually reached into Auschwitz. In any case, on September 3, 1941, about six hundred Soviet prisoners of war were killed in a cellar of Block 11 in the main camp. A few days later another nine hundred POWs were put to death in the morgue next to the crematorium. It seems that both times gas was used. The second time the local executioners probably asphyxiated their victims with the insecticide Zyklon B. Although there may have been some Jews among these victims, the bulk was not Jewish. Nor is there any reliable evidence to suggest that these killings were rehearsals for the subsequent mass gassing of Jews.

At Auschwitz this mass slaughter did not start until the summer of 1942. That was the time that Jews began to arrive to be consigned to work and die in Birkenau, whose inherent desolation just then was compounded by typhus. With the rates of sickness and death soaring, and with the installation of the new crematoriums many months away, the camp authorities decided to put together a gassing facility at Birkenau. Workmen converted two recently evacuated peasant houses into gas chambers by removing their interior walls, insulating their windows, and refitting their doors. These two converted dwellings, hereafter known as Bunker I and Bunker II, were of uneven size, and their respective killing capacities remain unknown. They became operative in mid-July 1942, possibly on July 17 or 18, during Himmler's second visit to Auschwitz. Presumably, these improvised facilities were intended to speed the death of the uncared-for, failing victims of the epidemic, which could no longer be handled by phenol injections. No real effort was made to stem the epidemic: the local authorities, including the physicians among them, neither organized emergency evacuations nor requested that all incoming transports be delayed or halted. Instead, they sought to contain and control the epidemic by imposing what they must have known to be totally ineffective quarantine measures.

The camp officials did not keep very accurate records of the inbound deportees. Untold thousands were "processed" without being signed in. Because of this, and because so many records were destroyed, there are no close approximations of the numbers and identities of the Jews checked into Auschwitz except for those sent there from western Europe. Their fate can be reconstructed not from the incomplete registers of inmates checked into the camps, but with the help of the shipping manifests of departing transports, which are reliable and have survived. As we saw, in the course of 1942 Himmler and Pohl ordered about 200,000 Jews sent from western Europe to Auschwitz as part of their extortion of forced labor for German war production. At the same time that Berlin pressed for the delivery of Jews, it intensified its drive for security and economic mobilization throughout German-dominated territories as well as for the transfer of laboring men and women for work in the Reich. By tightening its iron hold on the peoples of western Europe, the Third Reich and its collaborators numbed them, at least initially, to the particular plight of the Jews. Above all, the mounting drive for compulsory labor service in Germany made the deportation of the Jews seem less aberrant. And little, if anything, was known about the uniquely infernal conditions at Auschwitz and Majdanek.

Eventually, about 75,000 Jews were deported from France, about 25,000 from Belgium, and about 100,000 from Holland. The story of the deportations from France is typical of the countries and territories over which the Third Reich exercised less than complete control, or that were spared total subjugation like that inflicted on Poland and occupied Russia. The unfolding of these French deportations is also relatively well documented.

Both halves of France suffered the consequences of the military impasse on the eastern front. The captive nation with the greatest economic resources, France was expected and driven to make exceptionally heavy contributions to the Reich's war effort. Berlin made ever greater demands on French agriculture and industry. By 1944 very nearly all of France's output of automobiles, engineering products, and airplanes was going to Germany at cut-rate prices. France suffered growing shortages of oil, raw materials, and foods while much of its rolling stock was also commandeered for the Wehrmacht. During most of the four years of German mastery, French industrialists offered little if any resistance and, unlike in the east, there were enough political collaborators and collaborationists to obviate the need for massive coercion.

This is the context in which France was also stripped of labor. Between October 1940 and mid-1942 probably about 150,000 French men and women, most of them unskilled, went to work in the Reich of their own accord, drawn there by economic opportunities. Most of them, however, signed six-month contracts which they did not renew, and in September 1942 the number of volunteers in Germany stood at only 42,000. Meanwhile, the 1.6 million French officers and men taken prisoner in May and June 1940 remained in German captivity. Naturally, the labor supply began to tighten as soon as the economy was converted to production for the enemy. Sauckel's labor requisitions greatly aggravated the situation. In the spring of 1942, at the same time that the first Jews were being ordered deported to Auschwitz for labor, Sauckel asked Vichy to provide Germany with 250,000 workers, 60 percent of them skilled. This demand coincided with the return of Pierre Laval to the premiership on April 18, which reflected Hitler's growing pressure on Pétain to redouble his support of the Axis. At first, Laval sought to persuade Berlin to return one French prisoner of war in exchange for each worker, but on June 22, 1942, two years after the armistice, he had to settle for one prisoner for every three workers. Significantly, these negotiations overlapped with those bearing on the first delivery of Jews from France. In any case, Berlin practically ignored the agreement as it began to marshal French POWs for the German economy. About 900,000 of them were at work in the Reich by early 1944.

Despite intense propaganda, from July through September 1942 only about 17,000 workers volunteered to go to Germany, some of them hoping to facilitate the release of French prisoners. His patience tried, Sauckel threatened to replace the carrot with the stick and served notice that he would make additional demands. Presumably, to head off this move, Vichy began to wield its own whip, hoping to appease Berlin by meeting the original quota. The manpower law of September 4, 1942 introduced a first element of compulsion for men between eighteen and fifty and unmarried women between twenty-one and thirty-five. By the end of the year nearly 240,000 additional workers left for the Reich, about 135,000 of them skilled workers, and virtually all under compulsion. Sauckel promptly asked for an additional 220,000 workers. In turn, Laval saw to the adoption of a law on February 16, 1943, which drafted most men of twenty-one to twenty-three years of age for labor service in Germany. About 130,000 men were sent across the Rhine between early May and early August 1943, when Sauckel asked for another 150,000 workers. All told, during the ten months from October 1942 through July 1943 some 600,000 Frenchmen were sent to Germany, or about 2,000 per day and 61,500 per month. But then, with the tides of battle changing, the heavy flow was reduced to a trickle. Over the next eleven months, until June 1944, only about 91,000 additional conscripts left, or about 250 daily and 8,300 monthly. Indeed, as of late summer 1943, more and more young men dodged the labor service. With time and regional variations, a fair number of them joined the resistance, fewer of them the maquis, the armed underground. In an effort to counteract this trend, Speer arranged for the exemption of workers employed in French firms contracted to deliver 80 percent of their output to the Reich. But time was running out. Sauckel's demand for a further 1 million men in January 1944 was virtually delusory and was never met.

Of course, this general conscription for labor service in Germany differed radically from the deportation of Jews for labor in the east. The former involved drafting only healthy young males. Once in Germany they lived in labor camps whose conditions had nothing in common with those in concentration camps, and they worked under standard wartime conditions in regular industry. To be sure, although they fared much better than labor conscripts from the east, their circumstances were not ideal. In fact, scores of restive French workers wound up in concentration camps, where not a few must have perished. Others were killed in air raids. Even so, at least 90 percent of all non-Jewish Frenchmen who went to work in Germany, or were impressed to go there, returned after the war, and so did nearly all prisoners of war. But while the war lasted and the German furor and extortion mounted, this outcome was far from certain. Nazi Germany held the 2.3 million Frenchmen within its borders hostage for the good behavior of their compatriots and rulers, or so these last either feared or pretended, with disastrous consequences for French Jews.

In the meantime, starting soon after the French defeat in June 1940, the Jews of France were being deemancipated and persecuted in both halves of the country. France counted between 300,000 and 330,000 Jews, about half of them of foreign nationality or stateless, and this Jewish population was nearly evenly divided between the two zones. By early 1942 Jews on both sides of the demarcation line were rapidly being squeezed out of civic, political, and cultural life, and they were also being strangulated economically. Foreign and stateless Jews became the primary victims for arbitrary arrest. With the Gestapo pressing the seamless drive against communism, sabotage, and Jews, as part of the first of many security sweeps, in mid-May 1941 the French police readily rounded up over 3,700 foreign Jews in Greater Paris and interned them in nearby camps. The police staged its second such operation on August 20: to retaliate for Communist agitation following the German invasion of the Soviet Union, and as a measure of intimidation, the police remanded 4,200 Jews to Drancy, among them about 1,000 French Jews.

Before long, the deadlock of Barbarossa sparked an intensified security drive in both German-occupied and Vichy France. The third major police operation took place December 12 to 15, 1941, following several attacks on German military personnel. Almost without exception these assaults were executed by Communists, many of them by foreign-born Jewish Communists. At a time when France was still overwhelmingly collaborationist, these early urban maquisards were not about to be hailed as national heroes, and it was easy for the Germans to portray them as well as their fellow travelers and sympathizers as part of the "Judeobolshevik" world conspiracy. On December 12 German security and police operatives, assisted by French policemen, arrested 743 Jewish male hostages in Paris, nearly all of them French nationals who were businessmen and professionals. Together with 300 French Jews taken out of Drancy, they were interned at Compiègne. Two days later, on December 14, the local military authorities used placards to announce that in retribution for the recent outrages "the Jews of occupied France will be fined one billion francs; . . . a large number of criminal Judeobolshevik elements will be deported for forced labor in the east; . . . and 100 Jews, Communists, and anarchists, who have proven contacts with the perpetrators of these assassinations, will be executed." Of the hostages executed on December 15 at Mont-Valérien, 53 were Jews, nearly all of them selected from among over 8,000 Jews interned for being Communist or socialist militants. The first retaliatory transport of 1,112 young Jewish males left on March 27, 1942, and included many of the hostages held in Drancy and Compiègne. A second convoy followed on June 5.

Meanwhile, the Vichy government, on its own, had begun to harass and persecute the Jews in the southern zone. In early October 1941 it interned about 25,000 foreign Jews in refugee camps along with anti-Franco Spanish exiles. An additional 15,000 foreign and stateless Jews of both sexes and all ages were interned during the following four months, disastrously overcrowding Gurs and other camps. Concurrently, Pétain's Commissariat for Jewish Affairs kept narrowing the civil rights and freedoms of all Jews, both native and foreign. By mid-1942 the Jews of Vichy France were being deemancipated and ostracized on the German model, except that they were spared wearing the yellow star. But until June 1942 Vichy had not interned, executed, or deported any French Jews, nor had it executed or deported any foreign and stateless Jews. Their bondage was not part of a genocidal intention or project, certainly less so than in the occupied northern zone, in which the situation was already distinctly worse.

Himmler's original directive to prepare to send 100,000 Jewish men and 50,000 Jewish women from western Europe for work in concentration camps was issued in late January 1942, immediately after the Wannsee Conference. It would take six months to translate it into a firm order for deportation to Auschwitz. Having gathered preliminary information, the top security officials for Jewish affairs in Paris, Brussels, and The Hague were summoned to a meeting on June 11, 1942, in the Berlin offices of the RSHA. Probably under Eichmann's chairmanship, this conclave decided that during the next eight months 100,000 Jews were to be shipped to Auschwitz from both halves of France, 10,000 from Belgium, and 15,000 from Holland. The deportees were to be primarily able-bodied men and women between the ages of sixteen and forty, although these could be accompanied by up to 10 percent of Jews unfit for work.

SS Captain Theodor Dannecker, responsible for France, returned to Paris eager to fill his quota, if necessary by exerting pressure on Vichy. Just then the SS was strengthening its whip hand in Paris, while Laval, fully backed by Pétain, quickened the pace of compliant collaboration in Vichy. On both sides of the demarcation line the French authorities, prodded by Berlin, were willing, some of them even eager, to cooperate in the repression of resistance, in the infeudation of the French economy, in the dispatch of French workers to Germany, and in the deportation of Jews.

Even so, Dannecker soon discovered that the quota of 100,000 Jews between the ages of sixteen and forty was unrealistic. In a Jewish population of 300,000 to 330,000 only about 80,000 fell into this age group. Besides, since not all French officials were unconditional collaborators, the Germans could not afford to press too hard for fear of alienating some of their indispensable helpers. Assisted by SS Colonel Helmut Knochen, chief of the Sipo and the SD in Paris, and by SS Brigadier General Karl Oberg, chief of the SS, Dannecker took three weeks, until July 4, to work out a plan under which 35,000 to 40,000 Jews between sixteen and forty-five years of age would be deported to Auschwitz on relatively short order. About 30,000 were to come from the occupied zone where the Germans were the absolute masters. And Dannecker prevailed on Laval and his police chief, René Bousquet, to turn over 10,000 Jews from the southern zone. In exchange for the Vichy authorities ordering their own police to arrest, assemble, and deliver their own quota of Jews, the Germans agreed that Jews of French nationality could be exempted, to some extent north of the demarcation line as well. But then, between July 4 and 7, Laval voluntarily proposed to deport children between two and fifteen years of age either in the company of their parents or unaccompanied. Though nearly all the children in question were the offspring of foreign parents, as natives of France they were all but assured of citizenship in the future. How to explain Laval's unforced initiative? Although Louis Darquier de Pellepoix, his commissioner for Jewish affairs, was a confirmed anti-Semite, Laval himself was not anti-Jewish. He was, above all, a supreme expediency-monger. Determined to press Vichy's sovereignty and protofascist national interest, Laval lost all sense of moral and political limits. That he shared in the general ignorance about conditions in eastern Europe, and more particularly in Auschwitz, only marginally lessens the degree of his perfidy.

In any case, during 1942 a total of about 42,000 Jews were deported from France to Auschwitz, all but about 5,000 of them between July 17 and November 11 of that year. They were taken there in forty-three transports, of which thirty-two left from Drancy, the camp a few miles northeast of Paris. While about 26,500 were seized in the occupied zone, and 21,000 of them in Greater Paris alone, about 10,500 were picked up and handed over by Vichy. About 6,000 were French citizens, all the others foreigners. By the early fall of 1942 high Catholic and Protestant churchmen protested these "unselected" deportations, with the result that Vichy began to slow down its surrender of Jews. Though at a reduced rate, the deportations continued after the Germans occupied the southern zone in November 1942. In 1943 about 17,000 Jews were sent to the east in seventeen transports, thirteen of which went to Auschwitz, four to Sobibór. The following year seventeen transports took about 14,800 Jews to Auschwitz.

Approximately 75,000 Jews were deported from France during the war, about one-fifth of the total Jewish population. Among the victims there were about 2,000 children of under six years, about 8,700 children between six and seventeen, and about 9,700 adults over sixty. Not counting the children born in France to foreign parents, about 15,000 of all deportees were French citizens. Among the Jews deported from France there were about 24,000 Polish Jews, a sign that even in far-western Europe the *Ostjuden* were the most wretchedly abused. Of course, established French Jews had an easier time fleeing abroad and then avoiding the dragnets. They had higher status, more money, better connections, and a surer sense of place. All this helped them get timely information and find safe hideouts. In addition, indigenous Jewish notables all but controlled the main institutions of the Jewish community, which generally cooperated with the French authorities that were disposed to trade foreign Jews for native Jews, only to discover that all Jews were marked for death. At least 40 percent of all France's foreign Jews perished in the east, compared to "only" about 10 percent of all French Jews.

The overwhelming majority of the deportees from France were taken to Auschwitz, specifically to Birkenau. While the first few transports were made up almost exclusively of able-bodied young men, after a while this ceased to be the case. Henceforth, the mortality rate after arrival was doubtless highest among those selected as unfit for work. About 42,000 Jews, or more than half of the total, were deported in 1942, and most of these arrived during the typhus epidemic. It is not unreasonable to suppose, therefore, that large numbers died a "natural" death, their corpses burned on pyres. How many were gassed during the second half of 1942 is difficult to say. It should be remembered, though, that at this time only the two improvised gas chambers—Bunker I and Bunker II—were functioning at Birkenau, and their killing capacity is likely to have been limited. There is a much stronger presumption of massive gassings beginning with the second quarter of 1943, when the four large crematorium complexes became operative. But as of today it is impossible to give a close approximation of the number of deportees from France who were selected for gassing before or after entering Auschwitz, as opposed to the number who died of exposure, malnutrition, sickness, and overwork. Nor is it possible to say how many of the French deportees survived to suffer the torment of the forced marches and transfers following the dismantling of Auschwitz. But whatever the uncertainties and imprecisions about the circumstances and ways of death of the Jews deported from France, there are none about the general magnitude of the number of Jews from France who died and were murdered in the east.

The agony of the Jews of Hungary who were deported to Auschwitz was intrinsically similar to that of the Jews of France, but on an infinitely more massive scale. Both countries were satellites of Nazi Germany, though Horthy's Hungary was a much more willing and active partner than Pétain's France. As we saw, Budapest not only made a major direct military contribution to the eastern campaign but also rushed to send foreign Jews to their death in Kamenets-Podolsk, even if it did so with nonmurderous intentions. But though the ways and means of the French and Hungarian complicity in the Judeocide were essentially alike, there were great differences in timing and in the information available to Nazi Germany's collaborators. When the deportations to the east were imposed on France and other European countries, the east, including Auschwitz, was a dark and unknown continent and the Behemoth, though cornered, still loomed large and potentially ascendant. By the time the deportations were dictated to Hungary, Auschwitz was recognized for what it was and the Nazi regime forced the delivery of Jews, at gunpoint, as part of its final paroxysm of desperation, incoherence, and rage. Even as late as the spring and summer of 1944 this extortion of Jews was not uninfluenced by Berlin's frantic search for forced labor. By then the aeronautics industry in particular was vulnerable to enemy air raids. Desperate to maintain if not increase the output of fighter planes, Göring and Speer proposed to build an impregnable underground factory at Auschwitz. When Speer discussed this project with Hitler on April 7, 1944, the führer offered to urge Himmler to help procure the necessary manpower by impressing 100,000 Hungarian Jews. On May 11 Himmler notified Pohl that Hitler had ordered 10,000 officers and men of the Waffen-SS to be detached "to guard the 200,000 Jews . . . [about] to be transferred to the Reich's concentration camps for assignment to large construction projects of the Todt Organization or to other essential war work." From among the 300,000 to 400,000 Hungarian Jews shipped to Auschwitz, between 100,000 and 200,000 were to be selected to excavate and build the bunkers for the production of military aircraft. The transports from Hungary were, of course, packed with Jews unsuited for this work, let alone for hard labor, especially since Budapest continued to conscript Jewish males for its own labor battalions. Before long, the influx of Hungarian Jews contributed to the acute overcrowding of Auschwitz and to making the Jews for the first time the single largest group of inmates in the camp. Between April and August 1944 the population of Auschwitz rose from 67,000 to 135,000, to be decimated by undernourishment, disease, and gassing during the remainder of the year.

In the last chapter we will see that in 1944 the majority of Hungarian Jews suffered the same torment as the other Jews of eastern Europe. But we must first examine the absolutely unique enormity carried out in 1942–43 in the four out-and-out killing centers and in Majdanek—an enormity visited primarily on Poland's Jews.

CHAPTER XII

THE EXTERMINATION SITES
CHEŁMNO, BEŁŻEC, SOBIBÓR, TREBLINKA

The four out-and-out killing sites—Chełmno, Bełżec, Sobibór, Treblinka—have none of the ambiguities of Auschwitz and Majdanek. Paradoxically, this makes these sites that much more difficult to bring into historical focus. Notwithstanding its abject monstrosity, Auschwitz appears in some sense comprehensible in that it was a microcosmic reflection of the *Gleichzeitigkeit des Ungleichzeitigen* of the Nazi regime and presumption, including particularly its seething resentment fraught with avenging violence. The ultramodernity and specious rationality of I. G. Farben coexisted with the deadly productivism of the WVHA and the naked exterminism of the RSHA. In essence the complicity of Krauch and Ambros with Göring and Himmler was an extension, not to say consummation, of the co-optation of the non-Nazi elites by the Nazi leadership in 1933–34. As we have seen, this grand accommodation was grounded in antibolshevism, antileftism, and antiparliamentarism at home and expansionism abroad, notably in the east. Even the deportations of the Jews to Auschwitz fitted into the twisted logic of an immanent collaboration involving a full mobilization for total war as well as a resolute attack on the "Jewish problem," one which entailed forcibly evacuating it beyond the borders of Greater Germany.

There are no such factors to help explain the four killing sites, which had no function other than the mass murder of totally unarmed and helpless civilians—nearly 99 percent of them Jews, about 1 percent Gypsies. Although this slaughter occurred in a social field delimited in space and time, it had little, if anything, of the ritualism, contestation, or inversion of a social drama familiar to historians and anthropologists. In an arena that had no center stage, both the executioner and the victim were and remained strictly anonymous. The executioners carried out their infamous deeds without public ceremony, and the victims suffered their dehumanization in terrifying silence. The executioners ordained and enforced the way of perdition, leaving the victims no choice but to bend to their mortifying yoke. There were no bonds of common humanity between them. Theirs was an encounter of radical mutual exclusion and enmity which precluded both reintegration into society and defection from it. Besides, the "passage" of victims through a killing center was too rapid for them to develop social bonds either with their executioners or among themselves. Unlike the concentration camps, including Auschwitz and Majdanek, the death centers left no room and time for the growth of a civic and political culture of survival and resistance.

Seemingly discontinuous with the intrinsic social amalgam and tactical ambiguity of the Nazi project, as well as uninformed by precedent, the extermination sites defy explanation. The historian faces them with a poverty of critical theory and imagination. This analytic and speculative inadequacy is compounded by his deficient empathetic understanding of the behavior of both executioner and victim. Despite these handicaps, historians cannot avoid confronting the out-and-out killing installations that existed and operated in the most extreme moment of the Thirty Years War of the twentieth century. Attuned to the *longue* and *moyenne durée,* many "new" historians may be inclined to dismiss them as microscopic and evanescent phenomena unworthy of study, the more so since none of the four killing sites had a life span of more than seventeen to eighteen months. Perhaps the sites and their victims are more likely to come into the eye and field of the new historical vision once they are assimilated into the monstrous, even if receding, miseries and casualties of the two world conflicts. But their unique barbarity was not simply a matter of numbers. The Second World War was distinctive by reason of the preponderance of civilian casualties, among whom the damned of Chełmno, Bełżec, Sobibór, and Treblinka occupy a singular place. In addition, the ways of dying and death inflicted on these unjustly damned was unprecedented by any civilized standards. And for both of these reasons the killing centers may well be the touchstone for understanding the unique temper and cruelty of the recent catastrophe in world history in general, and in German and European history in particular.

The four annihilation centers were located in Poland. As we have seen, Poland was not only the heartland of European Jewry, but also the strategic staging area and passageway for the assault on Russia, and later the critical defensive glacis against the advancing Red Army. As the geopolitical hinge of the eastern campaign, it experienced both the flux and reflux of the Third Reich's formidable military and security machine. Auschwitz and Majdanek, also located on conquered Polish soil, one in the Warthegau, the other in the General Government, had been conceived as camps for political prisoners and POWs during the onrush of the *Drang nach Osten* and of Operation Barbarossa. By the time the four killing centers were established, however, this advancing tide had crested, which meant that their mission was at best marginally related to military and security operations. Admittedly, the original camp near Treblinka was for prisoners of war and political prisoners condemned to forced labor. But Polish Jews figured prominently among its inmates from its opening in the spring of 1941, and within a year the other infamous complex not far from this same village, Treblinka II, served exclusively to exterminate Jews.

The four annihilation sites were intended primarily for the decimation of the Jews of Poland and of certain occupied Soviet territories farther east. Of course, as at Auschwitz and Majdanek, some Jews from other parts of the Continent were also among the victims deported to these out-and-out murder mills. But these Jews from afar were never more than a distinct minority. For the most part, each site processed the Jews from a well-defined geographic area in the east: Chełmno took the Jews from the Warthegau, particularly from Łódź; Bełżec the Jews from Eastern and Western Galicia, notably of Lublin, Lvov, and Cracow; Sobibór the Jews from eastern Poland, including parts of the Lublin district; and Treblinka the Jews from the Warsaw, Radom, and Białystok districts.

Given the Nazi regime's resolve to desolate the Jewish heartland, no doubt it was cost-effective to locate the extermination sites in Poland. The distances for the transport of the victims would be relatively short and Poland had an adequate railway network. It may well be that the choice of Poland was also favored by the availability of large tracts of thickly forested and sparsely populated land, which would facilitate keeping the premeditated crime relatively secret. To the extent that this secret would be impossible to keep from surrounding rural populations, these were presumed to be so deeply infused with Judeophobia and anti-Semitism that they could be expected to be indifferent to, if not in favor of, the suffering of the Jews.

But these local advantages, identified by a hindsight colored by the logic of location-of-industry theory, are likely to have counted for less than the regional ascendancy of the SS, already firmly established in the east. As we have seen, beginning in the late thirties, and with Hitler's blessing, Himmler fixed on the east as the moving frontier for the expansion and exaltation of this sprawling state within the state. He deployed most of the SS's military, paramilitary, and security forces to help conquer, police, and Germanize the eastern *Lebens-raum.* The SS secured a firm and organized footing in Poland up to the German-Russian border of September 1939—in both the Warthegau and the General Government. After June 1941 they extended their hold to virtually the entire buffer zone ceded to Moscow under the Nazi-Soviet Pact, notably to the Baltic countries and eastern Poland. Of course, the SS followed the Wehrmacht and Waffen-SS deep into Russia, visiting the lion's share of Nazi Germany's nonmilitary wrath on civilians. In the forward zones, ahead of the Reich Commissariats Ostland (Baltic lands) and Ukraine, the SS remained essentially itinerant, their movements and actions correlated with, even dictated by, the ebb and flow of military operations. By way of contrast, further back, wherever the civil administration took over from military government, the SS clearly was in charge. Indeed, the territories within the boundaries of interwar Poland, as fixed in 1920–22, were not only the military hub of the Third Reich's drive for eastern *Lebensraum* and the center of the mass of European Jewry but also the only province in which Himmler ever managed to entrench the embryonic SS state. It is thus difficult to imagine circumstances under which the high command of the SS would have located the killing centers in any other place than Poland.

The impasse of the eastern campaign contributed to Poland's becoming the principal redoubt of the SS. Their élan broken, and denied their moving frontier, the forces of the SS became penned up within the former Pale of Jewish Settlement, their ranks permeated with embittered operatives of the retreating Einsatzgruppen and their adjuncts. As we saw, the slowdown of Barbarossa in the fall of 1941 had significantly affected the time, place, and scale of the Jewish massacres by the SS special commandos. The forced withdrawals of the winter of 1941–42 were no less decisive. Operating behind the front lines, the SS formations fell back even farther west than the Wehrmacht and the Waffen-SS. As if by reflex, Himmler's paramilitary units intensified their hunt for Bolshevik cadres and partisans while at the same time venting their rage on the Jews. As in the triumphant phase of Barbarossa, anti-Semitism and antibolshevism were as inseparable in the field propaganda against "Judeobolshevism" as they were in the razzias against Jews and partisans in the cities, forests, and marshlands of occupied Russia. But just as throughout Europe the impressment of Jews for forced labor was not merely a subterfuge for their "resettlement," so in the occupied Soviet territories the drive against party agents and partisans was not simply a pretext or a screen for the raids against the Jews.

During the first half of 1942 the Wehrmacht and the SS mounted a joint campaign to search out and destroy Bolshevik cadres, terrorists, and partisans immediately behind the front lines as well as in strategic communications, supply, and staging zones which the military command had turned over to civilian control. Many of these security sweeps turned disproportionately or completely against the Jews, who were a convenient and safe prey. Between December 1941 and July 1942 the Jewish communities of a host of cities which had been captured before the first retreat were ravaged with fire and sword: Riga, Minsk, Kharkov, Simferopol, Kerch, and Pyatigorsk. Certainly in Riga but probably also in other cities the special or regular SS units used mobile gas vans in their massacres of Jews.

When the Wehrmacht resumed its offensive in late June 1942 the security forces followed close behind. As they advanced, they came up against larger networks of political and partisan resistance but found smaller concentrations of Jews. The cities on the way to the Volga and the Caucasus had far smaller Jewish communities than those of the Pale, and many or most of the Jews in the far interior had fled or were evacuated ahead of the German troops. Soviet Jewry suffered much less from the second summer offensive than from the second major slowdown and retreat of the eastern campaign. For it was starting in the fall of 1942, shortly before the Red Army launched its counteroffensive from Stalingrad and the Caucasus, that the assaults on the Jews were renewed. In advance of the retreating divisions of the Central and Southern Army groups, the SS struck Jewish communities which they had struck once before, soon after they were captured in July and August 1941: Pinsk, Kobrin, and Brest-Litovsk in Belorussia; Rovno, Dubno, Łuck, and Kovel in the Ukraine. All these cities were just west of the critical Kiev-Korosten-Zhitomir triangle, where the Wehrmacht had encountered its first major obstacles and suffered its first serious delays. They were located along the vital transportation arteries linking the eastern front with its logistical base in Poland. The security specialists of both the Wehrmacht and the SS were convinced that the western confines of Belorussia and the Ukraine, and in particular the Pripet Marshes, were partisan-infested. Accordingly, in wracking the Jews the SS were moved not only by their visceral anti-Semitism but also by their fear of the underground in general and the partisan bands in particular, as well as by their eagerness to redeem their tarnished mission by smiting the trapped surrogates of their increasingly elusive and dangerous "common enemy."

But the main body of *Ostjuden* were trapped on the other side of the Russo-German border of 1941—west of the Niemen and the upper Bug rivers. After conquering Poland the Germans had set about concentrating and ghettoizing the Jews. Whatever its ultimate intent, this compression of the Polish Jews conceivably could have facilitated their resettlement beyond the Urals in the event of a Nazi German victory over Soviet Russia. But once this historical possibility disappeared, the Polish Jews were doubly vulnerable by virtue of being locked into ghettos. Contacts with the outside world, including the Polish resistance, became extremely difficult and hazardous. Only the economic utility of the Jews attenuated and delayed the decimation or liquidation of certain ghettos. Unlike in the occupied Soviet territories, in occupied Poland the pragmatists of the SS, in cooperation with the Wehrmacht, organized the productive forces of the Jews for the war effort, with the result that here and there they intermittently slowed down their exterminationist accomplices. Especially in Łódź, but in other large ghettos as well, the members of the *Judenrat* (Jewish council), supported by the bulk of the Jewish population, became frenetic champions of productivism, convinced that compliant overwork and labor certificates were the only passports to survival under conditions of absolute overcrowding, hunger, and disease. Even with the rising suspicion, if not certainty, that resettlement or evacuation meant almost inevitable death, this belief persisted and the Jewish councils continued to deliver the dictated quotas for transfers out of the ghettos.

But it must be stressed again that the economic calculus of the ghetto elders was justified, especially given the place of the Jews in the Polish economy. Well into 1943 Jewish artisanal labor continued to produce the bulk of Poland's manufactured goods destined for the Wehrmacht and the SS. Simultaneously, however—in other words, as of the winter of 1941–42—the populations of the major ghettos were being ravaged by starvation, exposure, and sickness. Acute wartime shortages combined with the Nazi resolve to torment the Jews produced utter deprivation, resulting in a death rate of exterminationist proportions. In turn, this deprivation reduced the productivity of the ghettos. With ever more Jews becoming unfit for work, they were condemned either to waste away in their ghettos or be deported to the killing centers.

The Nazi theory and practice of "mercy killing" prefigured these killing centers, making them conceivable, plausible, and practicable. This is not to suggest that the availability of the rationale, personnel, and technique of the preexisting euthanasia program accounts for the eventual resort to the mass gassing of Jews, which began at Chełmno. It is tempting to construe the Nazi regime's "mercy killing" as the precursor of the murder of Jews, not least because it is well documented: the euthanasia order, signed by Hitler, has survived; the project was directed from the führer's Chancellery; and the identity of its principal architects and executors is known. But whatever the tie between the euthanasia program and the Judeocide, it is not the ever elusive missing link in the chain of Hitler's sole and direct responsibility for the Jewish torment. It does, however, embody some of the underlying mainsprings and indeterminate circumstances of the "Final Solution."

In 1938 Hitler himself instructed Philipp Bouhler, chief of the Chancellery and a *Reichsleiter* of the Nazi Party, and Dr. Karl Brandt, his personal physician, to prepare a plan for the "mercy killing" first of incurably ill and deformed children, then of mentally and physically handicapped adults. From the very outset the führer, mindful of adverse reactions abroad and at home, stressed the need for absolute secrecy. Bouhler was an inveterate Nazi and so was his first assistant, SS Colonel Viktor Brack, who headed the new task force and soon became the supervisor of the euthanasia program. All alike were, of course, moved by tenets of specious race hygiene. But there was also a practical side to their scheme in that by disburdening Germany of *Ballastexistenzen,* or human ballast, they meant to free hospital beds, physicians, and nurses for the regime's upcoming wars. Bouhler, Brandt, and Brack invited leading physicians of the public health services to join their working group, which had some difficulty formulating a text that would render Hitler's oral instructions in writing. But eventually, they agreed on a one-sentence authorization, which the führer signed some time in October 1939: "Reichsleiter Bouhler and Dr. Brandt, M.D., are charged with the responsibility for broadening the authority of physicians, who are to be designated by name and empowered to grant a mercy death to incurably ill patients following a humanly discretionary critical and exhaustive evaluation of their medical condition." Typed on a letterhead of the Chancellery embossed with the party emblem, this secret warrant was not a government decree but an expression of Hitler's personal will. Equally noteworthy, its wording was so vague as to invite arbitrary discretion in a regime that had long since ceased to be a *Rechtsstaat,* or constitutional state. Most remarkably of all, Hitler backdated the order to September 1, 1939, the day of the invasion of Poland and the start of the war. He must have assumed that the excitements and perils of war would muffle possible criticism, distract attention, and make incurably handicapped lives less sacrosanct in Germany and beyond.

Bouhler and Brandt had no difficulty bringing together a corps of euthanasia physicians, though some of them, along with other officials in the program, chose to operate under cover names. Their assignment was to arrange for the "mercy killing" of about 20 percent of the mentally and physically handicapped in Germany's *Heilanstalten*, or sanatoriums, some 70,000 chronically ill patients who had been institutionalized for five years or more. The operation went by the code name T4, as its coordinating office was located in 4 Tiergartenstrasse in Berlin-Charlottenburg, the address of the Chancellery.

Six institutions in different parts of Germany began to "process" mental patients, each with its own geographic radius of activity: Grafeneck in Württemberg; Hadamar in Hessen; Brandenburg and Bernburg in central Prussia; Sonnenstein in Silesia; and Hartheim near Linz. The staff of Grafeneck eventually was sent to Hadamar, and that of Brandenburg was transferred to Bernburg. Between January 1940 and August 1941 the operatives of these institutions put to death about 70,000 patients by individual gassing, and they are estimated to have ended another 20,000 lives by lethal injections and overdoses of drugs. The corpses were cremated. The closest kin or guardians were sent notices of the passing away of their infirm relatives or wards, with invented and perfunctory explanations as to the cause of death.

These notifications soon aroused suspicion. By mid-1940 concerned relatives, functionaries, and, above all, Catholic and Protestant churchmen began to remonstrate, first through private channels, then in public. Among those who registered early objections were the archbishops of Freiburg, Breslau, Munich, and Berlin. Although the protest of Clemens August Count von Galen, archbishop of Münster, was far from the first, it may be taken as representative, especially since in other respects von Galen was not a critic of the Nazi regime.

The removal of mental patients from an asylum in Marienthal near Münster prompted him to submit questions formally to local judicial and police authorities. On August 3, 1941, after his inquiries had been ignored for a full week, von Galen confronted the issue in a sermon in Münster's Lamberti Church. He introduced his homily by quoting from a pastoral letter which had been read in Catholic churches on July 7 and which declared that "never, under any circumstances, was a human being permitted to kill an innocent being, except in war and in legitimate self-defense." It is worth pointing out that this incipient sacerdotal criticism of "mercy killing" coincided with the Church's—including von Galen's—unforced and ungrudging consecration of the crusading war against Soviet Russia and "Judeobolshevism." In any event, the bishop insisted that immediately after the pastoral letter had been issued he had voiced his "suspicion, if not certainty" that the death of many of the mentally ill who were reported "to have passed away on their own had in fact been deliberately induced."

Having primed his congregation, von Galen denounced ending the life of the mentally ill as mass murder and all but proclaimed "mercy killers" to be murderers. One of his principal concerns was that the rationale for doing away with the mentally ill would be expanded to apply to other categories of unproductive members of society.

> Have you, have I the right to live only as long as we are productive, as long as [some official or commission] certifies us to be productive? Once you establish and apply this principle that "unproductive" human beings may be killed, then woe to all of us when we grow old and infirm! If you allow individuals to be killed because they are unproductive, then woe to all invalids who exerted, sacrificed, and wasted their energy and healthy bones in the production process! Once you permit fellow creatures who are unproductive to be eliminated by brute force, then woe to those of our brave soldiers who will return home heavily wounded, crippled, or disabled. At bottom, to grant common mortals the right to kill "unproductive" fellow humans—even if for the moment only the unfortunate and defenseless mentally ill are targeted—is to license the murder of all unproductive individuals: the incurably sick; the invalids of work and war; and all of us who in our infirm old age will be unproductive.

Von Galen's sermon was widely disseminated by word of mouth, by handbill, and by fliers scattered by England's Royal Air Force. It encouraged prominent Catholic bishops of other cities to come out against euthanasia. Several prominent Protestant pastors and laymen spoke up as well. The secret was out.

On August 24, 1941, Hitler called off the wholesale euthanasia. He could not afford to have the morale of the Wehrmacht undermined by doubts about the fate of wounded war heroes. Nor did he want to provide grist for the enemy's propaganda mill. Besides, there was no way of silencing von Galen and other clerics without creating popular martyrs.

But to stop the sweeping killing operation inside the Reich was not to put an end to T4 altogether. Within Germany the euthanasia program continued on a reduced scale. Operation 14 f 13, its most characteristic extension, shifted its focus from asylums for the mentally ill and homes for the physically handicapped to concentration camps. Himmler prevailed on Bouhler to detach some of the euthanasia doctors to sort out all camp inmates who were physically and psychologically disabled.

This selection started some time around mid-1941. Bouhler's

physicians traveled to the different camps to administer medical examinations that were even more cursory than those administered heretofore. Before long, these doctors were charged with weeding out inmates who were unfit to work. The euthanasia doctors signed thousands of death warrants, though exactly how many is unclear. Between mid-1941 and mid-1943 close to 4,500 inmates were taken from Mauthausen, Gusen, and Dachau to Hartheim for gassing. About 830 inmates from Buchenwald suffered the same fate at Sonnenstein. Before the war was over the doctors of 14 f 13 selected many more inmates in these and other camps, most of them to be killed at Hartheim.

Meanwhile, the euthanasia program had expanded beyond Germany's borders, notably to occupied Poland and Russia. Like the SS, the so-called "mercy killers" made the conquered eastern territories their principal field of operation.

Soon after the defeat of Poland the euthanasiasts took charge of the major asylums in the district of Poznań in the Warthegau, displacing Polish personnel in favor of their own. Their objective was to rid these institutions of all Polish and Jewish mental patients. While the physicians of T4 made the selections, the SS did the killing. To carry out this task the RSHA made available a special commando. Headed by SS Captain Herbert Lange, in May and June 1940 this Sonderkommando is estimated to have gassed about 7,000 persons in improvised extermination trucks. Although there were some German nationals among those killed, the vast majority were Christian Poles, a smaller number Polish Jews. Probably the single largest operation involved about 1,500 mental patients who were brought to a transit camp at Dzialdowo (Soldau) before being taken to their death.

T4 personnel also moved into the Soviet Union. They operated either in conjunction with or alongside the Einsatzgruppen. It was hardly accidental that in reporting their exploits certain SS detachments listed the killing of mental patients along with the execution of Jews, Gypsies, Bolshevik cadres, partisans, and saboteurs. To make room for wounded German soldiers in the summer of 1941, security forces shot the inmates of mental institutions in Latvia, notably in Jelgava, Riga, and Dvinsk. For the same reason, and with the approval of local military authorities, incurable mental patients were executed in Poltava in September; in Minsk, Mogilev, and Kiev in October; and in Dnepropetrovsk in December.

Occupied Russia also became the testing ground for more effective methods of mass killing. In September 1941 euthanasia doctors collaborated with the SS in an experiment in which a group of mental patients from Minsk were killed with a charge of dynamite. The results were deemed unsatisfactory. T4 personnel were also involved in an experiment designed to test mass gassing in an asylum in Mogilev. In this instance a group of Soviet mental patients were asphyxiated by carbon monoxide fumes in a hermetically sealed room connected to the exhaust of a truck. Whatever the drawbacks, group gassing seemed a more efficient and practicable way of killing than mass shootings and dynamite charges. Besides, killing with gas could be practiced by introducing carbon monoxide fumes into either stationary structures or mobile vans. It appears that the first truck specially fitted for regular gassing was tested successfully in the late fall of 1941 in Sachsenhausen, a group of Soviet prisoners having served as guinea pigs. But by this time Himmler's men, and not T4 personnel, were fully in charge.

As it turned out, Hitler was only partially wrong in his assumption that the strains and exhilarations of war would help his euthanasia program pass unnoticed. Granted, within Germany he felt obliged to stop or curtail the selective mass killing of Gentiles. But he did so under the pressure of single-issue objectors who were otherwise perfectly loyal, particularly as to foreign policy and the war against the Soviet Union and bolshevism. Under the circumstances, Hitler need not have had any compunctions about continuing his selective mass murder in the conquered and occupied eastern territories. He was confident that there would be no opposition to the brutalization, including the mass murder, of Poles and Russians, be they Gentiles or Jews. He also knew that there was no one to protest the final persecution of Germany's own remnant of Jews, especially now that they were being deported to the east, to be disposed of there, as part of the Reich's "common enemy."

Jews, as we have seen, were certainly among the victims of the euthanasia operations in Germany, Poland, and the Soviet Union. They are also likely to have been among the subjects used in the test runs for mass murder by gassing in which T4 experts played an active but not controlling role. But neither the euthanasia operations in Poland and Russia nor the experiments spawned by them were solely or even primarily directed against the Jews. There is no denying, however, the links between the personnel and apparatus of the euthanasia program, including its extension and experimentation beyond Germany's eastern borders, and the Judeocide, which was centered in Poland. In late 1941 the Sonderkommando of SS Captain Herbert Lange was posted to Chełmno, where the first of the mass killings was to take place, in the newly designed gas vans, on or about December 8. At about this same time a first group of T4 men arrived in Lublin, to be followed by a second group in early 1942. They were assigned to work with SS Brigadier General Odilo Globocnik, chief of all security and police forces in the district of Lublin, who—as we shall see—was to direct Operation Reinhard against the Jews of eastern Poland. Probably, Christian Wirth was the most notorious of these deputized euthanasia operatives. A police captain, Wirth had been the bureau chief of three of the six euthanasia institutes before being posted to Lublin. Globocnik put him in charge of Belżec, which began to operate in mid-March 1942. In early August, Wirth became chief inspector of Belżec, Sobibór, and Treblinka, with offices in Lublin, which earned him a promotion to police major. In the meantime, Franz Stangl had become commandant of Sobibór. A simple policeman, he had assisted and then succeeded Wirth at Hartheim. Before long, Stangl was sent to replace Dr. Irmfried Eberl, the first commandant of Treblinka. An SS physician, Eberl formerly had been the director of the Brandenburg and Bernburg euthanasia institutions.

All told, Viktor Brack seems to have detached ninety-two men from T4 for service in Operation Reinhard. But few of these operatives were slated or qualified for executive positions. Many or most of them were truck drivers, guardsmen, cremators, and clerks. Although they wore the field uniform of the Waffen-SS, they were not on its payroll, and they were noncommissioned rather than commissioned officers.

The T4 men were mere ciphers in a regime of new and improbable men. Even Wirth and Stangl were at best small cogs in a formidable coercive machine that was anchored deeply in the civil and political society of the Third Reich. Moreover, the T4 men and their associates were few in number and widely dispersed. To fix excessively on them is to obscure the enabling conditions for their actions and to exculpate both the leaders who directed them and the elites that condoned them. While dregs of their sort fester in every society, it is rare for them to find governing and ruling classes to license and put them to use. Bouhler and Brack were certainly of considerable importance by virtue of their proximity to the highest spheres of government. Occupying important posts at the Chancellery, both of them, but particularly Bouhler, had direct access to the führer, which increased their aura of power. Just as important, Brack had a close working relationship with Himmler, notably in connection with Operation Reinhard. As in the cases of Hitler and Himmler, Bouhler and Brack did not rise to the top by themselves but were put there by Germany's upper ten thousand.

However, not only the Nazi leaders but also historical circumstances defined the time, venue, and form of the ultimate radicalization of the Judeocide. The domestic euthanasia action was discontinued at about the time that Barbarossa began to falter. This meant that the men and procedures of T4 were available to serve the barbarization of the war against the Soviets and the Jews. In the Nazi scheme of things such a transfer was not out of the ordinary. Bishop von Galen had rightly forewarned that the most likely abuse and expansion of euthanasia would issue from the reification of the criterion of human utility or productivity. Whatever the amalgam of ideas and motives underlying the decision to mass-murder Jews, it was justified and applied in terms of such a principle of utility. Or rather, exterminationists constantly invoked the *disutility* of most Jews, the burden they represented in the struggle for *Sein oder Nichtsein*.

This death-dealing calculus is mentioned in several of the rare documents that touch on the gestation of the mass slaughter of Jews. It surfaced as early as mid-July 1941 in a report on a discussion, in Poznań, by high SS and police officials of this province of "the solution of the Jewish question" in the Warthegau. According to SS Major Rolf-Heinz Höppner, writing to SS Lieutenant Colonel Adolf Eichmann, it was suggested that "all the Jews of the Warthegau be taken to a camp for 300,000 Jews" to be set up "as close as possible to the coal basin," their workshops to be relocated with them. If necessary, "Jews fit for work can be formed into labor commandos to be put to work outside such a camp." To concentrate the Jews in a single location would mean saving on guards to watch over them and reducing the danger of epidemics spreading from Łódź and other ghettos to neighboring populations. Besides, "there is the likelihood of no longer being able to feed all the Jews this coming winter." That being the case, "it should be seriously considered whether the most humane solution would not be to finish off all the Jews who are unfit for work by some quick-acting procedure." Such a process would certainly "be more pleasant than to let them starve to death." Meanwhile, the projected camp would also facilitate the "sterilization of Jewish women of childbearing age with a view to solving the Jewish problem for all time with this generation." There is no way of knowing whether the euthanasia agents who were operating in Poland influenced these deliberations in Poznań.

Similar ideas were under consideration in the Reich Ministry for the Occupied Eastern Territories, headed by Alfred Rosenberg. On October 25, 1941, Dr. Erhard Wetzel, his adviser for Jewish affairs, submitted to Rosenberg a draft of a letter intended for Gauleiter Heinrich Lohse, Reich commissar for the Ostland. According to the draft, Viktor Brack of the führer's Chancellery had "indicated his

readiness to expedite the construction of barracks and gassing facilities." Since it would be easier to put together the required equipment
on the spot than in Germany, Brack offered to send some of his own
men, including a chemist, Dr. Helmut Kallmeyer, to Riga, where they
could also help oversee safety procedures. Lohse was urged to contact
Brack through Himmler. The draft letter also informed him that
Eichmann, in charge of Jewish Affairs in the RSHA, agreed with this
course of action. Eichmann was said to propose setting up camps for
Jews in Riga and Minsk, to which Jews from the Old Reich were to be
sent. Just now, Jews were being "evacuated [from Germany] to Łódź
and other camps, and those fit for work could be assigned to labor
battalions in the east." At this point Wetzel's memorandum advanced
the principle of disutility:

> As things stand, there is no need for compunctions about disposing
> of Jews who are unfit for work by recourse to Brack's remedy. . . . On
> the other hand, Jews fit for work will continue to be sent to forced
> labor in the east. Of course, among the able-bodied Jews men and
> women will have to be kept apart.

Perhaps it should be stressed that Wetzel submitted his draft to
Rosenberg—it is uncertain whether he ever signed and mailed it—
while the Wehrmacht and Einsatzgruppen were being blocked by the
Red Army in the northern sector, but *before* the retreat from Moscow,
before the mobilization for total war, and *before* the Wannsee Conference.

But it was not until *after* the maddening winter of 1941–42 that
the deliberate mass murder of the Jews was set in motion. Of all the
killing centers Chełmno was the only one to begin functioning before
the spring of 1942. But even Chełmno's first gassing took place
around December 8, 1941, hence after the failure of Typhoon, and
the proportion of Jewish victims during the first few months remains
uncertain.

The General Government still held many times as many Jews as the
Warthegau, and Operation Reinhard was meant to reduce this
unique Jewish commonwealth. On March 27, 1942, Goebbels made
an entry in his diary which leaves no doubt that the inner circle of
the Nazi regime not only was fully implicated in this ultimate turn in
the persecution of Jews, but also calibrated it in accordance with the
productivity-disutility precept. According to Goebbels, the Jews of
the General Government were about to be "evacuated to the east,"
starting with Lublin. He noted that the procedure to be used would
be "quite barbarous," but he preferred "not to describe it in any

detail." Though usually a master of rhetorical hyperbole, in this instance Goebbels was sober and precise in his notation.

> Not many of these Jews will survive. On the whole, about 60 percent of them will have to be liquidated, while only about 40 percent can be put into labor battalions.

Goebbels was no longer a latter-day pogromist. He now wanted, and trusted, Odilo Globocnik, the former gauleiter of Vienna, to handle this large-scale operation without arousing too much attention. The ghettos "vacated" in the cities of the General Government "will be filled with Jews to be deported from the Reich," and this process would be "repeated many times over."

As Goebbels saw it, "although the retribution that the Jews are suffering is barbaric, it is fully deserved." The führer's prophecy was "beginning to be fulfilled in the most horrible ways." There was no room for "sentimentality," since not to fight the Jews would mean waiting to be "destroyed" by them in a "struggle of life and death between the Aryan race and the Jewish bacillus." Goebbels credited Hitler with being "the unflinching pacesetter and spokesman for a radical solution, dictated by current conditions and therefore ineluctable." Clearly, "there was nothing for Jewry to laugh at," and the Jews of continental Europe would be made to "pay dearly" for having their "proxies in England and America organize and propagate the war against Germany."

Starting in the winter of 1941–42, Poland became the country of slaughter for European Jewry. The first year was particularly devastating for the Polish Jews of both the Warthegau and the General Government.

The Jewish population of the Warthegau, which had stood at about 500,000 in September 1939, was radically reduced by January 1942, as many Jews had been transported to the General Government. Łódź remained the main metropolis of the Warthegau as well as the second biggest city and the principal industrial center of all of Poland. In early 1942 it still counted about 160,000 Jews, including about 20,000 who had been brought there from central and western Europe in late 1941. By comparison, there were many more Jews in the General Government. Of course, since June 1941 their numbers had also been reduced, by about 400,000: some had fled to the east, others had been massacred by action groups, and still others had died from deprivation. Even so, there remained about 1.5 million Jews, most of them in the major cities, including Warsaw, whose ghetto, by itself, held close to one quarter of this total, or about 380,000.

Chełmno was the first killing site to be set up, and it became a prototype for the other death centers. Renamed Kulmhof in German, Chełmno was an isolated village in the Warthegau, located halfway between Warsaw and Poznań. It was joined by a feeder line to the main Łódź–Poznań railway and by a good surface road to Łódź, thirty-five miles to the southeast. The site also may have been chosen because of the availability of a small abandoned castle with outlying farmhouses and a church, all set in a secluded park.

More than likely, Chełmno was set up with a view to making room in the ghettos of the Warthegau, especially in Łódź, for Jews being deported there from the core of the Reich. This goal was to be achieved by disposing of Jews who were unfit for work—primarily women, children, and the aged—in accordance with the ideas adumbrated during the Poznań parley in mid-July 1941 and in Wetzel's draft-memorandum three months later. It is not clear who gave the order to make Chełmno a site for the mass gassing of "unproductive" and "burdensome" civilians, above all Jews. As we have seen, sometime in November 1941 SS Captain Herbert Lange, the veteran of the euthanasia program in Poznań province, was asked to head up Sonderkommando Kulmhof. He supervised the construction of two wooden barracks on the abandoned estate, which was then also enclosed with a high wooden fence. Apparently, the villagers were deported, except for a group of men impressed for construction work.

Within a few months SS Captain Hans Johann Bothmann replaced Lange as commandant of Chełmno. Bothmann directed a commando of thirty-five policemen, detached from the police in Poznań, which included the drivers and operators of the mobile gas vans fitted for mass asphyxiation. These policemen in turn selected helpless Poles and, above all, Jews for the fatal work details which were to do their *basse besogne*. Bothmann reported to Arthur Greiser, gauleiter of the Warthegau, and Otto Bradfisch, mayor and chief of the Gestapo of Litzmannstadt (Łódź). Presumably, it was they who fixed the quotas, times, and places for the victims to be taken to slaughter. The victims were brought to Chełmno by both train and truck. After being "processed" on the estate, they were herded into the vans in which they were asphyxiated with carbon monoxide fumes and driven about two and a half miles to Rzuchowski Forest. There the bodies were dumped into mass graves. In the early spring of 1943 the corpses, including those previously interred in pits, were burned in the open, for there were no crematories. There was nothing particularly modern or industrial about either the installations or the operations at Chełmno-Rzuchow.

When this killing center began its lethal operations on or about December 8, 1941, the first victims seem to have been Jews from nearby towns and villages. But in January 1942 the initial transports from Łódź delivered not Jews but most of the 5,000 Austrian Gypsies who only recently had been deported there, where some of them had died of typhus. Hereafter, however, all the victims were Jews. In the course of less than fifteen months about 100,000 Jews of the Warthegau were murdered at Chełmno. Over 70,000 of them came from the Łódź ghetto, whose economic usefulness saved some 85,000 Jews until 1944. Its first mission completed, the Bothmann commando apparently dismantled Chełmno's installation in March 1943 before leaving for a special assignment to Dalmatia. The commando was brought back a year later to help decimate Łódź's remaining Jews.

While there is little reliable data for Chełmno, there is a fair amount for the Łódź ghetto, its primary source of victims. This ghetto was set up in February 1940, pending deportation of its population farther east. Almost at once rations and medicines were sharply cut. Material conditions did not, however, become disastrous until after the start and impasse of Barbarossa. During the first year of the eastern campaign the statisticians of the ghetto registered between 1,700 and 1,800 "natural" deaths per month. In June 1942 1,725 Jews died, as against 49 born, 5 of them stillborn. From the fall of 1942 to the spring of 1943, the monthly deaths averaged 4,658 in a rapidly shrinking population.

From mid-January through mid-September 1943 over 70,000 Jews were deported. According to the *Chronicle of the Łódź Ghetto,* at least 10,000 were taken away each month, but during the month of March alone the total reached 24,687, composed of 9,267 men and 15,420 women.

> The resettlement action continued through the month, Sundays excepted. Thus each of the transports, on the average, comprised 900 people per day. . . . March will long be remembered in the annals of the ghetto as the month of resettlement. From morning on, for twenty hours nonstop, processions of deportees headed on foot to Marysin.

Rather than make the cruel selections themselves, the SS officials fiendishly and confidently left it to the local *Judenrat* to fill their prescribed quotas. In March this Jewish council selected "for the most part . . . welfare recipients, including, in large measure, individuals who had recently been working . . . but had formerly been on welfare." With the help of an advisory committee, Mordecai Chaim Rumkowski, the overpresumptuous but unenviable president of

Łódź's Jewish council, also sacrificed "all persons listed on the rolls of the court or in the Bureau of Investigation and also in the office of administrative punishment." Above all, however, the Jewish leaders selected those unable to work, or those least fit or suited to do so, as the high proportion of women among the deportees attests.

This is not to say that Rumkowski and his associates knowingly sent the unemployed and unemployable to their death. In fact, given the appalling living and health conditions in the ghetto, resettlement at first was widely seen, if not welcomed, as a palliative. This view persisted despite irrepressible rumors about the fate of the deportees. It even prevailed until after the summer of 1942, when word filtered back about the mass killing at Chełmno. In the Łódź ghetto, as in virtually all other Jewish ghettos, there was a strong disposition to disbelieve the rumors and reports about the Nazi butchery, which was so totally beyond the bounds of common morality and historical experience as to be utterly unbelievable and unthinkable. Once the rumored outrages could no longer be denied altogether, the damned of the ghettos generally either explained them away or minimized them as unsystematic and wild local excesses.

Developments within the ghetto contributed to this widespread denial of the ultimate reality. From the outset, and almost to the very end, the Łódź ghetto was buffeted by an intense rivalry between the productivists and the exterminationists in the SS. Rumkowski resolved to collaborate with the former. Clinging to the hope that the economically useful would be spared, he strained to mobilize the ghetto economy for the German war effort in exchange for an alleviation of the suffering of the Jews, or just for a stay of execution. With time, and especially after September 1942, the Łódź ghetto became a cruelly caged manufacturing center of about 70,000 workers, since most or all "unusable" Jews had been removed. These immured slaves, many of them artisans, produced a wide range of soft goods, including urgently needed winter wear, for a Wehrmacht desperate for supplies.

But with the relentless paring of rations, which was pressed by the exterminists, conditions in this hellish workshop became grueling beyond belief. As early as July 2, 1942, local Gestapo officials sent a fiercely realistic assessment to headquarters.

> The productivity of the Jews is decreasing because of their declining stamina. To compensate, the Jewish Elder has put to work all children over 10 years of age with a view to meeting the delivery dates for all army contracts. Despite the bad food situation the Jews are straining to maintain the quality and quantity of their work. To fill the running

army contracts about 70,000 Jews are being employed in this ghetto. By the end of this year they can be exploited to the full by working them in three shifts.

Compared to last year the health of the Jews is three times worse, even though the Jewish Elder takes every imaginable measure to keep his *Rassengenosse* fit for work. Over the last months the number of Jewish deaths has risen to an average of 1,800, and it has not decreased with the onset of the warmer season. Of the 1,725 Jews who died in June, 397 died of tuberculosis, 368 of coronary problems, 425 of malnutrition, 14 of typhus, 24 of dysentery, and 497 of a variety of other illnesses.

Hereafter, the physical condition of the ghetto workers kept deteriorating and, as we have seen, the death rate rose to over 4,500 per month.

In April 1943 even Hans Biebow, the German administrator of the Łódź ghetto, reiterated his fear, which was that of all pragmatists, that the situation was rapidly approaching the point of no return.

The food rations for the Jews have become so inadequate as to threaten to reduce productivity at the expense of the Wehrmacht. In shops and factories in which the twelve-hour day has just been introduced (two shifts per day), in particular workers who labor standing up collapse on the job.

In September 1942 all the sick and infirm Jews were evacuated. Even so, since then and until March 31, 1943, the mortality [rate] has been 4,658 [per month(?)]. . . .

The food provided by the factory kitchens is unnourishing. Vegetables . . . of poor quality are boiled in water, . . . only a touch of oil being added. . . . There are no potatoes. Soups cannot be thickened with flour, which is reserved for the bakeries.

For months neither full nor skimmed milk has been distributed. The want of [fresh] meat is being offset by canned meat [which is not edible]. . . . The fact that in March only 0.30 RM were spent on the daily food of each Jew proves the inadequacy of the provisions sent to the Jewish quarter. . . . [Meanwhile,] the ghetto's contracts have risen at least fifteenfold over last year.

In closing, Biebow urged top officials of Łódź-Litzmannstadt to intercede with their superiors in Poznań.

In the face of the deteriorating military situation in the east, including the mounting partisan attacks, Himmler was increasingly hard-pressed to follow a coherent line. Instead of keeping a tight and balanced rein on the two rival factions within the SS, the productivists and the exterminationists, he oscillated between them. In June

1943 he ordered the major Polish ghettos closed down and transformed into concentration camps under the control of Pohl. As part
of this restructuring, and to appease the exterminationists, the workers and productive facilities of the Łódź ghetto were to be transferred
to Lublin, care being taken not to unduly damage the economic
capacity of the relocated ghetto. By early December 1942 Himmler
changed his mind, and decided or agreed that the Łódź ghetto should
not be moved, thereby satisfying Pohl. When Gauleiter Greiser
balked, Pohl urged Himmler to bring him into line, insisting that at
this time "for both technical and political reasons a relocation to
Lublin is now totally out of the question." In February 1944 Himmler
finally forced a compromise: the ghetto's economy was to be kept
intact and in place, but under Greiser's, not Pohl's jurisdiction.
Himmler ordered the number of Jewish workers reduced to the absolute minimum necessary for war production and recalled the Bothmann commando from Croatia to help with this additional
decimation.

Then, in early June of 1944, with the Red Army advancing upon
the 1939–41 border, Himmler had another change of mind: he instructed or authorized Greiser to proceed with the liquidation of the
Łódź ghetto. This time it was Albert Speer who tried to save what
remained of the ghetto for essentially economic reasons. Speer's efforts failed as the inevitable and quickening defeat on the eastern
front favored the exterminists at the expense of the pragmatists.
About 10,000 Jews were taken from Łódź to Chełmno between June
23 and July 14, 1944. But the final destruction of the Łódź ghetto was
put off until the early fall, when about 60,000 pitiful souls were sent
to Auschwitz. If the Łódź ghetto was the last Polish ghetto to be
liquidated, it was largely because of its residual economic value and
its geographic location far to the west. In mid-January 1945, when the
Red Army liberated Poland's second largest city, it found fewer than
1,000 Jewish survivors of what a few years before had been the second
largest Jewish community in Poland.

The drive against the Jews in the territories of the General Government started in the spring of 1942, a few months after the one in the
Warthegau. The 1.5 million Jews of these territories were concentrated in five districts centered around five cities of eastern Poland:
Warsaw, Radom, Lublin, Cracow, and Lvov. Warsaw was the largest
and most urbanized Jewish center, with about 380,000 Jews. The
Lublin district ranked third in size, after Warsaw and Lvov. But
100,000 of its 250,000 to 300,000 Jews lived in rural areas, some of
them having recently been deported there for settlement in the pro-

jected Lublinland Jewish Reserve. The city of Lublin itself had about 100,000 inhabitants of whom about 35,000 were Jews, enclosed in a ghetto since October 17, 1941. About two years earlier Majdan Tatarski, a suburb of Lublin, had become the site of a prisoner-of-war camp for Poles, which was later expanded to hold Soviet POWs as well.

Himmler ordered Globocnik, his deputy for the Lublin district with headquarters in Lublin, to take charge of the drive against the Jews of the General Government. It seems that from the very outset of his new assignment Globocnik had the help of Christian Wirth who, as we saw, had served in the euthanasia program. It took Globocnik close to six months to plan his operation and to set up three killing complexes: Bełżec began to function in mid-March 1942, Sobibór in May, and Treblinka in July. All this time the prison and camp at Majdan Tatarski was being expanded to become the Majdanek concentration camp, though its gassing facilities were not installed until considerably later.

Once under way, Globocnik's drive proceeded with great efficacy and speed. Soon after Reinhard Heydrich's assassination it was given the code name Operation Reinhard, which captured its implacable spirit. Even if, because of sparse evidence, there are some uncertainties about the fiery ordeal at Bełżec, Sobibór, and Treblinka, several official documents testify to its overall character and scope. Again, no enabling order has turned up thus far.

On June 18, 1942, top German administrative and security officials met in Cracow, the capital of the General Government, to discuss the progress of Operation Reinhard. Speaking for the governor of Lublin province, senior undersecretary Dr. Wilhelm Engler reported that the old Jewish quarter of the city of Lublin "has been evacuated and that all Jews fit for work have been settled in a special district outside the city." According to SS Major General Fritz Katzmann, security and police chief for Galicia, "a rather large number of Jews have already been evacuated" from his district. While there remained "85,000 Jews in Lemberg [Lvov], of whom 45,000 are integrated into the work process, more Jews will be forcibly resettled [ausgesiedelt] during the coming weeks." Dr. Herbert Hummel, delegate of the governor of the Warsaw district, claimed that contrary to expectations, for the time being the economy of the Warsaw ghetto was getting by without external subsidies.

> Within the ghetto about 25,000 Jews are working in firms important for war production. About 3,000 Jews are employed outside the ghetto [in external work commandos]. The second-largest furriery has its

workshops inside the ghetto, and it supplies the bulk of the Wehrmacht's fur requirements.

Since even under the best of circumstances, the ghetto economy could not support its swollen population, Hummel voiced the hope "that before long the city of Warsaw will be disburdened of its dead weight of unemployable Jews." When Dr. Josef Bühler, who had manifested his impatience at Wannsee, inquired about the prospects for "speeding up the reduction of the ghetto population" in the General Government, SS Major General Freidrich Wilhelm Krüger, the General Government's security and police chief, replied that it would take "until some time in August to answer this question." No doubt this was a veiled reference to the impending second summer offensive on the eastern front, whose outcome would be decisive. At any rate, Krüger asserted that for two weeks all nonmilitary rail traffic was suspended and it would be difficult to commandeer rolling stock "for the *Abtransport* of Jews."

At about this same time, on June 23, 1942, Viktor Brack informed Himmler that Bouhler had just met a request from Globocnik for additional T4 personnel. Brack reported that Globocnik urged that "the entire Jewish action be carried out as rapidly as possible in order to avoid the risk of having to stop halfway as a consequence of unforeseen circumstances." In passing, Brack reminded Himmler that Himmler himself had once told him "that for reasons of camouflage alone" there was need for haste. Of course, he added, the assignment was formidable. According to Brack, of Europe's 10 million Jews, about 2- to- 3 million were economically usable. But, he said, these 3 million able-bodied Jews should not be exploited without being simultaneously rendered incapable of reproducing themselves. To this end, the Jews could be either sterilized by individual injections, which would be "time-consuming and costly, . . . [or] castrated by X-ray treatment, which would be cheap and could be quickly administered to many thousands." Brack assured Himmler that should he choose the second option "in the interest of saving work Reichsleiter Bouhler stood ready to make available necessary physicians and [accessory] personnel."

In the meantime, Hans Frank, the head of the General Government, had become increasingly nervous about the impact of the taxing and long-drawn-out war on conditions in his captive province. Even Frank now advocated giving absolute priority to winning the war. As far as he was concerned, once the enemy was defeated, "the Poles and Ukrainians, as well as others, [could be made] into chopped meat or anything else." But until then, Frank considered it essential to maintain the "tranquility, order, work, and discipline" of some 15 million restless Poles.

With regard to the Jews, as of mid-1942 Frank was in a quandary. On the one hand, he was prepared to starve Poland's Jews to death in order to save food for German soldiers and civilians. On the other, he conceded that the Jews of the General Government "repaired nearly all the uniforms and boots and made all the furs for the eastern front." The order "to subject all Jews to destruction, . . . which comes from higher authority," could not help but be economically damaging.

Frank made no secret of his continuing aversion for the *Ostjuden*. On August 1, 1942, in a talk at Lvov, he declared that on his arrival in Posen (Poznań) in 1939 these Jews had struck him as so "horrible" and "unsightly" that he wondered how the world could have tolerated them through the centuries. Now that German soldiers were face-to-face with these masses of eastern Jews with "*Kaftan und Peies*," it should be clear "that European culture cannot be revitalized without a prior solution of the Jewish question." Eventually, the Reich would settle this problem by "no longer allowing [eastern] Jews into Germany." In the meantime, however, the Jews "will have to work for us," and it would do them good "at long last to do some useful work and come in contact with the serious side of life."

In this same spirit, on July 17, 1942, Lieutenant General Max Schindler, local representative of the Wehrmacht's Armament Inspectorate, urged SS Major General Krüger to keep Operation Reinhard from unduly interfering with war production. Stressing the intense need for Jewish labor, Schindler prevailed on Krüger to "build and operate camps for forced Jewish labor" in accordance with army needs. After also agreeing not to dissolve Jewish ghettos without prior consultation, Krüger ordered that the ghetto of Częstochowa not be broken up until a "camp with barracks [was ready to receive its] 3,000 Jewish workers."

Two days later, on July 19, 1942, Himmler sent a telegram to Krüger stipulating the deadline for the deportation of the Jews of the General Government and specifying those who were to be exempted.

> I direct that the resettlement [*Umsiedlung*] of the entire Jewish population of the General Government be carried out and completed by December 31, 1942. As of that day, individuals of Jewish origin no longer will be allowed to reside in the General Government, unless they reside in the *Sammellager* [work ghettos] of Warsaw, Cracow, Częstochowa, Radom, or Lublin. All other work places employing

Jewish labor must be phased out by then or, failing that, transferred to one of the *Sammellager.*

On this occasion Himmler accompanied his command with an exceptionally candid statement of purpose in which he conflated his racial and security concerns.

> These measures are essential for the ethnic separation of races and peoples in accordance with the spirit of the New Order in Europe. They are also necessary for the security and hygiene of the German Reich and its spheres of interest. To breach these prescripts is to jeopardize law and order throughout the entire German orbit and to create breeding places not only for resistance movements but also moral and physical epidemics.

Himmler insisted that "for all these reasons there is need for a thorough cleansing," to be carried out without delay.

Once the second summer offensive began to falter, the army worried more than ever about Operation Reinhard impeding war production. On September 18, 1942, General Curt Freiherr von Gienanth, commander of all troops stationed in the General Government, told his superiors of his concern about supplies for the coming winter. He was under instructions to put Jews to work in order to free Polish and Ukrainian workers for labor in the Reich. However, he maintained, to "resettle" Jews without proper coordination with military authorities, as Himmler had directed, was to complicate and delay this labor rotation along with vital production. The key problem was the shortage and deployment of skilled industrial labor. Of the slightly over 1 million workers in the General Government, 300,000 were Jews, and of these one-third were skilled workers. In the firms producing for the Wehrmacht, Gienanth pointed out, "the Jews provided between 25 percent and 100 percent of the skilled workers, the figure being 100 percent in textile firms making winter clothing." Jews were of critical importance in the production of vehicles and "with few exceptions all saddlers are Jewish." Of the 22,700 workers employed in the private manufacture of uniforms, "22,000 are Jews, 16,500 of them skilled textile and leather workers." To reassign or remove this skilled labor, without first training replacements, would "considerably reduce the war potential of the Reich and momentarily paralyze the provisioning of the troops at the front and in the General Government." In conclusion, General von Gienanth asked the OKW to convince Himmler not to uproot skilled Jews too rapidly, for fear of "damaging critical war production."

Even Himmler, who became more and more incoherent, could not ignore this plea, particularly given the renewed reverses on the eastern front, which promised another hard winter. Accordingly, on October 2, 1942, he notified Globocnik that he had ordered Krüger and Pohl "to collect [and relocate] all the so called [Jewish] armaments workers employed in garment, fur, and shoemaking workshops in concentration camps in Warsaw and Lublin." Hereafter, the Wehrmacht would place all contracts for clothing directly with the SS in charge of the camps, which would guarantee deliveries. As for the Jews working in "genuine armaments plants," they were to be concentrated within these plants until such time as they and their activities could be transferred to the work ghettos as well. The aim was to replace these Jews with Poles and to "aggregate the many Jewish enterprises in concentration camps into a few large firms to be transferred to the east of the General Government." But Himmler noted that "even there the Jews would disappear some day, in accordance with the führer's wishes."

The military disaster on the eastern front continued to unsteady Himmler. At the same time that for economic reasons he agreed to maintain or set up a host of work ghettos, he intensified the extrusion of all unemployable Jews. When he visited Warsaw on January 9, 1943, Himmler was informed that about 35,000 Jews remained in the ghetto, of whom about 20,000 were said to be armaments workers. Even this small residue struck him as excessive. Although he was told that these Jews were being kept at work following consultations between Krüger and Schindler, Himmler ordered the Warsaw ghetto dissolved by February 15, 1943. All genuinely "usable" Jews were to be transferred to Majdanek, where the SS would direct their economic activities. Claiming that Field Marshal Keitel had agreed to this transfer, Himmler indicated that "for reasons of security I mean to concentrate all Jews in only two camps, notably in Auschwitz and Lublin." Incidentally, Himmler did not suspect that at the time there remained not 35,000 but 70,000 Jews in Warsaw, half of them in hiding.

About two weeks before Himmler's visit, on November 15, 1942, the United Antifascist Organization in the Warsaw ghetto managed to send a sober but anguished report about the agony of the Jews in the General Government to the Polish government-in-exile in London.

    The tragedy of the Jews of Warsaw in no way exceeds that of hundreds of other Jewish settlements in the territories of the so-called

General Government. The Germans have not spared a single small town, village, or community in the districts of Warsaw, Lublin, Radom, Cracow, and Galicia. The *"Aussiedlungen* [evacuations]" are directed to Treblinka, the main murder installation . . . , but sometimes also to the *Vernichtungslager* [extermination camp] in Belzec. . . . Everywhere the technique is the same, the Germans resorting to lies and deception. In addition, they take advantage of the fact that on the whole the Jews do not believe in the possibility of their total destruction. . . . Everywhere the action is carried out by the *Einsatz* [Operation] Reinhard, that terrible *Vernichtungskommando* [extermination commando].

This report gave an incomplete list of thirty-six cities and towns ravaged by *"Aussiedlungen."* In Częstochowa only 4,000 out of 40,000 Jews were said to remain; in Cracow 6,000 out of 60,000; and in Piotrków 600 out of 15,000.

The German authorities had, of course, more accurate and detailed statistics than the Jewish underground. On January 18, 1943, Himmler asked Dr. Richard Korherr, the chief statistician of the SS, to prepare a detailed report on "The Final Solution of the Jewish Question in Europe." According to this accounting, submitted to him on March 23, 1943, between 1937 and the end of 1942 the number of Jews in Europe had been reduced by about 4 million by emigration, excess mortality, and "evacuations, above all in the heavily [Jewish] eastern territories." According to Korherr, by December 31, 1942, 145,301 Jews had been "sent, passed, or channeled through [*durchgeschleust*]" the camps in the Warthegau, 1,274,166 through the camps in the General Government. These figures did not include the Jews taken to Auschwitz or Majdanek. Korherr was also quite precise about the Jews remaining in the major ghettos. There were still "87,100 Jews in the Litzmannstadt [Łódź] ghetto, 83,133 of them formerly of Polish nationality." As for the General Government, it still counted 297,914 Jews in its five major districts, "the bulk of them in *Rest-Ghettos* [rump-ghettos]": 37,000 in Cracow; 29,400 in Radom; 20,000 in Lublin; 50,000 in Warsaw; 161,415 in Lvov.

By Korherr's own accounting, 1,274,166 Jews of the General Government were processed by "the camps." There is a strong presumption that most of these Jews were slaughtered in Belzec, Sobibór, and Treblinka. It is difficult to imagine where and how else they could have been "resettled." Of course, there are no exact figures for the number of Jews killed at each of these three sites, most local and central registers and archives having been either destroyed or hidden. Since Treblinka was set up, in the first instance, to handle the Jews of the Warsaw ghetto, which was by far the largest Jewish settlement, it is likely to have had the largest facilities and to have devoured the greatest number of victims. Pending the discovery of incontrovertible data, it is pointless to make or dispute round-figure estimates about the number of Jews processed through each of the three outright extermination centers of Operation Reinhard. Even allowing for an error of a few hundred thousand victims either way, Korherr's authoritative figures testify to the general magnitude of Nazi Germany's willful mass murder of Jews in the General Government during the year 1942.

Bełżec was the second killing center to be set up, after Chełmno. Situated about a hundred miles southeast of Warsaw, it was connected by a feeder track to a main railway line at a point halfway between Lublin and Lvov. Christian Wirth was appointed commandant in the second half of December 1941, but his adjutant, Josef Oberhauser, was responsible for all construction work. It appears that at Bełżec, unlike at Chełmno, the gassing facilities were stationary. They were installed in three wooden barracks. After using bottled carbon monoxide at the outset, the operatives switched to feeding exhaust fumes from trucks into the chambers. The first phase of killing began in mid-March and lasted three months, until mid-June, when new and larger facilities were built.

It seems that when operations resumed in mid-July, the wooden barracks had been replaced by a brick structure holding six gas chambers. The dimensions and capacities of these chambers remain as uncertain as those of the original ones. The new facilities were in use until December 1942, when they were destroyed. At this time the nearby mass graves were presumably opened for the corpses to be burned in the open.

During both phases the victims were brought to Bełżec from southeastern Poland, particularly from the districts and cities of Lublin and Lvov, but also from Cracow. The Jews of Eastern Galicia had the highest survival rate as of late 1942, no doubt largely because of their economic utility. The majority of Jews who "passed through" Bełżec were considered "unfit" and "unusable."

While Bełżec was southeast of Lublin, Sobibór was to the northeast, not far from the Chełm–Wlodawa rail line. Globocnik appointed Franz Stangl to direct the camp. Sobibór was a variant of Bełżec, which Stangl took as his model. From May through July 1942 the largest shipments of Jews came from Lublin province, though a certain number also came from Austria, the Protectorate, and Slovakia. During the second phase, which started after the installation of new equipment in September 1942, a large contingent of Dutch Jews figured among the victims.

Treblinka was the last of the four death centers to be established. It was located fifty miles northeast of Warsaw, not far from Małkinia on the Bug, whose railroad station was on the main Warsaw–Białystok rail line. SS Captain Richard Thomella came from Sobibór to supervise the construction at Treblinka II, which began in the late spring or early summer of 1942. He was assisted by SS Sergeant Erwin Lambert of the euthanasia program. With Dr. Eberl, already in charge of Treblinka I, in command, the installation started operating on July 23. Apparently, by then three gas chambers had been installed in a brick structure, which also contained a space for a diesel engine that generated asphyxiating fumes. In every other respect Treblinka's layout and operation followed the pattern set at Bełżec and Sobibór. Within a few weeks of early August, when Globocnik appointed Wirth inspector in chief of all three death centers, he also transferred Stangl from Sobibór to replace Eberl as commandant of Treblinka.

During the first five weeks, by late August 1942, over 250,000 Jews are estimated to have been "channeled through" Treblinka. Over 200,000 of them were brought there from Warsaw and environs, the others primarily from the city and district of Radom, and also from Kielce. When the transports delivered more Jews than the facilities of Treblinka could handle, local SS officials ordered the use of firing squads and urged their superiors to add to the existing plant. It seems that before long a new building with ten additional and larger gas chambers was added, considerably increasing Treblinka's overall killing capacity and enabling it to outperform the other death centers. Before the end of the year many thousands of Jews from the ghettos of the Białystok region were gassed in Treblinka, and so were many thousands of additional Jews from Warsaw.

About half the Jews of the Warsaw ghetto, or about 190,000, were "resettled" by mid-August, and another 120,000 by the end of the year. At least 200,000 of these 310,000 Jews are estimated to have been sent to Treblinka.

While there may be some questions about the destination and treatment of some of the Jews of Warsaw, Nazi German documents leave no doubt about the fact of their systematic, wholesale, and pitiless "relocation." On July 22, 1942, SS Major Hans Höfle, one of Globocnik's adjuncts, notified the *Judenrat* that beginning that day "all Jews resident in Warsaw, regardless of age and sex, will be resettled in the east." His edict went on to specify the categories of Jews to be "exempted" from this relocation: the employees of "German authorities or [their] firms"; the "members or employees of the *Judenrat*"; Jews "working for German firms"; Jews "fit for work but not yet integrated into the work process"; Jews "working for Jewish hospitals and disinfection teams"; Jews "confined to Jewish hospitals"; and "the wives and children" of all exempted Jews. Each deportee would be allowed to take along thirty-three pounds of baggage and all personal valuables, as well as food for three days.

As for the mechanics of the operation, the *Judenrat* was charged with seeing to it that "no later than 4:00 P.M. every day 6,000 Jews report to the assembly point . . . at the Jewish hospital on Stawkistrasse," which was to be cleared for this purpose within twenty-four hours. In order not to fall short in its daily consignments of 6,000 Jews, the *Judenrat* was expected to make use of "the Jewish order police (100 men)." Any Jew trying to escape from the ghetto "will be shot," and so would any Jew seeking or helping "to circumvent or obstruct the resettlement measures." Lastly, Höfle served notice that should "a quota not be met 100 percent, a corresponding number of new hostages will be taken and executed."

Three months later, on October 15, 1942, the governor of the Warsaw district, Dr. Ludwig Fischer, notified his superiors in Cracow that "for the time being the resettlement of the Jewish quarter of the city of Warsaw is completed." There remained only about "35,000 Jews . . . , nearly all of them workers in . . . armaments plants." While, as we have seen, he underestimated the remaining Jewish population by about one-half, he exaggerated the number of those resettled, reporting "400,000 . . . out of 540,000 Jews to have been evacuated." Fischer related correctly, however, that the economy of the Warsaw ghetto was at an end. In turn, the production of the city of Warsaw as a whole "was down by 50 percent," and if it was to return to normal "an adequate Aryan work force" would first have to be found.

In its previously cited message of November 15, to London, the internal antifascist organization made a special point of reporting the torment of what it called "the city of death." Warsaw had suffered "a depopulation" exceeding even that caused by the "epidemics of past centuries." During the summer 300,000 Jews were deported by an "international Nazi gang of Lithuanians, Latvians, Ukrainians, and ghetto policemen led by SS officers." They were taken to Treblinka to be "murdered by suffocation in gas chambers." Characterizing the operation "as a crime of unprecedented cruelty," the Jewish resistance warned that the "storm threatens [to ravage] the rest of European Jewry" along with "other oppressed peoples, especially the Poles." Except for a certain number of men fit for work, all Jews, including children, were deported, many of them so starved that the promise of "6 pounds of bread and 2 pounds of marmalade" induced them to volunteer.

The final liquidation of the Warsaw ghetto began soon after Himmler visited the Polish capital in early January 1943. This last move met with resistance perhaps largely because most of the remaining Jews, including those in hiding, were young, relatively fit, and uninhibited by concern for family members. They were able and free to go down fighting, and they were also ideologically primed to do so. In April, once the uprising of the Warsaw ghetto was snuffed out completely, the Germans deported many of the survivors—perhaps as many as 16,000 of them—to Majdanek.

Majdanek played an important auxiliary role in Operation Reinhard. An extension of the camp at Majdan Tatarski, it was situated two to three miles east of the center of the city of Lublin, on the road to Zamość and Lvov. Located on an open tract of land of over a hundred acres, Majdanek was visible from every direction, with neither forests nor trees to shield it.

Himmler stopped off in Lublin on July 20–21, 1941, at the height of Barbarossa, to instruct Globocnik to establish a concentration camp for 25,000 to 50,000 inmates. Here, as at Auschwitz a few months earlier, the idea was to provide the Thousand-Year Reich, particularly the SS, with a forward bastion in the east. On September 22 an order came down to build a stockade for 5,000 inmates, who were to construct a camp to house ten times that number. Within five days there was a follow-up order sacrificing this unhurried plan for a confident future to the pressing demands of the trying eastern campaign: Berlin called for the double-quick construction of two prisoner-of-war camps, each with a capacity of 50,000 prisoners, one in Lublin-Majdanek, the other in Auschwitz.

At Majdanek the original work crews consisted of Polish-Jewish and Soviet prisoners of war. By late November 1941, these POWs and local construction workers had built facilities to hold about 20,000 prisoners. Eventually, by late 1943, these facilities held four or five times that many inmates. But by then most of the detainees were not POWs but civilians.

During 1942, while untold numbers of "unusable" Jews were being "channeled through" Bełżec, Sobibór, and Treblinka, scores of Jews fit for labor were brought to Majdanek, most of them from the Lublin district, but also from other regions. During the late winter and early spring of 1943, Majdanek took in many of the still employable Warsaw Jews as well as Jews from the remaining work ghettos of the

General Government. Unlike the four all-out killing centers, but like Auschwitz, Majdanek continued to have an economic and political mission. Throughout 1943 many thousands of non-Jews from the General Government and from occupied Russian territories were deported to Majdanek. Most of them were seized for aiding and abetting partisans or as hostages for those who did. Over the three-year life of Majdanek, and counting Soviet POWs, probably half of its inmates were Gentile Poles, Belorussians, Ukrainians, and Great Russians.

Once in Majdanek, these prisoners became slave laborers under the general direction of Pohl's WVHA. Unlike Auschwitz, which was an industrial redoubt, Majdanek became a center for the manufacture and processing of soft goods. The relocation of the ghetto of Radom to Majdanek contributed to this development. Jews were also assigned to Majdanek's satellite camps, or external work commandos, of which there were only a few. Some Jews were selected to work in a nearby Heinkel aircraft factory. Others were sent to demolish the buildings of the emptied Warsaw ghetto with a view to salvaging valuable construction materials.

The wrack of the inmates of Majdanek was in every way comparable to that of the inmates of Auschwitz. Living and working conditions were catastrophic, and so were medical facilities. About 60 percent of the loss of life at Majdanek was due to starvation, disease, sickness, and overwork, which may well represent the highest "natural" death rate of any of the savage camps in Nazi Germany's penal universe.

The other 40 percent were killed by mass shootings and mass gassings, though in which proportions remains uncertain. The bulk of the executions were carried out in nearby forests. After the shooting of a group of Soviet POWs, most of the victims were Jews brought to Majdanek from Lublin province, including the Lublin ghetto, as well as from Slovakia and the Protectorate. Presumably, the Jews selected to be shot were considered unfit for work. The worst of the executions coincided with a typhus epidemic.

In September or October 1942 the gassings started. Initially, Majdanek had only two gas chambers, but additional, larger chambers were installed in 1943, as were additional cremating facilities. The gassings continued until the fall of that year, most if not all of the victims Jews who were "worn to the bones." After a brief hiatus mass executions resumed. By now the Red Army, after blocking the Wehrmacht's third summer offensive in the Kursk salient, was rolling back the armies of von Kluge and von Manstein. Simultaneously, the partisans stepped up their attacks, operating behind the lines far back into Poland. The uprising in the Warsaw ghetto must have added to the SS's sense of embattlement and rancor, and so did the flashes of elemental resistance among the Jewish work commandos in Treblinka and Sobibór in late August and mid-October 1943 respectively, which prompted the closing of both of these death centers. Besides, since Majdanek was located next door to the headquarters of Operation Reinhard, and was the most easterly of the major camps, it was a caldron of Nazi frenzy and frustration.

It appears that on November 3, 1943, Majdanek was the scene of an outburst of pogromlike Nazi rage and violence. A large number of SS and policemen stationed throughout eastern Poland assembled in Lublin to participate in a collective massacre code-named *"Erntefest* [Harvest Festival]." They came from Warsaw, Cracow, Radom, and Lvov to join their local accomplices in shooting most of the Jewish inmates of Majdanek as well as most of the Jews in neighboring work camps, including in Poniatowa and Trawniki. All told, within a day or two these frenzied zealots put to death between 20,000 and 40,000 Jews. Himmler, who customarily preferred his and his men's violence to be of an impersonal kind, must nevertheless have turned a blind eye to this uncharacteristic saturnalia of blood, which was an explosion of avenging fury, of growing disenchantment within the Nazi world. At the same time he gave the order to remove all embers and ashes left by this fiery ordeal before the arrival of the dreaded Red Army.

By early 1944 the Soviets crossed the prewar Polish border and came to within a hundred miles of Lublin. But then, with the logistics of battle momentarily shifting in favor of the Wehrmacht, their advance was slowed until midyear. The camp authorities used this respite to carry out additional executions and to begin evacuating the remaining inmates of Auschwitz and camps further west. On July 23, 1944, two days after crossing the Bug, the Red Army finally liberated Majdanek.

Taking prewar Poland as a whole, the Jews of Lublin-Majdanek were the first to be all but totally victimized, and those of Łódź were the last. Clearly, the timing of the destruction of each Jewish remnant was influenced by its geographic location in relation to the battle lines of the eastern front. Since Lublin and Lvov were furthest east and of vital strategic importance, the Red Army and the partisans threatened and attacked them many months earlier than Łódź. Not that the devastation of the ghettos and work camps of the General Government, the Białystok region, the Baltic lands, and the Reichskommissariat Ostland can be closely correlated with particular military developments. For example, the Jews of the ghetto of Sosnowiec-

Będzin, an important textile center near Katowice in incorporated eastern Upper Silesia, were sent to Auschwitz in August 1943, almost a year ahead of Łódź, which was located due north. Still, the impact of Nazi Germany's failing war-cum-crusade was omnipresent, and fired the frenzied violence of the Nazi regime's final convulsions. While the retreating Wehrmacht scorched the earth of the eastern territories before yielding them, the hopelessly cornered SS subjected the inmates of their concentration camps to the hellish marches of the eleventh hour.

CHAPTER XIII

IN THE MAELSTROM OF
FINAL DEFEAT

THE DEATH MARCHES AND THE WRACK OF
HUNGARIAN JEWRY

Just as the war against the Jews did not end with Operation Reinhard, so the war against the Soviets did not end with Operation Blue. Both wars continued, each with its own momentum and autonomy. But whereas the course and outcome of World War Two, notably in the east, continued to determine the fate of the Jews, the war against the Jews had no effect on the military and diplomatic termination of the Thirty Years War of the twentieth century. When the Wehrmacht launched its third and last summer offensive in early July 1943, millions of Jews were still alive throughout the Continent. Until this moment the "Final Solution" had consumed principally the Jews of the Polish-Russian Pale. Of course, outside this Pale Jews had also been cruelly victimized, notably in Greater Germany, Serbia, and Croatia. But the Jews of the Rumanian Regat and of Hungary remained essentially unharmed, and so did the bulk of the Jews of other European countries. By mid-1943, except for those saved by the Soviets, the Jews in and near the Pale had been reduced to pitiful remnants immured in deadly *Rest-Ghettos.* There as elsewhere the future of all surviving Jews depended on military and political developments which were entirely beyond their influence and control.

The tide of war having turned decisively against the Axis, the Third Reich found it increasingly difficult to hold in line its allies and satellites, none of whom were committed to Hitler's precept of all or nothing, of *Sein oder Nichtsein.* Berlin faced the outright defection of Italy and Rumania, the gradual disengagement of Hungary, and the quickening desertion of pragmatic collaborators in western and northern Europe. The Third Reich lacked the human and material resources to keep all of Europe under its iron heel while fighting against ever greater odds. But wherever it did manage to intervene directly to shore up its sagging military and economic position, the

SS made the Jews pay for the Nazi regime's continuous setbacks and looming downfall. The Wehrmacht, bolstered by the Waffen-SS, continued to provide the space, the time, and a shield that enabled the Nazi security forces, in league with their local ideological collaborationists, to set upon the Jews. Such was the case in Italy in 1943, until liberation by the Western Allies, and in Hungary in 1944, until liberation by the Soviets. By virtue of certain geopolitical advantages and the fast approach of the Red Army, Rumania succeeded in abandoning the Axis for the Allies without the Wehrmacht stepping in, and this became the salvation of most of Rumanian Jewry. Even before the landing of the Allied forces in Italy and France, the Reich also lost its capacity to press its war against the Jews in western Europe, in part because of the erosion of support among local collaborators but above all because the elites of Nazi Germany, both new and old, continued to give first priority to the eastern war against the Soviet Union, bolshevism, and the *Ostjuden*.

In every respect Germany was less well placed for Operation Citadel, its third summer offensive, than it had been for Operation Blue the year before, let alone for Operation Barbarossa in June 1941. Granted, the Wehrmacht still stood a few hundred miles west of Moscow and east of Kiev. But these forward positions were not without their drawbacks, since they created enormous logistical problems. Above all, however, Nazi Germany suffered serious shortages of matériel and manpower. Because of irreducible industrial bottlenecks the Nazi regime was hard-pressed to make good the Ostheer's losses of tanks, trucks, guns, and aircraft. For obvious reasons, motor fuel also became very scarce.

As for the shortfall of about 1 million soldiers, it could only be partially alleviated by levying inadequately trained foreign recruits. Meanwhile, after the disastrous winter of 1942–43, rather than recommit their severely battered troops for a new offensive, Berlin's allies strained to extricate themselves from a losing cause. Finland, Rumania, and Hungary fought shy of any further military effort, and so did Slovakia. Even before the Allied landing in Sicily on July 10, 1943, Mussolini began to repatriate Italy's legions and to urge a negotiated end to the war. Franco similarly begged off by recalling Spain's Blue Division.

Compared to the weakening Axis, the Grand Alliance was on the upswing. After Stalingrad the strategic and tactical initiative was with the Soviets. The Red Army easily replenished and expanded its ranks by drawing on Russia's vast reserves of manpower. There was a distinct qualitative improvement as well. The increase in Soviet tank production and the timely arrival of American motor vehicles combined to increase the overall mobility of the Soviet forces. Moscow also benefited from the fact that Germany had to face a second front and that its cities were being pounded from the air. An additional advantage was that by mid-1943 Russia's shadow army was a reality, the bulk of its partisans centered around the forests and marshlands of strategically vital zones in the Ukraine and Belorussia. These partisans excelled at sabotaging communications behind enemy lines. They also collected crucial military information for forward Soviet commands, thereby robbing the Wehrmacht of the element of surprise.

Operation Citadel was launched on July 4, 1943. It was designed to deliver a paralyzing blow to the Red Army before the Kremlin's Western Allies could land in force on the Continent. The attack was centered two hundred miles east of Kiev, in the Kursk salient, bounded by Orel to the north and Kharkov to the south. For this assault the Wehrmacht deployed two-thirds of its armored strength on the eastern front, or about 2,500 tanks, supported by 1,800 aircraft. Even more so than the year before, the Red Army was ready and waiting. Generals Konstantin Rokossovsky and N. F. Vatutin all but stopped the tanks of Generals von Kluge and von Manstein in their tracks, and within a few weeks the Wehrmacht was being pushed back along the entire eastern front. After being driven out of Orel and Kharkov in mid-August, the Germans were forced to yield Smolensk on September 24, Gomel on September 25, and Kiev on November 6.

Indeed, this was the start of the Third Reich's humiliating retreat from Russia. Admittedly, the German armies, including the Waffen-SS, were still powerful, and their fallback was disciplined and orderly. But they had lost the strategic initiative, and this fallback became irreversible. In the early fall of 1943 the Red Army fielded at least twice as many soldiers as the Ostheer, and it had a three-to-one edge in tanks and guns. According to Major General Reinhard Gehlen, who monitored the balance of forces on the eastern front for the OKH, the Soviets were certain to maintain if not increase their advantage in both manpower and equipment in preparation for a major winter offensive.

This imbalance was all the more serious since following the Anglo-American landing in Sicily the German High Command began to divert considerable resources to the west. As of this moment Hitler and his generals were locked into incessant and inconclusive wrangles over the division of limited supplies of men and equipment between the two major theaters. On November 3, 1943, Hitler issued a directive giving first priority to strengthening the German forces in the west to meet the imminent Anglo-American invasion. Confident that the generals of the Ostheer did not need major reinforcements to hold the line against the Red Army, he ordered them to stand firm all along the front, without taking any steps backward. The idea was to keep the Soviet forces at bay long enough to repulse or trap the British and American forces. The ultimate hope was that the defeat or high cost of the amphibious invasion would cause the Western Allies to fall out with their Soviet partner and prompt them to either condone or join Nazi Germany's drive to crush Bolshevik Russia.

But Hitler underestimated Stalin's timetable and agenda. Determined to keep the Wehrmacht in retreat and off balance, he and his generals mounted a powerful winter offensive. Rather than disperse their forces up and down the entire front, they focused their attack on the southern sector. It was there, between the Pripet Marshes and the Black Sea, that nearly half of the Ostheer's infantry and at least 75 percent of its panzers were concentrated under the expert command of von Manstein and von Kleist. To breach or rout these forces would be to advance toward southern Poland and northern Rumania as well as to reclaim the population and resources of the western Ukraine.

General Vatutin attacked on Christmas 1943. Within a fortnight he overran Korosten, Zhitomir, Berdichev, and Vinnitsa. This was the second time these cities were ravaged by war, since they had seen heavy fighting in the summer of 1941, when the Soviet forces had first slowed the Wehrmacht's race toward Kiev. All four cities and many other western Ukrainian towns which were recaptured by mid-April had once had large Jewish populations: Kovel, Lutsk, Kovno, Brody, Tarnopol, and Uman. Farther south, Generals Ivan S. Konev and Rodion I. Malinovsky launched their offensive in the direction of the Carpathian Mountains and the Balkans during the first week of January. Konev forced von Kleist to keep reeling back, with heavy losses, across the Bug, the Dniester, and the Prut. Within less than three months the Red Army drew near Bukovina, Bessarabia, and Moldavia. At the same time, with the Black Sea as his chief objective, Malinovsky ran the Germans and Rumanians out of Nikolaev, Kherson, and Odessa. These three cities also had been battered once before, during the late surge of Barbarossa, when their large Jewish populations had suffered their unique torment. In the meantime, on the extreme northern flank, in late January Soviet troops broke General von Küchler's blockade of Leningrad, repossessed Pskov, and by mid-March pushed the Northern Army Group back to the Estonian and Latvian border. On the far southern flank General Polkovnik

Tolbukhin crashed into the Crimea in early April, liberating first Simferopol and then Sevastopol.

Obviously, Hitler and most of his senior generals had once again underrated the Red Army. On the whole, the Wehrmacht still avoided encirclements and executed orderly disengagements and withdrawals. But even the best German units and officers could no longer do so without paying a heavy price. Particularly in the southern theater the Soviets exacted a high toll. There the Red Army virtually wiped out ten enemy divisions, including seasoned panzer units, and severely mangled forty to fifty others. Overall, Stalin's winter offensive inflicted close to 1 million casualties and important material losses on the Germans and their allies. True to form, and understandably, Hitler dismissed von Manstein and von Kleist for having failed to hold the Ukraine and von Küchler for having pulled back from Leningrad. Major General Gehlen, whose estimates had been ignored the previous fall, submitted a new reading of the balance of forces. He now estimated that the Soviets had the capacity to resume their advance after a short respite. Gehlen considered it most likely that Stalin would aim the principal thrust of his second summer offensive against the Central Army Group with a view to liberating Belorussia, the most direct passageway to East Prussia and northeastern Poland.

Relying on the relatively unimpaired strength of its northern and central armies, the German command focused on bolstering its weakened and weary southern front, which by now also was farthest to the west and closest to the homeland. But as if to confirm Gehlen's warning, General Zhukov was getting ready to storm Field Marshal Ernst Busch's Central Army Group, the Wehrmacht's most powerful and critical rampart on Russian soil, with Minsk as its pivot. For this offensive the Soviets deployed 166 divisions or over 1.5 million men; 30,000 guns, mortars, and rocket launchers; 5,000 tanks; 70,000 trucks; and 6,000 planes. By now, in the Belorussian sector, the Red Army had an advantage of 2 to 1 in men, 3 to 1 in guns, 4.5 to 1 in planes. To boot, this was the sector in which the Soviet command could count on considerable partisan support. There were an estimated 140,000 partisans in Belorussia, among them an uncertain number of Jews. Most of the partisans were clustered near the forests west of Vitebsk and Minsk and around the marshlands along the Ushachi and Berezina rivers between Polotsk and Borisov. They were, of course, subjected to cold-blooded punitive expeditions by German military and security forces. Even so, the partisans managed to step up their sabotage of critical railway lines immediately before the summer offensive.

The Soviets fixed the start of this defiant and risky assault for June 22–23, 1944, the third anniversary of the irruption of Barbarossa. Generals I. D. Chernyakhovsky and Matrei V. Zakharov attacked along a three-hundred-mile front. Their armored units were to take Minsk in a pincer movement before moving northwest to Vilna and Kovno, straight ahead toward Lida and Grodno, and southwest toward Baranovichi, Pinsk, and Brest-Litovsk. To reach and envelop the capital of Belorussia they needed to first capture or bypass and encircle Vitebsk, Orsha, Mogilev, and Bobruisk. These four cities, which were vital communication hubs, were like a chain of military redoubts that Hitler wanted held at all cost. To the surprise of both sides, the Soviet forces overran all four cities within a week. Well over 100,000 Germans were killed and over 60,000 taken prisoner, primarily near Vitebsk and Bobruisk. Having broken through this formidable defensive barrier, the Soviets forged ahead to surround and take Minsk on July 3, 1944. The battle of Minsk was hard-fought. Sworn to scorched-earth tactics, the Germans left the city in almost complete ruins, at a cost of 40,000 dead and wounded of their own. Moreover, east of Minsk the Red Army captured another 100,000 prisoners. On July 17 half of these prisoners were paraded through the streets of Moscow to dramatize the sweep of the Soviet advance and the resignation of the retreating enemy.

The fall of Minsk was the signal for a three-pronged drive to expel what remained of the enemy on Soviet soil. By the end of July the Germans abandoned Dvinsk and Kovno in the north, and Vilna, Grodno, Białystok, and Brest-Litovsk in the center. Having crossed the Polish-Soviet border of 1941 General Rokossovsky's troops captured Lublin on July 22, Majdanek on July 23. That was also the time that on the far southern flank General Konev completed the liberation of the western Ukraine, captured Lvov, and established several bridgeheads on the western bank of the lower Vistula. Warsaw seemed within reach of both Rokossovsky and Konev.

Within six weeks of the start of Stalin's second summer offensive, the situation on the eastern front was transformed radically. The roles were totally reversed, now that the Red Army had the upper hand and was forcing the Wehrmacht to keep retreating. The Northern Army Group was all but encircled on the Baltic region. The Central Army Group was severely battered, with its back to East Prussia and the Vistula. The Southern Army Group was unable to halt or delay the Soviet advance toward Rumania. After the fall of Jassy, Kishinev, and Czernowitz, on August 23, 1944, the Third Reich's principal military ally on the eastern front surrendered unconditionally. Within a few weeks Bulgaria and Finland followed suit.

But the Germans were not put to rout. They fought fiercely every inch of their forced withdrawal from Russia. There was little combat in open field. During the retreat of the German armies, as during their advance, the principal battles centered on and around cities, with the result that most of them were ravaged twice. Many of the cities of western Russia and eastern Poland that had been spared in the early summer of 1941 were devastated three years later. Benefiting from shortened supply lines and fearful of Soviet vengeance, the German armies fought to the last ditch of every town and city. While the military resorted to scorched-earth practices, the security forces stepped up their drive against partisans and their impressment of desperately needed labor. Wherever Jews had survived until this terminal paroxysm, they were disproportionately wracked by it.

Except for the thirty German divisions trapped in Courland, the westernmost province of Latvia, by early fall 1944 the Wehrmacht had been thrown back to the Soviet borders of 1941. In the meantime, the Allies had landed in Normandy on June 6, two days after capturing Rome. Within less than two months the Americans broke through the German lines at Avranches to begin their drive to the Rhine. The Western Allies could not have invaded Europe at the time they did without the Red Army tying down and pushing back the bulk of the Wehrmacht. For all these reasons, Hitler continued to divert scarce resources to the west, eventually to the extent necessary to mount a counterattack. Even so, the eastern front remained his first and ultimate preoccupation, if not obsession. It was there that the German troops were ordered to keep fighting with the destructive zeal that was characteristic of their crusade against the Soviet Union but that never informed their fighting against the Western Allies. During its great retreat from its continental conquests the Wehrmacht, including the Waffen-SS, scorched the provinces and cities of eastern, not western Europe. Similarly, the regular SS all but confined their final fury to the eastern front. Characteristically, Warsaw was drenched in blood and laid waste while Paris came through the war practically undamaged. In the east the SS massacred Jews and mercilessly evacuated Jews for deadly forced labor ahead of the approaching Red Army. The atrocities against the Jews ahead of the advancing Western armies were on a distinctly smaller scale.

In December Major General Gehlen submitted a third estimate, in anticipation of a massive Soviet offensive in the first half of January 1945. Close to 6 million well-equipped Soviet soldiers were drawn up along a front shortened to 1,300 miles between the Baltic Sea and the Carpathian Mountains and opposite some 3 million German troops, many of them exhausted and undersupplied. Instead of taking the shortest route to Berlin, which would require breaking through the heavily defended center at great cost, the Red Army was preparing to attack to the south in the direction of Budapest, Bratislava, and Vienna, as well as to the north, in the direction of Danzig and Königsberg. With the center forced to send reinforcements to both flanks, General Zhukov would unleash his frontal drive to the German capital.

Despite the enormous losses inflicted on the Wehrmacht during the previous year—over 1.5 million men, 6,500 tanks, 28,000 guns, and 12,000 planes—Hitler continued to underestimate the Red Army, as he always had. He dismissed reports about its capability to launch yet another winter drive. Against the advice of several senior generals, the führer decided to gamble on a surprise offensive in the west, convinced that there the Wehrmacht would be able to achieve a momentary numerical and logistic advantage. His idea was to hit the Western Allies at their weakest point, once again in the hope of shocking them into distancing themselves from Moscow.

Hitler and his chief military advisers decided to strike at a sector held by the Americans in the Ardennes Mountains in southern Belgium and northern Luxembourg. Marshal von Rundstedt took charge of the operation, spearheaded by the Sixth SS Panzer Army of SS General Josef "Sepp" Dietrich and the Fifth Panzer Army of General Hasso von Manteuffel. The U.S. forces were caught off guard, with the result that the Wehrmacht made a deep dent in the Allied forces that were on the verge of breaking into the German heartland. But within less than four weeks General George S. Patton decisively reversed the situation to win the Battle of the Bulge, thereby enabling Generals Dwight D. Eisenhower and Field Marshal Bernard Montgomery to order the resumption of the Allied advance. Characteristically, early in the Rundstedt offensive Sepp Dietrich displayed the brutality that was common on the eastern front, where he had served before coming west. The First Panzer Regiment of his SS division massacred seventy American prisoners of war at Malmédy, raising outcries throughout the Allied world, particularly in Washington. No less typically, Hitler's last gamble having failed in the west, Dietrich and his units were rushed to Hungary in a last-minute effort to help block the Red Army's southern drive into Austria and Germany, and to do so by bringing to bear their particular brand of ferocity.

In the meantime, partly in response to Allied urgings, Stalin pushed forward the date of the winter offensive that Hitler had discounted: it would now start on January 12, 1945. The Red Army broke into central and western Poland with remarkable speed. It did so partly because it was well prepared, partly because the enemy was drained. Konev easily cracked the German lines to liberate Cracow on January 19 and nearby Auschwitz on January 22. After taking Katowice and Częstochowa, the heart of the Silesian industrial basin, his armored units captured Breslau on May 6, putting them within 285 kilometers of Berlin. On January 14, Zhukov's forces made their frontal assault in the direction of Warsaw, which fell to them three days later. Having overrun Łódź on January 19, Soviet tanks pressed ahead to seize Poznań on February 23, bringing them to only 250 kilometers from the German capital. Only the northern drive into East Prussia ran into effective resistance and took a heavy toll of Soviet lives. Overall, however, the momentum of the Red Army was such that there was no stopping it. On April 25 Zhukov completed the encirclement of Berlin, whose garrisons capitulated on May 2.

The continuous reverses of the Wehrmacht set the stage for the self-inflicted death agony of the Nazi regime. The military debacle also galvanized a cabal of members of the old elite into trying to assassinate Hitler in order to shorten this agony and reclaim the German nation for themselves. Since the military and diplomatic situation was all but hopeless, prominent conservative collaborators at long last resolved to jettison the führer in the hope of salvaging certain foreign conquests along with the core of their own socioeconomic order and values. These oppositionists lacked and discounted popular support. By predilection they stood upon the primacy of foreign policy, which was their area of greatest agreement not only among themselves but also with their weaker liberal-democratic associates. Nearly the entire opposition considered the removal of Hitler the sine qua non for an opening to the Western Allies. The idea was to offer them a timely and mutually advantageous military surrender as well as cooperation in the containment of the expansive Russian colossus and Bolshevik ideology. In exchange, London and Washington were expected to maintain Germany as a great power, with mastery over the small states of eastern, east-central, and southeastern Europe. Contrary to the "stab in the back" of 1918, which had come from below, the plot of 1944 was orchestrated by a venerable elite operating from above. It must be stressed that this elite was moved to action by national, class, and status interests, not by concern for the torment of the Jews, which they continued to virtually ignore even at this late hour.

The tragic but peculiar failure of the tyrannicide of July 20, 1944, spelled the liquidation of the conservative *fronde*, the only potential internal brake on Nazi Germany's terminal fury. Himmler was destined to be the principal beneficiary of this abortive putsch, much as he had been of the Röhm purge. In 1934 Hitler had rewarded the SS for decimating the leadership of the SA and cowing the fledgling regime's conservative partners by making the chief of the SS the undisputed master of all police and security forces. This had been the start of the steady expansion of the SS's power and ambitions, first within the Reich and then throughout the conquered territories, but most especially in the east. As we have seen, as of early 1942, following the impasse of the Russian campaign, Himmler drove his far-flung terror apparatus both to help the unexpectedly taxing war effort and at the same time to further its murderous ideological mission. This dual effort became particularly fatal for the Jews, who were victimized by both the productivist and exterminationist zealots. Paradoxically, the economic push by Pohl, Sauckel, and Speer had the effect of facilitating the torment of the Jews.

As of the winter of 1943–44, the mortifying retreat out of the eastern *Lebensraum* and the growing fear of the approaching Red Army, compounded by the heightened aerial punishment and chaos of the homefront, intensified the Nazi rage and incoherence still further. The failed attempt on Hitler's life crystallized and accelerated the ultimate hardening of the regime, reflected in the enhanced power of Himmler, Goebbels, and Bormann. The führer turned to the Nazi faithful as he set to purging and eviscerating the old elites, which he had never ceased to resent and distrust, even at the height of their mutually beneficial collaboration. He did so not with a view to completing the Nazi counterrevolution but in order to steel the nation to struggle to the finish.

Himmler became the man of the hour. Hitler put him in charge of rooting out the conservative *fronde* by mercilessly and brutally liquidating over 4,000 real and imagined conspirators, many of them distinguished notables and their totally innocent relatives. This furious and vengeful retribution was intended to deter all future resistance. And by having Himmler act as the grand executioner, the führer confirmed him as his first and most fearsome paladin. Himmler was chief of the SS, the police, and the Interior Ministry. He also wielded considerable authority as Reich commissar for the strengthening of Germandom and as head of the Waffen-SS.

Admittedly, the Waffen-SS fought under the command of the Wehrmacht. Even so, Himmler's military power was more than nominal. In addition to helping to endow the Waffen-SS with the ethos of the parent black order, Himmler was in a position to see that they received preferential allocations of scarce manpower and matériel.

This was confirmed on July 15, 1944, just before the attempted putsch, when Hitler ordered Himmler to raise and equip fifteen new Waffen-SS divisions to serve on the crumbling eastern front. Then, following his narrow escape on July 20, at the same time that Hitler charged Himmler with liquidating the conspirators, he appointed him commander in chief of the reserve army. Shaken in what remained of his confidence in the military establishment, the führer also decided to create the party-army that Röhm had once urged upon him. This is not to say that he expected such an army to replace or control the regular Wehrmacht, including its regular though purged officer corps. But Hitler did want Himmler to raise politically reliable popular legions to reinforce and embolden the troops on the eastern front, particularly the Waffen-SS, which set the pace in brazen bravery and tenacity.

Of course, at this late date it would be difficult to muster a National Socialist army, to be known as the Volksgrenadiers, complete with political commissars on the model of those of the Red Army. Given the manpower shortage, Himmler was reduced to recruiting older men, underaged boys, and partially disabled veterans. He also combed the home front and the army for idlers and shirkers. In the fall of 1944 Himmler mobilized an estimated 500,000 additional fighters of uneven quality for the Volksgrenadiers, primarily to help stem the Soviet tide. At about the same time, Himmler, in close cooperation with Bormann, began to organize the Volkssturm, or Home Guard, a militia of all remaining males between the ages of fifteen and sixty-one for the last-ditch defense of the German *Heimat*, chiefly along its eastern borders. Party officials were expected to become the recruiters and political officers of this makeshift *levée en masse*. But because of across-the-board shortages and mounting chaos, the Volkssturm remained nearly as embryonic as the Werwolf, the zealots Himmler meant to train for partisan warfare in the event of an enemy occupation. In the meantime, the führer also entrusted Himmler with two successive theater commands. Himmler was sent to command Army Group Rhine from December 10, 1944, through mid-January 1945, when Hitler reassigned him to take charge of Army Group Vistula. Since Himmler was without military experience and the situation on both fronts was hopeless, it is hardly surprising that he met his Waterloo.

As important as the scope of Himmler's newest powers was the fact that Hitler chose and trusted him to exercise them in the vicious spirit of "all or nothing," which Goebbels did his best to lash into a fury. Ever since Stalingrad, Goebbels had been urging Hitler to mobilize all idle and underused forces, a position which Speer, backed by top industrialists, also pressed on the führer. The eruption of the Soviet summer offensive and of the plot of July 20 prompted Hitler to follow their counsel, which stressed the need for a stricter delegation and concentration of authority. At the same time that the führer increased Himmler's military sway, he charged Goebbels with mobilizing the state apparatus and public opinion, Speer with tightening his rein on the economy, and Bormann with taking in hand the party. On July 25 Hitler issued a decree ordering total mobilization and appointing Goebbels Reich plenipotentiary for total war.

The next day, in a major address, Goebbels proclaimed the absolute primacy of "total war," which called for the freeing of maximum manpower and resources for the front as well as for war production. In early August he told a conference of party leaders that in this eleventh hour they were fighting "not only for the life of the nation but also for their own lives." Although it was just short of midnight and there was need to drive home the awareness that "the enemy stood at Germany's gates," it was important not to become "hysterical." Instead, with its customary "revolutionary élan," the party should concentrate on raising "one million soldiers or roughly one hundred divisions" so as to turn around the situation and "stabilize the eastern front."

In late February 1945, after the Red Army had forced open the doors of the *Heimat*, Goebbels tried to whip up a hysterical fear of bolshevism to bolster the fight to the last ditch. The Soviets were perpetrating "indescribable atrocities" throughout the eastern lands, including in the east of "our own fatherland." Millions of "bodies and souls" were being "tortured and raped." According to Goebbels, "every German knows that many of the horrors . . . are so gruesome that pens refuse to register and report them." Germany needed to fight this "bloodthirsty and vengeful enemy with *every* means at its disposal, but above all with unvarnished hatred." Turning reality upside down, Goebbels swore that "the enemy would have to pay for making thousands of German women cry and beg in vain for the lives of their defenseless children." After "shamelessly" mistreating many of these women, the "ruthless horde from the steppe was battering their sucklings and throwing them at their feet, in jeering and satanic contempt." This they dared do to "us *Germans!*" Goebbels vowed that inspired by their forefathers, all Germans would rally to "break this Mongol irruption into the European heartland . . . with the fanatic fury as well as intractable and cold hatred of which we [alone] are capable." It would never have come to this critical pass, he said, without "western Europe and the plutocratic-Jewish leadership of the USA covering the flanks of the Soviet *Soldateska* and tying our hands." Indeed, to the "eternal shame" of the twentieth century, as a result of "international Jewry's relentless and systematic subversion," the western countries "infamously left Europe in the lurch."

In the meantime, on August 1, 1944, Hitler had also acted on Speer's advice to create a general staff for all war-related production. The membership of this economic war council, headed by Speer himself, included top executives of AEG, BMW, Flick, and Messerschmitt. Before long, this last-minute drive to further rationalize the output of arms faltered in the face of rapidly spreading economic chaos due to the aerial pounding of vital production and transport facilities as well as to scorched-earth practices. Eventually, on March 19, 1945, Hitler issued his Nero edict ordering the continued scorching of the homeland ahead of the advancing armies. But in the final weeks the military and economic high command, supported by big industry, honored this order only in the breach, especially in the west, with an eye to saving factories, bridges, and railways for after the war.

The failure to capture Moscow in late 1941 had prefigured the Wehrmacht's inability to defeat the Red Army. Desperate to prevail, the Nazi leaders had proceeded to intensify not only the war in the east but also the exploitation and oppression of occupied Europe and the persecution of the Jews. The disaster at Stalingrad in late 1942 had merely redoubled their resolve to persist in this course. Starting with the fiasco of the Reich's third summer offensive in June 1943, it became clear that the war not only could not be won but would almost certainly be lost. Instead of chastening the highest circles of the Third Reich, this realization drove them to battle on with undiminished fury, above all in the east. Hitler and his closest acolytes swore to fight to the end, prepared to immolate themselves, along with much of Europe, including Germany, in the death throes of a regime condemned to total entropy. Jews were destined to be among the chief victims of this unconscionable *guerre à mort*.

As noted, between the summer of 1944 and the spring of 1945 the Wehrmacht executed its retreat and suffered its defeat in a perfectly orderly fashion. There was neither panic nor mutiny. But this military self-possession and discipline went hand in hand with unrelenting barbarity and destruction both at the front and in the rear. Party and security officials summoned soldiers and civilians to fanatical resistance. They orchestrated a wanton defense, determined to capitalize on the turmoil and misery of defeat to prolong the final crisis of the regime. In this terminal phase of the war most Nazi leaders, like most traditional conservatives, including the oppositionists among them, saw only one way of avoiding total disaster: to play on the latent tensions in the enemy coalition, and concentrate on persuading the Western Allies that the survival of a strong Germany was in their own best interest. This diplomatic strategy called for exaggerating the Russian threat, playing on the Allied fear of bolshevism, and giving first priority to fighting the crusade on the eastern front. It was in this same context that Himmler eventually ordered an end to the mass murder of Jews. In the west, meanwhile, the Wehrmacht would put up an essentially conventional defense designed to secure an accommodation or selective capitulation with the United States and Great Britain.

Eastern Europe thus became the principal arena for this asymmetrical life-or-death struggle of the Nazi Behemoth. Soviet and Polish lands were scorched savagely and became the scene of the ruthless pursuit of real and imagined partisans, the massive impressment and deportation of labor, the wholesale pillage of food and raw materials, and the pitiless evacuation to the west of inmates of concentration and labor camps. These extreme measures were deliberate acts of policy and not the wild excesses of individual soldiers and security men.

The nearer the Red Army moved first to Poland and then to the *Altreich,* the more ferocious the German defense became. With their calculated and merciless violence during the Reich's death throes, the Nazis exacerbated the avenging spirit of the Soviet troops, which had to fight their way through the ravaged and blood-drenched villages, towns, and cities of the Ukraine, Belorussia, and Poland. It became a self-fulfilling prophecy that the approaching Red Army was nothing less than a terror-breathing horde.

Ilya Ehrenburg—leading Soviet novelist, journalist, propagandist—overstepped the bounds of normal retaliation with his injunction to exact "not an eye for an eye, but two eyes for one eye." But it was neither sheer exaggeration nor cheap agitprop for Ehrenburg to claim that "all the trenches, graves, and ravines filled with corpses of the innocents are advancing on Berlin, [along with] the boots and shoes and babies' slippers of those murdered and gassed at Majdanek." By early February of 1945 Soviet authorities made efforts to dampen the avenging fury of their troops. Both the *Red Star* and *Pravda,* following Stalin, criticized Ehrenburg's call for blind vengeance, warning against breaches of discipline and insisting that not all Germans were Nazis. The officers and men of the Red Army were, however, hard to restrain in the midst of the most lacerated provinces of Europe's second Thirty Years War. Besides, Soviet soldiers discovered and liberated concentration and death camps nearly nine months earlier than the Allied forces.

As we saw, the Red Army liberated Majdanek on July 24, 1944. Starting in April, the local SS authorities had marched and shipped large numbers of inmates, many of them Jews, from Lublin to camps farther west. Some of these unfortunates wound up in Auschwitz, others in Gross-Rosen, Natzweiler, and Ravensbrück. Although their ultimate fate remains unknown, not many of them are likely to have survived. The Soviets reached Majdanek with such unexpected speed that the SS did not have the time to evacuate all inmates and raze all installations before taking flight. The troops of General Rokossovsky's Eighth Guards Army liberated about 1,000 captives, most of them Polish and Russian POWs, and seized many barracks, a crematorium, and a gas chamber intact. This capture of Majdanek provided the world with the first concrete evidence of the barbarous conditions and practices in Nazi Germany's concentration-camp universe.

The SS had multiple reasons for evacuating their helpless charges, including the sick and the invalids among them. They were under strict orders not to let the Red Army or Polish partisans liberate witnesses of mass murder or capture incriminating installations and documents. This firm resolve to leave no traces of their unspeakable crimes was altogether compatible with the SS's other assignment, which was to keep raising scarce labor by force and violence. In the vortex of defeat Germany's labor shortage became incurable. The Nazi leaders could not make up for the staggering casualties of the Wehrmacht and the defection of the satellites on the eastern front at the same time that they were being overwhelmed on the western front. The war economy could spare little manpower, especially now that Sauckel's push for foreign labor was no longer effective.

Under the circumstances, the forced labor in the eastern concentration and work camps became a particularly valuable reserve of manpower, as did the workers that the Wehrmacht continued to commandeer before surrendering occupied Soviet and Polish territories. The army resorted to forced labor to repair roads, railway tracks, and bridges as well as to construct earthworks. After meeting its own needs the Wehrmacht helped the security forces round up and deport men, women, and children for labor in German concentration and work camps. The number of these unidentified deportees is difficult to estimate, and so is the number who succumbed to mistreatment.

By and large, this last-minute impressment of Gentile Russians and Poles, despite its inhumanity, was motivated by pragmatic rather than punitive considerations, and it was relatively effective. This was not the case with the concurrent deportations and evacuations of Jews.

Not that the work potential of the Jews was discounted. But the rivalry between the productivists and the exterminationists in the SS continued to mark the hyperexploitation and torment of the Jews during the violent twilight of the Nazi regime.

Especially after the shaming capture of Majdanek, which was the easternmost camp in occupied Poland, Himmler's SS and police speeded up the evacuation of Jews who had been kept alive in work camps and residual ghettos. Many of these Jews were shipped to Auschwitz. All in all, the SS sent some thirty overcrowded transports of Jews from different parts of the General Government and the Warthegau to Auschwitz. This was also the moment when over 18,000 Jews were brought there from Theresienstadt. At the same time that the slave labor force of Auschwitz-Monowitz continued to be replenished, large numbers of these deportees, notably the "unproductive elements" among them, were willfully murdered by starvation, disease, and gassing.

Even as these Jews were being delivered to Auschwitz-Birkenau, thousands of others were being shipped out by train to camps in Germany, including Buchenwald, Dachau, Flossenbürg, and Sachsenhausen. These evacuations were part of the frantic effort to remove valuable labor and incriminating evidence from the path of the Red Army. During the second half of 1944 about 400,000 foreigners were forcibly taken to Germany, most of them from the east and a large number of them Jews. Not coincidentally, between August 1944 and January 1945 the population of Germany's concentration and work camps rose from about 524,000 (379,000 men, 145,000 women) to about 713,000 (511,000 men, 202,000 women), a large but uncertain number of them Jews. Many large firms, desperate for labor, hired inmates, organized in external work commandos, from the major camps: AEG, Braunkohle-Benzin, Friedrich Flick, and Argus from Sachsenhausen; Gelsenberg-Benzin, Braunkohle-Benzin, Junkers, Siebel-Flugzeugwerke, Friedrich Flick, Friedrich Krupp, Rheinmetall-Borsig, and Ernst Heinkel from Buchenwald; Messerschmitt, Norddeutsche Hydrierwerke, BMW, and Agfa from Dachau; Siemens, Friedrich Flick, Auto-Union, and Zeiss-Ikon from Flossenbürg; Hugo Schneider and Siemens from Ravensbrück. During the last year of war in particular, some of the major producers of aircraft, motor vehicles, and chemicals recruited concentration-camp labor to build underground factories and tunnels safe from air attacks.

The final evacuations were as senseless and erratic as they were cruel and deadly. To the very end the SS and police pursued the dual goal of keeping the enemy from liberating foreign non-German camp inmates and preserving and regimenting this precious but expendable slave labor for the crumbling war economy of the Nazi regime's reckless last stand. With the contraction of the Third Reich's borders, ever more evacuees were crammed into the concentration camps in the interior of Germany, originally intended for political prisoners. The forced treks on foot, by train, and by boat were murderous and dehumanizing beyond imagining. In turn, the camps became more and more overcrowded, resulting in massive death from exposure, starvation, disease, and ill-treatment. Jews were vastly overrepresented in the marches and transports as well as among the dead and dying.

Between January 17 and 22, 1945, with Soviet troops closing in, the Germans ruthlessly evacuated about 50,000 inmates from Auschwitz to Gross-Rosen, Bergen-Belsen, Buchenwald (including some of its satellite camps), Dachau, and Ravensbrück. This was the start of a wild whirl of brutal relocations ahead of the Red Army. The inmates of Stutthof were moved out beginning in late January, those of Gross-Rosen in early February, those of Sachsenhausen in April, and the women prisoners of Ravensbrück in March and April. In turn, eager to propitiate the Western Allies, Nazi officials became desperate about a fatal consequence of these transfers: the radical deterioration of conditions in camps likely to fall to British and American—as opposed to Soviet—troops. During April tens of thousands of prisoners were shunted from Dora to Bergen-Belsen as well as from Buchenwald and Flossenbürg to Dachau. There was no rhyme or reason to these savage moves, except that the SS guards—some 40,000 of them—spared no effort to keep themselves and their captives beyond the reach of the Red Army.

From the start of the final drive into Germany on the western and eastern fronts in January 1945, to the capture of Berlin four months later, well over 200,000 camp inmates were relocated to camps inside Germany. During these same months probably as many as 150,000 died or were murdered in these same camps. When units of the 60th Soviet Army freed the Auschwitz complex between January 22 and 27, they found about 7,000 infirm inmates left behind by their tormentors. For their part, the British troops who took over Bergen-Belsen on April 15 found about 50,000 hollow-eyed and emaciated inmates and some 13,000 unburied corpses, most of them dead of typhus. More than a quarter of the survivors were too devitalized to live on more than a few weeks, victims of disease and the effects of malnutrition. Upon occupying Buchenwald on April 11 and Dachau on April 29, the American forces freed about 20,000 and 30,000 inmates respectively, most of them no less spent but in marginally better physical condition than the survivors of Bergen-Belsen.

. . .

The brutal repression of the Warsaw uprising in August and September 1944 and the ordeal of Hungarian Jewry were an integral part of the monstrous wages of Hitler's *guerre à mort*. Both enormities were committed as part of the Wehrmacht's desperate effort to block the advance of the Red Army toward Germany's eastern and southern borders. While Warsaw was the most direct gateway to Berlin, Budapest was the critical passageway to Vienna. Fast-moving military and diplomatic developments framed the timing of the Polish uprising and of Horthy's efforts to extricate Hungary from the Axis. The defiance of both Warsaw and Budapest was actuated by political and ideological considerations, and so was Berlin's response. In this terminal stage of the second Thirty Years War, the politics and diplomacy of liberation and disengagement, cramped by the imperative of unconditional surrender on both sides, unwittingly added fuel to the fires and miseries of total war.

The Polish resistance took courage from the attack on Hitler's life and from the rapid approach of the Red Army. But it was also spurred to action by the resolve to liberate Warsaw ahead of the Red Army with a view to limiting the Soviet and Communist influence in postwar Poland. General Count Tadeusz Bór-Komorowski and his chief advisers misread the short-run consequence of the abortive coup in Germany, which strengthened the last-ditchers and the *enragés* there. They also overestimated the Red Army's ability to cross the Vistula, Stalin's readiness to lend support to an essentially anti-Soviet initiative, and the Western Allies' willingness to prevail on Stalin to do so.

With Soviet troops drawing close to the Vistula General Bór-Komorowski ordered the underground in Warsaw to rise on August 1, 1944. In a population of close to 1 million this Polish Home Army counted between 25,000 and 30,000 potential combatants, of whom about 10 percent were adequately armed. This ill-equipped, untrained, and poorly led popular militia faced a German garrison of about 15,000 professional troops, backed up by the full weight of nearby German battle units. Soon additional German forces were brought in, but these did not consist primarily of conventional soldiers. With the Ninth Army straining to stem the advance of the Red Army, Field Marshal Walter Model was reluctant to divert any of his troops to suppress the uprising, which was not without serious military perils. Indeed, both he and General Guderian, now chief of the General Staff of the Army High Command, were alarmed at the prospect of their troops on the eastern bank of the Vistula being cut off and facing enemy forces to their rear. But whereas Model urged calling in security forces to crush the uprising in Warsaw, Guderian had misgivings about using them. He not only doubted their effectiveness but also took exception to their savage ways.

Hitler decided in favor of Himmler's taking charge of crushing the Warsaw insurrection in the same spirit in which he was just then liquidating the conspirators of July 20. Accordingly, although the regular army played an important role, the SS and the police set the pace and tone. Himmler enjoined his men to take no prisoners and to level the city, partly as an object lesson to the rest of occupied Europe.

Himmler rushed twelve police companies from the Warthegau to Warsaw. He also sent two SS units whose officers and men were typical of the *canaille* that the Third Reich enlisted to impose and defend its eastern positions, to root out partisans, and to man concentration camps and extermination sites. One of these SS brigades was led by Dr. Oskar Dirlewanger, a miscreant who had served in the Condor Legion in Spain and who now had hardened criminals under his command. The other was led by Mieczysław Kamiński. A Belorussian villain, he had become a confirmed and opportunistic Nazi collaborator deep in Russia before retreating into Poland with his volunteer and conscript legion of non-Germans. Both Dirlewanger and Kamiński were SS generals. In Warsaw they reported to SS General Heinz Reinefarth.

The Nazi move to quell the rising began on August 5. Following air strikes reminiscent of 1939, about 6,500 regular police and SS moved into two central districts of Warsaw. Within a few days they murdered several thousand civilians in an assault marked by pillage and rape. Not surprisingly, this indiscriminate and wild violence left countless innocent victims and martyrs without breaking or even weakening the revolt.

For reasons of efficiency, Himmler turned the operation over to Erich von dem Bach-Zelewski, a general in both the regular and the Waffen SS. Between the wars Bach-Zelewski had become a seasoned expert in the use of naked violence: in 1919 he had served in the Freikorps; in 1932–33 he had killed several Communists in street fighting; and in 1934 he had participated actively in the Röhm purge. Following the conquest of Poland, he had become a high security official in the Warthegau. Then, with Barbarossa, Bach-Zelewski went to Russia, where he served as a top SS and police official in the rear of the Central Army Group answerable, *inter alia,* for the massacre of Jews in Minsk and Mogilev. In late 1942, after Bach-Zelewski had recovered from a nervous breakdown, Himmler appointed him chief of antipartisan warfare for the entire eastern front. Directly responsible to Himmler, he had no troops of his own. Rather, he ordered and coordinated punitive drives that were executed by the Wehrmacht, the Waffen-SS, or the police. For these antiguerrilla operations Bach-Zelewski typically relied heavily on locally recruited auxiliaries or mercenaries.

Once he arrived in Warsaw, he set about using more rational methods to repress the uprising. He moderated Himmler's warrant for absolute liquidation and destruction, regimented his rampaging shock troops, and pulled out the frenzied and badly mauled Kamiński Brigade, whose commander he summarily executed. Even so, the battle lasted a full nine weeks, until early October. Being both cunning and overextended, the Soviets provided little aid, and that reluctantly, leaving the rebels to their fate, much like that which befell the insurgents of the Jewish ghetto the year before. At least 10,000 Polish freedom fighters sacrificed their lives and 6,000 were wounded. Well over 150,000 civilians are estimated to have been killed. Several hundred thousand citizens of Warsaw were arrested during and immediately after the fighting. Of these at least 150,000 were deported to the Reich for forced labor, and over 50,000 of these were locked into concentration camps. There was enormous physical damage to the city as well. Warsaw's central districts were nearly completely laid waste, as the Jewish ghetto districts had been earlier. The capital of Poland had become the most martyred and desolate capital of Europe's second Thirty Years War.

Shortly after the capitulation on October 2, Hitler commended Bach-Zelewski for his accomplishment and posted him to Budapest, where Himmler expected the approaching Red Army to precipitate another uprising.

While the Polish national and conservative resistance had a broad popular base, Hungary's temporization was orchestrated by an ingrown governing class contemptuous and fearful of the lower orders. After the first Soviet summer offensive and the Anglo-American landing in Sicily, Horthy and his inner circle no longer had any illusions about the possibility of a German victory. They sought to distance Budapest from Berlin in an effort to limit their losses. But this would not be an easy task. As part of their stubborn battle to save their old world, they had become complicit in the war against both the Soviet Union and the Jews. Characteristically, in 1941 the government of László Bárdossy had enacted Hungary's most flagrant anti-Jewish measures in conjunction with its eager enlistment in the crusade against "Judeobolshevism." In addition to issuing Nuremberg-type decrees, Bárdossy had enacted a law excluding Jews from regular military service but making them liable to service in auxiliary labor battalions. Attached to regular army divisions for noncombatant duty, Jewish labor conscripts were commanded by far-rightist officers who drove them with a special venom. Between June 1941 and December 1943 at least 40,000 Jews were sent to the eastern theater. Eventually, the single largest concentration of Jewish laborers saw service with the Second Hungarian Army. In early 1943, when the Soviets counterattacked on the Don, this army had about one-half of its 200,000 men killed and wounded. Though the Jewish laborers were not in the front lines, they are estimated to have suffered proportionately even heavier losses, and large numbers of them were captured by the Red Army.

Until October 15, 1944, official Hungary all but ignored its own anti-Jewish laws. Likewise, there was nothing intentionally murderous about the confinement of Jews to special labor detachments or even, as we saw, about the deportation of Jews to Kamenets-Podolsk. Nevertheless, the discriminatory policies did serious harm by legitimating and stimulating age-old anti-Jewish hatreds and by creating bureaucratic structures to act on them. But above all, once Horthy and his ultraconservative associates faced military defeat, they discovered that they were no longer free to raise or lower the sluice gates of official anti-Semitism at will. For the Nazi leaders in Berlin and for the fascist opposition within Hungary, the Magyar establishment's treatment of the "Jewish question" became a test of its continuing commitment to the crusade against Soviet Russia and bolshevism in all its dimensions.

By early 1943 Premier Miklós Kállay, Bárdossy's pragmatically minded successor, looked for ways to free Hungary from Hitler's increasingly deadly hold. The prospect of a Soviet victory made him tremble for the future of his country and class. Like the conservative *fronde* in Germany, the conservative leadership in Hungary sought a diplomatic opening to the Western powers, convinced that Churchill and Roosevelt shared their concern for keeping the Soviet Union and communism out of southeastern Europe and the Balkans. But unlike their German counterparts, the Hungarian conservatives still had over 700,000 Jews living in their country to be used to conciliate the Western Allies. In sum, while Bárdossy had supererogatorily resorted to anti-Semitic measures to *advance* the national and class interests of Old Hungary, Kállay meant to shield Hungarian Jewry in a delicate and risky effort to *salvage* some of its values and interests.

To avert a breakup of the Axis, Hitler summoned first Marshal Antonescu and then Admiral Horthy to confer with him at Klessheim Castle near Salzburg. On April 12–13, 1943, he complained to Antonescu about certain disloyal diplomatic soundings by King Michael and other prominent Rumanians. Hitler stressed that the choice was between "clear-cut victory or total destruction," particularly at the hands of the Soviets. He insisted that unlike in 1918–19, when bolshevism had been in its infancy, it now had "enormous military power." In addition, not to win the war would mean perpetuating the "Jewish danger, either in the form of pure bolshevism or in the disguise of liberalism." Hence the need to continue the struggle to the finish with "fanatic resolve." After expressing his agreement about the Bolshevik peril, Antonescu reassured Hitler of Rumania's steadfastness, attested by the 200,000 Rumanians killed and 180,000 wounded on the eastern front, 11,000 officers among them.

Before Antonescu took his leave, Hitler broached the "Jewish question." He insisted that unlike Antonescu and Horthy, he was convinced that their countries were in need of the same "energetic measures" as Germany. The situation was particularly troublesome in Hungary, where "the Jews are the natural allies of bolshevism and candidates for the posts vacated by the intelligentsia who would be murdered in case of Bolshevization." To avoid this outcome, "the more radical the treatment of the Jews, the better." Hitler told Antonescu that just as in military battle he would rather risk all than court a stalemate, so in the drive against the Jews he would prefer "to burn all bridges behind me, since the hatred of the Jews is boundless in any case." The Jewish question had been solved in Germany, making for a united nation, even if, "having taken this path, there is no turning back."

A few days later, on March 16 and 17, 1943, Hitler lectured Horthy in similar terms. He began again by warning of the danger that Bolshevik power would sweep over all of Europe, "unless the Germans manage to crush the Russians." Mindful of Hungary's efforts to pull out of the Axis, Hitler told Horthy that it was "totally naive and childish" to suppose that "if 200 German divisions" could not provide protection from the Bolsheviks "a few English or American divisions" could. Besides, even assuming such divisions were ever in the offing, "the Jews in London and Washington will block any drive against the Jews in Moscow." There simply was no denying that this was "a total war, admitting of no distinction between East and West, between Russians and Anglo-Saxons." Kállay's hope to avoid Soviet occupation by changing camps was specious. Budapest should know that "Germany and its allies are sitting in the same boat on stormy seas," which meant that whoever "tries to jump ship, will drown instantly."

Horthy sought to placate Hitler in terms similar to Antonescu's. Protesting his loyalty, he claimed that to date Hungary had had

146,000 soldiers killed and 30,000 wounded on the eastern front, not counting 36,000 Jewish laborers sent to help fight the Bolshevik enemy. Furthermore, Hungary contributed "80 percent of its industrial production and 60 percent of its agricultural output" to the Axis war effort, leaving bread rations "smaller" in Hungary than in Germany. Hitler replied that while he had full confidence in Horthy, he had none in Kállay, who was doing great harm abroad by creating the impression that "Hungary no longer believed in [an Axis] victory."

Hitler then turned to the subject of the Jews, affirming that "Hungary's pro-Jewish attitude" was altogether incomprehensible. It should be self-evident, he maintained, that for Horthy "not to expel the Jews," as Germany had done, meant to leave them free to once again "destroy [Hungary's] economy, currency, and morale," as they had done in 1918–19. Why of all people should the Jews be "handled with kid gloves"? After all, having "instigated the First World War, they were responsible for the millions of lives that were sacrificed." Thereafter, they had "unleashed the revolution" in Hungary, which took a heavy toll as well. The Jews were no less to blame for the present war, in particular for the "form it has taken," notably the "bombing of civilian populations, which victimized so many women and children."

Horthy conceded that Hungary had a particularly difficult "Jewish problem." He stressed that "as a small country it has 200,000 more Jews" than Germany had at the time of the Nazi takeover. But Hungary had to take some of the blame itself, since "for a thousand years Hungarians took the view that money was too dirty to be touched by gentlemen." This explained the importance of Jews in Hungary, with "no adequate substitute for them in the Hungarian economy." Even so, the Hungarian regent claimed credit for the anti-Jewish measures of his governments, which excluded Jews from universities, the press, cultural life, and "all important [public] positions." In point of fact, he had "done everything that could decently be done against the Jews, short of murdering or otherwise disposing of them, which was, after all, impossible." The führer's retort was that there was no need to murder them, since they could be "committed to concentration camps . . . or made to work in mines." But Hitler also seized on Horthy's passing reference to the "murder of Jews" to remind him that the Jews themselves were "the chief murderers, since it is they who have brought on the war and used [their] influence to have it directed against civilians, women, and children."

Horthy responded by asking what he should do with the Jews whom he had "all but deprived of their livelihood, but whom he could not, after all, beat to death." Von Ribbentrop interjected that the choice was to "either destroy [*vernichten*] them or put them in concentration camps." Justifying this radical course with the charge that the Jews were "pure parasites," Hitler invoked the example of Poland, where "Jews who refuse to work are shot [while] those unable to do so are left to waste away." Overall, the Jews should be "treated as tubercle bacilli, contagious for healthy organisms." This prescription was not particularly "cruel, considering that even innocent natural creatures like rabbits and deer have to be decimated to prevent spoliation." Indeed, "why should beasts bent on inflicting bolshevism on us be treated with greater forbearance?"

Horthy resisted Hitler. He did so because his own anti-Semitism was not murderous and above all because of his own reluctance to burn his bridges behind him. Horthy refused to join in the Judeocide in order to avoid becoming irrevocably tied to the Third Reich, especially since the safekeeping of Hungarian Jewry remained central to his stratagem for courting the Western Allies.

With Budapest increasingly recalcitrant and Soviet troops pressing their advance, the OKW made contingency plans for the occupation of Hungary. The defection of Italy in early September 1943 strengthened Hitler's resolve to hold on to his strategically vital eastern satellite. He rightly calculated that since the Hungarian leaders continued to fear the Soviet Union more than the Third Reich, the approach of the Red Army would bring them to their senses. But once Soviet troops pulled close to Eastern Galicia, the Dniester, and the Prut, it became too risky to continue to trust Budapest.

In early March 1944, after consulting von Ribbentrop and Himmler, as well as his military advisers, the führer decided to move troops into Hungary to impose a government that would stand fast with Germany. Acute shortages of military and civilian personnel circumscribed this operation. Only eight divisions were sent in, but Hitler was confident that the Hungarian army could be counted on to garrison the country. Berlin proposed to exercise indirect control. Pro-German officials would be placed in commanding positions, and otherwise, Hungary's civil and military bureaucracy would be asked to carry on. Rather than press the new government for additional divisions to battle against the Red Army, Hitler meant to stop Hungary's furtive diplomacy and increase its industrial output. He also expected it to tackle the "Jewish problem," the quickest and easiest yardstick of Budapest's forced collaboration, a course which was favored by local ultraconservatives and fascists.

Hitler once again summoned Horthy to Klessheim Castle, where they met on March 18, 1944. Without mentioning the military intervention begun that very morning, the führer peremptorily demanded that the regent install a trustworthy government loyal to Germany. After some hesitation, Horthy agreed. He did so out of fear of the Soviet Union and bolshevism, as well as concern for Hungary's future borders. Under German guns he dismissed Kállay and chose Döme Sztójay to head a government of the extreme and fascist right. Horthy resisted only to the point of refusing to take Béla Imrédy, leader of the Party of Hungarian Revival, as his prime minister. While Imredy remained in the wings, several of his associates and fellow travelers were given cabinet positions. László Endre and László Baky, of the local National Socialist Party, became state secretaries for Jewish affairs in the Interior Ministry.

As expected, the Wehrmacht was welcomed, particularly by the Hungarian military and police. With their help the German security forces instantly arrested hundreds of refractory conservatives, democrats, leftists, and Jews. While the German High Command took full military control of the country, including the Hungarian armed forces, SS Major General Dr. Edmund Veesenmayer, the plenipotentiary of the Third Reich in Hungary, became the supreme master of civil affairs. Under von Ribbentrop's orders Veesenmayer had acted as the advance man of the German intervention, establishing close contacts with local collaborationists, including key members of the Arrow Cross. Now that he was Nazi Germany's proconsul, he reported to both Ribbentrop and Kaltenbrunner. Indeed, Veesenmayer became a prime mover of the Jewish deportation by virtue of his influence over both the German and Hungarian security forces.

At Klessheim Hitler had extracted from Horthy a pledge to bear down on the Jews. It is unclear whether Horthy agreed to the actual systematic persecution of the Jews right then and there or only after it was initiated by Premier Sztójay, acting in concert with Veesenmayer. What is certain, however, is that at Klessheim the regent promised to deliver 100,000 Jews to Greater Germany for forced labor in war-related projects. The plan was to rush Jewish laborers to the Protectorate to help in the construction of underground aircraft factories. Two weeks after the Klessheim meeting Hitler notified interested Luftwaffe officials that this labor would soon be delivered. In mid-April Sztójay promised to make available 50,000 Jewish workers by the end of that month, and an additional 60,000 by the end of May. If these chained workers were to be accompanied by their families, the number deported would greatly exceed this total of 110,000.

Military as well as labor considerations influenced the Nazis in planning these deportations. The Jews were seen as a potential security risk and, as we shall see, the SS began with the removal of Jews from Carpathian Ruthenia and northern Transylvania, the two provinces that were most immediately threatened by advancing units of the Red Army, which at one point along the front were less than forty miles away.

Meanwhile, entirely on its own initiative, the Sztójay cabinet hastened to enforce and stiffen Hungary's existing anti-Semitic laws. By the end of March, Jews were forced to wear the yellow star, which facilitated their arrest and deportation. Indeed, Nazi Germany's full range of discriminatory measures were now put into practice in Hungary.

Soon SS Lieutenant Colonel Adolf Eichmann and several of his associates arrived in Budapest. They were charged with accelerating and streamlining the deportation of Jews. Fully backed by Veesenmayer, Eichmann had wide latitude and could count on the enthusiastic collaboration of Endre and Baky, as well as of the Hungarian police, gendarmerie, and army. As a matter of course, Eichmann infused the agreement to deliver a limited number of Jews for forced labor with the nihilistic spirit of the exterminists. The built-in but fatal ambiguity which had facilitated the "Final Solution" all along began to inform the deportation of Hungarian Jewry. At first, and with dire consequences, not only Horthy but the Jews themselves believed in the economic or productivist purpose of Nazi Germany's imperative for impressment, which even at this late date could not be dismissed as mere subterfuge.

On April 23 Veesenmayer informed the chief operatives of the deportation that the Jews were to be transported not to the Protectorate but to Auschwitz and other concentration camps. Two transports carrying about 3,800 able-bodied male Jews left from near Budapest for Auschwitz at the end of April. Veesenmayer specified that beginning May 15, 1944, about 3,000 Jews were to be shipped out daily.

The chief architects of the deportation divided Hungary into six zones, to be emptied of Jews one after the other. As noted, the operation began in the two frontier zones—Carpathian Ruthenia and northern Transylvania—most exposed to the approaching Red Army. Starting in mid-April the Jews of these two provinces were concentrated in makeshift internment camps on the outskirts of towns and cities with or near railway connections. After this brutal relocation, they were deported under typically atrocious conditions. Between May 15 and June 7 close to 290,000 Jews were packed into ninety-two freight trains, each train carrying over 3,000 victims to their tragic destiny. Veesenmayer and Eichmann could not have filled their outrageous quotas without the unstinting cooperation of the Hungarian authorities.

The deportations from the three other provincial zones proceeded in the same ruthless fashion and just as quickly. Between June 10 and July 10, 1944, 148,000 Jews were deported to the Reich from northern, western, and southern Hungary. Accordingly, in two months, from mid-May to mid-July, over 435,000 Jews were taken away. There remained the sixth zone, Greater Budapest. The capital counted over 250,000 Jews, many of them assimilated, educated, and wealthy, with close ties to the nation's traditional ruling and governing elites.

The Jewish council of Budapest was slow to comprehend the full extent of the tragedy befalling the Jews of Hungary. The members of this council were, of course, relentlessly pressured by Veesenmayer and Eichmann, by Sztójay and Baky. But at first they also complied or collaborated because they believed or wanted to believe that as long as they did so, the deportations would be rigidly circumscribed. In addition, they were more inclined to cede, however reluctantly, the Jews of the provinces, most of whom were less assimilated and acculturated than the Jews of the capital.

The noose kept tightening around the Jews of Greater Budapest, who were beginning to be ghettoized. On June 22, 1944, the Jewish council implored Premier Sztójay to protect not only the Jews of the capital but those who had already been deported. This supplication stressed that the extension of the deportations from the frontier zones to the interior "invalidated the assumption that the removal of the Jews was necessitated by military considerations." Likewise, the deportation of Jews "irrespective of age, sex, and health" destroyed the hope that they were being "removed from the country . . . for labor." To date "427,000 Jews, or about half the Jews of Hungary," had been taken away under the most inhumane conditions. After being assembled in internment camps, "the physically and spiritually broken people were taken to deportation trains to be crowded 70 to 80 into a freight car, in many cases . . . after undergoing severe interrogations and physical abuse." During their long voyage in cars that were sealed and barely ventilated, "these unfortunates . . . were deprived of everything . . . [except] a few loaves of bread and two buckets, one full of water and the other for sanitary needs."

Tormented by this extreme suffering of the Jews from the provinces, the Central Council of Hungarian Jewry now faced the stark reality "that the deportation of the Jews of the capital was also to begin within the next few days." Conceding that there were sinners "among us" as there were sinners "in every community," the Jewish leaders protested that, nevertheless, "every just man, whatever his affiliation, has to cry out in pain at innocent children and infants being taken to destruction in their mother's arms, and at helpless invalids, old people, and pregnant women being taken on their fateful journey . . . from which there was hardly any return." Invoking the "1,000-year-old history . . . that has tied local Jewry to the Hungarian nation . . . since [its] founding," in this "last hour" the Jewish notables "ask for mercy for those still at home and beg for the lives of innocent children."

The bulk of the Jews deported from Hungary were taken to Auschwitz, and many of them died en route. Upon arrival there, an uncertain percentage were selected as fit for work. All the others were condemned either to waste away from exposure, malnutrition, and sickness, or to be killed outright, mostly by gassing. It is impossible to give an accurate breakdown of the number selected to work, to languish in conditions that spelled "natural" death, or to be murdered. With the influx of the Hungarian Jews, the always execrable living and sanitary facilities of Auschwitz became even more atrociously overloaded, turning Birkenau particularly into a hell on earth and into "the journey's end" for those unfit for labor—for infants, children, the aged, the sick, the disabled.

The fate of those Hungarian Jews designated fit for work is difficult to reconstruct. Many of the able-bodied men and women who were set apart for slave labor were kept in or near Auschwitz. This was, of course, the time that extreme efforts were being made to boost production as well as to locate and construct industrial plants safe from enemy air attacks. Within Auschwitz proper the I. G. Farben complex at Monowitz was operating full blast while new facilities were being built both above ground and below. Hungarian Jews were used to supply the reserve army of expendable forced labor assigned to these and other tasks. Hungarian Jews also became slaves in factories and mines of the greater Auschwitz region. In addition to being condemned to backbreaking tasks in or around Auschwitz, able-bodied Hungarian Jews were sent to be hyperexploited in the concentration camps of Greater Germany, which meant that many of them eventually also were consigned to the deadly forced marches and transports of the Third Reich's final days.

The ordeal of Hungarian Jewry was impossible to hide. For one thing, it was too massive and public to go undetected. For another, pragmatic collaborators within Hungary and compromised neutral nations exposed and denounced it as part of their search for a rapprochement with tomorrow's victors. Besides, though a satellite,

Hungary had all along remained a sovereign state open to neutral diplomats, journalists, and businessmen. These foreigners, with contacts among local dissident conservatives, informed the outside world about the Jewish nightmare, with special emphasis on the role and complicity of the Hungarian authorities. The dispatches to the foreign offices and newspapers of Switzerland, Sweden, Portugal, and Spain provided a reasonably full and accurate picture, except that they lacked precision about the victims' final destination and fate, which remained inscrutable. The Vatican was similarly informed. All these reports corroborated testimony already brought out by Jews and disseminated by Jewish agencies, whose accounts still tended to be discounted as exaggerated and self-serving.

This incontrovertible evidence combined with the certainty that the Axis was doomed roused the outside world to remonstrate. Neutral governments, the pope, and the International Red Cross issued caveats, petitions, and protests, most of them addressed to Horthy. As for the Allies, they not only cautioned Budapest but also directed protests and warnings of reprisals to Berlin.

Not surprisingly, these admonitions from abroad had a powerful and immediate effect on the conservative wing of Hungary's inveterate upper class, which had long since recognized the need for a turnabout. Typically, in late June Count István Bethlen, the elder statesman of this momentarily recessive but far from innocent political caste, cautioned Horthy that the Jewish deportations were "irreparably soil[ing] the name of Hungary before the world."

The regent finally realized that the moment had come to risk standing up to Nazi Germany and its local collaborators, perhaps by using the "Jewish question" as a pretext. At the same time, however, the fear of an imminent breakthrough by the Red Army continued to feed his irresolution.

Still, on June 26, 1944, Horthy urged the Crown Council to dismiss Baky and Endre and put a stop to the deportation of Budapest's Jews. In turn, Baky planned a coup for early July to head off this resurgence of the old elite. But this coup failed, as Horthy had ordered timely countermeasures. On July 7 the regent took it upon himself to order the arrest of Baky and a halt to all deportations, thereby testing his residual authority not just to reign but to govern as well. Von Ribbentrop and Veesenmayer reacted by threatening to tighten Germany's military grip. But Horthy stood his ground, with considerable backing from within Hungary's political society. The deportations were suspended.

Soon thereafter, on August 23, Soviet troops captured Kishinev and Jassy in their drive through Bessarabia and Moldavia to the

Carpathian Mountains. To avoid total disaster King Michael capitulated unconditionally and ordered the Rumanian army to switch sides. For joining the Soviets in battle Bucharest secured first claim on northern Transylvania. Close to the breaking point, the German command was unable to prevent or contain this reversal on the doorsteps of Hungary and Czechoslovakia, which also meant that about 60 percent of Rumanian Jews remained beyond the reach of the SS.

The situation became more critical than ever for Hungary and the Jews of Budapest. Now that King Michael had wrecked Horthy's revisionist territorial ambitions, the regent became all the more determined to avoid Rumania's fate of falling under Soviet control. On August 24 he appointed a new cabinet headed by General Géza Lakatos, who was much more of Kállay's than of Sztójay's bent. Horthy instructed Lakatos to collaborate with the Wehrmacht in holding back Soviet and Rumanian divisions, while at the same time defying Berlin's political demands, particularly its insistence on the continuing surrender of Jews. This refusal to deport any more Jews was an integral part of Horthy's primary objective, which was to prevail on the Western Allies to grant Hungary a separate armistice and peace. In sum, the strategy was to help block the Russo-Rumanian advance in the vain hope of gaining time for the Anglo-Americans to break into the Balkans and shield Hungary from the Soviets. Saving Budapest's Jews was meant to prove the bona fides of the Hungarian government and to preserve hostages for diplomatic purposes.

Lakatos asked Berlin to withdraw Eichmann at the same time that Hungarian emissaries, both official and private, sought to make overtures to the Allies in Berne, Lisbon, Stockholm, and Istanbul. But time was running out. Soviet and Rumanian troops broke through Carpathian Ruthenia and Transylvania to cross into Hungary in late September 1944. With the Western Allies lacking military leverage in east-central Europe and refusing separate negotiations, Horthy could not continue to shun Stalin. With great hesitation and reluctance he ordered the start of negotiations with Moscow. But unlike King Michael, he had to reckon with both Berlin and local fascists blocking his efforts. With the Wehrmacht about to fall back to bolster the defense of the strategically vital Danubian basin, a coalition of Hungary's traditional and new right resolved to stage a fascist takeover as part of a mad effort to salvage the old regime. At this critical pass the fate of the Jews was at best of only marginal importance for Horthy, Hitler, and Ferenc Szálasi, leader of the Arrow Cross.

Once again, the Third Reich prepared its intervention carefully.

But compared to six months ago, the stress was on tightening the political reins, especially since by now German troops were expertly deployed and the Hungarian military, notably the officer corps, still favored a last stand against the Soviets. Accordingly, while emboldening the Arrow Cross and unregenerate army officers to obstruct the conservative trimmers, Berlin exerted direct pressure on Horthy. Hitler sent a special envoy to give additional weight to Veesenmayer's dire warnings and threats. In addition SS General Bach-Zelewski was on hand, and so was SS Major General Otto Skorzeny. A daring commando specialist, on September 12, 1943, Skorzeny had rescued Mussolini from the government of Marshal Pietro Badoglio, which, after capitulating to the Allies, had declared war on Germany. Now, in Hungary, he planned to take Horthy's son hostage for the good behavior of his father.

The regent knew what was afoot, except for the projected capture of his son. Pressured by the Soviets, and once again determined to preempt a German-orchestrated coup, on October 14 Horthy decided to announce Hungary's capitulation the next day. To head off this prospect, Veesenmayer precipitated a showdown on October 15. With both military units and the Arrow Cross on alert, he warned Horthy that unless he backed off from surrendering to the Soviets his son would be killed and Germany would seize full control of Hungary. Horthy once again bent his knee to Hitler. In exchange for the life of his son and protection for himself and his retinue, Horthy reluctantly asked Szálasi to form a coalition cabinet in which new rightists had ascendancy over old conservatives. Simultaneously, but altogether less grudgingly, he summoned the Hungarian people to continue fighting the Red Army alongside the Third Reich. Horthy resigned as head of state and agreed to go live in forced residence in Germany. But he did so only after first legitimating the successor fascist regime and the continuation of the crusading war alongside Nazi Germany.

By mid-October Soviet and Rumanian troops had seized most of Hungary east of the Danube, and by early November they had advanced to within a few miles of Budapest. As of then, and until liberation on February 13, 1945, over 200,000 Jews were trapped in a quasi-captive metropolis which was subjected to eruptions by local fascists as well as to Soviet cannonades. Budapest, unlike Warsaw, never spawned an effective popular underground, either Christian or Jewish. Since Szálasi's police arrested and hounded the old conservatives, foreign diplomats were the only ones left to intervene on behalf of the Jews.

On October 16 the paramilitary zealots of the Arrow Cross confirmed the new regime with a massacre of several hundred Jews, which may have been the first anti-Jewish pogrom in the history of Budapest. This carnage was followed by thousands of Jews being herded like cattle through city streets and on open roads. After three days Szálasi himself put an end to this wanton savagery. Forthwith, Veesenmayer, under instructions from Berlin, pressed for the delivery of 50,000 fit Jews for forced heavy labor near Vienna and in other parts of the Greater Reich. Men from sixteen to sixty and women up to forty years of age were rounded up to be marched to distant and undetermined work stations. By mid-November between 25,000 and 30,000 able-bodied Jews were trekking westward under extreme conditions, scores of them collapsing from exhaustion and exposure. At about this time Szálasi ordered these forced marches stopped, presumably because he was troubled, even appalled, by the toll they took on women. For the time being, he restricted his regime's drive against the Jews to stigmatizing and ghettoizing them, which meant that he denied the Germans the collaboration without which further deportations became increasingly difficult.

Perhaps Szálasi and his clique were also influenced by the proximity of the Red Army as well as by the active intervention of foreign emissaries in Budapest. Representatives of the neutral nations, the Vatican, and the International Red Cross provided Jews not only with protection but also with emigration papers and avenues of escape. Raoul Wallenberg became exemplary in this regard. The young scion of a prominent Swedish family, Wallenberg resolved to use his position as attaché of the Swedish legation to extend unstinting help to the imperiled Jews of Greater Budapest. He managed to turn Swedish diplomatic offices into sanctuaries for Jews while arranging to issue special travel papers for them. The Swiss, Spanish, and Portuguese envoys engaged in similar if less intensive efforts, and so did the papal nuncio, especially on behalf of baptized Jews.

More than likely, Szálasi and local Nazi officials cast a blind eye to such attempts to help Budapest's Jews, in part because of their total absorption with holding back the Red Army and maneuvering for separate negotiations with the Western Allies, which involved using Hungarian Jews as diplomatic coin. As we saw, despite his resolve to stand fast on all fronts, Hitler hoped for a breakup of the Grand Alliance. As he had told Antonescu on March 23, 1944, "world history had seen few wars in which coalitions held together for five years if all its members were not equally determined to fight for *Sein oder Nichtsein.*" Hitler reiterated this view on December 12, insisting on the ultimate incompatibility of "the ultracapitalist states on the one hand . . . and the ultra-Marxist state on the other." As usual, he played on the Western world's fear of Soviet expansion and Bolshevik subversion with a view to splitting London and Washington from Moscow, all the time traducing the Jews for supposedly working against such a rupture and against the formation of an anti-Soviet block as part of a self-serving scheme for unconditional surrender.

Eventually, all the senior Nazi leaders, like the leaders of the abort-ive *fronde,* put out feelers to the Western Allies for a separate strategic surrender contingent on a shared interest in stopping the Red tide as far east as possible and in maintaining a strong Germany as a bulwark against Soviet Russian power and world communism. Using different official and unofficial channels, Goebbels, von Ribbentrop, and Göring worked to this end, and so did Himmler.

Paradoxically, Himmler became most directly involved in trying to harness the labor of Hungarian Jews while also seeking to use them as a pawn in the search for an opening to the Western Allies. At the very time that he became the supreme advocate and executor of the Nazi regime's political and military fight to the death, Himmler began to side with the pragmatists within the SS who proposed to harness Slavs, Jews, and concentration-camp labor for this reckless effort, which was—as we saw—directed against the surging Red Army. A lifelong anti-Bolshevik, Himmler increasingly blamed the Soviets for the disastrous plight of the Third Reich. He became so incensed that he considered exchanging what remained of the hated Jewish enemy for help in holding Soviet power and bolshevism at bay.

This was the military, ideological, and diplomatic setting for the ruthlessly opportunistic and ill-fated efforts to ransom Hungarian Jewry. Actually, the idea originated with Rezsö Kasztner and Joel Brand, two Hungarian labor Zionists who in early 1943 had organized the Jewish Rescue Committee of Budapest to help Jews from Nazi-occupied countries make their way to Palestine via Hungary. But they did not really become active until late March 1944, immediately after the installation of the Sztójay Cabinet, when the Hungarian Jews themselves became imperiled. Kasztner tried to bribe or convince a member of Eichmann's staff to allow six hundred Jews to emigrate to Palestine in exchange for 4 million marks. Although this attempt failed, in early April Brand used his contacts with the German Ab-wehr to revive the idea of ransoming the Jews. It soon came to the attention of SS Captain Otto Clages, chief of the local SD. Hard-headed in the face of seemingly endless military reverses, Clages urged Himmler to consider using the Jewish Rescue Committee as a go-between to trade Jews for weapons for the Waffen-SS. The suggestion struck a responsive chord. Given his warped preconceptions about the enormous power of Jews in London and Washington, Himmler was inclined to view Kasztner and Brand as providing potentially valuable access to the Western Allies for vital supplies and diplomatic soundings.

Eichmann was busy planning the deportations when in mid-May Himmler ordered him to contact Joel Brand to propose the release of Hungarian Jews in exchange not for cash but for critical war materials and consumer goods. Specifically, Eichmann was told to ask for 10,000 trucks, 2 million cases of soap, and 200 tons of tea and coffee. It is not impossible that the demand for soft staples was intended either to shroud the extortion of trucks and other strategic materials or to signal a fallback position, should the Allies balk at the idea of supplying Germany with war matériel. Indeed, ultimately the bid to barter Jews was designed to tempt the Western powers and split them from the Soviets. Accordingly, Himmler instructed Eichmann to assure his contacts that the trucks would be used exclusively on the eastern front. For his part, Brand asked that as a pledge of good faith the SS should authorize the prompt departure of a preliminary convoy of between 600 and 1,200 Hungarian Jews to a neutral country, to which Eichmann agreed.

On May 17, just after the start of the deportations, and with a German safe-conduct, Joel Brand left for Istanbul, where he arrived on May 19. He was accompanied on his mission by Andor "Bandi" Grosz. A christened Jew in the pay of the Axis secret services, Grosz had contacts with Allied intelligence operatives. While Brand was to mobilize Zionist and Jewish circles for the ransom plan, Grosz was to convince British and American agents that powerful German officials were eager to negotiate a separate armistice for the western front.

Fully aware of the urgency of their mission, Brand and Grosz rushed from neutral Turkey to Syria, which was British-controlled. Both men were taken into custody upon crossing the border. But whereas Grosz's efforts ended with his arrest, on June 10, in Aleppo, Brand was allowed to confer with Moshe Shertok, head of the political department of the Jewish Agency, with headquarters in Palestine. After stressing the growing torment of Hungarian Jewry, Brand must have told Shertok that although the Western Allies were unlikely to trade trucks for Jews, everything should be done to convince them to hold out the prospect for early negotiations, which alone could slow or halt the deportations. In sum, however innocently, Brand spoke to Shertok as Grosz had been instructed to speak to Allied agents. Whatever the avowed pretext or actual substance of the overture from Berlin, its end purpose was to press the Western Allies to relax their demand for unconditional surrender, and to do so at the Soviet Union's expense.

All the time the Hungarian Jews, except those of Greater Budapest, were being deported, the British kept Brand in prison in Cairo. It was left to Zionist leaders in Palestine to implore British officials not to spurn Eichmann's overture and to send Brand back with a message designed to temporize or to elicit a more acceptable hostage deal. Although Washington, informed of Brand's mission, was inclined to follow such a course, London and Moscow insisted that the German feeler be rejected outright. Not that the Allied leaders were indifferent or insensitive to the plight of Hungarian Jewry. But Stalin and Churchill in particular were not about to further strain the Grand Alliance over a hostage scheme that they quite rightly assumed was calculated to do just that.

Between mid-May and mid-July the deportations from Hungary were in full swing, and the SS did nothing to advance the proposed barter of Jews. When the model convoy of between 600 and 1,200 Jews did not leave as promised, Kasztner sought ways to circumvent Eichmann, who seemed to be blocking it. He approached SS Major Kurt Becher, responsible for procurement at the local headquarters of the Waffen-SS. In mid-May, Becher arranged for the SS to secure a 55 percent interest in the Jewish-owned Manfred-Weiss Works, a large industrial complex, in exchange for exit visas for forty-eight members of the extended Weiss family, thirty-five of them Jewish, and 3 million reichsmarks. Impressed by Becher's practical-mindedness, Kasztner urged him to expedite the pilot transport to help along the Brand mission. After checking back with Himmler, Becher agreed to release a train of close to 1,700 Jews against payment of $1,000 per hostage. The train left Budapest for Spain on June 30, but Eichmann, acting without Himmler's and Becker's knowledge, had it diverted to Bergen-Belsen. By this time the Nazi hardliners were taking courage from the fact that Brand had not reported back. Once the British publicly leaked and rejected the proposed trucks-for-Jews deal, even Himmler withdrew his support, momentarily.

Even so, Kasztner redoubled his efforts. He resumed contact with Clages, who agreed to transmit a revised proposal to Himmler. Drafted by Andreas Biss, a local businessman and cousin of Brand's, the new scheme intimated that the American Jewish Joint Distribution Committee, a major overseas relief organization, might participate in the financing. On July 26 Himmler responded favorably, more than ever eyeing the Western connection. At Himmler's behest Becher approved the release of five hundred Jews before leaving for

Switzerland on August 21 to negotiate with Saly Mayer, a Swiss banker who was also the Joint Distribution Committee's local representative. Instructed to play for time, Mayer made the end of all deportations and the release of part of the Bergen-Belsen convoy a precondition for substantive talks. He also pressed Becher to substitute nonmilitary items for the trucks on Germany's ransom note. Mayer's credibility with the SS was bolstered in late September, when Roosevelt appointed Roswell G. McClelland, head of the American Quakers and close to the War Refugee Board, his personal emissary to Switzerland. Himmler seized upon this appointment to hint at the phasing out of Auschwitz and to clear part of the Bergen-Belsen transport to leave for Switzerland. On November 5 Becher conferred with McClelland in Zurich, but he, too, refused to pay ransom, even after the arrival of the hostages from Bergen-Belsen in Switzerland.

In the meantime, SS Brigadier General Walter Schellenberg had started a parallel set of initiatives which were also calculated to probe the terrain for a separate capitulation or peace in the west. Chief of military intelligence for the SS with particular responsibility for political affairs abroad, Schellenberg ranked immediately after Himmler in the Gestapo. Like his superior, he, too, considered Germany's remaining captive Jews in the east and in the camps as a major diplomatic asset. Schellenberg exploited a connection to two American orthodox Jewish rabbis who were in Montreux and were in contact with McClelland. Through them he persuaded Dr. Jean-Marie Musy, former president of Switzerland, to come to Berlin in early October to confer with Himmler and explore the payment of a fixed ransom for each Jewish hostage. To show his appreciation, Himmler allegedly ordered that all Jews in camps were to be kept alive, and their treatment raised to the level of non-Jewish forced laborers from the east. But Musy's intercession got no further, despite a second visit to Berlin in mid-January. By then, as we saw, the Nazi leaders had their own reasons for sparing Jews and Slavs for forced labor, and they did so without regard for the outside world.

Schellenberg's second major approach was to Count Folke Bernadotte, nephew of the king of Sweden and vice president of the Swedish Red Cross. In a meeting that Schellenberg set up with Himmler for February 18, Bernadotte sought to save all Danish and Norwegian concentration-camp inmates from the fallout of nazism's final convulsions by having them transferred for safekeeping to Neuengamme, before being repatriated. He also proposed that Sweden supply all camps with provisions and become a haven for those inmates who were liberated, including Jews. Bernadotte came to Berlin for a second meeting with Himmler on April 2. Off the record, Schellenberg asked Bernadotte to intercede with General Eisenhower for a separate German capitulation in the west. Bernadotte refused to do so except at the official request of Himmler, which, given the führer's intransigence, would have required the prior overthrow of Hitler. Himmler and Bernadotte met for a third time in Lübeck on April 23, 1945, two days before Soviet and American troops met near Torgau on the Elbe. According to Bernadotte, even at five minutes to midnight Himmler affirmed that "to save as great a part of Germany as possible from a Russian invasion . . . [and] to save millions of Germans from Russian occupation . . . [he was] willing to capitulate on the western front in order to enable the Western Allies to advance rapidly toward the east." On this same occasion Himmler asserted that he was "not prepared to capitulate on the eastern front," insisting that he had "always been, and . . . [would] always remain, a sworn enemy of bolshevism."

Grand Admiral Karl Dönitz, the man Hitler designated as his successor before committing suicide on April 30, took exactly the same position. As a naval warrior, he was an anomalous choice to lead and liquidate an imploding land empire, except that he was a steadfast Nazi loyal to his führer. On the evening of May 1 Dönitz announced that Hitler had "fallen fighting to his last breath against bolshevism" and hailed him "as one of the greatest heroes of German history." In an appeal to the German people he stressed that his "first duty was to save Germans from destruction [Vernichtung] by the advancing Bolshevik enemy" and that "in so far and as long as the British and Americans" interfered with this effort the Reich would also have "to continue to defend itself and fight against them." In like manner, in a proclamation to the armed forces, Dönitz extolled the führer for dying "a hero's death" fighting for his "great idea of protecting the peoples of Europe from bolshevism." He wanted the Wehrmacht to know that he was assuming full command, "determined to continue the struggle against bolshevism until the field armies and hundreds of thousands of families in Germany's eastern provinces are saved from enslavement and destruction." He also vowed to keep fighting the English and Americans as long as they "hinder me in carrying through the war against the Bolsheviks."

Until the very end the Jews remained the primary victims of this relentless eastward-turning crusade, which ultimately precluded any separate and negotiated surrender coupled with the ransom of hostages, despite the efforts of top Nazi officials. Although Hitler discouraged and eventually condemned all overtures to the Western Allies, he was nevertheless incensed that they should be so scornfully spurned. With no way out he more than ever fixed the blame for his impending doom on others, particularly the Jews.

From his last radio address of January 30, 1945, which marked the twelfth anniversary of his accession to power, to his political testament of April 29, 1945, on the eve of his suicide, Hitler relentlessly lashed out against his enemies in terms consistent with Nazi ideology and propaganda. Throughout this time he sought to accuse others and vindicate himself for the fiasco of the Reich's crusade against bolshevism. Hitler castigated the Western Powers, especially England, for forcing the two-front war that he had worked to prevent. Churchill, he claimed, had thwarted a search for compromise by "traditional Britain" because he was "bound hand and foot to the Jewish chariot." The war had been brought on by "international statesmen who either were of Jewish origin or worked for Jewish interests." In his last will and testament Hitler also charged that ultimately "international Jewry and its helpmates are responsible" for Germany's plight and for this "murderous struggle."

Not that he felt the situation had become irreversible with the outbreak of war in September 1939. Hitler claimed that after the defeat of France he had once more tried to come to an accommodation with Britain, but again "the Jews would have none of it, their lackeys Churchill and Roosevelt being there to prevent it." Instead of giving up, however, he then "attacked eastward, in the hope that by lancing the Communist abscess I would rekindle a spark of common sense in the minds of the Western Powers," which could safely have trusted the "disinfection of the west" to the Third Reich. Indeed, Hitler insisted that with "my rear secure I could have thrown myself heart and soul into the destruction of bolshevism, which is Germany's essential task, the ambition of my life, and the *raison d'être* of National Socialism." This drive to destroy bolshevism "would have been coupled with the conquest of vast spaces in the east, . . . to ensure the future well-being of the German people."

On February 24 and March 11, 1945, in proclamations marking the anniversary of the birth of the Nazi Party and observing the Third Reich's Memorial Day, Hitler execrated the Jews for forging the alliance between "exploitative capitalism and murderous bolshevism" whose ultimate aim was the "extermination [*Ausrottung*] of the German nation." On April 13 he summoned the soldiers on the eastern front to stand fast against the final attack of the "mortal enemy Judeobolshevism . . . whose masses are determined to destroy Germany and exterminate our people." Unless the Ostheer fought off this horde "old men and children will be murdered, while women and girls will be forced into military whorehouses," except for the unserviceable ones, who would be "marched off to Siberia."

On February 4, 1945, Hitler had berated the Western powers for having thwarted his drive to "lance the Bolshevik abscess," but a week later, on February 13, he boasted that he had successfully "lanced the Jewish abscess, [for which] the world of the future will be eternally grateful to us." The Jews had, he said, brought this fate upon themselves. The führer once again claimed that "on the eve of war" he had given the Jews "one final warning," to the effect that should "they precipitate another war, they will not be spared and . . . [I] will exterminate the [Jewish] vermin throughout Europe, and this time for good." Courting disaster, the Jews "countered with a declaration of war."

Unlike Hitler's past formulations of the prophecy or warning of destruction, this one spoke of the Jews as "vermin," "parasites," and "poison." As part of its effort to fend off the "Jewish bid for world domination," Hitler said, National Socialism had resolved to "purge the Germanic world of the Jewish poison" which threatened to "asphyxiate and destroy" it. Having completed this "vital process of disinfection" within Germany "there was a good chance to extend it farther afield." In one final instance of total inversion, Hitler charged that because the Jews were "quick to realize the danger facing them [they] decided to go to all lengths in the life-and-death struggle which they launched against us." The Jews had set out to destroy National Socialism at any cost, if necessary by "destroying the whole world in the process," with the result that there had never "been a war so typically and at the same time so exclusively Jewish."

In his last days Hitler kept execrating the Jews in racial terms. On April 2 he again stressed that "after the war, in the [white] world only peoples showing themselves capable of eradicating the deadly Jewish poison from their system" would have the strength to face an emergent Asia, Africa, and South America. This same venomous spirit informed the closing sentence of Hitler's political testament of April 29, 1945: "Above all, I put the [successor] leadership of the nation and its followers under obligation to strictly uphold the racial laws and to mercilessly resist international Jewry, the universal poisoner of all nations."

But Hitler also spoke in another idiom. On February 13, in the same discourse in which he used racial catchwords and racist sophisms to revile the Jews, Hitler conceded that he "uses the term Jewish race as a matter of convenience, for in reality and from the genetic point of view there is no such thing as the Jewish race." The "appellation of Jewish race" should, he said, be given to what was, and to what the Jews themselves admitted to be, "a community" consisting of a "spiritually homogeneous group." This community was neither a "religious entity" nor "a collection of groups, united by the bond of a common religion," though the Hebrew religion had "a certain influence in molding its general characteristics," as did the "bond that has been forged by centuries of persecution." In sum, "the Jewish race was first and foremost an abstract race of the mind." Of course, "every Jew in the world has some drops of purely Jewish blood in him," for otherwise "it would be impossible to explain the presence of certain physical characteristics which are permanently common to all Jews from the ghetto of Warsaw to the bazaars of Morocco—the offensive nose, the cruel vicious nostrils, and so on." Still, "a race of the mind is something more solid, more durable than just a race, pure and simple." The fact that a "Jew remains a Jew wherever he goes and is impervious to the processes of assimilation . . . is proof of the superiority of the mind over the flesh."

With his own world collapsing all around him, Hitler's excoriation of the Jews became altogether incoherent and absurd, but no less venomous. He prided himself on having "opened the eyes of the whole world to the Jewish peril." Of course, should he "win the war," which by February 13, 1945, even he no longer believed possible, he would "put an end to Jewish world power and . . . deal the Jews a mortal blow from which they will not recover." But even if "I lose the war . . . [and] our endeavors . . . end in failure," the "triumph" of the Jews would only be temporary. Nazism had not only unmasked the Jews but had caused them "to become aggressive." Paradoxically, "the Jew" was "less dangerous in that frame of mind than when he is sly and cunning, . . . shifty and shamefaced." Should they survive, the Jews would become so "arrogant, . . . vainglorious, and bombastic" as to "evoke a violent reaction against them." In short, they could be trusted to remain a danger, and "as long as they survive, anti-Semitism will never fade," since "the Jews themselves will add fuel to its flames and . . . [keep these flames] well stoked."

Although Hitler's anti-Semitism was distinctive, it was not entirely new, nor was it coherent and constant. It became murderous not because it was any of these things, not because it was obsessive, but because it was polymorphous and found a fertile soil in the General Crisis and Thirty Years War of the twentieth century. Had it been narrower in focus and had not only Germany but Europe been balanced and thus immune, Nazi anti-Semitism would have been dismissed for its irrationality, not to mention its archaic conjurations and rabid violence. As it was, the Jews became the all-purpose scapegoats for the multiple ills of severely torn civil and political societies before becoming the chosen victims of the vengeful fury generated in the course of a monstrous and disastrous "holy war." And just as Hitler would have been inconceivable and ineffectual without his conservative underpinnings and apologists, so his anti-Semitism prevailed only because it was part and parcel of a syncretistic ideology combining key tenets of conservatism, reaction, and fascism.

BIBLIOGRAPHY

Abraham, David. *The Collapse of the Weimar Republic: Political Economy and Crisis.* 2nd ed., New York: Holmes & Meier, 1986.

Abramsky, Chimen; Jachimczyk, Maciej; and Polonsky, Antony (eds.). *The Jews in Poland.* Oxford: Basil Blackwell, 1986.

Ach, Manfred, and Pentrop, Clemens. *Hitlers "Religion": Pseudoreligiöse Elemente im nationalsozialistischen Sprachgebrauch.* Augsburg: Asgard-Edition 3, 1977.

Ackermann, Josef. *Heinrich Himmler als Ideologe.* Göttingen: Musterschmidt, 1970.

Adam, Uwe Dietrich. *Judenpolitik im Dritten Reich.* Düsseldorf: Droste, 1972.

Adler, H. G. *Theresienstadt, 1941–1945: Das Antlitz einer Zwangsgemeinschaft.* 2nd ed., Tübingen: J. C. B. Mohr (Paul Siebeck), 1960.

———. *Die verheimlichte Wahrheit: Theresienstädter Dokumente.* Tübingen: J. C. B. Mohr (Paul Siebeck), 1958.

———. *Der verwaltete Mensch: Studien zur Deportation der Juden aus Deutschland.* Tübingen: J. C. B. Mohr (Paul Siebeck), 1974.

Adler, Jacques. *Face à la Persécution: Les Organisations juives à Paris de 1940 à 1944.* Paris: Calmann-Lévy, 1985.

Adonyi-Naredy, Franz v. *Ungarns Armee im Zweiten Weltkrieg: Deutschlands letzter Verbündeter.* Neckargemünd: Kurt Vowinckel Verlag, 1971.

Agthe, M., and Pöhl, G. v. *Das Judentum: Das wahre Gesicht der Sowjets.* Berlin: Verlagsanstalt Otto Stollberg, 1941(?).

Ainsztein, Reuben. *Jewish Resistance in Nazi-Occupied Eastern Europe* (with a historical survey of the Jew as fighter and soldier in the Diaspora). London: Paul Elek, 1974.

Alderman, Geoffrey. *The Jewish Community in British Politics.* Oxford: Clarendon, 1983.

Allen, William S. "Die deutsche Öffentlichkeit und die 'Reichskristallnacht': Konflikte zwischen Werthierarchie und Propaganda im Dritten Reich." In Detlev Peukert and Jürgen Reulecke (eds.), *Die Reihen fest geschlossen: Beiträge zur Geschichte des Alltags unterm Nationalsozialismus,* pp. 397–411. Wuppertal: Hammer Verlag, 1981.

———. *The Nazi Seizure of Power: The Experience of a Single German Town, 1922–1945.* Rev. ed. New York: Franklin Watts, 1984.

452

American Council on Soviet Relations. *The Molotov Paper on Nazi Atrocities.* New York: American Council on Soviet Relations, 1942.

Angebert, Jean-Michel. *The Occult in the Third Reich: The Mystical Origins of Nazism and the Search for the Holy Grail.* New York: Macmillan, 1974.

Antoni, Ernst. *KZ von Dachau bis Auschwitz: Faschistische Konzentrationslager, 1933–1945.* Frankfurt am Main: Röderberg, 1979.

Arasse, Daniel. *La Guillotine et l'Imaginaire de la Terreur.* Paris: Flammarion, 1987.

Arendt, Hannah. *Eichmann in Jerusalem: A Report on the Banality of Evil.* Rev. ed. London: Penguin, 1977.

———. *The Origins of Totalitarianism.* New ed. with added prefaces. New York: Harcourt Brace Jovanovich, 1973.

Arndt, Monika. "Das Kyffhäuser-Denkmal: Ein Beitrag zur politischen Ikonographie des Zweiten Kaiserreiches." In Wallraf-Richartz-Jahrbuch, *Jahrbuch für Kunstgeschichte,* Vol. XL (1978), pp. 75–126.

Arnheim, Rudolf. *The Genesis of a Painting: Picasso's Guernica.* Berkeley: University of California Press, 1962.

Aron, Raymond. *The Century of Total War.* Boston: Beacon Press, 1955.

———. *Penser la Guerre: Clausewitz.* 2 vols. Paris: Gallimard, 1976.

Aschenauer, Rudolf (ed.). *Ich, Adolf Eichmann: Ein historischer Zeugenbericht.* Leoni am Starnberger See: Druffel-Verlag, 1980.

Aschheim, Steven E. *Brothers and Strangers: The East European Jew in German and German Jewish Consciousness, 1800–1923.* Madison: University of Wisconsin Press, 1982.

Aston, Trevor (ed.). *Crisis in Europe: 1560–1660.* New York: Basic Books, 1965.

Bach, Jürgen A. *Franz von Papen in der Weimarer Republik.* Düsseldorf: Droste, 1977.

Bahne, Siegfried. *Die KPD und das Ende von Weimar: Das Scheitern einer Politik, 1932–1935.* Frankfurt and New York: Campus Verlag, 1976.

Baird, Jay W. *The Mythical World of Nazi War Propaganda, 1939–1945.* Minneapolis: University of Minnesota Press, 1974.

Baranowski, Shelley. *The Confessing Church, Conservative Elites, and the Nazi State.* Lewiston, N.Y.: Edwin Mellen Press, 1986.

———. "Continuity and Contingency: Agrarian Elites, Conservative Institutions and East Elbia in Modern German History." *Social History,* Vol. 12, No. 3 (1987), pp. 285–308.

Bardy, Roland. *1919: La Commune de Budapest.* Paris: Tête de Feuilles, 1972.

Barkun, Michael. *Disaster and Millennium.* New Haven: Yale University Press, 1974.

Baron, Salo W. *The Russian Jew under Tsars and Soviets.* 2nd ed. New York: Macmillan, 1976.

Bartoszewski, Wladyslaw. *Das Warschauer Getto: Wie es wirklich war.* Frankfurt am Main: Fischer Taschenbuch, 1983.

Bartov, Omer. *The Eastern Front, 1941–45: German Troops and the Barbarization of Warfare.* London: Macmillan, 1985.

Bauer, Yehuda. *A History of the Holocaust.* New York: Franklin Watts, 1982.

———. *The Holocaust in Historical Perspective.* Seattle: University of Washington Press, 1978.

Baumgart, Winfried. "Zur Ansprache Hitlers vor den Führern der Wehrmacht im August 1939." *Vierteljahrshefte für Zeitgeschichte*, Vol. 16, No. 2 (April 1968), pp. 120–49.

Becker, Josef, and Becker, Ruth (eds.). *Hitlers Machtergreifung, 1933*. Munich: Deutscher Taschenbuch Verlag, 1983.

Behrens, Manfred; Bosch, Herbert; Elfferding, Wieland; et al. *Faschismus und Ideologie*. 2 vols. Berlin: Argument-Verlag, 1980.

Bein, Alexander. *Die Judenfrage*, Vol. II. Stuttgart: Deutsche Verlags-Anstalt, 1980.

Belperron, Pierre. *La Croisade contre les Albigeois et l'Union du Languedoc à la France, 1209–1249*. Paris: Plon, 1948.

Benjamin, Walter. *Illuminationen: Ausgewählte Schriften*. Frankfurt am Main: Suhrkamp, 1977.

Bennathan, Esra. "Die demographische und wirtschaftliche Struktur der Juden." In Werner E. Mosse (ed.), *Entscheidungsjahr 1932: Zur Judenfrage in der Endphase der Weimarer Republik*, pp. 87–131. Tübingen: J. C. B. Mohr, 1965.

Ben-Sasson, H. H.; Ettinger, S.; et al. *A History of the Jewish People*. Cambridge: Harvard University Press, 1976.

Berenstein, Tatiana; Eisenbach, Artur; Mark, Bernard; and Rutkowski, Adam (eds.). *Faschismus—Getto—Massenmord: Dokumentation über Ausrottung und Widerstand der Juden in Polen während des Zweiten Weltkrieges*. Berlin: Rütten & Loening, 1961.

Berghahn, Volker R. "Der Streit um die weltanschauliche Führung in der Wehrmacht, 1939–1943." *Vierteljahrshefte für Zeitgeschichte*, Vol. 17, No. 1 (January 1969), pp. 17–71.

Bernstein, Herman. *The Truth about "The Protocols of Zion."* New York: Covici Friede, 1935.

Besymenski, Lew. *Sonderakte "Barbarossa": Dokumente, Darstellung, Deutung*. Stuttgart: Deutsche Verlags-Anstalt, 1968.

Bettelheim, Bruno. *The Informed Heart: Autonomy in a Mass Age*. Glencoe, Ill.: Free Press, 1960.

Beyerchen, Alan D. *Scientists under Hitler: Politics and the Physics Community in the Third Reich*. New Haven: Yale University Press, 1977.

Bezwińska, Jadwiga, and Czech, Danuta (eds.). *KL Auschwitz Seen by the SS: Höss, Broad, Kremer*. Publications of Państwowe Muzeum w Oświecimiu, 1972.

Biddiss, Michael D. *Father of Racist Ideology: The Social and Political Thought of Count Gobineau*. London: Weidenfeld & Nicolson, 1970.

Billig, Joseph. *Les Camps de concentration dans l'économie du reich hitlérien*. Paris: Presses Universitaires de France, 1973.

———. "The Launching of the 'Final Solution.' " In Serge Klarsfeld (ed.), *The Holocaust and the Neo-Nazi Mythomania*, pp. 1–104. New York: Beate Klarsfeld Foundation, 1978.

Binion, Rudolph. *Hitler among the Germans*. New York: Elsevier, 1976.

Birn, Ruth Bettina. *Die höheren SS- und Polizeiführer: Himmlers Vertreter im Reich und in den besetzten Gebieten*. Düsseldorf: Droste, 1986.

Black, Edwin. *The Transfer Agreement: The Untold Story of the Secret Agreement Between the Third Reich and Jewish Palestine*. New York: Macmillan, 1984.

Black, Peter R. *Ernst Kaltenbrunner: Ideological Soldier of the Third Reich*. Princeton: Princeton University Press, 1984.

Blank, Alexander S. *Die deutschen Kriegsgefangenen in der UdSSR.* Cologne: Pahl-Rugenstein, 1979.

Bloch, Ernst. *Erbschaft dieser Zeit.* Frankfurt am Main: Suhrkamp, 1962.

———. *Vom Hasard zur Katastrophe: Politische Aufsätze aus den Jahren 1934–1939.* Frankfurt am Main: Suhrkamp, 1972.

Boelcke, Willi A. (ed.). *"Wollt ihr den totalen Krieg?": Die geheimen Goebbels-Konferenzen, 1939–1943.* Stuttgart: Deutsche Verlags-Anstalt, 1967.

Böhme, Kurt W. *Die deutschen Kriegsgefangenen in sowjetischer Hand: Eine Bilanz.* Bielefeld: Ernst und Werner Gieseking, 1966.

Boog, Horst; Förster, Jürgen; Hoffman, Joachim; et al. *Der Angriff auf die Sowjetunion.* Vol. IV of *Das Deutsche Reich und der Zweite Weltkrieg.* Stuttgart: Deutsche Verlags-Anstalt, 1983.

Borkin, Joseph. *The Crime and Punishment of I. G. Farben.* New York: Free Press, 1978.

Botz, Gerhard. *Wohnungspolitik und Judendeportation in Wien, 1938 bis 1945: Zur Funktion des Antisemitismus als Ersatz nationalsozialistischer Sozialpolitik.* Vienna and Salzburg: Geyer Edition, 1975.

Bracher, Karl Dietrich. *The German Dictatorship: The Origins, Structure, and Effects of National Socialism.* New York: Praeger, 1970.

———. "Die Gleichschaltung der deutschen Universität." In *Universitätstage 1966: Nationalsozialismus und die deutsche Universität,* pp. 126–42. Berlin: Walter de Gruyter, 1966.

———; Sauer, Wolfgang; and Schulz, Gerhard. *Die nationalsozialistische Machtergreifung: Studien zur Errichtung des totalitären Herrschaftssystems in Deutschland 1933/34.* Cologne: Westdeutscher Verlag, 1960.

Braham, Randolph L. *The Politics of Genocide: The Holocaust in Hungary.* 2 vols. New York: Columbia University Press, 1981.

Braudel, Fernand. *Écrits sur l'Histoire.* Paris: Flammarion, 1969.

Brenner, Lenni. *Zionism in the Age of the Dictators.* London: Croom Helm, 1983.

Broszat, Martin. "Hitler und die Genesis der 'Endlösung': Aus Anlass der Thesen von David Irving." *Vierteljahrshefte für Zeitgeschichte,* Vol. 25, No. 4 (October 1977), pp. 739–75.

———. *Nationalsozialistische Polenpolitik, 1939–1945.* Stuttgart: Deutsche Verlags-Anstalt, 1961.

———; Buchheim, Hans; Jacobsen, Hans-Adolf; and Krausnick, Helmut. *Anatomie des SS-Staates.* 2 vols. 2nd ed. Munich: Deutscher Taschenbuch Verlag, 1967.

Browning, Christopher. *Fateful Months: Essays on the Emergence of the Final Solution.* New York: Holmes & Meier, 1985.

———. *The Final Solution and the German Foreign Office: A Study of Referat D III of Abteilung Deutschland, 1940–43.* New York: Holmes & Meier, 1978.

———. "Zur Genesis der 'Endlösung': Eine Antwort an Martin Broszat." *Vierteljahrshefte für Zeitgeschichte,* Vol. 29, No. 1 (1981), pp. 97–109.

Brüdigam, Heinz. *Faschismus an der Macht: Berichte, Bilder, Dokumente über das Jahr 1933.* Frankfurt am Main: Röderberg-Verlag, 1982.

Bryon, Robert J. *The Jewish Intelligentsia and Russian Marxism: A Sociological Study of Intellectual Radicalism and Ideological Divergence.* London: Macmillan, 1978.

Buchbender, Ortwin. *Das tönende Erz: Deutsche Propaganda gegen die Rote Armee im Zweiten Weltkrieg.* Stuttgart: Seewald Verlag, 1978.

Bullock, Alan. *Hitler: A Study in Tyranny.* Rev. ed. New York: Harper Torch-books, 1964.

Bunzl, John. *Klassenkampf in der Diaspora.* Vienna: Europaverlag, 1975.

Burckhardt, Carl J. *Meine Danziger Mission 1937–1939.* Munich: Verlag Georg D. W. Callwey, 1960.

Burckhardt, Jacob. *Judgments on History and Historians.* Boston: Beacon Press, 1958.

Burden, Hamilton T. *The Nuremberg Party Rallies: 1923–39.* New York: Praeger, 1967.

Butz, A. R. *The Hoax of the Twentieth Century.* Torrance, Calif.: Noontide Press, 1977.

Bytwerk, Randall L. *Julius Streicher.* New York: Stein & Day, 1983.

Caffier, Michel. *L'Univers de Jacques Callot.* Paris: Scrépel, 1986.

Cahen, Claude. *Orient et Occident au temps des croisades.* Paris: Aubier, 1983.

Cardoza, Anthony L. *Agrarian Elites and Italian Fascism: The Province of Bologna, 1901–1926.* Princeton: Princeton University Press, 1982.

Carell, Paul. *Unternehmen Barbarossa: Der Marsch nach Russland.* Frankfurt am Main: Ullstein, 1973.

Cecil, Robert. *Hitler's Decision to Invade Russia, 1941.* London: Davis-Poynter, 1975.

Cerf, Paul. *L'Étoile juive au Luxembourg.* Luxembourg: RTL Edition, 1986.

Chaliand, Gerard, and Ternon, Yves. *Le Génocide des Arméniens.* Brussels: Édi-tions Complexe, 1984.

Chary, Frederick B. *The Bulgarian Jews and the Final Solution, 1940–1944.* Pitts-burgh: University of Pittsburgh Press, 1972.

Childers, Thomas. *The Nazi Voter: The Social Foundations of Fascism in Germany, 1919–1939.* Chapel Hill: University of North Carolina Press, 1983.

Clark, George. *War and Society in the Seventeenth Century.* Cambridge: Cam-bridge University Press, 1958.

Clark, Ronald W. *The Life and Times of Einstein.* New York: World Publishing, 1971.

Claussen, Detlev. *Grenzen der Aufklärung: Zur gesellschaftlichen Geschichte des mod-ernen Antisemitismus.* Frankfurt am Main: Fischer Taschenbuch, 1987.

Cohen, Carl. "The Road to Conversion." *Leo Baeck Institute Year Book,* Vol. 6 (1961), pp. 259–79.

Cohen, J. Bernard. *Revolution in Science.* Cambridge: Harvard University Press, 1985.

Cohen, Jeremy. *The Friars and the Jews: The Evolution of Medieval Anti-Judaism.* Ithaca: Cornell University Press, 1982.

Cohen, Stuart A. *English Zionists and British Jews: The Communal Politics of Anglo-Jewry, 1895–1920.* Princeton: Princeton University Press, 1982.

Cohn, Norman. *The Pursuit of the Millennium: Revolutionary Messianism in Medie-val and Reformation Europe and its Bearing on Modern Totalitarian Movements.* 2nd ed. New York: Harper Torchbooks, 1961.

————. *Warrant for Genocide: The Myth of the Jewish World-Conspiracy and the Protocols of the Elders of Zion.* New York: Harper Torchbooks, 1969.

Collingwood, R. G. *An Autobiography.* Oxford: Oxford University Press, 1939.

Colloque de l'École des Hautes Études en Sciences Sociales. *L'Allemagne nazie et le génocide juif.* Paris: Seuil/Gallimard, 1985.

Conquest, Robert. *The Great Terror: Stalin's Purge of the Thirties.* New York: Macmillan, 1968.

Conway, J. S. *The Nazi Persecution of the Churches, 1933–45.* New York: Basic Books, 1968.

Cooper, Matthew. *The Nazi War Against Soviet Partisans, 1941–1944.* New York: Stein & Day, 1979.

Council for the Protection of Monuments of Struggle and Martyrdom. *Auschwitz: Nazi Extermination Camp.* Warsaw: Interpress Publishers, 1978.

Cramer, Erich. *Hitlers Antisemitismus und die Frankfurter Schule.* Düsseldorf: Droste, 1979.

Crépon, Pierre. *Les Réligions et . . . la guerre.* Paris: Éditions Ramsay, 1982.

Czech, Danuta; Iwaszka, Tudeusz; Piper, Franciszek; et al. *Auschwitz: Geschichte und Wirklichkeit des Vernichtungslagers.* Reinbek bei Hamburg: Rowohlt, 1980.

Czerniaków, Adam. *Im Warschauer Getto: Das Tagebuch des Adam Czerniaków, 1939–1942.* Munich: C. H. Beck, 1986. (Hilberg, Raul, et al. (eds.). *The Warsaw Diary of Adam Czerniaków.* Briarcliff Manor, N.Y.: Stein & Day, 1982.)

Czollek, Roswitha. *Faschismus und Okkupation: Wirtschaftspolitische Zielsetzung und Praxis des faschistischen deutschen Besatzungsregimes in den baltischen Sowjetrepubliken während des Zweiten Weltkrieges.* Berlin: Akademie-Verlag, 1974.

Dallin, Alexander. *German Rule in Russia, 1941–1945: A Study of Occupation Policies.* New York: Macmillan, 1957.

Damus, Martin. *Sozialistischer Realismus und Kunst im Nationalsozialismus.* Frankfurt am Main: Fischer Taschenbuch, 1981.

Dász, Stephan. *Das Berner Fehlurteil über die Protokolle der Weisen von Zion.* Erfurt: U. Bodung-Verlag, 1935.

Davey, Owen A. "The Origins of the Légion des Volontaires Français contre le Bolchevisme." *Journal of Contemporary History,* Vol. 6, No. 4 (1971), pp. 29–45.

Davies, Norman. *God's Playground: A History of Poland.* 2 vols. Oxford: Clarendon, 1981.

Dawidowicz, Lucy S. *The War Against the Jews, 1933–1945.* New York: Holt, Rinehart & Winston, 1975.

De Felice, Renzo. *Storia degli ebrei italiani sotto il fascismo.* Turin: Einaudi, 1972.

Deist, Wilhelm; Messerschmidt, Manfred; Volkmann, Hans-Erich; and Wette, Wolfram. *Ursachen und Voraussetzungen der deutschen Kriegspolitik.* (Vol. I of *Das Deutsche Reich und der Zweite Weltkrieg.*) Stuttgart: Deutsche Verlags-Anstalt, 1979.

Denzler, Georg, and Fabricius, Volker. *Die Kirchen im Dritten Reich: Christen und Nazis Hand in Hand?* 2 vols. Frankfurt am Main: Fischer Taschenbuch, 1984.

Des Pres, Terrence. *The Survivor: An Anatomy of Life in the Death Camps.* New York: Oxford University Press, 1976.

Deutscher, Isaac. *The Non-Jewish Jew and Other Essays.* London: Oxford University Press, 1968.

Dickmann, Fritz. "Machtwille und Ideologie in Hitlers aussenpolitischen Zielsetzungen vor 1933." In Konrad Repgen and Stephan Skalweit (eds.), *Spiegel der Geschichte: Festgabe für Max Braubach,* pp. 915–41. Münster: Aschendorff, 1964.

Dipper, Christof. "Der Widerstand und die Juden." In Jürgen Schmädeke and

Peter Steinbach (eds.), *Der Widerstand gegen den Nationalsozialismus: Die deutsche Gesellschaft und der Widerstand gegen Hitler*, pp. 598–616. Munich: Piper, 1985.

Długoborski, Waclaw (ed.). *Zweiter Weltkrieg und sozialer Wandel: Achsenmächte und besetzte Länder*. Göttingen: Vandenhoeck & Ruprecht, 1981.

Dobroszycki, Lucjan (ed.). *The Chronicle of the Łódź Ghetto, 1941–1944*. New Haven: Yale University Press, 1984.

Domarus, Max (ed.). *Hitler: Reden und Proklamationen, 1932–1945*. 2 vols. Neustadt: Schmidt, 1962–63.

Döscher, Hans-Jürgen. *Das Auswärtige Amt im Dritten Reich: Diplomatie im Schatten der 'Endlösung.'* Berlin: Siedler, 1987.

Dower, John W. *War Without Mercy: Race and Power in the Pacific War*. New York: Pantheon, 1986.

Drapkin, Israel, and Viano, Emilio (eds.). *Victimology: A New Focus*. Vol. IV: *Violence and Its Victims*. Lexington, Mass.: D. C. Heath, 1975.

Drobisch, Klaus. "Der Freundeskreis Himmler." *Zeitschrift für Geschichtswissenschaft*, Vol. VIII, No. 2 (1960), pp. 304–28.

———; Goguel, Rudi; and Müller, Werner (eds.). *Juden unterm Hakenkreuz: Verfolgung und Ausrottung der deutschen Juden, 1933–1945*. Frankfurt am Main: Röderberg, 1973.

Dülffer, Jost. "Aufrüstung, Kriegswirtschaft und soziale Frage im Dritten Reich, 1936–1939." In Klaus Hildebrand and Karl Ferdinand Werner (eds.), *Deutschland und Frankreich, 1936–1939*. Munich: Artemis, 1981.

———. "Der Beginn des Krieges 1939: Hitler, die innere Krise und das Mächtesystem." *Geschichte und Gesellschaft*, Vol. 2, No. 4 (1976), pp. 443–70.

Dupront, Alphonse. *Du Sacré: Croisades et pèlerinages—images et langages*. Paris: Gallimard, 1987.

Dupuy, T. N., and Martell, Paul. *Great Battles on the Eastern Front: The Soviet-German War, 1941–1945*. Indianapolis: Bobbs-Merrill, 1982.

Duroselle, J.-B. *La Décadence, 1932–1939*. Paris: Imprimerie Nationale, 1979.

Eckman, Lester Samuel. *Soviet Policy Towards Jews and Israel, 1917–1974*. New York: Shengold, 1975.

Edelman, Marek, and Krall, Hanna. *Mémoires du Ghetto de Varsovie*. Paris: Éditions du Scribe, 1983.

Ehrenburg, Ilya, and Grossman, Vasily (eds.). *The Black Book: The Ruthless Murder of Jews by German-Fascist Invaders Throughout the Temporarily Occupied Regions of the Soviet Union and in the Death Camps of Poland During the War of 1941–1945*. New York: Holocaust Library, 1981.

Eichholtz, Dietrich, and Schumann, Wolfgang. *Anatomie des Krieges: Neue Dokumente über die Rolle des deutschen Monopolkapitals bei der Vorbereitung und Durchführung des Zweiten Weltkrieges*. Berlin: VEB Deutscher Verlag, 1969.

Eidelberg, Shlomo (ed.). *The Jews and the Crusaders: The Hebrew Chronicles of the First and Second Crusades*. Madison: University of Wisconsin Press, 1977.

Elissar, Eliahu Ben. *La Diplomatie du IIIe Reich et les Juifs, 1933–1939*. Paris: Julliard, 1969.

Elliot, Gil. *Twentieth Century of the Dead*. London: Penguin, 1972.

Erbstösser, Martin. *Die Kreuzzüge: Eine Kulturgeschichte*. Leipzig: Verlag für Kunst und Wissenshaft, 1977.

Erdmann, Carl. *Die Entstehung des Kreuzzugsgedankens*. Stuttgart: W. Kohlhammer, 1935.

Erdmann, Karl Dietrich, and Schulze, Hagen (eds.). *Weimar: Selbstpreisgabe einer Demokratie*. Düsseldorf: Droste, 1980.

Erickson, John. *The Road to Berlin: Continuing the History of Stalin's War with Germany*. Boulder, Colo.: Westview Press, 1983.

———. *The Road to Stalingrad: Stalin's War with Germany*. New York: Harper & Row, 1975.

Ertel, Rachel. *Le Shtetl: La bourgade juive de Pologne*. Paris: Payot, 1982.

Etringer, Norbert. *Das Kriegsgeschehen an der Dreiländerecke, 1939–1940*. Luxembourg: J. P. Krippler-Müller, 1983.

Evans, Jon. *The Nazi New Order in Poland*. London: Victor Gollancz, 1941.

Fargion, Liliana Picciotto. *L'occupazione tedesia e gli ebrei di Roma*. Rome: Carucci Editore, 1979.

Farias, Victor. *Heidegger et le Nazisme*. Paris: Verdier, 1987.

Feig, Konnilyn G. *Hitler's Death Camps: The Sanity of Madness*. New York: Holmes & Meier, 1981.

Fein, Helen. *Accounting for Genocide: National Responses and Jewish Victimization During the Holocaust*. New York: Free Press, 1979.

Feingold, Bernard. *The Politics of Rescue: The Roosevelt Administration and the Holocaust, 1938–1945*. New Brunswick, N.J.: Rutgers University Press, 1970.

Feingold, Henry L. *Zion in America: The Jewish Experience from Colonial Times to the Present*. New York: Twayne Publishers, 1974.

Fenyo, Mario D. *Hitler, Horthy, and Hungary: German-Hungarian Relations, 1941–1944*. New Haven: Yale University Press, 1972.

Ferencz, Benjamin B. *Less Than Slaves: Jewish Forced Labor and the Quest for Compensation*. Cambridge: Harvard University Press, 1979.

Fest, Joachim C. *Hitler*. New York: Vintage, 1975.

Field, Geoffrey G. *Evangelist of Race: The Germanic Vision of Houston Stewart Chamberlain*. New York: Columbia University Press, 1981.

Finucane, Ronald C. *Soldiers of the Faith: Crusaders and Moslems at War*. London and Melbourne: J. M. Dent, 1983.

Fischer, Conan. *Stormtroopers: A Social, Economic and Ideological Analysis, 1929–35*. London: Allen & Unwin, 1983.

Fisher, Julius S. *Transnistria: The Forgotten Cemetery*. New York: Thomas Yoseloff, 1969.

Flannery, Edward H. *The Anguish of the Jews: Twenty-three Centuries of Anti-Semitism*. New York: Macmillan, 1965.

Fleischhauer, Ingeborg. *Die Chance des Sonderfriedens: Deutsch-sowjetische Geheimgespräche, 1941–1945*. Berlin: Siedler, 1986.

Fleming, Gerald. *Hitler und die Endlösung: "Es ist des Führers Wunsch . . ."* Wiesbaden: Limes Verlag, 1982.

Förster, Jürgen. "The Wehrmacht and the War of Extermination Against the Soviet Union." *Yad Vashem Studies*, Vol. XIV (1981), pp. 7–34.

Foster, J. "Croisade de l'Europe contre le bolchevisme." *Revue d'Histoire de la Deuxième Guerre Mondiale*, Vol. 118 (April 1980), pp. 1–26.

Fraenkel, Ernst. *The Dual State*. New York: Oxford University Press, 1941.

Frei, Norbert. *Der Führerstaat: Nationalsozialistische Herrschaft, 1933–1945*. Munich: Deutscher Taschenbuch, 1987.

Fresco, Nadine. "Les Redresseurs de morts." *Les Temps Modernes*, June 1980, pp. 2150–211.

Friedländer, Saul. "From Anti-Semitism to Extermination: A Historiographical

Study of Nazi Policies Toward the Jews." *Yad Vashem Studies,* Vol. XVI (1984), pp. 1–50.

Friedman, Philip. *Roads to Extinction: Essays on the Holocaust.* New York: Jewish Publication Society, 1980.

Friedman, Saul S. *No Haven for the Oppressed: U.S. Policy Toward Jewish Refugees, 1938–1945.* Detroit: Wayne State University Press, 1973.

Fuld, Werner. *Walter Benjamin: Zwischen den Stühlen.* Frankfurt am Main: Fischer Taschenbuch, 1981.

Funke, Manfred (ed.). *Hitler, Deutschland und die Mächte.* 2nd ed. Düsseldorf: Droste, 1978.

Gager, John. *Origins of Christian Anti-Semitism.* New York: Oxford University Press, 1983.

Geiss, Imanuel, and Jacobmeyer, Wolfgang (eds.). *Deutsche Politik in Polen 1939–1945: Aus dem Diensttagebuch von Hans Frank, Generalgouverneur in Polen.* Opladen: Leske & Budrich, 1980.

Gérard-Libois, J., and Gotovitch, José. *L'An 40: La Belgique occupée.* Brussels: CRISP, n.d.

Gerns, Ditti (ed.). *Hitlers Wehrmacht in der Sowjetunion.* Frankfurt am Main: Verlag Marxistische Blätter, 1985.

Geyer, Michael. *Aufrüstung oder Sicherheit: Die Reichswehr in der Krise der Machtpolitik, 1924–1936.* Wiesbaden: Franz Steiner, 1980.

Gheorghe, Ion. *Rumäniens Weg zum Satellitenstaat.* Heidelberg: Kurt Vowinckel, 1952.

Gilbert, Felix. *A European Past: Memoirs 1905–1945.* New York: Norton, 1988.

Gilbert, Martin. *Atlas of the Holocaust.* New York: Macmillan, 1982.

———. *Exile and Return.* London: Weidenfeld & Nicolson, 1978.

———. *The Holocaust: A History of the Jews of Europe During the Second World War.* New York: Holt, Rinehart & Winston, 1986.

Gilboa, Yehoshua A. *The Black Years of Soviet Jewry, 1939–1953.* Boston: Little, Brown, 1971.

Gitelman, Zvi N. *Jewish Nationality and Soviet Politics: The Jewish Sections of the CPSU, 1917–1930.* Princeton: Princeton University Press, 1972.

Goebbels, Joseph. *Goebbels-Reden, 1932–1945.* 2 vols. Düsseldorf: Droste, 1972.

———. *Das Tagebuch von Joseph Goebbels, 1925–6.* Stuttgart: Deutsche Verlags-Anstalt, 1960.

Golczewski, Frank. *Polnisch-Jüdische Beziehungen, 1881–1922: Eine Studie zur Geschichte des Antisemitismus in Osteuropa.* Wiesbaden: Franz Steiner, 1981.

Goldhagen, Erich. "Weltanschauung und Endlösung: Zum Antisemitismus der nationalsozialistischen Führungsschicht." *Vierteljahrshefte für Zeitgeschichte,* Vol. 24, No. 4 (1976), pp. 379–405.

Gordon, Sarah. *Hitler, Germans, and the "Jewish Question."* Princeton: Princeton University Press, 1984.

Gosztony, Peter. *Deutschlands Waffengefährten an der Ostfront, 1941–1945.* Stuttgart: Motorbuch Verlag, 1981.

Gouldner, Alvin W. "Stalinism: A Study of Internal Colonialism." *Telos,* Vol. 34 (Winter 1977–78), pp. 5–84.

Graber, G. S. *The Life and Times of Reinhard Heydrich.* New York: David McKay, 1980.

Graf, Christoph. *Politische Polizei zwischen Demokratie und Diktatur.* Berlin: Colloquium Verlag, 1983.

Graml, Hermann, and Henke, Klaus-Dietmar (eds.). *Nach Hitler: Der schwierige Umgang mit unserer Geschichte: Beiträge von Martin Broszat.* Munich: Oldenburg, 1987.

——, Mommsen, Hans, et al. *The German Resistance to Hitler.* Berkeley: University of California Press, 1970.

Green, Nancy L. *The Pletzle of Paris: Jewish Immigrant Workers in the Belle Epoque.* New York: Holmes & Meier, 1986.

Greive, Hermann. *Geschichte des modernen Antisemitismus in Deutschland.* Darmstadt: Wissenschaftliche Buchgesellschaft, 1983.

Grill, Johnpeter Horst. *The Nazi Movement in Baden, 1920–1945: The Origins and Functions of Hitler's Party in Southwestern Germany.* Chapel Hill: University of North Carolina Press, 1983.

Gross, Jan Thomasz. *Polish Society under German Occupation: The Generalgouvernement, 1939–1944.* Princeton: Princeton University Press, 1979.

Gstrein, Heinz. *Jüdisches Wien.* Munich: Herold Wien, 1984.

Guiraud, Jean. *L'Inquisition médiévale.* Paris: Tallendier, 1978.

Gumkowski, Janusz, and Leszczynski, Kasimierz. *Poland under Nazi Occupation.* Warsaw: Polonia Publishing House, 1961.

Haffner, Sebastian. *Anmerkungen zu Hitler.* Munich: Kindler, 1978.

Halder, Franz. *Kriegstagebuch: Tägliche Aufzeichnungen des Chefs des Generalstabes des Heeres, 1939–1942.* 3 vols. Stuttgart: W. Kohlhammer, 1962–64.

Hayes, Peter. *Industry and Ideology: I. G. Farben in the Nazi Era.* New York: Cambridge University Press, 1987.

Heiber, Helmut (ed.). *Hitlers Lagebesprechungen: Die Protokollfragmente seiner militärischen Konferenzen, 1942–1945.* Stuttgart: Deutsche Verlags-Anstalt, 1962.

Heidegger, Martin. *Die Selbstbehauptung der deutschen Universität: Das Rektorat 1933/34.* Frankfurt am Main: Vittorio Klostermann, 1983.

Heifetz, Elias. *The Slaughter of the Jews in the Ukraine in 1919.* New York: Thomas Seltzer, 1921.

Heilbut, Iwan. *Die öffentlichen Verleumder: Die "Protokolle der Weisen von Zion" und ihre Anwendung in der heutigen Weltpolitik.* Zurich: Europa, 1937.

Heineman, John L. *Hitler's First Foreign Minister: Constantin Freiherr von Neurath.* Berkeley: University of California Press, 1979.

Heister, Hanns-Werner, and Klein, Hans-Günter (eds.). *Musik und Musikpolitik im faschistischen Deutschland.* Frankfurt am Main: Fischer Taschenbuch, 1984.

Heller, Celia S. *On the Edge of Destruction: Jews of Poland Between the Two World Wars.* New York: Schocken Books, 1977.

Herbert, Ulrich. *Fremdarbeiter: Politik und Praxis des "Ausländer-Einsatzes" in der Kriegswirtschaft des Dritten Reiches.* Berlin: Dietz, 1985.

Herbst, Ludolf. "Die Krise des NS-Regimes 1938/39: Zu den Thesen von T. W. Mason." *Vierteljahrshefte für Zeitgeschichte,* Vol. 26, No. 3 (1978), pp. 347–92.

——. *Der Totale Krieg und die Ordnung der Wirtschaft: Die Kriegswirtschaft im Spannungsfeld von Politik, Ideologie und Propaganda, 1939–1945.* Stuttgart: Deutsche Verlags-Anstalt, 1982.

Herf, Jeffrey. *Reactionary Modernism: Technology, Culture, and Politics in Weimar and the Third Reich.* Cambridge: Cambridge University Press, 1984.

Hermann, Armin. *Max Planck.* Hamburg: Rowohlt, 1973.

Herneck, Friedrich. *Albert Einstein.* Leipzig: Teubner, 1974.

——. *Einstein und sein Weltbild.* Berlin: Buchverlag der Morgen, 1976.

Hesse, Erich. *Der sowjetrussische Partisanenkrieg im Spiegel deutscher Kampfanweisungen und Befehle, 1941–1944.* Göttingen: Musterschmidt, 1969.

Hilberg, Raul. *The Destruction of the European Jews.* 3 vols. Rev. ed. New York: Holmes & Meier, 1985.

Hildebrand, Klaus. *Deutsche Aussenpolitik, 1933–1945: Kalkül oder Dogma?* Stuttgart: W. Kohlhammer, 1971.

———. *Das Dritte Reich.* Munich: Oldenburg, 1979.

———. "Weltmacht oder Untergang: Hitlers Deutschland, 1941–1945." In Oswald Hauser (ed.), *Weltpolitik II 1939–1945,* pp. 286–314. Göttingen: Musterschmidt, 1975.

Hillgruber, Andreas. "Die 'Endlösung' und das deutsche Ostimperium als Kernstück des rassenideologischen Programms des Nationalsozialismus." *Vierteljahrshefte für Zeitgeschichte,* Vol. 20, No. 2 (April 1972), pp. 133–53.

———. *Hitlers Strategie: Politik und Kriegführung, 1940–1941.* Frankfurt am Main: Bernard & Graefe Verlag, 1965.

———. (ed.). *Staatsmänner und Diplomaten bei Hitler.* 2 vols. Frankfurt am Main: Bernard & Graefe Verlag, 1970.

———. *Zweierlei Untergang: Die Zerschlagung des Deutschen Reiches und das Ende des europäischen Judentums.* Berlin: Siedler, 1986.

Hirschfeld, Gerhard (ed.). *The Policies of Genocide: Jews and Soviet Prisoners of War in Nazi Germany.* London: Allen & Unwin, 1986.

Historikerstreit: Die Dokumentation der Kontroverse um die Einzigartigkeit der nationalsozialistischen Judenvernichtung. Munich: Piper, 1987.

Hitler, Adolf. *Hitlers zweites Buch: Ein Dokument aus dem Jahr 1928.* Stuttgart: Deutsche Verlags-Anstalt, 1961.

———. *Mein Kampf.* 2 vols. Munich: F. Eher, 1925–27.

———. *Monologe im Führerhauptquartier, 1941–1944: Die Aufzeichnungen Heinrich Heims.* Munich: Wilhelm Heyne, 1982.

———. *The Testament of Adolf Hitler: The Hitler-Borman Documents of February–April 1945.* London: Cassell, 1959.

Hobsbawm, E. J. *The Age of Empire, 1875–1914.* New York: Pantheon, 1987.

Hoffmann, Peter. *Widerstand gegen Hitler und das Attentat vom 20. Juli 1944: Probleme des Umsturzes.* Munich: Piper, 1979.

Höhne, Heinz. *Der Orden unter dem Totenkopf: Die Geschichte der SS.* Munich: C. Bertelsmann, 1984.

Hollstein, Dorothea. *"Jud Süss" und die Deutschen: Antisemitische Vorurteile im nationalsozialistischen Spielfilm.* Frankfurt am Main: Ullstein, 1983.

Homze, Edward L. *Foreign Labor in Nazi Germany.* Princeton: Princeton University Press, 1967.

Horkheimer, Max. "Die Juden und Europa." *Zeitschrift für Sozialforschung,* Vol. 8 (1939), pp. 115–37.

Horowitz, Irving Louis. *Taking Lives: Genocide and State Power.* New Brunswick: Transaction Books, 1980.

Hörster-Philipps, Ulrike (ed.). *Grosskapital und Faschismus, 1918–1945: Dokumente.* Cologne: Pahl-Rugenstein, 1981.

Höss, Rudolf. *Kommandant in Auschwitz: Autobiographische Aufzeichnungen.* Edited by Martin Broszat. Munich: Deutscher Taschenbuch Verlag, 1979.

Howard, Michael. *War in European History.* London: Oxford University Press, 1976.

Hubatsch, Walther (ed.). *Hitlers Weisungen für die Kriegführung, 1939–1945: Dokumente des Oberkommandos der Wehrmacht.* Frankfurt am Main: Bernard & Graefe Verlag, 1962.

Huberband, Shimon. *Kiddush Hashem: Jewish Religious and Cultural Life in Poland During the Holocaust.* New York: Yeshiva University Press, 1987.

Hughes, H. Stuart. *Prisoners of Hope: The Silver Age of the Italian Jews, 1924–1974.* Cambridge: Harvard University Press, 1983.

Hyman, Paula. *From Dreyfus to Vichy: The Remaking of French Jewry, 1906–1939.* New York: Columbia University Press, 1979.

Institut zum Studium der Judenfrage (ed.). *Die Juden in Deutschland.* Munich: F. Eher, 1936.

International Military Tribunal. *Trial of the Major War Criminals Before the International Military Tribunal, Nuremberg 14 November 1945–1 October 1946.* 42 vols. Washington, D.C. 1947–49.

Isaac, Jules. *Jésus et Israël.* Paris: Fasquelle, 1959.

———. *The Teaching of Contempt: Christian Roots of Anti-Semitism.* New York: Holt, Rinehart, & Winston, 1964.

Israel, Jonathan I. *European Jewry in the Age of Mercantilism, 1550–1750.* Oxford: Clarendon, 1985.

Jäckel, Eberhard. *Hitler in History.* Hanover, N.H., and London: University Press of New England, 1984.

———. *Hitler's World View: A Blueprint for Power.* Cambridge: Harvard University Press, 1981.

———, and Kuhn, Axel (eds.). *Hitler's sämtliche Aufzeichnungen, 1905–1924.* Stuttgart: Deutsche Verlags-Anstalt, 1980.

Jacobsen, Hans-Adolf (ed.). *Kriegstagebuch des Oberkommandos der Wehrmacht.* Vol. I (1940–41). Frankfurt am Main: Bernard & Graefe Verlag, 1965.

———. *Nationalsozialistische Aussenpolitik, 1933–1938.* Frankfurt am Main: Alfred Metzner, 1968.

Jäger, Herbert. *Verbrechen unter totalitärer Herrschaft: Studien zur nationalsozialistischen Gewaltkriminalität.* Olten and Freiburg: Walter-Verlag, 1967.

James, Harold. *The German Slump: Politics and Economics, 1924–1936.* Oxford: Clarendon, 1986.

Janos, Andrew C. *The Politics of Backwardness in Hungary, 1825–1945.* Princeton: Princeton University Press, 1982.

Jelinek, Yeshayahu. "The 'Final Solution': The Slovak Version." *East European Quarterly,* Vol. IV, No. 4 (1970), pp. 431–41.

Jick, Leon A. "The Holocaust: Its Use and Abuse Within the American Public." *Yad Vashem Studies,* Vol. XIV (1981), pp. 303–12.

Juhász, Gyula. *Hungarian Foreign Policy, 1919–1945.* Budapest: Akadémiai Kiadó, 1979.

Kalow, Gert. *The Shadow of Hitler: A Critique of Political Consciousness.* London: Rapp & Whiting, 1968.

Kamenetsky, Ihor. *Secret Nazi Plans for Eastern Europe: A Study of Lebensraum Policies.* New York: Bookman Associates, 1961.

Kamiński, Andrzej J. *Konzentrationslager 1896 bis heute.* Stuttgart: W. Kohlhammer, 1982.

Kantorowicz, Ernst. *Frederick the Second, 1194–1250.* New York: Richard R. Smith, 1931.

Karady, Victor. "Les Juifs de Hongrie sous les lois antisémites: Étude d'une conjoncture sociologique, 1938–1943." *Actes de la Recherche en Sciences Sociales*, No. 56 (March 1985), pp. 3–30.

Karbaum, Michael. *Studien zur Geschichte der Bayreuther Festspiele, 1876–1976.* Regensburg: Gustav Bosse, 1976.

Kater, Michael H. *The Nazi Party: A Social Profile of Members and Leaders, 1919–1945.* Cambridge: Harvard University Press, 1983.

Katz, Jacob. *From Prejudice to Destruction: Anti-Semitism, 1700–1933.* Cambridge: Harvard University Press, 1980.

Kaul, F. K. *Nazimordaktion T4: Ein Bericht über die erste industriemässig durchgeführte Mordaktion des Naziregimes.* Berlin: VEB Verlag Volk und Gesundheit, 1973.

Keegan, John. *Barbarossa: Invasion of Russia, 1941.* New York: Ballantine, 1971.

Kelman, Herbert C. "Violence Without Moral Restraint." *Journal of Social Issues*, Vol. 29, No. 4 (1973), esp. pp. 38–49.

Kenrick, Donald, and Puxon, Grattan. *The Destiny of Europe's Gypsies.* London: Chatto-Heinemann, 1972.

Kershaw, Ian. *The Nazi Dictatorship: Problems and Perspectives of Interpretation.* London: Edward Arnold, 1985.

———. "The Persecution of the Jews and German Popular Opinion in the Third Reich." *Leo Baeck Institute Year Book*, Vol. XXVI (1981), pp. 261–89.

———. *Popular Opinion and Political Dissent in the Third Reich: Bavaria, 1933–1945.* Oxford: Clarendon, 1983.

Klarsfeld, Serge. *Auschwitz: Le Rôle de Vichy dans la Solution finale de la question juive en France, 1942–1944.* 2 vols. Paris: Fayard, 1983, 1986.

———. *Le Mémorial de la Déportation des Juifs de France.* Paris: Klarsfeld, 1978.

Klee, Ernst (ed.). *Dokumente zur "Euthanasie."* Frankfurt am Main: Fischer Taschenbuch, 1985.

Klee, Ernst. *"Euthanasie" im NS-Staat: Die "Vernichtung lebensunwerten Lebens."* Frankfurt am Main: S. Fischer, 1983.

Kleinfeld, Gerald R., and Tambs, Lewis A. *Hitler's Spanish Legion: The Blue Division in Russia.* Carbondale: Southern Illinois University Press, 1979.

Klemperer, Viktor von. *L. T. I.: Notizbuch eines Philologen.* 7th ed. Leipzig: Reclam, 1975.

Klessmann, Christoph. *Die Selbstbehauptung einer Nation: Nationalsozialistische Kulturpolitik und polnische Widerstandsbewegung im Generalgouvernement, 1939–1945.* Düsseldorf: Bertelsmann-Universitätsverlag, 1971.

Knütter, Hans-Helmuth. *Die Juden und die deutsche Linke in der Weimarer Republik, 1918–1933.* Düsseldorf: Droste, 1971.

Koehl, Robert Lewis. *The Black Corps: The Structure and Power Struggles of the Nazi SS.* Madison: University of Wisconsin Press, 1983.

Kogon, Eugen. *The Theory and Practice of Hell.* New York: Farrar, Straus, 1950.

———; Langbein, Hermann; and Rückerl, Adalbert (eds.). *Nationalsozialistische Massentötungen durch Giftgas: Eine Dokumentation.* Frankfurt am Main: S. Fischer, 1983.

Komitee der Antifaschistischen Widerstandskämpfer in der DDR. *Sachsenhausen: Dokumente, Aussagen, Forschungsergebnisse und Erlebnisberichte.* Berlin: VEB Deutscher Verlag der Wissenschaften, 1974.

———. *SS im Einsatz: Eine Dokumentation über die Verbrechen der SS.* Berlin: Deutscher Militärverlag, 1967.

Kommoss, Rudolf. *Juden hinter Stalin: Die jüdische Vormachtstellung in der Sowjetun-*

ion, auf Grund amtlicher Sowjetquellen dargestellt. Berlin: Nibelungen-Verlag, 1938.

Koonz, Claudia. *Mothers in the Fatherland: Women, the Family, and Nazi Politics.* New York: St. Martin's, 1987.

Korman, Gerd. "The Holocaust in American Historical Writing." *Societas,* Vol. II, No. 3 (1972), pp. 251–70.

Korzec, Pawel. *Juifs en Pologne: La question juive pendant l'entre-deux-guerres.* Paris: Presses de la Fondation Nationale des Sciences Politiques, 1980.

Korzen, Meir. "Problems Arising out of Research into the History of Jewish Refugees in the USSR during the Second World War." *Yad Vashem Studies,* Vol. III (1975), pp. 119–40.

Koselleck, Reinhart. *Futures Past: On the Semantics of Historical Time.* Cambridge: MIT Press, 1985.

Koshar, Rudy. *Social Life, Local Politics, and Nazism: Marburg, 1880–1935.* Chapel Hill: University of North Carolina Press, 1986.

Kovács, Mária M. "Luttes professionnelles et Antisémitisme: Chronique de la montée du fascisme dans le corps médical hongrois, 1920–1944." *Actes de la Recherche en Sciences Sociales,* No. 56 (March 1985), pp. 31–44.

Kraus, Ota, and Kulka, Erich. *Massenmord und Profit: Die faschistische Ausrottungspolitik und ihre ökonomischen Hintergründe.* Berlin: Dietz, 1963.

Krausnick, Helmut. "Kommissarbefehl und 'Gerichtsbarkeitserlass Barbarossa' in neuer Sicht." *Vierteljahrshefte für Zeitgeschichte,* Vol. 25, No. 4 (October 1977), pp. 683–738.

————, and Wilhelm, Hans-Heinrich. *Die Truppe des Weltanschauungskrieges: Die Einsatzgruppen der Sicherheitspolizei und des SD, 1938–1942.* Stuttgart: Deutsche Verlags-Anstalt, 1981.

Kris, Ernst, and Speier, Hans. *German Radio Propaganda: Report on Home Broadcasts During the War.* London: Oxford University Press, 1944.

Kube, Alfred. *Pour le Mérite und Hakenkreuz: Hermann Göring im Dritten Reich.* Munich: Oldenburg, 1986.

Kuby, Erich. *Als Polen deutsch war: 1939–1945.* Munich: Max Heuber Verlag, 1986.

Kulka, Otto. " 'Public Opinion' in Nazi Germany and the Jewish Question." *The Jerusalem Quarterly,* Vol. 25 (1982), pp. 121–44, and Vol. 26 (1983), pp. 34–45.

Kuper, Leo. *Genocide: Its Political Use in the Twentieth Century.* New Haven: Yale University Press, 1981.

Kupferman, Fred. *Laval: 1883–1945.* Paris: Balland, 1987.

Kuznetsov, Anatolii Vasil'evich. *Babi Yar: A Document in the Form of a Novel.* London: Jonathan Cape, 1970.

Lambert, Raymond-Raoul. *Carnet d'un Témoin, 1940–1943.* Paris: Fayard, 1985.

Lamberti, Marjorie. *Jewish Activism in Imperial Germany: The Struggle for Civil Equality.* New Haven: Yale University Press, 1978.

Lang, Jochen von. *Das Eichmann Protokoll: Tonbandaufzeichnungen der israelischen Verhöre.* Frankfurt am Main: Ullstein, 1985.

Langbein, Hermann. *Menschen in Auschwitz.* Vienna: Europa Verlag, 1972.

Langer, Herbert. *The Thirty Years' War.* London: Blandford Press, 1980.

Langmuir, Gavin I. "From Ambrose of Milan to Emicho of Leiningen: The Transformation of Hostility Against Jews in Northern Christendom." In *Gli*

Ebrei Nell'alto Medioevo, Vol. I, pp. 313–68. Spoleto: Presso La Sede Del Centro Italiano di Studi Sull'alto Medioevo, 1980.

Lanzmann, Claude. *Shoah.* 1985. Film. (Full text of film published, New York: Pantheon, 1985.)

Lapeyre, Henri. *Géographie de l'Espagne morisque.* Paris: S.E.V.P.E.N., 1959.

Laqueur, Walter. *The Terrible Secret: Suppression of the Truth about Hitler's "Final Solution."* London: Penguin Books, 1982.

Lavi, Th. "The Background to the Rescue of Romanian Jewry During the Period of the Holocaust." In Bela Vago and George L. Mosse (eds.), *Jews and Non-Jews in Eastern Europe, 1918–1945,* pp. 177–86. New York: John Wiley, 1974.

Leach, Barry A. *German Strategy Against Russia, 1939–1941.* Boulder: Westview Press, 1983.

Lebzelter, Gisela C. *Political Anti-Semitism in England, 1918–1939.* London: Macmillan, 1978.

Le Chêne, Evelyn. *Mauthausen: The History of a Death Camp.* London: Methuen, 1971.

Legters, Lyman H. (ed.). *Western Society After the Holocaust.* Boulder: Westview Press, 1983.

Leopold, John A. *Alfred Hugenberg: The Radical Nationalist Campaign Against the Weimar Republic.* New Haven: Yale University Press, 1977.

Levi, Primo. *The Drowned and the Saved.* New York: Summit, 1988.

———. *If This Is a Man.* New York: Orion Press, 1959. (Subsequently republished under the title *Survival in Auschwitz: The Nazi Assault on Humanity.*)

Levin, Dov. "The Attitude of the Soviet Union to the Rescue of Jews." In *Rescue Attempts During the Holocaust: Proceedings of the Second Yad Vashem International Historical Conference* (Jerusalem, April 8–11, 1974), pp. 225–42. Jerusalem: Yad Vashem, 1977.

Levy, Richard S. *The Downfall of the Anti-Semitic Political Parties in Imperial Germany.* New Haven: Yale University Press, 1975.

Lewis, D. S. *Illusions of Grandeur: Mosley, Fascism and British Society, 1931–81.* Manchester: Manchester University Press, 1987.

Lewy, Guenter. *The Catholic Church and Nazi Germany.* New York: McGraw-Hill, 1964.

Libaridian, Gerald J. "Objectivity and the Historiography of the Armenian Genocide." *Armenian Review,* Vol. 31, No. 1 (Spring 1978), pp. 79–87.

Liddell Hart, B. H. *History of the Second World War.* London: Cassell, 1970.

Lifton, Robert Jay. *The Nazi Doctors: Medical Killing and the Psychology of Genocide.* New York: Basic Books, 1986.

Lipman, V. D. *Social History of the Jews in England, 1850–1950.* London: Watts, 1954.

Littell, Franklin H. *The Crucifixion of the Jews.* New York: Harper & Row, 1975.

Lochner, Louis P. (ed.). *The Goebbels Diaries, 1942–1943.* Garden City, N.Y.: Doubleday, 1948.

Löwe, Heinz-Dietrich. *Antisemitismus und reaktionäre Utopie: Russischer Konservatismus im Kampf gegen den Wandel von Staat und Gesellschaft, 1890–1917.* Hamburg: Hoffmann und Campe, 1978.

Lowenthal, E. G. "Die Juden im öffentlichen Leben." In Werner E. Mosse (ed.), *Entscheidungsjahr 1932: Zur Judenfrage in der Endphase der Weimarer Republik,* pp. 51–85. Tübingen: J. C. B. Mohr (Paul Siebeck), 1965.

Lukács, Georg. *Die Zerstörung der Vernunft.* 3 vols. Darmstadt and Neuwied: Hermann Luchterhand, 1974.

Lukas, Richard C. *The Forgotten Holocaust: The Poles under German Occupation, 1939–1944.* Lexington: University Press of Kentucky, 1986.

Lumer, Hyman (ed.). *Lenin on the Jewish Question.* New York: International Publishers, 1974.

Lyttelton, Adrian. *The Seizure of Power: Fascism in Italy, 1919–1929.* 2nd ed. Princeton: Princeton University Press, 1987.

Maalouf, Amin. *Les Croisades vue par les Arabes.* Paris: Éditions J.-C. Lattès, 1983.

Macksey, Kenneth. *The Partisans of Europe in the Second World War.* New York: Stein & Day, 1975.

Mannheim, Karl. *Essays on the Sociology of Knowledge.* New York: Oxford University Press, 1952.

Marcus, Joseph. *Social and Political History of the Jews in Poland, 1919–1939.* New York and Amsterdam: Mouton, 1983.

Mark, Bernard. "The Study of the Jewish Resistance Movement." *Yad Vashem Studies,* Vol. XI (1975), pp. 49–65.

Marrus, Michael R. *The Holocaust in History.* Hanover, N.H., and London: University Press of New England, 1987.

———. *The Politics of Assimilation: A Study of the French Jewish Community at the Time of the Dreyfus Affair.* Oxford: Clarendon, 1971.

———, and Paxton, Robert O. *Vichy France and the Jews.* New York: Basic Books, 1981.

Marszalek, Jósef. *Majdanek: Geschichte und Wirklichkeit des Vernichtungslagers.* Reinbek bei Hamburg: Rowohlt, 1982.

Martin, Bernd, and Schulin, Ernst (eds.). *Die Juden als Minderheit in der Geschichte.* Munich: Deutscher Taschenbuch Verlag, 1981.

Marwick, Arthur. *War and Social Change in the Twentieth Century: A Comparative Study of Britain, France, Germany, Russia, and the United States.* London: Macmillan, 1974.

Maser, Werner. *Adolf Hitler: Legende, Mythos, Wirklichkeit.* Munich: Bechtle, 1971.

———. *Adolf Hitler: Mein Kampf—Geschichte, Auszüge, Kommentare.* Munich: Moewig, 1981.

———. *Hitlers Mein Kampf.* Munich: Bechtle, 1966.

Mason, Timothy W. "The Primacy of Politics: Politics and Economics in National Socialist Germany." In S. J. Woolf (ed.), *The Nature of Fascism,* pp. 165–95. New York: Random House, 1968.

———. *Sozialpolitik im Dritten Reich: Arbeiterklasse und Volksgemeinschaft.* 2nd ed. Opladen: Westdeutscher Verlag, 1978.

Mayer, Arno J. "Internal Crisis and War Since 1870." In Charles L. Bertrand (ed.), *Revolutionary Situations in Europe, 1917–1922: Germany, Italy, Austria-Hungary,* pp. 201–33. Montreal: University Center for European Studies, 1977.

———. "The Lower Middle Class as Historical Problem." *Journal of Modern History,* Vol. 47 (1975), pp. 409–36.

Mayer, Hans Eberhard. "Probleme moderner Kreuzzugsforschung." *Vierteljahrschrift für Sozial- und Wirtschaftsgeschichte,* Vol. 50, No. 4 (1964), pp. 505–13.

Medding, P. J. "Towards a General Theory of Jewish Political Interests and Behavior." *Jewish Journal of Sociology,* Vol. XIX, No. 2 (1977), pp. 115–44.

Medvedev, Roy A. *Let History Judge: The Origins and Consequences of Stalinism.* New York: Knopf, 1971.

Mendelsohn, Ezra. *The Jews of East Central Europe Between the World Wars.* Bloomington: Indiana University Press, 1983.

Mermet, Pierre, and Danan, Yves Maxime. "Les Thèmes de la Propagande allemande après le 22 juin 1941." *Revue d'Histoire de la Deuxième Guerre Mondiale,* Vol. XVI, No. 64 (October 1966), pp. 39–62.

Merson, Allan. *Communist Resistance in Nazi Germany.* London: Lawrence and Wishart, 1985.

Mertens, Dieter. "Christen und Juden zur Zeit des ersten Kreuzzuges." In Bernd Martin and Ernst Schulin (eds.), *Die Juden als Minderheit in der Geschichte,* pp. 46–67. Munich: Deutscher Taschenbuch Verlag, 1982.

Michaelis, Meir. *Mussolini and the Jews: German-Italian Relations and the Jewish Question in Italy, 1922–1945.* Oxford: Clarendon, 1978.

Michel, Jean. *Dora.* Paris: Éditions J.-C. Lattès, 1975.

Milano, Attilio. *Storia degli ebrai in Italia.* Turin: Einaudi, 1963.

Milton, Sybil. "The Expulsion of Polish Jews from Germany, October 1938–July 1939: A Documentation." *Leo Baeck Institute Year Book,* Vol. XXIX (1984), pp. 169–99.

Milward, Alan S. *The German Economy at War.* London: Athlone Press, 1965.

———. *War, Economy and Society, 1939–1945.* London: Allen Lane, 1977.

Minuth, Karl-Heinz (ed.). *Akten der Reichskanzlei: Regierung Hitler, 1933–1938. Part 1: 1933/34.* Vols. 1 and 2. Boppard am Rhein: Harald Boldt Verlag, 1983.

Moltmann, Günter. "Goebbels' Rede zum totalen Krieg am 18. Februar 1943." *Vierteljahrshefte für Zeitgeschichte,* Vol. 12, No. 1 (1964), pp. 13–43.

Mommsen, Hans. "Hitlers Stellung im nationalsozialistischen Herrschaftssystem." In Gerhard Hirschfeld and Lothar Kettenacker (eds.). *Der 'Führerstaat': Mythos und Realität,* pp. 47–70. Stuttgart: Ernst Klett, 1981.

———. "National Socialism: Continuity and Change." In Walter Laqueur (ed.), *Fascism: A Reader's Guide,* pp. 179–210. Berkeley: University of California Press, 1976.

———. "Der Nationalsozialismus, kumulative Radikalisierung und Selbstzerstörung des Regimes." In *Meyers Enzyklopädisches Lexikon,* Vol. 16, pp. 785–90. Mannheim: Lexikonverlag, 1976.

———. "The Realization of the Unthinkable: The 'Final Solution of the Jewish Question' in the Third Reich." In Gerhard Hirschfeld (ed.). *The Policies of Genocide: Jews and Soviet Prisoners of War in Nazi Germany,* pp. 93–144. London: Allen & Unwin, 1986.

Mommsen, Wolfgang J. *Max Weber und die deutsche Politik, 1890–1920.* Tübingen: J. C. B. Mohr, 1959.

Moritz, Erhard (ed.). *Fall Barbarossa: Dokumente zur Vorbereitung der faschistischen Wehrmacht auf die Aggression gegen die Sowjetunion, 1940–41.* Berlin: Deutscher Militärverlag, 1970.

Morse, Arthur D. *While Six Million Died: A Chronicle of American Apathy.* New York: Random House, 1968.

Mosse, George L. *The Nationalization of the Masses: Political Symbolism and Mass Movements in Germany from the Napoleonic Wars Through the Third Reich.* New York: New American Library, 1975.

Mühsam, Erich. *Von Eisner bis Levine: Die Entstehung und Niederlage der bayrischen Räterepublik.* Berlin: Lutz Schulenburg, 1976.

468

Müller, Ingo. *Furchtbare Juristen: Die unbewältigte Vergangenheit unserer Justiz.* Munich: Kindler, 1987.

Müller, Norbert (ed.). *Deutsche Besatzungspolitik in der UdSSR, 1941–1944.* Cologne: Pahl-Rugenstein, 1980.

Münster, Arno. *Utopie, Messianismus und Apokalypse im Frühwerk von Ernst Bloch.* Frankfurt am Main: Suhrkamp, 1982.

Munro, D. C. "The Speech of Pope Urban II at Clermont, 1095." *American Historical Review,* Vol. XI, No. 2 (January 1905), pp. 231–42.

Munz, Peter. *Frederick Barbarossa: A Study in Medieval Politics.* Ithaca: Cornell University Press, 1969.

Murphy, Thomas Patrick (ed.). *The Holy War: Conference on Medieval and Renaissance Studies, Ohio State University, 1974.* Columbus: Ohio State University Press, 1976.

Nagy-Talavera, Nicholas M. *The Green Shirts and the Others: A History of Fascism in Hungary and Rumania.* Stanford: Hoover Institution Press, 1970.

Nationalsozialistische Deutsche Arbeiterpartei. *Der Parteitag der Freiheit, vom 10. bis 16. September 1935: Offizieller Bericht über den Verlauf des Reichsparteitages mit sämtlichen Kongressreden.* Munich: Zentralverlag der NSDAP, 1935.

———. *Der Parteitag der Ehre, vom 8. bis 14. September 1936: Offizieller Bericht über den Verlauf des Reichsparteitages mit sämtlichen Kongressreden.* Munich: Zentralverlag der NSDAP, 1936.

———. *Der Parteitag der Arbeit, vom 6. bis 13. September 1937: Offizieller Bericht über den Verlauf des Reichsparteitages mit sämtlichen Kongressreden.* Munich: Zentralverlag der NSDAP, 1938.

Neebe, Reinhard. *Grossindustrie, Staat, und NSDAP, 1930–1933.* Göttingen: Vandenhoeck & Ruprecht, 1981.

Nekritch, Alexandre. *L'Armée Rouge assassinée: 22 juin 1941.* Paris: Bernard Grasset, 1968.

Neumann, Franz. *Behemoth: The Structure and Practice of National Socialism.* London: Victor Gollancz, 1942.

Niewyk, Donald L. *The Jews in Weimar Germany.* Baton Rouge: Louisiana State University Press, 1980.

———. *Socialist, Anti-Semite, and Jew: German Social Democracy Confronts the Problem of Anti-Semitism, 1918–1933.* Baton Rouge: Louisiana State University Press, 1971.

Nolte, Ernst. *Der Faschismus in seiner Epoche: Die Action française, der italienische Faschismus, der Nationalsozialismus.* Munich: Piper, 1963.

Oberman, Heiko A. *Wurzeln des Antisemitismus: Christenangst und Judenplage im Zeitalter von Humanismus und Reformation.* Berlin: Severin & Siedler, 1981.

Oduev, S. F. *Auf den Spuren Zarathustras: Der Einfluss Nietzsches auf die bürgerliche deutsche Philosophie.* Berlin: Akademie-Verlag, 1977.

Ophir, Baruch Z., and Wiesemann, Falk (eds.). *Die jüdischen Gemeinden in Bayern, 1918–1945: Geschichte und Zerstörung.* Munich: Oldenburg, 1979.

Ory, Pascal. *Les Collaborateurs, 1940–1945.* Paris: Seuil, 1976.

Overy, R. J. *The Nazi Economic Recovery, 1932–1938.* London: Macmillan, 1982.

Parker, Geoffrey. "Some Recent Work on the Inquisition in Spain and Italy." *Journal of Modern History,* Vol. 54, No. 3 (September 1982), pp. 520–26.

———. *The Thirty Years' War.* London: Routledge & Kegan Paul, 1985.

———, and Smith, Lesley M. (eds.). *The General Crisis of the Seventeenth Century.* London: Routledge & Kegan Paul, 1978.

Pätzold, Kurt. *Faschismus, Rassenwahn, Judenverfolgung: Eine Studie zur politischen Strategie und Taktik des faschistischen deutschen Imperialismus, 1933–1935.* Berlin: VEB Deutscher Verlag der Wissenschaften, 1972.

———. "Von der Vertreibung zum Genozid: Zu den Ursachen, Triebkräften und Bedingungen der antijüdischen Politik des faschistischen deutschen Imperialismus." In Klaus Drobisch, Dietrich Eichholtz, Kurt Gossweiler, et al. (eds.), *Faschismus in Deutschland: Faschismus der Gegenwart,* pp. 209–46. Cologne: Pahl-Rugenstein, 1980.

———, and Weissbecker, Manfred. *Geschichte der NSDAP, 1920–1945.* Cologne: Pahl-Rugenstein, 1981.

Paucker, Arnold (ed.). *Die Juden im Nationalsozialistischen Deutschland.* Tübingen: J. C. B. Mohr, 1986.

Pawelczyńska, Anna. *Values and Violence in Auschwitz: A Sociological Analysis.* Berkeley: University of California Press, 1979.

Paxton, Robert O. *Vichy France: Old Guard and New Order, 1940–1944.* New York: Knopf, 1972.

Penkower, Monty Noam. *The Jews Were Expendable: Free World Diplomacy and the Holocaust.* Urbana: University of Illinois Press, 1983.

Petzold, Joachim. *Die Demagogie des Hitlerfaschismus: Die politische Funktion der Naziideologie auf dem Wege zur faschistischen Diktatur.* Frankfurt am Main: Röderberg-Verlag, 1983.

Pfahlmann, Hans. *Fremdarbeiter und Kriegsgefangene in der deutschen Kriegswirtschaft, 1939–1945.* Darmstadt: Wehr & Wissen Verlagsgesellschaft, 1968.

Philippi, Alfred, and Heim, Ferdinand. *Der Feldzug gegen Sowjetrussland, 1941 bis 1945.* Stuttgart: W. Kohlhammer, 1962.

Pinchuk, Ben-Cion. "Soviet Media on the Fate of Jews in Nazi-Occupied Territory, 1939–1941." *Yad Vashem Studies,* Vol. XI (1975), pp. 221–33.

Poliakov, Léon. *Bréviaire de la Haine: Le Troisième Reich et les Juifs.* Paris: Calmann-Lévy, 1979.

———. *Histoire de l'Antisémitisme.* 4 vols. Paris: Calmann-Lévy, 1956–77.

Polišenský, J. V. *War and Society in Europe, 1618–1648.* Cambridge: Cambridge University Press, 1979.

Pollins, Harold. *Economic History of the Jews in England.* Rutherford, N.J.: Fairleigh Dickinson Press, 1982.

Porter, Jack Nusan (ed.). *Jewish Partisans: A Documentary of Jewish Resistance in the Soviet Union During World War II.* Washington, D.C.: University Press of America, 1982.

Präg, Werner, and Jacobmeyer, Wolfgang (eds.). *Das Diensttagebuch des deutschen Generalgouverneurs in Polen, 1939–1949.* Stuttgart: Deutsche Verlags-Anstalt, 1975.

Prel, Max Freiherr du (ed.). *Das General-Gouvernement.* Würzburg: Konrad Triltsch, 1942.

Presser, J. *The Destruction of the Dutch Jews.* New York: Dutton, 1969.

Rabb, Theodore K. *The Struggle for Stability in Early Modern Europe.* New York: Oxford University Press, 1975.

Rajsfus, Maurice. *Des Juifs dans la Collaboration: L'UFIG, 1941–1944.* Paris: Études et Documentation Internationales, 1980.

Rassinier, Paul. *Le Mensonge d'Ulysse.* 6th ed. Paris: La Vieille Taupe, 1979.

Rauschning, Hermann. *Gespräche mit Hitler.* New York: Europa Verlag, 1940.

Rein, Hans. *Franz von Papen im Zwielicht der Geschichte*. Baden-Baden: Nomos Verlagsgesellschaft, 1979.

Reinhardt, Klaus. *Die Wende vor Moskau: Das Scheitern der Strategie Hitlers im Winter 1941/42*. Stuttgart: Deutsche Verlags-Anstalt, 1972.

Reinharz, Jehuda. *Fatherland or Promised Land: The Dilemma of the German Jew, 1893–1914*. Ann Arbor: University of Michigan Press, 1975.

Reitlinger, Gerald. *The Final Solution: The Attempt to Exterminate the Jews of Europe, 1939–1945*. New York: A. S. Barnes, 1961.

———. *The House Built on Sand: The Conflicts of German Policy in Russia, 1939–1945*. London: Weidenfeld, 1960.

Rémond, René. *Les Droites en France*. 4th ed. Paris: Aubier Montaigne, 1983.

Rhodes, James M. *The Hitler Movement: A Modern Millenarian Revolution*. Stanford: Hoover Institution Press, 1980.

Richardi, Hans-Günter. *Schule der Gewalt: Die Anfänge des Konzentrationslagers Dachau, 1933–1945*. Munich: C. H. Beck, 1983.

Riley-Smith, Jonathan. *The First Crusade and the Idea of Crusading*. London: Athlone Press, 1986.

Ringelblum, Emmanuel. *Notes from the Warsaw Ghetto*. New York: McGraw-Hill, 1958.

Robertson, Esmonde M. (ed.). *The Origins of the Second World War: Historical Interpretations*. London: Macmillan, 1971.

Robinson, Jacob. *And the Crooked Shall Be Made Straight: The Eichmann Trial, the Jewish Catastrophe, and Hannah Arendt's Narrative*. New York: Macmillan, 1965.

Rodinson, Maxime. *Peuple juif ou Problème juif?* Paris: François Maspero, 1981.

Rohman, Fernand. *Hitler, le Juif et le troisième homme*. Paris: Presses Universitaires de France, 1983.

Rosenblit, Marsha L. *The Jews of Vienna, 1867–1914: Assimilation and Identity*. Albany: State University of New York Press, 1983.

Rosenhaft, Eve. *Beating the Fascists?: The German Communists and Political Violence, 1929–1933*. Cambridge: Cambridge University Press, 1983.

Roskies, David G. *Against the Apocalypse: Responses to Catastrophe in Modern Jewish Culture*. Cambridge: Harvard University Press, 1984.

Roth, Cecil. *The History of the Jews of Italy*. Philadelphia: Jewish Publication Society, 1946.

———. *The Spanish Inquisition*. New York: Norton, 1964.

Rothfels, Hans, and Eschenburg, Theodor (eds.). *Studien zur Geschichte der Konzentrationslager*. Stuttgart: Deutsche Verlags-Anstalt, 1970.

Rothschild, Joseph. *East Central Europe Between the Two World Wars*. Seattle: University of Washington Press, 1974.

Rousset, Paul. *Histoire d'une Idéologie: La Croisade*. Lausanne: Éditions l'Age d'Homme, 1983.

Rubenstein, Richard L. *The Cunning of History*. New York: Harper & Row, 1978.

Rückerl, Adalbert (ed.). *Nationalsozialistische Vernichtungslager im Spiegel deutscher Strafprozesse: Belzec, Sobibór, Treblinka, Chelmno*. Munich: Deutscher Taschenbuch, 1977.

Ruether, Rosemary Radford. *Faith and Fratricide: The Theological Roots of Anti-Semitism*. New York: Seabury Press, 1974.

Runciman, Steven. *A History of the Crusades*. 3 vols. Cambridge: Cambridge University Press, 1951–54.

Rürup, Reinhard. *Emanzipation und Antisemitismus.* Göttingen: Vandenhoeck & Ruprecht, 1975.

Sadoul, Georges. *Jacques Callot: Miroir de son temps.* Paris: Gallimard, 1969.

St. George, George. *The Road to Babi-Yar.* London: Neville Spearman, 1967.

Samuel, Maurice. *The Great Hatred.* New York: Knopf, 1948.

Sartre, Jean-Paul. *Réflexions sur la Question juive.* Paris: Gallimard, 1954.

Sauder, Gerhard (ed.). *Die Bücherverbrennung, 10. Mai 1933.* Frankfurt am Main: Ullstein, 1985.

Schachter, Marc. "The Origins and Failure of the Schacht-Rublee Plan: A Case Study in German Jewish Policy, 1938–1939." Senior thesis, Princeton University, 1985.

Schiller, Friedrich. *The History of the Thirty Years War.* London: G. Bell, 1916.

Schleunes, Karl A. *The Twisted Road to Auschwitz: The Nazi Policy Toward German Jews, 1933–1939.* Urbana: University of Illinois Press, 1970.

Schmädeke, Jürgen, and Steinbach, Peter (eds.). *Der Widerstand gegen den Nationalsozialismus: Die deutsche Gesellschaft und der Widerstand gegen Hitler.* Munich: Piper, 1985.

Schmid, Hans-Dieter; Schneider, Gerhard; and Sommer, Wilhelm (eds.). *Juden unterm Hakenkreuz: Dokumente und Berichte zur Verfolgung und Vernichtung der Juden durch die Nationalsozialisten, 1933 bis 1945.* 2 vols. Düsseldorf: Schwann, 1983.

Schmidt, Matthias. *Albert Speer: Das Ende eines Mythos [und] Aufdeckung einer Geschichtsfälschung.* Munich: Wilhelm Goldmann, 1982.

Schneeberger, Guido. *Nachlass zu Heidegger: Dokumente zu seinem Leben und Denken.* Bern: Suhr, 1962.

Schoenbaum, David. *Hitler's Social Revolution: Class and Status in Nazi Germany, 1933–1939.* Garden City, N.Y.: Doubleday, 1966.

Schreiner, Klaus. "Führertum, Rasse, Reich: Wissenschaft von der Geschichte nach der nationalsozialistischen Machtergreifung." In Peter Lundgreen (ed.), *Wissenschaft im Dritten Reich,* pp. 163–253. Frankfurt am Main: Suhrkamp, 1985.

Schubert, Kurt, and Moser, Jonny (eds.). "Der Gelbe Stern in Österreich: Katalog und Einführung zu einer Dokumentation." In *Studia Judaica Austriaca,* Vol. V. Eisenstadt: Edition Roetzer, 1977.

Schüler, Winfried. *Der Bayreuther Kreis von seiner Entstehung bis zum Ausgang der Wilhelminischen Ära: Wagnerkult und Kulturreform im Geiste völkischer Weltanschauung.* Münster: Aschendorff, 1971.

Schumann, Wolfgang (ed.). *Konzept für die "Neuordnung" der Welt: Die Kriegsziele des faschistischen deutschen Imperialismus im Zweiten Weltkrieg.* Berlin: Dietz, 1977.

———, and Groehler, Olaf (eds.). *Deutschland im Zweiten Weltkrieg.* Vol. 6: *Die Zerschlagung des Hitlerfaschismus und die Befreiung des deutschen Volkes (Juni 1944 bis zum 8. Mai 1945).* Cologne: Pahl-Rugenstein, 1985.

Schweitzer, Arthur. *Big Business in the Third Reich.* Bloomington: Indiana University Press, 1964.

Schwerin von Krosigk, Lutz Graf. *Memoiren.* Stuttgart: Seewald Verlag, 1977.

Seaton, Albert. *The Russo-German War, 1941–45.* London: Arthur Barker, 1971.

Sedlmayr, Hans. *Verlust der Mitte: Die bildende Kunst des 19. und 20. Jahrhunderts als Symptom und Symbol der Zeit.* Frankfurt am Main: Ullstein, 1973.

Seeber, Eva. *Zwangsarbeiter in der faschistischen Kriegswirtschaft: Die Deportation *und Ausbeutung polnischer Bürger unter besonderer Berücksichtigung der Lage der Arbeiter aus dem sogenannten Generalgouvernement, 1939–1945.* Berlin: VEB Deutscher Verlag der Wissenschaften, 1964.

Seifert, Hermann Erich. *Der Jude an der Ostgrenze.* Berlin: Zentralverlag der NSDAP, 1940.

Seraphim, Hans-Günther (ed.). *Das politische Tagebuch Alfred Rosenbergs, 1934–5 und 1939–40.* Munich: Deutscher Taschenbuch Verlag, 1956.

Sereny, Gitta. *Into that Darkness: From Mercy Killing to Mass Murder.* New York: McGraw-Hill, 1974.

Sherman, Ari Joshua. *Island Refuge: Britain and Refugees from the Third Reich, 1933–1939.* London: Paul Elek, 1973.

Showalter, Dennis E. *Little Man, What Now?: "Der Stürmer" in the Weimar Republic.* Hamden, Conn.: Archon Books, 1982.

Siegfried, Klaus-Jörg. *Rüstungsproduktion und Zwangsarbeit im Volkswagenwerk, 1939–1945: Eine Dokumentation.* Frankfurt am Main: Campus Verlag, 1986.

Silberner, Edmund. *Kommunisten zur Judenfrage: Zur Geschichte von Theorie und Praxis des Kommunismus.* Opladen: Westdeutscher Verlag, 1983.

Silverman, Dan P. "National Socialist Economics: The *Wirtschaftswunder* Reconsidered." In Barry Eichengreen and Tim Hatton (eds.), *Interwar Unemployment in International Perspective.* The Hague: Martinus Nijhoff, forthcoming.

Simon, Ernst. *Brücken: Gesammelte Aufsätze.* Heidelberg: Lambert Schneider, 1965.

Smith, Bradley F., and Peterson, Agnes F. (eds.). *Heinrich Himmler: Geheimreden 1933 bis 1945 und andere Ansprachen.* Frankfurt am Main: Ullstein, 1974.

Sombart, Werner. *Krieg und Kapitalismus.* New York: Arno Press, 1975.

Sorokin, Pitrim A. *Social and Cultural Dynamics.* Vol. III: *Fluctuation of Social Relationships, War, and Revolution.* New York: American Book Company, 1937.

Speer, Albert. *Inside the Third Reich: Memoirs.* New York: Macmillan, 1970.

Stalin, Joseph. *The Great Patriotic War of the Soviet Union.* New York: International Publishers, 1945.

Stein, George H. *The Waffen SS: Hitler's Elite Guard at War, 1939–1945.* Ithaca: Cornell University Press, 1966.

Stein, Leonard. *The Balfour Declaration.* New York: Simon & Schuster, 1961.

Steinberg, Maxime. *Le Dossier Bruxelles-Auschwitz: La police SS et l'extermination des Juifs de Belgique.* Brussels, 1980.

Steiner, George. *In Bluebeard's Castle: Some Notes Towards the Redefinition of Culture.* New Haven: Yale University Press, 1971.

Steinert, Marlis G. *Hitlers Krieg und die Deutschen: Stimmung und Haltung der deutschen Bevölkerung im Zweiten Weltkrieg.* Düsseldorf: Econ Verlag, 1970.

Sternhell, Zeev. *Ni droite, ni gauche: L'idéologie fasciste en France.* Paris: Seuil, 1983.

Stern, J. P. *Hitler: The Führer and the People.* Berkeley: University of California Press, 1975.

Stokes, Lawrence D. "The German People and the Destruction of the European Jews." *Central European History,* Vol. VI, No. 2 (1973), pp. 167–91.

Strauss, Herbert A. "Jewish Emigration from Germany: Nazi Policies and Jewish Responses." Part I in *Leo Baeck Institute Year Book,* Vol. XXV (1980), pp. 313–61; Part II in *ibid.,* Vol. XXVI (1981), pp. 343–409.

Streim, Alfred. *Sowjetische Gefangene in Hitlers Vernichtungskrieg: Berichte und Dokumente, 1941–1945.* Heidelberg: C. F. Müller Juristischer Verlag, 1982.

Streit, Christian. *Keine Kameraden: Die Wehrmacht und die sowjetischen Kriegsgefangenen, 1941–1945.* Stuttgart: Deutsche Verlags-Anstalt, 1978.

Sumption, Jonathan. *The Albigensian Crusade.* London: Faber & Faber, 1978.

Sydnor, Charles W., Jr. *Soldiers of Destruction: The SS Death's Head Division, 1933–1945.* Princeton: Princeton University Press, 1977.

Tal, Uriel. *Christians and Jews in Germany: Religion, Politics, and Ideology in the Second Reich, 1870–1914.* Ithaca: Cornell University Press, 1975.

————. "On the Study of the Holocaust and Genocide." *Yad Vashem Studies,* Vol. XIII (1979), pp. 7–52.

Talmon, Shemaryahu, and Siefer, Gregor (eds.). *Religion und Politik in der Gesellschaft des 20. Jahrhunderts.* Bonn: Keil Verlag, 1978.

Taylor, Fred (ed.). *The Goebbels Diaries, 1939–1941.* New York: Putnam, 1983.

Tenenbaum, Joseph. "The Crucial Year 1938." *Yad Vashem Studies,* Vol. II (1975), pp. 49–77.

Termois, Daniel. *L'Art de Jacques Callot.* Paris: F. De Nobele, 1962.

Thalmann, Rita, and Feinermann, Emmanuel. *La Nuit de Cristal: 9–10 novembre 1938.* Paris: Robert Laffont, 1972.

Thies, Jochen. *Architekt der Weltherrschaft: Die "Endziele" Hitlers.* Düsseldorf: Droste, 1976.

Thoss, Bruno. *Der Ludendorff-Kreis, 1919–1923: München als Zentrum der mitteleuropäischen Gegenrevolution zwischen Revolution und Hitler-Putsch.* Munich: Stadtarchiv, 1978.

Thurlow, Richard. *Fascism in Britain: A History, 1918–1985.* Oxford: Basil Blackwell, 1987.

Toland, John. *The Last 100 Days.* New York: Random House, 1966.

Trachtenberg, Joshua. *The Devil and the Jews: The Medieval Conception of the Jew and Its Relation to Modern Anti-Semitism.* New Haven: Yale University Press, 1943.

Treue, Wilhelm (ed.). "Hitlers Denkschrift zum Vierjahresplan 1936." *Vierteljahrshefte für Zeitgeschichte,* Vol. V, No. 2 (April 1955), pp. 184–210.

Trunk, Isaiah. *Judenrat: The Jewish Councils in Eastern Europe under Nazi Occupation.* New York: Macmillan, 1972.

Tuchel, Johannes, and Schattenfroh, Reinold. *Zentrale des Terrors: Prinz-Albrecht-Strasse 8—Das Hauptquartier der Gestapo.* Berlin: Siedler, 1987

Tucker, Robert C. (ed.). *Stalinism.* New York: Norton, 1977.

Turner, Henry Ashby, Jr. *German Big Business and the Rise of Hitler.* New York: Oxford University Press, 1985.

Vago, Bela. *The Shadow of the Swastika: The Rise of Fascism and Anti-Semitism in the Danube Basin, 1936–1939.* London: Saxon House, 1975.

————, and Mosse, George (eds.). *Jews and Non-Jews in Eastern Europe, 1918–1945.* New York: Wiley, 1974.

Valentin, Hugo. *Antisemitism Historically and Critically Examined.* New York: Viking Press, 1936.

Van Greveld, Martin. *Supplying War: Logistics from Wallenstein to Patton.* Cambridge: Cambridge University Press, 1977.

Venner, Dominique. *Baltikum dans le Reich de la défaite: Le combat des corps-francs, 1918–1923.* Paris: Laffont, 1974.

474

Vidal-Naquet, Pierre. *Les Assassins de la Mémoire*. Paris: Éditions la Découverte, 1987.

Vittori, Jean-Pierre. *Eux, les S.T.O.* Paris: Messidor/Temps Actuels, 1982.

Volkov, Shulamit. "Antisemitism as a Cultural Code: Reflections on the History and Historiography of Antisemitism in Imperial Germany." *Leo Baeck Institute Year Book*, Vol. 23 (1978), pp. 25–46.

Vondung, Klaus. *Magie und Manipulation: Ideologischer Kult und politische Religion des Nationalsozialismus.* Göttingen: Vandenhoeck & Ruprecht, 1971.

Vorländer, Herwart (ed.). *Nationalsozialistische Konzentrationslager im Dienst der totalen Kriegführung: Sieben württembergische Aussenkommandos des Konzentrationslagers Natzweiler/Elsass.* Stuttgart: W. Kohlhammer, 1978.

Wagner, Richard. *Sämtliche Schriften und Dichtungen.* Vols. 4–6. Leipzig: Hesse und Becker, 1914.

Waite, Robert G. L. *Vanguard of Nazism: The Free Corps Movement in Postwar Germany, 1918–1923.* Cambridge: Harvard University Press, 1952.

Walberer, Ulrich (ed.). *10. Mai 1933: Bücherverbrennung in Deutschland und die Folgen.* Frankfurt am Main: Fischer Taschenbuch, 1983.

Warlimont, Walter. *Im Hauptquartier der deutschen Wehrmacht, 1939–1945: Grundlagen, Formen, Gestalten.* Frankfurt am Main: Athenäum Verlag, 1964.

Wasserstein, Bernard. *Britain and the Jews of Europe, 1939–1945.* Oxford: Clarendon, 1979.

Watt, Donald C. *Too Serious a Business: European Armed Forces and the Approach of the Second World War.* Berkeley: University of California Press, 1975.

Weber, Reinhold W. *Die Entstehungsgeschichte des Hitler-Stalin-Paktes 1939.* Frankfurt am Main: Peter D. Lang, 1980.

Wedgwood, C. V. *The Thirty Years War.* London: Penguin, 1957.

Wegner, Bernd. *Hitlers politische Soldaten: Die Waffen-SS, 1933–1945.* Paderborn: Ferdinand Schöningh, 1982.

Wehler, Hans-Ulrich. *Entsorgung der deutschen Vergangenheit?: Ein polemischer Essay zum "Historikerstreit."* Munich: C. H. Beck, 1988.

Wehner, Bernd (ed.). *Die polnischen Greueltaten: Kriminalpolizeiliche Ermittlungsergebnisse.* Berlin: E. Jaedicke, 1942.

Weinberg, David H. *A Community on Trial: The Jews of Paris in the 1930s.* Chicago: University of Chicago Press, 1977.

Weinberg, Gerhard. *The Foreign Policy of Hitler's Germany: Starting World War II, 1937–1939.* Chicago: University of Chicago Press, 1980.

Weingartner, James J. *Crossroads of Death: The Story of the Malmédy Massacre and Trial.* Berkeley: University of California Press, 1979.

Weinstein, Fred. *The Dynamics of Nazism: Leadership, Ideology, and the Holocaust.* New York: Academic Press, 1980.

Wellers, Georges (ed.). *La France et la Question juive, 1940–1944: Actes du Colloque du Centre de Documentation Juive Contemporaine.* Paris: Éditions Sylvie Messinger, 1981.

Wendt, Bernd-Jürgen. *Grossdeutschland: Aussenpolitik und Kriegsvorbereitung des Hitler-Regimes.* Munich: Deutscher Taschenbuch, 1987

Werth, Alexander. *Russia at War, 1941–1945.* New York: Dutton, 1964.

Wertheimer, Jack. *Unwelcome Strangers: East European Jews in Imperial Germany.* New York: Oxford University Press, 1987.

West, Benjamin. *Struggles of a Generation: The Jews under Soviet Rule.* Tel Aviv: Massada Publishers, 1959.

Westwood, J. D. *Eastern Front: The Soviet-German War, 1941–45.* New York: Crown Publishers, 1984.

Whaley, Barton. *Codeword Barbarossa.* Cambridge: MIT Press, 1973.

Wiesel, Elie. *La Nuit.* Paris: Editions de Minuit, 1958. *Night.* New York: Hill and Wang, 1960.

Wilson, Charles. *The Transformation of Europe, 1558–1648.* London: Weidenfeld & Nicolson, 1976.

Winckler, Lutz. *Studie zur gesellschaftlichen Funktion faschistischer Sprache.* Frankfurt am Main: Suhrkamp, 1970.

Wistrich, Robert. *Hitler's Apocalypse: Jews and the Nazi Legacy.* New York: St. Martin's, 1985.

———. *Who's Who in Nazi Germany.* London: Weidenfeld & Nicolson, 1982.

Wormser-Migot, Olga. *Le Système concentrationnaire nazi, 1933–45.* Paris: Presses Universitaires, 1968.

Wykes, Alan. *Heydrich.* New York: Ballantine, 1973.

Wyman, David S. *The Abandonment of the Jews: America and the Holocaust, 1941–1945.* New York: Pantheon, 1984.

Wynot, Edward D. " 'A Necessary Cruelty': The Emergence of Official Anti-Semitism in Poland, 1936–39." *American Historical Review,* Vol. 76, No. 4 (October 1971), pp. 1034–58.

Wysocki, Gerd. *Zwangsarbeit im Stahlkonzern: Salzgitter und die Reichswerke "Hermann Göring," 1937–1945.* Braunschweig: Magni-Buchladen, 1982.

Wytwycky, Bohdan. *The Other Holocaust: Many Circles of Hell.* Washington, D.C.: Novak Report, 1980.

Yahil, Leni. "Raoul Wallenberg: His Mission and Activities in Hungary." *Yad Vashem Studies,* Vol. XV (1984), pp. 7–53.

Yerushalmi, Yosef Hayim. *Zakhor: Jewish History and Jewish Memory.* Seattle: University of Washington Press, 1982.

Zahn, Gordon C. *German Catholics and Hitler's Wars.* New York: Dutton, 1969.

Zeman, Z. A. B. *Nazi Propaganda.* 2nd ed. London: Oxford University Press, 1973.

Ziemke, Earl F. *Stalingrad to Berlin: The German Defeat in the East.* Washington, Office of the Chief of Military History, United States Army. New York: Dorset Press, 1968.

Zischka, Johannes. *Die NS-Rassenideologie: Machttaktisches Instrument oder handlungsbestimmendes Ideal?* Frankfurt am Main: Peter Lang, 1986.

Zorn, Gerda. *Nach Ostland geht unser Ritt: Deutsche Eroberungspolitik zwischen Germanisierung und Völkermord.* Berlin: Dietz, 1980.

Zuccotti, Susan. *The Italians and the Holocaust: Persecution, Rescue, and Survival.* New York: Basic Books, 1987.

INDEX

480

490

About the Author

Arno J. Mayer was born in Luxembourg in 1926. Currently the Dayton-Stockton Professor of European History at Princeton University, he received his B.B.A. from City College of New York and his Ph.D. from Yale University, and went on to teach at Brandeis, Harvard, Columbia and New York universities. He is fellow of the American Academy of Arts and Sciences, and his previous books are: *Political Origins of the New Diplomacy, 1917–1918*; *Politics and Diplomacy of Peacemaking: Containment and Counterrevolution at Versailles, 1918–1919*, which was awarded the American Historical Association's Herbert Baxter Adams Prize; *Dynamics of Counterrevolution in Europe, 1870–1956*; and *The Persistence of the Old Regime: Europe to the Great War.*